GRAMMAR

FOR THE WELL-TRAINED MIND

KEY TO BLUE WORKBOOK

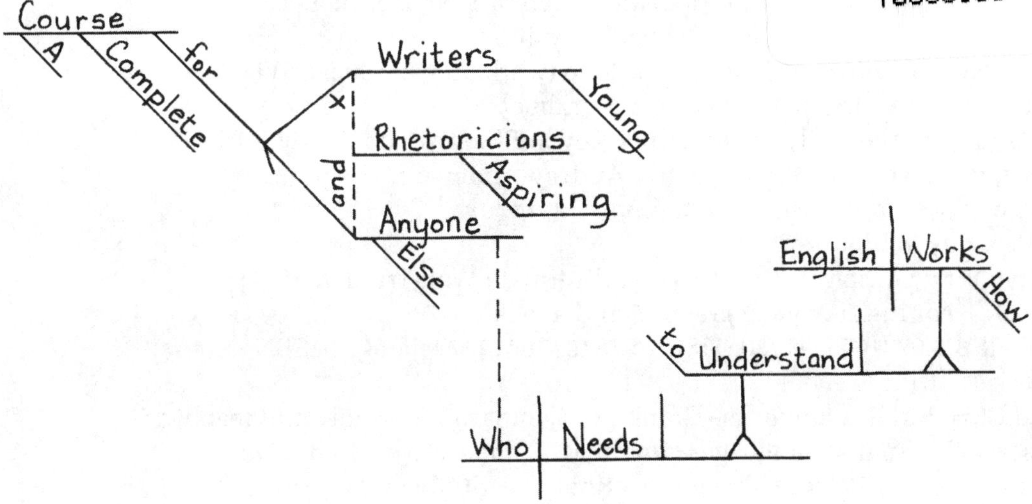

By Susan Wise Bauer

with Amanda Saxon Dean and Audrey Anderson,

Diagrams by Patty Rebne

Layout and Design by Shannon Zadrozny

WELL-TRAINED MIND PRESS

Publisher's Cataloging-In-Publication Data
(Prepared by The Donohue Group, Inc.)

Names: Bauer, Susan Wise, author. | Dean, Amanda Saxon, author. | Anderson, Audrey, 1986- author. | Rebne, Patty, illustrator. | Zadrozny, Shannon, book designer. | Guide to (work): Bauer, Susan Wise. Grammar for the well-trained mind. Blue workbook.
Title: Grammar for the well-trained mind. Key to Blue workbook / by Susan Wise Bauer, with Amanda Saxon Dean & Audrey Anderson ; diagrams by Patty Rebne ; layout and design by Shannon Zadrozny.
Other Titles: Key to Blue workbook
Description: First edition. | [Charles City, Virginia] : Well-Trained Mind Press, [2020] | For instructors of grades 5 and above.
Identifiers: ISBN 9781945841330 | ISBN 9781945841347 (ebook) | ISBN 9781945841613 (Kindle ebook)
Subjects: LCSH: English language--Grammar, Comparative--Study and teaching (Middle school) | English language--Grammar, Comparative--Study and teaching (Secondary) | English language--Rhetoric--Study and teaching (Middle school) | English language--Rhetoric--Study and teaching (Secondary)
Classification: LCC LB1631 .B3942 2020 (print) | LCC LB1631 (ebook) | DDC 428.00712--dc23

For a list of corrections, please visit **www.welltrainedmind.com/corrections**.

TABLE OF CONTENTS

WEEK 1

Introduction to Nouns and Adjectives

— LESSON 1 —

Introduction to Nouns
Concrete and Abstract Nouns

Exercise 1A: Abstract and Concrete Nouns

Decide whether the underlined nouns are abstract or concrete. Above each noun, write *A* for abstract or *C* for concrete. If you have difficulty, ask yourself: Can this noun be touched or seen, or experienced with another one of the senses? If so, it is a concrete noun. If not, it is abstract.

The sentences below are from Benjamin Franklin's *Poor Richard's Almanack*.

C A
At the working man's house hunger looks in but dares not enter.

> **Note to Instructor:** Although *hunger* can be felt, in this sentence *hunger* is an abstract principle; it is the idea of hunger, not a real sensation being experienced by a specific person.

A A A
Trouble springs from idleness and grievous toil from needless ease.

C C C C
A child and a fool imagine twenty shillings and twenty years can never be spent.

> **Note to Instructor:** *Years* has been marked as concrete, but arguments could be made for either response. If the student marks it as abstract and can support her decision, accept it.

A C C C
The wise man draws more advantage from his enemies than the fool from his friends.

C C
Men and melons are hard to know.

C C C
Beware of little expenses; a small leak will sink a great ship.

A C
There are lazy minds as well as lazy bodies.

> **Note to Instructor:** While *brains* would be concrete, *minds* is abstract.

A A A A
Great beauty, great strength, and great riches are really and truly of no great use; a right heart exceeds all.

> **Note to Instructor:** *Heart* is not used here in its concrete sense—Franklin is not referring to the rightness of an internal organ! *Heart* in this sentence refers to a person's center of emotion, which is abstract.

Employ thy time (C) well, if thou meanest to gain leisure (A).

Note to Instructor: As with *years* above, *time* could also be considered abstract. If the student chooses abstract and can explain her answer, accept it.

Exercise 1B: Using Concrete and Abstract Nouns

Identify each noun as concrete or abstract. Write a sentence that includes the given noun *and* at least one noun of the opposite type (so, if the given noun is a concrete noun, you must use it and also include an abstract noun of your choice).

Underline the additional noun in your sentence and label it as *C* for concrete or *A* for abstract. (It's fine to use more than one extra noun, but you only need to label one.)

The first is done for you.

Note to Instructor: The answers below are only samples.

	C or *A*?	Your Sentence
danger	A	Danger seemed to follow the lad (C) wherever he went.
hat	C	Wearing the new hat filled the girl with happiness (A).
melody	C	The haunting melody reminded me of the mystery (A) we were trying to solve.
reality	A	In reality, the spooky shadow was caused by a squirrel (C).
anticipation	A	The sight of that chocolate cake (C) filled me with hungry anticipation.
potato	C	A familiar feeling of dread (A) came over me as I saw the potato on my plate.

— LESSON 2 —

Introduction to Adjectives
Descriptive Adjectives, Abstract Nouns
Formation of Abstract Nouns from Descriptive Adjectives

Exercise 2A: Descriptive Adjectives, Concrete Nouns, and Abstract Nouns

Decide whether the underlined words are concrete nouns, abstract nouns, or descriptive adjectives. Above each, write *DA* for descriptive adjective, *CN* for concrete noun, or *AN* for abstract noun.

The sentences below were taken from *Mrs. Frisby and the Rats of NIMH*, by Robert C. O'Brien. Some have been slightly adapted.

A little later the last (DA) bit of wire (CN) disappeared behind them like a thin (DA) black (DA) snake (CN), and Mrs. Frisby climbed down from the asparagus (DA) bush (CN).

Note to Instructor: *Asparagus* can also be a noun, but if the student labels it as *CN*, ask "What kind of bush was it?"

CN CN AN AN
I had been in what is called a maze, a device to test intelligence and memory.

CN AN DA CN
When Mrs. Frisby thought of the danger she would face in just a few more hours, she wanted to
CN
kiss her children all goodbye.

> **Note to Instructor:** *Hour* can be an abstract noun, in such usages as "We have come to an evil hour." In this case, *a few more hours* is a specific span of time that Mrs. Frisby will experience, so we have labeled it as a concrete noun. However, if the student can make a good argument for labeling it as abstract, you may accept the answer (and also point out that abstract vs. concrete is not always an easy distinction!).

CN CN DA CN DA DA CN
It was in the kitchen, near her cage, a small scuffling on the hard linoleum floor.

> **Note to Instructor:** *Scuffling* is a gerund—a present participle acting as a noun. If the student has covered gerunds in a previous year, you may point this out. If not, and if the student is confused, say "*Scuffling* is a kind of noise—a thing that Mrs. Frisby could hear. Things are nouns. If a thing can be experienced by the senses, what kind of noun is it?"

DA CN CN DA CN CN
Some field mice find their way to barn lofts; some even creep into people's houses and live under
CN CN AN CN
the eaves or in attics, taking their chances with mousetraps.

> **Note to Instructor:** *Field* can also be a concrete noun. If the student mislabels it, ask "What kind of mice were they?"

CN CN DA CN CN AN
He continued the training, with new words and new pictures every day; but the fact is, once we
AN DA CN CN
had grasped the idea and learned the different sounds each letter stood for, we leaped way ahead of him.

Exercise 2B: Descriptive Adjectives and Abstract Nouns

For each sentence, identify the underlined word as *DA* for descriptive adjective or *AN* for abstract noun. Then change the underlined word to the other form (adjective to noun or noun to adjective) and rewrite the sentence with the new form. You may rearrange, add, or subtract words as necessary to make a sensible sentence. Your new sentence doesn't have to match the original exactly in meaning, but it should be close.

The first is done for you.

> **Note to Instructor:** Student answers may vary; accept reasonable answers as long as the noun or adjective in question has been properly transformed. The transformed words bolded below must be included in the answers.

AN
The store had a quaintness that made me smile.

The **quaint** store made me smile.

DA
Amy is a lively child, isn't she?

Amy is full of **liveliness**, isn't she?

I'm beginning to question the usefulness (AN) of this particular rule.

I'm beginning to question whether this particular rule is **useful**.

The cloudiness (AN) worried us on the morning of the picnic, but by noon the sky was clear.

The **cloudy** sky worried us on the morning of the picnic, but by noon it was clear.

Peter's bashfulness (AN) disappears the moment he steps on stage.

Peter's **bashful** nature disappears the moment he steps on stage.

The manager was pleased to hear that he had such a helpful (DA) employee.

The manager was pleased to hear about his employee's **helpfulness**.

Exercise 2C: Color Names

Underline all the color words in the following sentences. Then write *A* for adjective or *N* for noun above each underlined color word.

These sentences are taken from L. Frank Baum's *The Marvelous Land of Oz*. Some have been slightly adapted.

The boy found several lines clearly written in red (A) ink.

They soon regained the road of yellow (A) brick.

She wore a costume that struck the boy as being remarkably brilliant: her silken waist being of emerald green (N) and her skirt of four distinct colors—blue (N) in front, yellow (N) at the left side, red (N) at the back and purple (N) at the right side.

These flowers were almost blinding in their vivid hues of red (N) and gold (N).

The powder sifted down from Jack's head and scattered over the red (A) shirt and pink (A) waistcoat and purple (A) trousers Tip had dressed him in.

The front was striped with alternate bands of light brown (N) and white (N), blending together at the edges.

He was clothed all in green (N) and wore a high, peaked green (A) hat upon his head and green (A) spectacles over his eyes.

The tent of the Sorceress was larger than the others, and was composed of pure white (A) silk, with scarlet (A) banners flying above it.

— LESSON 3 —

Common and Proper Nouns
Capitalization and Punctuation of Proper Nouns

Exercise 3A: Capitalizing Proper Nouns

Write a proper noun for each of the following common nouns. Don't forget to capitalize all of the important words of the proper noun. If the proper noun requires quotation marks, include them.

You may either write your answers below or use a computer. If you are handwriting your answers, underline any proper noun that should be italicized.

Note to Instructor: Sample answers are given below; answers will vary. The proper nouns for *television show* and for *newspaper* should either be italicized or underlined to indicate italics; the proper noun for poem should be in quotation marks.

Common Noun	Proper Noun
television series	*Once Upon a Time* or Once Upon a Time
poem	"Jabberwocky"
newspaper	*The New York Times* or The New York Times
author	J. K. Rowling
city	Bangkok
school	Greenway Preparatory Academy

Exercise 3B: Proper Names and Titles

On your own paper, rewrite the following sentences properly. Capitalize and punctuate all names and titles correctly.

Note to Instructor: The corrected sentences are provided first. The original sentences follow. If the student is using a computer, underlined titles should be italicized.

Anna Sewell wrote Black Beauty.
My favorite of Robert Frost's poems is "Stopping by Woods on a Snowy Evening."
The Miracle Worker is a movie about Anne Sullivan, who was Helen Keller's teacher.
The words to "Take Me Out to the Ball Game" were written by Jack Norworth.
The television show I Love Lucy began airing in October 1951.

anna sewell wrote black beauty.
My favorite of robert frost's poems is stopping by woods on a snowy evening.
the miracle worker is a movie about anne sullivan, who was helen keller's teacher.
The words to take me out to the ball game were written by jack norworth.
The television show i love lucy began airing in october 1951.

Exercise 3C: Proofreading for Proper Nouns

In the following sentences, indicate which proper nouns should be capitalized by underlining the first letter of the noun three times. This is the proper proofreading mark for "capitalize." The first noun is done for you.

jackie robinson was born in cairo, georgia, in 1919.

robinson played second base for the brooklyn dodgers and was the first african american to play major league baseball in the modern era.

He was part of the team when the dodgers won the 1955 world series.

In 1962, robinson was inducted into the baseball hall of fame.

— LESSON 4 —

Proper Adjectives
Compound Adjectives (Adjective-Noun Combinations)

Exercise 4A: Forming Proper Adjectives from Proper Nouns

Form adjectives from the following proper nouns. (Some will change form and others will not.) Write each adjective into the correct blank below. If you are not familiar with the proper nouns, you may look them up online on Encyclopaedia Britannica, Wikipedia, or some other source (this will help you complete the sentences as well). This exercise might challenge your general knowledge! (But you can always ask your instructor for help.)

April	Hungary	Aquinas	Maine	Augusta
Ptolemy	Chile	Songkran	Elizabeth	Spain

Hungarian goulash is one of my favorite comfort foods.

My sister thought it would be funny to take some Spanish moss she found on the ground and put it on her head—until I informed her that it often has bugs in it!

The Chilean flamingo, which is native to western and southern South America, can be distinguished from other species by its gray legs with pink joints.

In her argumentative essay, Kimberly supported an Aquinian position on lending money at interest.

Our picnic was ruined by one of those famous April showers.

For over 1500 years, astronomers used the Ptolemaic system, which places Earth at the center of the universe.

William Shakespeare penned his plays and poems during England's Elizabethan era.

The Augusta National Golf Club, which hosts the Masters Tournament every spring, was founded by Bobby Jones and Clifford Roberts.

Held every August, the Maine Lobster Festival attracts visitors from around the world.

In the Songkran Water Festival, the people of Thailand celebrate the new year with water fights.

Exercise 4B: Capitalization of Proper Adjectives

In the following sentences, correct each lowercase letter that should be capitalized by underlining it three times.

Then, underline each proper adjective. Finally, circle each proper adjective that has not changed its form from the proper noun.

hans janssen and his son zacharias were dutch spectacle makers who may have developed the first compound microscope.

Note to Instructor: Although natives of the Netherlands are often known as Netherlanders, they are also known as the Dutch, so Dutch is a proper noun that does not change its form when it acts as an adjective.

esperanto, developed by a polish-jewish ophthalmologist named l. l. zamenhof, is a constructed language, but there are between 1000 and 2000 native esperanto speakers today.

a new york law in 1910 was the first north american law to require a license for driving a motor vehicle, but it only required this for professional chauffeurs.

jordan romero, an american mountain climber, is on record as the youngest person to complete a mount everest climb, having done so at the age of thirteen.

Exercise 4C: Hyphenating Attributive Compound Adjectives

Hyphens prevent misunderstanding! Explain to your instructor the differences between each pair of phrases. The first is done for you. If you're confused, ask your instructor for help.

Note to Instructor: These are intended to be fun, not frustrating. Use the suggestions below to help the student, and give answers if the student is stumped. There may be other ways to interpret these beyond the suggestions provided!

heavy-metal detector
heavy metal detector

a heavy-metal detector detects heavy metals

a heavy metal detector detects all metal, and is heavy to carry (a heavy detector and a metal detector)

good-morning wave
good morning wave

a good-morning wave is a hand motion that means "good morning"

a good morning wave is a hand motion in the morning that's done particularly well (a good wave and a morning wave)

slow-motion video
slow motion video

a slow-motion video is a video where the movement has been slowed down

a slow motion video is a video about motion, but it doesn't progress very quickly (a motion video and a slow video)

dog-friendly restaurant
dog friendly restaurant

a dog-friendly restaurant is a restaurant that's friendly to dogs

a dog friendly restaurant is a restaurant for dogs that's friendly (a dog restaurant and a friendly restaurant)

grape-flavored medicine
grape flavored medicine

grape-flavored medicine is medicine that has been given a grape flavor

grape flavored medicine is medicine with an unknown flavor added, made out of grapes (flavored medicine and grape medicine)

WEEK 2

Introduction to Personal Pronouns and Verbs

— LESSON 5 —

Noun Gender
Introduction to Personal Pronouns

Exercise 5A: Introduction to Noun Gender

How well do you know your animals? Fill in the blanks with the correct name (and don't worry too much if you don't know the answers . . . this is mostly for fun).

Animal	Male	Female	Baby	Group of Animals
bear	boar	sow	cub	sleuth OR sloth of bears
water buffalo	bull	cow	calf	pot of water buffalo
mallard	greenhead	hen	duckling	flush of mallards
ferret	hob	jill	kit	business of ferrets
hare	buck	doe	leveret	band OR down of hares
peafowl	peacock	peahen	peachick	ostentation of peafowls
raccoon	boar	sow	cub	gaze of raccoons
dolphin	bull	cow	calf	school OR pod of dolphins

Exercise 5B: Nouns and Pronouns

Write the correct pronoun above the underlined word(s). The first is done for you.

After Thomas Edison invented the phonograph, Thomas Edison [he] became known as the Wizard of Menlo Park.

Massachusetts legislators did not want Edison's invention of a device that would count their votes quickly; Massachusetts legislators [they] wanted to be able to change their colleagues' minds before the votes were tallied.

Although Alexander Graham Bell invented the telephone, the telephone [it] was not something Alexander Graham Bell [he] particularly liked. Alexander Graham Bell [He] refused to have a telephone [it] in his study because a telephone would allow the outside world to interfere with the time Alexander Graham Bell [he] spent thinking and working.

Mary Anderson invented the windshield wiper and was granted a patent in 1903, but Mary Anderson [she] was unable to sell the rights to her invention. After the patent expired in 1920, automobile manufacturers began including windshield wipers; windshield wipers [they] became standard equipment starting in 1922.

Margaret E. Knight invented a machine that would make flat-bottomed paper bags, but Margaret E. Knight [she] had to file a lawsuit when her design was stolen and her patent was granted to the thief. Margaret E. Knight [She] won the rights to her patent [it], and her patent allowed her to start up the Eastern Paper Bag Company.

Exercise 5C: Substituting Pronouns

The following passage is from a nineteenth-century translation of the Welsh myth cycle called the *Mabinogion*. The translation, made by Charlotte Guest, sounds a little bit stiff and formal to us, because it is over a hundred years old. But in this version, it sounds even odder because the pronouns *I*, *you*, *he*, *she*, *it*, *we*, and *they* have all been replaced by nouns.

Choose the nouns that can be replaced by pronouns, cross them (and any accompanying words such as "the") out, and write the appropriate pronouns above them.

You may also need to cross out and replace some verbs or helping verbs if necessary to maintain agreement.

Note to Instructor: The original text (very slightly adapted) is below, followed by the version provided to the student. Show the original to the student so she can compare her work to it. The two may not match perfectly, but if the student has done a reasonable job replacing nouns with pronouns to make a more readable passage, accept her work.

ORIGINAL

So they rode forth together joyfully towards the place where Arthur was; and when Kai saw them coming, he said, "I knew that Gwalchmai did not need to fight the knight. No wonder that he should gain fame; he can do more by his fair words, than I by the strength of my arm." And Peredur went with Gwalchmai to his tent, and they took off their armour. And Peredur put on garments like those that Gwalchmai wore; and they went together to Arthur, and saluted him. "Behold, lord," said Gwalchmai, "him whom you have sought so long."

"Welcome to you, Peredur," said Arthur. "With me you shall remain; and had I known thy valour had been such, you would not have left me as you did. Nevertheless, this was predicted of you by the dwarf and the dwarfess, whom Kai ill treated, and whom you have avenged."

And hereupon, behold there came the Queen and her handmaidens, and Peredur saluted them. And they were rejoiced to see him, and bade him welcome. And Arthur did him great honour and respect, and they returned towards Caerlleon.

STUDENT WORKBOOK VERSION

So Gwalchmai and Peredur rode forth together joyfully towards the place where Arthur was; and when Kai saw them coming, Kai said, "I knew that Gwalchmai did not need to fight the knight. No wonder that Gwalchmai should gain fame; Gwalchmai can do more by his fair words, than Kai by the strength of my arm." And Peredur went with Gwalchmai to his tent, and Peredur and Gwalchmai took off their armour. And Peredur put on garments like those that Gwalchmai wore; and Peredur and Gwalchmai went together to Arthur, and saluted him.

"Behold, lord," said Gwalchmai, "him whom Arthur has sought so long."

"Welcome to Peredur, Peredur," said Arthur. "With me Peredur shall remain; and had Arthur known thy valour had been such, Peredur would not have left me as Peredur did. Nevertheless, this was predicted of Peredur by the dwarf and the dwarfess, whom Kai ill treated, and whom Peredur has avenged."

And hereupon, behold there came the Queen and her handmaidens, and Peredur saluted the Queen and her handmaidens. And the Queen and her handmaidens were rejoiced to see him, and bade him welcome. And Arthur did him great honour and respect, and Arthur, Peredur, Gwalchmai, Kai, and the Queen and her handmaidens returned towards Caerlleon.

Exercise 5D: Pronouns and Antecedents

Circle the personal pronouns in the following sentences, and draw an arrow from each pronoun to its antecedent. If the noun and pronoun are masculine, write *m* in the margin. If they are feminine, write *f*; if neuter, write *n*. Look carefully: Some sentences may have more than one personal pronoun, and some personal pronouns may share an antecedent! In addition, some antecedents may not actually appear in the sentences provided.

If the antecedent is the speaker or the listener, simply write "speaker" or "listener" above the pronoun. In such cases, if the gender of the noun and pronoun are unknown, write *u* in the margin.

These sentences are from *David Copperfield*, by Charles Dickens. Some have been slightly adapted.

The servant was seen along with—our poor girl—last night. He's been in hiding about here, this week or over. m

Mr. Spenlow had stepped out, old Tiffey said, to get a gentleman sworn for a marriage
speaker
license; but as I knew he would be back directly, our place lying close to the Surrogate's, u, m
speaker
and to the Vicar-General's office too, I told Peggoty to wait. u

"Not, of course, but that Sophy is beautiful too in my eyes," said Traddles, "and would be
one of the dearest girls that ever was, in anybody's eyes I should think). But when I m, m
say the eldest is a Beauty, I mean she really is a—" he seemed to be describing clouds m, f, m
listener
about himself, with both hands: "Splendid, you know," said Traddles, energetically. u

speaker

This gave my aunt such unspeakable satisfaction, that I believe she took a delight in prowling up and down, with her bonnet insanely perched on the top of her head, at times when Mrs. Crupp was likely to be in the way. u, f

"I found out an English gentleman as was in authority," said Mr. Peggotty, "and told m

him I was a going to see my niece. He got me them papers as I wanted fur to carry me m, m, m

through—I don't rightly know how they're called—and he would have given me money, m, n, m

but that I was thankful to have no need on." m

speaker speaker

I doubt whether two young birds could have known less about keeping house, than I and u, u

my pretty Dora did. We had a servant, of course. She kept house for us. u&f, f

speaker

I made the toast on the usual infallible principles. When it was ready for my aunt, she u, n, f

was ready for it. n

— LESSON 6 —

Review Definitions

Introduction to Verbs
Action Verbs, State-of-Being Verbs
Parts of Speech

Exercise 6A: Identifying Action Verbs

Circle the action verbs in the following passage. Underline the state-of-being verbs.

This passage has been slightly adapted from a piece written by Mary Mapes Dodge in 1873, when smallpox was still a common disease.

The last known case of smallpox was in 1975. In 1980, the World Health Organization declared that smallpox had been eradicated—completely removed from the human population.

In the days when young Edward Jenner worked and studied in a surgeon's office in the town of Sodbury, in Gloucestershire, he heard a good deal of talk about the small-pox. This disease makes great trouble in our own time, and people fear it more than any other sickness; but it is not so bad now-a-days as it was in Jenner's time. It was a frightful plague, and carried, in England alone, away 45,000 people every year! Kings died of it, queens, princes, princesses, the rich and the poor, the high and the low, the learned and the ignorant. When it appeared in an army, it often slew more than the sword, and our soldiers suffered grievously from this pestilence in the beginning of the War of Independence.

Thirty-one years before Edward Jenner's birth, a bright, witty lady, with a sharp tongue but a good heart,—Lady Mary Wortley Montague,—discovered that in Turkey, where the small-pox raged terribly every year, they treated healthy people so they caught the disease,—but in a lighter and less dangerous form than if they took it in the common way. Well persons agreed to this treatment, because they knew that smallpox very rarely comes to a person more than once. They called this treatment inoculation. Lady Mary, who believed in the treatment, inoculated her own son in 1718, and with perfect success.

People thought this a great discovery, but the small-pox raged on, as badly as ever.

Exercise 6B: Choosing Verbs

Provide both an appropriate action and state-of-being verb for each of the following nouns or pronouns. The first is done for you.

Note to Instructor: The words provided are sample answers; the student's answers may be different.

	State-of-Being	Action
The beginner	is (or was)	attempted
A snail	is/was	creeps
She	is/was	jumped
My observations	are/were	suggested
The rules	are/were	demand
The jail	is/was	holds
His property	is/was	extends
Apple trees	are/were	bloom
It	is/was	startled
Donkeys	are/were	bray

Exercise 6C: Strong Action Verbs

Good writers use descriptive and vivid verbs!

In the following sentences, replace the underlined state-of-being and action verbs, which are bland and general, with more vigorous and colorful action verbs. The first is done for you.

Write your new verbs above the underlined verbs. You may use a thesaurus if necessary.

Mary Roach, the author of these sentences, used much more interesting verbs! Your instructor will show you her original sentences when you're finished.

Note to Instructor: Accept any appropriate verbs, but ask the student to compare her answers with the original sentences below.

Shooting stars streak past below you, and the sun rises in the middle of the night.

Antarctica is a useful analogue for space, and people who thrive there are thought to be psychologically well equipped for the isolation and confinement of space travel.

As gravity fades out on the twenty-eighth parabola, I pull up my legs, crouch on the windowpane, and then gently uncoil, launching myself across the cabin of the plane.

You can't control the weather or gravity, but you can control the shoes your visitor wears and the amount of water that falls onto the floor from her umbrella.

Gravity disappears again, and we rise off the floor like spooks from a grave.

Mary Roach, *Packing for Mars: The Curious Science of Life in Space*

The mortician ushered us into a large, dim, hushed room with heavy drapes and too much air-conditioning.

I explain that the surgeon in charge of the symposium invited me to observe.

She strides into her office and dials the phone, staring at me while she talks, like security guards in bad action movies just before Steven Seagal clubs them on the head from behind.

Though the surgeons clearly do not relish dissection of dead people's heads, they just as clearly value the opportunity to practice and explore on someone who isn't going to wake up and look in the mirror anytime soon.

He introduced me to Ben the cadaver, who, despite having by then been reduced to a head, lungs, and arms, retained an air of purpose and dignity.

Mary Roach, *Stiff: The Curious Lives of Human Cadavers*

— LESSON 7 —

Helping Verbs

Exercise 7A: Action and Helping Verbs

Underline the action verbs in both columns of sentences once. The sentences in the second column each contain at least one helping verb. Underline these helping verbs twice. These sentences are adapted from the *Biggle Poultry Book*, by Jacob Biggle.

COLUMN 1	COLUMN 2
A chicken rearer begins his work early.	The successful chicken rearer must begin his operations long before the advent of the chickens.
People built incubators for hatching eggs during colder months.	Mammoth incubators are now built with a capacity of as high as 20,000 eggs at a hatching.
The market for broiler chickens opens soon after the New Year but is not at its best until asparagus appears.	Broilers must all be hatched and reared during the most unfavorable season for such operations, winter.
The most successful hen farms consist mainly of houses with yards of only moderate size.	With proper care a flock will produce a fifth more eggs in confinement than when at liberty.

COLUMN 1	COLUMN 2
Farmers sometimes, though rarely, make the mistake of keeping too small a number of fowls.	Fowls, if allowed the privileges of the premises, will utilize much that would otherwise go to waste.
Persons living in towns and villages sometimes keep too many in their flock.	Attention should be paid to the variety of fowls kept, and to the yard fences.

Exercise 7B: Providing Missing Helping Verbs

Fill in each blank with a helping verb. Sometimes, more than one helping verb might be appropriate. This excerpt is adapted from William Makepeace Thackeray's *The Rose and the Ring*.

Note to Instructor: Accept any reasonable answers

The Fairy Blackstick, by whose means this young King and Queen had certainly won their respective crowns back, would come not unfrequently to pay them a little visit—as they were riding in their triumphal progress toward Giglio's capital—change her wand into a pony, and travel by their Majesties' side, giving them the very best advice. I am not sure that King Giglio did not think the Fairy and her advice rather a bore, fancying that it was his own valor and merits which had put him on his throne, and conquered Padella; and, in fine, I fear he rather gave himself airs toward his best friend and patroness. She exhorted him to deal justly by his subjects, to draw mildly on the taxes, never to break his promise when he had once given it—and in all respects to be a good King.

"A good King, my dear Fairy!" cries Rosalba. "Of course he will. Break his promise! Can you fancy my Giglio would ever do anything so improper, so unlike him? No! never!" And she looked fondly toward Giglio, whom she thought a pattern of perfection.

"Why is Fairy Blackstick always advising me, and telling me how to manage my government, and warning me to keep my word? Does she suppose that I am not a man of sense, and a man of honor?" asks Giglio, testily. "Methinks she rather presumes upon her position."

"Hush! dear Giglio," says Rosalba. "You know Blackstick has been very kind to us, and we must not offend her." But the Fairy was not listening to Giglio's testy observations: she had fallen back, and was trotting on her pony now, by Master Bulbo's side—who rode a donkey, and made himself generally beloved in the army by his cheerfulness, his kindness, and good-humor to everybody. He was eager to see his darling Angelica. He thought there never was such a charming being. Blackstick did not tell him it was the possession of the magic rose that made Angelica so lovely in his eyes. She brought him the very best accounts of his little wife, whose misfortunes and humiliations had indeed very greatly improved her; and you see, she could whisk off on her wand a hundred miles in a minute, and be back in no time, and so carry polite messages from Bulbo to Angelica, and from Angelica to Bulbo, and comfort that young man upon his journey.

When the Royal party arrived at the last stage before you reach Blombodinga, who should be in waiting, in her carriage there, with her lady of honor by her side, but the Princess Angelica?

A splendid luncheon was served to the Royal party, of which all our friends partook. You could hear the joy-bells ringing in the capital, and the guns which the citizens were firing off in honor of their Majesties.

"What can have induced that hideous old Gruffanuff to dress herself up in such an absurd way? Did you ask her to be your bridesmaid, my dear?" says Giglio to Rosalba. "What a figure of fun Gruffy is!"

— LESSON 8 —

Personal Pronouns

First, Second, and Third Person
Capitalizing the Pronoun *I*

Exercise 8A: Capitalization and Punctuation Practice

Correct the following sentences. Mark through any incorrect small letters and write the correct capitals above them. Insert quotation marks if needed. Use underlining to indicate any italics.

Note to Instructor: The correct sentences are below.

Noah McVicker, who worked for the soap company Kutol Products in Cincinnati, Ohio, developed a product for cleaning soot off wallpaper. After World War II, when wallpaper and heat sources had changed, there was less of a market for McVicker's wallpaper cleaning putty.

A schoolteacher named Kay Zufall thought her students might enjoy playing with the putty, and she convinced McVicker's nephew to try producing it as a toy called Play-Doh.

In the mid-1950s, Play-Doh was introduced at an educational convention, stores in New York and Chicago began selling it, and advertisements for it were played during such programs as *Captain Kangaroo* and *Romper Room*.

Peg Solitaire is known to have existed at least since the time of Louis XIV of France. The game may have been invented by a mathematician named Pelisson in Louis's court. A 1687 engraving of the Princess of Soubise, Anne de Rohan-Chabot, includes the game on a table beside the princess.

An edition of the magazine *Mercure Galant* from the same year includes a description of the game and its rules. By 1710, it had caught the attention of Gottfried Wilhelm Leibniz, who wrote that he preferred to play the game backwards, replacing pegs in empty holes that had been leaped over.

In 1883, Heyliger de Windt, who lived in Chicago, filed a patent for a board to be used in a game called Parlor Quoits. De Windt's board was angled and had a square hole, into which the players of Parlor Quoits would try to toss a bag filled with beans.

"In some cases," wrote de Windt in his patent application, "I propose to suspend a bell" at the end of the board; a player whose bag struck the bell would lose ten points.

A version of his game sold by a toy manufacturer in Massachusetts was called Faba Baga. Faba Baga had two round holes, worth different point values for the players, and one larger bag to toss each round.

Today, the game is known as Cornhole and is played with boards with one round hole. The American Cornhole Organization establishes rules and organizes tournaments for the game.

Exercise 8B: Person, Number, and Gender

Label each personal pronoun in the following selection with its person (*1*, *2*, or *3*) and number (*S* or *PL*). For third-person-singular pronouns only, indicate gender (*m*, *f*, or *n*). The first is done for you.

The selection below is adapted from Anna Sewell's *Black Beauty*.

> **Note to Instructor:** We have only addressed subject personal pronouns so far, but this passage contains personal pronouns that act as objects and possessives as well. The student may or may not mark these additional personal pronouns; the key below indicates these in parentheses. Answers NOT in parentheses are subject pronouns, which the student should be sure to mark.

The longer I [1s] lived at Birtwick, the more proud and happy I [1s] felt at having such a place. Our [(1p)] master and mistress were respected and beloved by all who knew them [(3p)]. They [3p] were good and kind to everybody and everything; not only men and women, but horses and donkeys, dogs and cats, cattle and birds. If any of the village children were known to treat any creature cruelly, they [3p] soon heard about it [3sn] from the Hall.

The Squire and Farmer Grey had worked together, as they [3p] said, for more than twenty years, to get bearing-reins on the cart-horses done away with, and in our [(1p)] parts you [2s] seldom saw them [(3p)]; but sometimes if mistress met a heavily laden horse, with his [(3sm)] head strained up, she [3sf] would stop the carriage; and get out, and reason with the driver in her [(3sf)] sweet, serious voice, and try to show him [(3sm)] how foolish and cruel it [3sn] was.

I [1s] don't think any man could withstand our [1p] mistress. I [1s] wish all ladies were like her [(3sf)]. Our [(1p)] master, too, used to come down very heavy sometimes. I [1s] remember he [3sm] was riding me [(1s)] towards home one morning, when we [1p] saw a powerful man begin to lash his [(3sm)] pony furiously. I [1s] knew what fearful pain it [3sn] gave that delicate little creature; but master gave me [(1s)] the word, and we [1p] were up with him [(1sm)] in a second.

"Do you [2s] think," said master sternly, "that treatment like this will make him [(3sm)] fond of your [(2s)] will? I [1s] must say, Mr. Sawyer, that more unmanly, brutal treatment of a little pony it [3sn] was never my [(1s)] painful lot to witness; and by giving way to such passion, you [2s] injure your [(2s)] own character as much, nay more, than you [2s] injure your [(2s)] horse; and remember, we [1p] shall all have to be judged according to our [(1p)] works, whether they [3p] be towards man or towards beast."

WEEK 3

Introduction to the Sentence

— LESSON 9 —

The Sentence
Parts of Speech and Parts of Sentences
Subjects and Predicates

Exercise 9A: Parts of Speech vs. Parts of the Sentence

Label each underlined word with the correct part of speech AND the correct part of the sentence.

part of speech — noun, verb

This strawberry is delicious.

part of the sentence — subject, predicate

part of speech — noun, verb

A cardinal landed on the bird feeder.

part of the sentence — subject, predicate

part of speech — pronoun, verb

She canceled our reservation.

part of the sentence — subject, predicate

part of speech — pronoun, verb

They snarled at us.

part of the sentence — subject, predicate

Exercise 9B: Parts of Speech: Nouns, Adjectives, Pronouns, and Verbs

Label each underlined word with the correct part of speech. Use *N* for noun, *A* for adjective, *P* for pronoun, and *V* for verb.

These sentences are from *Tarzan of the Apes*, by Edgar Rice Burroughs.

Had they (P) known that the child (N) had seen (V) thirteen moons before it (P) had come into Kala's possession (N) they would have considered (V) its case as absolutely hopeless (A), for the little (A) apes (N) of their own tribe (N) were as far advanced in two (A) or three moons (N) as was this little stranger (N) after twenty-five.

Tublat, Kala's husband, was sorely vexed, and but for the female's careful watching would have put the child out of the way.

"He will never be a great ape," he argued. "Always will you have to carry him and protect him. What good will he be to the tribe? None; only a burden."

"Let us leave him quietly sleeping among the tall grasses, that you may bear other and stronger apes to guard us in our old age."

"Never, Broken Nose," replied Kala. "If I must carry him forever, so be it."

Exercise 9C: Parts of the Sentence: Subjects and Predicates

In each of the following sentences, underline the subject once and the predicate twice. Find the subject by asking, "Who or what is this sentence about?" Find the predicate by saying, "Subject what?"

Manatees are large mammals.
Manatees live in the water.
They eat water plants.
Sometimes people call manatees "sea cows."
That name arose due to similarities in behavior between manatees and cows.
Manatees have good memories.
Florida's Wakulla Springs State Park is a good place for manatee sightings.

— LESSON 10 —

Subjects and Predicates

Diagramming Subjects and Predicates
Sentence Capitalization and Punctuation
Sentence Fragments

Exercise 10A: Sentences and Fragments

If a group of words expresses a complete thought, write *S* for sentence in the blank. If not, write *F* for fragment.

because it's raining outside	F
we ate three pieces of candy each	S
nightmares interrupting her sleep	F
the umbrella opened with a pop	S
a jealous child wants his sister's ice cream	S
the sleepy little town by the river	F
or inside the dilapidated barn	F

Exercise 10B: Proofreading for Capitalization and Punctuation

Add the correct capitalization and punctuation to the following sentences. In this exercise you will use proofreader's marks. Indicate letters which should be capitalized by underlining three times. Indicate ending punctuation by using the proofreader's mark for inserting a period: ⊙ Indicate words which should be italicized by underlining them and writing *ital* in the margin.

in 1949, george lerner invented a toy for children that involved sticking face parts into a potato or other vegetable or fruit⊙

lerner's toy required the use of actual produce, which was seen as wasteful following the years of food rationing in world war ii⊙

finally, lerner found a food company that would include the plastic parts as prizes in cereal boxes⊙

in 1951, lerner showed his toy to henry and merrill hassenfeld, who owned a toy company called hassenfeld brothers ⊙

the company, which has since changed its name to hasbro, decided to buy the rights to the toy, and mr⊙ potato head made his debut on may 1, 1952 ⊙

mr⊙ potato head was the first toy to be advertised on television⊙

mr⊙ potato head (and his wife, mrs⊙ potato head) appeared in disney's toy story movies⊙ ital

in 1998, the first and only season of the mr⊙ potato head show aired on the fox television network⊙ ital

Exercise 10C: Diagramming

Find the subjects and predicates in the following sentences. Diagram each subject and predicate on your own paper. You should capitalize on the diagram any words that are capitalized in the sentence, but do not put punctuation marks on the diagram. If a proper name is the subject, all parts of the proper name go onto the subject line of the diagram.

The raucous raccoons ran right into the river.

Cecily celebrated the centennial.

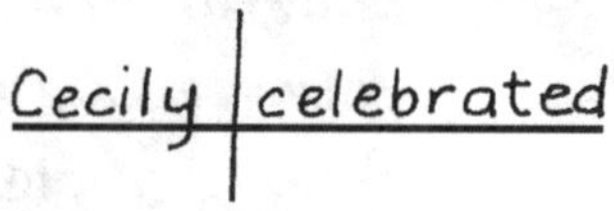

A heartbroken hedgehog hijacked the helicopter!

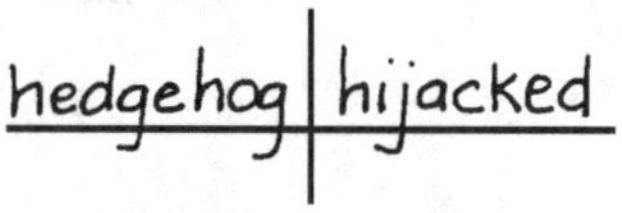

The preferred present for the precocious preschooler is a pretend prairie dog.

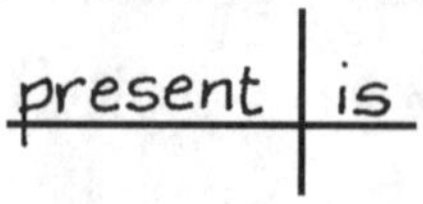

Dana Daniels dutifully danced to the drumbeats.

Annie's anaconda answers to Anthony.

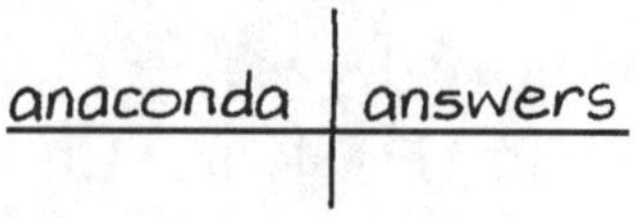

The garrulous goose gossiped with Gloria about the gawky gatekeeper.

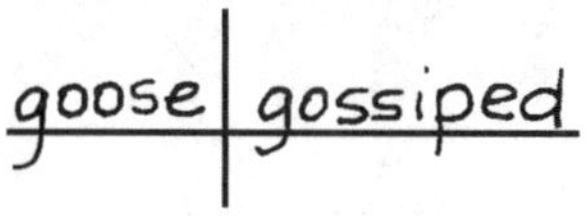

Jennifer jettisoned her jacket—in January!

— LESSON 11 —

Types of Sentences

Exercise 11A: Types of Sentences: Statements, Exclamations, Commands, and Questions

Identify the following sentences as *S* for statement, *E* for exclamation, *C* for command, or *Q* for question. Add the appropriate punctuation to the end of each sentence.

	Sentence Type
Put the toys in the basket.	C
Where did you get your new shirt?	Q
Remember to clean up your dishes after dinner.	C
Is the game tonight or tomorrow?	Q
Please call me when you get this message.	C
What a beautiful day!	E
I can't wait to go ice skating!	E
We were both at the library yesterday.	S
I'd like to see that movie.	S
Would you like the last piece of bread?	Q

Exercise 11B: Proofreading for Capitalization and Punctuation

Proofread the following sentences. If a lowercase letter should be capitalized, draw three lines underneath it. Add any missing punctuation by writing it into the sentence.

she has been in the hospital for a whole week!

several people came to visit yesterday.

did they bring these flowers?

put them in a vase.

add a little water.

that's too much water!

will you help me clean up this mess?

Exercise 11C: Diagramming Subjects and Predicates

On your own paper, diagram the subjects and predicates of the following sentences. Remember that the understood subject of a command is "you," and that the predicate may come before the subject in a question.

Mail the letter.

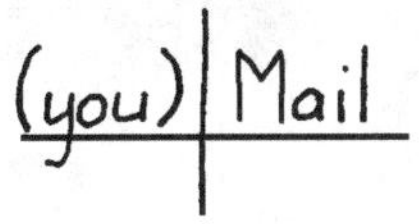

Am I awake?

I remember this movie.

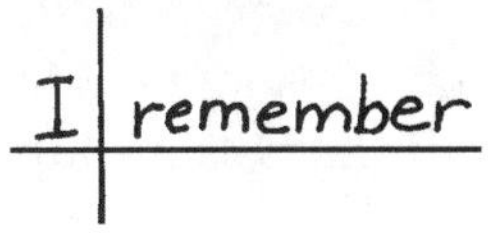

Philip ascended the stairs.

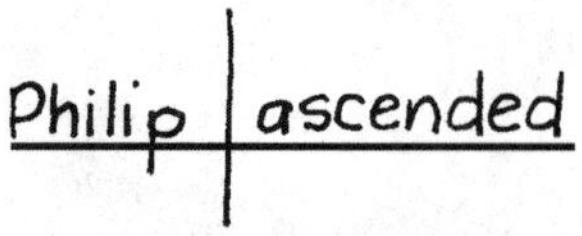

Quietly take your seat.

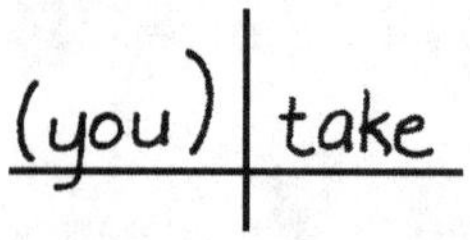

You look fabulous!

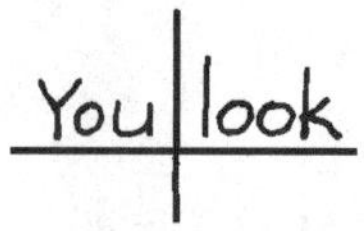

Are your sisters nearby?

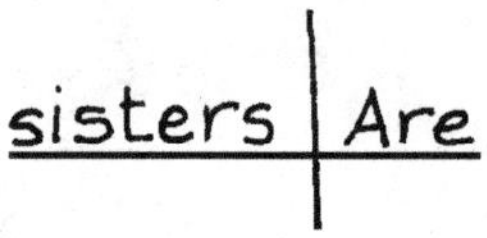

The show begins in two minutes!

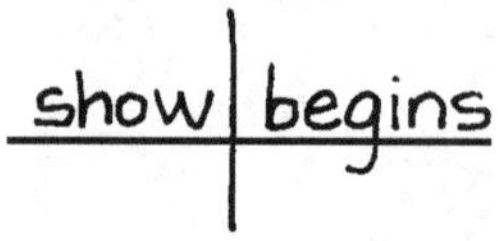

— LESSON 12 —

Subjects and Predicates
Helping Verbs
Simple and Complete Subjects and Predicates

Exercise 12A: Complete Subjects and Complete Predicates

Match the complete subjects and complete predicates by drawing lines between them.

Note to Instructor: Our solutions are listed below, but accept any reasonable answers.

A dishonest magician	sees the sultan's daughter.
Inside the cave, the boy	rubs a magic ring, revealing a genie.
The ring genie	provides food and prosperity to Aladdin and his mother for many years.
Back at home, Aladdin's mother	eventually lives happily ever after.
The lamp genie	manages to marry the sultan's daughter.
One day, Aladdin	tricks Aladdin into going into a cave to fetch a lamp.
Determined to marry the a princess, Aladdin	rubs at the lamp, revealing a more powerful genie.
With a few more tricks, Aladdin	uses wealth provided by the genie to amaze the sultan.
Although some misfortunes befall them, the couple	frees Aladdin from the cave.

Exercise 12B: Simple and Complete Subjects and Predicates

In the following sentences, underline the simple subject once and the simple predicate twice. Then, draw a vertical line between the complete subject and the complete predicate. The first is done for you.

These sentences are adapted from Norton Juster's *The Phantom Tollbooth.*

An ominous silence | dropped like a curtain around them.

Five very tall, thin gentlemen regally dressed in silks and satins, plumed hats, and buckled shoes | rushed up to the car.

A slavish concern for the composition of words | is the sign of a bankrupt intellect.

Most people | have forgotten me entirely.

My cabinet members | can do all sorts of things.

I | am quite ordinary.

The hours | passed.

He | stood bravely at the fortress door.

Exercise 12C: Diagramming Simple Subjects and Simple Predicates

On your own paper, diagram the simple subjects and simple predicates from Exercise 12B.

An ominous silence dropped like a curtain around them.

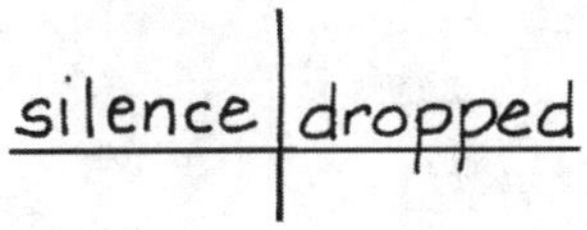

Five very tall, thin gentlemen regally dressed in silks and satins, plumed hats, and buckled shoes rushed up to the car.

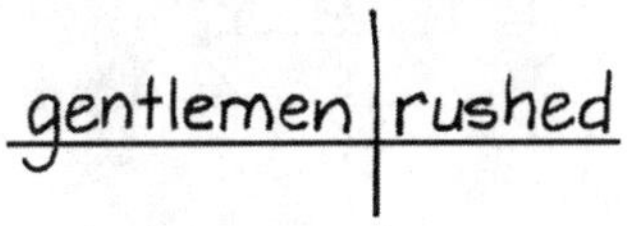

A slavish concern for the composition of words is the sign of a bankrupt intellect.

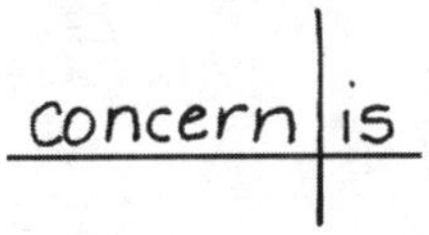

Most people have forgotten me entirely.

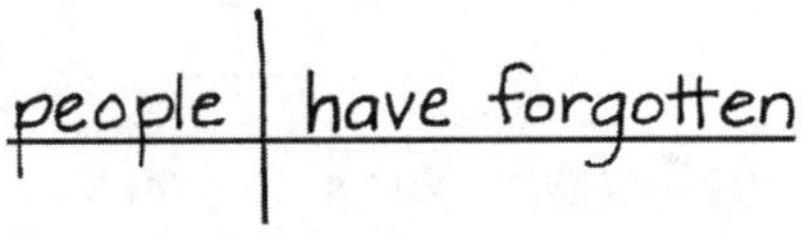

My cabinet members can do all sorts of things.

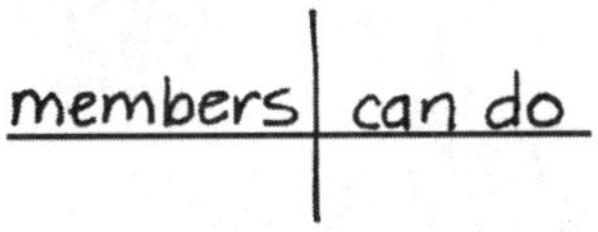

I am quite ordinary.

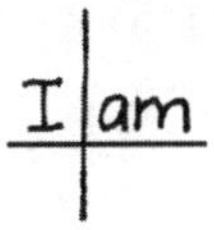

The hours passed.

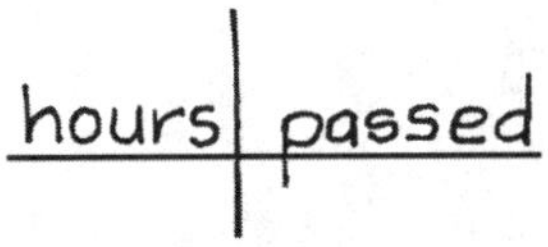

He stood bravely at the fortress door.

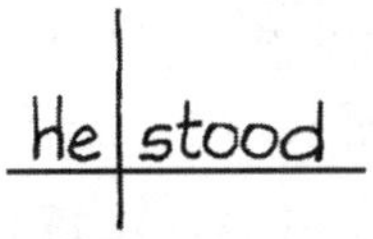

— REVIEW 1 —

Weeks 1-3

Topics
Concrete/Abstract Nouns
Descriptive Adjectives
Common/Proper Nouns
Capitalization of Proper Nouns and First Words in Sentences
Noun Gender
Pronouns and Antecedents
Action Verbs/State-of-Being Verbs
Helping Verbs
Subjects and Predicates
Complete Sentences
Types of Sentences

Review 1A: Types of Nouns

Fill in the blanks with the correct description of each noun. The first is done for you.

	Concrete / Abstract	Common / Proper	Gender (M, F, N)
Clara Barton	C	P	F
uncle	C	C	M
eye	C	C	N
incredulity	A	C	N
queen	C	C	F
Pythagoras	C	P	M
Lake Victoria	C	P	N
snore	C	C	N
New York Times	C	P	N
education	A	C	N
artistry	A	C	N

Review 1B: Types of Verbs

Underline the complete verbs in the following sentences. Identify any helping verbs as *HV*. Identify the main verb as *AV* for action verb or *BV* for state-of-being verb.

Magnets attract (AV) certain metals.

Every magnet has (AV) a positive pole and a negative pole.

The opposite poles are (HV) attracted (AV) to each other.

You can (HV) turn (AV) an iron object into a temporary magnet!

Rub (AV) a magnet on the item repeatedly in the same direction.

Inside the item, the poles will (HV) line (AV) up.

The item has (HV) been (HV) magnetized (AV)!

The poles do (HV) not remain (AV) that way.

The object will not be a magnet after a while.

Review 1C: Subjects and Predicates

Draw one line under the simple subject and two lines under the simple predicate in the following sentences. Remember that the predicate may be a verb phrase with more than one verb in it. If the subject is an understood "you" in a command, write "(you)" in the left margin and underline it once to indicate that it is the simple subject.

You can also make a magnetic compass.

(you) First, magnetize a needle by rubbing a magnet on it many times.

The needle should be inserted into a thin piece of cork.

A bowl of water is the next thing needed.

(you) Place the magnetized needle (with the cork) in the water.

The needle will point toward the north.

You can spin the needle around.

Because of the earth's magnetic poles, the needle will spin itself back toward the north.

(you) Just keep the needle away from the sides of the bowl.

The sides can interfere with the needle's rotation.

Review 1D: Parts of Speech

Identify the underlined words as *N* for noun, *P* for pronoun, *A* for adjective, *AV* for action verb, *HV* for helping verb, or *BV* for state-of-being verb.

The following passage is from Norton Juster's *The Phantom Tollbooth.*

"He (P) looks friendly enough," thought (AV) Milo (N), not sure just how friendly a friendly (A) bumblebee (N) should (HV) be (BV), and tried (AV) to think of a very difficult (A) word (N). "Spell (AV) 'vegetable,'" he suggested, for it (P) was (BV) one that always troubled (AV) him at school (N).

"That is a difficult one," said (AV) the bee (N), winking at the letter man (N). "Let (AV) me see (AV) now . . . hmmmmmm . . ." He frowned (AV) and wiped (AV) his brow (N) and paced (AV) slowly back and forth on top (N) of the wagon (N). "How much time (N) do (HV) I (P) have (AV)?"

"Just ten (A) seconds (N)," cried (AV) Milo excitedly. "Count (AV) them off, Tock (N)."

Review 1E: Capitalization and Punctuation

Use proofreading marks to indicate correct capitalization and punctuation in the following sentences. Be careful: Some of these may have more than one sentence, so ending punctuation will need to be inserted to split sentences correctly!

Small letter that should be capitalized: ≡ beneath the letter.

Italics: single underline

insert period: ⊙

insert exclamation point: ^!

insert question mark: ^?

insert quotation marks: ^"

ernest thayer wrote the famous baseball poem "casey at the bat" in 1888 ⊙

have you seen the beautiful work of the paper artist yulia brodskaya?

how beautiful you look today!

adriana caselotti starred as the title character's voice in snow white and the seven dwarfs.

after the 2000 summer olympics in sydney, australia, the international table tennis federation set a new standard size for balls at 40 millimeters. these balls moved more slowly than the 38-millimeter balls used previously, making the game easier to watch on television.

ray bradbury, who wrote fahrenheit 451 and many other works in a variety of genres, also wanted to be a magician.

the national anthem of canada is "o canada," composed and written in 1880.

on that famous 1492 voyage, christopher columbus captained the santa maria. brothers martín alonso pinzón and vicente yáñez pinzón captained the pinta and the niña, respectively.

Review 1F: Types of Sentences

Identify the following sentences as *S* for statement, *C* for command, *E* for exclamation, or *Q* for question. If the sentence is incomplete, write *I*.

The following sentences are from *The House on Mango Street*, by Sandra Cisneros. Some have been slightly adapted.

	Sentence Type
The boys and the girls live in separate worlds.	S
The boys in their universe and we in ours.	I
That does it!	E
Come here.	C
Which one is your house?	Q
Okay, I'll be your friend.	S
But only till next Tuesday.	I
How do I know this is so?	Q
Wait a minute.	C
Meme won.	S
And broke both arms.	I
The green metal cage, the porcelain table top, the family that spoke like guitars.	I
I like to tell stories.	S

WEEK 4

Verb Tenses

— LESSON 13 —

Nouns, Pronouns, and Verbs

Sentences

Simple Present, Simple Past, and Simple Future Tenses

Exercise 13A: Simple Tenses

	Simple Past	Simple Present	Simple Future
I	whispered	whisper	will whisper
You	boasted	boast	will boast
She	preserved	preserves	will preserve
We	sneezed	sneeze	will sneeze
They	stirred	stir	will stir

Exercise 13B: Using Consistent Tense

When you write, you should use consistent tense—if you begin a sentence in one tense, you should continue to use that same tense for any other verbs in the same sentence. The following sentences use two verb tenses. Cross out the second verb and rewrite it so that the tense of the second verb matches the tense of the first one.

The first sentence is done for you.

For a bit of fun, see if you can guess which board game each of these sentences is referring to!

The monsters will attack the castle and ~~knocked~~ will knock down the walls. *(Castle Panic)*

On her turn, Amy built a settlement and ~~trades~~ traded wool to Kendra in exchange for ore. *(Settlers of Catan)*

Everyone visits a variety of places in Japan and ~~kept~~ keeps track of his or her experiences. *(Tokaido)*

This city will be hit by an epidemic soon, and then we ~~have~~ will have another outbreak! *(Pandemic)*

Sean places trains on the board, and Amelie ~~will groan~~ groans at the disruption of her planned route. *(Ticket to Ride)*

I will reserve this sapphire card worth two points on this turn, and on my next turn I ~~purchased~~ will purchase it. *(Splendor)*

James chose fishing as his final action before the harvest and ~~will have~~ had plenty of food for his family. *(Agricola)*

Exercise 13C: Forming the Simple Past Tense

Using the rules for forming the simple past, put each one of the verbs in parentheses into the simple past. Write the simple past form in the blank. Be sure to spell the past forms of regular verbs correctly, and to use the correct forms of irregular verbs.

These sentences are taken from *What Katy Did*, by Susan Coolidge.

Of course Katy __was__ too young to understand these whispers, or the reasons why people were not disposed to think well of Mr. Spenser. The romance of the closed door and the lady whom nobody __saw__, __interested__ her very much. She __used__ to stop and stare at the windows, and wonder what was going on inside, till at last it __seemed__ as if she *must* know. So, one day she __took__ some flowers and Victoria, her favorite doll, and boldly __marched__ into the Spensers' yard.

She __tapped__ at the front door, but nobody __answered__. Then she tapped again. Still nobody answered. She __tried__ the door. It was locked. So shouldering Victoria, she __trudged__ round to the back of the house. As she __passed__ the side-door she saw that it was open a little way. She __knocked__ for the third time, and as no one __came__, she __went__ in, and passing through the little hall __began__ to tap at all the inside doors.

There __seemed__ to be no people in the house. Katy __peeped__ into the kitchen first. It was bare and forlorn. All sorts of dishes were standing about. There was no fire in the stove. The parlor was not much better. Mr. Spenser's boots __lay__ in the middle of the floor. There were dirty glasses on the table. On the mantle-piece was a platter with bones of meat upon it. Dust lay thick over everything, and the whole house __looked__ as if it hadn't been lived in for at least a year.

Katy __tried__ several other doors, all of which were locked, and then she __went__ up stairs. As she __stood__ on the top step, grasping her flowers, and a little doubtful what to do next, a feeble voice from a bed-room __called__ out:

"Who is there?"

— LESSON 14 —

Simple Present, Simple Past, and Simple Future Tenses

Progressive Present, Progressive Past, and Progressive Future Tenses

Exercise 14A: Forming the Simple Past and Simple Future Tenses

Form the simple past and simple future of the following regular verbs.

Past	Present	Future
stayed	stay	will stay
whispered	whisper	will whisper
scared	scare	will scare
troubled	trouble	will trouble
turned	turn	will turn
sinned	sin	will sin
stretched	stretch	will stretch
jammed	jam	will jam
hurried	hurry	will hurry

Exercise 14B: Progressive Tenses

Circle the ending of each verb. Underline the helping verbs.

is camping

were gluing

has been interrupting

was avoiding

am reaching

will be collecting

were suggesting

was polishing

Exercise 14C: Forming the Progressive Past, Present, and Future Tenses

Complete the following chart. Be sure to use the spelling rules above.

Note to Instructor: This exercise drills progressive verbs and also prepares the student for the introduction of person in next week's lessons. If the student asks why the helping verbs change, you may either say, "You'll find out next week" or turn to Lesson 18 and do it out of order. (The first method is recommended for students who are doing this course for the first time; person has not yet been covered in order to allow the student to concentrate on the tenses being introduced.)

	Progressive Past	Progressive Present	Progressive Future
I stitch	I was stitching	I am stitching	I will be stitching
I mourn	I was mourning	I am mourning	I will be mourning
I manage	I was managing	I am managing	I will be managing
I borrow	I was borrowing	I am borrowing	I will be borrowing
You communicate	You were communicating	You are communicating	You will be communicating
You visit	You were visiting	You are visiting	You will be visiting
You remain	You were remaining	You are remaining	You will be remaining
You step	You were stepping	You are stepping	You will be stepping
We belong	We were belonging	We are belonging	We will be belonging
We serve	We were serving	We are serving	We will be serving
We plan	We were planning	We are planning	We will be planning
We melt	We were melting	We are melting	We will be melting

Exercise 14D: Simple and Progressive Tenses

Fill in the blanks with the correct form of the verb in parentheses.

In 1928, Dr. Alexander Fleming __was returning__ from vacation when he __saw__ the mess in his petri dishes.

When he __looked__ at the dishes under his microscope, he __realized__ that a mold __was keeping__ the bacteria from growing.

This discovery __led__ to the development of penicillin.

In 1945, Fleming predicted that overusing penicillin could lead to resistant bacteria, and today, doctors are discovering that Fleming was correct.

Dr. Percy Spencer was working with a magnetron, which generated microwaves.

Spencer discovered that the waves from the magnetron were melting the chocolate he had in his pocket.

He also learned that popcorn popped when it was brought close to the magnetron.

People all over the world are enjoying the convenience of microwave ovens today because of Spencer's affinity for chocolate.

— LESSON 15 —

Simple Present, Simple Past, and Simple Future Tenses
Progressive Present, Progressive Past, and Progressive Future Tenses
Perfect Present, Perfect Past, and Perfect Future Tenses

Exercise 15A: Perfect Tenses
Fill in the blanks with the missing forms.

Simple Past	Perfect Past	Perfect Present	Perfect Future
I packed	I had packed	I have packed	I will have packed
I wailed	I had wailed	I have wailed	I will have wailed
I fried	I had fried	I have fried	I will have fried
I traveled	I had traveled	I have traveled	I will have traveled
We reflected	We had reflected	We have reflected	We will have reflected
We offered	We had offered	We have offered	We will have offered
We batted	We had batted	We have batted	We will have batted
We unlocked	We had unlocked	We have unlocked	We will have unlocked
He camped	He had camped	He has camped	He will have camped
He dreamed	He had dreamed	He has dreamed	He will have dreamed
He haunted	He had haunted	He has haunted	He will have haunted
He encouraged	He had encouraged	He has encouraged	He will have encouraged

Exercise 15B: Identifying Perfect Tenses

Identify the underlined verbs as perfect past, perfect present, or perfect future. The first one is done for you.

perfect present
I have decided to make an edible model of an animal cell.

perfect past
I had learned about the different parts of a cell before making my decision.

perfect present / perfect present
I have studied diagrams of cells, and I have looked at a few different cells under a microscope.

perfect past
Yesterday I needed to go to the grocery store because we had run out of eggs for my cake.

perfect present
Now I have baked the cake.

perfect present
Once the cake has cooled, I will use icing and candy to represent the parts of the cell.

perfect future
In a few hours, I will have created a beautiful—and tasty—cell model!

Exercise 15C: Perfect, Progressive, and Simple Tenses

Each underlined verb phrase has been labeled as past, present, or future. Add the label *perfect*, *progressive*, or *simple* to each one. The first one has been done for you.

This passage is adapted from Robert Lawson's *Robbut: A Tale of Tails.*

simple PAST / perfect PRESENT
"Goodness gracious, Robbut!" the Snake cried, "whatever's happened to you, and

simple PRESENT / simple PRESENT
what's wrong with your tail, or whoever's tail it is? It can't be yours, but it seems to be

simple PRESENT
on you. It looks like a Cat's, but no Cat would have that mussy a tail. What's this all about anyway?"

simple PAST / perfect PAST
Robbut rather sheepishly explained about it; how he had saved the Little Old Man

perfect PAST
from the trap and how the Little Old Man had given him a new tail.

simple PAST / simple PAST
"Well, I must say you made an awfully poor choice," exclaimed the Snake. "Of all the

perfect PRESENT
stupid things I've ever heard, that's about the stupidest—even for a Rabbit. What would anyone, especially you, want with a long, furry nuisance like that?

"Now there—" and he was twitching (progressive PAST) his own tail in the sunshine—"there's what I call (simple PRESENT) a tail. It's clean cut, useful, no trouble, and if I do say so, quite handsome. What's more, it will never get (simple FUTURE) muddy, stained, or spotted—or stuck up with burrs or pine needles. It sheds (simple PRESENT) water like a Duck and has (simple PRESENT) real life and style to it."

His tail was flickering (progressive PAST) and quivering in the sunshine, and it really did look most attractive and extremely lively. It certainly was neat and clean. Robbut eyed (simple PAST) it with envy and his unfortunate tail with regret.

— LESSON 16 —

Simple Present, Simple Past, and Simple Future Tenses
Progressive Present, Progressive Past, and Progressive Future Tenses
Perfect Present, Perfect Past, and Perfect Future Tenses
Irregular Verbs

Exercise 16A: Irregular Verb Forms: Simple Present, Simple Past, and Simple Future
Fill in the chart with the missing verb forms.

Note to Instructor: If this is the student's first time through the course, she has not yet covered number and person of verbs, which affects some irregular forms. If the student uses an incorrect form, simply tell her the correct form. Have her cross out the incorrect answer and write the correct answer in its place.

	Simple Past	Simple Present	Simple Future
I	overtook	overtake	will overtake
You	drew	draw	will draw
She	arose	arises	will arise
We	knelt	kneel	will kneel
They	said	say	will say
I	left	leave	will leave
You	drank	drink	will drink
He	bore	bears	will bear

	Simple Past	Simple Present	Simple Future
We	rang	ring	will ring
They	won	win	will win
I	heard	hear	will hear
You	fed	feed	will feed
It	stuck	sticks	will stick
We	bent	bend	will bend
They	stole	steal	will steal
I	stung	sting	will sting
You	shot	shoot	will shoot
We	beat	beat	will beat
They	slept	sleep	will sleep

Exercise 16B: Irregular Verbs, Progressive and Perfect Tenses

Fill in the remaining blanks. The first row is done for you.

Note to Instructor: This is only the first practice run with irregular verbs, designed to increase the student's familiarity—give all necessary help. Since we have not yet covered person and number in this workbook, the student should follow the pattern established in the first line of the chart.

Simple Present	Progressive Past	Progressive Present	Progressive Future	Perfect Past	Perfect Present	Perfect Future
overtake	was overtaking	am overtaking	will be overtaking	had overtaken	have overtaken	will have overtaken
draw	was drawing	am drawing	will be drawing	had drawn	have drawn	will have drawn
arise	was arising	am arising	will be arising	had arisen	have arisen	will have arisen
kneel	was kneeling	am kneeling	will be kneeling	had knelt	have knelt	will have knelt
say	was saying	am saying	will be saying	had said	have said	will have said
leave	was leaving	am leaving	will be leaving	had left	have left	will have left

Simple Present	Progressive Past	Progressive Present	Progressive Future	Perfect Past	Perfect Present	Perfect Future
drink	was drinking	am drinking	will be drinking	had drunk	have drunk	will have drunk
bear	was bearing	am bearing	will be bearing	had borne	have borne	will have borne
ring	was ringing	am ringing	will be ringing	had rung	have rung	will have rung
win	was winning	am winning	will be winning	had won	have won	will have won
hear	was hearing	am hearing	will be hearing	had heard	have heard	will have heard
feed	was feeding	am feeding	will be feeding	had fed	have fed	will have fed
stick	was sticking	am sticking	will be sticking	had stuck	have stuck	will have stuck
bend	was bending	am bending	will be bending	had bent	have bent	will have bent
steal	was stealing	am stealing	will be stealing	had stolen	have stolen	will have stolen
sting	was stinging	am stinging	will be stinging	had stung	have stung	will have stung
shoot	was shooting	am shooting	will be shooting	had shot	have shot	will have shot
beat	was beating	am beating	will be beating	had beaten	have beaten	will have beaten
sleep	was sleeping	am sleeping	will be sleeping	had slept	have slept	will have slept

WEEK 5

More About Verbs

— LESSON 17 —

Simple, Progressive, and Perfect Tenses
Subjects and Predicates
Parts of Speech and Parts of Sentences
Verb Phrases

Exercise 17A: Simple, Progressive, and Perfect Tenses

All the bolded verbs are in the past tense. Label each bolded verb as simple (*S*), progressive (*PROG*), or perfect (*PERF*). These sentences are adapted from George MacDonald's *At the Back of the North Wind.*

I cannot tell whether Diamond **knew** [S] what his mother **was thinking** [PROG], but I think I know. She **had heard** [PERF] something at church the day before, which **came** [S] back upon her—something like this, that she hadn't to eat for tomorrow as well as for today; and that what was not wanted couldn't be missed. So, instead of saying anything more, she **stretched** [S] out her hand for the basket, and she and Diamond **had** [S] their dinner.

And Diamond did enjoy it. For the drive and the fresh air **had made** [PERF] him quite hungry; and he did not, like his mother, trouble himself about what they should dine off that day week. The fact was he **had lived** [PERF] so long without any food at all at the back of the north wind, that he **knew** [S] quite well that food **was** [S] not essential to existence; that in fact, under certain circumstances, people could live without it well enough.

His mother did not speak much during their dinner. After it was over she **helped** [S] him to walk about a little, but he was not able for much and soon got tired. He did not get fretful, though. He was too glad of having the sun and the wind again, to fret because he could not run about. He **lay** [S] down on the dry sand, and his mother **covered** [S] him with a shawl. Then, as she **was sitting** [PROG] by his side, she **took** [S] a bit of work from her pocket. But Diamond **felt** [S] rather sleepy, and **turned** [S] on his side and **gazed** [S] sleepily over the sand. A few yards off he **saw** [S] something; it **was fluttering** [PROG].

Exercise 17B: Identifying and Diagramming Subjects and Predicates; Identifying Verb Tenses

Underline the subject once and the predicate twice in each sentence. Be sure to include both the main verb and any helping verbs when you underline the predicate. Identify the tense of each verb or verb phrase (*simple past*, *present*, or *future*; *progressive past*, *present*, or *future*; *perfect past*, *present*, or *future*) on the line. Then diagram each subject and predicate on your own paper.

These sentences are adapted from George MacDonald's *At the Back of the North Wind.*

His father had shut the door of his cab upon a fare. perfect past

father | had shut

Mr. Raymond took the little book. simple past

Mr. Raymond | took

That van is moving now. progressive present

van | is moving

I will tell my father about your goodness to me. simple future

I | will tell

He carried with him one pound one shilling and sixpence. simple past

He | carried

She was thinking of her twenty-one shillings and sixpence. progressive past

She | was thinking

With the help of the stone he scrambled out by the opening. simple past

he | scrambled

Why, that girl has been to the back of the north wind! perfect present

girl | has been

I will write it down. simple future

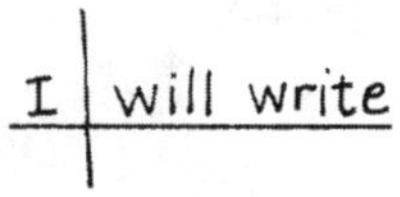

Nobody has ever heard it before? perfect present

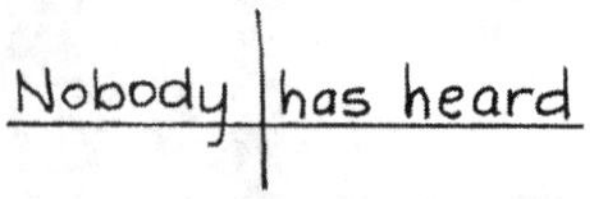

You will be sailing against me. progressive future

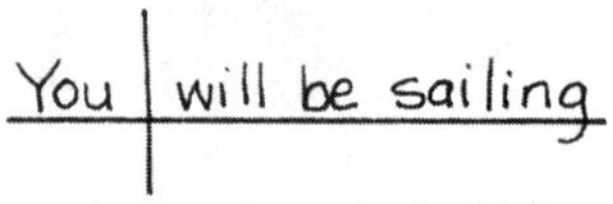

My older readers will have already discovered this. perfect future

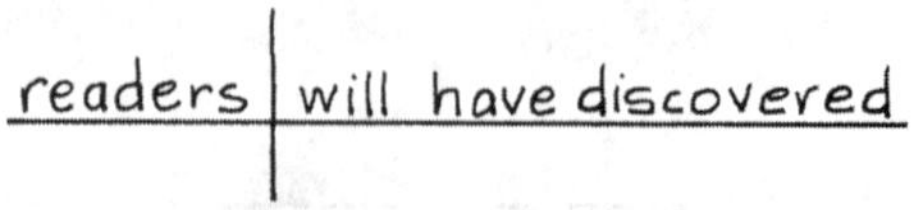

They were sweeping with the speed of the wind itself towards the sea. progressive past

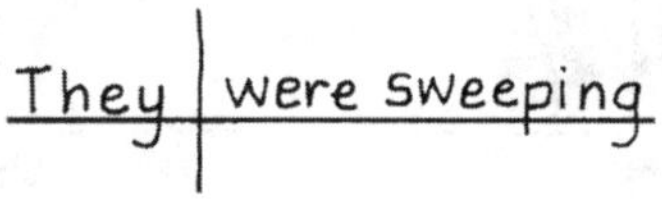

— LESSON 18 —

Verb Phrases

Person of the Verb

Conjugations

Exercise 18A: Third Person Singular Verbs

In the simple present conjugation, the third person singular verb changes by adding an *-s*. Read the following rules and examples for adding *-s* to verbs in order to form the third person singular. Then, rewrite the first person verbs as third person singular verbs. The first of each set is done for you.

Usually, add *-s* to form the third person singular verb.

First Person Verb	Third Person Singular Verb	
I battle	he	battles
I weigh	she	weighs
I inform	it	informs

Add *-es* to verbs ending in *-s*, *-sh*, *-ch*, *-x*, or *-z*.

First Person Verb	Third Person Singular Verb	
we bless	she	blesses
we attach	it	attaches
we mix	he	mixes

If a verb ends in *-y* after a consonant, change the *y* to *i* and add *-es*.

First Person Verb	Third Person Singular Verb	
I multiply	it	multiplies
I dry	he	dries
I fancy	she	fancies

If a verb ends in *-y* after a vowel, just add *-s*.

First Person Verb	Third Person Singular Verb	
we pay	he	pays
we annoy	she	annoys
we prey	it	preys

If a verb ends in *-o* after a consonant, form the plural by adding *-es*.

First Person Verb	Third Person Singular Verb	
I lasso	she	lassoes
I veto	it	vetoes
I undo	he	undoes

Exercise 18B: Simple Present Tenses

Choose the correct form of the simple present verb in parentheses, based on the person. Cross out the incorrect form.

Thea and her brother Nazim (want / ~~wants~~) to surprise their parents.

Thea (~~tidy~~ / tidies) her room while Nazim (~~clean~~ / cleans) the bathroom.

They (work / ~~works~~) together to clean all the floors.

Nazim (~~start~~ / starts) dinner right before their parents (call / ~~calls~~) to say they'll be home soon.

"I (think / ~~thinks~~) we should have some flowers on the table," (~~say~~ / says) Thea.

"If you (pick / ~~picks~~) some from the back yard, I will get a vase ready," (~~reply~~ / replies) Nazim.

Thea (~~get~~ / gets) the flowers and (~~come~~ / comes) back inside.

When their parents (arrive / ~~arrives~~) a few minutes later, the siblings (wish / ~~wishes~~) them a happy anniversary.

Exercise 18C: Perfect Present Tenses

Write the correct form of the perfect present verb in the blank. These sentences are from Jules Verne's *Around the World in Eighty Days.*

"You have forgotten [forget] nothing?" asked he.

I'm off, you see; and if you will examine my passport when I get back, you will be able to judge whether I have accomplished [accomplish] the journey agreed upon.

But the East India Company has now passed [pass] away, leaving the British possessions in India directly under the control of the Crown.

You have been [be] serviceable and devoted. I have paid [pay] for your service, but not for your devotion.

He has not made [make] his appearance since yesterday.

At least I have not missed [miss] the steamer, which is the most important thing.

— LESSON 19 —

Person of the Verb

Conjugations

State-of-Being Verbs

Exercise 19A: Forming Progressive Present Tenses

Fill in the blanks with the correct helping verbs.

Regular Verb, Progressive Present

	Singular	Plural
First person	I am commanding	we are commanding
Second person	you are commanding	you are commanding
Third person	he, she, it is commanding	they are commanding

Exercise 19B: Forming Progressive Past and Future Tenses

Regular Verb, Progressive Past

	Singular	Plural
First person	I was commanding	we were commanding
Second person	you were commanding	you were commanding
Third person	he, she, it was commanding	they were commanding

Regular Verb, Progressive Future

	Singular	Plural
First person	I ___will be___ commanding	we ___will be___ commanding
Second person	you ___will be___ commanding	you ___will be___ commanding
Third person	he, she, it ___will be___ commanding	they ___will be___ commanding

— LESSON 20 —

Irregular State-of-Being Verbs

Helping Verbs

Exercise 20A: Simple Tenses of the Verb *Have*

Try to fill in the missing blanks in the chart below, using your own sense of what sounds correct as well as the hints you may have picked up from the conjugations already covered. Be sure to use pencil so that any incorrect answers can be erased and corrected!

Simple Present

	Singular	Plural
First person	I ___have___	we ___have___
Second person	you ___have___	you ___have___
Third person	he, she, it ___has___	they ___have___

Simple Past

	Singular	Plural
First person	I ___had___	we ___had___
Second person	you ___had___	you ___had___
Third person	he, she, it ___had___	they ___had___

Simple Future

	Singular	Plural
First person	I will ___have___	we ___will have___
Second person	you ___will have___	you ___will have___
Third person	he, she, it ___will have___	they ___will have___

Exercise 20B: Simple Tenses of the Verb *Do*

Try to fill in the missing blanks in the chart below, using your own sense of what sounds correct as well as the hints you may have picked up from the conjugations already covered. Be sure to use pencil so that any incorrect answers can be erased and corrected!

Simple Present

	Singular	Plural
First person	I ___do___	we ___do___
Second person	you ___do___	you ___do___
Third person	he, she, it ___does___	they ___do___

Simple Past

	Singular	Plural
First person	I did	we did
Second person	you did	you did
Third person	he, she, it did	they did

Simple Future

	Singular	Plural
First person	I will do	we will do
Second person	you will do	you will do
Third person	he, she, it will do	they will do

WEEK 6

Nouns and Verbs in Sentences

— LESSON 21 —

Person of the Verb
Conjugations
Noun-Verb/Subject-Predicate Agreement

Exercise 21A: Person and Number of Pronouns

Identify the person and number of the underlined pronouns. Cross out the incorrect verb(s) in parentheses. The first one is done for you.

These sentences are adapted from L. M. Montgomery's *Anne of the Island.*

	Person	Singular/Plural
You (remember / ~~remembers~~), Marilla, what a consuming desire I had to sleep in the spare room bed.	second	singular
They (~~am~~ / ~~is~~ / are) all nice, kind, motherly souls.	third	plural
Wherever I (go / ~~goes~~),	first	singular
they (confront / ~~confronts~~) me.	third	plural
It (~~am~~ / is / ~~are~~) just the end of the beginning.	third	singular
She (~~were~~ / was) the prettiest freshette I saw to-day.	third	singular
We (~~am~~ / ~~is~~ / are) going for a walk in the park.	first	plural
He (~~have~~ / has) always been crazy about you.	third	singular
You all (do / ~~does~~) well to remember him.	second	plural

Exercise 21B: Identifying Subjects and Predicates

Draw two lines underneath each simple predicate and one line underneath each simple subject in the following sentences. If a phrase comes between the subject and the predicate, put parentheses around it to show that it does not affect the subject-predicate agreement.

The sentences below are taken or adapted from *Creatures of the Sea: Rays* by Kris Hirschmann.

About five hundred species (of rays) exist around the world.

The skate family, (a type of ray), has about two hundred species.

A ray's flat body is called a disc.

At only four inches across, the smallest ray is the shortnose electric ray.

Because of the position of its eyes, a ray cannot see anything directly below itself.

Other senses compensate for this.

A tail (with spikes and venomous barbs) serves as a defense mechanism for some rays.

Exercise 21C: Subject-Verb Agreement

Cross out the incorrect verb in parentheses so that subject and predicate agree in number and person. Be careful of any confusing phrases between the subject and predicate.

Ravi and Philip (want/~~wants~~) to see what plant cells look like.
Ravi's mother, after a bit of instruction, (~~allow~~/allows) them to use her microscope.
Philip (~~tear~~/tears) a small bit of the skin off an onion and (~~place~~/places) it on a slide.
The boys (remember/~~remembers~~) that they (need/~~needs~~) to add a drop of water.
Then Ravi, working carefully, (~~put~~/puts) a cover slip on top.
Once the slide (~~am~~/is/~~are~~) under the microscope, the two boys (take/~~takes~~) turns looking at it.
Each boy (~~draw~~/draws) a picture of what he (~~see~~/sees).

— LESSON 22 —

Formation of Plural Nouns
Collective Nouns

Exercise 22A: Collective Nouns

Write the collective noun for each description. Then fill in an appropriate singular verb for each sentence. (Use the simple present tense!) The first one is done for you.

Description		Collective Noun	Verb	
a group of teachers working at a school	The	faculty	instructs	the students.
several dancers performing together	The	troupe OR company	dances	beautifully.
a group of listeners	The	audience	applauds	loudly.
several experts	The	panel	debates	animatedly.
many sailors on a ship	The	crew	navigates	well.
two shoes	This	pair	is	too tight.
several bananas together	This	bunch	is	brown.

Exercise 22B: Plural Noun Forms

Read each rule and the example out loud. Then rewrite the singular nouns as plural nouns in the spaces provided.

Note to Instructor: Make sure that the student reads the rules and examples out loud, not to herself!

Usually, add -*s* to a noun to form the plural.

Singular Noun	Plural Noun
beginner	beginners
snail	snails
airport	airports
morning	mornings

Add -*es* to nouns ending in -*s*, -*sh*, -*ch*, -*x*, or -*z*.

Singular Noun	Plural Noun
kiss	kisses
crash	crashes
watch	watches
mailbox	mailboxes
klutz	klutzes

If a noun ends in -*y* after a consonant, change the *y* to *i* and add -*es*.

Singular Noun	Plural Noun
activity	activities
spy	spies
tendency	tendencies
memory	memories

If a noun ends in -*y* after a vowel, just add -*s*.

Singular Noun	Plural Noun
tray	trays
boy	boys
monkey	monkeys
railway	railways

Some words that end in -*f or -fe* form their plurals differently. You must change the *f* or *fe* to *v* and add -*es*.

Singular Noun	Plural Noun
half	halves
loaf	loaves
wolf	wolves
calf	calves

Words that end in -*ff* form their plurals by simply adding -*s*.

Singular Noun	Plural Noun
muff	muffs
handcuff	handcuffs
knockoff	knockoffs

Some words that end in a single *-f* can form their plurals either way.

Singular Noun	Plural Noun
hoof	hoofs/hooves
wharf	wharfs/wharves

If a noun ends in *-o* after a vowel, just add *-s*.

Singular Noun	Plural Noun
video	videos
embryo	embryos

(note that the "y" makes a vowel sound in this word!)

Singular Noun	Plural Noun
stereo	stereos
kazoo	kazoos

If a noun ends in *-o* after a consonant, form the plural by adding *-es*.

Singular Noun	Plural Noun
torpedo	torpedoes
peccadillo	peccadilloes
volcano	volcanoes
embargo	embargoes

To form the plural of foreign words ending in *-o*, just add *-s*.

Singular Noun	Plural Noun
bonobo	bonobos
taco	tacos
chorizo	chorizos
piccolo	piccolos
silo	silos

Irregular plurals don't follow any of these rules!

Singular Noun	Irregular Plural Noun
cactus	cacti
vertex	vertices
shrimp	shrimp
bison	bison
datum	data
offspring	offspring
parenthesis	parentheses
criterion	criteria

Exercise 22C: Plural Nouns

Complete the following excerpt by filling in the plural form of each noun in parentheses. The following passage is condensed from Frances Hodgson Burnett's *The Secret Garden*.

Mary asked no more (question) questions but waited in the darkness of her corner, keeping her (eye) eyes on the window. The carriage (lamp) lamps cast (ray) rays of light a little distance ahead of them and she caught (glimpse) glimpses of the (thing) things they passed. After they had left the station they had driven through a tiny village and she had seen whitewashed (cottage) cottages and the (light) lights of a public house. Then they had passed a church and a vicarage and a little shop-window or so in a cottage with (toy) toys and (sweet) sweets and odd (thing) things set out for sale. Then they were on the highroad and she saw (hedge) hedges and (tree) trees. After that there seemed nothing different for a long time—or at least it seemed a long time to her.

At last the (horse) horses began to go more slowly, as if they were climbing up-hill, and presently there seemed to be no more (hedge) hedges and no more (tree) trees. She could see nothing, in fact, but a dense darkness on either side. She leaned forward and pressed her face against the window just as the carriage gave a big jolt.

"Eh! We're on the moor now sure enough," said Mrs. Medlock.

The carriage (lamp) lamps shed a yellow light on a rough-looking road which seemed to be cut through (bush) bushes and low growing (thing) things which ended in the great expanse of dark apparently spread out before and around them. A wind was rising and making a singular, wild, low, rushing sound.

"It's—it's not the sea, is it?" said Mary, looking round at her companion.

"No, not it," answered Mrs. Medlock. "Nor it isn't (field) fields nor (mountain) mountains, it's just (mile) miles and (mile) miles and (mile) miles of wild land that nothing grows on but heather and gorse and broom, and nothing lives on but wild (pony) ponies and (sheep) sheep."

They drove into a clear space and stopped before an immensely long but low-built house which seemed to ramble round a stone court. At first Mary thought that there were no (light) lights at all in the (window) windows, but as she got out of the carriage she saw that one room in a corner up-stairs showed a dull glow.

The entrance door was a huge one made of massive, curiously shaped (panel) panels of oak studded with big iron (nail) nails and bound with great iron (bar) bars. It opened into an enormous hall, which was so dimly lighted that the (face) faces in the (portrait) portraits on the (wall) walls and the (figure) figures in the (suit) suits of armor made Mary feel that she did not want to look at them.

— LESSON 23 —

Plural Nouns
Descriptive Adjectives
Possessive Adjectives
Contractions

Exercise 23A: Introduction to Possessive Adjectives

Read the following nouns. Choose a person that you know to possess each of the items. Write that person's name, an apostrophe, and an *s* to form a possessive adjective.

Note to Instructor: Even if the person's name ends in -*s*, the student should still add 's to form the possessive: "Marcus's football."

Example: Cecily	Cecily's	encyclopedia
	[Name]'s	water bottle
	[Name]'s	ticket to *Phantom of the Opera*
	[Name]'s	capybara
	[Name]'s	calculator
	[Name]'s	growl

Exercise 23B: Singular and Plural Possessive Adjective Forms

Fill in the chart with the correct forms. The first row is done for you. Both regular and irregular nouns are included.

Noun	Singular Possessive	Plural	Plural Possessive
pencil	pencil's	pencils	pencils'
grass	grass's	grasses	grasses'
robin	robin's	robins	robins'
creator	creator's	creators	creators'
bison	bison's	bison	bison's
potato	potato's	potatoes	potatoes'
island	island's	islands	islands'
motion	motion's	motions	motions'
knife	knife's	knives	knives'
fireman	fireman's	firemen	firemen's
fairy	fairy's	fairies	fairies'

Exercise 23C: Common Contractions

Drop the letters in grey print and write the contraction in the blank. The first one is done for you.

Full Form	Common Contraction	Full Form	Common Contraction
you had	you'd	would not	wouldn't
I will	I'll	we would	we'd
could not	couldn't	it has	it's
have not	haven't	I had	I'd

they will	they'll	what has	what's
he had	he'd	does not	doesn't
when is	when's	she will	she'll
they would	they'd	should not	shouldn't

— LESSON 24 —

Possessive Adjectives
Contractions
Compound Nouns

Exercise 24A: Using Possessive Adjectives Correctly

Cross out the incorrect word in parentheses.

(~~Its~~ / It's) very icy out there; I'm not sure if the car will be able to make (its / ~~it's~~) way up the hill.
I want to put (his / ~~he's~~) hat back before (~~his~~ / he's) had a chance to miss it.
(~~Your~~ / You're) the famous detective, right? I've read (your / ~~you're~~) book!
(Their / ~~They're~~) alibis prove that (~~their~~ / they're) innocent.
(~~Hers~~ / She's) adamant that the jacket is not (yours / ~~your's~~); (~~its~~ / it's) (hers / ~~she's~~).
(~~His~~ /He's) trying to adjust (their/ ~~they're~~) microphones; (~~their~~ /they're) starting the conference soon.
(Its / ~~It's~~) head drooping, the dog walked through the rain toward (its / ~~it's~~) favorite hole.
When (~~your~~ / you're) feeling sleepy, (your / ~~you're~~) bed is a welcome sight.
(~~Its~~ / It's) almost time; (~~hers~~ / she's) going to be here any minute.
If (yours / ~~your's~~) is the red car, you should know that (your / ~~you're~~) lights were left on.

Exercise 24B: Compound Nouns

Underline each simple subject once and each simple predicate (verb) twice. Circle each compound noun.

The restrooms are down the hallway.

I have selected new curtains for the living room.

Captain Picard is my favorite character on *Star Trek: The Next Generation*.

I enjoy our city's fireworks on Independence Day.

The queen's lady-in-waiting was standing on the other side of the drawbridge.

Monday's earthquake startled my great-aunt.

A grand jury has found sufficient evidence for the indictment of the ninety-three-year-old.

Hazel remembered her password.

Exercise 24C: Plurals of Compound Nouns

Write the plural of each singular compound noun in parentheses in the blanks to complete the sentences.

Marie Curie was the first person to win two (Nobel Prize) Nobel Prizes.

My friend and I discovered that both our (mother-in-law) mothers-in-law live in (cul-de-sac) culs-de-sac in this neighborhood.

> **Note to Instructor:** Although culs-de-sac is the correct plural, cul-de-sacs will also be listed as an acceptable alternative in some dictionaries.

All the (washing machine) washing machines are already in use.

Indoor (swimming pool) swimming pools are a great place to exercise in the winter.

Last night, I dreamed that (truckful) truckfuls of (catfish) catfish were being delivered to my house!

The women talking over there are not medical doctors, but (doctor of philosophy) doctors of philosophy.

How many (cupful) cupfuls of sugar did you put in these cookies?

The (lieutenant colonel) lieutenant colonels agreed to take the issue to their (higher-up) higher-ups.

— REVIEW 2 —

Weeks 4-6

Topics
Simple, Progressive, and Perfect Tenses
Conjugations
Irregular Verbs
Subject/Verb Agreement
Possessives
Compound Nouns
Contractions

Review 2A: Verb Tenses

Write the tense of each underlined verb phrase on the line in the right-hand margin: simple past, present, or future; progressive past, present, or future; or perfect past, present, or future. Watch out for words that interrupt verb phrases but are not helping verbs (such as *not*).

These sentences are adapted from Sir Walter Scott's *Ivanhoe*.

	Verb Tense
The date of our story refers to a period towards the end of the reign of Richard I, when his return from his long captivity had become an event rather wished than hoped for by his despairing subjects.	simple present perfect past
Reginald Front-de-Boeuf is coming down to this country in person, and we shall soon see how little Cedric's trouble will avail him.	progressive present simple future simple future
The upper dress of this personage resembled that of his companion.	simple past
Silk and embroidery distinguished their dresses.	simple past
These were forming, at the same time, a striking contrast with the martial simplicity of his own attire.	progressive past
I have seen no maiden so beautiful since Pentecost was a twelve-month.	perfect present
Prior, your collar is in danger; I will wear it over my gorget in the lists at Ashby-de-la-Zouche.	simple present simple future
One grisly old wolf-dog alone had planted himself close by the chair of state, and was occasionally putting his large hairy head upon his master's knee.	perfect past progressive past
He had exchanged his shirt of mail for an under tunic of dark purple silk.	perfect past

He <u>followed</u> modestly the last	simple past
of the train which <u>entered</u> the hall.	simple past
My vow <u>binds</u> me to advance no farther upon this floor of my fathers.	simple present
My steward <u>has expounded</u> to you the cause of my seeming discourtesy.	perfect present
I <u>will have marred</u> his archery.	perfect future
But our bards <u>are</u> no more;	simple present
our deeds <u>are</u> lost in those of another race—our	simple present
language—our very name <u>is hastening</u> to decay,	progressive present
and none <u>mourns</u> for it save one solitary old man.	simple present

Review 2B: Verb Formations

Fill in the charts with the correct conjugations of the missing verbs. Identify the person of each group of verbs.

PERSON: Third

	Past	Present	Future
SIMPLE	she carried	she carries	she will carry
PROGRESSIVE	she was carrying	she is carrying	she will be carrying
PERFECT	she had carried	she has carried	she will have carried

PERSON: First

	Past	Present	Future
SIMPLE	I cycled	I cycle	I will cycle
PROGRESSIVE	I was cycling	I am cycling	I will be cycling
PERFECT	I had cycled	I have cycled	I will have cycled

PERSON: Second

	Past	Present	Future
SIMPLE	you gathered	you gather	you will gather
PROGRESSIVE	you were gathering	you are gathering	you will be gathering
PERFECT	you had gathered	you have gathered	you will have gathered

PERSON: Third

	Past	Present	Future
SIMPLE	they walked	they walk	they will walk
PROGRESSIVE	they were walking	they are walking	they will be walking
PERFECT	they had walked	they have walked	they will have walked

Review 2C: Person and Subject/Verb Agreement

Cross out the incorrect verb or contraction in parentheses. The following sentences are taken or adapted from the Irish story "Deirdre and the Sons of Uisneach" as retold by Una Leavy in *Irish Fairy Tales and Legends.*

The stars never (~~lies~~ / lie)!
We (~~has~~ / have) looked at the stars to see this baby's future.
She (is / ~~are~~) only a little baby!
When she (grows / ~~grow~~) up, I will marry her myself.
Naoise, son of Uisneach, (is / ~~are~~) the only such man in the world.
I only (~~wants~~ / want) to be with you, Naoise.
Conor's men (~~is~~ / are) just behind us!
When morning came, they (~~was~~ / were) near the sea again.
King Conor (has / ~~have~~) forgiven you! He (wants / ~~want~~) you to come home.
You (~~doesn't~~ / don't) know how I (~~has~~ / have) longed for this news!
The king (has / ~~have~~) asked you to his fort at once. You, Fergus, (~~has~~ / have) been invited to a harvest feast.

Review 2D: Possessives and Compound Nouns

Complete the chart below, writing the singular possessive, plural, and plural possessive of each singular pronoun or compound noun. The first one has been done for you.

Noun	Possessive	Plural	Plural Possessive
nightmare	nightmare's	nightmares	nightmares'
dragonfly	dragonfly's	dragonflies	dragonflies'
she	her	they	their
has-been	has-been's	has-beens	has-beens'
I	my	we	our
grapefruit	grapefruit's	grapefruit	grapefruits'
toothbrush	toothbrush's	toothbrushes	toothbrushes'
you	your	you	your
father-in-law	father-in-law's	fathers-in-law	fathers-in-law's
congresswoman	congresswoman's	congresswomen	congresswomen's
it	its	they	their
crybaby	crybaby's	crybabies	crybabies'
he	his	they	their
runner-up	runner-up's	runners-up	runners-up's

Review 2E: Plurals and Possessives

In the following sentences, provide the possessive, the plural, or the plural possessive for each noun in parentheses as indicated. These sentences are from *The Wind in the Willows,* by Kenneth Grahame.

Why can't (fellow, plural) fellows be allowed to do what they like when they like and as they like, instead of other (fellow, plural) fellows sitting on (bank, plural) banks and watching them all the time and making (remark, plural) remarks and poetry and (thing, plural) things about them?

Some ten (minute, plural possessive) minutes' hard work, and the point of the (Rat, possessive) Rat's cudgel struck something that sounded hollow.

In accordance with the kindly (Badger, possessive) Badger's (injunction, plural) injunctions, the two tired (animal, plural) animals came down to breakfast very late next morning.

The (hedgehog, plural) hedgehogs dropped their (spoon, plural) spoons, rose to their (foot, plural) feet, and ducked their (head, plural) heads respectfully as the two entered.

The (Mole, possessive) Mole's thoughts ran a good deal on supper.

Your own idea, those little (sleeping-bunk, plural) sleeping-bunks in the wall? Capital!

The result was not so very depressing after all, though of course it might have been better; a tin of (sardine, plural) sardines —a box of (captain, possessive) captain's (biscuit, plural) biscuits, nearly full—and a German sausage encased in silver paper.

Mole saw his little (friend, plural possessive) friends' (face, plural) faces brighten and beam as they fell to without delay.

Review 2F: Contractions

In the following sentences, form contractions from the words in parentheses. These sentences are adapted from Andrew Peterson's *The Warden and the Wolf King.*

I never thought I'd (I would) see ye again!
I guess that's (that is) the downward fork.
Why don't (do not) you love me?
Of course it's (it is) real.
And we're (we are) going to fight.
You'd (You had) better have that dagger ready.
You're (You are) still a Throne Warden.
The sight made Sara's heart ache like it hadn't (had not) in years.
She didn't (did not) allow herself to hope that she might see her own parents again.
Who's (Who is) hungry?
I think you'll (you will) find that many of us at Clovenfast have...quirks.
And yes, he's (he is) alive.
If what Cadwick said is true, they'll (they will) be wilder.
There's (There is) one just ahead.
And once we're (we are) out, what then?
I've (I have) done my best to teach the replacements the messenger posts.
"Let's (Let us) eat," Kal said.
Janner couldn't (could not) see his eyes.
And I'm (I am) proud to be your brother.
We'll (We will) eat on the way.

WEEK 7

Compounds and Conjunctions

— LESSON 25 —

Contractions
Compound Nouns
Diagramming Compound Nouns
Compound Adjectives
Diagramming Adjectives
Articles

Exercise 25A: Contractions Review

Write the two words that form each contraction on the blanks to the right. Some contractions have more than one correct answer. The first is done for you.

Contraction	Helping Verb	Other Word
we'd	would OR had	we
she'll	will	she
I'm	am	I
didn't	did	not
you've	have	you
isn't	is	not
weren't	were	not
it'll	will	it
they're	are	they

Exercise 25B: Diagramming Adjectives and Compound Nouns

On your own paper, diagram every word of the following sentences.

Our solar system moves.

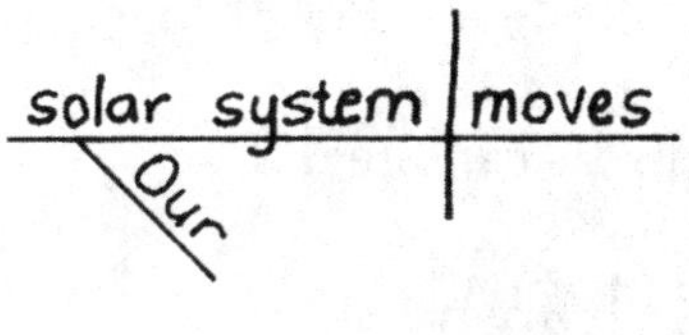

Louisa May Alcott wrote.

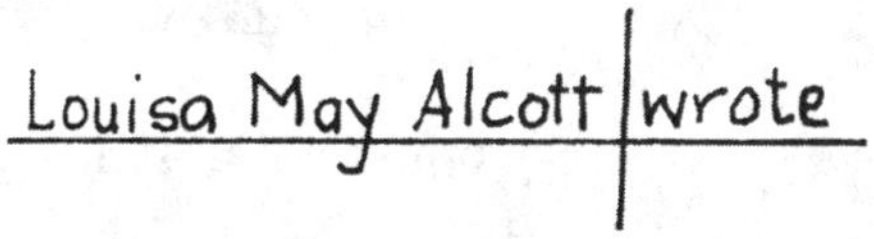

Melissa's high school instructs.

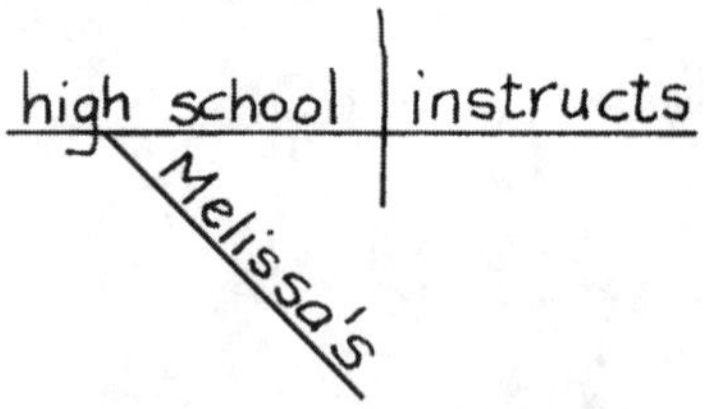

Good hearing aids assist.

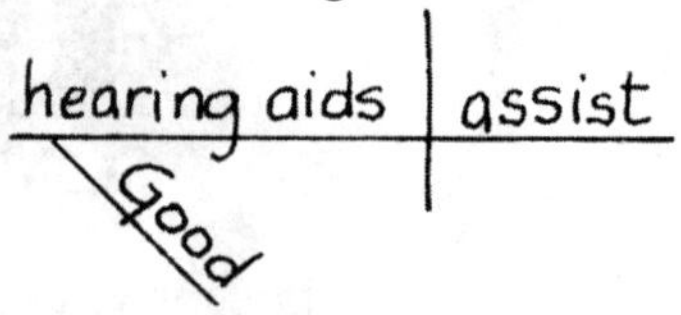

Exercise 25C: Compound Nouns

Using the list of words below, make as many single-word compound nouns as you can. Each word in the list can be used *at least* twice.

Note to Instructor: Accept any word that can be found in the dictionary!

ball	book	case	cut	fall
foot	mark	rest	room	suit
store	snow	water	work	

ballroom	bookcase	bookmark	bookstore
bookwork	casebook	casework	cutwater
cutwork	football	footfall	footrest
footwork	restroom	snowball	snowfall
snowsuit	storeroom	suitcase	waterfall
watermark	waterwork	workbook	workroom

Exercise 25D: Compound Adjectives

Correctly place hyphens in the following phrases.

four hundred fifty-one degrees Fahrenheit

the mixed-up files

the life-changing magic

a fifty-year friendship

twenty-two high-end watches

a two-day-old lamb

a germ-destroying air purifier

Exercise 25E: Diagramming Adjectives, Compound Nouns, and Compound Adjectives

On your own paper, diagram every word in the following sentences.

The old two-story house collapsed.

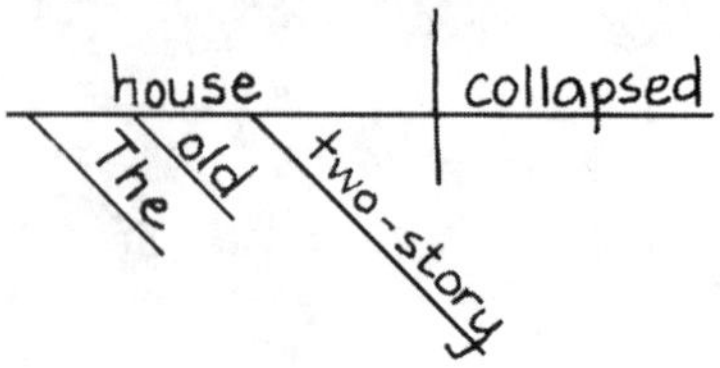

Fragile eggshells can break.

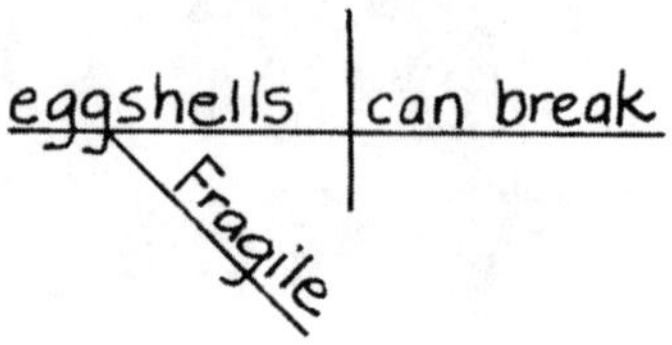

An out-of-breath police officer hurried.

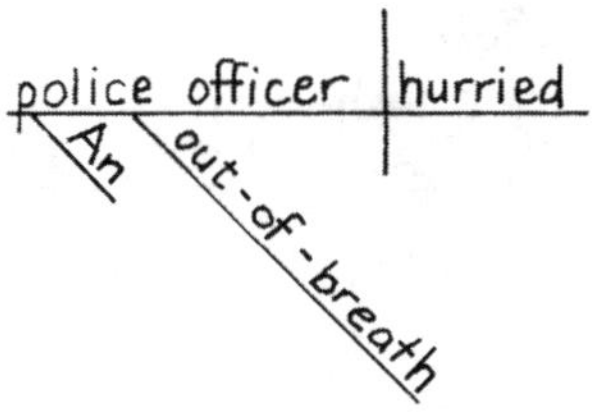

A sweet-smelling yellow flower had opened.

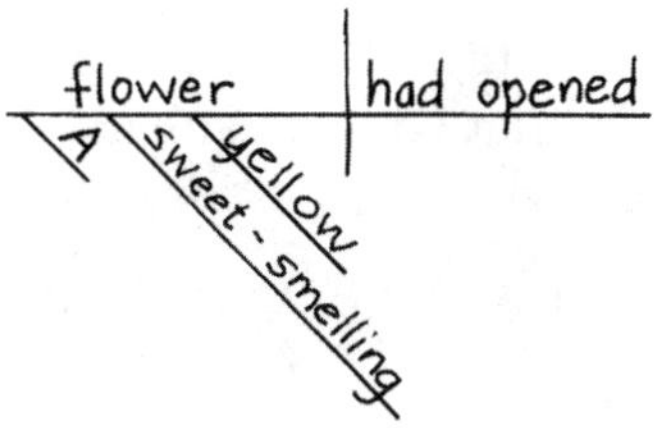

Sixty-three left-handed men responded.

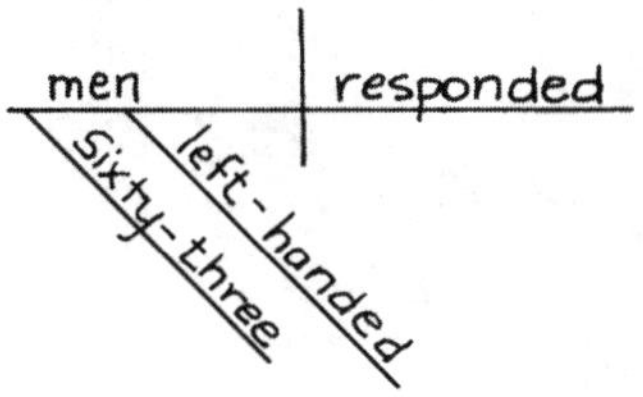

— LESSON 26 —

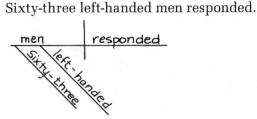

Compound Subjects
The Conjunction *And*
Compound Predicates
Compound Subject-Predicate Agreement

Exercise 26A: Identifying Subjects, Predicates, and Conjunctions

Underline the subjects once and the predicates twice in each sentence. Circle the conjunctions that join them. The first one is done for you.

These sentences are adapted from Jack London's *The Call of the Wild.*

He drank eagerly, and later bolted a generous meal of raw meat.

All passiveness and unconcern had dropped from them.

An oath from Perrault, the resounding impact of a club upon a bony frame, and a shrill yelp of pain, heralded the breaking forth of pandemonium.

Here were many men, and countless dogs.

The hair rose along his back and stood on end across his shoulders and up his neck.

He whittled and listened and gave monosyllabic replies and terse advice.

Exercise 26B: Diagramming Compound Subjects and Predicates

Draw one line under the subject[s] and two lines under the predicate[s] in the following sentences. Circle any conjunctions that connect subjects and/or predicates. When you are finished, diagram the subjects, predicates, and conjunctions ONLY of each sentence on your own paper.

These sentences are adapted from the Britannica Illustrated Science Library's *Plants, Algae, and Fungi.*

The gametes, spores, and seeds of plants can move about, especially with the help of water and wind.

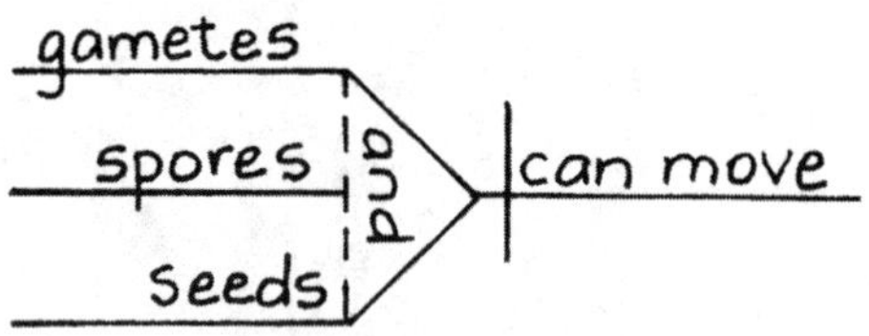

Grasses grow and reproduce in the long hours of summer daylight.

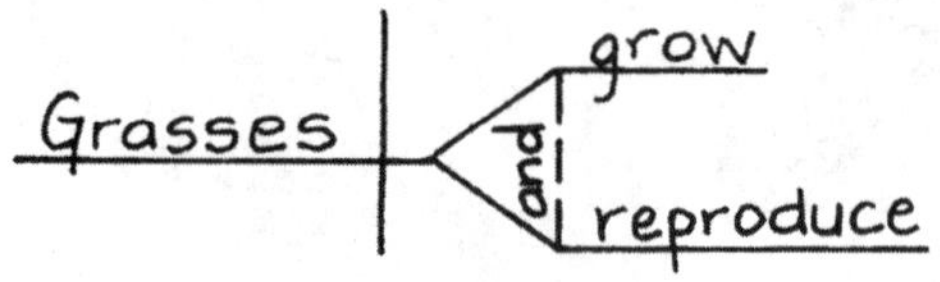

Red algae can thrive at relatively high temperatures and live inside thermal water vents.

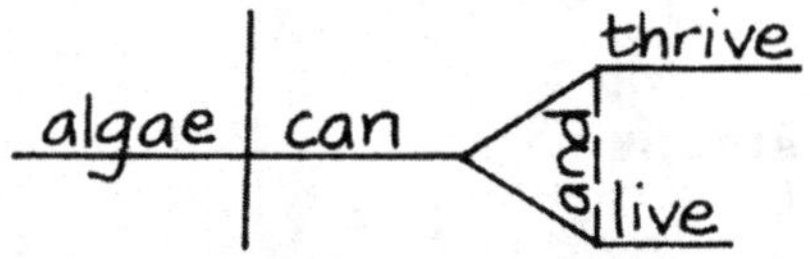

Optimal temperature and appropriate quantities of water and air are the important factors for a seed's awakening.

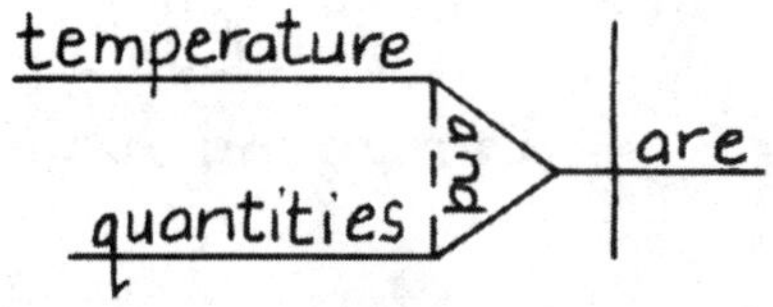

Orchids' flowers are large and very colorful and secrete a sugary nectar.

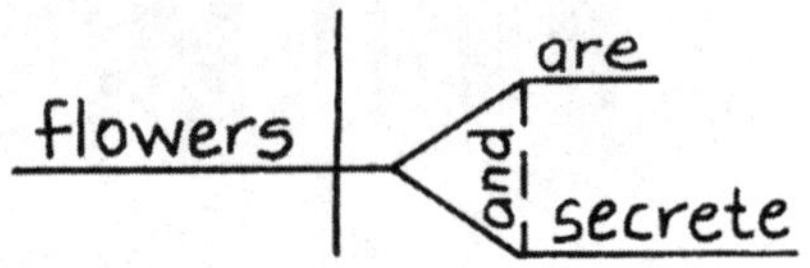

Water and nutrients are sufficient for the cultivation of tomatoes.

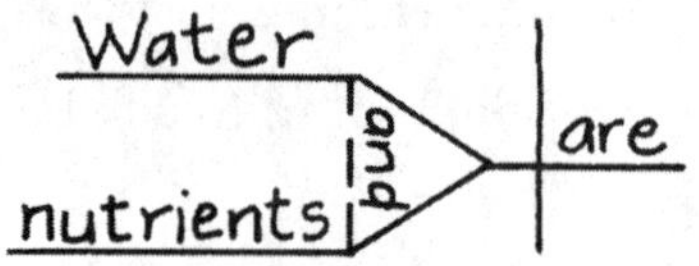

Exercise 26C: Forming Compound Subjects and Verbs

Combine each of these sets of simple sentences into one sentence with a compound subject and/or a compound predicate joined by *and.* Use your own paper.

The boy plays with the ball.
The dog plays with the ball.

The boy and the dog play with the ball.

The engineer studies the problem.
The engineer develops a solution.
The engineer searches for ways to improve the solution.

The engineer studies the problem, develops a solution, and searches for ways to improve the solution.

Paul runs up onto the stage.
Janice runs up onto the stage.
Yuan runs up onto the stage.
Paul sings.
Janice sings.
Yuan sings.

Paul, Janice, and Yuan run up onto the stage and sing.

After the science fair, Josué packed up his project.
After the science fair, Josué went home.
After the science fair, I packed up my project.
After the science fair, I went home.

After the science fair, Josué and I packed up our projects and went home.

Exercise 26D: Subject-Verb Agreement with Compound Subjects

Choose the correct verb in parentheses to agree with the subject. Cross out the incorrect verb.

Amaya (~~dash~~/ dashes) down the street and (~~dart~~/ darts) into a shop.

The baker and his assistant (stop / ~~stops~~) talking and (stare / ~~stares~~) at Amaya.

Amaya (~~catch~~/ catches) her breath and (~~look~~/ looks) at the display case.

She (~~order~~/ orders) a cake and (~~tell~~/ tells) the baker that it will be a surprise for her sister.

The baker (~~prepare~~/ prepares) and (~~decorate~~/ decorates) the cake.

Amaya (~~pay~~/ pays) for the cake and (~~thank~~/ thanks) the baker.

— LESSON 27 —

Coordinating Conjunctions
Complications in Subject-Predicate Agreement

Exercise 27A: Using Conjunctions

Fill the blanks in the sentences below with the appropriate conjunctions. You must use each conjunction (*and, or, nor, for, so, but, yet*) at least once. (There is more than one possible answer for many of the blanks!)

These sentences are adapted from Sir Walter Scott's *Ivanhoe*.

Note to Instructor: The answers below are the conjunctions found in the original text, but you should accept any conjunction that makes sense, as long as the student uses each conjunction at least once.

It becomes not one wearing this badge to answer, __yet__ to whom, besides the sworn champions of the Holy Sepulchre, can the palm be assigned among the champions of the Cross?

There was a stranger at the gate, imploring admittance __and__ hospitality.

Cedric hastened to meet her, and to conduct her, with respectful ceremony, to the elevated seat at his own right hand.

Replacing his javelin, he resumed his seat, bent his looks downward, and appeared to be absorbed in melancholy reflection.

It was the Knight of Ivanhoe; nor was there one of the six that, for his years, had more renown in arms.

Pride and jealousy there was in his eye, for his life had been spent in asserting rights which were constantly liable to invasion.

I can guess thy want, so I can supply it.

If I had a horse, I would be your guide, for the way is somewhat intricate, though perfectly well known to me.

The path soon led deeper into the woodland, and crossed more than one brook, the approach to which was rendered perilous by the marshes through which it flowed; but the stranger seemed to know, as if by instinct, the soundest ground and the safest points of passage.

In this dress I am vowed to poverty, nor do I change it for aught save a horse and a coat of mail.

Exercise 27B: Subject-Predicate Agreement: Troublesome Subjects

Circle the correct verb in parentheses so that it agrees with the subject noun or pronoun in number.

The mirrors on the shelf (reflect/reflects) the candlelight.

Half of the milk (has/have) spilled on the counter and (is/are) dripping onto the floor!

The kindergarten class (wreck/wrecks) the art room on a daily basis, but the teacher and the aide (clean/cleans) things up afterward.

The crew (was/were) alerted to the danger by the captain's loud cry.

The flock of birds (was/were) flying in all directions.

Two-thirds of the students (describe/describes) the visitor as a good storyteller.

Kenneth and Dawson (dislike/dislikes) pumpkin pie but (love/loves) brownies.

The staff (entertain/entertains) themselves during slow times by creating art with sticky notes.

One million gallons of water (was/were) brought onto the hurricane-battered island.

The jar of cookies (tempt/tempts) me.

My brother or sister (has/have) been experimenting with recipes again—cookies should be sweet, but four cups of sugar for two dozen cookies (is/are) just too much!

One-fourth of the fence (has/have) been painted.

One-fourth of the fences (has/have) been painted.

Five years (remain/remains) before the next election.

The panel of experts (disagree/disagrees) on how to solve this issue.

The guide or some tourists usually (spot/spots) a manatee around this part of the boat ride.

Exercise 27C: Fill In the Verb

Choose a verb in the present tense that makes sense to complete each sentence. Be sure the verb agrees in number with its subject!

Note to Instructor: Sample answers are inserted below, but accept any reasonable answer as long as it is in the correct person and number (indicated in parentheses after each sentence).

The fury of the people incites a riot. **(3rd singular)**

My brother and I find snails and worms under those rocks all the time. **(3rd plural)**

Either the bus or one of the vans arrives late for the retreat every year. **(3rd singular)**

Your observations about the painting sound very astute. **(3rd plural)**

The class holds elections for officers in October. **(3rd singular)**

The mayor, the city council, and the police department claim credit for the decrease in violent crimes over the last year. **(3rd plural)**

The ink in all of my pens disappears too quickly! **(3rd singular)**

Either the berries or the milk causes me to have an allergic reaction, so I will avoid both! **(3rd singular)**

Half of the pages in this book are covered with pencil marks. **(3rd plural)**

— LESSON 28 —

Further Complications in Subject-Predicate Agreement

Exercise 28A: Subject-Verb Agreement: More Troublesome Subjects

Find the correct verb (agrees with the subject in number) in parentheses. Cross out the incorrect verb.

Gymnastics (is / ~~are~~) Maria's favorite activity of the week.

Every part in the play (has / ~~have~~) been cast.

In *The Lord of the Rings*, there (is / ~~are~~) one ring more powerful than all the rest.

The vertices of a regular polygon (~~lies~~ / lie) on the circle that can be drawn around the polygon.

The teacher and technology director (is / ~~are~~) running late for his meeting.

Biscuits and gravy (was / ~~were~~) not on the menu today.

There (~~is~~ / are) only six Wonder Gadgets left—you'd better order yours now!

Each fork, knife, and spoon (was / ~~were~~) placed in precisely the right spot.

"Each of the dresses (has / ~~have~~) something wrong with it," complained Julia.

Green Eggs and Ham (was / ~~were~~) written as the result of a bet Dr. Seuss's publisher made with him; the publisher believed Dr. Seuss could not write a book using no more than fifty unique words.

My new binoculars (~~allows~~ / allow) me to observe birds all the way across the lake!

Today's news (is / ~~are~~) not good.

The alumni of our campus organization (~~supports~~ / support) us financially.

Jane Austen's *Pride and Prejudice* (was / ~~were~~) published in 1813.
Billiards (is / ~~are~~) a game with many variations.
Science and Nature (is / ~~are~~) my favorite category in Trivial Pursuit.
Here on the handout (~~is~~ / are) the criteria for this project.
Each of the poisons (has / ~~have~~) a unique antidote.
Trinidad and Tobago (has / ~~have~~) been an independent nation since 1962.
Every minute (brings / ~~bring~~) us closer to the deadline.

Exercise 28B: Correct Verb Tense and Number

Complete each of these sentences by writing the correct number and tense of the verb indicated in the blank. The sentences are taken or adapted from Nathaniel Hawthorne's *The Scarlet Letter.*

Externally, the jollity of aged men (simple present of *have*) has much in common with the mirth of children.

This rose-bush, by a strange chance, (perfect present of *am*) has been kept alive in history.

In some two years, or less, that the woman has been a dweller here in Boston, no tidings (simple present of *have*) have come of this learned gentleman, Master Prynne.

Here, to witness the scene which we are describing, (simple past of *am*) was Governor Bellingham himself.

The discipline of the family, in those days, (simple past of *am*) was of a far more rigid kind than now.

Physical compulsion or restraint (simple past of *am*) was effectual, of course, while it lasted.

The children of the settlement (progressive past of *play*) were playing at going to church.

All the powers of nature (simple present of *call*) call so earnestly for the confession of sin.

A knowledge of men's hearts (simple present of *am*) is needful to the completest solution of that problem.

There (simple present of *am*) is no law nor reverence for authority mixed up with that child's composition.

Here (simple present of *am*) is a child of three years old, and she cannot tell who made her!

Their wide, short trousers (simple past of *am*) were confined about the waist by belts, often clasped with a rough plate of gold.

A sluggish bond-servant or an undutiful child (simple past of *am*) was to be corrected at the whipping-post.

The Governor and gentlemen (progressive present of *come*) are coming!

WEEK 8

Introduction to Objects

— LESSON 29 —

Action Verbs

Direct Objects

Exercise 29A: Direct Objects

In the following sentences, underline the subjects once and the predicates twice. Circle each direct object. These sentences are adapted from Daniel Defoe's *Robinson Crusoe*.

I had lived a dreadful life.

We never see the true state of our condition.

I had no powder or shot left.

I would build another *Periagua* or *Canoe*.

I had thus laid the scheme of my design.

The floor had a sort of small loose gravel upon it.

I took him up, and made much of him, and encouraged him.

In this voyage I visited my colony in the island, saw my successors, and had the whole story of their lives.

They must run out and see the battle.

However, they used some caution too.

They soon outdid their masters.

I cut the thread of his comforts and shortened his days.

We made signals of distress to the ship.

I got much money by the first adventure, and an insight into the method of getting more.

The tree effectually shaded him over the head.

Exercise 29B: Diagramming Direct Objects

On your own paper, diagram the subjects, verbs, and direct objects ONLY in the sentences from Exercise 29A.

I had lived a dreadful life.

I had no powder or shot left.

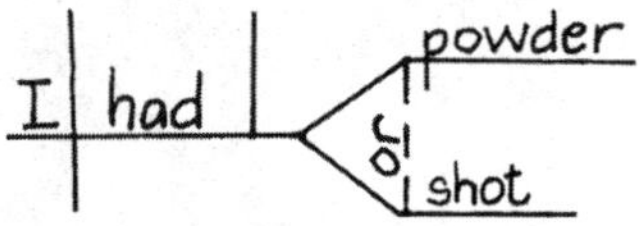

I had thus laid the scheme of my design.

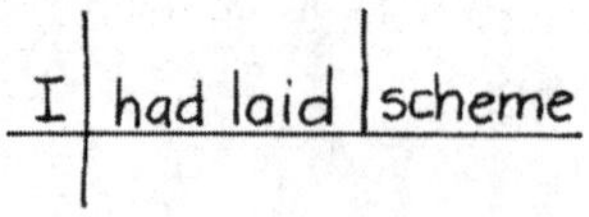

I took him up, and made much of him, and encouraged him.

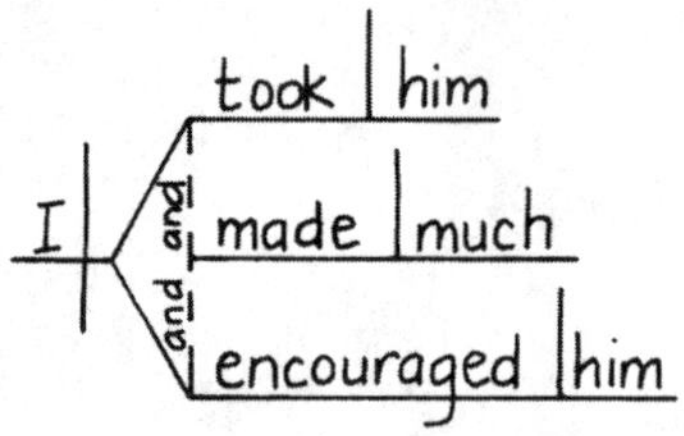

They must run out and see the battle.

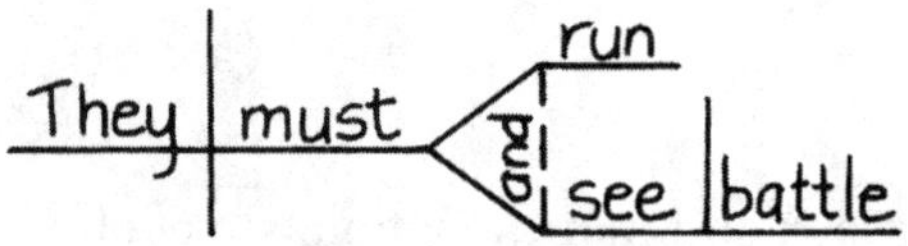

They soon outdid their masters.

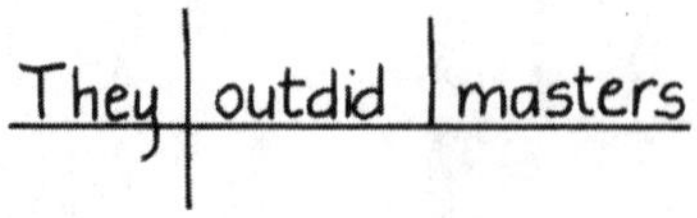

We made signals of distress to the ship.

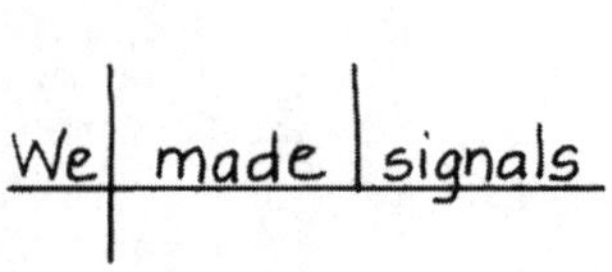

The tree effectually shaded him over the head.

We never see the true state of our condition.

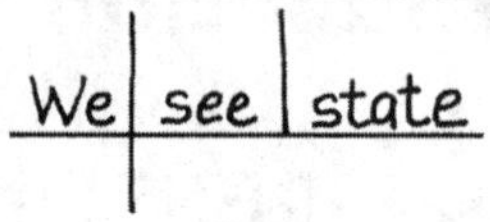

I would build another *Periagua* or *Canoe*.

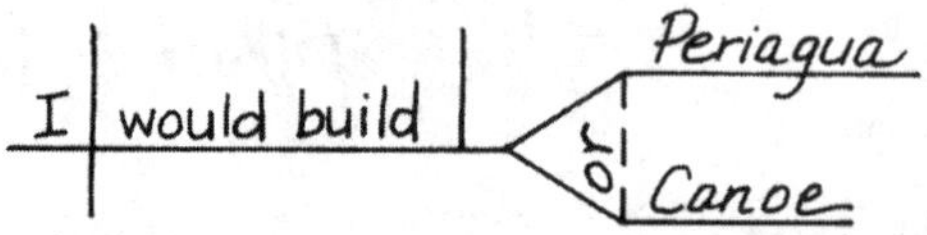

The floor had a sort of small loose gravel upon it.

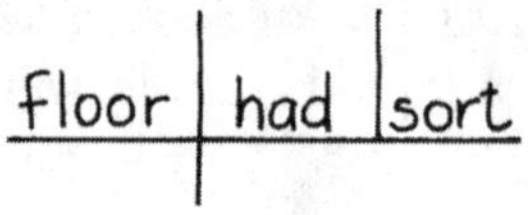

In this voyage I visited my colony in the island, saw my successors, and had the whole story of their lives.

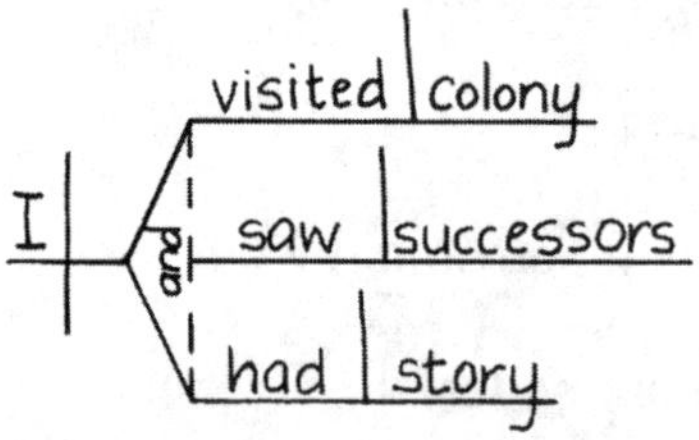

However, they used some caution too.

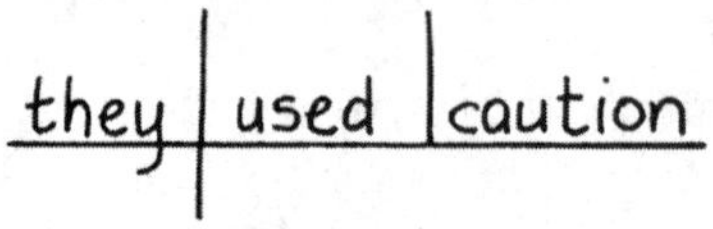

I cut the thread of his comforts and shortened his days.

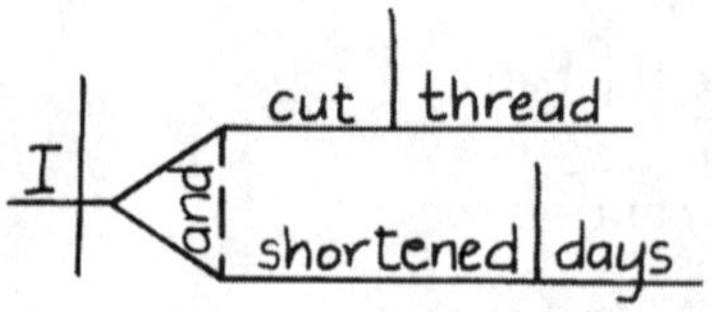

I got much money by the first adventure, and an insight into the method of getting more.

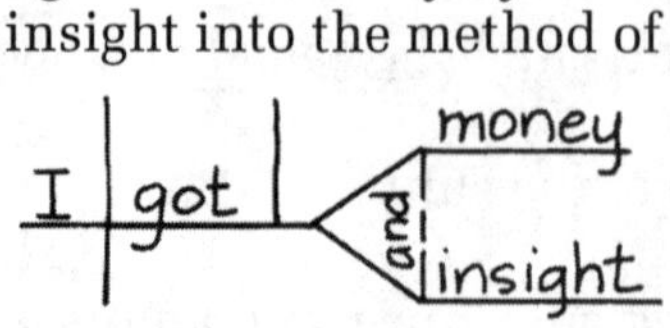

— LESSON 30 —

Direct Objects
Prepositions

Exercise 30A: Identifying Prepositions

In the following sentences (adapted from Oscar Wilde's *The Picture of Dorian Gray*), find and circle each preposition.

> **Note to Instructor:** *Up* is acting as an adverb in he *suddenly started up*, not as a preposition. If the student is confused about this, review the definition of a preposition with him. There is no noun or pronoun that *up* is relating to another word in this sentence.

In the centre of the room, clamped to an upright easel, stood the full-length portrait of a young man of extraordinary personal beauty, and in front of it, some little distance away, was sitting the artist himself, Basil Hallward, whose sudden disappearance some years ago caused, at the time, such public excitement, and gave rise to so many strange conjectures.

As the painter looked at the gracious and comely form he had so skilfully mirrored in his art, a smile of pleasure passed across his face. But he suddenly started up, and, closing his eyes, placed his fingers upon the lids, as though imprisoning within his brain some curious dream from which he feared he might awake.

Exercise 30B: Word Relationships

The following sentences all contain action verbs. Underline each subject once and each action verb twice. If the sentence has an action verb followed by a direct object, write *DO* above the direct object.

If the sentence contains a preposition, circle the preposition and draw a line to connect the two words that the preposition shows a relationship between. The first two are done for you.

Mathieu apologized to me for his mistake.

Zoey collected the trash. (DO: trash)

This new strategy will double our profit. (DO: profit)

I burned my finger on the cookie sheet. (DO: finger)

Three children in shabby clothes shivered pitifully in the snow.

Our cousins arrived on the early flight from Atlanta.

The computer at the end of the row works slowly.

The kingdom's borders extend beyond the mountain.

Amina laughed heartily at my joke.

The exhausted heroes stepped warily into the cave.

Someone must change the baby's diaper!

This key will unlock any door in the building.

Gleefully, the soldiers obeyed the evil queen's orders.

Harold sheepishly grinned at his sister.

Exercise 30C: Diagramming Direct Objects

On your own paper, diagram the subjects, predicates, and direct objects ONLY from the sentences above. If a sentence does not have a direct object, do not diagram it.

Zoey collected the trash.

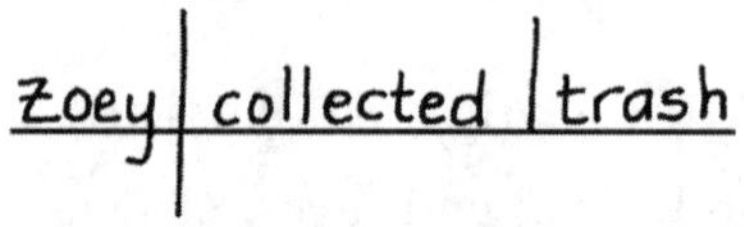

This new strategy will double our profit.

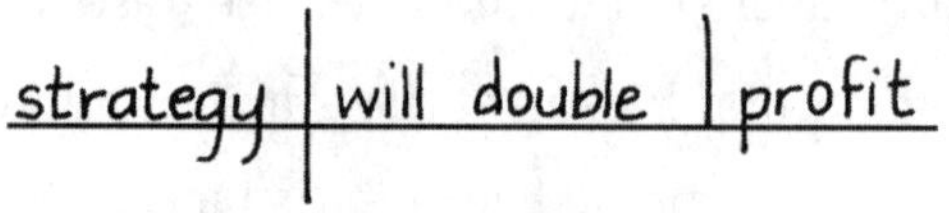

I burned my finger on the cookie sheet.

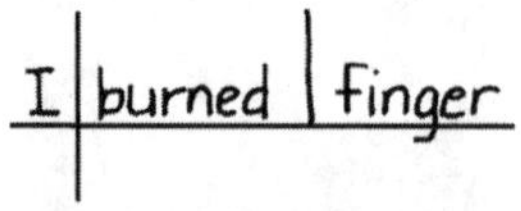

Someone must change the baby's diaper!

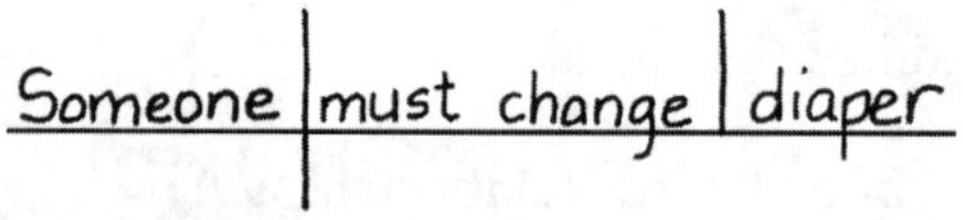

This key will unlock any door in the building.

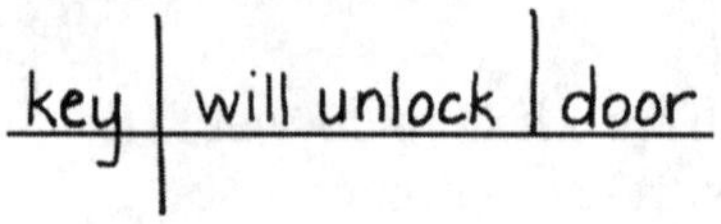

Gleefully, the soldiers obeyed the evil queen's orders.

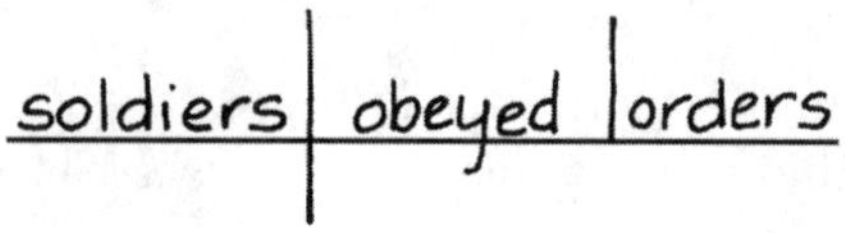

— LESSON 31 —

Definitions Review
Prepositional Phrases
Object of the Preposition

Exercise 31A: Objects of Prepositional Phrases

Fill in the blanks with a noun as the object of the preposition to complete the prepositional phrases.

Note to Instructor: Answers will vary. Suggestions are provided.

Somehow, a library book ended up behind the refrigerator.

You can find more pretzels in the pantry.

We raced down the corridor to deliver the news.

Throughout the land, the people rejoiced to hear about the victory.

Suzanne enjoyed the documentary about flowers.

I like my pizza with cheese and pepperoni. *(Use as many objects as you'd like for this one!)*

Exercise 31B: Identifying Prepositional Phrases

Can you find all eleven of the prepositional phrases in the following excerpt, adapted from *The Time Machine* by H. G. Wells? (Beware words that can be prepositions but can also function as other parts of speech!)

Underline each complete prepositional phrase. Circle each preposition. Draw a box around each object of a preposition. One preposition has a compound object.

Note to Instructor: The word *by* in this excerpt ("dashed by too fast") is acting as an adverb.

I saw the sun hopping swiftly across the sky, leaping it every minute, and every minute marking a day. I supposed the laboratory had been destroyed, and I had come into the open air. I had a dim impression of scaffolding, but I was already going too fast for consciousness of any moving things. The slowest snail that ever crawled dashed by too fast for me. The twinkling succession of darkness and light was excessively painful to the eye. Then in the intermittent darkness, I saw the moon spinning swiftly through her quarters, and had a faint glimpse of the circling stars.

Exercise 31C: Remembering Prepositions

Can you remember all forty-six prepositions without looking back at your list? The first letter of each preposition has been given for you.

A	B	D	E	F	I	L
aboard	before	down	except	for	in	like
about	behind	during		from	inside	
above	below				into	
across	beneath					
after	beside					
against	between					
along	beyond					
among	by					
around						
at						

N	O	P	S	T	U	W
near	of	past	since	through	under	with
	off			throughout	underneath	within
	on			to	until	without
	over			toward	up	
					upon	

— LESSON 32 —

Subjects, Predicates, and Direct Objects
Prepositions
Object of the Preposition
Prepositional Phrases

Exercise 32A: Identifying Prepositional Phrases and Parts of Sentences

In the following sentences, circle each prepositional phrase. Once you have identified the prepositional phrases, underline subjects once, underline predicates twice, and label direct objects with *DO*.

Things to watch out for:

1) Words that could be prepositions but are acting as other parts of speech instead. If it doesn't have an object, it's not a preposition!
2) In some of these sentences, subjects and predicates are inverted so that the predicate comes first. Find the verb first, then ask, "Who or what [verb]?" to find the subject. Remember that the subject will not be the object of a preposition!

These sentences are adapted from "The Padishah of the Forty Peris," from *Turkish Fairy Tales and Folk Tales*, collected by Ignácz Kunos and translated by R. Nisbet Bain.

The first is done for you.

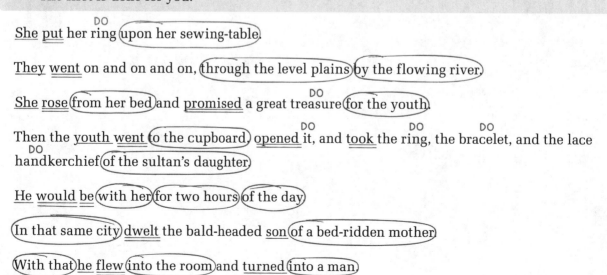

She put her ring (DO) (upon her sewing-table).

They went on and on and on, (through the level plains) (by the flowing river).

She rose (from her bed) and promised a great treasure (DO) (for the youth).

Then the youth went (to the cupboard), opened it (DO), and took the ring (DO), the bracelet (DO), and the lace handkerchief (DO) (of the sultan's daughter).

He would be (with her) (for two hours) (of the day).

(In that same city) dwelt the bald-headed son (of a bed-ridden mother).

(With that) he flew (into the room) and turned (into a man).

He was filled with joy at the sight of his child.

He looked to the right of him and to the left.

Exercise 32B: Diagramming

On your own paper, diagram all of the uncircled parts of the sentences from Exercise 32A. EXCEPTION: Do not diagram the *and* in the last sentence, since its only function is to connect two prepositional phrases.

DO

She put her ring upon her sewing-table.

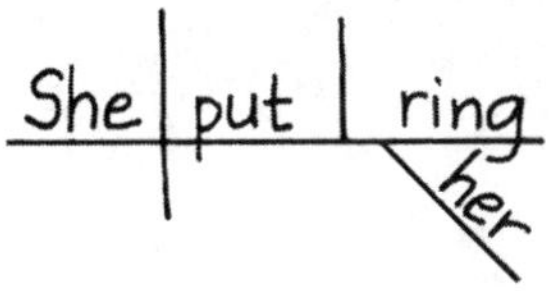

They went on and on and on, through the level plains by the flowing river.

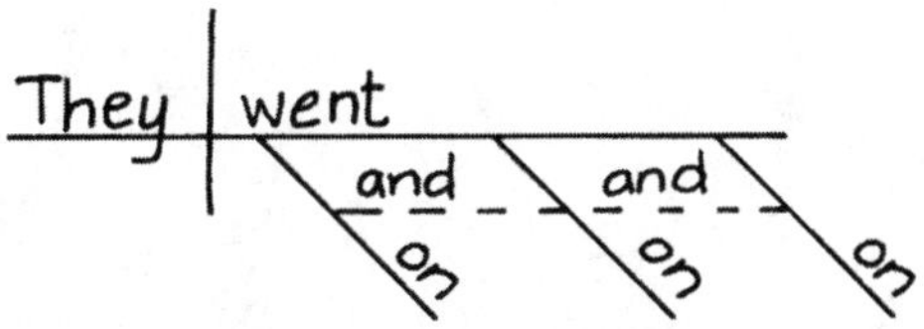

DO

She rose from her bed and promised a great treasure for the youth.

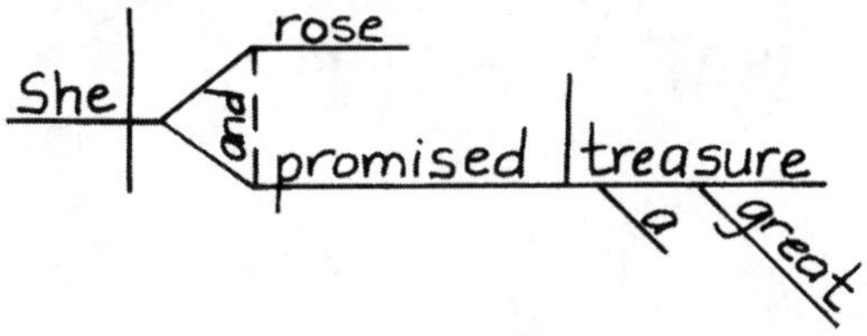

DO DO DO

Then the youth went to the cupboard, opened it, and took the ring, the bracelet, and the lace

DO

handkerchief of the sultan's daughter.

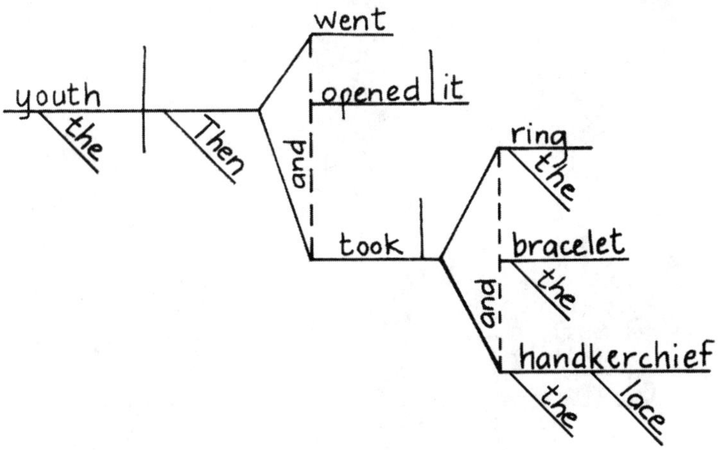

He would be with her for two hours of the day

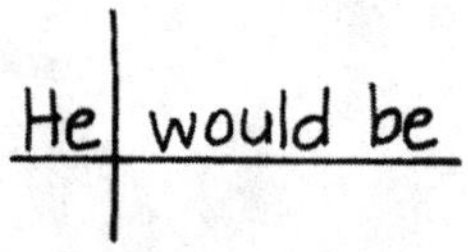

In that same city dwelt the bald-headed son of a bed-ridden mother

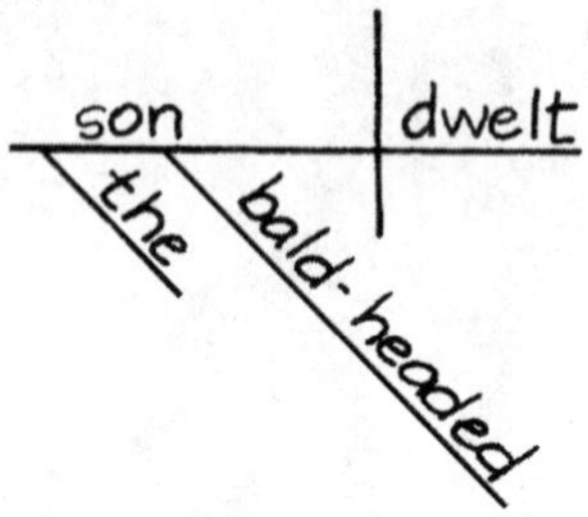

With that he flew into the room and turned into a man

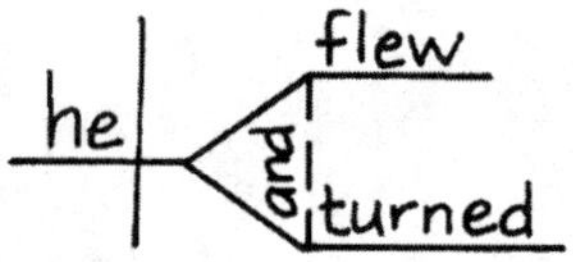

He was filled with joy at the sight of his child

He looked to the right of him and to the left

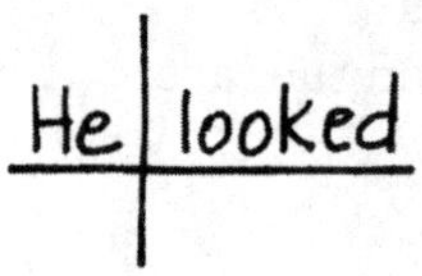

WEEK 9

Adverbs

— LESSON 33 —

Adverbs That Tell How

Exercise 33A: Identifying Adverbs That Tell *How*

Underline the adverbs telling *how* in the following sentences, and draw arrows to the verbs that they modify.

"May I have another cookie?" the child asked sweetly.

The captured spy glared defiantly as the enemy soldiers roughly pushed her toward the interrogation room.

Absentmindedly, Elissa stirred the soup on the stove.

Eamon spoke with us frankly about his desire to join the circus.

The coach dealt justly with the conflict between the teammates.

"If you can make a bed properly, you're hired," said the hotel manager exhaustedly.

When Akari's stage fright threatened to overcome her, the director spoke reassuringly to her.

Truly, I believe this is the best choice.

His shield and sword lying in the field behind him, the knight courageously—and rather foolishly—rode toward the monster's lair.

I called my parents to tell them I'd arrived home safely.

Exercise 33B: Forming Adverbs from Adjectives

Turn the following adjectives into adverbs.

Adjective	Adverb	Adjective	Adverb
thoughtful	thoughtfully	dizzy	dizzily
sore	sorely	languid	languidly
spotty	spottily	hideous	hideously
decorous	decorously	bouncy	bouncily
flagrant	flagrantly		

Exercise 33C: Diagramming Adverbs

Diagram the following sentences on your own paper.

I dearly love this place.

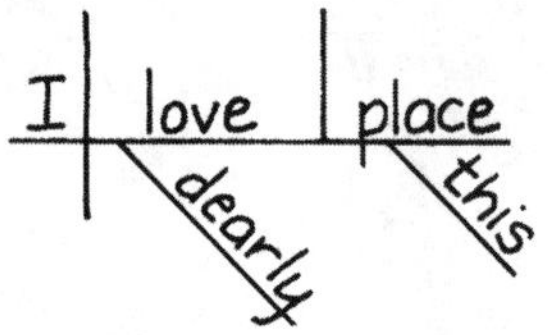

Violet thankfully accepted the gift.

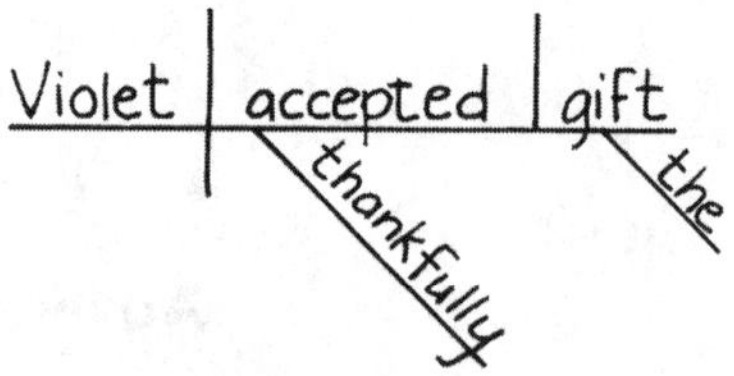

My adorable new kitten mewed questioningly.

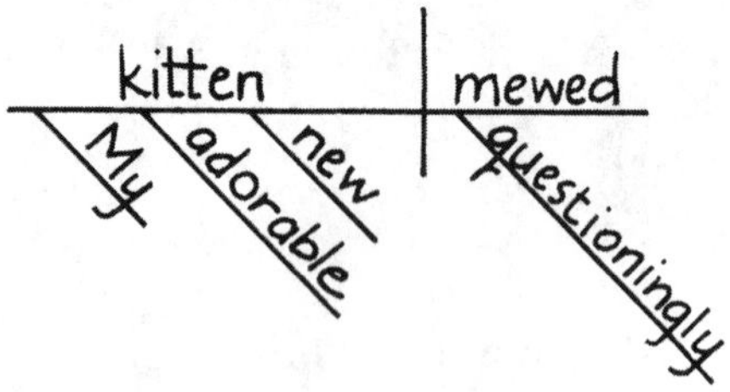

Has she answered knowledgeably?

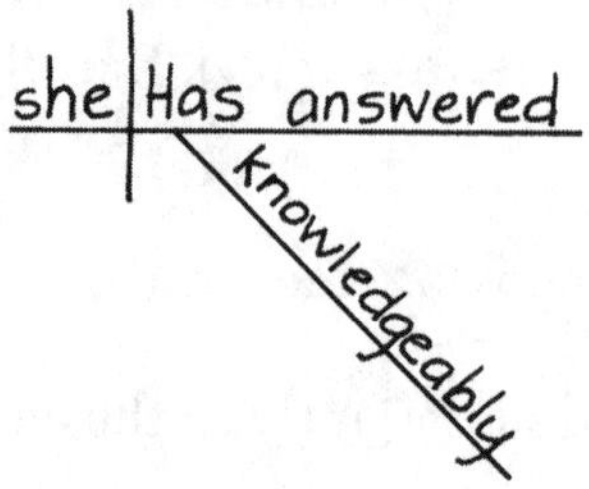

Nervously, we entered the decrepit old house.

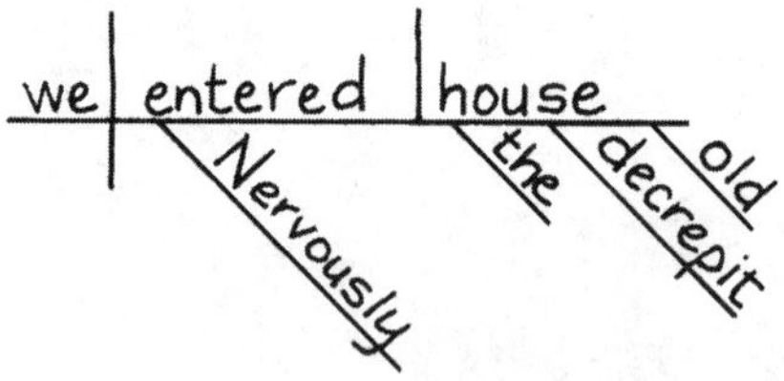

Toby completed the application thoroughly.

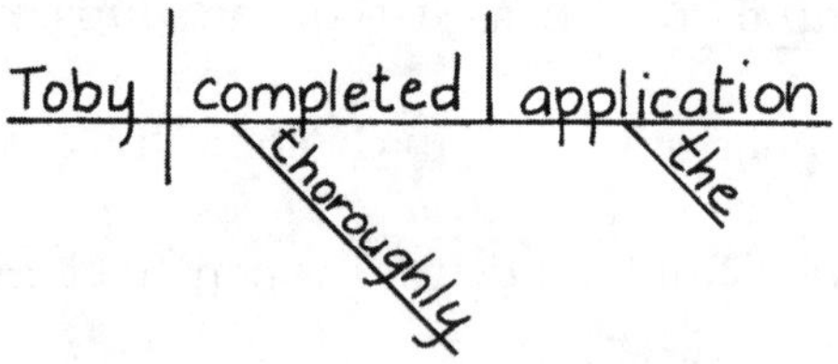

— LESSON 34 —

Adverbs That Tell When, Where, and How Often

Exercise 34A: Telling When

Tim dropped his recipe cards for chocolate chip cookies. Help him get organized by numbering the following sentences from 1 to 5 so he can make the cookies.

2 Second, add the salt, vanilla, and applesauce.

4 Later, chill the dough for at least an hour.

1 First, cream together the butter and sugars.

5 Finally, bake for about 10 minutes in a 350° oven.

3 Next, mix in the flour and baking soda before adding the chocolate chips.

Exercise 34B: Distinguishing Among Different Types of Adverbs

Put each of the following adverbs in the correct category, according to the question each one answers.

below	greedily	then	rarely
today	kindly	outside	yearly
daily	earlier	angrily	down

When	Where	How	How Often
then	below	greedily	rarely
today	outside	kindly	yearly
earlier	down	angrily	daily

Exercise 34C: Identifying Adverbs of Different Types

Underline the adverbs in the following sentences that tell *when, where*, or *how often*.

I lost my way once yesterday.

Sometimes Shanika plays her saxophone outdoors.

Nikki talked incessantly during the movie.

Let's go downstairs now.

That piano key occasionally sticks.

I usually sit there.

Winston will visit his grandfather tomorrow.

Mrs. Lee always arrives early.

Unless that cough improves soon, you should see a doctor.

Where did Miguel put his keys?

Exercise 34D: Diagramming Different Types of Adverbs

Diagram the following sentences on your own paper.

Lenore will eat these leftovers later.

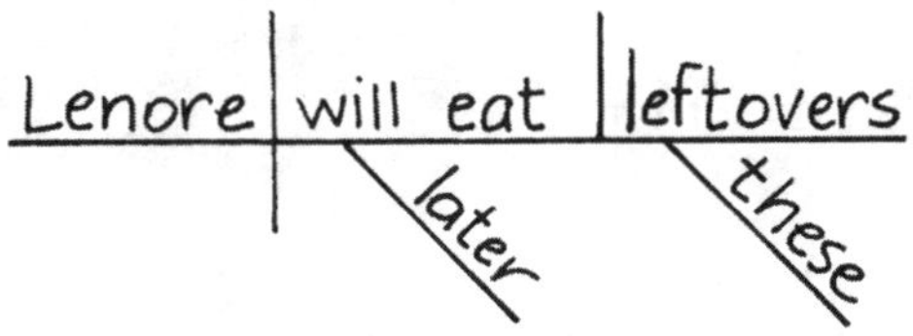

When is Dad going outside?

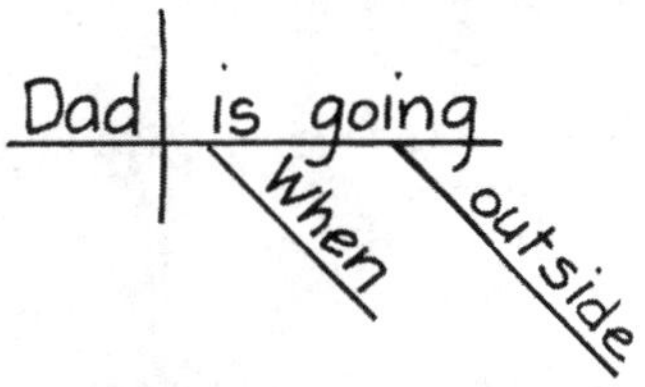

Today I breakfasted late.

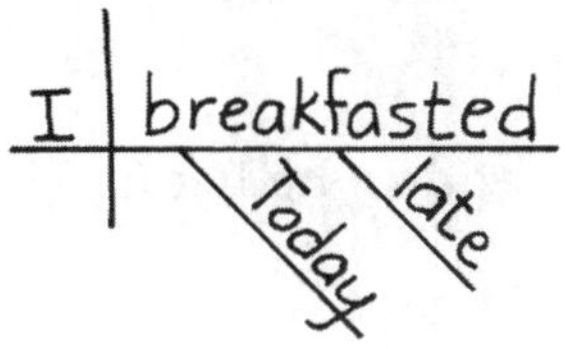

Complete your exercises now.

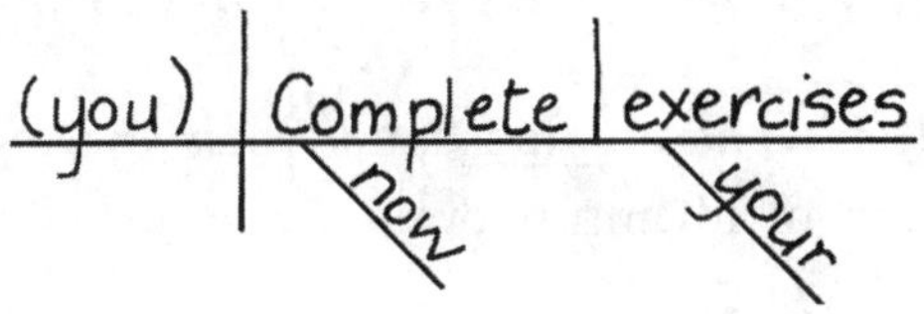

Gloria and Caleb clapped enthusiastically and then stood.

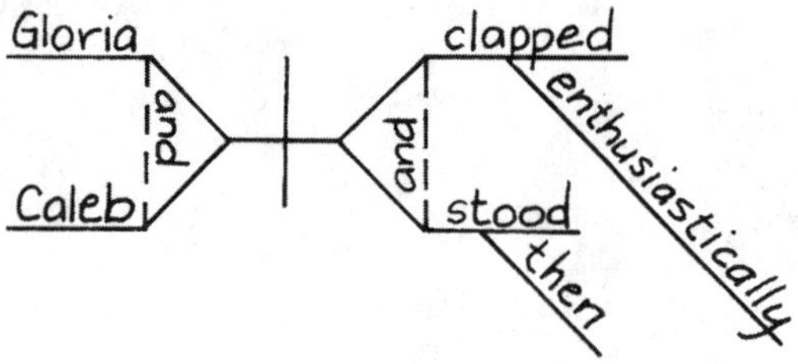

You left your hat here yesterday.

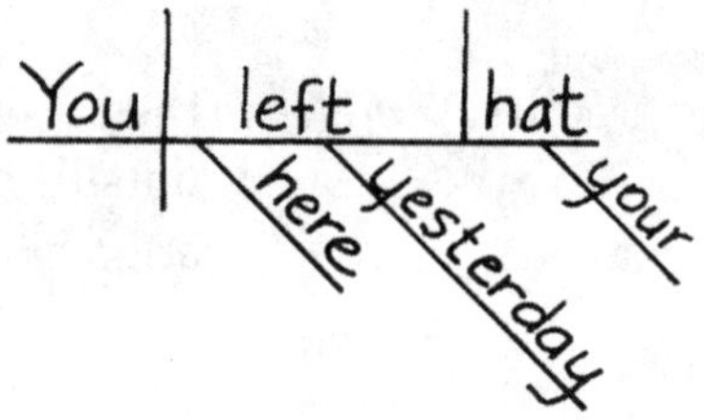

— LESSON 35 —

Adverbs That Tell To What Extent

Exercise 35A: Identifying the Words Modified by Adverbs

Draw an arrow from each underlined adverb to the word it modifies. These sentences are from J. M. Barrie's *Peter Pan*.

No nursery could possibly have been conducted more correctly.

It had begun so uneventfully, so precisely like a hundred other evenings.

The little stars are not really friendly to Peter, who had a mischievous way of stealing up behind them and trying to blow them out; but they are so fond of fun that they were on his side tonight.

Of course I'm very sorry, but how could I know you were in the drawer?

I nipped a bit out of that eagle's mouth pretty neatly, Wendy.

Of course this was rather unsatisfactory.

Tink was not all bad; or, rather, she was all bad just now, but, on the other hand, sometimes she was all good.

Then they had to tell Peter of Tink's crime, and almost never had they seen him look so stern.

And how ardently they grew to love their home under the ground.

He often went out alone, and when he came back you were never absolutely certain whether he had had an adventure or not.

She was really glad for the sake of his reputation that no one heard him except herself.

She had to admit that she was too tired.

"It is sweet, Peter, isn't it?" Wendy said, frightfully gratified.

The awful cynicism of this made an uncomfortable impression, and most of them began to look rather doubtful.

Exercise 35B: Diagramming Different Types of Adverbs

Diagram the following sentences on your own paper.

Your new puppy is almost unbearably cute!

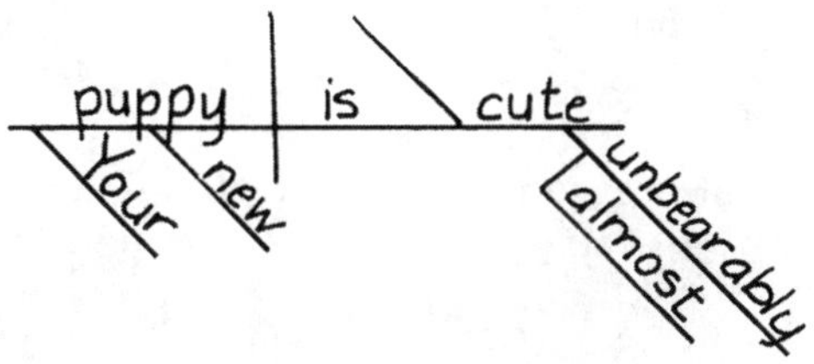

Zoe regarded the overly eager salesman suspiciously.

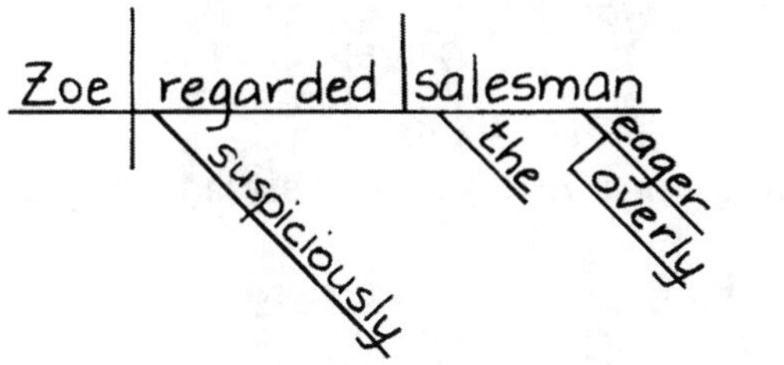

Currently, skies are partly cloudy.

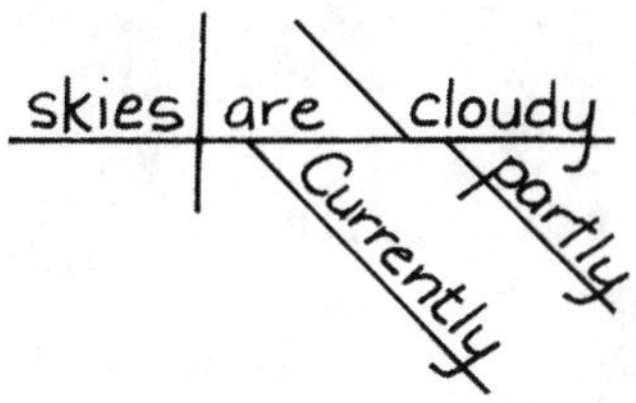

Rafael will soon attempt a surprisingly difficult feat.

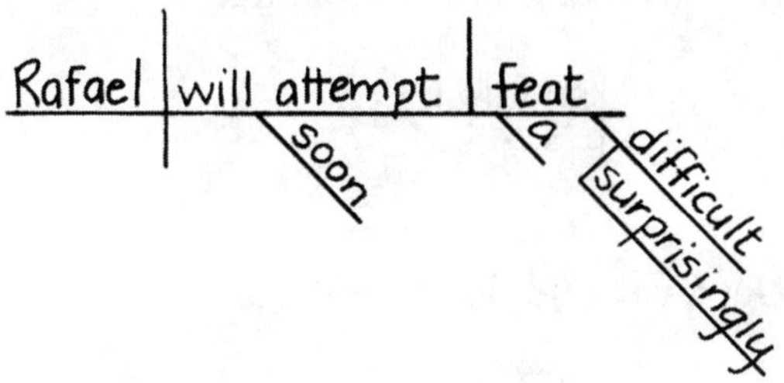

The freshman rather nervously addressed the senior class.

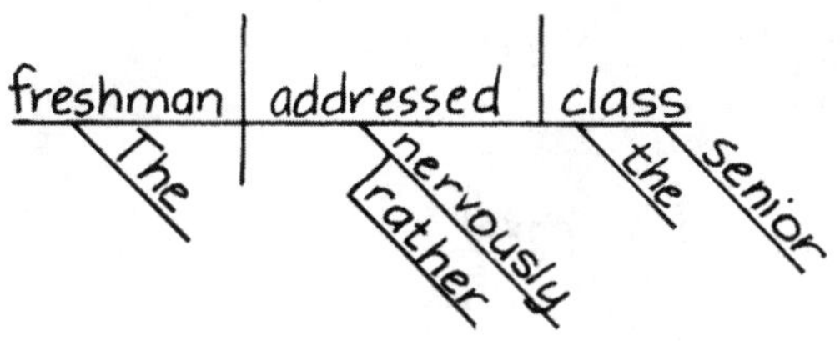

A fairy appeared quite suddenly and waved her wand mysteriously.

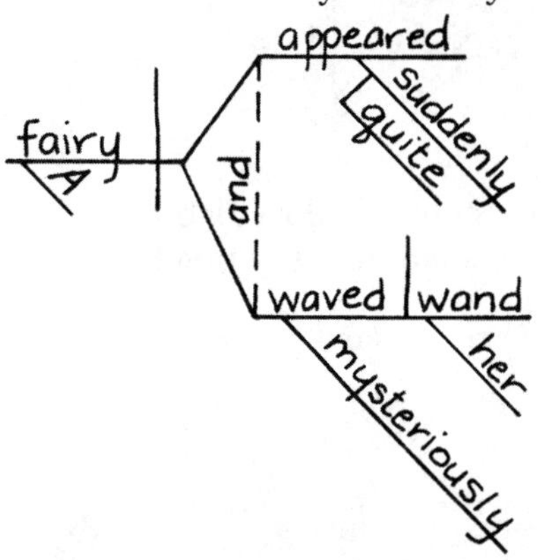

— LESSON 36 —

Adjectives and Adverbs

The Adverb *Not*

Diagramming Contractions

Diagramming Compound Adjectives and Compound Adverbs

Exercise 36A: Practice in Diagramming

On your own paper, diagram every word of the following sentences. They are adapted from Johanna Spyri's *Heidi*.

If this is your first time through this course, you may skip #1, #4 and #8. If not, diagram them!

She was so hot and uncomfortable.

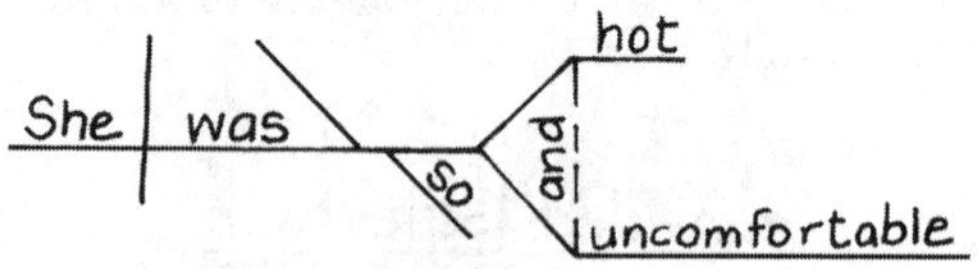

Here a neat little bed was already prepared.

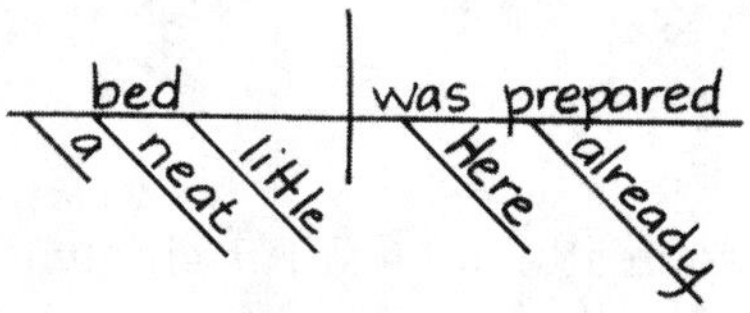

Why should there be a change?

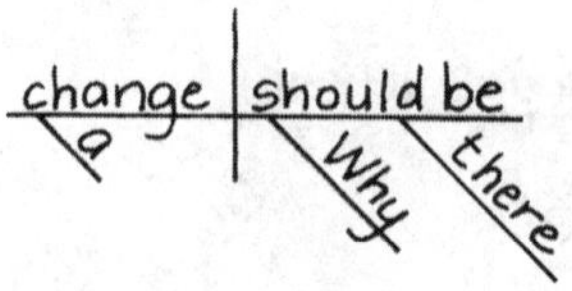

Get away and don't try it again.

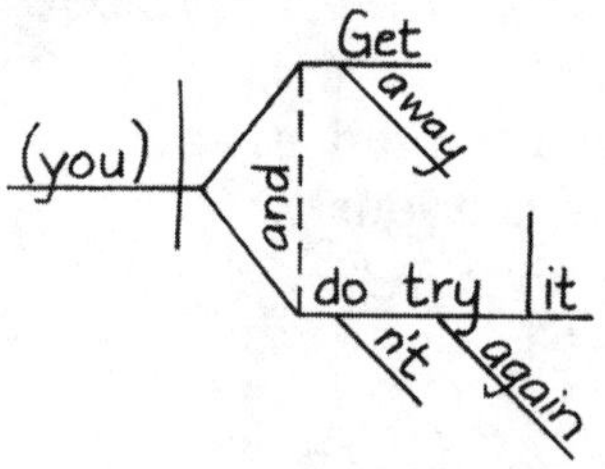

This little incident had ruffled Miss Rottenmeier's temper very much.

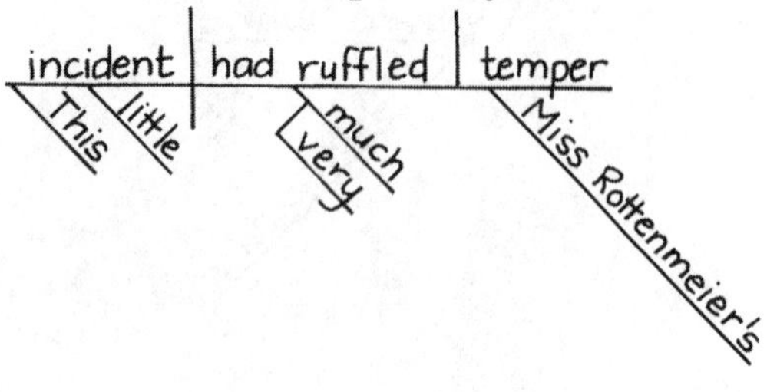

She ran busily to and fro.

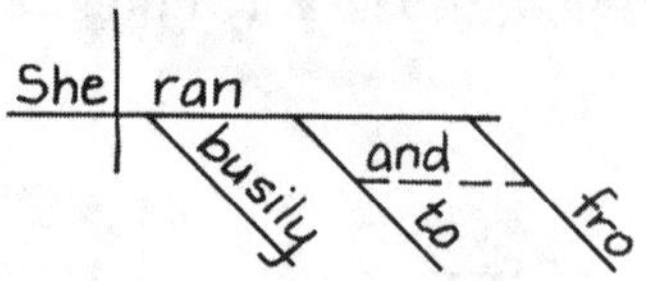

The little goat pressed close and became perfectly quiet.

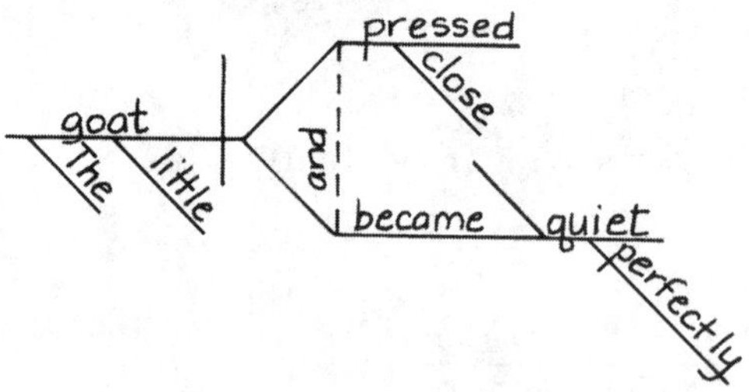

People only half believed these reports.

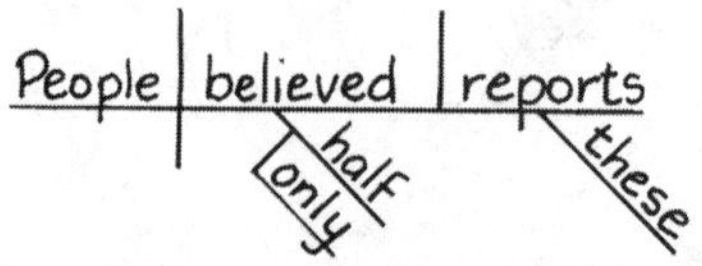

The child does not look very terrible.

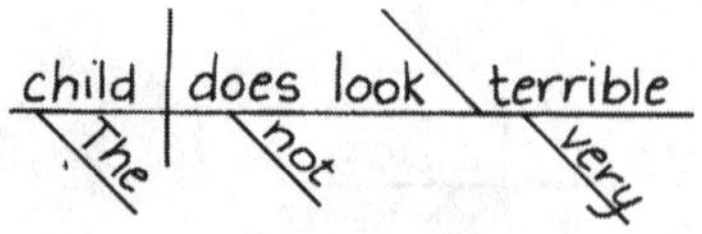

A large hall came next.

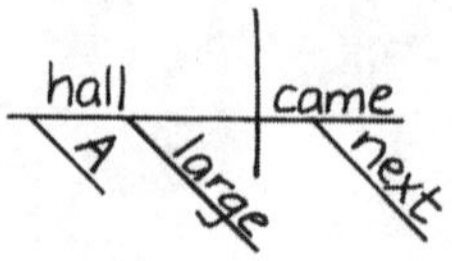

— REVIEW 3 —

Weeks 7-9

Topics
Parts of Speech
Compound Parts of Sentences
Prepositions
Prepositional Phrases
Objects of Prepositions
Subjects and Predicates
Subject-Verb Agreement
Verbs and Direct Objects

Review 3A: Parts of Speech

In the passage below from Orson Scott Card's *Ender's Game*, identify the underlined words as *N* for noun, *ADJ* for adjective, *ADV* for adverb, *PREP* for preposition, or *CONJ* for conjunction. The first is done for you.

N ADV ADV N
The monitor lady smiled very nicely and tousled his hair and said, "Andrew, I suppose by

ADV ADJ ADJ PREP
now you're just absolutely sick of having that horrid monitor. Well, I have good news for you. That

N ADV ADV
monitor is going to come out today. We're going to take it right out, and it won't hurt a bit."

PREP CONJ N ADV
Ender nodded. It was a lie, of course, that it wouldn't hurt a bit. But since adults always

N ADJ N
said it when it *was* going to hurt, he could count on that statement as an accurate prediction of the

N ADV ADV ADJ N
future. Sometimes lies were more dependable than the truth.

CONJ ADV ADV ADV ADV ADV N
"So if you'll just come over here, Andrew, just sit right up here on the examining table. The

N ADV PREP N
doctor will be in to see you in a moment."

N ADJ N PREP N
The monitor gone. Ender tried to imagine the little device missing from the back of his

ADV PREP ADV
neck. I'll roll over on my back in bed and it won't be pressing there. I won't feel it tingling and

ADV N
taking up the heat when I shower.

Review 3B: Recognizing Prepositions

Circle the forty-six prepositions from your list in the following bank of words. Try to complete the exercise without looking back at your list of prepositions.

up among then until side
and my around you above
before through from there into
down throughout within pen much
jump they but aboard without
like between most near off
toward about of play beyond
with however along behind to
by on paper then except
sort during nor for less
eat against below air since
where underneath inside beside across
in when kind at spot
beneath after over well his
whom past upon move under

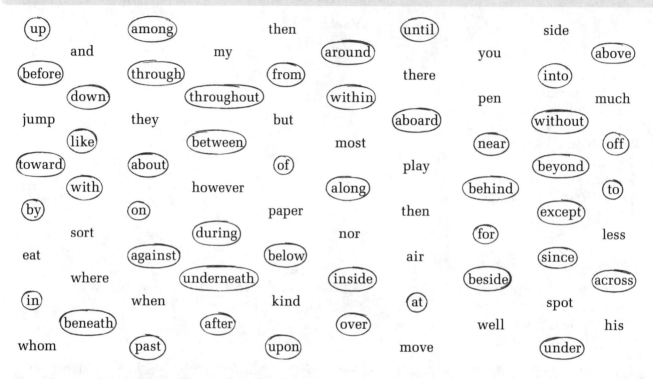

Review 3C: Subjects and Predicates

Draw one line under the simple subject and two lines under the simple predicate. Watch out for compound subjects or predicates! Also, remember that in poetry, sometimes the order of words is different than in normal speech—once you have found the verb, ask "who or what" before it to find the subject.

The following lines are from the poem "The Tyger," by William Blake.

What immortal hand or eye could frame thy fearful symmetry?

In what distant deeps or skies burnt the fire of thine eyes?

And what shoulder, and what art, could twist the sinews of thy heart?

In what furnace was thy brain?

The following lines are from the poem "Buttercups," by Wilfrid Thorley.

There must be fairy miners just underneath the mould.

They take the shining metals and beat them into shreds.

Sometimes they melt the flowers to tiny seeds like pearls and store them up in bowers for little boys and girls.

And still a tiny fan turns above a forge of gold.

The following lines are from the poem "The Ingenious Little Old Man," by John Bennett.

A little old man of the sea went out in a boat for a sail.

The water came in almost up to his chin.

But this little old man of the sea just drew out his jack-knife so stout.

And a hole with its blade in the bottom he made.

All of the water ran out.

Review 3D: Complicated Subject-Verb Agreement

Circle the correct verb form in parentheses.

My extended family (is / are) scattered around the country.

Twenty dollars (is / are) a great deal for this dress!

The pianist or the flautists (needs / need) to play louder.

Three-fourths of the employees (has / have) donated to this month's charity.

Julian's family (is / are) arriving in three hours.

The judging criteria for the art competition (is / are) available on the website.

The plants near the window (requires / require) frequent watering.

There (is / are) two buttons missing from this shirt.

Books and papers (covers / cover) a writer's desk.

A painted rocking chair (sits / sit) invitingly in the corner of the playroom.

Cristina or Isobel (times / time) each runner in the race.

Aleksandra and Madeline (counts / count) the money after the bake sale.

Newsies (is / are) a musical.

My clothes (was / were) not in the blue suitcase.

Review 3E: Objects and Prepositions

Identify the underlined words as *DO* for direct object or *OP* for object of preposition. For each direct object, find and underline twice the action verb that affects it. For each object of a preposition, find and circle the preposition to which it belongs.

These sentences are from *The Giver*, by Lois Lowry.

Now, thinking about the feeling (OP) of fear (OP) as he pedaled home along the river path (OP), he remembered that moment (DO) of palpable, stomach-sinking terror (OP) when the aircraft had streaked above.

But his mind was still on December (OP) and the coming Ceremony (OP).

OP DO
It was effortless for Jonas, and even boring, though Asher enjoyed it.

DO OP
He had held a magnifying glass to it.

OP DO
They all listened carefully and discussed with Lily the warning that the dream had given.

OP OP
Now Father sat beside Mother in the audience.

OP DO OP
In each dwelling tonight they would be studying the instructions for the beginning of
OP
their training.

OP DO OP
Jonas grinned with delight, and blew his own steamy breath into view.

DO OP
He could see an odd look on The Giver's face.

OP DO OP
In one ecstatic memory he had ridden a gleaming brown horse across a field that smelled of damp
OP OP
grass, and had dismounted beside a small stream from which both he and the horse drank cold,
DO
clear water.

DO OP
He waved his hand in the familiar gesture.

WEEK 10

Completing the Sentence

— LESSON 37 —

Direct Objects
Indirect Objects

Exercise 37A: Identifying Direct Objects

Underline the action verbs and circle the direct objects in these sentences. Remember that you can always eliminate prepositional phrases first if that makes the task easier.

The sentences are adapted from May R. Berenbaum's *Bugs in the System: Insects and Their Impact on Human Affairs.*

Linnaeus described only about 2,000 species of insects.

Some insects carry metamorphosis to an extreme and undergo major anatomical modification with each and every molt.

Like most higher animals, insects perceive information about their environment through the nervous system.

These alarm pheromones can evoke different responses through the content and composition of the secretion.

With all the cooperative workers, a queen bee can raise literally thousands of offspring.

Bees have provided useful services.

Exercise 37B: Identifying Direct Objects and Indirect Objects

Underline the direct and indirect objects in the following sentences. Write *DO* for direct object and *IO* for indirect object.

Please bring me (IO) the mail (DO).

Marcella will leave George (IO) a few cookies (DO).

Will Nermin play us (IO) a song (DO) on her harp?

That will cost you (IO) an arm (DO) and a leg (DO)!

We are offering Shivani (IO) the job (DO) tomorrow.

After class, I can teach you (IO) the new dance (DO).

Exercise 37C: Diagramming Direct Objects and Indirect Objects

On your own paper, diagram the following sentences.

Buy me a new toy!

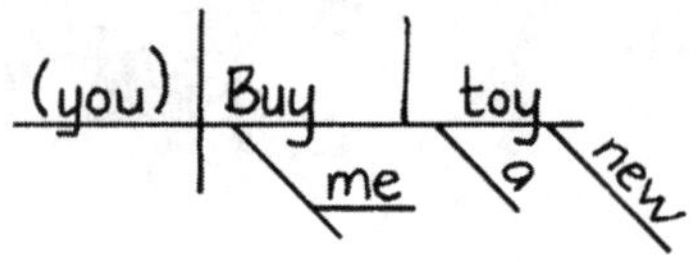

I made you a quilt.

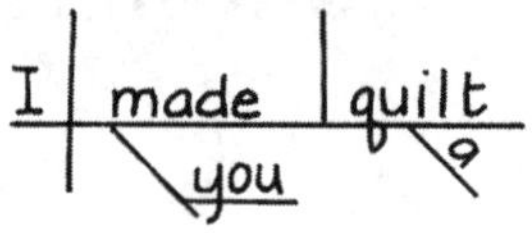

He has promised her the moon.

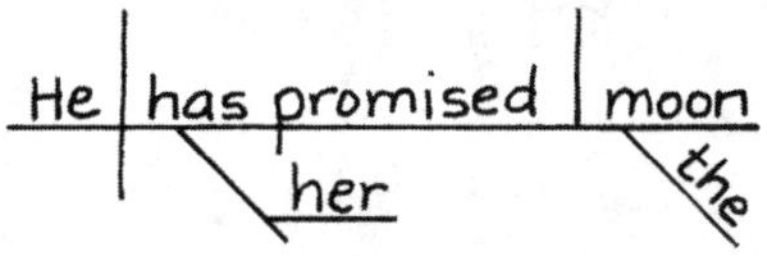

Asher got us some doughnuts.

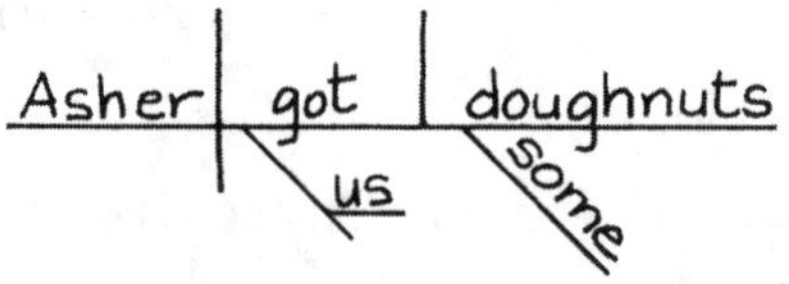

You owe me a favor.

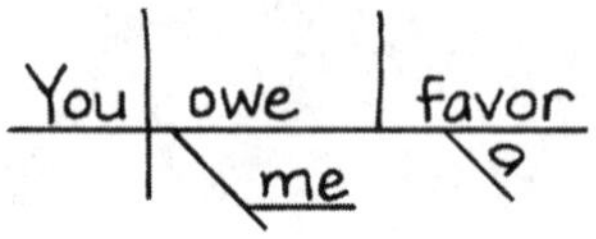

Can you tell me another story and sing me another song?

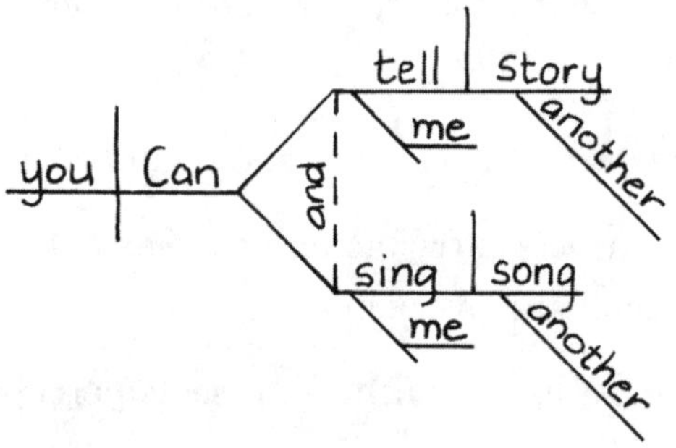

Purnama has written her father a long letter.

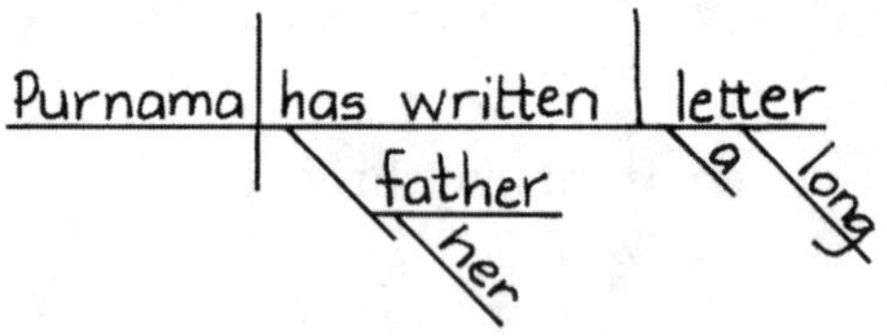

— LESSON 38 —

State-of-Being Verbs
Linking Verbs
Predicate Adjectives

Exercise 38A: Action Verbs and Linking Verbs

In the following sentences, underline the subjects once and the predicates twice. If the predicate is a linking verb, write *LV* over it, circle the predicate adjective, and label it *PA*. If the predicate is an action verb, write *AV* over it, circle the direct object, and label it *DO*. The first is done for you.

These sentences are slightly condensed from *Flatland: A Romance of Many Dimensions*, by Edwin A. Abbott.

AV DO
I admit the truth of your critic's facts.

AV DO
During my slumber I had a dream.

All our lines are EQUALLY and INFINITESIMALLY thick.

Straight Lines are in many important respects superior to the Circles.

> **Note to Instructor:** You may accept just Lines as the subject. Straight Lines is underlined because in *Flatland* it serves as a proper name, but the student may not realize this.

Many-sidedness was almost essential as a pretext for the Innovators.

All, except the Isosceles, were either neutral or averse to the Bill.

I heard the sound of many voices in the street.

The sights tantalized and tempted me to outspoken treason.

BRIGHTNESS, as well as length, is necessary to the existence of a Line.

On the reply to this question I am ready to stake everything.

Once or twice I even spoke the forbidden terms "the Third and Fourth Dimensions."

A third appeal on my part was equally ineffectual.

The Working Men they spared but decimated.

Exercise 38B: Diagramming Direct Objects and Predicate Adjectives

On your own paper, diagram ONLY the subjects, predicates, and direct objects or predicate adjectives (along with any conjunctions used to connect compounds) from the sentences in Exercise 38A.

I admit the truth of your critic's facts.

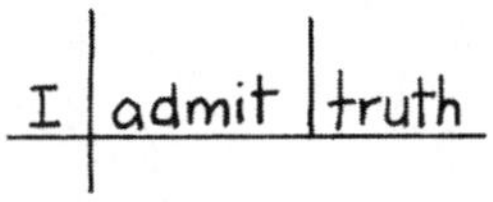

During my slumber I had a dream.

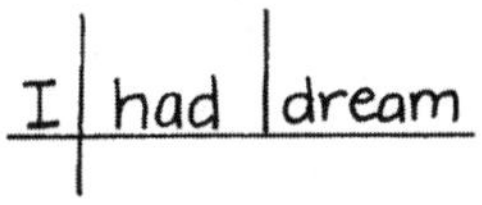

All our lines are EQUALLY and INFINITESIMALLY thick.

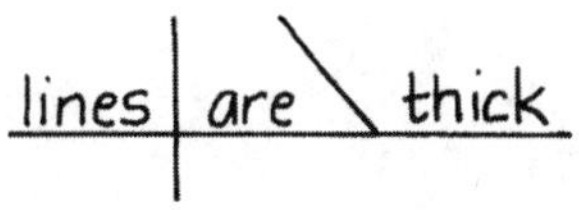

Straight Lines are in many important respects superior to the Circles.

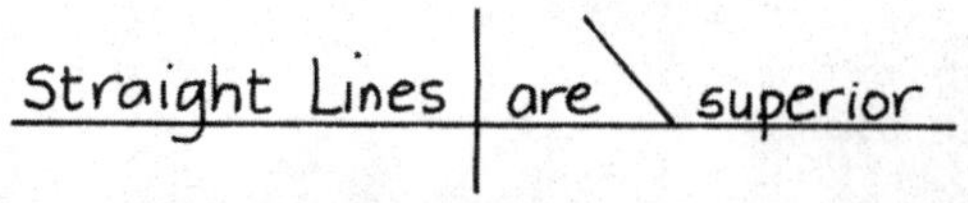

Note to Instructor: You may accept just Lines as the subject of the diagram.

LV PA
Many-sidedness was almost essential as a pretext for the Innovators.

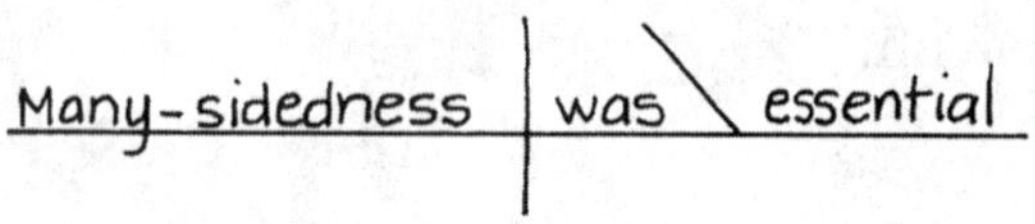

PA PA
All, except the Isosceles, were either neutral or averse to the Bill.

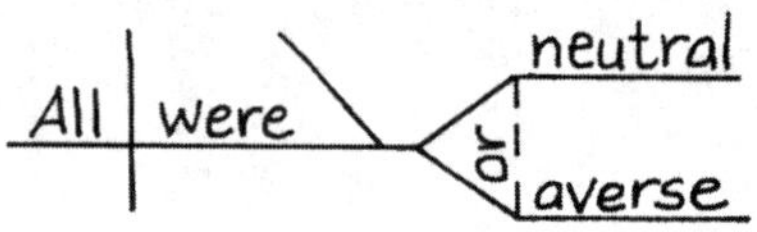

AV DO
I heard the sound of many voices in the street.

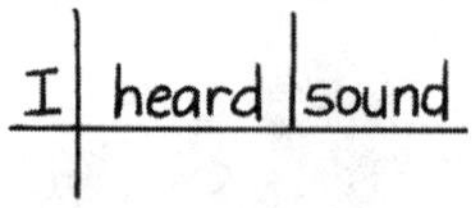

AV AV DO
The sights tantalized and tempted me to outspoken treason.

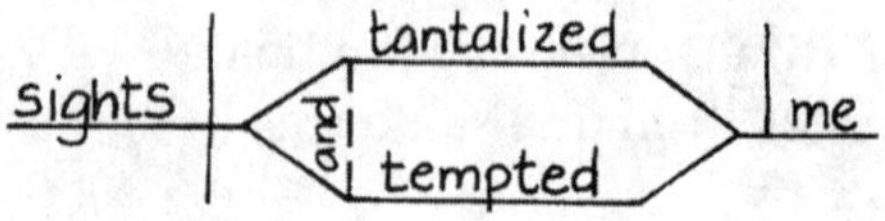

LV PA
BRIGHTNESS, as well as length, is necessary to the existence of a Line.

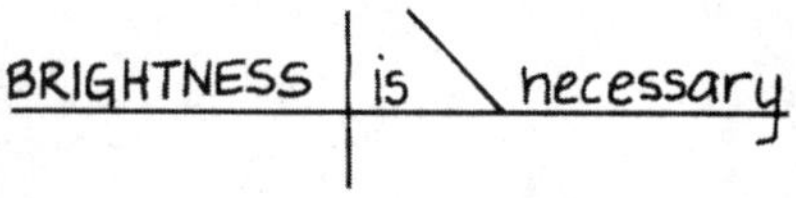

LV PA
On the reply to this question I am ready to stake everything.

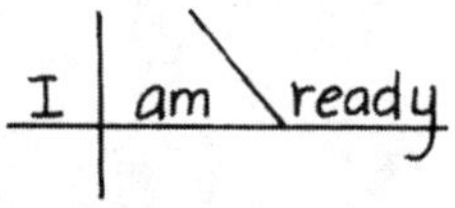

AV DO
Once or twice I even spoke the forbidden terms "the Third and Fourth Dimensions."

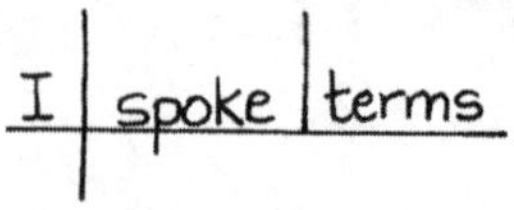

LV PA
A third appeal on my part was equally ineffectual.

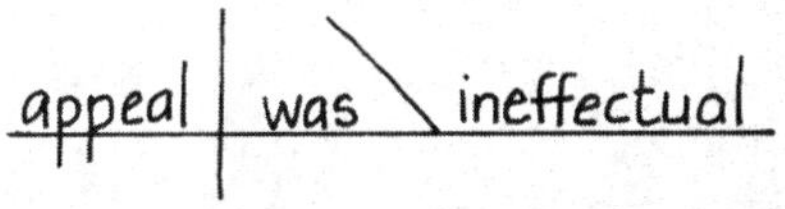

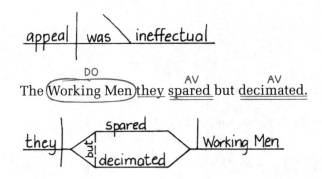

The Working Men they spared but decimated.

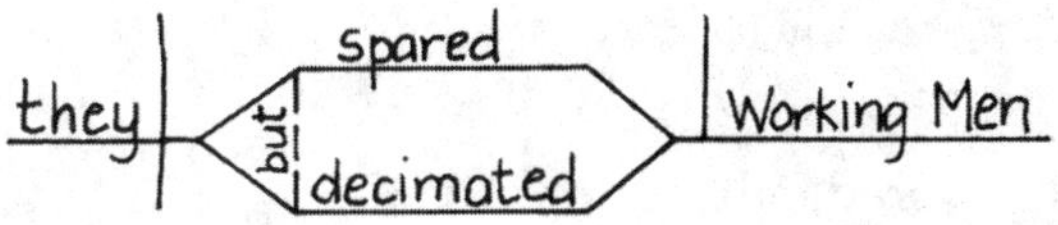

— LESSON 39 —

Linking Verbs
Predicate Adjectives
Predicate Nominatives

Exercise 39A: Identifying Predicate Nominatives and Adjectives

In the following sentences, underline the subjects once and the predicates twice. Circle the predicate nominatives or adjectives and label each one *PN* for predicate nominative or *PA* for predicate adjective. Draw a line from the predicate nominative or adjective to the subject that it renames or describes. There may be more than one of each.

These sentences are adapted from Noel Streatfeild's *Theater Shoes.*

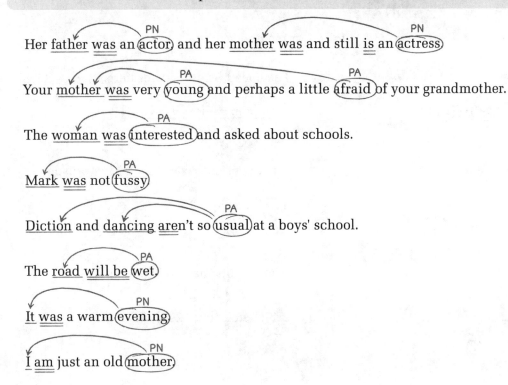

Her father was an actor and her mother was and still is an actress.

Your mother was very young and perhaps a little afraid of your grandmother.

The woman was interested and asked about schools.

Mark was not fussy.

Diction and dancing aren't so usual at a boys' school.

The road will be wet.

It was a warm evening.

I am just an old mother.

Exercise 39B: Writing Predicate Nominatives and Adjectives

Finish each sentence in two ways: with a predicate nominative and with a predicate adjective. If you need to use more than one word in a blank to complete your sentence, circle the word that is the predicate nominative or predicate adjective.

The first is done for you.

Note to Instructor: Sample answers are found below; accept any grammatically correct solutions in the blanks!

Football is ___my favorite (sport)___. (predicate nominative)

Football is ___entertaining___. (predicate adjective)

My grandmother's jewels are ___rubies___. (predicate nominative)

My grandmother's jewels are ___beautiful___. (predicate adjective)

The elderly passenger was ___Mr. Gregory___. (predicate nominative)

The elderly passenger was ___asleep___. (predicate adjective)

The proposed tax is ___a great (idea)___. (predicate nominative)

The proposed tax is ___unjust___. (predicate adjective)

All the girls at the party were ___flautists___. (predicate nominative)

All the girls at the party were ___terrified___. (predicate adjective)

That thunder was ___a (surprise)___. (predicate nominative)

That thunder was ___loud___. (predicate adjective)

Exercise 39C: Diagramming

On your own paper, diagram every word of the following sentences.

Science can be fascinating.

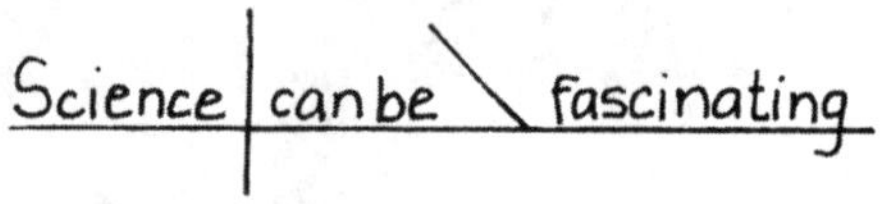

The speed limit is lower here.

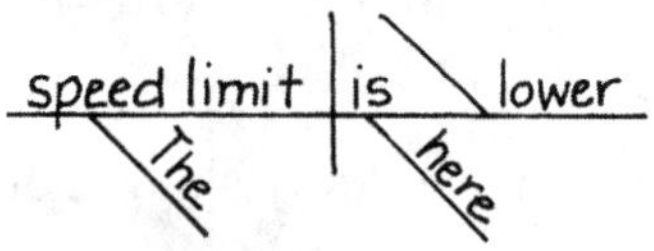

The dark cellar was not inviting.

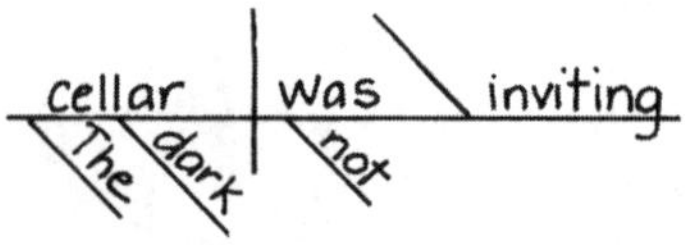

A golden ticket was an exciting prospect.

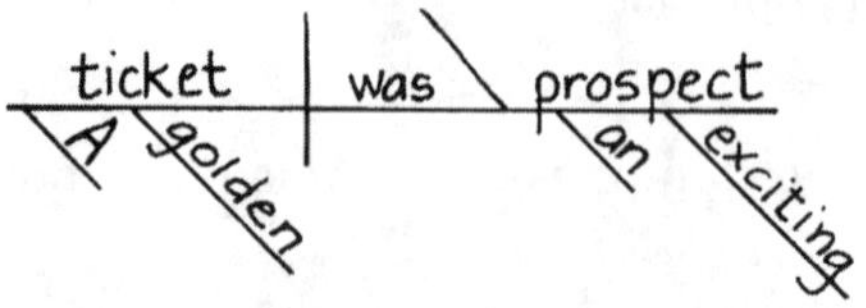

Is this book the right one?

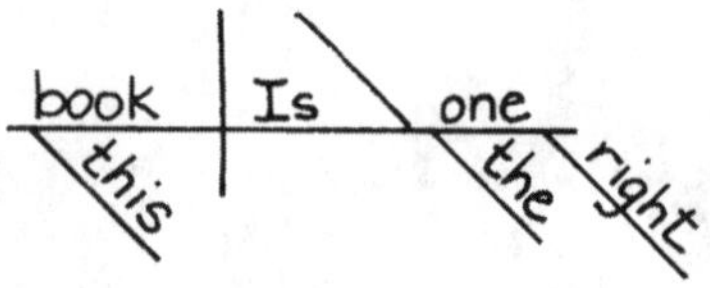

Some giants may be friendly.

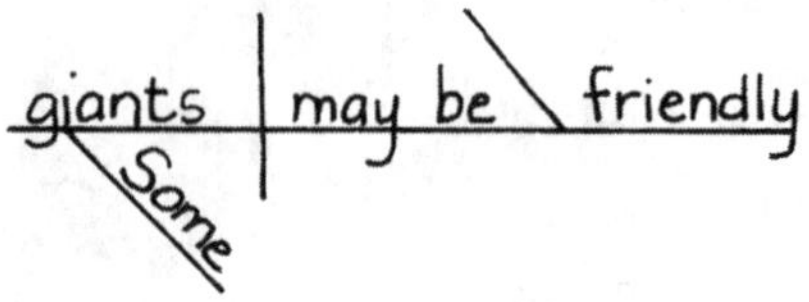

Be a participant!

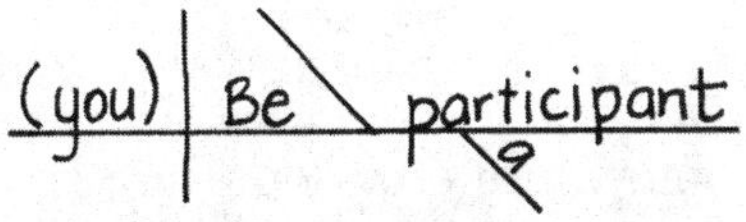

Her errors were minor.

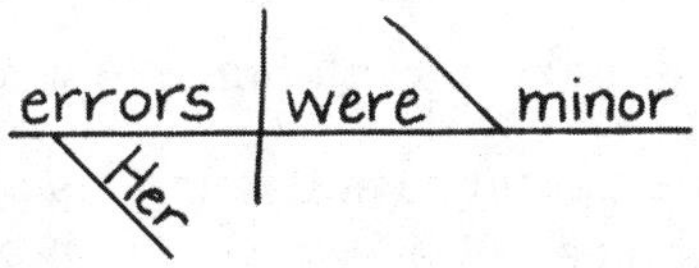

— LESSON 40 —

Predicate Adjectives and Predicate Nominatives
Pronouns as Predicate Nominatives
Object Complements

Exercise 40A: Reviewing Objects and Predicate Adjectives and Nominatives

Identify the underlined words as *DO* for direct object, *IO* for indirect object, *OP* for object of preposition, *PN* for predicate nominative, or *PA* for predicate adjective.

- For each direct object (or direct object/indirect object combination), find and underline twice the action verb that affects it.
- For each object of the preposition, find and circle the preposition to which it belongs.
- For each predicate nominative and predicate adjective, find and draw a box around the linking verb that it follows.
- When you are finished, fill in the blank in the statement at the end of the selection.

The following passage is from *Where the Red Fern Grows*, by Wilson Rawls. It has been condensed and slightly adapted.

It was always a pleasure to prowl where fishermen had camped. I usually could find things: a fish line, or a forgotten fish pole. On one occasion, I found a beautiful knife stuck in the bark of a sycamore tree, forgotten by a careless fisherman. But on that day, I found a great treasure, a sportsman's magazine, discarded by the campers. It was a real treasure for a country boy.

... The advertisement was from a kennel in Kentucky. I read it over and over. By the time I had memorized the ad, I was seeing dogs, hearing dogs, and even feeling them. The magazine was forgotten. I was lost in thought. The brain of an eleven-year-old boy can dream some fantastic dreams.

... I took the magazine from my pocket and again I read the ad. Slowly a plan began to form. I'd save the money. I could sell the fishermen stuff: crawfish, minnows, and fresh vegetables. In berry season, I could sell all the berries I could pick at my grandfather's store. I could trap in the winter. There was the way to get those pups—save my money.

DO OP DO

I could almost <u>feel</u> the <u>pups</u> (in) my <u>hands</u>. I <u>planned</u> the little <u>doghouse</u>, and where to put it.

DO

<u>Collars</u> I could <u>make</u> myself. Somehow, some way, I was determined to have those dogs.

Find the compound adjective in this passage. Write it in the blank below and cross out the incorrect choice. eleven-year-old is in the (attributive/~~predicative~~) position.

Exercise 40B: Parts of the Sentence

Label the following in each sentence: *S* (subject), *LV* (linking verb), *AV* (action verb), *DO* (direct object), *OC-A* (object complement-adjective), *OC-N* (object complement-noun), *IO* (indirect object), or *PN* (predicate nominative).

AV DO OC-A
Leave me alone.

AV IO DO
Leave me some pizza money.

S AV DO OC-N
Arnold pronounced the event a success.

S AV DO
We found the old house easily.

S AV DO OC-A
We found the old house empty.

S LV PA
The old house was empty.

S AV DO OC-A
Clarice prefers her tea hot.

S AV DO
Clarice prefers water occasionally.

Now for a challenge. A man finds a genie and gives the first order he can think of: "Make me a sandwich!" The genie smiles and replies, "Done! You're a sandwich."

Label (as above) the man's order in two ways—first, how the man intended it, and second, how the genie interpreted it.

AV IO DO
Make me a sandwich. (intended meaning)

AV DO OC-N
Make me a sandwich. (genie's interpretation)

Exercise 40C: Diagramming

On your own paper, diagram the sentences from Exercise 40B, including both versions of the final sentence.

Leave me alone.

Leave me some pizza money.

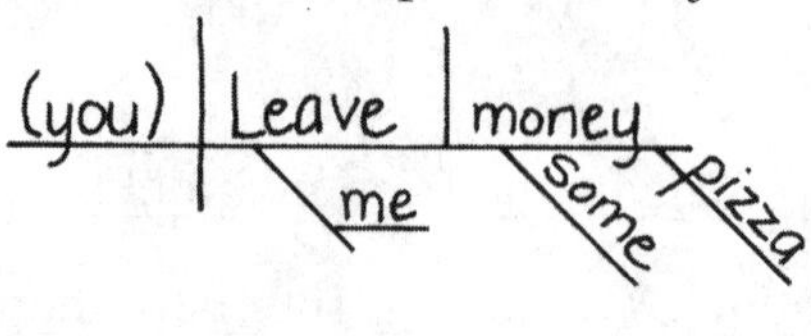

Arnold pronounced the event a success.

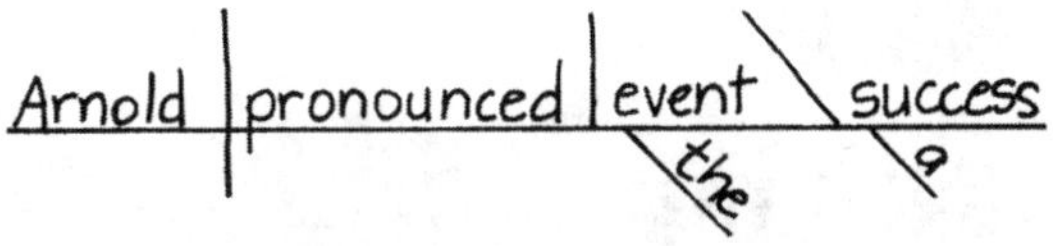

We found the old house easily.

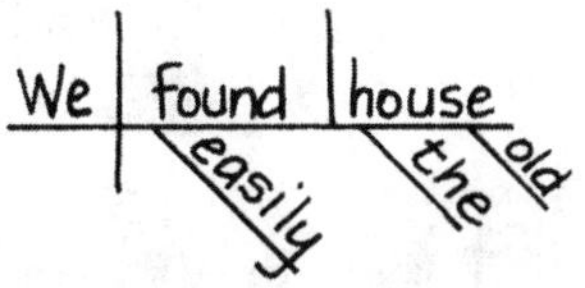

We found the old house empty.

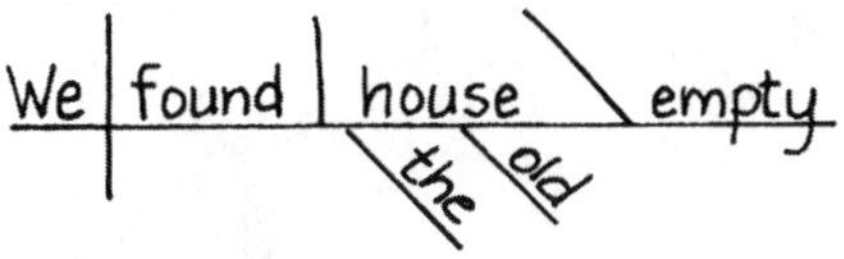

The old house was empty.

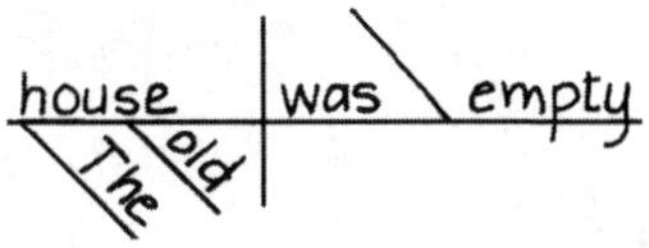

Clarice prefers her tea hot.

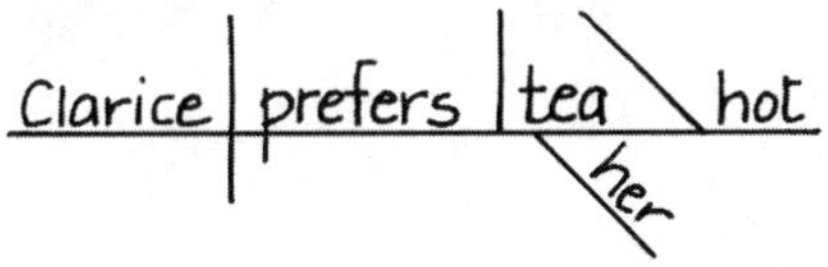

Clarice prefers water occasionally.

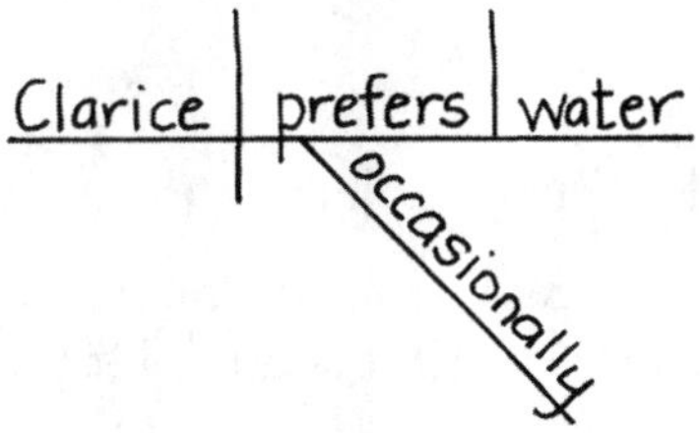

Make me a sandwich. (intended meaning)

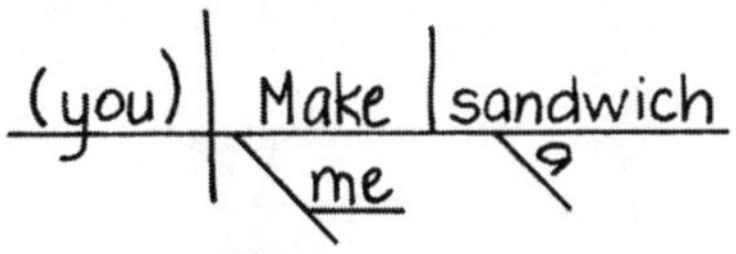

Make me a sandwich. (genie's interpretation)

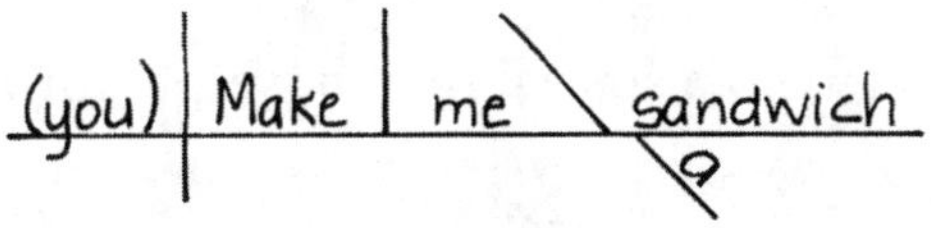

WEEK 11

More About Prepositions

— LESSON 41 —

Prepositions and Prepositional Phrases
Adjective Phrases

Exercise 41A: Identifying Adjective Phrases

Underline the adjective phrases in the following sentences. Draw an arrow from each phrase to the word it modifies. The first is done for you.

These sentences are adapted from *What the Robin Knows*, by Jon Young.

Her mother had a special relationship with a robin in her yard.

The feathers of the spotted towhee have little black and white patterns.

Some of it may be more desirable, high-rent terrain, with good access to food, water, and cover, and with relatively less danger from nest robbers and other predators.

You will see the mink and the fox in repose.

Note to Instructor: In the sentence above, the book's context makes it clear that "in repose" describes both *mink* and *fox*. However, without that context, it could be viewed as describing only *fox*—meaning "you will see the mink, and you will see the fox in repose," rather than meaning "you will see both animals in repose." Accept either response from the student.

The current mystery was the identification of a new woodpecker.

Speed of delivery, intensity, volume, position on landscape, and body language will confirm the alarm.

Knowledge of the territories will clear up any confusion about the alarm responses.

Exercise 41B: Diagramming Adjective Phrases/Review

Diagram each sentence from Exercise 41A on your own paper. Follow this procedure, and ask yourself the suggested questions if necessary.

1. Find the subject and predicate and diagram them first.
   What is the verb?
   Who or what [verb]?
2. Ask yourself: Is the verb an action verb? If so, look for a direct object.
   Who or what receives the action of the verb?

   If there is a direct object, check for an indirect object.
   To whom or for whom is the action done?

   Remember that there may be no direct object or no indirect object—but you can't have an indirect object without a direct object. If there is an indirect object, it will always come between the verb and the direct object.
3. Ask yourself: Is the verb a state-of-being verb? If so, look for a predicate nominative or predicate adjective.
   Is there a word after the verb that renames or describes the subject?
4. Find all prepositional phrases. Ask yourself: Whom or what do they describe?
5. Place all other adjectives and adverbs on the diagram. If you have trouble, ask for help.

Her mother had a special relationship with a robin in her yard.

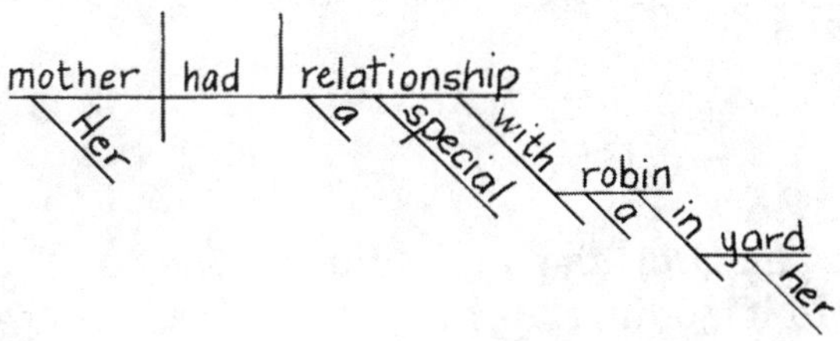

The feathers of the spotted towhee have little black and white patterns.

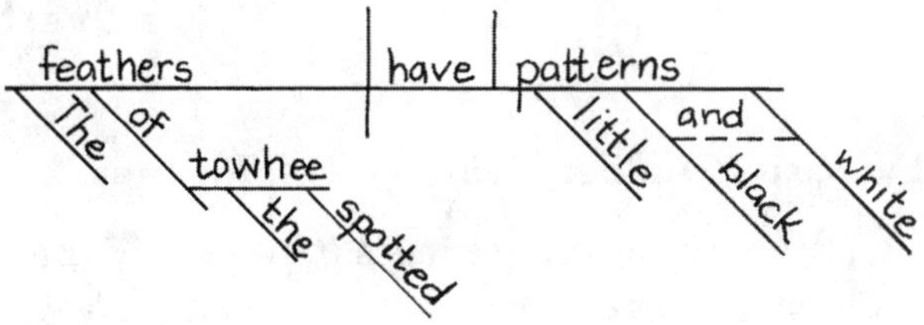

Some of it may be more desirable, high-rent terrain, with good access to food, water, and cover, and with relatively less danger from nest robbers and other predators.

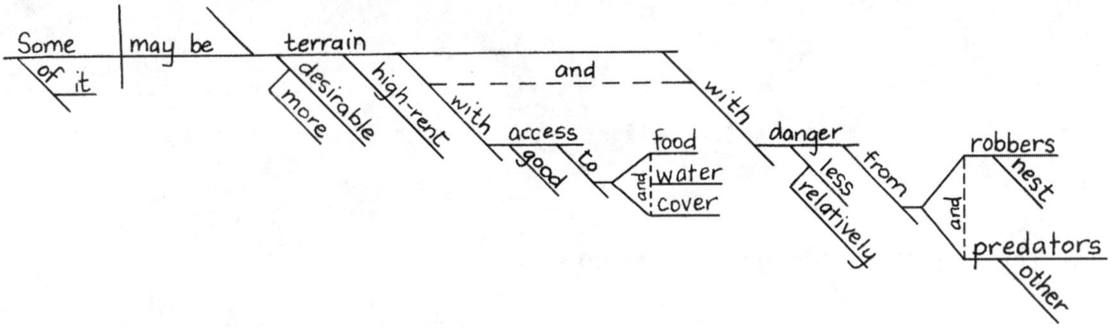

You will see the mink and the fox in repose.

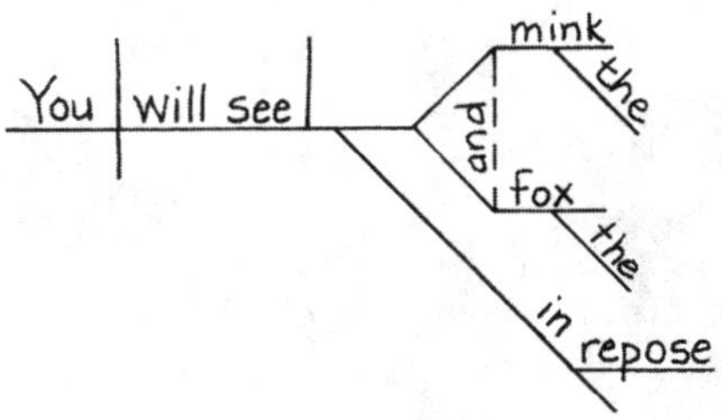

The current mystery was the identification of a new woodpecker.

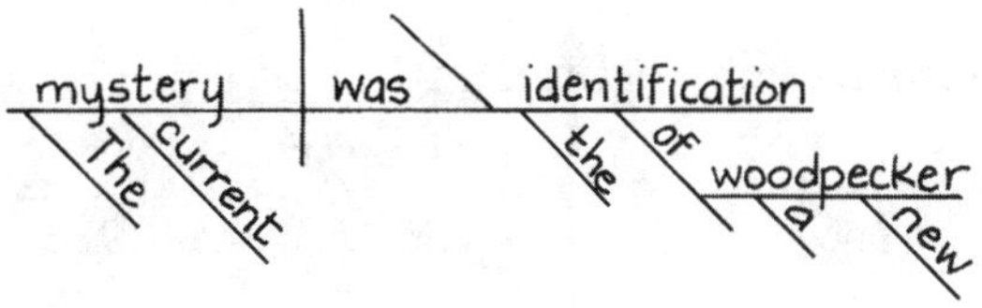

Speed of delivery, intensity, volume, position on landscape, and body language will confirm the alarm.

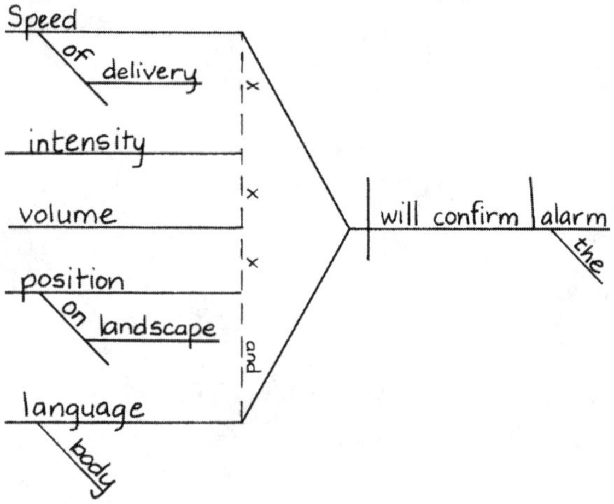

Knowledge of the territories will clear up any confusion about the alarm responses.

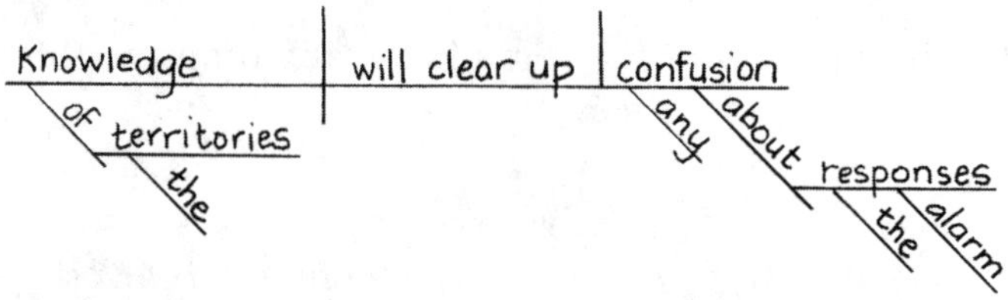

Note to Instructor: *Clear up* is a compound ("phrasal") verb; the word *up* is functioning as part of the verb. If the student diagrams *up* as an adverb, accept the answer, but show the student the diagram in this Key and point out that *clear up* has a single meaning.

— LESSON 42 —

Adjective Phrases

Adverb Phrases

Exercise 42A: Identifying Adverb Phrases

Underline the adverb phrases in the following sentences and circle the preposition that begins each phrase. Draw an arrow from each phrase to the word it modifies. Be careful! There are three adjective phrases hiding in these sentences as well. Don't mistake them for adverbs!

These sentences are adapted from *Pompeii: The Living City*, by Alex Butterworth and Ray Laurence.

The first is done for you.

Note to Instructor: The prepositional phrases in italics below are the three adjective phrases. The student should NOT mark these.

Tombs have also been found outside the Herculaneum gate.

Abroad, two new provinces had been added to the Empire through skilful diplomacy and well-weighted military pressure.

Jucundus had competitors in Pompeii.

Note to Instructor: The phrase isn't an adjective describing *competitors*; if the student asks why, point out that it answers the question *where*, and also can be placed at the beginning of the sentence, whereas an adjective phrase has to stay with the noun it modifies.

Elite life was conducted within a shame culture.

Amongst the statues, two figures would have caught the eye.

The family gladiators would doubtless have been used in the games.

Bursts *of colour* exploded beside the city's thoroughfares.

Unlike Augustus's organizations, Nero's new club did not revolve around piety, obedience, conformity, and respect.

Amid the bewilderment, for hours and days there would have been little realistic sense *of the eventual final death toll.*

On his arrival he befriended Julius Polybius.

In the past these fish had shoaled in large numbers around the rocky headlands *of Italy.*

> **Note to Instructor:** The student may include *of Italy* in the underlined adverb phrase *around the rocky headlands*, since it's technically an element of the phrase.

At one point, a suit was brought by the entire district against a tax-collector.

Exercise 42B: Diagramming Adverb Phrases

On your own paper, diagram the following five sentences from Exercise 42A.

Jucundus had competitors in Pompeii.

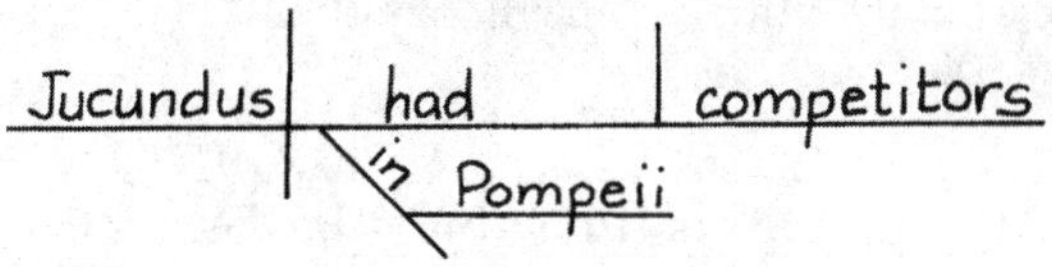

Amongst the statues, two figures would have caught the eye.

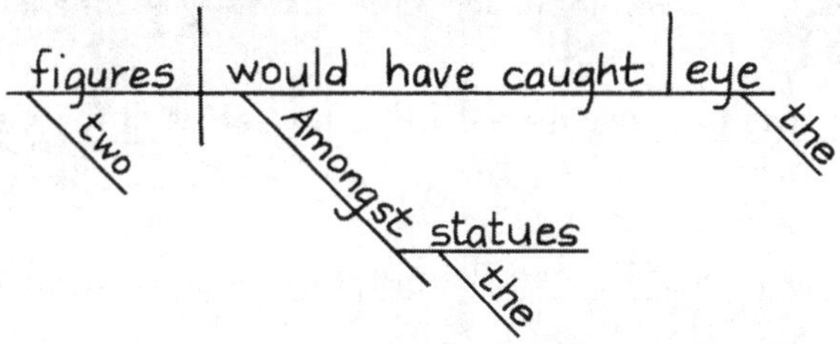

Unlike Augustus's organizations, Nero's new club did not revolve around piety, obedience, conformity, and respect.

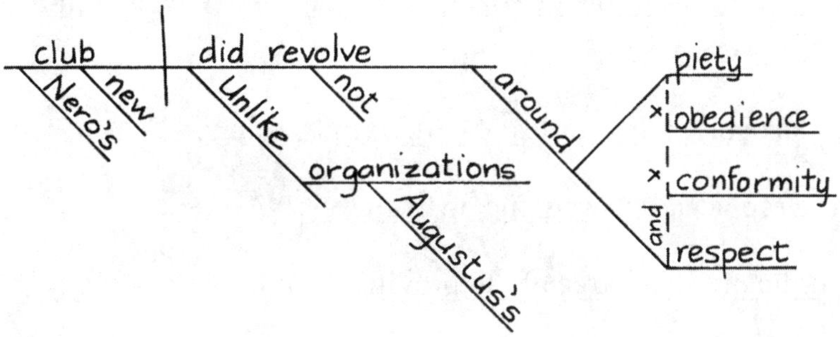

On his arrival he befriended Julius Polybius.

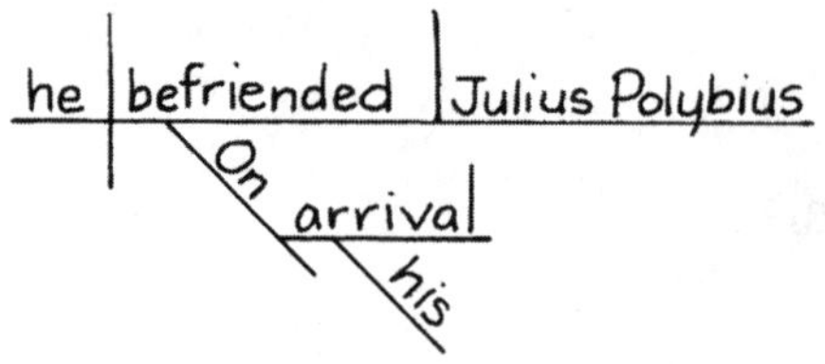

At one point, a suit was brought by the entire district against a tax-collector.

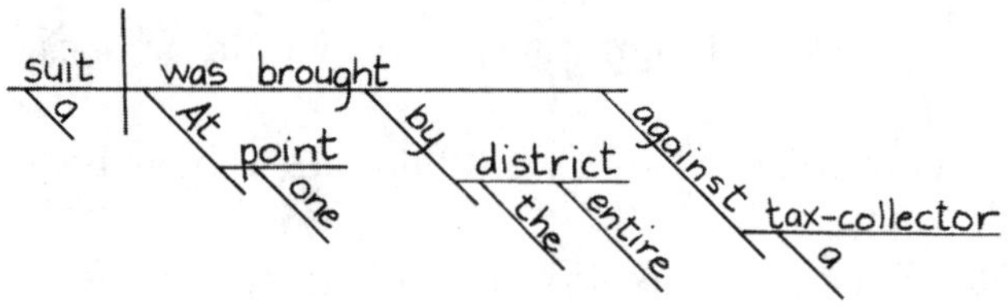

— LESSON 43 —

Definitions Review
Adjective and Adverb Phrases
Misplaced Modifiers

Exercise 43A: Distinguishing Between Adjective and Adverb Phrases

Underline all the prepositional phrases in the following sentences. Write *ADJ* above the adjective phrases and *ADV* above the adverb phrases. These sentences are adapted from R. G. Collingwood's *Roman Britain.*

The army was permanently distributed along the frontiers (ADV).

The Vallum ran from the Tyne (ADV) above Newcastle (ADJ) to the Solway (ADV) below Burgh-by-Sands (ADJ).

Note to Instructor: The student may wonder why the adjective clauses, which also seem to express *where*, are not adverbs. *From the Tyne* and *to the Solway* describe the verb *ran* and tells *where* the Vallum (wall) ran (adverbial). *Above Newcastle* describes at *which* part of the Tyne river the Vallum began, and *below Burgh-by-Sands* describes at *which* part of the Solway it ended, so both are acting as adjectives (describing nouns and answering the question *which*).

For this purpose (ADV) an entirely new series of forts (ADJ) was created at about this time (ADV) along the "Saxon Shore." (ADV)

The towns of Roman Britain (ADJ) may be conveniently divided into three classes (ADV).

Note to Instructor: *Into three classes* describes *how* the division is done, not the towns directly.

Sculptural and architectural fragments of unusually fine quality (ADJ) give an impressive idea of the artistic development (ADJ) of Romanized British taste (ADJ).

In 367 (ADV) practically the whole of Britain (ADJ) was overrun by hordes (ADV) of barbarian invaders (ADJ).

Sharp angles in the profile (ADJ) of a vessel (ADJ) are replaced by sweeping open curves (ADV).

We find a real Romano-British art not in the civilized area (ADV) of the province (ADJ), but in the outlying military fringe (ADV).

ADV ADV ADJ ADJ ADJ
The same desire was certainly at work in the mind of the carver of the tombstone of Flavinus.

ADJ ADJ ADV ADJ ADV
The temple of Nodens at Lydney was built on the site of a prehistoric hill-fort in the fourth century.

Exercise 43B: Correcting Misplaced Modifiers

Circle the misplaced adjective and adverb phrases in the following sentences. Draw an arrow to show where the phrase should be.

For some of the sentences, the phrase may make sense where it is—but if a phrase doesn't communicate what the author wants it to, it is misplaced. Assume that each sentence contains a phrase that is misplaced (that is, a different meaning was intended), correct as instructed above, and explain to your instructor how the placement changes the meaning.

The first is done for you, with a sample explanation provided.

Inside the clock Daniel watched the huge pendulum swinging back and forth.

Inside the clock as initially placed indicates the place from which Daniel did the watching. In the corrected position, the phrase answers the question "which pendulum?"

The girl fell down on the skating rink in the yellow dress.

As placed, the phrase indicates that the skating rink is in the yellow dress. It's much more likely that the girl is the one in the yellow dress, as the corrected position indicates.

The bird above the trees escaped the predator by flying.

As placed, the phrase answers the question "which bird?" In the corrected version, the phrase is acting as an adverb that answers "flying where?"

I saw six huge birds flying through my car window.

As placed, the phrase tells where the birds are flying. As corrected, the phrase tells where I saw the birds. The phrase could also be inserted after "saw" for the same corrected meaning.

The woman with the worn keys selected the piano.

Who or what has worn keys—the woman, or the piano? As placed, the phrase indicates that it's the woman. As corrected, it's the piano.

The man with the fluffy tail tossed the dog a ball.

As placed, the one with the fluffy tail is the man. As corrected, it's the dog.

The student on the flute played "Hot Cross Buns."

As placed, the phrase answers the question "which student?" As corrected, it answers the question "played how?" The phrase could also be inserted at the beginning of the sentence for the same corrected meaning.

Behind the desk the teacher knocked over the trash can.

This phrase could have three different meanings, depending on its position in the sentence! As placed, it answers the question of where the teacher was when he knocked over the trash can. As corrected, it answers the question "which trash can?" It could also have been moved to just after the word "teacher" to answer the question "which teacher?"

The tiny ship beyond the horizon has sailed to a far-off land.

This one also has three possible meanings. As placed, the phrase answers the question "which ship?" As corrected, it answers the question "which far-off land?" Alternatively, the phrase could be moved to the beginning of the sentence or to after the word "sailed"; in either of those positions, it would answer the question "sailed where?"

My friend during the test jumped out of her seat at the sound of the fire alarm.

And another one with three possibilities! As placed, the phrase answers the question "which friend?" As corrected, it answers the question "jumped when?" It could also be moved to the space after "alarm" to answer the question "which fire alarm?"

We followed the narrow path to a quaint cottage through the woods.

As placed, the phrase answers the question "followed where?," or possibly "which cottage?" It's kind of hard to tell! As corrected, it answers "which path?" If the phrase were moved to the beginning of the sentence, it would be a clearer "followed where?" answer.

— LESSON 44 —

Adjective and Adverb Phrases

Prepositional Phrases Acting as Other Parts of Speech

Exercise 44A: Prepositional Phrases Acting as Other Parts of Speech

In each sentence below, circle any prepositional phrases. Underline the subject of the sentence once and the predicate twice. Then label the prepositional phrases as *ADJ* (adjective phrase), *ADV* (adverb phrase), *S* (subject), *PA* (predicate adjective), *PN* (predicate nominative), or *OP* (object of a preposition).

S

In her mother's arms is the newborn baby's favorite place.

A book about unicorns is on order.

With a timid voice, Iris answered the question from the teacher.

Among the trees in the deepest part of the forest lives the wise old owl.

Toward those trees is your path. OR Toward those trees is your path.

Note to Instructor: This sentence could be understood in two ways. If the speaker is identifying the path (not the "in the valley" path or the "along the riverbank" path, but the "toward those trees" path), *Toward those trees* acts as the subject and *path* is a predicate nominative renaming *Toward those trees*. If the speaker is pointing out *where* the path is, *toward those trees* could be identified as an adverb, and the subject and predicate of the sentence are *path is*.

Accept either answer, but discuss the alternate possibility as well.

The scariest place to be is in very deep dark woods.

Laura has been smiling since before the beginning of class.

The steps in the hallway seem steep to me.

Allan is in love with Rita.

I will listen to the children in a moment.

Exercise 44B: Diagramming

On your own paper, diagram these sentences from Exercise 44A.

In her mother's arms is the newborn baby's favorite place.

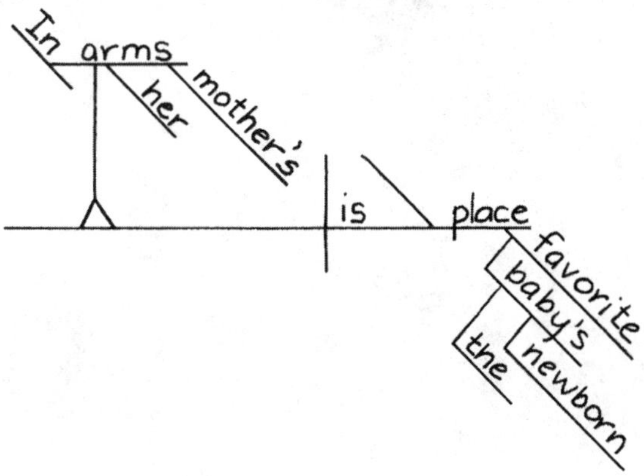

A book about unicorns is on order.

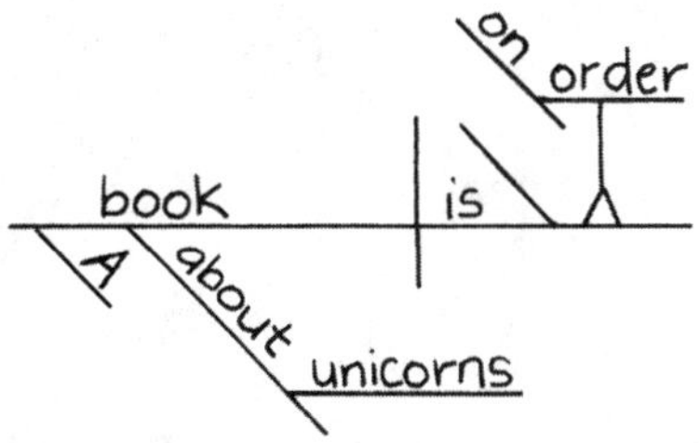

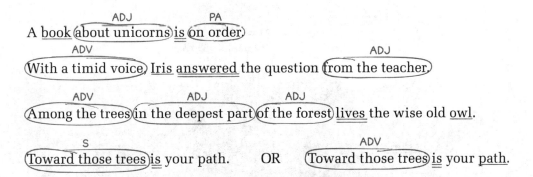

With a timid voice, Iris answered the question from the teacher.

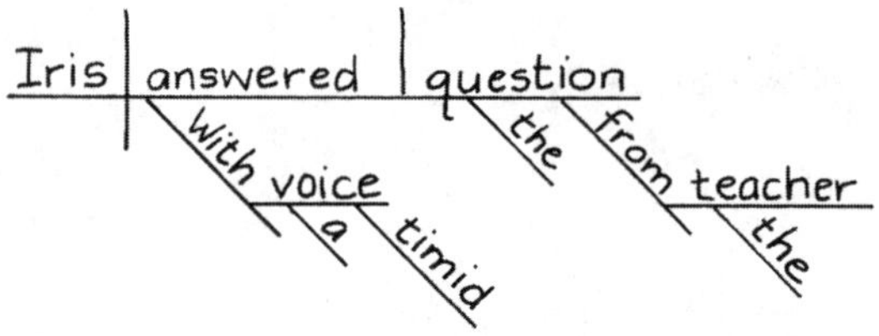

Among the trees in the deepest part of the forest lives the wise old owl.

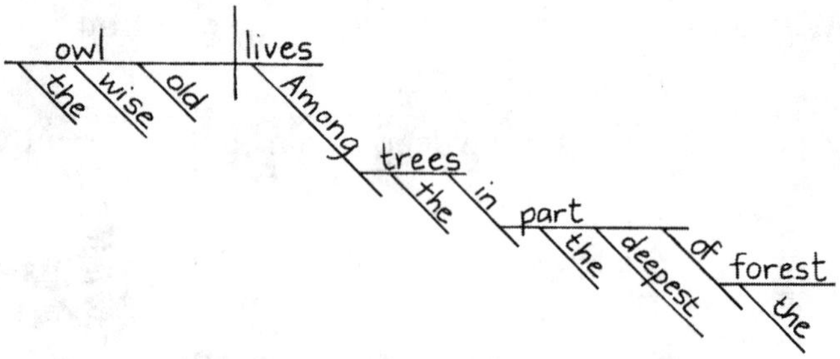

Toward those trees is your path.

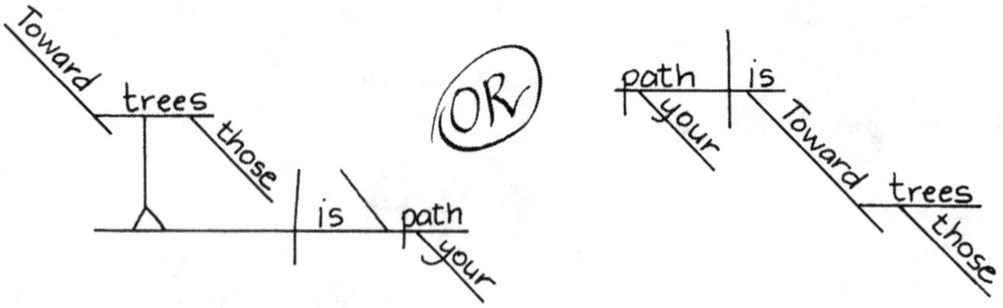

Note to Instructor: As noted above, *Toward those trees* can be diagrammed as the subject or as an adverb phrase. Accept either answer, but show the student the alternate diagram.

Laura has been smiling since before the beginning of class.

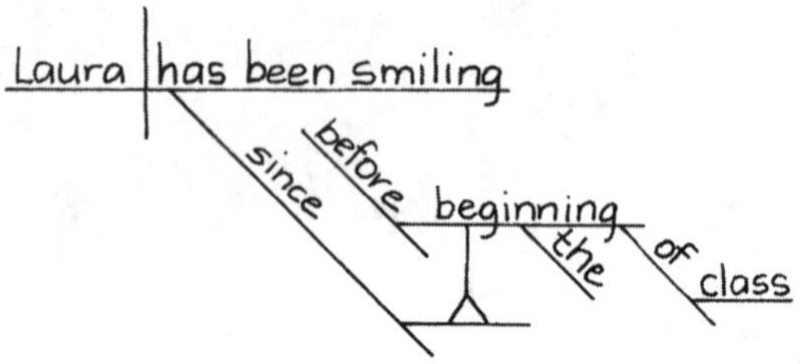

The steps in the hallway seem steep to me.

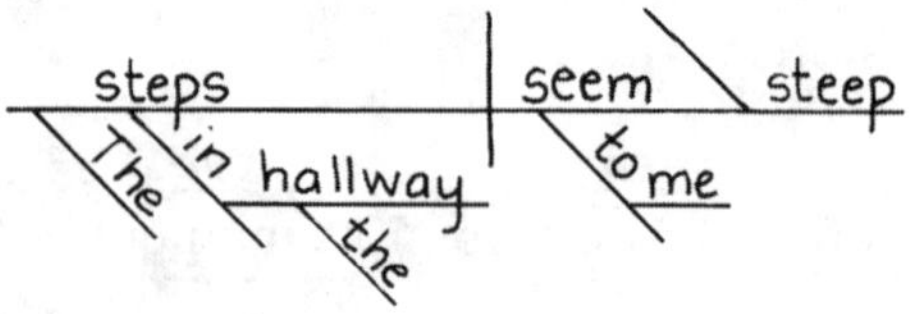

Allan is in love with Rita.

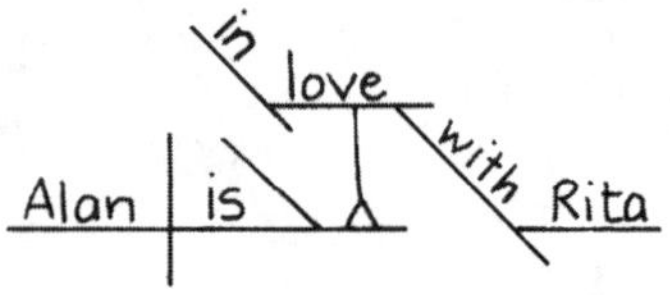

I will listen to the children in a moment.

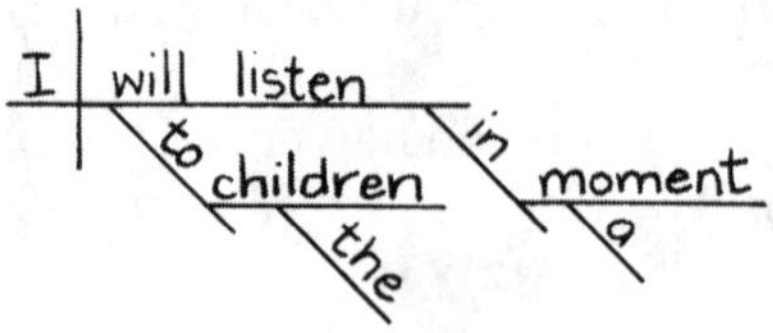

WEEK 12

Advanced Verbs

— LESSON 45 —

Linking Verbs

Linking/Action Verbs

Exercise 45A: Distinguishing Between Action Verbs and Linking Verbs

Underline the verbs in the following sentences. Identify them as *AV* for action verb or *LV* for linking verb. If the verb is followed by a direct object (*DO*), predicate adjective (*PA*), or predicate nominative (*PN*), label it.

Remember that a verb with *no* direct object, predicate adjective, or predicate nominative will be an action verb, unless it is a state-of-being verb. Also remember that direct objects, predicate adjectives, and predicate nominatives are never found within prepositional phrases.

AV DO
Do not turn another page in this book!

LV PA
Your nose will turn green!

AV
Turn around now.

AV
Ethan looked around the room quickly.

LV PA
He looked nervous.

LV PN
She may become the next president of our club.

AV DO
Does the dog smell bacon?

LV PA
Does the dog smell bad?

LV PA
Her boots were purple.

AV DO
Can you prove me wrong?

Note to Instructor: "Wrong" in the sentence above is an object complement.

LV PN
Your son will prove a strong manager.

LV PA
Elyse remained awake throughout the night.

LV PA
Tavi grows taller with every passing week!

AV DO
Tavi grows zucchini in his garden.

Exercise 45B: Distinguishing Among Different Kinds of Nouns

Underline all the nouns in the following sentences. Identify them as *S* for subject, *OP* for object of a preposition, *IO* for indirect object, *DO* for direct object, or *PN* for predicate nominative.

These sentences are adapted from *A Dog on Barkham Street*, by M. S. Stolz.

Mrs. Frost (S) gave the mailman (IO) a sweet bun (DO) with his coffee (OP).

Edward (S) hadn't seen a sign (DO) of a wren (OP).

The sun (S) burned right through that glass (OP) and set the leaves (DO) on fire (OP).

But Toad (S) was a problem (PN) to all his friends (OP).

On the afternoon (OP) of assembly day (OP), all the classes (S) would have a dress rehearsal (DO).

Maybe a genie (S) will come out and give my father (IO) the answer (DO).

Buffalo (S) have never been considered good pets (PN).

Exercise 45C: Diagramming Action Verbs and Linking Verbs

Diagram the following sentences.

Sophia is a cat.

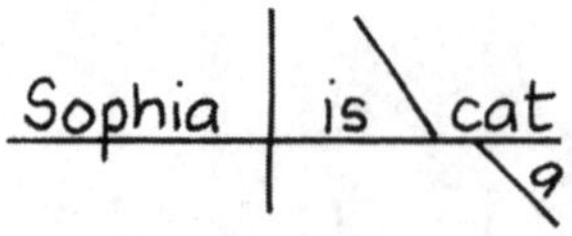

Jordan gave Sophia a treat.

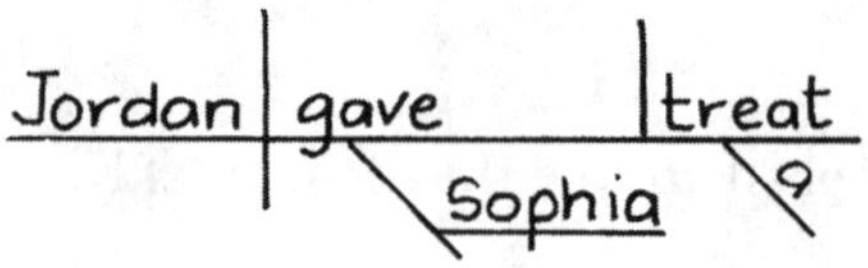

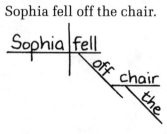

Sophia tasted the treat.

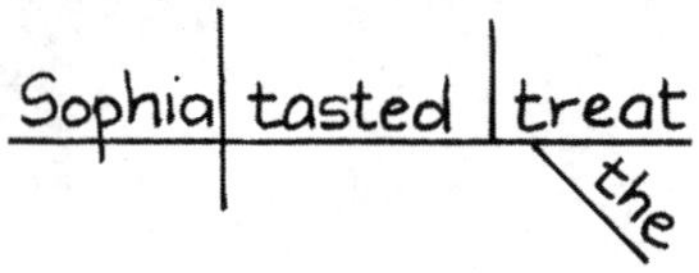

The treat tasted delicious.

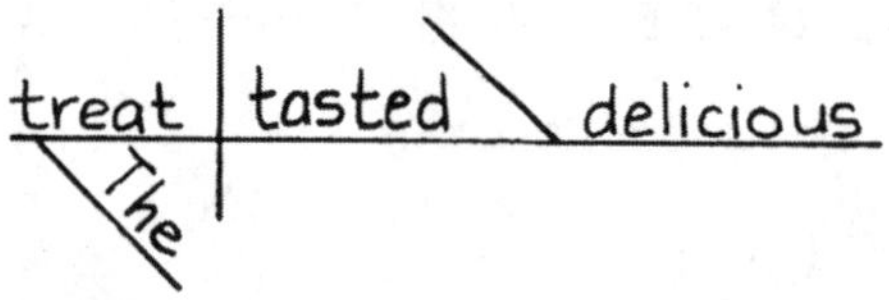

Sophia is sleepy.

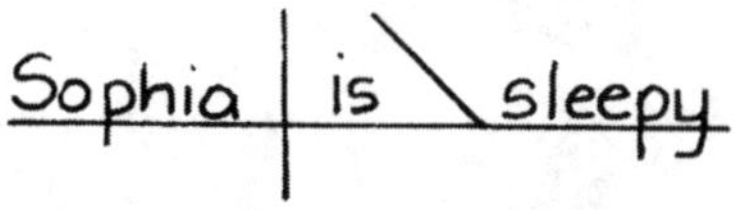

Sophia fell asleep.

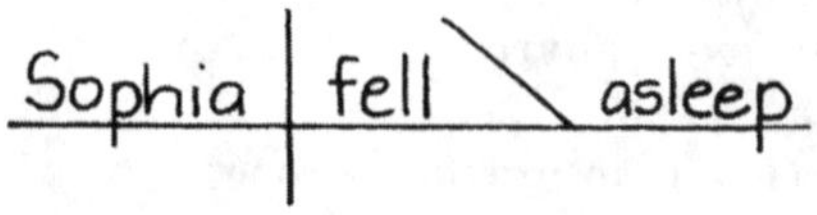

Sophia fell off the chair.

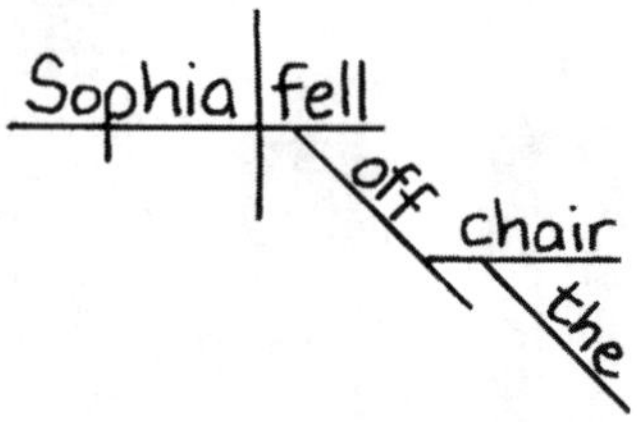

— LESSON 46 —

Conjugations
Irregular Verbs
Principal Parts of Verbs

Exercise 46A: Forming Simple, Perfect, and Progressive Tenses

Fill in the missing blanks in the chart below.

Simple Present

	Singular	Plural
First person	I blink	We blink
Second person	You blink	You blink
Third person	He, she, it blinks	They blink

Simple Past

	Singular	Plural
First person	I blinked	We blinked
Second person	You blinked	You blinked
Third person	He, she, it blinked	They blinked

Simple Future

	Singular	Plural
First person	I will blink	We will blink
Second person	You will blink	You will blink
Third person	He, she, it will blink	They will blink

Perfect Present

	Singular	Plural
First person	I have blinked	We have blinked
Second person	You have blinked	You have blinked
Third person	He, she, it has blinked	They have blinked

Perfect Past

	Singular	Plural
First person	I had blinked	We had blinked
Second person	You had blinked	You had blinked
Third person	He, she, it had blinked	They had blinked

Perfect Future

	Singular	Plural
First person	I will have blinked	We will have blinked
Second person	You will have blinked	You will have blinked
Third person	He, she, it will have blinked	They will have blinked

Progressive Present

	Singular	Plural
First person	I am blinking	We are blinking
Second person	You are blinking	You are blinking
Third person	He, she, it is blinking	They are blinking

Progressive Past

	Singular	Plural
First person	I was blinking	We were blinking
Second person	You were blinking	You were blinking
Third person	He, she, it was blinking	They were blinking

Progressive Future

	Singular	Plural
First person	I will be blinking	We will be blinking
Second person	You will be blinking	You will be blinking
Third person	He, she, it will be blinking	They will be blinking

Exercise 46B: Spanish and English Words

Draw lines to match each English word with its Spanish equivalent. Because English and Spanish have similar backgrounds, you should be able to complete this exercise easily, even if you've never learned any Spanish!

English	**Spanish**
adventure	pingüino
traffic	paciencia
giraffe	voleibol
patience	jirafa
fascinate	aventura
penguin	preparar
leader	sorpresa
prepare	tráfico
volleyball	líder
surprise	fascinar

Exercise 46C: Principal Parts of Verbs

Fill in the chart with the missing forms.

	First Principal Part Present	Second Principal Part Past	Third Principal Part Past Participle
I	launch	launched	launched
I	bury	buried	buried
I	compete	competed	competed
I	enter	entered	entered
I	correct	corrected	corrected
I	imagine	imagined	imagined
I	hurry	hurried	hurried
I	tip	tipped	tipped
I	brake	braked	braked
I	betray	betrayed	betrayed

Exercise 46D: Distinguishing Between First and Second Principal Parts

Identify each underlined verb as *1* for first principal part or *2* for second principal part. These sentences are from Steven Ujifusa's *A Man and His Ship*.

On March 28, 1918, the men of the 301st Heavy Tank Battalion joined [2] some six thousand other troops on *Olympic* bound for Europe.

We note [1] with great interest the suggestion made that future construction should be of steel largely in place of wood.

The liners traveled [2] alone because they were too fast for escorts to keep up with them.

"On behalf of myself and the people of the United States," he said [2] in closing, "I thank [1] you from the bottom of my heart."

In stark contrast to most employers of the time, William Francis Gibbs based [2] his hires not on background, but on ability.

— LESSON 47 —

Linking Verbs
Principal Parts
Irregular Verbs

No exercises this lesson.

— LESSON 48 —

Linking Verbs
Principal Parts
Irregular Verbs

Exercise 48A: Principal Parts

Fill in the blanks in the following chart of verbs.

Present	Past	Past Participle
bear	bore	born or borne (depending on meaning)
breed	bred	bred
feel	felt	felt
have	had	had
overtake	overtook	overtaken
show	showed	shown
spread	spread	spread
sweep	swept	swept
win	won	won
beat	beat	beaten
broadcast	broadcast	broadcast
forbid	forbade	forbidden
hold	held	held
pay	paid	paid
sink	sank	sunk
stand	stood	stood
swell	swelled	swollen or swelled
arise	arose	arisen
blow	blew	blown
eat	ate	eaten
hang	hung	hung
spit	spat	spat
swear	swore	sworn
mow	mowed	mown or mowed
weep	wept	wept
bend	bent	bent
burst	burst	burst
forgive	forgave	forgiven
kneel	knelt	knelt
put	put	put
sit	sat	sat

Present	Past	Past Participle
stick	stuck	stuck
swing	swung	swung
bet	bet	bet
cling	clung	clung
get	got	gotten
leave	left	left
saw	sawed	sawn or sawed
slide	slid	slid
sting	stung	stung
wake	woke	woken
bind	bound	bound

Exercise 48B: Forming Correct Past Participles

Write the correct third principal part (past participle) in each blank. The first principal part is provided for you in parentheses. The first is done for you.

I have __drawn__ (draw) you a beautiful picture!

The bell has not __rung__ (ring) on time at all this week.

By the time I realized I had __stolen__ (steal) the wrong suitcase, the right one had __set__ (set) off for France.

Hattie has __ridden__ (ride) her horse for three hours already.

Louis had __shown__ (show) me the plan, but I hadn't __thought__ (think) it would work.

Since that bad experience, Hyung has never __eaten__ (eat) at that restaurant again.

I have __given__ (give) you too many chances already!

What has __led__ (lead) you to this conclusion?

Exercise 48C: Forming Correct Past Tenses

Write the correct second principal part (past) in each blank. The first principal part is provided for you in parentheses. The first is done for you.

The little fish __swam__ (swim) upstream.

Yesterday, I __ran__ (run) all the way from the post office to the park.

Maria's pencil __fell__ (fall) off her desk, but she __caught__ (catch) it before it __hit__ (hit) the floor.

I __chose__ (choose) the design for my new bookcase, and my father __built__ (build) it.

We __went__ (go) hiking and __lost__ (lose) our way.

The squirrel __hid__ (hide) ten nuts and __kept__ (keep) searching for more.

Jamil __read__ (read) the contract and __paid__ (pay) the membership fee.

Exercise 48D: Proofreading for Irregular Verb Usage

In the passage below, from Dorothy Canfield Fisher's *Understood Betsy*, you will find seven errors in irregular verb usage. Cross out the incorrect forms and write the correct ones above them.

But it ~~haved~~ had a weighty, satisfying ring to it. The little girl ~~feeled~~ felt the importance of having her statement recognized. She turned back to her driving.

The slow, heavy plow horses had stopped during her talk with Uncle Henry. They ~~standed~~ stood as still now as though their feet had ~~growed~~ grown to the road. Elizabeth Ann looked up at the old man for instructions. But he ~~beed~~ was deep in his figures. She had been ~~teached~~ taught never to interrupt people, so she ~~sitted~~ sat still and waited for him to tell her what to do.

Exercise 48E: Diagramming

On your own paper, diagram the following four sentences.

When did we elect Jim president?

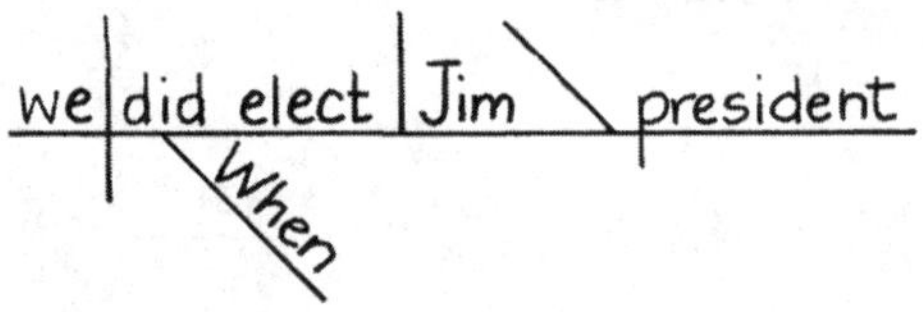

Abigail and Joanna look adorable in their new dresses.

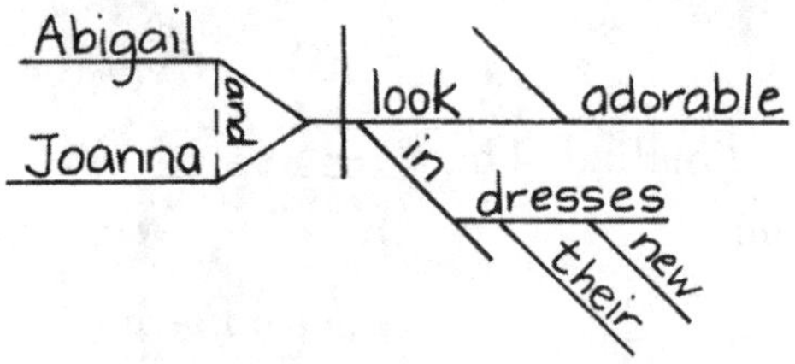

The bird looked questioningly at the little boy.

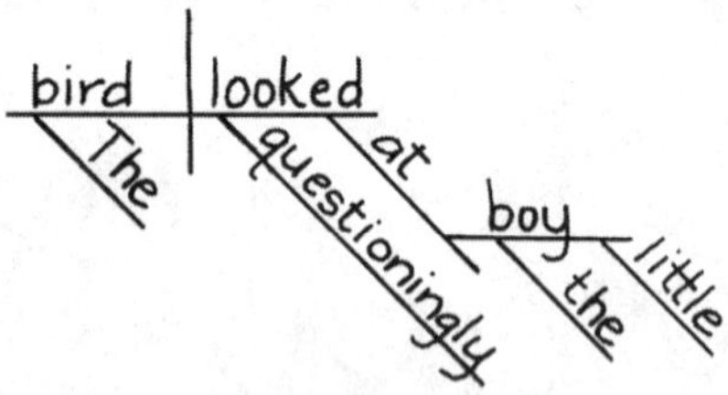

After nine is an acceptable time for a phone call.

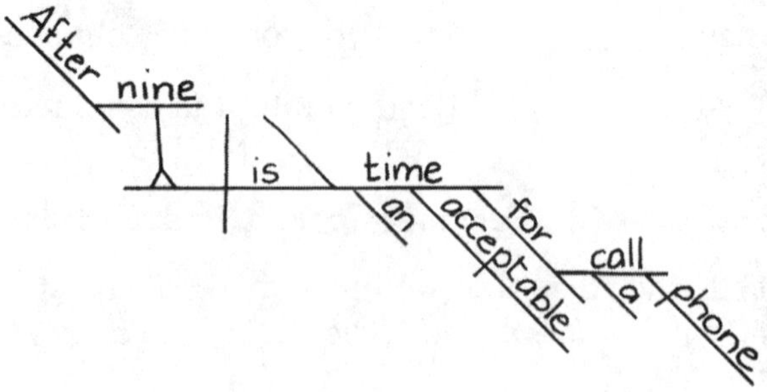

— REVIEW 4 —

Weeks 10-12

Topics:
Direct and Indirect Objects
Linking Verbs
Predicate Adjectives
Predicate Nominatives
Articles
Adjective Phrases
Adverb Phrases
Action vs. Linking Verbs
Irregular Verbs
Principal Parts (Present, Past, Past Participle)

Review 4A: Action vs. Linking Verbs

Identify the underlined verbs as *A* for *action* or *L* for *linking.*

Zebras are [L] not tame like horses.

A baby zebra smells [A] its mother.

The mother smells [L] familiar, so the foal follows [A] her.

Lions and painted hyenas are [L] predators of the zebra.

The spotted hyena usually scavenges [A] for leftovers from another's meal, but it can kill [A] zebras as well.

The stripes on a zebra protect [A] it from predators; they make the zebra look [L] blurry when it runs [A].

Mother zebras look [A] carefully at unfamiliar animals to make sure that they pose no threat.

If the animal is a predator, the mother sounds [A] an alarm.

Although the zebra seems [L] gentle, it can kick [A] and bite [A] attackers when needed.

The zebra's whinny, or bray, sounds [L] odd, a little like the bark of a small dog.

Mountain zebras, which live [A] in southern Africa, are [L] a protected species.

The quagga, a subspecies of zebra with stripes on the front half of its body and brown on the back half, has become [L] extinct.

Scientists in the Quagga Project are trying [A] to use DNA from a quagga to breed new animals that resemble the extinct ones.

Review 4B: Predicate Adjectives and Predicate Nominatives

Underline the linking verb in each of the following sentences. If the sentence concludes with a predicate nominative or predicate adjective, circle each and write *PA* for predicate adjective or *PN* for predicate nominative above it.

Miles is my best (friend) [PN]

Rehema looked nervous (PA) but excited (PA).

My cousin's birthday party was a sleepover (PN).

That pizza smells wonderful (PA), but I am not very hungry (PA).

Glory will become a famous athlete (PN) one day.

Jacob remained a computer programmer (PN) for the university until his retirement.

Will Sora look older (PA) with her new hairstyle?

These cookies from your new recipe taste weird (PA); macaroni is a strange ingredient (PN) for cookies!

Review 4C: Adjective and Adverb Phrases

In the following excerpt from Aldous Huxley's *Brave New World*, identify each underlined prepositional phrase as *ADJ* for adjective phrase or *ADV* for adverb phrase.

Lenina and Henry climbed into their machine (ADV) and started off. At eight hundred feet (ADV) Henry slowed down the helicopter screws, and they hung for a minute or two (ADV) poised above the fading landscape (ADV). The forest of Burnham Beeches (ADJ) stretched like a great pool (ADV) of darkness (ADJ) towards the bright shore (ADV) of the western sky (ADJ). Crimson at the horizon (ADV), the last of the sunset (ADJ) faded, through orange (ADV), upwards into yellow and a pale watery green (ADV). Northwards, beyond and above the trees (ADV), the Internal and External Secretions factory glared with a fierce electric brilliance (ADV) from every window (ADV) of its twenty stories (ADJ). Beneath them (ADV) lay the buildings of the Golf Club.

Review 4D: Forming Principal Parts

Complete the following excerpt (from Anna Sewell's *Black Beauty*) by writing the correct principal part (*PP*) of the verb (first, second, or third) in parentheses.

"I am the best friend and the best riding-master those children have (have, 1st PP). It is not them; it is the boys. Boys," said (say, 2nd PP) he, shaking his mane, "are quite different; they must be broken (break, 3rd PP) in, as we were broken (break, 3rd PP) in when we were colts, and just be taught (teach, 3rd PP) what's what. The other children had ridden (ride, 3rd PP) me about for nearly two hours, and then the boys thought (think, 2nd PP) it was their turn; and so it was, and I was quite agreeable. They rode (ride, 2nd PP) me by turns, and I galloped (gallop, 2nd PP) them about up and down the fields and all about the orchard for a good hour. They had each cut (cut, 3rd PP) a great hazel stick for a riding-whip, and laid (lay, 2nd PP) it on a little too hard, but I took (take, 2nd PP) it in good part, till at last I thought (think, 2nd PP) we had had (have, 3rd PP) enough, so I stopped (stop, 2nd PP) two or three times by way of a hint."

Review 4E: Irregular Verbs

Find and correct the SIX errors in irregular verb usage in the following excerpt from *Five Little Peppers and How They Grew*, by Margaret Sidney. Cross out the incorrect form and write the correct form above it.

But Jasper didn't come! Thursday ~~comed~~ [came] and ~~goed~~ [went]; a beautiful, bright, sunny day, but with no signs of the merry boy whom all had ~~beginned~~ [begun] to love, nor of the big black dog. The children had ~~maked~~ [made] all the needful preparations with much ostentation and bustle, and ~~beed~~ [were] in a state of excited happiness, ready for any gale. But the last hope had to be ~~gived~~ [given] up, as the old clock ticked away hour after hour.

Review 4F: Misplaced Modifiers

Circle the misplaced adjective and adverb phrases in the following sentences. Draw an arrow to the place where each phrase should be.

Sierra Leone (with a green, white, and blue flag) is the only country ↓.

(Inside the oven) Frank checked on the casserole ↓.

↓ Mr. Gutiérrez explained to us how his mother taught him to ride a bike (in homeroom).

The book ↓ belongs to my cousin (on the highest shelf).

The children (in the nest) watched the eggs hatching ↓.

The gift ↓ is for the wonderful coach (inside this beautifully wrapped box).

The little rabbit ↓ lives in our classroom (with the floppy ears).

Annabel handed a pen ↓ to the very tall man (from her purse).

Review 4G: Diagramming

Diagram the following sentences.

The children stomp their feet in unison.

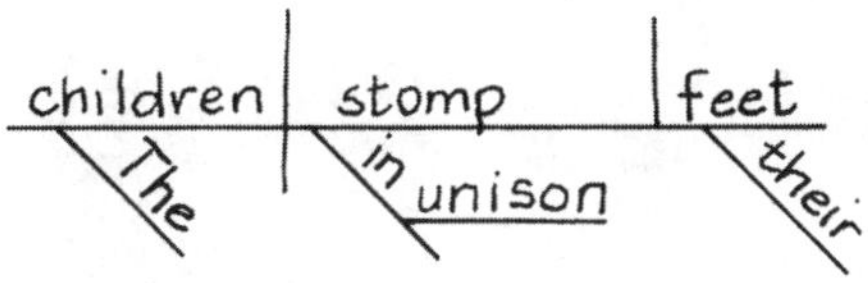

Johanna told her brother a secret.

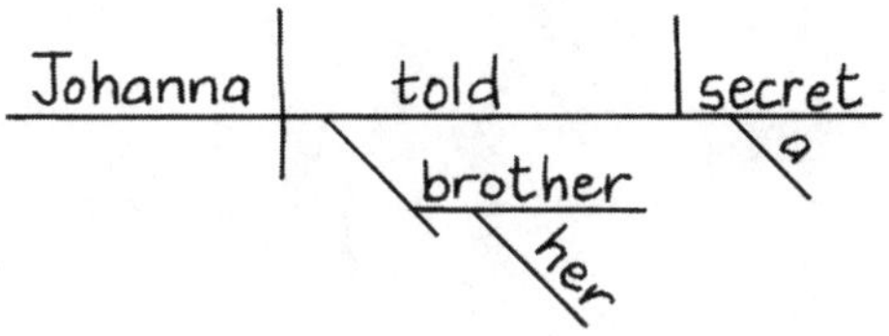

After three consecutive victories, our team is looking great!

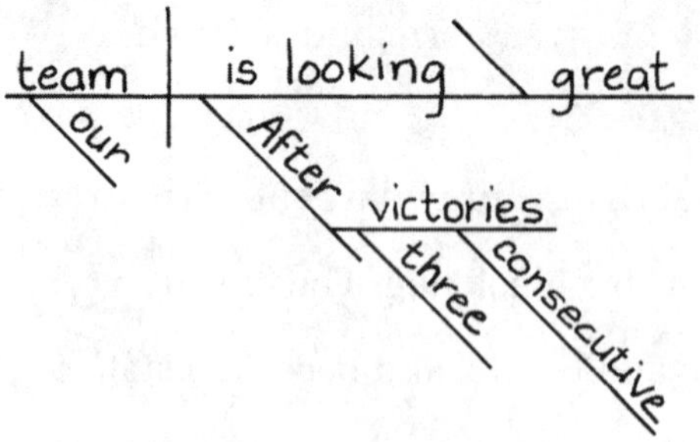

Did Jeff and Kristen name their new baby Luna?

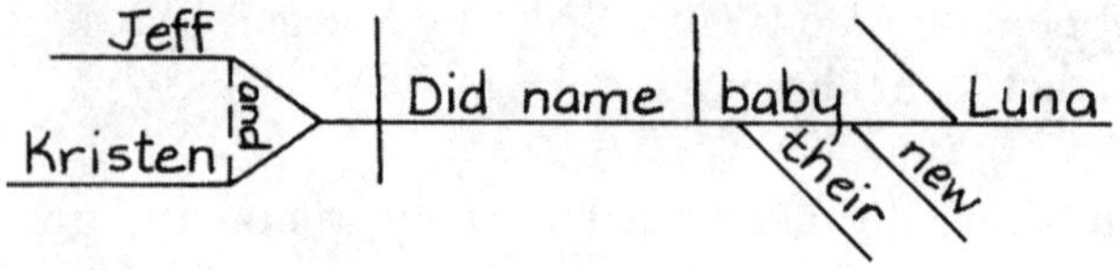

Dr. Gonzales looked at the students in the back of the room.

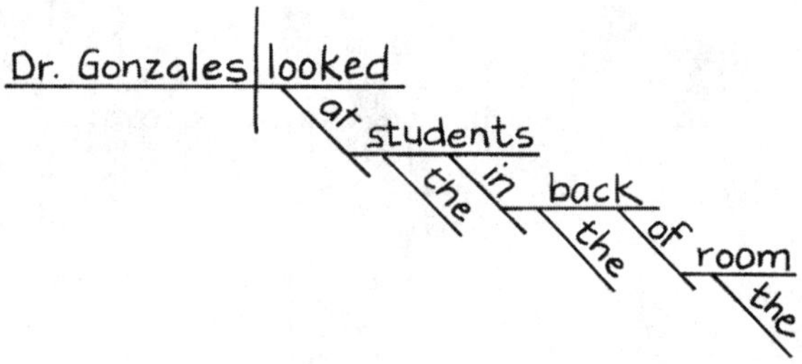

Our neighbors in the yellow house fed their pet turtle cucumbers.

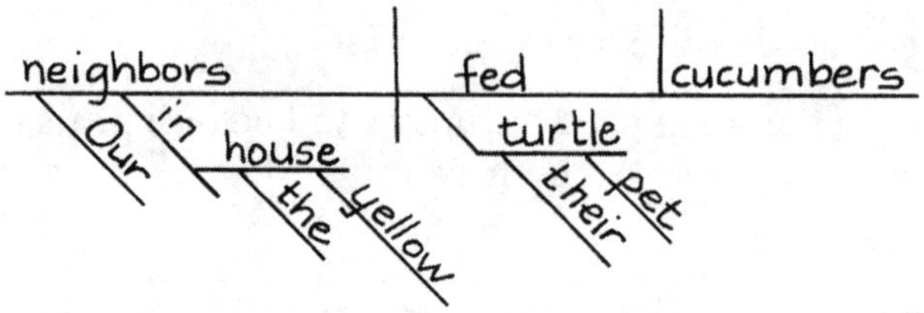

Pet turtles can live for a long time!

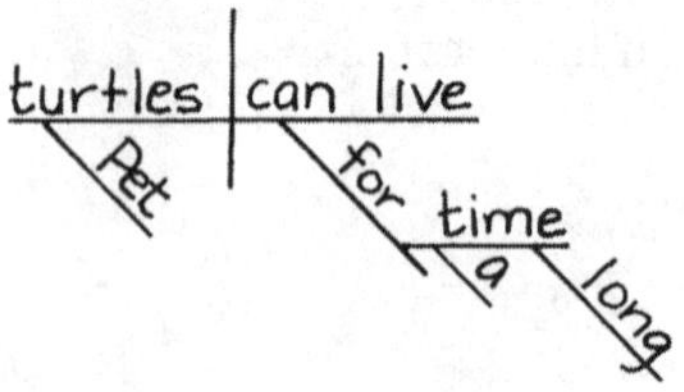

A turtle with a flaky shell may be sick.

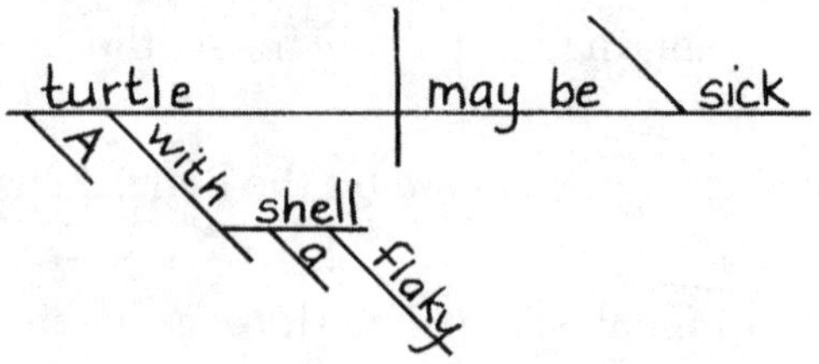

WEEK 13

Advanced Pronouns

— LESSON 49 —

Personal Pronouns

Antecedents

Possessive Pronouns

Exercise 49A: Personal Pronouns and Antecedents

Circle the personal pronouns in the following sentences, adapted from *Parachuting into Poland, 1944: Memoir of a Secret Mission with Józef Retinger*, by Marek Celt, trans. Jan Chciuk-Celt. Draw an arrow from each pronoun to the antecedent. In the margin, write the gender (*f*, *m*, or *n*) and number (*S* or *PL*) of each pronoun.

My companion practically never left the house. He did a lot of reading, and listened to the radio often. mS

The men who went on these missions were an elite group of special forces called the *Cichociemni*, literally "the silent Dark Ones." They've become something of a heroic legend in Polish war lore. mPL

The airplane landed, and the little old man ran to it in a hurry, but he only got a good look at the taillights as it flew off. nS mS nS

We, the passengers of the Third Air Bridge, had run a gauntlet of difficulties and dangers, and we were met and greeted joyously in Brindisi. nPL nPL

Exercise 49B: Identifying Possessive Pronouns

Underline the possessive pronouns in the following sentences from *Silk Parachute*, by John McPhee. Each possessive pronoun is acting as an adjective. Draw an arrow from the pronoun to the noun that is the pronoun's antecedent. There may be more than one pronoun in each sentence.

In the first game, an English midfielder, sprinting up his left sideline to take a pass on a clear, looked over his shoulder and saw that the ball was headed wide, low, and out of bounds.

On hulks and barges, boatmen serving the ships lived on the river with their families and with their cats, dogs, chickens, sheep, and cows.

Such river runes are not beyond the grasp of Livia Svenvold McPhee, who is six and quick to learn, but they're off the scale for her two-year-old brother, Jasper, and their father and mother.

The puffin is among the nation's emblematic birds. With <u>its</u> bright-white chest, <u>its</u> orange webbed feet, and <u>its</u> big orange scimitar bill, it could be an iced toucan.

Exercise 49C: Using Possessive Pronouns

In the following sentences, taken from *Bird Dream: Adventures at the Extremes of Human Flight,* by Matt Higgins, write the correct possessive pronoun above the underlined noun(s).

The 1991 movie *Point Break*...depicted a group of California surfer/skydivers who robbed banks to
their
fuel <u>the group's</u> lifestyle, a story that struck a chord with males of a certain age and bent.

its
By 1995 this generation would get <u>this generation's</u> Woodstock when ESPN created a festival for radical sports in Providence, Rhode Island, called the Extreme Games, soon to be rechristened the X Games.

his
Finally, on <u>Jeb's</u> fourth jump, Jeb pitched in full flight and swung into severe line twists, requiring
his
a nasty cutaway to <u>Jeb's</u> reserve.

his your
Afterwards, the officer gave Jeb a lift back to <u>Jeb's</u> hotel and asked casually, "Who was <u>Jeb's</u> friend?"

our
Clinicians tell us that <u>all humanity's</u> brain's occipital lobe, which processes visual information, becomes highly active during sleep.

Exercise 49D: Diagramming Possessive Pronouns

On your own paper, diagram every word in the following sentences, slightly adapted from *Barbarian Days: A Surfing Life,* by William Finnegan.

The wide white board was mine.

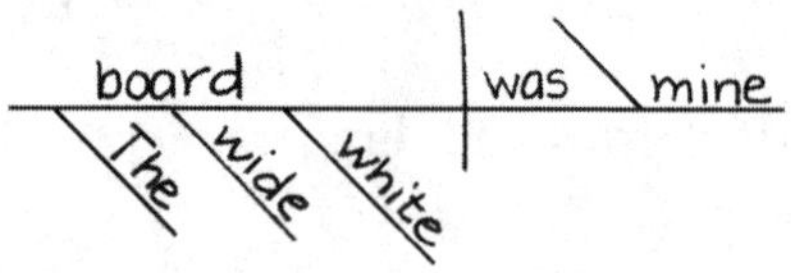

I took my next wave far too lightly.

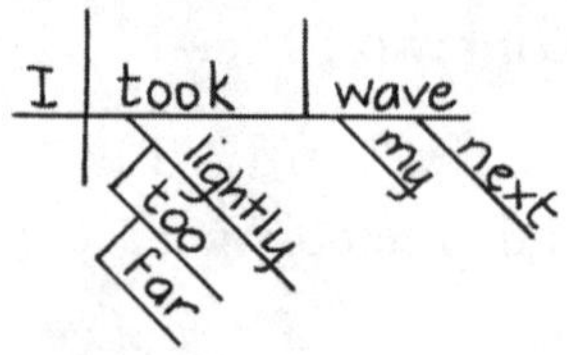

Our street and our lane formed a main funnel for local storm runoff.

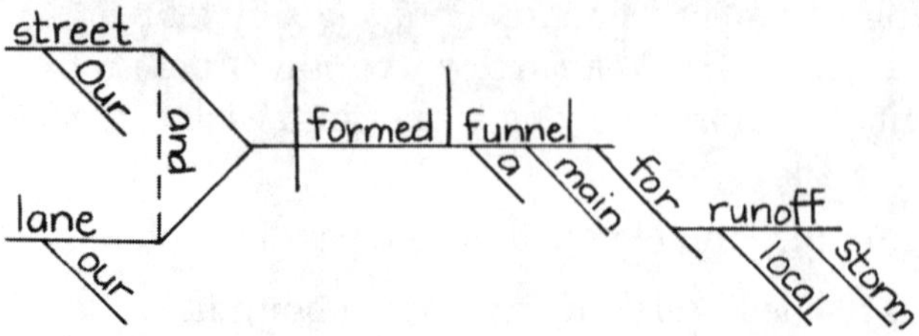

We murmured our business with Sina Savaiinaea to her young assistant.

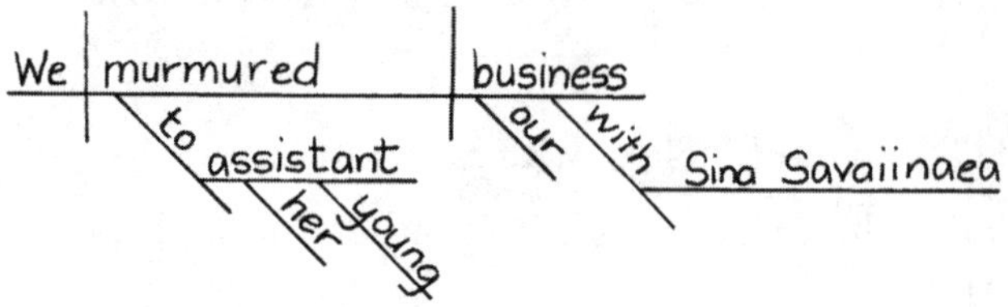

The waves were the object of your deepest desire and adoration.

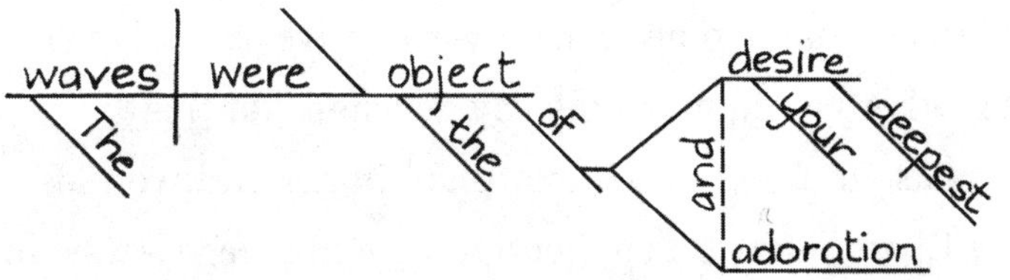

At the same time, they were your adversary, your nemesis, your mortal enemy.

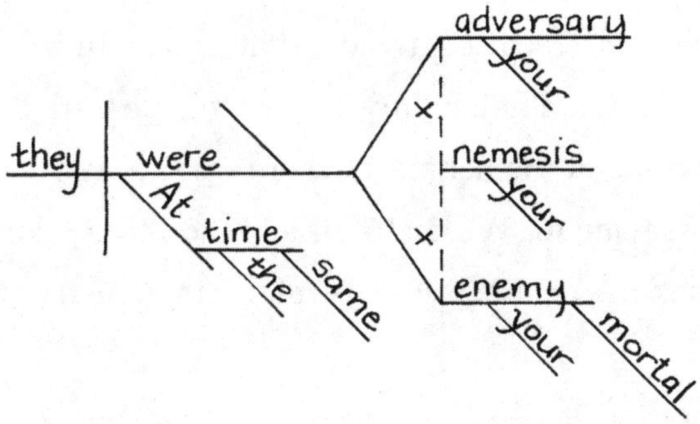

Its clear prose and subtle wit make it a must-read for all surfers.

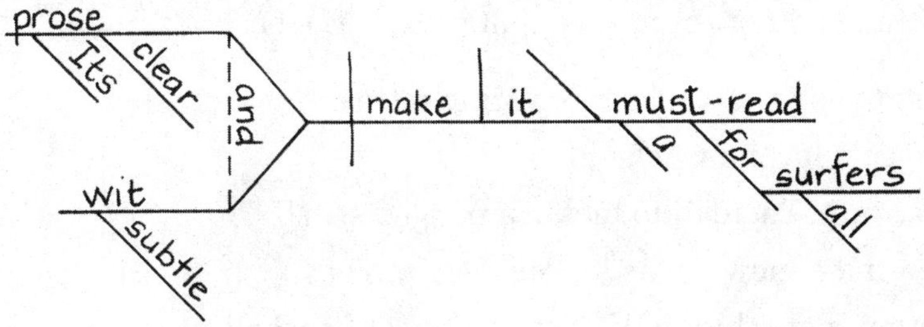

It's the only book for all surfers.

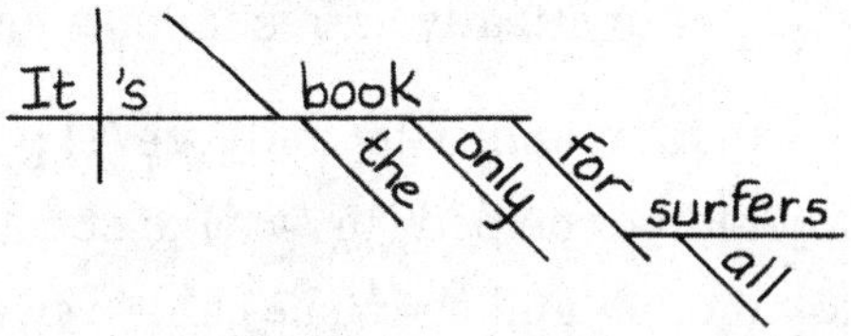

— LESSON 50 —

Pronoun Case

Exercise 50A: Subject and Object Pronouns

Underline all the personal pronouns in the following sentences. Identify them as *S* for subject, *O* for object, or *P* for possessive.

These sentences are from *Will in the World: How Shakespeare Became Shakespeare*, by Stephen Greenblatt.

If before his [P] success with the *Henry VI* plays Shakespeare had not already met Marlowe, he [S] would certainly have met him [O] soon afterward, and along with Marlowe he [S] would have met many of the other playwrights—poets, as they [S] were then called—who were writing for the London stage.

The small revision makes a large point: the dead are completely dead. No prayers can help them [O]; no messages can be sent to them [O] or received from them [O]. Hamnet was beyond reach.

Anne Hathaway represented an escape in another sense: she was in the unusual position of being her own woman. Very few young, unmarried Elizabethan women had any executive control over their own lives; the girl's watchful father and mother would make the key decisions for their daughter, ideally, though not always, with her consent. But Anne—an orphan in her midtwenties, with some resources left to her by her father's will and more due to her upon her marriage—was, in the phrase of the times, "wholly at her own government."

In his old age, a man named Willis, born the same year as Will, recalled a play…that he saw in Gloucester…when he was a child…" At such a play, Willis remembered, "my father took me with him, and made me stand between his legs, as he sat upon one of the benches, where we saw and heard very well." The experience was a remarkably intense one for Willis: "This sight took such an impression in me," he wrote, "that when I came towards man's estate, it was as fresh in my memory as if I had seen it newly acted."

Exercise 50B: Using Personal Pronouns Correctly

Choose the correct word(s) in parentheses and cross out the incorrect choice(s). Be sure to choose the grammatically correct choice for writing and not the choice that sounds the best.

My mother and sister and (~~me~~/I) planned to go on a weekend knitting retreat.
My mother helped (us/~~we~~) to choose projects for the weekend.
My mother and (~~her~~/she) chose sweaters, and I decided to tackle a fringed scarf.
Mom bought (my sister and me/~~my sister and I~~) new yarns for our new projects.
At the end of the retreat, (~~us~~/we) had gotten more than half of each project finished.
My mother gave my sister and (me/~~I~~) a huge compliment.
She said that the best company she'd ever had on a retreat were (~~us~~/we).

Exercise 50C: Diagramming Personal Pronouns

On your own paper, diagram the following sentences. Personal pronouns are diagrammed exactly like the nouns or adjectives they replace.

They threw us a life-line.

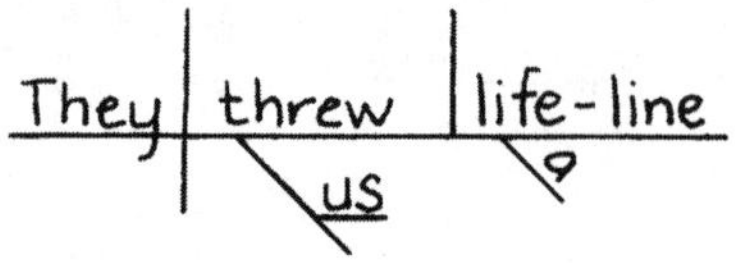

We thanked them profusely.

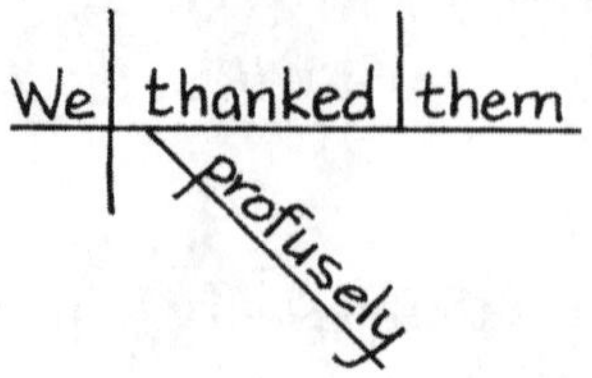

Where am I?

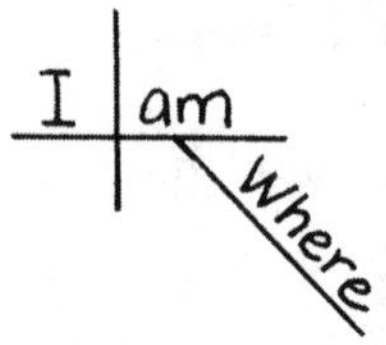

He gave me a dry towel.

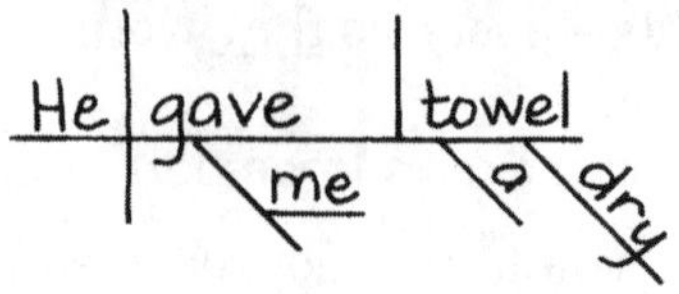

I hear you!

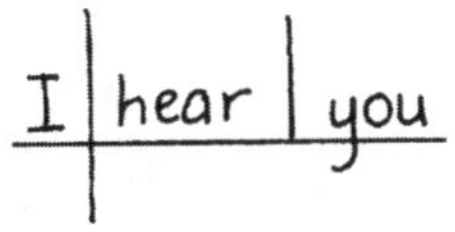

The recipients of their help were we.

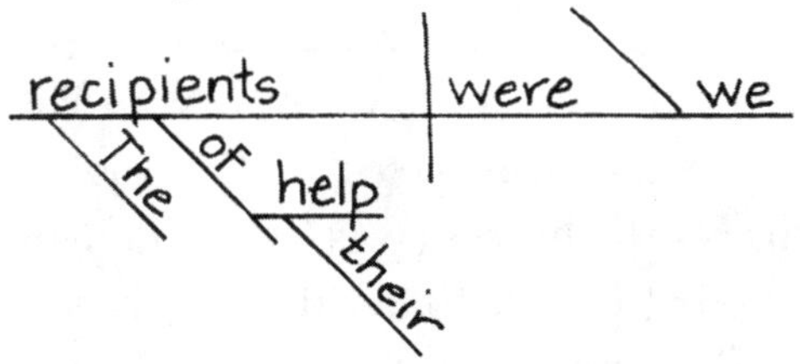

— LESSON 51 —

Indefinite Pronouns

Exercise 51A: Identifying Indefinite Pronouns

Underline all of the indefinite pronouns in the following sentences. Each sentence may contain more than one pronoun.

These sentences are drawn from *Don Quixote*, by Miguel de Cervantes, trans. John Ormsby.

Don Quixote, without uttering a word or imploring aid from anyone, once more dropped his buckler and once more lifted his lance.

But there was nobody now to listen to these words of Don Quixote's.

Master Nicholas, the village barber, however, used to say that neither of them came up to the Knight of Phoebus, and that if there was any that could compare with him it was Don Galaor, the brother of Amadis of Gaul, because he had a spirit that was equal to every occasion.

Yesterday was the first day of our coming here; we have a few of what they say are called field-tents pitched among the trees on the bank of an ample brook that fertilises all of these meadows.

In the meantime Sancho had recounted to them several of the adventures and accidents that had happened to his master.

All or most of the knights-errant in days of yore were great troubadours and great musicians, for both of these accomplishments, or more properly speaking gifts, are the peculiar property of lovers-errant.

Exercise 51B: Subject-Verb Agreement: Indefinite Pronouns

Choose the correct verb in parentheses. Cross out the incorrect verb.

Everyone (has/~~have~~) agreed to go trail riding in the mountains!

All of the company (is/~~are~~) going on this exciting adventure.

Note to Instructor: The entire company, as a single group, is going, so the verb is singular: It is going.

All of the horses (~~is~~/are) guaranteed to be gentle and calm.

Note to Instructor: Each horse in the group (and there are multiple horses) is guaranteed, so the verb is plural: They are guaranteed.

A few of the guests (~~has~~/have) ridden before, but some of them (~~is~~/are) just a little bit nervous.

Most of the horses (~~has~~/ have) been saddled already.
Most of the group (is / ~~are~~) mounting up.
One of the horses (was / ~~were~~) named Volcano.
Nobody (~~want~~/ wants) to ride Volcano!
Another of the horses (was / ~~were~~) named Sleepyhead.
Everybody (asks / ~~ask~~) to ride Sleepyhead.
(Does / ~~Do~~) anyone know which horse is named Killer?
None of us (want / ~~wants~~) to ride Killer either!

Exercise 51C: Diagramming Indefinite Pronouns

On your own paper, diagram the following sentences, slightly adapted from *The Knights Hospitaller: A Military History of the Knights of St John*, by John C. Carr.

By now, Rome and most of Italy had become insecure.

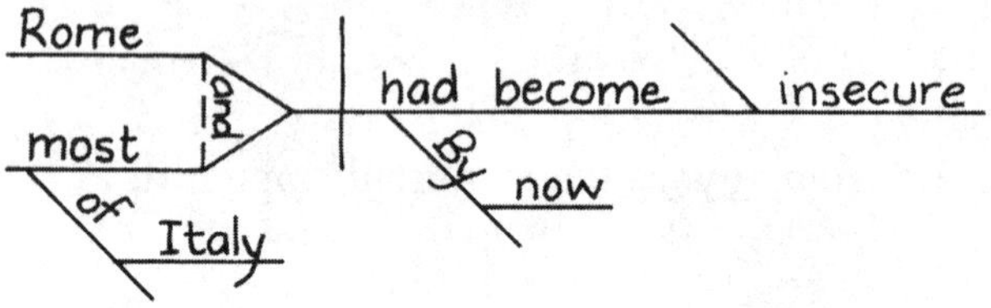

Turanshah demanded all of Outremer.

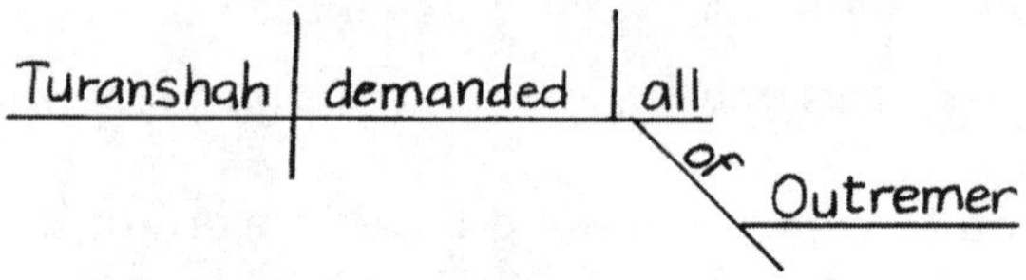

To his surprise and chagrin, everyone did not agree with him.

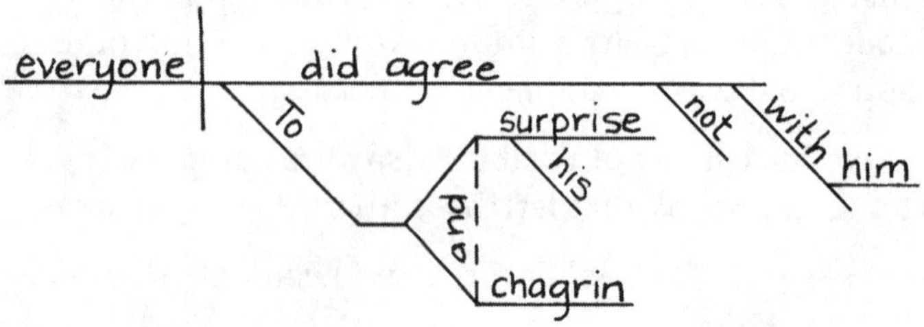

In 1309, the papacy had split into one in Rome and the other in Avignon.

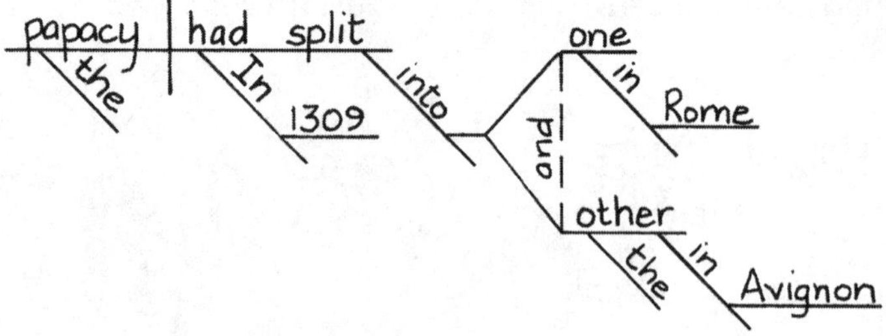

A few refused, on the grounds of conscience.

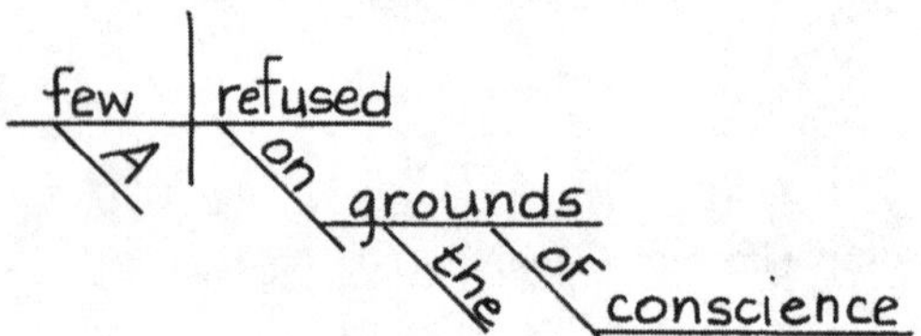

Nothing came of the move.

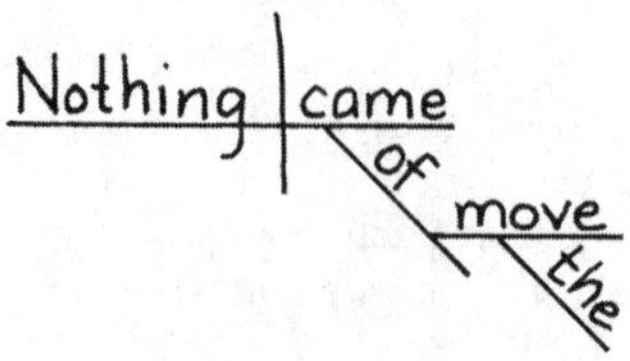

— LESSON 52 —

Personal Pronouns
Indefinite Pronouns

Exercise 52A: Subject and Object Pronouns

In the following sentences, cross out the incorrect pronoun.

This first set of sentences is from *Number the Stars*, by Lois Lowry.

But if (they/~~them~~) are watching (~~we~~/us)—if (they/~~them~~) see all of (~~we~~/us) leave?

And (I/~~me~~) have named (~~he~~/him) Thor, for the God of Thunder.

"Soon (we/~~us~~) will have to add another blanket to your bed," Mama said one morning as (~~her~~/she) and Annemarie tidied the bedroom.

(She/~~Her~~) remembered how (she/~~her~~) had stared at the others, frightened, when (~~them~~/they) had stopped (~~she~~/her) on the street.

Annemarie called to (him/~~he~~) and (~~him~~/he) came to the side, his face worried when (~~him~~/he) recognized (~~she~~/her) on the dock.

This second set of sentences is from *The Tenant of Wildfell Hall*, by Anne Brontë.

(~~Me~~/I) am very much attached to my little friend, and so is (~~her~~/she) to (me/~~I~~).

"Oh, yes! come in," said (she/~~her~~) (for (~~me~~/I) had met (them/~~they~~) in the garden).

Millicent told (me/~~I~~) (I/~~me~~) was the life of the party.

It is (I/~~me~~) who have left (~~they~~/them).

When (~~us~~/we) did meet, it was (he/~~him~~) that sought (~~I~~/me) out.

But what is (~~him~~/he) doing—what is it that keeps (him/~~he~~) away?

(I/~~Me~~) would not believe (~~they~~/them), for (~~me~~/I) knew (~~she~~/her) better than (~~them~~/they).

Oh, it would be cruel to make (her/~~she~~) feel as (~~me~~/I) feel now, and know what (~~me~~/I) have known!

(~~Me~~/I) was annoyed at the continual injustice (~~her~~/she) had done (me/~~I~~) from the very dawn of our acquaintance.

(~~Him~~/He) and Lord Lowborough were accompanying Annabella and (~~I~~/me) in a long, delightful ride.

Exercise 52B: Possessive and Indefinite Pronouns

In these sentences, taken from *The House of Mirth,* by Edith Wharton, cross out the incorrect word in each set of parentheses.

"Do let us go and take a peep at the presents before everyone else (leaves/~~leave~~) the dining-room!" suggested Miss Farish, linking her arm in her friend's.

I always say no one (~~do~~/does) things better than cousin Grace!

Each of them (~~want~~/wants) a creature of a different race.

But at this point one or two belated passengers from the last station forced (~~his~~/their/~~his or her~~) way into the carriage, and Lily had to retreat to her seat.

The landscape outspread below her seemed an enlargement of her present mood, and she found something of herself in (its/~~their~~) calmness, (its/~~their~~) breadth, (its/~~their~~) long free reaches.

The topmost shelf of every closet (~~were~~/was) made to yield up (its/~~their~~) secret, cellar and coal-bin (were/~~was~~) probed to (~~its~~/their) darkest depths and, as a final stage in the lustral rites, the entire house (~~were~~/was) swathed in penitential white and deluged with expiatory soapsuds.

Her discretions interested him almost as much as her imprudences: he was so sure that both (were/~~was~~) part of the same carefully-elaborated plan.

Under the Georgian porch she paused again, scanning the street for a hansom. None (~~were~~/was) in sight.

And I suppose most of the owners of Americana (are/~~is~~) not historians either?

To the lady and her acquaintances there (~~were~~/was) something heroic in living as though one were much richer than one's bank-book denoted.

It (~~were~~/was) the last week in June, and none of her friends (were/~~was~~) in town.

Every one (knows/~~know~~) you're a thousand times handsomer and cleverer.

The fire, like the lamps, (~~were~~/was) never lit except when there (~~were~~/was) company.

And there (~~were~~/was) everybody talking about you.

There (~~were~~/was) something to be done before she left the house.

None of the desultory interests which she dignified with the name of tastes (~~were~~/was) pronounced enough to enable her to live contentedly in obscurity.

Some (were/~~was~~) in small fragments, the others merely torn in half.

And there (~~is~~/are) others who (~~is~~/are) afraid of me.

In the center of the table, between the melting marrons glaces and candied cherries, a pyramid of American Beauties lifted (~~its~~/their) vigorous stems.

Exercise 52C: Writing Sentences from Diagrams

Use the diagrams below to reconstruct these sentences from Simon Schama's *The Story of the Jews: Finding the Words (1000 BCE–1492).*

Write the original sentence on the blank below each diagram. Pay careful attention to each part of speech! Punctuate each sentence properly.

Note to Instructor: You may need to remind the student to pay attention to which words are capitalized, in order to begin each sentence properly!

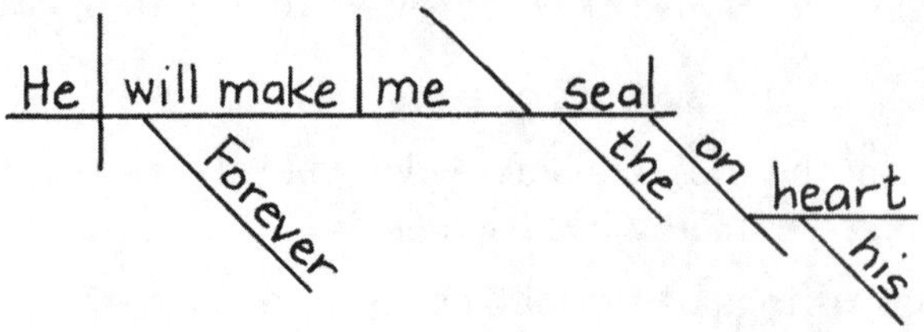

Forever will He make me the seal on his heart.

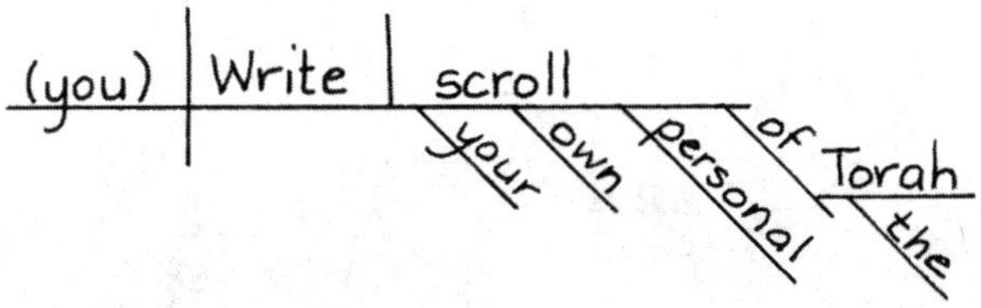

Write your own personal scroll of the Torah.

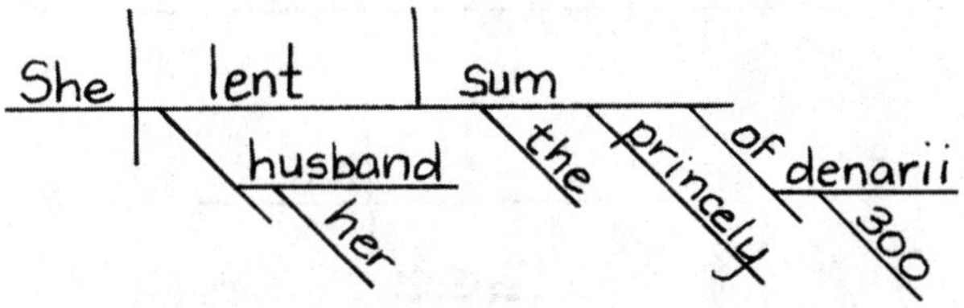

She lent her husband the princely sum of 300 denarii.

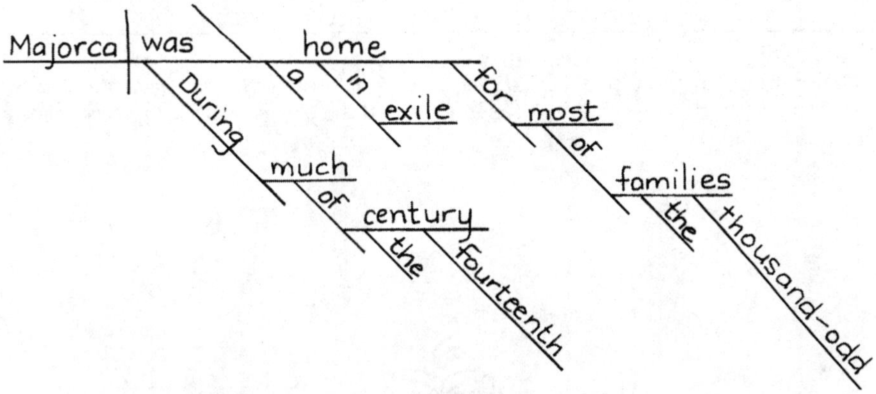

During much of the fourteenth century, Majorca was a home in exile for most of the thousand-odd families.

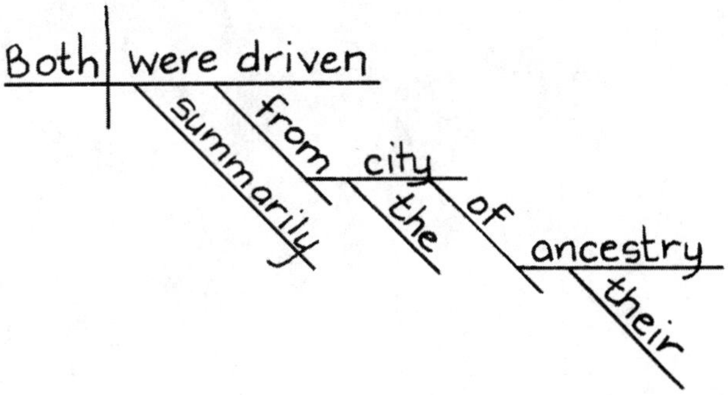

Both were summarily driven from the city of their ancestry.

Note to Instructor: You may also accept *summarily were driven* or *were driven summarily.* Ask the student to read both her version of the sentence and the original out loud, so that she can hear the difference in rhythm.

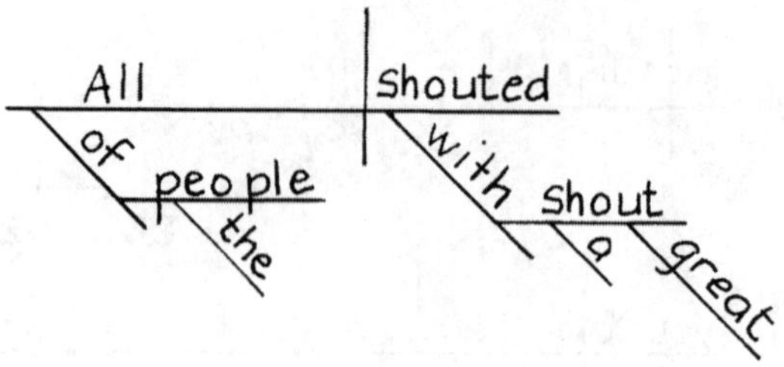

All of the people shouted with a great shout.

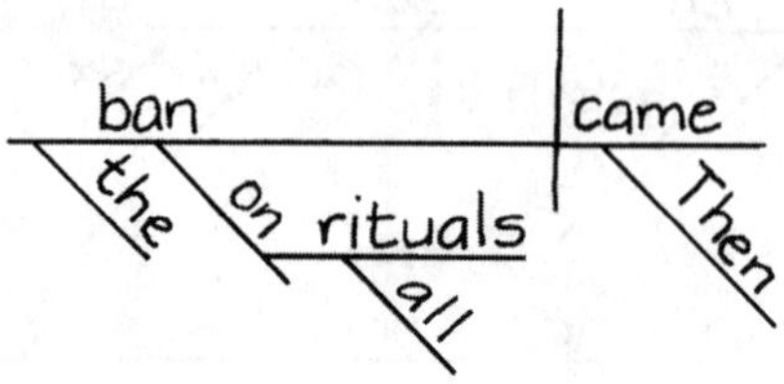

Then came the ban on all rituals.

Note to Instructor: You may also accept *the ban came on all rituals* or *the ban on all rituals came*. Ask the student to read both her version of the sentence and the original out loud, so that she can hear the difference in rhythm.

WEEK 14

Active and Passive Voice

— LESSON 53 —

Principal Parts
Troublesome Verbs

Exercise 53A: Principal Parts of Verbs

Fill in the chart with the missing forms.

	First Principal Part Present	Second Principal Part Past	Third Principal Part Past Participle
I	provide	provided	provided
I	split	split	split
I	drive	drove	driven
I	try	tried	tried
I	watch	watched	watched
I	fly	flew	flown
I	live	lived	lived
I	play	played	played

Exercise 53B: Using Correct Verbs

Choose the correct verb in parentheses. Cross out the incorrect verb.

First thing in the morning on July 1, Lea's father (~~rose~~/ raised) the flag outside their Whistler house.

He (~~let~~/ left) Lea alone until ten o'clock and (let / ~~left~~) her sleep late.

Lea loves to (~~lay~~/ lie) in bed a little longer on holiday mornings.

Her father (rose / ~~raised~~) early to celebrate Canada Day!

Lea's father (~~lay~~/ laid) out a special breakfast of beaver tails—fried dough with cinnamon and sugar.

Lea had (laid / ~~lain~~) out her favorite red and white clothes the night before.

Lea and her father (~~set~~/ sat) at the table, eating breakfast and listening to Leonard Cohen and Feist.

Afterwards, Lea (set / ~~sat~~) out cupcakes for her friends to decorate.

Sprinkles, red and white frosting, candy maple leafs, and tiny Canadian flags all (lay / ~~laid~~) ready to be used!

Exercise 53C: Correct Forms of Troublesome Verbs

Fill in the blanks with the correct form of the indicated verb.

He went to work in a foundry pouring molten iron where the work was steady and backbreaking, but he simply could not be home often and yet he still raised his boys responsibly. (raise, simple past)

Bill was raised in the segregated South and saw strict limitations for black people there compared to when he moved to Oakland, California. (raise, past participle)

After being incarcerated, he converted to Islam through his brother's encouragement and then rose within the ranks of Elijah Muhammad's Nation of Islam organization called Black Muslims. (rise, simple past)

Despite his hard work, Bill left the university in 1956, 16 credits shy of graduation. (leave, simple past)

But Swegle let the players play and his coaching really involved merely substituting. (let, simple past)

—Murry R. Nelson, *Bill Russell: A Biography*

He wondered what Iktomi would do, thus he lay still where he fell. (lie, simple past)

Saying this, he laid a firm hand upon the muskrat's shoulder, and started off along the edge of the lake. (lay, simple past)

A man in buckskins sat upon the top of a little hillock. (sit, simple past)

Wordless, the avenger ate in silence the food set before him on the ground. (set, past participle)

She did not wish a guest in her dwelling to sit upon the bare hard ground. (sit, present infinitive)

—Zitkala-Sa, *Old Indian Legends: Stories from the Dakotas*

Exercise 53D: Proofreading for Correct Verb Usage

The following excerpts are from *Prairie Gothic: The Story of a West Texas Family,* by John R. Erickson. Find and correct sixteen errors in verb usage by crossing out the incorrect verbs and writing the correct forms above them. Be careful—some sentences might not have any errors at all, and others might have more than one!

The original house ~~set~~ sat on several acres of land where a windmill provided water for the house as well as for chickens and several milk cows, a big garden, and an orchard of fruit trees.

We ~~rose~~ raised ducks, rabbits, and chickens in the back yard, and from her I ~~was learned~~ learned to wring a chicken's neck and pluck the feathers after dipping the bird into boiling water, skills she had ~~been learned~~ learned from her mother and grandmother. We ~~rose~~ raised a garden, collected horned toads, and ~~hanged~~ hung out the weekly wash on the clothesline.

On thousands of nights we have unrolled our bedrolls, ~~lying~~ laying them side by side, out under the stars.

Olive had been ~~risen~~ raised on a ranch that had plenty of rattlers and she should have known what to do: ~~set~~ sit down, stay calm, grit your teeth and look the other way while a rescuer went through the gory process of trying to save your life.

Into her eighties, she ~~writted~~ wrote letters that would be the envy of any college graduate: words ~~wrote~~ written in a precise hand, lines that couldn't have been straighter if they had been ~~lain~~ laid out with a ruler, and whole pages that contained no misspellings, ink smudges, coffee stains, or cross-outs.

Neither lawman had a chance to ~~saw~~ see what was coming, and both ~~laid~~ lay dead on the floor.

I had arrived just in time for supper and Mrs. Tennill had already ~~sat~~ set two places at Grandmother's big rectangular dining table, which looked out on the green expanse of the back yard.

I soon realized that the death of Martha Sherman, a story that had lain half-forgotten in the memory of my family, was a major news event on the Texas frontier in the winter of 1860-1861.

But make that same drive in a drought year and you might see snowplows pushing dunes of red sand off the highways, and tumbleweed cannonballs snapping power lines and ~~lying~~ laying barbed wire fence on the ground—this my mother remembered during the drought of the 1930s.

— LESSON 54 —

Verb Tense

Active and Passive Voice

Exercise 54A: Reviewing Tenses

Write the tense of each underlined verb above it. These two excerpts are from the Sherlock Holmes story "A Scandal in Bohemia," by Arthur Conan Doyle. The first is done for you.

One night—it was on the twentieth of March, 1888—I was returning [progressive past] from a journey to a patient (for I had now returned [perfect past] to civil practice), when my way led [simple past] me through Baker Street. As I passed [simple past] the well-remembered door, which must always be associated in my mind with my wooing, and with the dark incidents of the Study in Scarlet, I was seized with a keen desire to see Holmes again, and to know how he was employing [progressive past] his extraordinary powers.

I was already deeply interested in his inquiry, for, though it was surrounded by none of the grim and strange features which were associated with the two crimes which I have already recorded [perfect present], still, the nature of the case and the exalted station of his client gave [simple past] it a character of its own.

We both thought [simple past] the best resource was flight, when pursued by so formidable an antagonist; so you will find [simple future] the nest empty when you call [simple present]. As to the photograph, your client may rest in peace. I love [simple present] and am loved by a better man than he. The King may do what he will without hindrance from one whom he has cruelly wronged [perfect present].

Exercise 54B: Distinguishing Between Active and Passive Voice

Identify the following sentences, from Doyle's "A Scandal in Bohemia," as *A* for active or *P* for passive. If you're not sure, ask yourself: Is the subject *doing* the verb, or is the verb *happening* to the subject?

I am loved by a better man than he.	P
Godfrey Norton came running as hard as he could towards me.	A
A blow was struck.	P
She responded beautifully.	A
Your task is confined to that.	P
We will be shown into the sitting-room.	P
I was just balancing whether I should run for it.	A
The lamps were just being lighted.	P
It widened the field of my inquiry.	A
Twice she has been waylaid.	P
Five attempts have been made.	P
I have been too busy to think of food.	A
I am following you closely.	A
The paper was made in Bohemia.	P
I was still balancing the matter in my mind.	A
I will rejoin you in ten minutes.	A

Exercise 54C: Forming the Active and Passive Voice

Fill in the chart below, rewriting each sentence so that it appears in both the active and the passive voice. Be sure to keep the tense the same. The first is done for you.

Note to Instructor: The last two sentences have two active verbs each. If the student only transforms the first verb and not the second, accept the answer, but show the student the completely rewritten sentences below.

ACTIVE	PASSIVE
Modern detectives, unlike policemen, don't wear uniforms.	Uniforms aren't worn by modern detectives, unlike policemen.
Detectives interview suspects and witnesses as part of case investigation.	Suspects and witnesses are interviewed by detectives as part of case investigation.
Homicide units assign murder cases to detectives.	Detectives are assigned murder cases by homicide units.
Detectives often set aside cases that have no evidence, no witnesses, and no suspects.	Cases that have no evidence, no witnesses, and no suspects are often set aside by detectives.
Detectives "clear" cases when they arrest a suspect and send them to trial.	Cases are "cleared" by detectives when suspects are arrested and sent to trial.
Modern detectives often use DNA to help the perpetrators of crimes to be identified.	In modern detective work, DNA is often used to help identify the perpetrators of crimes.

— LESSON 55 —

Parts of the Sentence
Active and Passive Voice

Note to Instructor: You should adapt the following review to the student's level of knowledge. If the student is clear on the concepts learned so far and is able to diagram the sentences correctly, you do not need to follow every line of dialogue for every sentence. However, the student should be able not only to diagram the sentences, but to name the parts of the sentence and explain their use (for example, in the second sentence, if you ask the student "What kind of phrase is *of their own*, and what does it do?" the student should be able to answer "a prepositional phrase acting as an adjective").

These sentences are adapted from Jonathan Swift's satirical essay *A Modest Proposal.*

Sentence #1

Instructor: Read me the first sentence from your workbook.
Student: Many other advantages were enumerated.
Instructor: What is the predicate?

Note to Instructor: In the dialogues that follow, prompt the student whenever necessary.

Student: Were enumerated.
Instructor: Who or what was enumerated?
Student: Advantages.
Instructor: Diagram the subject and the predicate.
Does the subject perform the action? (Are the advantages enumerating something?)
Student: No.
Instructor: *Advantages* receives the action of the verb. Is *were enumerated* an active or passive verb?
Student: Passive.
Instructor: Repeat after me: In a sentence with a passive verb, the subject receives the action.
Student: In a sentence with a passive verb, the subject receives the action.
Instructor: How many advantages were enumerated?
Student: Many.
Instructor: *Many* is an adjective, describing *advantages* and answering the question "how many." What questions do adjectives answer?
Student: Which one, what kind, how many, whose.
Instructor: What kind of advantages are the many advantages?
Student: Other.
Instructor: *Many* and *other* are both adjectives describing *advantages.* Place them on your diagram now.

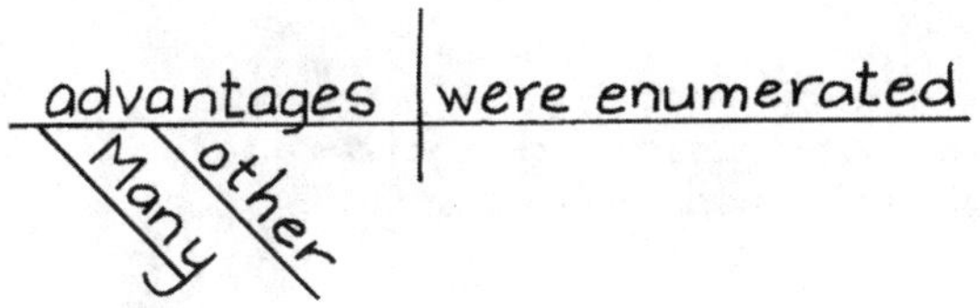

Sentence #2

Instructor: Read the second sentence out loud.

Student: The poorer tenants will have something valuable of their own.

Instructor: What are the subject and predicate of the sentence?

Student: Tenants will have.

Instructor: Tenants will have what?

Student: Something.

Instructor: *Something* receives the action of the verb *will have.* What part of the sentence is *something*?

Student: Direct object.

Instructor: When a sentence has a direct object, you can be pretty sure that the subject is performing the action! Repeat after me: In a sentence with an active verb, the subject performs the action.

Student: In a sentence with an active verb, the subject performs the action.

Instructor: Diagram the subject, predicate, and direct object on your own paper. *Something* is the direct object. What part of speech is *something*? What kind of word is it? (Hint: You learned about this word in Lesson 51.)

Student: Indefinite pronoun.

Instructor: What are indefinite pronouns?

Student: Indefinite pronouns are pronouns without antecedents.

Instructor: Although *something* is indefinite, meaning that we don't know exactly what it *is*, we do know *what kind* and *whose* the *something* is! What kind of *something* do the tenants have?

Student: A valuable something.

Instructor: Diagram *valuable* as an object describing *something.* What phrase tells you *whose* the something is?

Student: Of their own.

Instructor: What kind of phrase is this?

Student: It is a prepositional phrase.

Instructor: Since the phrase modifies the pronoun *something*, does it act as an adjective or adverb?

Student: Adjective.

Instructor: What is the preposition?

Student: Of.

Instructor: What is the object of the preposition?

Student: Own.

Instructor: What kind of pronoun is *their*?

Student: Possessive pronoun.

Instructor: What are possessive pronouns also known as?

Student: Possessive adjectives.

Instructor: *Their* modifies the object of the preposition *own.* Place that prepositional phrase on your diagram.

> **Note to Instructor:** *Own* is a word that can act as multiple parts of speech: adjective, noun, and verb (*own place, my own, I own that*). If the student asks, you may explain that a single word can play different parts within a sentence, something that will be covered in more detail in Lesson 107.

Instructor: There are two more words to be classified and diagrammed in this sentence. What word do they describe?

Student: Tenants.

Instructor: What part of speech is *The*?

Student: Article.

Instructor: The articles are *a*, *an*, and *the*. Diagram *The* beneath the word it modifies. What other words describes *tenants*?

Student: Poorer.

Instructor: What adjective question does this word answer?

Student: What kind.

Instructor: Add that to your diagram now.

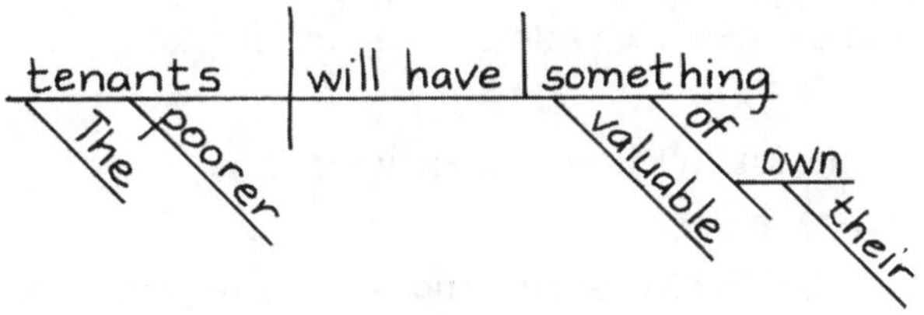

Sentence #3

Instructor: Read the third sentence out loud.

Student: The proposal is wholly new and has something solid and real.

Instructor: What are the two predicates in this sentence?

Student: Is and has.

Instructor: What is the subject?

Student: Proposal.

Instructor: Go ahead and diagram the subject and compound predicates on your paper now. What coordinating conjunction links them?

Student: And.

Instructor: Put the coordinating conjunction on your diagram as well. *Is* and *has* are two different kinds of verbs. What sort of verb is *is*?

Student: Linking verb.

> **Note to Instructor:** If the student says *state-of-being verb*, ask "Does the verb link *proposal* with a word that describes or renames it?"

Instructor: What word does the linking verb link to *proposal*?

Student: New.

Instructor: Is this a noun or an adjective?

Student: An adjective.

Instructor: Since it comes after the predicate, what kind of adjective is it?

Student: A predicate adjective.

Instructor: Put the predicate adjective on your diagram. There's a word that describes the predicate adjective *new*. How new is the proposal?

Student: Wholly.

Instructor: What do we call a word that describes an adjective?

Student: An adverb.

Instructor: What other two kinds of words can an adverb describe?

Student: A verb or another adverb.

Instructor: Put *wholly* on your diagram. Now let's look at the verb *has.* Is this a linking verb, a state-of-being verb, or an action verb?

Student: An action verb.

> **Note to Instructor:** If the student is unsure, ask "What does the proposal have?" Prompt the student if necessary to answer "Something." Then point out that since the verb has a direct object, it must be an action verb.

Instructor: What does the proposal have?

Student: Something.

Instructor: *Something* is the direct object of the verb *has.* What kind of word is *something*? Hint: you first learned about it in Lesson 51. And you don't know exactly what that *something* is!

Student: Indefinite pronoun.

Instructor: Repeat after me: Indefinite pronouns are pronouns without antecedents.

Student: Indefinite pronouns are pronouns without antecedents.

Instructor: Add *something* to your diagram. Two more adjectives describe the indefinite pronoun. What are they?

Student: Solid and real.

Instructor: Add both adjectives to the diagram, along with the coordinating conjunction that connects them. There's one word left to add. What is it?

Student: The.

Instructor: Finish your diagram now.

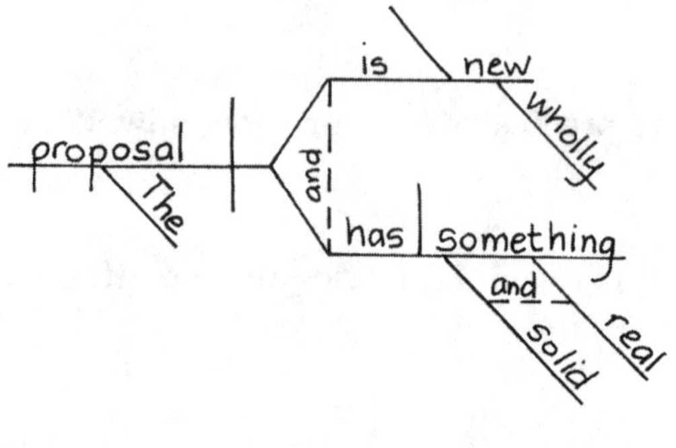

Sentence #4

Instructor: Read the fourth sentence out loud.

Student: The squire will grow popular among his tenants.

Instructor: Now read me just the subject and predicate.

Student: Squire will grow.

Instructor: Diagram those three words and add the article that describes *squire.* What kind of verb is *will grow*?

Student: Linking verb.

> **Note to Instructor:** If the student cannot identify *will grow* as a linking verb, ask "Does the squire grow something himself?" Then point out that there is no direct object, just a word that refers *back* to the squire. Try not to use the term *predicate adjective* so that you can complete the dialogue below.

Instructor: What word follows the linking verb?

Student: Popular.
Instructor: Is this a predicate adjective or predicate nominative?
Student: Predicate adjective.
Instructor: It describes the squire—it doesn't rename him. Add *popular* to your diagram. Now tell me about *among his tenants*. What kind of phrase is this, and what does it describe?

Note to Instructor: Prompt the student as necessary for the following information.

Student: Among his tenants is a prepositional phrase. It describes the adjective popular. It acts as an adverb.
Instructor: What is the preposition?
Student: Among.
Instructor: What is the object of the preposition?
Student: Tenants.
Instructor: What kind of adjective is *his*? Hint: you first learned about it in Lesson 49.
Student: Possessive adjective.
Instructor: Is it in the attributive or predicate position?
Student: Attributive.
Instructor: Add the prepositional phrase to your diagram.

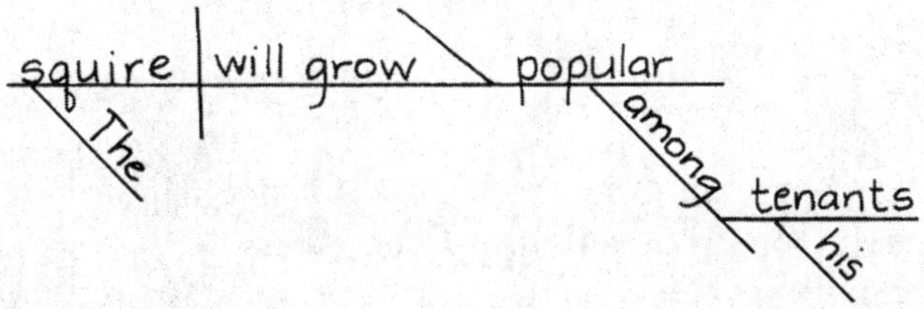

Sentence #5
Instructor: Read the final sentence out loud.
Student: I have no personal interest in the promotion of the necessary work.
Instructor: It should be easy to find the subject and predicate of this sentence—just two words! What are they?
Student: I have.
Instructor: Diagram those on your paper. *Have* is the first-person, simple-present form of this verb. What is the third-person, simple-present form of it? Hint: you've just seen it in Sentence #3.
Student: Has.
Instructor: What is the direct object of the verb *have* in this sentence?
Student: Interest.
Instructor: Add the direct object to your diagram. What are the two adjectives that describe the direct object?
Student: No *and* personal.
Instructor: Add those to the diagram as well. Now, tell me everything you can about the two phrases that end the sentence. Hint: they are both the same kind of phrase, doing the same kind of thing!

Note to Instructor: Prompt the student as necessary for the answers below.

Student: In the promotion *and* of the necessary work *are both prepositional phrases. They are adjectives that describe* interest.

Instructor: Explain the function of each word within the phrases.
Student: In *is a preposition.* Promotion *is the object of the preposition.* The *describes* promotion. Of *is a preposition.* Work *is the object of the preposition.* The *and* necessary *both describe* work.
Instructor: Complete your diagram.

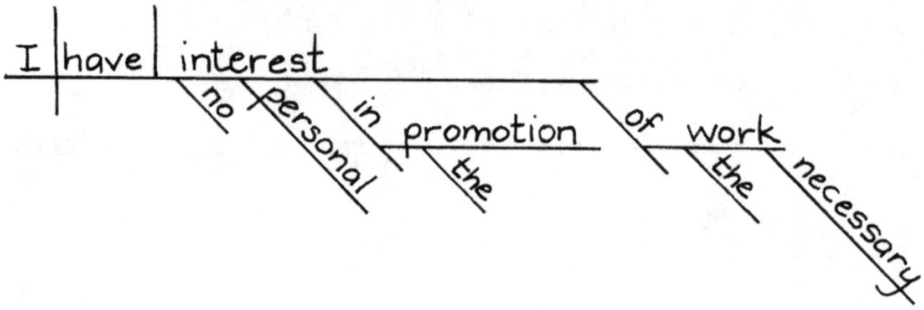

— LESSON 56 —

Active and Passive Voice

Transitive and Intransitive Verbs

Exercise 56A: Transitive and Intransitive Verbs

Find each verb serving as a predicate in the following sentences and underline it twice. Underline each subject of the predicate once. Write *T* above each transitive verb and *IT* above each intransitive verb. Circle the direct object of each transitive verb.

These sentences are adapted from *Viet Nam: A History from Earliest Times to the Present*, by Ben Kiernan.

Beginning around 14,000 BCE, the Hoabinhian people ate (T) wild cattle, water buffalo, rhinoceros, forest birds, turtles, tortoise, shellfish, and uncultivated, or "wild," rice.

In happier times, carefree, they ate (IT) and slept (IT).

Now, robbed of water, they fear (IT) for their land.

The catfish confessed (T) its theft, paid (T) the frogs' cost, and submitted (IT) to exile.

Dinh Bo Linh enjoyed (T) less success in his effort to win domestic legitimacy.

Dinh Bo Linh governed (IT) by fear.

Dinh Bo Linh's people feared (T) him.

The scene was set (T) for the brief emergence of a new, separate kingdom.

Note to Instructor: You may need to remind the student that passive verbs have to be transitive, because the subject is receiving the action of the verb.

Its Confucian elite ran (T) its own affairs and challenged (T) imperial control.

The Ming invasion of 1406-7 came (IT) on the pretext of restoring the Tran dynasty.

Imperial armies overthrew (T) and captured (T) Ho Quy Ly.

The Ming destroyed (T) all records of Dai Viet governance.

A flood of neo-Confucianism washed (IT) over the country.

Inland, Chinese ran (T) mining enterprises near the northern border.

Over the ensuing centuries Jiao's population adopted (T) more of the northern culture and system of government.

> **Note to Instructor:** The direct object of the transitive verb *adopted* is *more,* which here is serving as a noun.

These two regimes fought (T) wars on other fronts.

The weekly newspaper *Trung Bac Tan Van* (Central and Northern News) ran (IT) continuously from 1919 until 1945.

> **Note to Instructor:** *Trung Bac Tan Van* is an appositive, renaming the subject noun *newspaper.* Appositives are covered in Lesson 94; if this is the student's first time through the course, you may accept either *newspaper* or *Trung Bac Tan Van* as an underlined subject.

By early 1968, the 80,000 PAVN troops in the South were fighting (IT) alongside 160,000 NLF infantry and service troops.

Exercise 56B: Active and Passive Verbs

In the blanks below, rewrite each sentence with an active verb so that the verb is passive. Rewrite each sentence with a passive verb so that the verb is active. You may need to add or rearrange words or phrases to make the sentences grammatical!

These sentences are slightly adapted from *Vietnam: Journeys of Body, Mind, and Spirit,* by Van Huy Nguyen and Laurel Kendall.

The Kinh welcome the solar new year with people all over the globe.

The solar new year is welcomed by the Kinh and people all over the globe.

OR The solar new year is welcomed by the Kinh, along with people all over the globe.

Each person, each family, and Vietnamese society as a whole approach the new year as a time of fresh aspiration and hope.

The new year is approached by each person, each family, and Vietnamese society as a whole as a time of fresh aspiration and hope.

OR The new year is approached as a time of fresh aspiration and hope by each person, each family, and Vietnamese society as a whole.

If the solar new year can be considered the government's Tet, the lunar new year is considered the family's Tet.

If the government considers the solar new year to be its Tet, the family considers the lunar new year to be its Tet.

OR If the government can consider the solar new year its Tet, the family considers the lunar new year as its Tet.

Each family prepares offerings to worship ancestors.

Offerings are prepared by each family to worship ancestors.

OR Offerings are prepared to worship ancestors by each family.

According to tradition, visits are made and gifts are distributed during the week before Tet.

According to tradition, the Kinh make visits and distribute gifts during the week before Tet.

> **Note to Instructor:** Accept any reasonable plural subject for the sentence (for example, "families" or "the Vietnamese").

On New Year's Eve they will burn votive paper money.

On New Year's Eve, votive paper money will be burned by them.

OR On New Year's Eve, votive paper money will be burned by families.

Vendors set their wares on the pavement under red banners declaring "Tet Shop" or "Happy New Year."

Wares are set on the pavement by vendors, under red banners declaring "Tet Shop" or "Happy New Year."

Exercise 56C: Diagramming

On your own paper, diagram every word in the following sentences. They are slightly condensed from *Vietnam (Cultures of the World)*, by Audrey Seah and Charissa M. Nair.

The water level has been raised by silt deposits on the riverbeds.

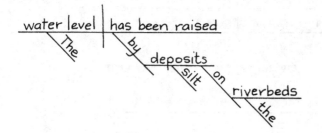

> **Note to Instructor:** It is acceptable for the student to diagram *water* beneath *level* as an adjective; it is also acceptable for the student to treat *silt deposits* as a single compound noun. Note that *on the riverbeds* is an adjective phrase describing *deposits*; it is not an adverb phrase and should not be diagrammed beneath *has been raised*.

Subsequent dynasties repaired and added more canals to the network and created a system of irrigation and flood control.

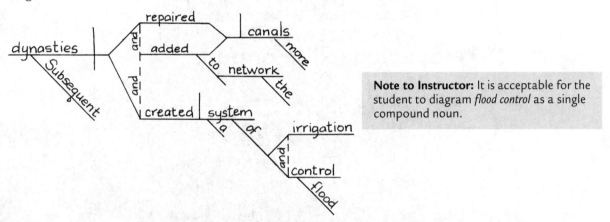

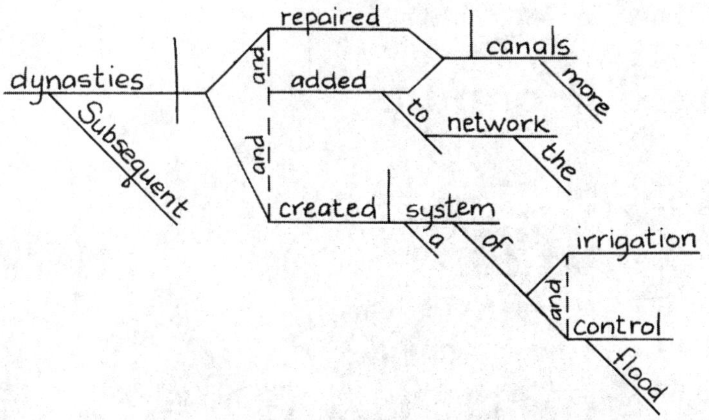

Note to Instructor: It is acceptable for the student to diagram *flood control* as a single compound noun.

Vietnam's indented eastern coastline extends from the Gulf of Tonkin to the South China Sea, past the Mekong delta, and reaches the Gulf of Thailand.

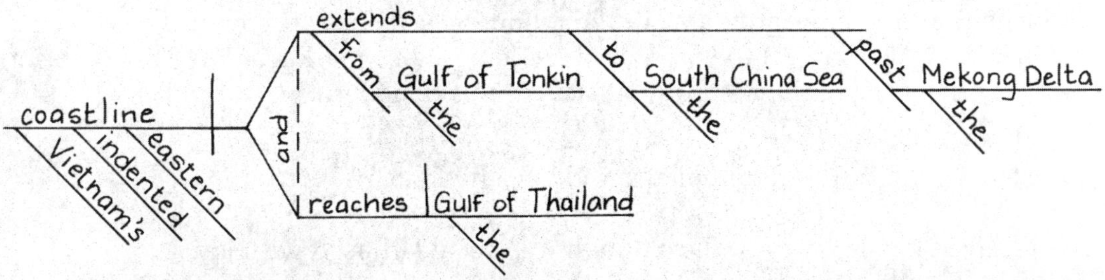

Note to Instructor: It is acceptable for the student to diagram *Mekong* as an adjective modifying *delta.*

At its narrowest point, the distance between its border with Laos in the west and the South China Sea in the east is only 31 miles.

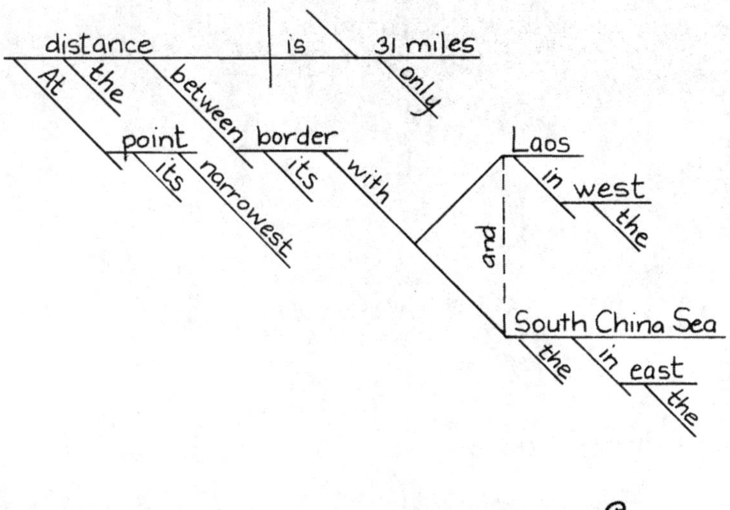

Note to Instructor: *31 miles* should be diagrammed as a single compound noun, since it represents a specific distance as the predicate nominative renaming *distance* (the distance isn't *miles*, it's specifically *31 miles*). *At its narrowest point* has been diagrammed as an adjective describing *distance* rather than an adverb phrase describing *is* and answering the question *where* because of its placement in the sentence, but the phrase's function is ambiguous and you may accept either placement on the diagram.

WEEK 15

Specialized Pronouns

— LESSON 57 —

Parts of Speech
Parts of the Sentence
Intensive and Reflexive Pronouns

Exercise 57A: Identifying Intensive and Reflexive Pronouns

Underline the intensive and reflexive pronouns in the following sentences. Above each pronoun, write *I* for intensive or *R* for reflexive. If the pronoun is reflexive, also mark it as *DO* (direct object), *IO* (indirect object), or *OP* (object of the preposition). The first is done for you.

The good woman let go with a smile, and Louise found herself (R DO) alone.

But when the son received his father well, the old man was beside himself (R OP) with joy.

They would also cook themselves (I), and wait upon each other.

Note to Instructor: Context should tell the student that *themselves* is not the direct object of the verb *cook*!

Throughout the work are feeble poetic epigrams composed by the compiler himself (I).

The race lies between Master Schummel and yourself (R OP).

No one knows me better than I know myself (R DO).

How comes it that you have produced nothing of value yourself (I)?

He convicted of ignorance those who had a great opinion of themselves (R OP).

I made up my mind to go myself (I).

Between ourselves (R OP), you owe your wife a great deal.

It would be strange indeed if I should torture myself (R DO), and make of myself (R OP) something which I am not, and hide myself (R DO) beneath a character foreign to me.

Exercise 57B: Using Intensive and Reflexive Pronouns Correctly

Each of the following sentences contains errors in the usage of intensive and reflexive pronouns. Cross out the incorrect word and write the correction above it.

He was quite beside ~~hisself~~ himself.

We had seated ~~ourselfs~~ ourselves round the table.

You yourself did ~~myself~~ me the honor to say that you wished ~~myself~~ me to be *fully* informed.

Then I go away for a little time and leave them to ~~theirselves~~ themselves.

Our assignment of ~~himself~~ him to the third century is based merely on the fact that he quotes writers of the second, and is ~~hisself~~ himself in turn cited by somewhat later authors.

On the contrary, ~~himself~~ he thought the ideal and the practical life perfectly compatible, and ~~himself~~ he strove to unite in himself the poet and the man of affairs.

Exercise 57C: Diagramming Intensive and Reflexive Pronouns

On your own paper, diagram every word in the following sentences, taken from *The Library of the World's Best Literature, Ancient and Modern*, Vol. 12, ed. Charles Dudley Warner.

I myself suffer from a different kind of education.

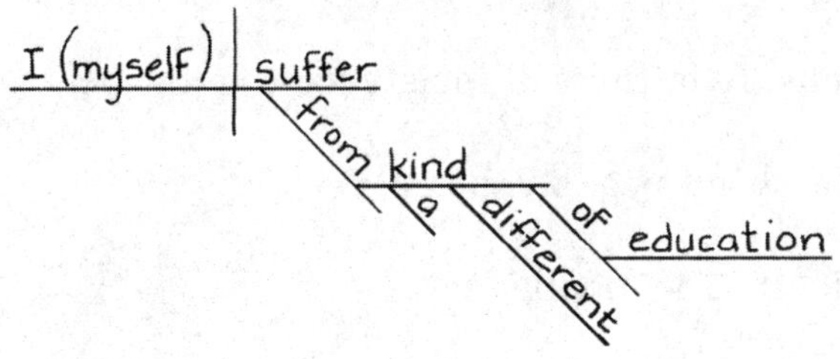

In the first place, I was ashamed of myself.

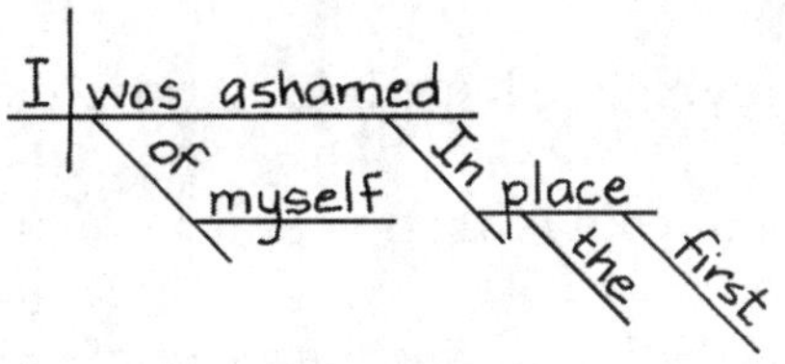

He prided himself on his simple manner of living, and never exacted any pay.

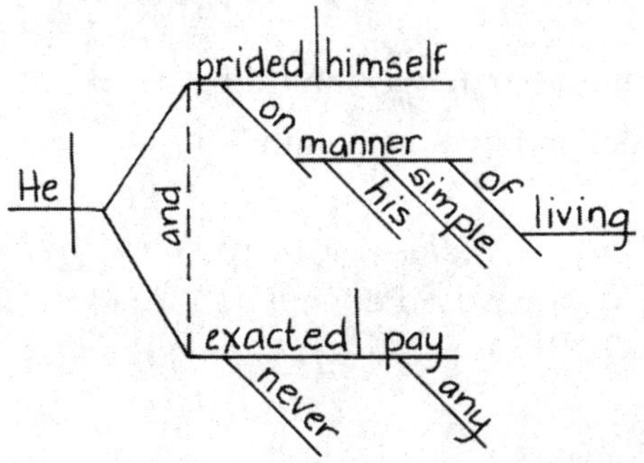

His love for the Northern seas shows itself in his poetry and prose.

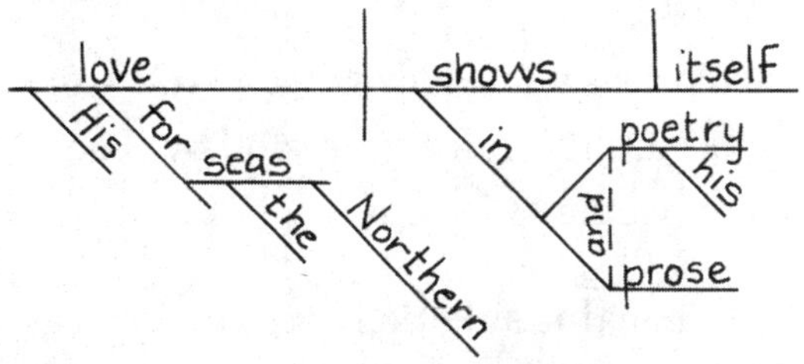

— LESSON 58 —

Demonstrative Pronouns
Demonstrative Adjectives

Exercise 58A: Demonstrative Pronouns and Demonstrative Adjectives

In the sentences below, label every occurrence of *this, that, these,* and *those* as either *DP* (demonstrative pronoun) or *DA* (demonstrative adjective). Draw an arrow from each demonstrative adjective to the noun it modifies. Label each demonstrative pronoun as *S* (subject), *DO* (direct object), *IO* (indirect object), or *OP* (object of the preposition).

These sentences are taken from *World of Warcraft and Philosophy: Wrath of the Philosopher King*, ed. Luke Cuddy and John Nordlinger.

DP S
And this is when weird things can happen.

DP OP
How can we even begin to think of this?

DA
Thus they are no longer "non-specified members of that other community," making their fights more personal than political.

DA
Plato then proceeds to discuss what it would be like for one of these people to be freed, and roam outside of the cave.

DA
I want to know what's on the other side of those hills.

DP S
Those occupying the hypothetical "original position" ensure fairness of society for all citizens.

DP S
However, these only function as driving licenses for the shiny siege weapons.

DP OP
Boredom, he believed, was the worst of these, calling it "the root of all evil."

DP OP
The story of *Warcraft II* is obviously a continuation of that.

DP S
That is guided by the game mechanics.

DP OP
Since prices and goods within WoW are so similar to those seen on Earth, we should be able to measure the value generated by Blood Elves just like we measure the value generated by actual people.

DA
Of course, this situation is unrealistic, as no reasonable entrepreneur would open a hobby store surrounded by eleven others.

DP DO
But if Ner'zhul knew this, he would have no reason to trust Kil'jaeden.

DA
These two models are very troublesome.

Exercise 58B: Demonstrative Pronouns

In the blank beneath each sentence, write a possible description of the thing or person that the underlined demonstrative pronoun stands for. Make sure to choose the correct number. (And use your imagination.)

Note to Instructor: The answers below are just examples—accept any description that fits the sentence and is the correct number!

Those are my least favorite ever.

Black pepper and chili jelly beans

That is the most spectacular thing I have ever seen.

The white stallion leading a herd of mares across the plains

This is truly horrifying.

The dead rat lying in the middle of the kitchen floor

These should just be thrown away immediately.

The ancient sneakers soaked in turpentine and swamp mud

Exercise 58C: Diagramming

On your own paper, diagram every word in the following three sentences, taken from *What Is Your Quest?: From Adventure Games to Interactive Books*, by Anastasia Salter.

In text-only games, this is the only description available.

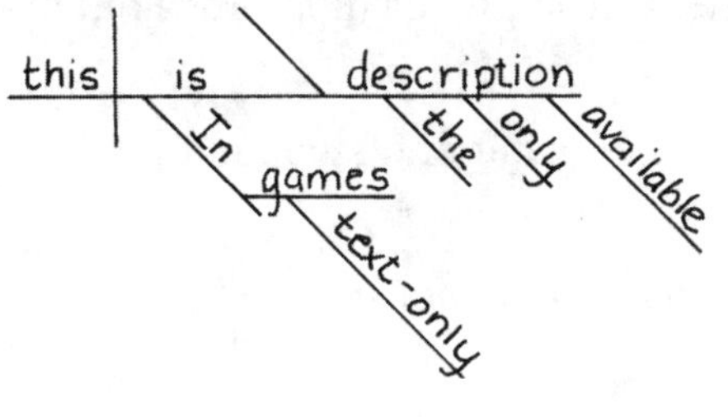

This take-it-or-leave-it avatar is not typical of other styles of games.

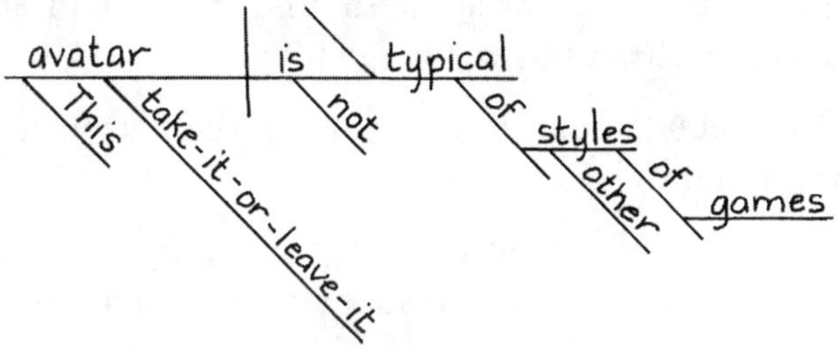

The campaign focused on the involvement of those creators and a return to the narrative.

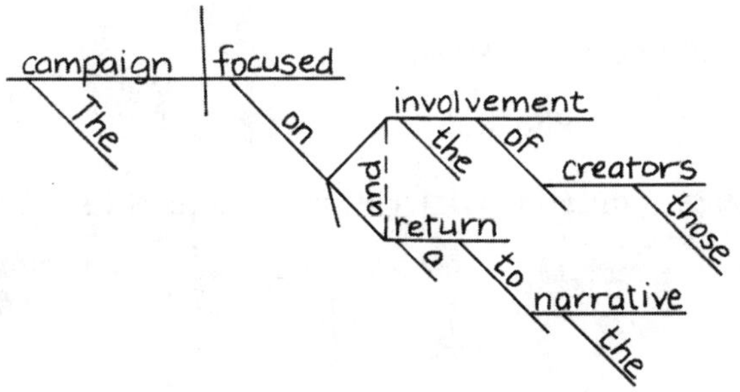

— LESSON 59 —

Demonstrative Pronouns
Demonstrative Adjectives
Interrogative Pronouns
Interrogative Adjectives

Exercise 59A: Identifying Demonstrative and Interrogative Pronouns

Underline all of the demonstrative and interrogative pronouns in the sentences. There may be more than one in each sentence.

These sentences are taken from *Japanese Fairy Tales*, compiled by Yei Theodora Ozaki.

"They have stood outside this house through the winter and the summer, often denying themselves food and sleep so they may win you. What more can you demand?"

"I shall soon take my leave if you will give me the big box—that is all I want!"

The insignia of the great Japanese Empire is composed of three treasures. These are the Yata-no-Kagami or the Mirror of Yata, the Yasakami-no-Magatama or the Jewel of Yasakami, and the Murakumo-no-Tsurugi or the Sword of Murakumo.

"This is no ordinary child. Whose can he be? I will find out before this day is done."

All the animals, those he had tamed to serve him, the bear, the deer, the monkey, and the hare, came to ask if they might attend him as usual.

But which was the way? He could not find it alone!

Slowly, very slowly, he untied the red silk cord, slowly and wonderingly he lifted the lid of the precious box. And what did he find? Strange to say only a beautiful little purple cloud rose out of the box in three soft wisps.

"That is good," said the old man. He then washed his feet in a basin of water and stepped up to the veranda.

These were placed before the old man, and the Lady Sparrow asked him to choose whichever he liked for a present, which she wished to give him.

"But next to you then, who is the strongest?"

Exercise 59B: Using Interrogative and Demonstrative Pronouns Correctly

Choose the correct word in parentheses. Cross out the incorrect word.

(These / ~~Those~~) are my suitcases right here, so (~~these~~ / those) must be Akari's suitcases next to the check-in counter.

(~~Whose~~ / Who's) excited about flying to Tokyo tonight?

(Who's / ~~Whose~~) sitting in the exit row of the plane?

(Who / ~~Whom~~) is planning to take the day trip to Mount Fuji with me?

(This / ~~These~~) is Akari's favorite travel pillow.

(Whose / ~~Who's~~) are these blankets?
(~~Who~~/ Whom) did she ask to meet us at the airport?
(~~Who~~/ Whom) did you invite to dinner?
(Who / ~~Whom~~) is leading the Tokyo biking tour on Thursday?
(~~Who~~/ What) is the name of the guide of the walking tour of Omoide Yokocho?
With (~~who~~/ whom) will you eat dinner on Friday?
(This / ~~These~~) has been a very smooth plane ride.

Exercise 59C: Diagramming Interrogative and Demonstrative Pronouns

On your own paper, diagram the following sentences.

Whose are these lovely summer yukatas?

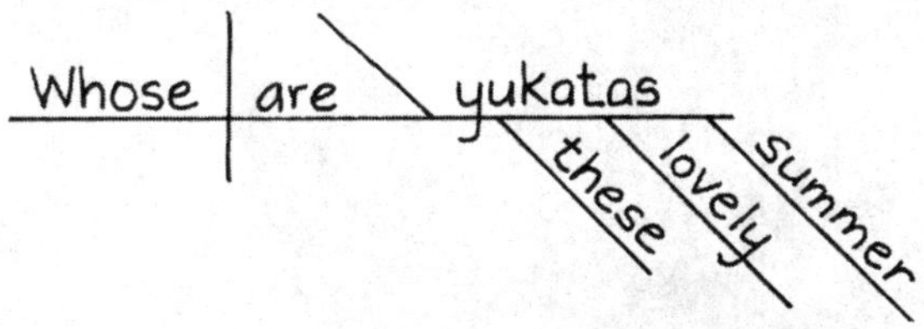

She bought what?

She carefully packed a suitcase of this and that.

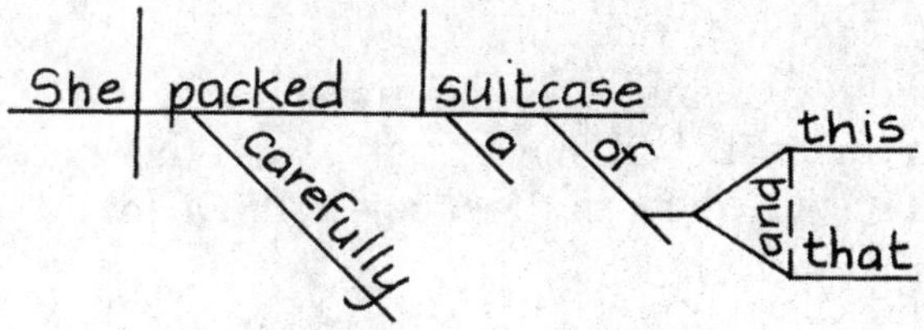

Who wore this?

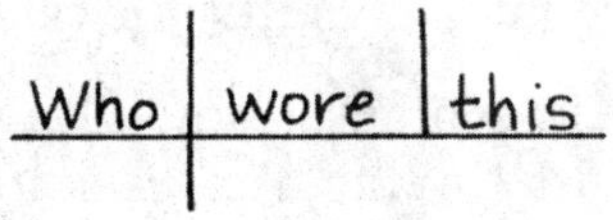

For whom were these shoes made?

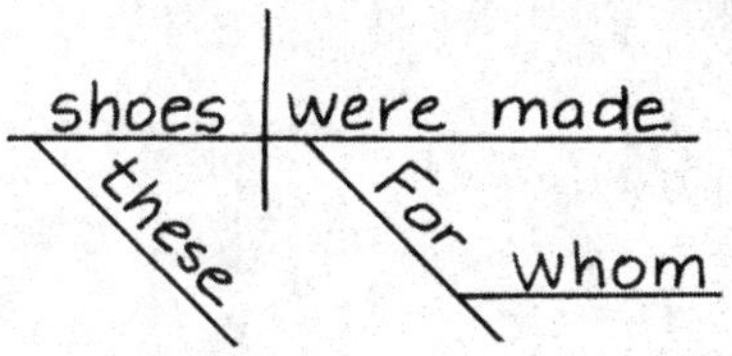

Which is the best fish market in Tokyo?

You must try this octopus and those shrimp!

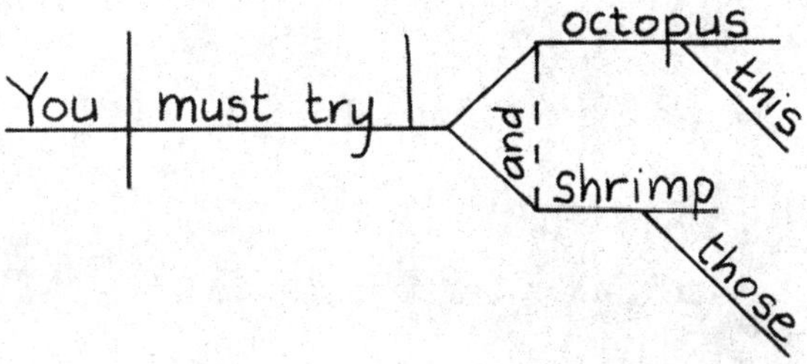

— LESSON 60 —

Pronoun Review

Sentences Beginning with Adverbs

Exercise 60A: Singular/Plural Indefinite Pronouns

Cross out the incorrect verb in each sentence. These are slightly adapted from *The Autobiography of Benjamin Franklin*, which is (you'll be surprised to hear) by Benjamin Franklin.

Not all of the wagons (were / ~~was~~) in serviceable condition.

None of the provisions (are / ~~is~~) left.

Some of them (were / ~~was~~) very unhappy.

Some of the hasty pudding (~~were~~ / was) left.

Some of my faults (were / ~~was~~) corrected.

I put down on paper my thoughts as they occurred. Most (are / ~~is~~) now lost.

Most (were / ~~was~~) men of property.

I asked for reassurance, but none (was / ~~were~~) forthcoming.

Exercise 60B: Interrogatives and Demonstratives

In each of the following sentences, underline the interrogatives and demonstratives. If they are acting as adjectives, draw a line from each to the noun it modifies. If they are acting as other parts of the sentence, label them (*S* for subject, *DO* for direct object, *IO* for indirect object, or *OP* for object of the preposition).

These sentences are also from *The Autobiography of Benjamin Franklin*.

DO What do you intend to infer from OP that?

What good shall I do this day?

S That amounts to nothing.

Whose shop is next door?

S These were not the governor's letters!

And, perhaps, S this might be one occasion of the differences we began to have about this time.

My time for these exercises and for reading was at night, after work or before it began in the morning,

I will give you what account I can of them at this distance from my papers, and if S these are not lost in my absence, you will among them find many more particulars.

Exercise 60C: Diagramming Practice

On your own paper, diagram every word of the following sentences, also taken from *The Autobiography of Benjamin Franklin.*

Some of my descendants may follow this example, and reap the benefit.

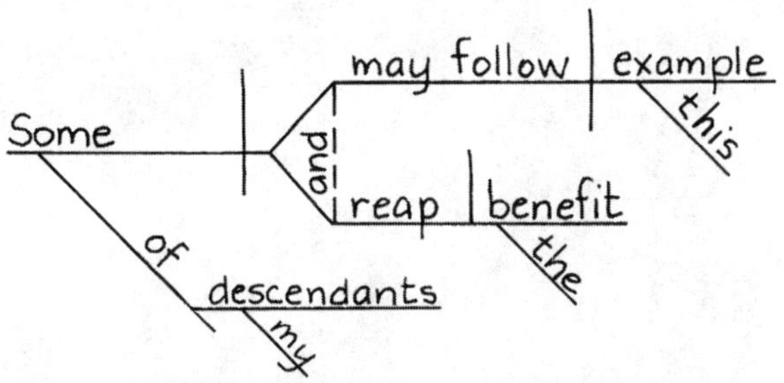

Where should I look for my night's lodging?

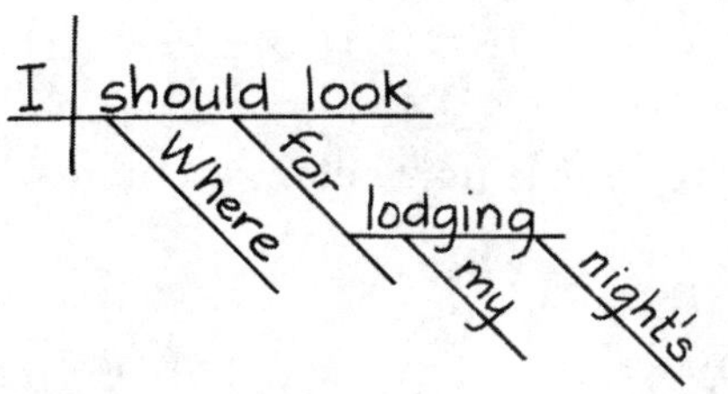

There are no gains without pains.

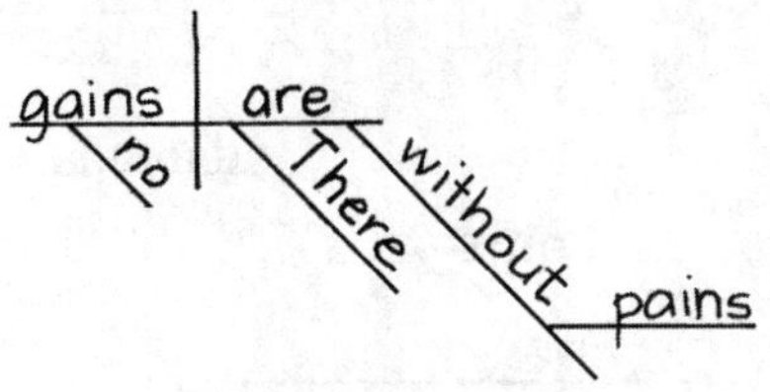

Our mutual affection was revived, but there were now great objections to our union.

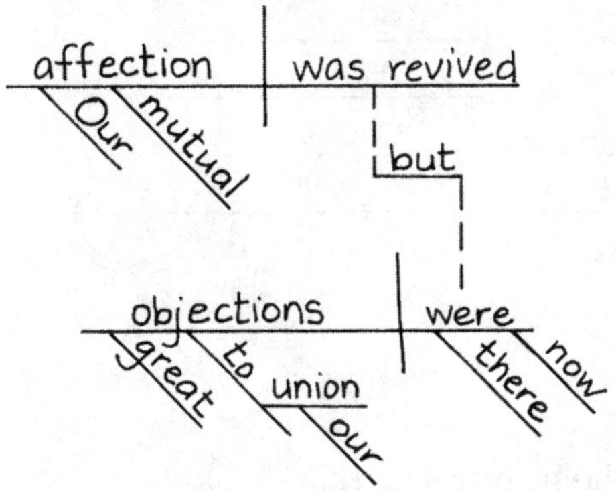

— REVIEW 5 —

Weeks 13-15

Topics
Pronouns and Antecedents
Possessive Pronouns
Subject and Object Pronouns
Indefinite Pronouns (and Subject-Verb Agreement)
Troublesome Verbs
Active and Passive Voice
Conjugating Passive Voice
Intensive and Reflexive Pronouns
Demonstrative and Interrogative Pronouns

Review 5A: Types of Pronouns

Put each pronoun from the word bank in the correct category. Some words may belong in more than one category.

this my many who
himself her which
those myself we none
all us its
whose it them ouselves
he these ours

Personal Subject	he	we	it
Personal Object	her	us	them
Personal Possessive	its	my	ours
Indefinite	many	none	all
Demonstrative	this	those	these
Interrogative	who	which	whose
Intensive/Reflexive	himself	ourselves	myself

Review 5B: Using Correct Pronouns

Cross out the incorrect pronoun in parentheses.

(~~Whose~~/Who's) going to help my mother and (~~I~~/me) shop at the farmer's market?

(Whose/~~Who's~~) basket is sitting over (there/~~their~~) with the gooseberries in it?

The first person to suggest we make gooseberry fool was (he/~~him~~).

My mother, my sister, and (he/~~him~~) were all arguing about (whose/~~who's~~) recipe for gooseberry fool is the best.

(There/~~their~~) was too much whipped cream in all of (~~there~~/their) recipes, and (~~their~~/they're) not sure how to fix (their/ ~~they're~~) soupy desserts.

(Who/~~Whom~~) would like to use (my/~~mine~~) recipe instead?

My father and (I/~~myself~~) would prefer to make the new gooseberry fool recipe by (~~ourself~~/ourselves).

(Who/~~Whom~~) are (they/~~them~~) cooking with tomorrow?

The last two people to finish cooking were (he/~~him~~) and (I/~~me~~).

(I/~~me~~) and (he/~~him~~) are cooking the next meal with (~~who~~/whom)?

Review 5C: Pronouns and Antecedents

Circle the nineteen personal pronouns (subject, object, and possessive) in the following excerpts from *Sideways Stories from Wayside School*, by Louis Sachar. Draw arrows to each pronoun's antecedent.

Mrs. Jewls hit her head against the wall five times. "How many times did I hit my head against the wall?" she asked.

"One, two, three, four, five, six, seven, eight, nine, ten. You hit your head against the wall ten times," said Joe.

The bell rang, and all the other children came back from recess. The fresh air had made them very excited, and they were laughing and shouting.

"Oh, darn," said Joe. "Now I missed recess."

"Hey, Joe, where were you?" asked John. "You missed a great game of kickball."

"Boy, am I hungry," said Louis. "I don't think Mrs. Gorf would mind if I ate this apple. After all, she always has so many."

He picked up the apple, which was really Mrs. Gorf, shined it up on his shirt, and ate it.

Review 5D: Agreement with Indefinite Pronouns

Choose the correct word in parentheses to agree with the indefinite pronouns. Cross out the incorrect word.

Hardly anyone can park (her or his/~~their~~) car close to the restaurant.

No one (enjoys/~~enjoy~~) a roast chicken more than I do.

(~~Is~~/Are) all of the peaches gone?

(Is/~~Are~~) all of the peach cobbler gone?

Some of these containers (hold/~~holds~~) cooking oil.

Both (~~was~~/ were) silent as the meal was served.

(Is / ~~Are~~) someone paying the bill?

Most of the talking (was / ~~were~~) done by our host.

Most of the meal (is / ~~are~~) gone by now.

(~~Has~~/ Have) all of you finished eating?

(Has / ~~Have~~) all of the wine been drunk as well?

Review 5E: Distinguishing Between Active and Passive Voice

Identify each underlined verb as *A* for active voice or *P* for passive voice. These sentences were taken from *Yes, Chef: A Memoir*, by Marcus Samuelsson.

I have never seen a picture of my mother. ___A___

The words seem meaningless, except the last is a clue because even today, in rural Ethiopia, girls are not encouraged to go to school. ___P___

I know this is what she fed us because this is what poor people eat in Ethiopia. ___A___

I have taught myself the recipes of my mother's people because those foods are for me, as a chef, the easiest connection to the mysteries of who my mother was. ___A___

When Mom, Dad, and Anna arrived at the customs area, they learned that our flight had been delayed for several hours. ___P___

In his application, my father promised to raise his adopted children in a good family, one with a dog and a cat, "both very friendly towards children." ___A___

Mr. Ljungqvist was shaped like a bowling ball, with thick white hair curling from under his black fisherman's cap. ___P___

Tram conductors who carried trolleys full of commuters were called herring packers. ___P___

Ljungqvist's customers bought lots and lots of herring—to poach, pickle, bake, and layer into cheesy, creamy casseroles with leeks and tomatoes. ___A___

Review 5F: Troublesome Verbs

Choose the correct verb form in parentheses. Cross out the incorrect forms. These sentences were taken from *Life, on the Line: A Chef's Story of Chasing Greatness, Facing Death, and Redefining the Way We Eat*, by Grant Achatz and Nick Kokonas.

Before she could agree Michael glided over to the light, (raised / ~~rose~~) his arm to the bulb, and snapped his fingers.

I fired up the stove, (~~sat~~/ set) my cutting board in place, and composed a couple of bains-marie with essential tools.

And of course, the ice cream had to be made, spun, (laid/~~lain~~) out in trays, frozen, and then punched out with a ring cutter and immediately refrozen.

After (~~setting~~/sitting) in Central Park for a bit we made our way to Cru.

It is the story of a man who (~~raised~~/rose) to the top of his chosen profession by working incredibly long hours and paying meticulous attention to detail to produce food in the best way he could.

He flopped his coat on the back of one of my dining room chairs and (~~lay~~/laid) out a few sheets of paper.

But the genius of the dish (lay/~~laid~~) in the use of the warmed vanilla bean as an aromatic handle.

A group of burgundy books (sat/~~set~~) on the shelf like a red siren flashing at me.

Without breaking stride he slid over to the dish machine, and again using his free hand, squeegeed the water off the rack, and starting (~~lying~~/laying) plates down.

I have been looking for about six months for a spot that would (let/~~leave~~) me produce my own food.

My overall plan for (raising/~~rising~~) the money for the restaurant was pretty simple.

He said good morning as he passed, began (~~sitting~~/setting) up his station, and then slid next to me.

WEEK 16

Imposters

— LESSON 61 —

Progressive Tenses
Principal Parts
Past Participles as Adjectives
Present Participles as Adjectives

Exercise 61A: Identifying Past Participles Used as Adjectives

Underline the past participles used as adjectives in the following sentences, taken from *Where the Red Fern Grows*, by Wilson Rawls. Draw a line to the noun or pronoun that each one modifies.

It was too much for him and he took off down the street, squalling like a scalded cat.

I went off to bed with my heart all torn up in little pieces, and cried myself to sleep.

However, many was the time I'd find my vegetables left in the abandoned camp.

Early the next morning, with the can jammed deep in the pocket of my overalls, I whistled and sang.

He saw the faded yellow piece of paper sticking out from the coins.

The country was new and sparsely settled.

Note to Instructor: The past participle *settled* is a predicate adjective, as is *new*, both of them linked to the subject *country* by the linking verb *was*.

Exercise 61B: Identifying Present Participles Used as Adjectives

Underline the present participles used as adjectives in the following sentences, taken from *Because of Winn-Dixie*, by Kate DiCamillo. Draw a line to each word modified.

There were just a lot of vegetables rolling around on the floor, tomatoes and onions and green peppers.

You are a suffering dog, so maybe he will take to you right away.

I couldn't do anything about his crooked yellow teeth because he got into a sneezing fit every time I started brushing them with my toothbrush, and I finally had to give up.

> **Note to Instructor:** The present participle *brushing* is an adverb modifying *started*, not an adjective.

But the first time Miss Franny Block saw Winn-Dixie standing up on his hind legs like that, looking in the window, she didn't think he was a dog.

Miss Franny sat there trembling and shaking.

Exercise 61C: Diagramming Participles Used as Adjectives

On your own paper, diagram the following sentences.

Barking dogs keep us awake.

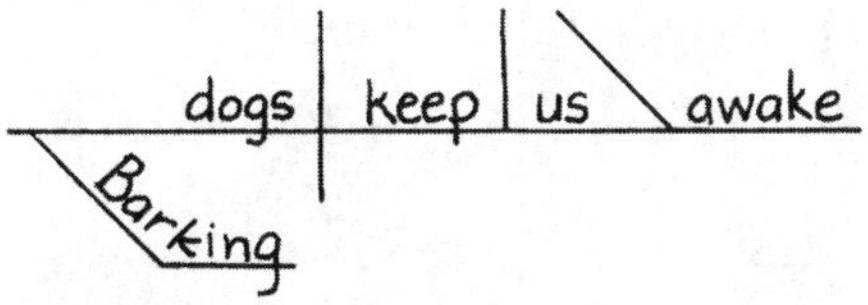

Shut windows don't keep out the sound.

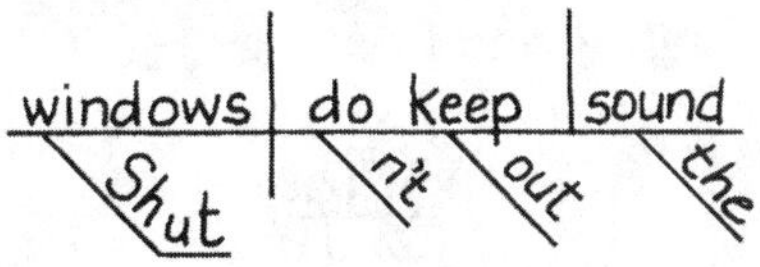

My complaining father calls our neighbors.

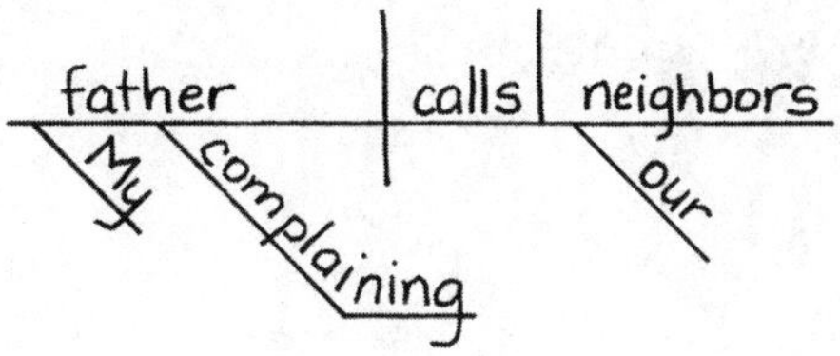

Our embarrassed neighbors bring their dogs into the house.

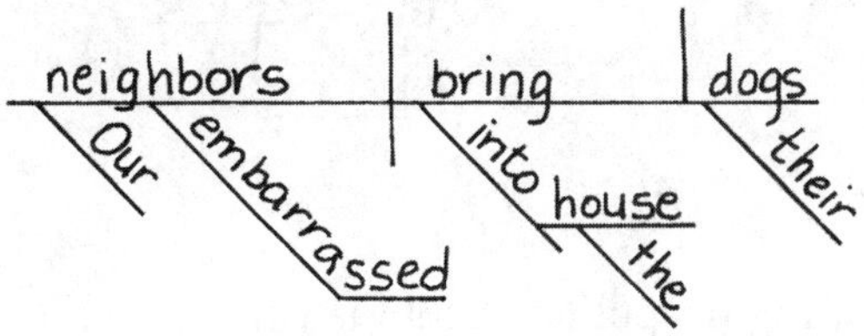

— LESSON 62 —

Parts of Speech and Parts of Sentences

Present Participles as Nouns (Gerunds)

Exercise 62A: Identifying Gerunds

In the following sentences, adapted from *Thor: Viking God of Thunder*, by Graeme Davis, underline each subject once and each predicate twice. Write *DO* above any direct objects of the predicate, *IO* above any indirect objects of the predicate, *OP* above any objects of prepositions, and *PN* above any predicate nominatives. Then, circle each gerund.

OP OP DO OP

Reading between the lines of the myths reveals Thor to be a model for pagan warriors.

PN

Thor's favorite pastime is slaying giants.

OP

Thor was known for slaughtering giants left and right.

DO

The stories emphasize his fighting.

OP PN

Protecting Asgard from encroaching giants was his primary task.

> **Note to Instructor:** *Encroaching* is not a gerund! It is a present participle acting as an adjective (modifying *giants*), not a noun.

IO DO OP

The gloves gave Thor the necessary strength for defending Asgard.

Exercise 62B: Diagramming Gerunds, Present Participles, and Progressive Verbs

On your own paper, diagram every word in the following sentences.

A giant loves eating and fighting!

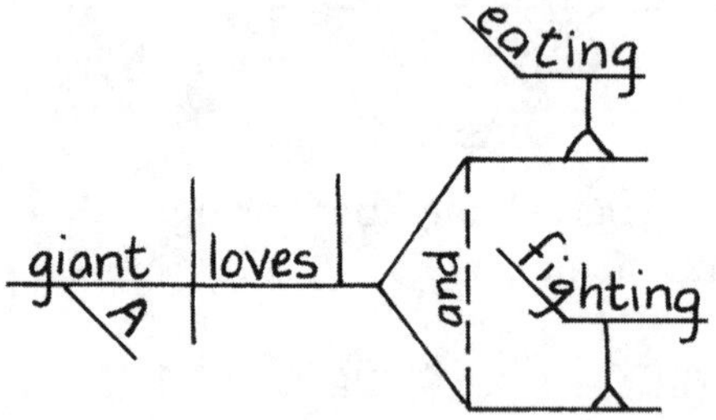

They were speaking to the farmer.

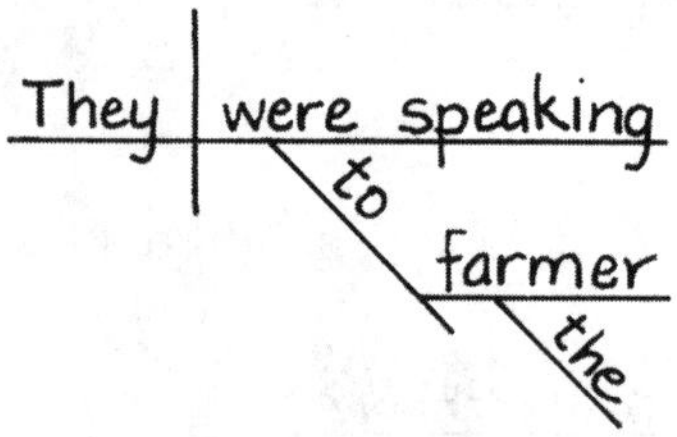

Hoping propelled them forward.

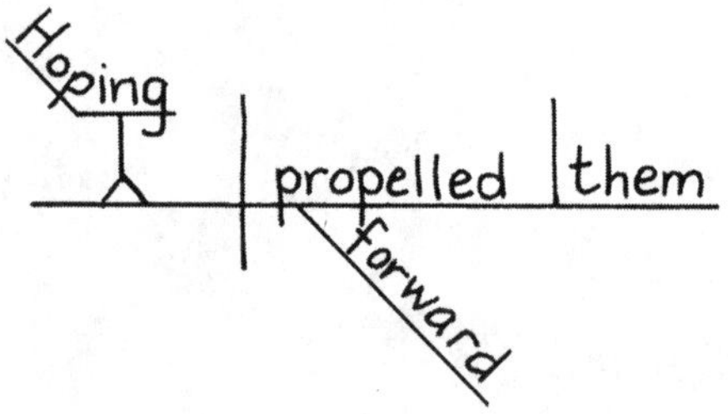

I am pointing this out.

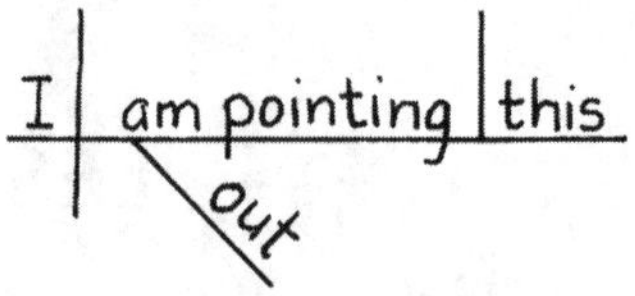

I am very tired of travelling.

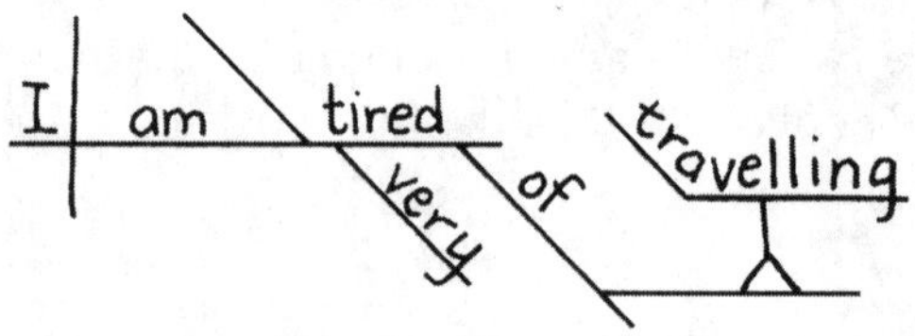

Please stop shouting about the flying hammer!

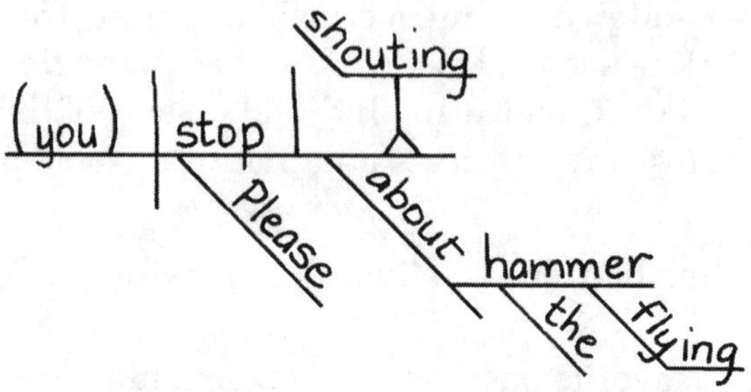

— LESSON 63 —

Gerunds
Present and Past Participles as Adjectives
Infinitives
Infinitives as Nouns

Exercise 63A: Identifying Gerunds and Infinitives

Underline the gerunds and infinitives in the following quotes about the twentieth century. Identify the imposters as *G* for gerund or *I* for infinitive. Then, identify each gerund or infinitive as a subject (*S*), predicate nominative (*PN*), direct object (*DO*), or object of a preposition (*OP*).

One of the really notable achievements of the twentieth century has been to make (I PN) the young old before their time.

—Robertson Davies

. . . [M]an began to study (I DO) himself as a scientific phenomenon.

—Timothy Leary

Pilots generally take pride in a good landing (G OP), not in getting (G OP) out of the vehicle.

—Neil Armstrong

Avoiding (G S) danger is no safer in the long run than outright exposure. The fearful are caught as often as the bold.

—Helen Keller

The major task of the twentieth century will be to explore (I PN) the unconscious, to investigate (I PN) the subsoil of the mind.

—Henri Bergson

Public policy in the twentieth century was about protecting (G OP) and expanding (G OP) the social compact, based on recognition that effective government at the federal level provides rules and services and safety measures that contribute to a better society.

—Carl Bernstein

Twentieth-century man must . . . purposefully strive to discover (I DO) the hidden secrets of our universe.

—John Young

. . . [T]he iconoclast . . . refuses to acknowledge (I DO) any . . . rules or hierarchy.

—Peter Sloterdijk

. . . [P]eople . . . think they're doing a great job of hiding (G OP) stuff, and it just keeps leaking (G DO) out.

—Harry Shearer

I DO
I like <u>to think</u> of my behavior in the sixties as a learning experience.

—P. J. O'Rourke

> **Note to Instructor:** *Learning* is not a gerund; it is a present participle serving as an adjective, modifying *experience*.

I DO
I have a lifetime appointment and I intend <u>to serve</u> it.

—Thurgood Marshall

I PN
The thing the sixties did was <u>to show</u> us the possibilities and the responsibility that we all had.

—John Lennon

I DO I DO
Everyone wants <u>to be</u> Cary Grant. Even I want <u>to be</u> Cary Grant.

—Cary Grant

I S I PN
<u>To say</u> "I accept," in an age like our own, is <u>to say</u> that you accept concentration-camps, rubber truncheons, Hitler, Stalin, bombs, aeroplanes, tinned food, machine guns, putsches, purges, slogans, Bedaux belts, gas-masks, submarines, spies, provocateurs, press-censorship, secret prisons, aspirins, Hollywood films and political murder.

—George Orwell

Exercise 63B: Diagramming Gerunds and Infinitives

On your own paper, diagram the following sentences.

We start to rock.

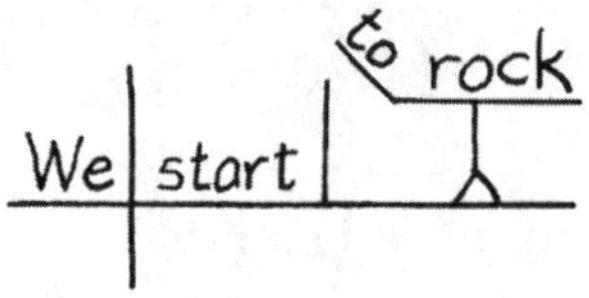

Stop shouting.

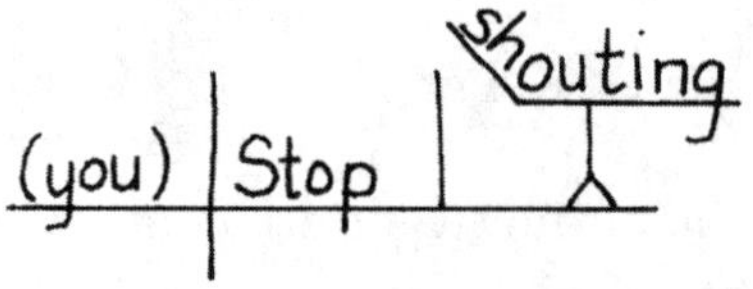

To live is to die.

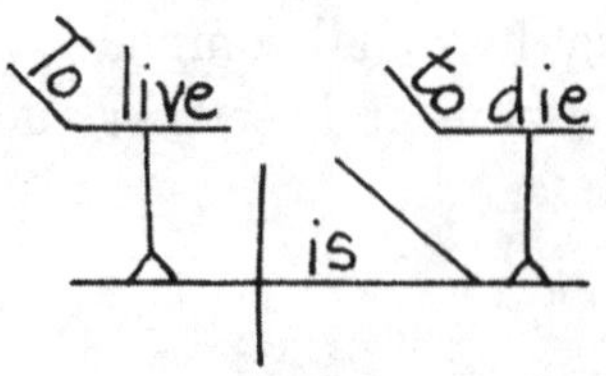

I cannot bear to witness any longer.

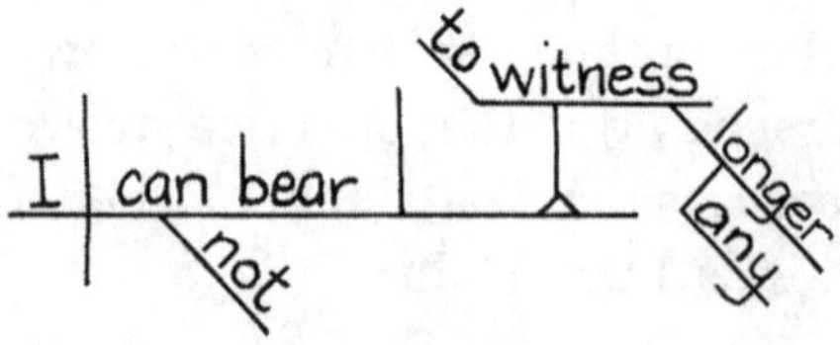

Running and shrieking are very bad ideas.

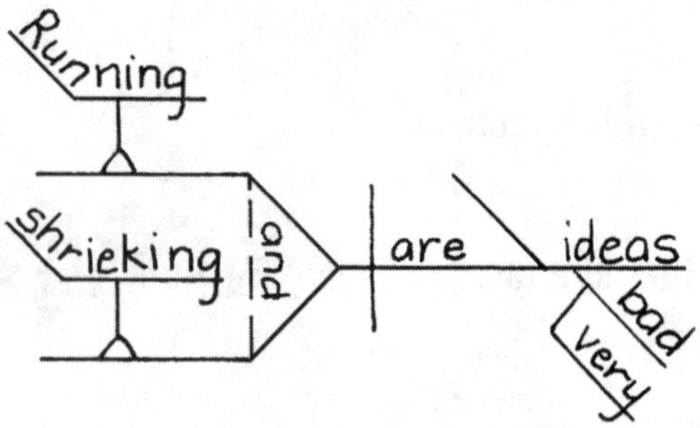

— LESSON 64 —

Gerunds
Present and Past Participles
Infinitives
Gerund, Participle, and Infinitive Phrases

Exercise 64A: Identifying Phrases that Serve as Parts of the Sentence

In the following sentences, begin by underlining each prepositional phrase.

- Then, circle each group of words that contains a gerund, infinitive, or past participle.
- Each one serves as a part of the sentence. (Those circled phrases might include some of your prepositional phrases!) Label each circled phrase. Your options are: *ADJ* (adjective), *ADV* (adverb), S (subject), *IO* (indirect object), *DO* (direct object), *OC* (object complement), *OP* (object of the preposition), *PN* (predicate nominative), or *PA* (predicate adjective).

These sentences are taken from *Otto of the Silver Hand*, by Howard Pyle.

ADV

Why had he talked about churning butter?

DO

No knight in those days dared to ride the roads without full armor.

ADV ADV

He left the room to give the needful orders, bearing the babe with him.

PA PA

He was to leave the happy, sunny silence of the dear White Cross, and to go out into that great world.

DO

The light from the oriel window behind the old man shed broken rays of light upon him, and

PA

seemed to frame his thin gray hairs with a golden glory.

He was a great lover of books, and had under lock and key wonderful and beautiful volumes,

ADJ ADJ OP

bound in hog-skin and metal, and with covers inlaid with carved ivory, or studded with

ADJ

precious stones.

He stood intently, motionlessly, listening, listening; but all was silent except for the monotonous dripping of water in one of the nooks of the court-yard, and the distant murmur of the river borne upon the breath of the night air.

ADV — listening, listening; OP — the monotonous dripping … court-yard; ADJ — borne upon the breath of the night air

Note to Instructor: *Except for* acts as a single compound preposition. *Borne* is the passive past participle of *bear,* acting as an adjective and describing *murmur.*

Oftentimes the good Father Abbot, coming into the garden, would find the poor, simple Brother sitting under the shade of the pear-tree, rocking the little baby in his arms, singing strange, crazy songs to it, and gazing far away into the blue, empty sky with his curious, pale eyes.

ADJ — coming into the garden; ADJ — sitting under the shade of the pear-tree; ADJ — rocking the little baby in his arms; ADJ — singing strange, crazy songs to it; ADJ — gazing far away into the blue, empty sky with his curious, pale eyes

Exercise 64B: Diagramming

On your own paper, diagram all of the sentences from Exercise 64A.

Why had he talked about churning butter?

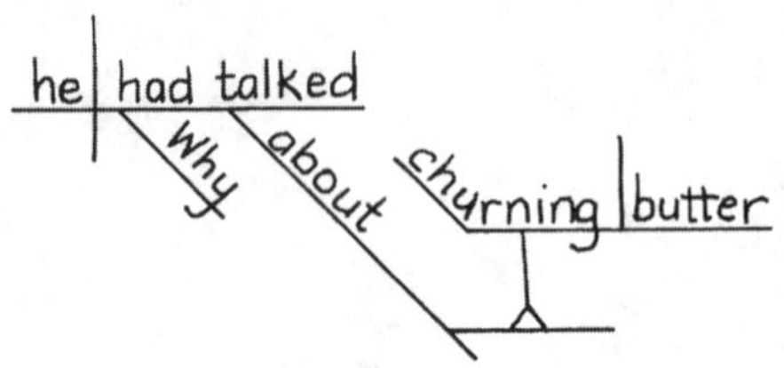

No knight in those days dared to ride the roads without full armor.

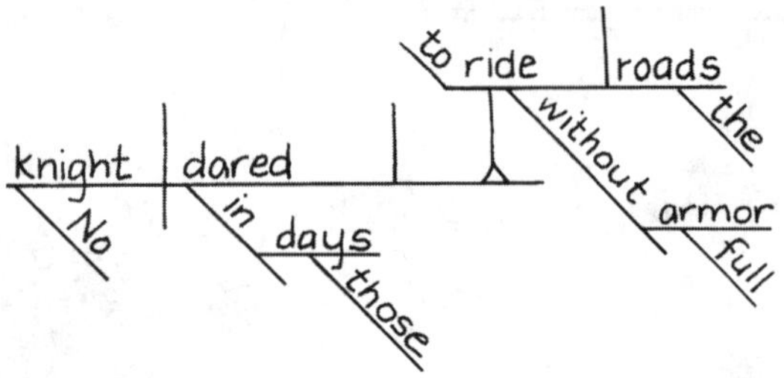

He left the room to give the needful orders, bearing the babe with him.

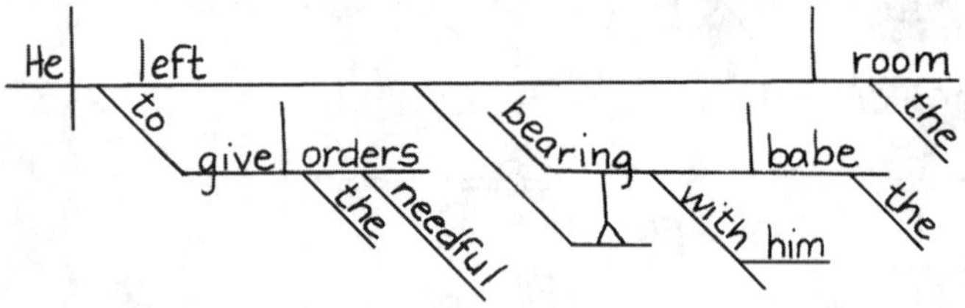

He was to leave the happy, sunny silence of the dear White Cross, and to go out into that great world.

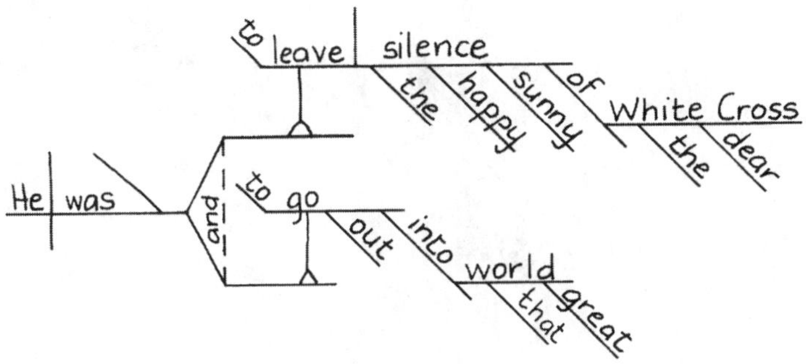

The light from the oriel window behind the old man shed broken rays of light upon him, and seemed to frame his thin gray hairs with a golden glory.

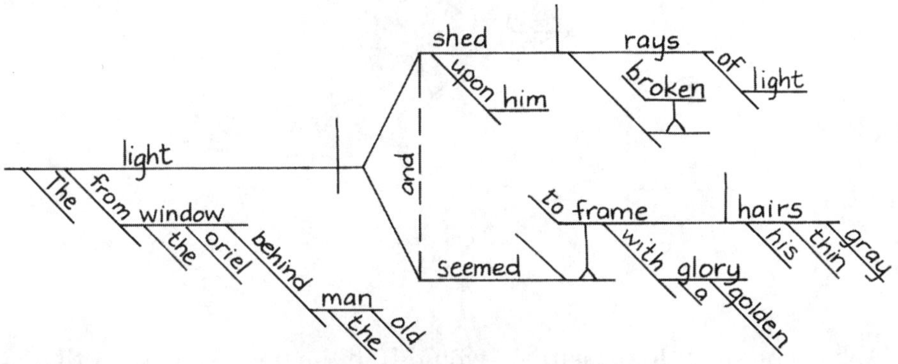

He was a great lover of books, and had under lock and key wonderful and beautiful volumes, bound in hog-skin and metal, and with covers inlaid with carved ivory, or studded with precious stones.

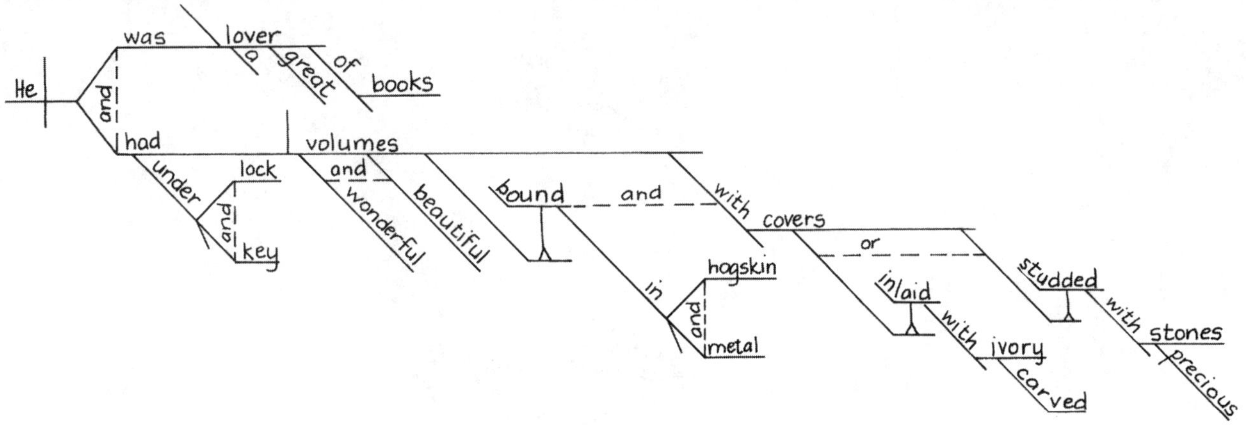

He stood intently, motionlessly, listening, listening; but all was silent except for the monotonous dripping of water in one of the nooks of the court-yard, and the distant murmur of the river borne upon the breath of the night air.

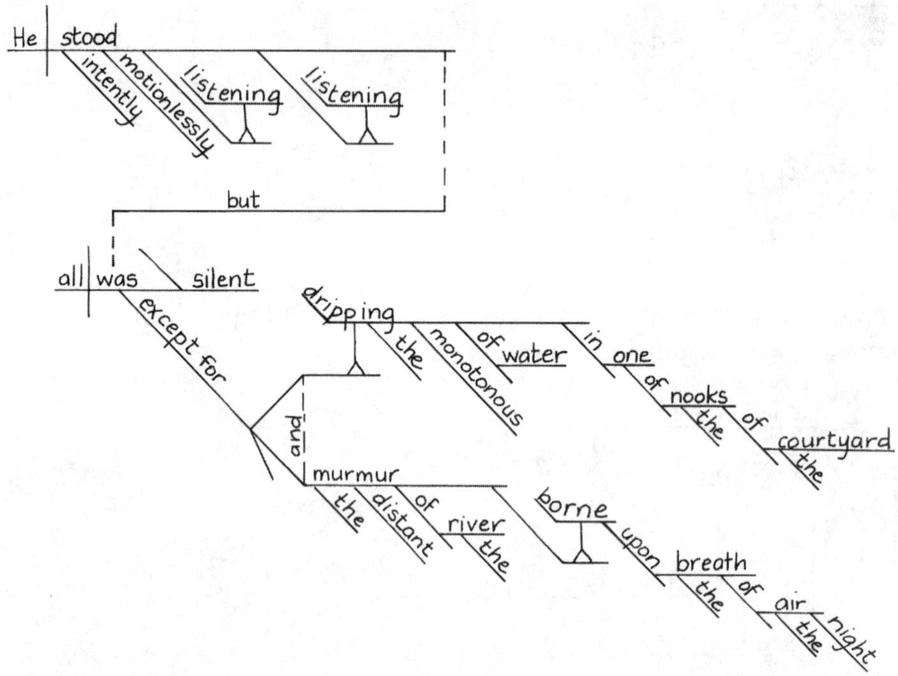

Oftentimes the good Father Abbot, coming into the garden, would find the poor, simple Brother sitting under the shade of the pear-tree, rocking the little baby in his arms, singing strange, crazy songs to it, and gazing far away into the blue, empty sky with his curious, pale eyes.

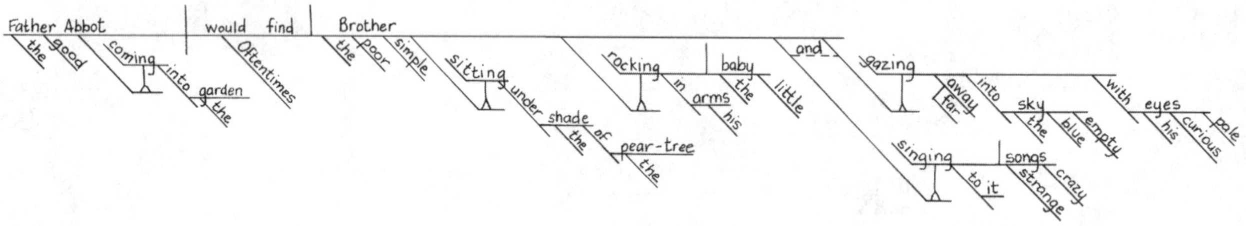

WEEK 17

Comparatives and Superlatives, Subordinating Conjunctions

— LESSON 65 —

Adjectives

Comparative and Superlative Adjectives

Exercise 65A: Identifying Positive, Comparative, and Superlative Adjectives

Identify the underlined adjective forms as *P* for positive, *C* for comparative, or *S* for superlative. These sentences are from *Modern Painters,* Volume I, by John Ruskin.

If we stand for a little [P] time before any of the more celebrated [C] works of landscape, listening to the comments of the passers-by, we shall hear numberless [P] expressions relating to the skill of the artist, but very few [P] relating to the perfection of nature.

The particularization of flowers by Shakespeare and Shelley affords us the most frequent [S] examples of the exalted [P] use of these inferior [P] details.

The same [P] faults must be found with his present [P] painting of foliage, neither the stems nor leafage being ever studied from nature; and this is the more to be regretted, because in the earlier [C] works of the artist there was much admirable [P] drawing.

The picture which has the nobler [C] and more numerous [C] ideas, however awkwardly expressed, is a greater [C] picture than that which has the less noble [C] and less numerous [C] ideas, however beautifully expressed.

If this then be the definition of great [P] art, that of a great [P] artist naturally follows. He is the greatest [S] artist who has embodied, in the sum of his works, the greatest [S] number of the greatest [S] ideas.

Leonardo's landscape has been of unfortunate [P] effect on art, so far as it has had effect at all. In realization of detail he verges on the ornamental, in his rock outlines he has all the deficiencies and little of the feeling of the earlier [C] men.

Exercise 65B: Forming Comparative and Superlative Adjectives

Fill in the blank with the correct form of the adjective in parentheses. These sentences are from *Women Painters of the World: From the Time of Caterina Vigri, 1413–1463, to Rosa Bonheur and the Present Day*, edited by W. S. Sparrow.

The work of Matilda Heming is interesting in a more special way. (comparative of *special*)

Older than the authenticated history of Greek art is a tradition that connects a girl's name with the discovery of a great craft, the craft of modelling portraits in relief. (comparative of *old*)

Lavinia Fontana and Elisabetta Sirani were the ablest women painters whose travels did not extend beyond Italy. (superlative of *able*)

Note to Instructor: *Most able* is also acceptable; this adjective can be formed in more than one way.

Elisabetta's health gave way, a painful disease of the stomach assailed her; and yet to the last day but one of her short life, she remained true to her colours, and was one of art's truest soldiers. (superlative of *true*)

There is some work of Mary Beale's in the National Portrait Gallery, London; it is work of the quiet, genuine kind, and better than most of the painting that came for some time afterwards. (comparative of *good*)

Marianne Stokes is made of sterner stuff. (comparative of *stern*)

Caterina Vigri was the earliest of these nuns, and the picture "St. Ursula and her Maidens" was painted in the year 1456. (superlative of *early*)

The work of each has great interest, but that of Mary Cassatt is the more attractive and the more enduring; it is richer with the emotions of the painter's own heart. (comparative of *attractive*, comparative of *enduring*, comparative of *rich*)

There are higher and more subtle qualities in the quiet wisdom of Julie Wolfthorn, a Berlin painter of note. (comparative of *high*, comparative of *subtle*)

Her attainments, her wit, and her eminent merits made Cornélie Lamme one of the most remarkable women of her day. (superlative of *remarkable*)

Exercise 65C: Diagramming Comparative and Superlative Adjectives

On your own paper, diagram the following four sentences from *A History of Art for Beginners and Students: Painting, Sculpture, Architecture*, by Clara Erskine Clement.

A second and even more serious fault in Egyptian architecture is a want of proportion.

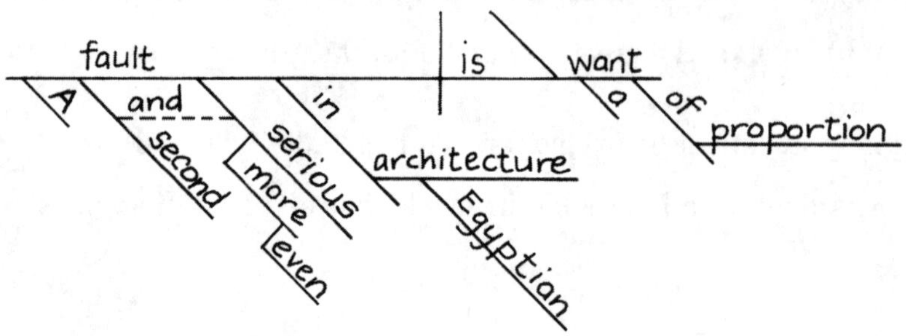

Of these pyramids, the three at Giza are best known, and that of Cheops is most remarkable.

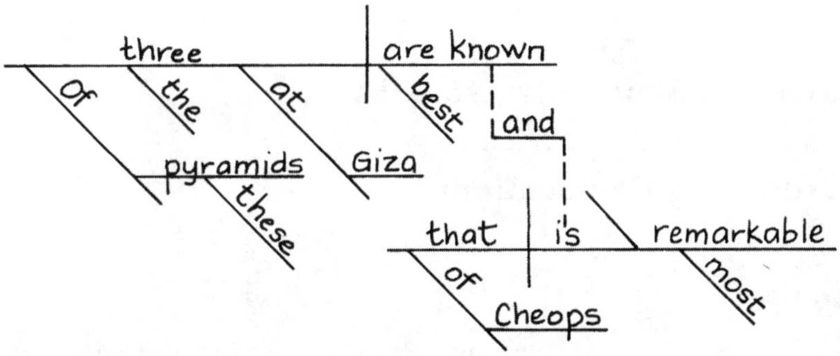

The great cathedral of Cologne is one of the largest and most famous churches in all of Europe.

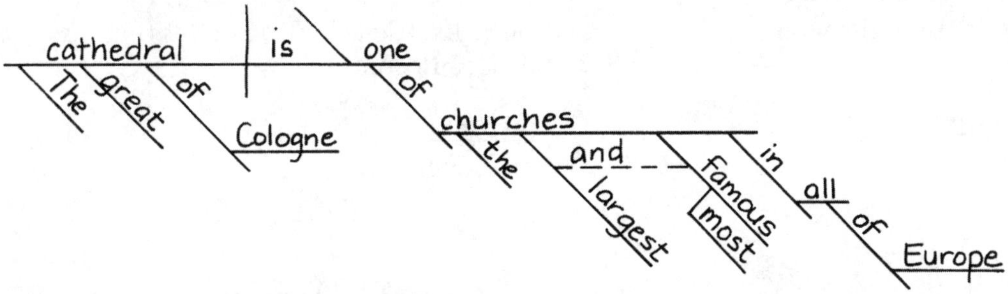

This basilica had four rows of Corinthian columns; many of these pillars were taken from more ancient edifices, and were composed of very beautiful marbles.

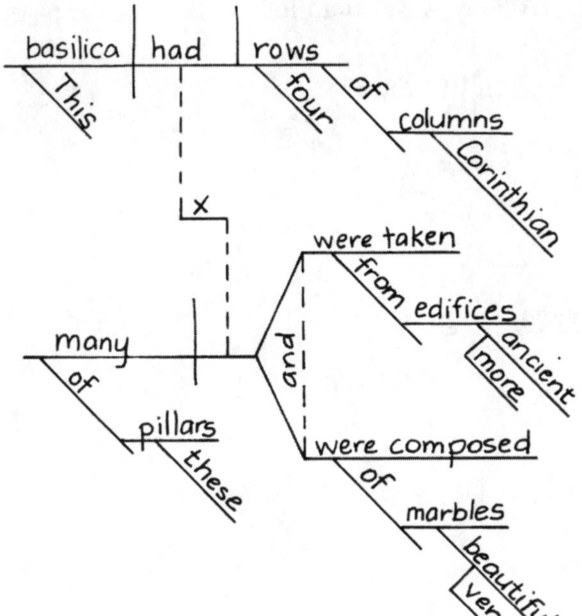

— LESSON 66 —

Adverbs
Comparative and Superlative Adverbs
Coordinating Conjunctions
Subordinating Conjunctions

Exercise 66A: Diagramming Comparatives

Diagram the first two sentences on the frames provided. Diagram the remaining sentences on your own paper.

The sun seems brighter than the moon.

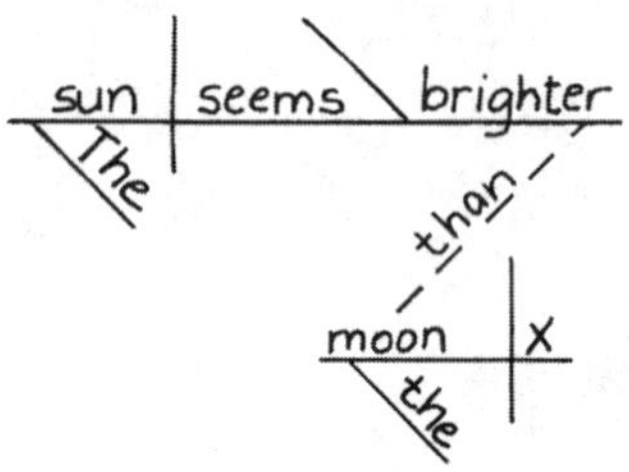

The red kettle is boiling hotter than the black cauldron.

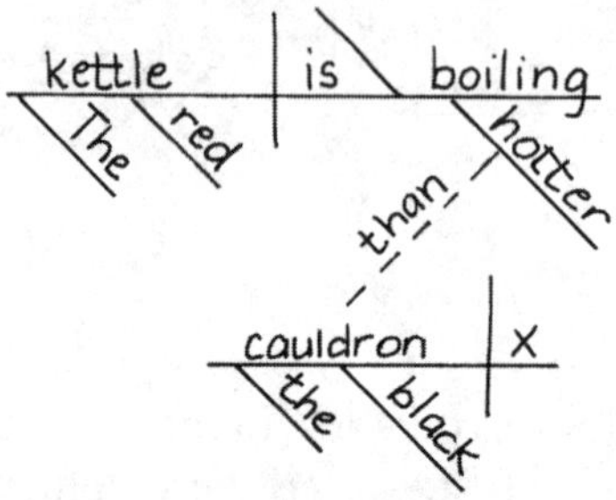

Courage is a better choice than cowardice.

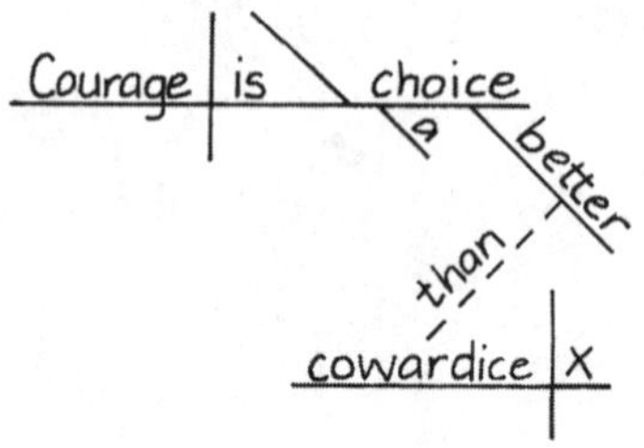

You are wiser than he.

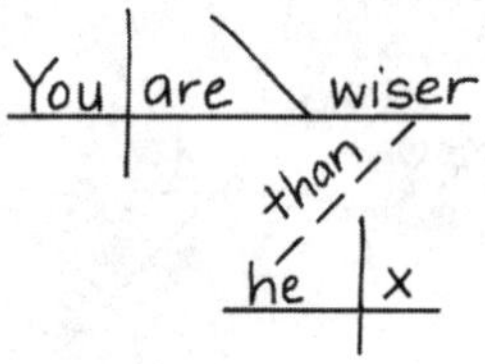

That young woman was taller and older than the others.

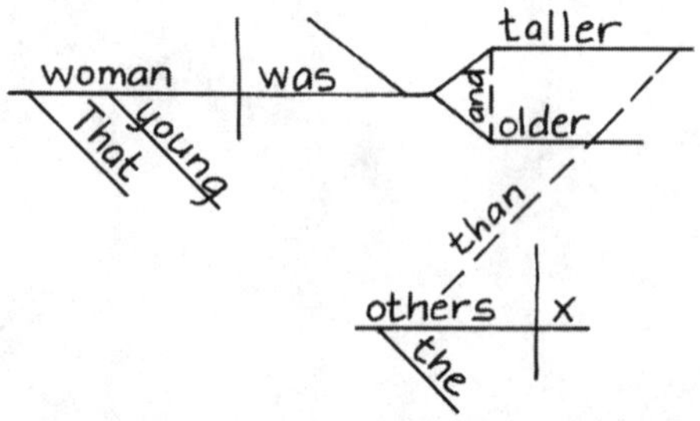

Exercise 66B: Identifying Positive, Comparative, and Superlative Adverbs

Identify the underlined adverb forms as *P* for positive, *C* for comparative, or *S* for superlative. These sentences are taken from *Wonder Stories*, by Carolyn Sherwin Bailey.

P

The waters were very heavy and took the lowest place where the earth held them safely in its hollows.

He made the daytime brighter and the gold rays of the sun shine more gloriously. (C)

With these he chained Prometheus to a rock and sent a vulture to eat his flesh, which grew again continually (P) so that Prometheus suffered most terrible pain as the vulture returned each day.

What a pair of shoulders they must have been, for they were, later (C), to uphold the sky!

"No doubt he intended it for me," Pandora said, "and most probably (S) it contains pretty dresses for me to wear, or toys for us both, or something nice for us to eat."

Both of them had been painfully (P) stung.

He dropped his lyre and ran after her, but she eluded him, running more swiftly (C) than the wind.

"Pray run slower (C) and I will follow more slowly (C)!"

She sang to the lyre, the most beautifully (S) of all the sisters.

Exercise 66C: Forming Comparative and Superlative Adverbs

Fill in the blank with the correct form of the adverb in parentheses.

Of all of the heroes, Hercules stood the tallest. (tall)

Mercury could travel faster than thought flies. (fast)

Daedalus loved his son Icarus more fervently than any other being in the world. (fervent)

Of the two hammers, Thor's was by far the heavier. (heavy)

The ram with a fleece of gold leaped highest of any animal on Mount Olympus. (high)

Vulcan forged tools for the gods more skillfully than the best of earthly blacksmiths. (skillfully)

Vulcan forged tools for the gods most skillfully of all blacksmiths in the universe. (skillfully)

— LESSON 67 —

Irregular Comparative and Superlative Adjectives and Adverbs

Exercise 67A: Best and Worst Ice Cream Flavors

Put the following ice cream flavors in the columns according to your opinion. (There are no correct answers—it all depends on you.)

bacon avocado	mint chocolate chip	rum raisin
salted caramel	bubblegum	cherry cheesecake

Note to Instructor: Accept any answers!

good: ______	**bad:** ______
better: ______	**worse:** ______
best: ______	**worst:** ______

Exercise 67B: Using Comparatives and Superlatives Correctly

Choose the correct form in parentheses. Cross out the incorrect form. These sentences are from *Newton's Football: The Science Behind America's Game*, by Allen St. John and Ainissa G. Ramirez.

The man who would come to be known as "Bootin' Ben" quickly discovered that with his injured foot and his modified boot, he could actually kick (farther/~~more far~~) and (~~accurater~~/more accurately) than he ever could with his toes.

No position relies (~~heavier~~/more heavily) on the applied physics of perfect technique.

This somewhat elongated ball could be cradled (~~easier~~/more easily), and even today, the rugby ball remains largely watermelon-shaped.

For example, drivers behind the wheel of large new SUVs with four-wheel drive and air bags tend to drive (faster/~~more fast~~) and (~~aggressiver~~/more aggressively) on snowy roads than they would if they were driving a tiny old economy car.

Like Hornung, Bart Starr had yet to establish himself fully, and the coach obliged by defining his role (~~tighter~~/more tightly).

Despite the NFL's ongoing efforts to make the kicker's job (harder/~~more hard~~) and thus reduce the number of field goals, there isn't a player whose success—or failure—is reflected (~~more direct~~/more directly) on the scoreboard.

Despite that, if we examine the numbers (~~closer~~/more closely), Gibson's supremacy still makes a certain kind of sense.

The player who used this strategy (~~more successfully~~/most successfully) was Patriots linebacker Mike Vrabel, who lined up at tight end in short-yardage situations and caught ten passes in his career, all for touchdowns.

When a player is feeling (~~well~~/good), rested, and ready for the next play, Wyche explains, he stands up straight in a posture with more than a little Superman-style swagger: hands on hips, fingers across his belly, thumbs pointing back.

"Losses seem to hurt (more/~~most~~) than a win feels (~~well~~/good)," explains Keith Chen, a Yale economist who has worked with Santos.

"It's an amazing thing. It feels so (easy/~~easily~~)," says Jim Breech.

In 1988, the Bengals started the season 6–0 on their way to a 12–4 regular season, the (~~better~~/best) record in football.

He considered that Miami's two (~~better~~/best) players were running backs Ronnie Brown and Ricky Williams.

Piedmont's second A-11 game was somewhat (better/~~best~~) from an execution standpoint, but the score was still lopsided.

It's not that the leather helmet was surprisingly (~~well~~/good) at protecting players from concussion. It's that the modern helmet was surprisingly (bad/~~badly~~).

The helmets currently in use don't seem to protect players particularly (well/~~good~~) from concussions.

Game theory works (well/~~good~~) in explaining actual games and especially ones that are conceptually tidy, if not actually simple.

Most of the way through the 2011 season, the Carolina Panthers were a (bad/~~badly~~) team getting (~~more better~~/better). The Tampa Bay Buccaneers were a (bad/~~badly~~) team getting (worse/~~more worse~~).

Exercise 67C: Using Correct Adverbs and Adjectives

Choose the correct word in parentheses. Cross out the incorrect word.

We ran so (~~good~~/ well)! We were much faster than the other cross-country team.

The opponents did not run (~~slow~~/ slowly), but we are extremely (good / ~~well~~) at middle distances.

The baby doesn't feel (~~good~~/ well) today. She has a cold.

The gangster looks (bad / ~~badly~~). He's not a very nice man!

The gangster looks (~~bad~~/ badly). He's not wearing his glasses and he has to squint.

The young thief is growing (~~good~~/ well). He's getting larger by the day.

The young thief is growing (good / ~~well~~). He is returning what he stole and making amends.

She remains (bad / ~~badly~~); she only thinks about herself and is cruel to others.

She remains (~~bad~~/ badly); she hates to stay in one spot and keeps leaving!

— LESSON 68 —

Coordinating and Subordinating Conjunctions
Correlative Conjunctions

Exercise 68A: Coordinating and Subordinating Correlative Conjunctions

In each of the following sentences, circle the correlative conjunctions. Underline the words or groups of words that the conjunctions connect. In the blank, write *C* for coordinating or *S* for subordinating.

These sentences have been slightly adapted from *A Brief History of Pakistan*, by James Wynbrandt.

Once they seize a plain, no one escapes, (neither) men (nor) cattle. C

Yet the passages that breached the guarding massifs served as funnels through which invaders (both) hostile (and) friendly have poured for millennia. C

Now old and nonthreatening, he was unable to keep (either) his officers (or) the Mongols in check. C

(Though) an independent state only since 1947, (yet) its homeland has a history unique from the rest of the subcontinent it shares with India. S

(Though) the Mughal Empire would survive for another century, (yet) it was increasingly subservient to Britain's agenda. C

Note to Instructor: In the sentence above, *though . . . yet* link two complete sentences, which are equal elements, so the compound conjunction is coordinating. In the previous sentence, they link a phrase with a sentence—since these are unequal, the conjunction is subordinating.

If I were to follow your advice, then how could I show my face? C

Note to Instructor: *If. . . then* links two complete independent sentences. One is a statement and the other a question, but grammatically they are equal.

Gandhi had come, he said, on a personal mission, and not as a representative of either Congress or the Hindus. C

Though rich in minerals, including iron ore and copper, yet Baluchistan has lagged in development of these resources. S

These new leaders not only hardened the league's stance against the British but advocated greater cooperation with Hindus through the Congress Party as well. C

If he agreed, then Pakistan stood to gain substantial benefits. C

Note to Instructor: Although the second independent sentence is longer, the conjunction links two independent sentences, which are grammatically equal.

Although many leading Muslims supported Great Britain during the war, still some backed the Ottoman Empire. C

Both the loss of territory and the war with India shook the soul of Pakistanis. C

Exercise 68B: Subject-Verb Agreement

Cross out the incorrect verb in each set of parentheses.

Either the farmer and the barber or the farmer's wife (is/~~are~~) going to win the bet.
Both the king and his two soldiers (~~was~~/were) agreed that the sound was a jackal, not a tiger.
Not only the old woman's foot but also the cords (~~was~~/were) cut by the prince's sword.
Both the parrots and the starling (~~was~~/were) hanging in cages in the apartments.
Neither scars nor sign (is/~~are~~) visible on the queen's hands.
Not only one ring, but also three precious anklets (~~was~~/were) presented to the princess.
Bracelets of emeralds and a chain of rubies (~~is~~/are) more glorious than anything the prince has ever seen.

Exercise 68C: Diagramming

On your own paper, diagram every word of the following sentences.

Neither the jackal nor the peacock was able to pass the test.

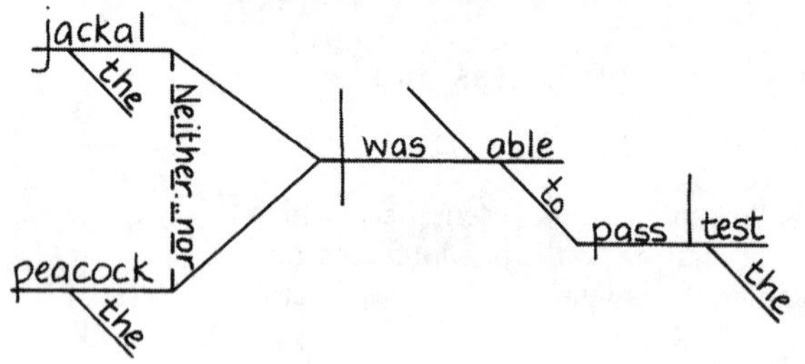

Either air or water will penetrate the cunningly carved great chest.

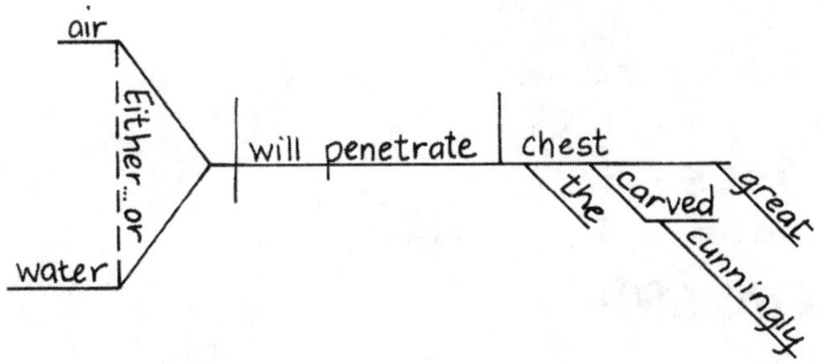

Both the yogi and his pupils were amazed to see the chest floating.

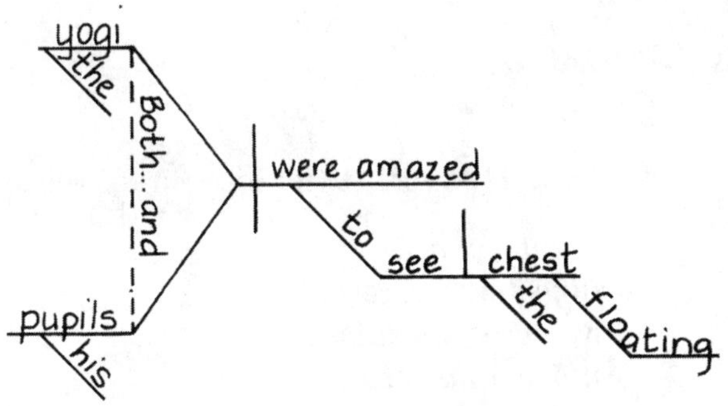

Not only beauty but also wisdom were hers.

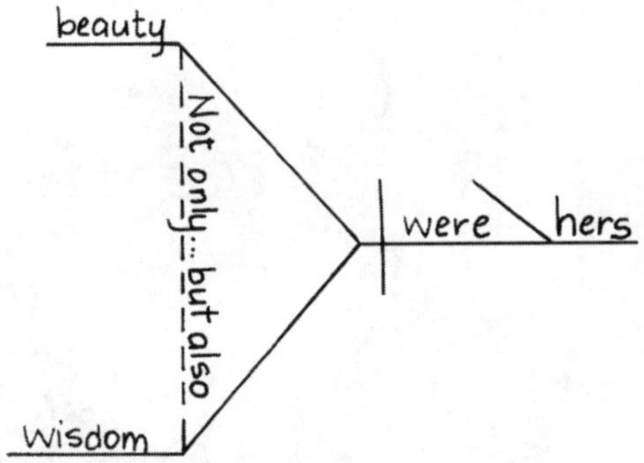

The fine horse had both a skin like snow and a neigh like thunder.

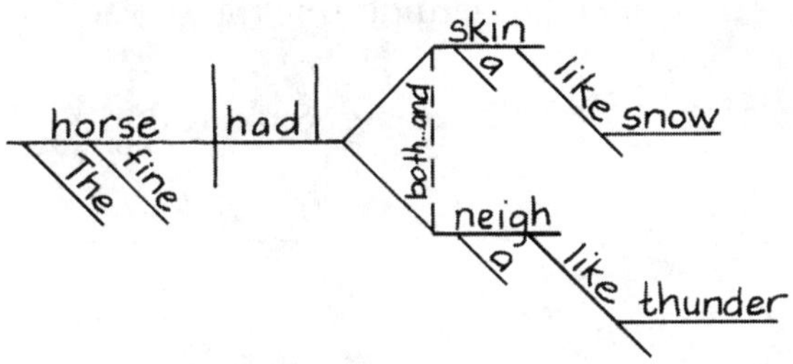

WEEK 18

Clauses

— LESSON 69 —

Phrases
Sentences
Introduction to Clauses

In the phrases and clauses below, the subjects are underlined once and the verbs twice for your reference.

Behind the dusty wardrobe.	***phrase***	*no subject or verb*
Lucy opened the door.	***clause***	*subject and verb*
Leaping and bounding.	***phrase***	*two verbs, no subject*
They did not believe her.	***clause***	*subject and verb*
He tasted the delicious candy.	***clause***	*subject and verb*
Because he wanted more.	***clause***	*subject and verb*

Although Jamie didn't mean to eat the entire cake.	D
Whether they won or lost.	D
He picked up the pieces.	I
That milk is from Uncle Louie's cow.	I
Since she was already covered in mud.	D

Exercise 69A: Distinguishing Between Phrases and Clauses

Identify the following groups of words as phrases or clauses. The clauses may be independent or dependent, but you only need to identify them as clauses. In each clause, underline the subject once and the verb twice.

These phrases and clauses are taken from *Kingdoms of the Yoruba*, by Robert Sydney Smith.

Whose sources are largely unwritten.	clause
However rich in primary and secondary material.	phrase
The past of the Yoruba of West Africa.	phrase
Who form the population of the Western State of Nigeria.	clause
All having specific and complex traditions.	phrase
Although these traditions are often of a legendary and miraculous kind.	clause
They may be sifted, correlated, and cross-checked.	clause

From ceremonies recalling and re-enacting the past. phrase

All these preserve fragments. clause

It is a platitude. clause

Working from tradition. phrase

Reconstructing the Yoruba past. phrase

Nigeria exemplifies this contrast. clause

Exercise 69B: Distinguishing Between Independent and Dependent Clauses

Identify the following clauses as independent (*IND*) or dependent (*DEP*). These clauses are drawn from *Yoruba Legends,* by M. I. Ogumefu.

When he returned home DEP

Who returned to his father after some time DEP

In due course they returned IND

Wherever he went DEP

The weapon glanced off his hide IND

A great king sent his various sons IND

Two women quarrelled IND

The King employed the charm IND

As he sat gloomily on the ground DEP

The whole earth was covered with water IND

Exercise 69C: Turning Dependent Clauses into Complete Sentences

Choose three of the dependent clauses in Exercise 69B and attach independent clauses to them to form complete thoughts. Write your three new sentences on your own paper. (The dependent clause can go before or after the independent clause.)

Note to Instructor: The original sentences from *Yoruba Legends* are found below. Accept any reasonable answers!

But his youngest grandson, Oranyan, was at that time away hunting, and *when he returned home* he learnt that his brothers and cousins had inherited the old King's money.

All of the sons were satisfied but one, the youngest and most ambitious, *who returned to his father after some time* with the complaint that his territory was much too small and his subjects too few.

Wherever he went, he sang his triumphant wrestling-song, and everyone feared and respected him.

As he sat gloomily on the ground, the king saw a little mouse running across the hut.

— LESSON 70 —

Adjective Clauses
Relative Pronouns

Intro 70: Introduction to Adjective Clauses

The following sentences describe famous ghost sightings! Complete each sentence by filling in the blank with the appropriate letter from the clauses below.

You can learn more about these haunts in *Famous Ghost Stories: Legends and Lore*, by Brian Haughton.

The village of Brill, in Buckinghamshire, boasted five different headless horsemen __C__.

She fell in love with a handsome stableboy __E__.

He is the ghost of a knight, killed in battle with the Scots, __A__.

The deathly paleness of the faces was an omen __D__.

The phantom London bus, __B__, tears down the middle of the road towards startled drivers and then disappears.

A. whose horse brought his headless body home
B. which appears between the Cambridge Gardens and Chesterton Road junctions on St. Mark's Road
C. who roamed the four roads and one field track leading into the village
D. that Lincoln would not live through his last term
E. whom she then threw over for a more eligible suitor

Exercise 70A: Identifying Adjective Clauses and Relative Pronouns

Underline the adjective clauses in the following sentences, and circle the relative pronouns. Draw an arrow from each relative pronoun to its antecedent.

These sentences are taken from *Ghosts: True Tales of Eerie Encounters*, by Robert C. Belyk.

The ghosts that haunt the Cherry Bank hotel are rarely seen.

One incident frightened a guest who had come with a group of friends.

As her eyes adjusted to the light, she was aware of a bearded man, whom she later described as wearing old-fashioned clothing, floating above her.

There was nothing on the tape but a noise that sounded like someone walking heavily across the floor.

The three chandeliers that lit the banquet room had been turned off and the room was in darkness.

Local children would turn the stones over to reveal the names of the children whose graves they had marked.

He was a bully whose manners were uncouth.

The best spot was near a stream which eventually tumbled over the cliff to the beach below.

When he returned, however, the person who had been sitting on the hearth was gone.

Exercise 70B: Choosing the Correct Relative Pronoun

In each sentence, cross out the incorrect relative pronoun. Above the correct pronoun, write *S* for subject, *OP* for object of the preposition, or *DO* for direct object to show how the relative pronoun is used within the dependent clause.

These sentences are adapted from *Ghost Stories of an Antiquary*, by the classic horror writer M. R. James.

DO
"Good heavens!" said the little man, (~~who~~/ whom) the suggestion threw into a state of unaccountable terror.

OP
He had some talk upon the matter with the Vicar of his parish, with (~~who~~/ whom) he travelled home.

OP
The Templars, to (~~who~~/ whom) this site had belonged, were in the habit of building round churches.

S S
The little boy (who / ~~whom~~) was the only passenger in the chaise, and (who / ~~whom~~) jumped out as soon as it had stopped, looked about him with the keenest curiosity.

S
The picture lay face upwards on the table where the last man (who / ~~whom~~) looked at it had put it.

OP
He made tea for the friend with (~~who~~/ whom) he had been playing golf.

S
He was a man (who / ~~whom~~) liked to be on pleasant terms with those about him.

S
Lady Fell was with her mother, (who / ~~whom~~) was dangerously ill.

DO
Mrs. Bunch was the most comfortable and human person (~~who~~/ whom) Stephen had as yet met.

Exercise 70C: Diagramming Adjective Clauses

On your own paper, diagram every word of the following sentences, adapted from M. R. James's *A Thin Ghost and Others.*

Saul, whose face expressed great anger, hastily picked the object up.

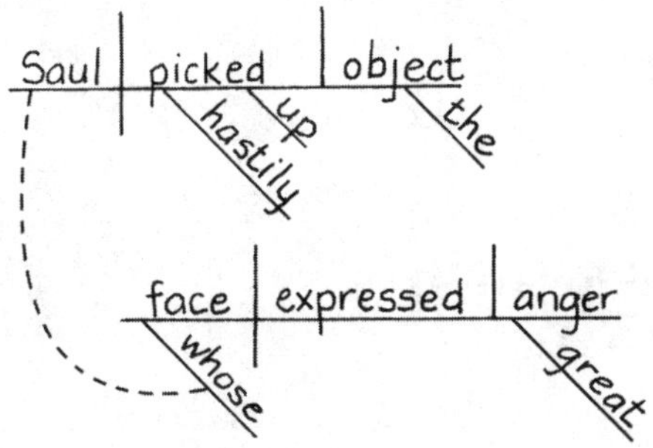

The ground rose to a field that was park-like in character.

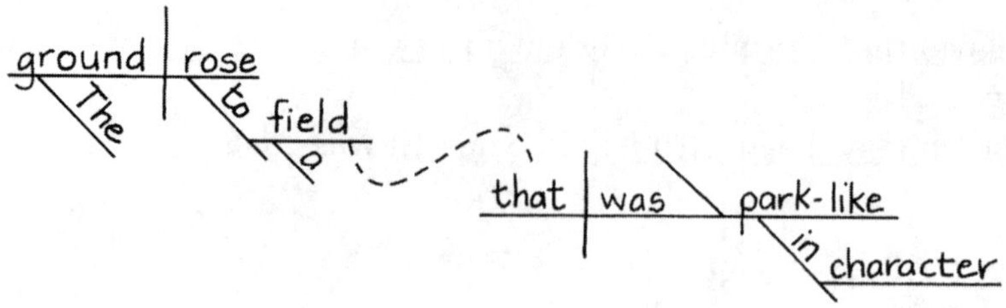

He held several long conversations with old women whom we met.

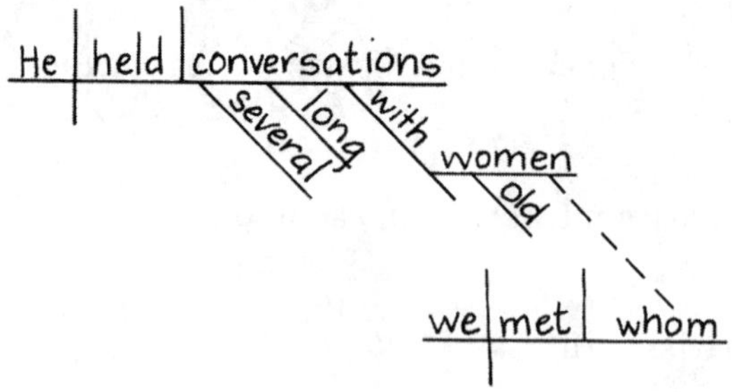

Dr. Quinn was a plain, honest creature, and a man to whom I would have gone.

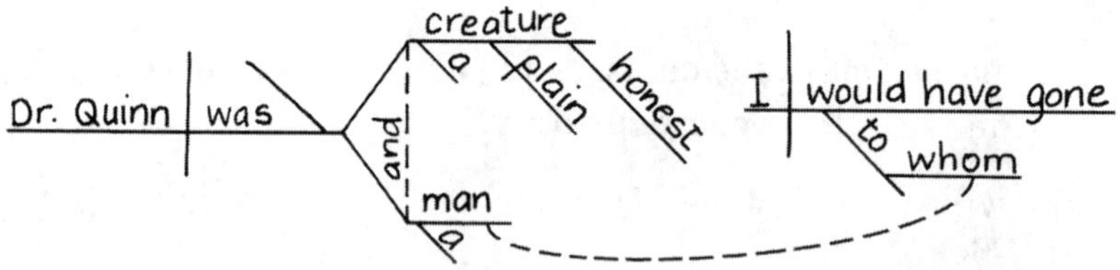

His wife, who accompanied him, was to make a series of illustrative drawings for his report.

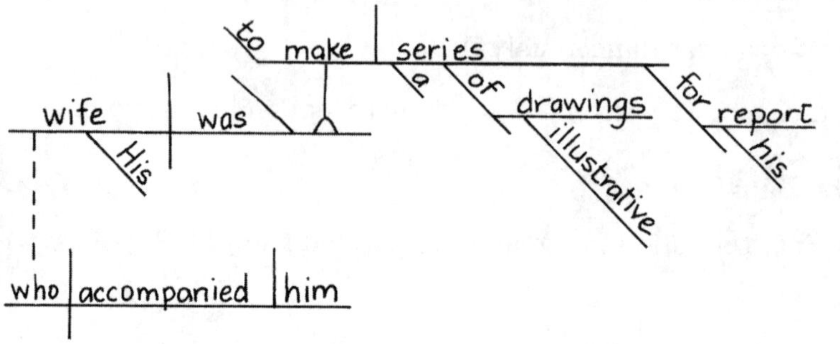

— LESSON 71 —

Adjective Clauses
Relative Adverbs
Adjective Clauses with Understood Relatives

Exercise 71A: Relative Adverbs and Pronouns

In the following sentences, underline each adjective clause. Circle each relative word and label it as *RP* for relative pronoun or *RA* for relative adverb. Draw an arrow from each relative word back to its antecedent in the independent clause.

These sentences are taken from *Bartleby, The Scrivener*, a novel by Herman Melville, who also wrote *Moby Dick*. Some have been slightly adapted or condensed.

He was afflicted by a continual discontent with the height of the table (where)RA he worked.

On a cold morning (when)RA business was dull, Turkey would gobble up scores of these cakes.

What is the reason (why)RA I should do no more writing?

He is a wanderer (who)RP refuses to budge.

He received visits from certain ambiguous-looking fellows in seedy coats, (whom)RP he called his clients.

He was a man (whom)RP prosperity harmed.

What was the time (when)RA he departed?

I procured a high green folding screen, (which)RP might entirely isolate Bartleby from my sight.

There are two scriveners in the office, (where)RA they assist each other.

It was 6 PM, after (which)RP I saw no more of the proprietor.

"Then sir," said the stranger, (who)RP proved a lawyer, "you are responsible for the man you left there."

As yet, nothing (that)RP I know of has ever been written.

Simply record the fact, (that)RP I was not unemployed in my profession.

It was the time (when)RA he must unconditionally leave the office.

Exercise 71B: Missing Relative Words

Draw a caret in front of each adjective clause and insert the missing relative pronoun. (For the purposes of this exercise, *which* and *that* may be used interchangeably.) These sentences are also loosely adapted from *Bartleby, The Scrivener*.

Note to Instructor: Accept any of the options listed.

The cake ^that / which he most enjoyed was small, flat, round, and very spicy.

He carefully considered each statement ^(that / which) I made.

The folio ^(that / which) he copied for me cost four cents.

You are responsible for the man ^(whom / that) you left there.

One report ^(that / which) I heard about will appear tomorrow.

It is a name ^(that / which) he loves to repeat.

He scorned all further words ^(that / which) I spoke.

Exercise 71C: Diagramming

On your own paper, diagram the following sentences from your first two exercises.

It was 6 PM, after which I saw no more of the proprietor.

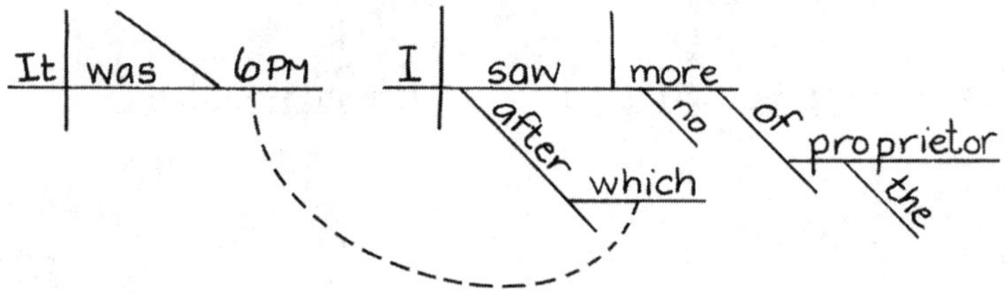

He was afflicted by a continual discontent with the height of the table where he worked.

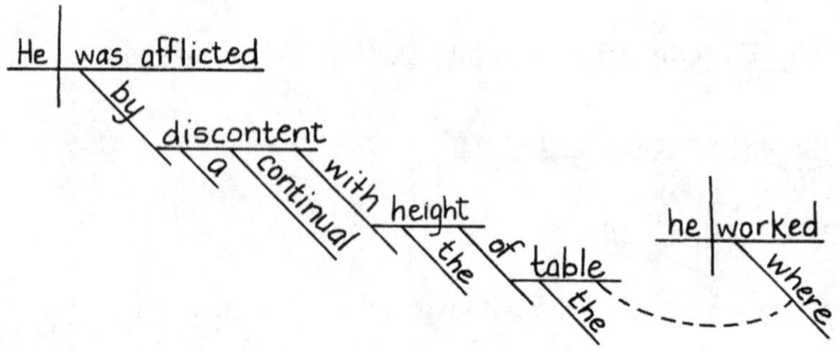

He received visits from certain ambiguous-looking fellows in seedy coats, whom he called his clients.

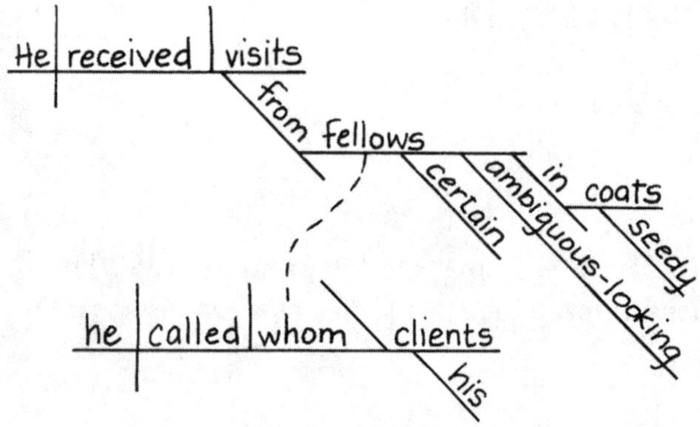

On a cold morning when business was dull, Turkey would gobble up scores of these cakes.

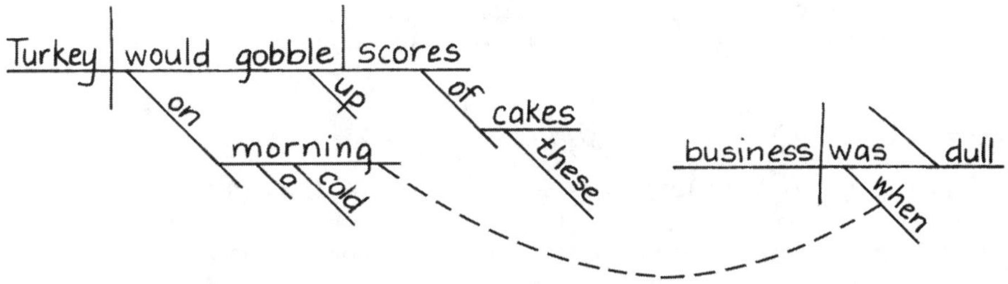

The cake he most enjoyed was small, flat, round, and very spicy.

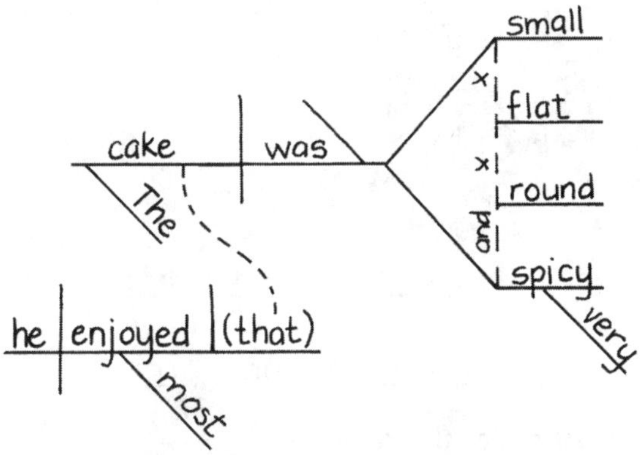

— LESSON 72 —

Adverb Clauses

Exercise 72A: Adverb Clauses

In the following sentences, underline each adverb clause. Circle the subordinating word(s) at the beginning of each clause and label it *ADV* for adverb or *SC* for subordinating conjunction. Draw an arrow from the subordinating word(s) back to the verb, adverb, or adjective that the clause modifies.

These sentences are slightly condensed from the Chinese classic *The Art of War*, by Sun Tzu, as translated by Lionel Giles.

SC
If I fail, I shall make myself a laughing-stock.

ADV
We can form a single united body, while the enemy must split up into fractions.

After that, you may crush him.

Note to Instructor: this is a trick sentence. *After that* is a prepositional phrase, not a clause (there is only one subject/predicate combination in the sentence, the main clause's *you may crush*.)

SC
We are not fit to lead an army on the march unless we are familiar with the face of the country.

Note to Instructor: You may also accept an arrow leading to *are*; the clause could be interpreted as modifying either the state of being, or the predicate adjective. We have connected it to the adjective because the fitness is directly associated with the condition laid out in the adverb clause.

SC

Although he had no practical experience of war, he was extremely fond of discussing the subject.

Note to Instructor: In this case, the clause should modify the verb, as it has to do with the subject's state of being, not the fondness.

ADV

He speaks as a man of Wu, a state which ceased to exist as early as 473 B.C.

Note to Instructor: This compound adverb based on *as* expresses *when*. Compounds of *as* can also work as subordinating conjunctions, but in this case, the expression of time makes this compound an adverb.

SC

I fully believe he was a good soldier, but I had him beheaded because he acted without orders.

ADV

The spirit of the enemy's soldiers will be keenest when they have newly arrived on the scene.

Note to Instructor: You may also accept an arrow leading to *will be*; the clause could be interpreted as modifying either the state of being, or the predicate adjective. We have connected it to the adjective because the keenness of the soldiers is directly associated with the time laid out in the adverb clause.

ADV

I attacked when their spirit was gone and ours was at its height.

Note to Instructor: The adverb *when* introduces the entire subordinate adverb clause, which is itself a compound sentence with two subjects (*spirit* and *ours*) and two predicates (*was gone* and *was*).

Throw your soldiers into positions whence there is no escape, and they will prefer death to flight.

Note to Instructor: This is a trick sentence; the clause *whence there is no escape* is an adjective phrase modifying the noun *positions*, introduced by the relative adverb *whence*.

ADV ADV

Attack him where he is unprepared, and appear where you are not expected.

SC SC

Though only eight days have passed since I threw off my allegiance, an army is already at the city-gates.

Note to Instructor: Technically, *since I threw off my allegiance* is a subordinate adverb clause within the larger adverb clause *Though only eight days have passed since I threw off my allegiance*, but encourage the student to identify both adverb clauses. She may also choose to underline the entire clause, and then double underline *since I threw off my allegiance*.

Exercise 72B: Descriptive Clauses

In the following sentences, underline each dependent clause. Above each, write *ADVC* for adverb clause or *ADJC* for adjective clause. Circle each subordinating word(s) and label it as *ADV* for adverb, *RP* for relative pronoun, or *SC* for subordinating conjunction. Draw an arrow from the subordinating word back (or forward) to the word in the independent clause that the dependent clause modifies.

These sentences are adapted from *Nonviolence: The History of a Dangerous Idea*, by Mark Kurlansky.

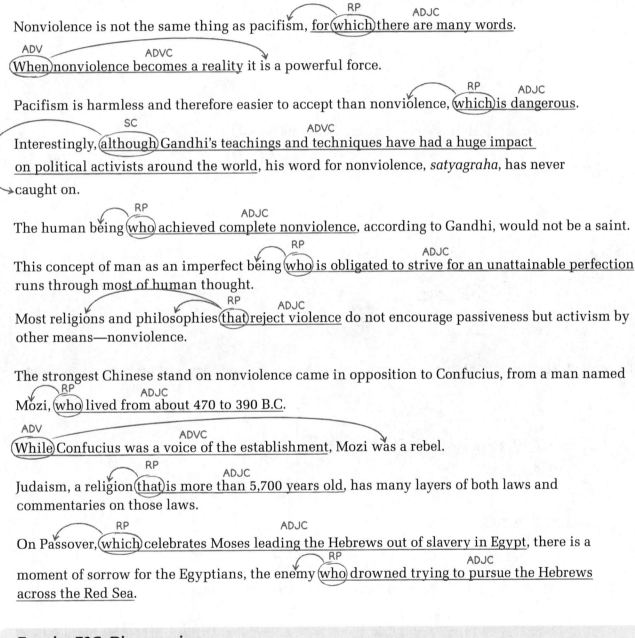

RP ADJC
Nonviolence is not the same thing as pacifism, for which there are many words.

ADV ADVC
When nonviolence becomes a reality it is a powerful force.

RP ADJC
Pacifism is harmless and therefore easier to accept than nonviolence, which is dangerous.

SC ADVC
Interestingly, although Gandhi's teachings and techniques have had a huge impact on political activists around the world, his word for nonviolence, *satyagraha*, has never caught on.

RP ADJC
The human being who achieved complete nonviolence, according to Gandhi, would not be a saint.

RP ADJC
This concept of man as an imperfect being who is obligated to strive for an unattainable perfection runs through most of human thought.

RP ADJC
Most religions and philosophies that reject violence do not encourage passiveness but activism by other means—nonviolence.

The strongest Chinese stand on nonviolence came in opposition to Confucius, from a man named RP ADJC
Mozi, who lived from about 470 to 390 B.C.

ADV ADVC
While Confucius was a voice of the establishment, Mozi was a rebel.

RP ADJC
Judaism, a religion that is more than 5,700 years old, has many layers of both laws and commentaries on those laws.

RP ADJC
On Passover, which celebrates Moses leading the Hebrews out of slavery in Egypt, there is a RP ADJC
moment of sorrow for the Egyptians, the enemy who drowned trying to pursue the Hebrews across the Red Sea.

Exercise 72C: Diagramming

On your own paper, diagram every word of the following sentences from the first two exercises.

Although he had no practical experience of war, he was extremely fond of discussing the subject.

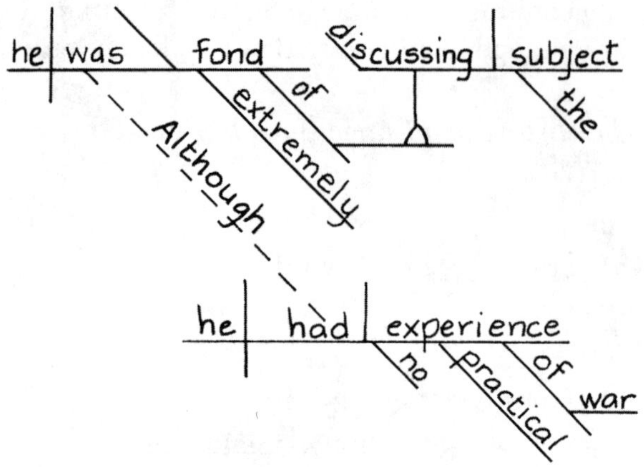

I attacked when their spirit was gone and ours was at its height.

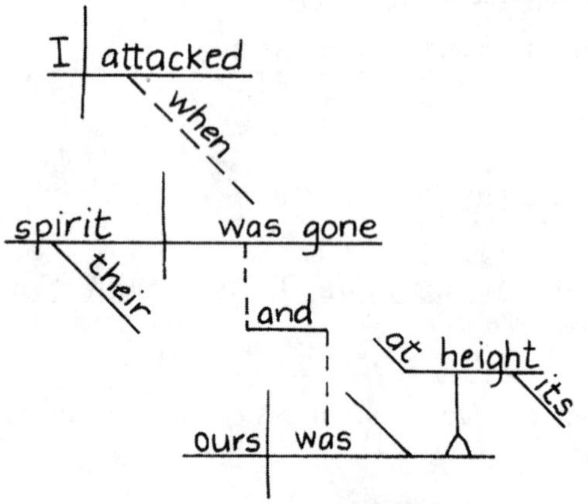

Throw your soldiers into positions whence there is no escape, and they will prefer death to flight.

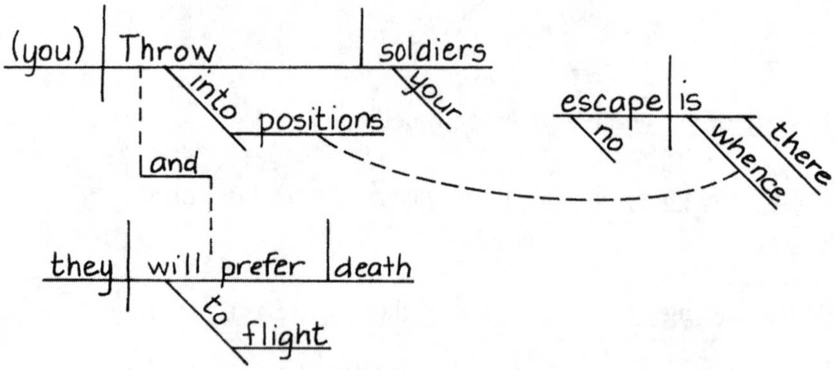

Nonviolence is not the same thing as pacifism, for which there are many words.

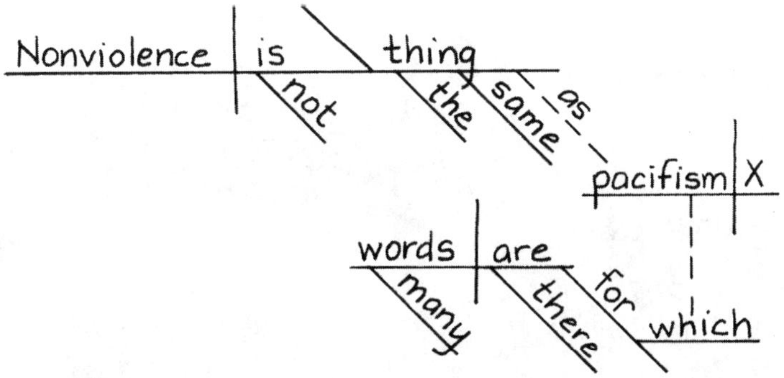

When nonviolence becomes a reality it is a powerful force.

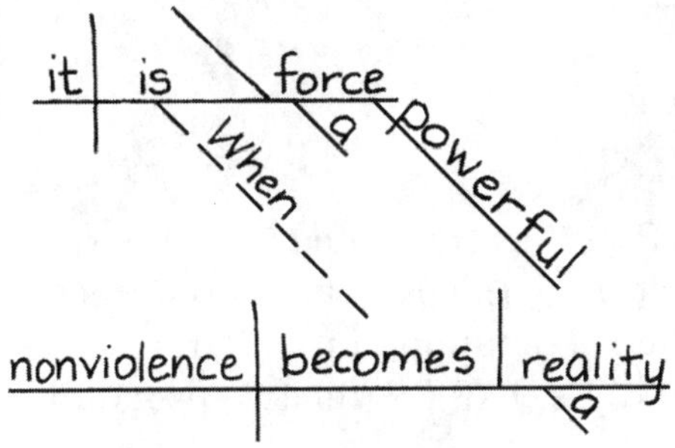

— REVIEW 6 —

Weeks 16-18

Topics

Personal Pronouns: Subject, Object, Possessive, Reflexive
Verb Voice (Active and Passive)
Verb Tense
Adjectives
Gerunds and Participles
Phrases
Clauses (Independent and Dependent)

Review 6A: Pronouns

In the following sentences, taken from Leo Tolstoy's *War and Peace* (as translated by Louise and Aylmer Maude), circle each pronoun. Label each as *S* (subject form of the personal pronoun), *O* (object form of the personal pronoun), *P* (possessive form of the personal pronoun), *R* (reflexive), *INT* (intensive), *I* (indefinite), *INTER* (interrogative), *D* (demonstrative), or *RP* (relative pronoun).

He [S] went up to Anna Pávlovna, kissed her [P] hand, presenting to her [O] his [P] bald, scented, and shining head, and complacently seated himself [R] on the sofa.

Another time, general attention was attracted by a small brown dog, coming heaven knows whence, which [RP] trotted in a preoccupied manner in front of the ranks with tail stiffly erect till suddenly a shell fell close by, when it [S] yelped, tucked its [P] tail between its [P] legs, and darted aside.

Nicholas expressed his [P] disapproval of the postponement of the marriage for a year; but Natásha attacked her [P] brother with exasperation, proving to him [O] that it [S] could not be otherwise, and that it [S] would be a bad thing to enter a family against the father's will, and that she [S] herself [INT] wished it [O] so.

Most of the time, by their [P] officers' order, the men sat on the ground. One [I], having taken off his [P] shako, carefully loosened the gathers of its [P] lining and drew them [O] tight again; another [I], rubbing some dry clay between his [P] palms, polished his [P] bayonet; another [I] fingered the strap and pulled the buckle of his [P] bandolier, while another [I] smoothed and refolded his [P] leg bands and put his [P] boots on again. Some [I] built little houses of the tufts in the plowed ground, or plaited baskets from the straw in the cornfield. All [I] seemed fully absorbed in these pursuits.

It[S] was evident that Kutúzov despised cleverness and learning and even the patriotic feeling shown by Denísov, but despised them[O] not because of his[P] own intellect, feelings, or knowledge—he[S] did not try to display any of these[D]—but because of something[I] else.

"Do you[S] know," he[S] said at last, evidently unable to check the sad current of his[P] thoughts, "that Anatole is costing me[O] forty thousand rubles a year? And," he[S] went on after a pause, "what[INTER] will it[S] be in five years, if he[S] goes on like this[D]?" Presently he[S] added: "That[D]'s what[RP] we[S] fathers have to put up with. . . . Is this princess of yours[P] rich?"

Note to Instructor: In the sentence *That's what we fathers have to put up with, That* is a demonstrative pronoun serving as the subject of the main clause (*That* is the subject, *'s* is the condensed form of the predicate *is*), and *what* is the relative pronoun serving as the subject of the dependent clause *what we fathers have to put up with* and referring back to the demonstrative pronoun *that*. (The clause is serving as a predicate nominative; if the student has not gone through this course before, she may not know that clauses can serve as nouns, since this is covered in Week 19. However, she should still be able to identify the pronouns.)

Review 6B: Using Comparative and Superlative Adjectives Correctly

Choose the correct form in parentheses. Cross out the incorrect form.

These sentences are taken from H. G. Wells's *A Short History of the World.*

In Sumeria the priest ruler was the (~~most great~~/greatest), (most splendid/~~splendidest~~) of beings.

People travelled about (more freely/~~most freely~~) than they had ever done before, and there were high roads and inns for them.

Travel is increasing and transport growing (~~more easy~~/easier) by reason of horses and roads.

Hiram established the very (~~most close~~/closest) relations both with David and with his son and successor Solomon.

Asoka made vast benefactions to the Buddhist teaching orders, and tried to stimulate them to a (~~more good~~/better) and (more energetic/~~energeticer~~) criticism of their own accumulated literature.

Sardanapalus's library has been unearthed and is perhaps the (~~more precious~~/most precious) store of historical material in the world.

The (~~bitterer~~/bitterest) rival of Athens in Greece was Sparta.

The power of the Roman republic came out of the west to subjugate one fragment after another and weld them together into a new and (more enduring/~~enduringer~~) empire.

The Trinitarian formula may be found in its (most complete/~~completest~~) expression in the Athanasian Creed.

Note to Instructor: This is a trick sentence—both forms are acceptable!

The steamboat was, if anything, a little ahead of the steam engine in its (~~more early~~/earlier) phases.

Review 6C: Verbs

Underline the main verb (along with any helping verbs) in every clause below (both independent and dependent).

In the space above each verb, write the tense (*SIMP PAST, PRES, FUT; PROG PAST, PRES, FUT; PERF PAST, PRES, FUT*) and voice (*ACT* for active or *PASS* for passive). For state-of-being verbs, write *SB* instead of voice.

If the verb is an action verb, also note whether it is transitive (*TR*) or intransitive (*INTR*).

The first is done for you.

These sentences are taken from the official government report on the Perry Expedition. In 1853–1854, Commodore Matthew Perry of the U.S. Navy was ordered, by President Millard Fillmore, to take warships to Japan. At that time, Japan's ports were closed—the country refused to trade with the United States. Perry's Expedition was ordered to open the ports and put trade into place—either through negotiation, or through force.

In 1854, Japan agreed to the terms the U.S. was offering, and trade with America began.

SIR: So soon as the steam frigate Mississippi shall be (SIMP FUT SB) in all respects ready for sea, you will proceed (SIMP FUT ACT INTR) in her, accompanied by the steamer *Princeton*, to Macao, or Hong Kong, in China, where the vessels of your command will rendezvous (SIMP FUT ACT INTR). . . . It has been deemed (PERF PRES PASS TR) necessary to increase the naval force of the United States in the East India and China seas, for reasons which will be found (SIMP FUT PASS TR) in the enclosed copy of a communication from the Secretary of State addressed to this department under date of November, 1852.

The special mission to Japan with which you have been charged (PERF PRES PASS TR) by the government will require (SIMP FUT ACT TR) all your firmness and prudence, in respect to which the department entertains (SIMP PRES ACT TR) the fullest confidence that they will be (SIMP FUT SB) adequate for any emergency.

Your attention is particularly invited (SIMP PRES PASS TR) to the exploration of the coasts of Japan and of the adjacent continent and islands.

The said officer shall detain (SIMP FUT ACT TR) him until the vessel in which he shall be serving (PROG FUT ACT INTR) shall return (SIMP FUT ACT INTR) to the United States.

Taking into view, also, the present disturbed state of China, and the need of one or more ships of the squadron in that quarter, and considering that not a single vessel which had been promised (PROG PAST ACT INTR) by the department had yet joined (SIMP PAST ACT TR) my force . . . I was (SIMP PAST SB) glad to have a good excuse for consenting to wait until the ensuing spring. . . . In the spring I shall have concentrated (PERF FUT ACT TR) my whole force, and will be (SIMP FUT SB) prepared with store and coal vessels, and all other conveniences for remaining, if it be necessary, an indefinite time, to secure such concessions as I believe (SIMP PRES ACT INTR) they will be constrained (SIMP FUT PASS TR) to make.

Review 6D: Identifying Dependent Clauses

Underline each dependent clause in the following sentences. Circle the subordinating word. Label each clause as either adjective (*ADJ*) or adverb clause (*ADV*), and draw a line from each subordinating word to the word it modifies.

These sentences are taken from *Breaking Open Japan: Commodore Perry, Lord Abe, and American Imperialism in 1853*, by George Feifer.

ADV ADJ

When the bluff fizzled, the tiny number who made Japan's political decisions could think of nothing else with which to counter the foreigners' threat.

ADJ

The harassed yet privileged Dutch traders who delivered the disturbing reports lived in a

ADJ

compound called Deshima, which can be translated as "island in front of the town."

ADJ

The Dutch East India Company, which traded in spices, tea, silk, and other much-wanted commodities, was the largest of its kind and—in keeping with Holland's commercial lead over Britain at the time—more successful than the British East India Company, founded two years earlier, in 1600.

ADJ ADV

The Dutch Factory, as its Japanese post was known, was moved to Deshima in 1641, after the other Western colonies had left the country, voluntarily or otherwise.

Note to Instructor: The adjective clause above is unusual—it begins with *as*, which is a subordinating conjunction rather than a relative pronoun, but describes a noun. Since it describes a place, it is a variation on the adjective clause introduced by a relative adverb (as seen in the next sentence).

ADJ

Smaller beacon fires were already burning all along the coast, where soldiers with pikes and "rusty flintlocks" stood guard, some additionally armed with war fans bearing the emblem of the rising sun.

ADV ADJ

While officers frantically drilled green troops, seacoast inhabitants, some of whose houses had already been razed for frenzied construction of new fortifications, were pressed into service.

ADV

With the panic and chaos swelling in the heat, the "whole city" succumbed to "uproar."

ADJ

Nothing had yet been reported to the Emperor in his Kyoto palace, where life continued unchanged in its detachment from political matters.

The court's big event during the week of panic was the first celebration of Boys' Day by the baby Prince who would become the Emperor Meiji.

ADJ

Review 6E: Present and Past Participles

Underline each present participle and past participle in the following sentences. Some are serving as nouns; others as adjectives. Label adjective forms as *ADJ* and draw a line to the word modified. Label noun forms as *N* and write the part of the sentence that the noun is serving as.

These sentences are taken from *On the Origins of Sports: The Early History and Original Rules of Everybody's Favorite Games*, by Gary Belsky and Neil Fine.

N subject ... N

Knowing the history and lore of our favorite sports can only enhance our experience of watching or competing in them.

N both are objects of the preposition

We are tribal by nature—genetically programmed to define "us" by "them"—and few things make that task easier than team jerseys. (ADJ)

Wiffle Ball was designed for use in congested areas. Because the ball will not travel far, ball chasing and base running have been eliminated. (ADJ; N subject; N subject)

The minimum number of players required to play Wiffle Ball are two—the pitcher and batter—one player to a side. (ADJ)

A cricket match is composed of two innings, with each team running through its eleven-man lineup twice. (ADJ)

N subject

Choosing the pitch offered an advantage.

Strikers, or batsmen, are "out" if a bowled ball knocks the bail off the stumps, or a fielder catches a batted ball in the air. (ADJ; ADJ)

Rules of Ancient Greek Wrestling: (N object of the preposition)

No intentional hitting or kicking is permitted. (N subject; N subject)

No gouging the eyes or biting is permitted. (N subject; N subject)

Infractions shall be punished by immediate whipping by the referee until the undesirable behaviour is stopped. (N object of the preposition)

Review 6F: Diagramming

On your own paper, diagram every word of the following sentences from *Moon Shot: The Inside Story of America's Apollo Moon Landings*, by Jay Barbree, Alan Shepard, and Deke Slayton.

It was a beautiful airfield, where pilots could come burning out of the sky and always have a place to land, where landing-speed restrictions were nonexistent.

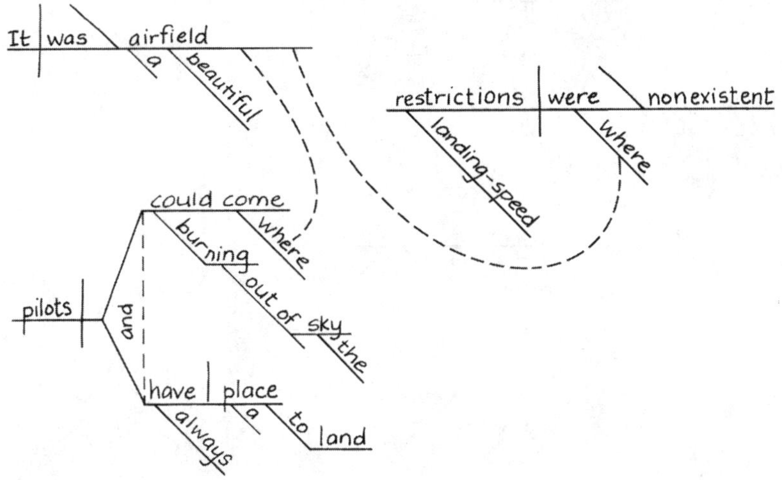

Note to Instructor: I have diagrammed *out of* as a single compound preposition, but the student can also diagram *out* as an adverb modifying *burning* and *of the sky* as the prepositional phrase.

Although the United States recruited the cream of the German rocket scientists, the Soviets captured many of those left behind and began their own missile program.

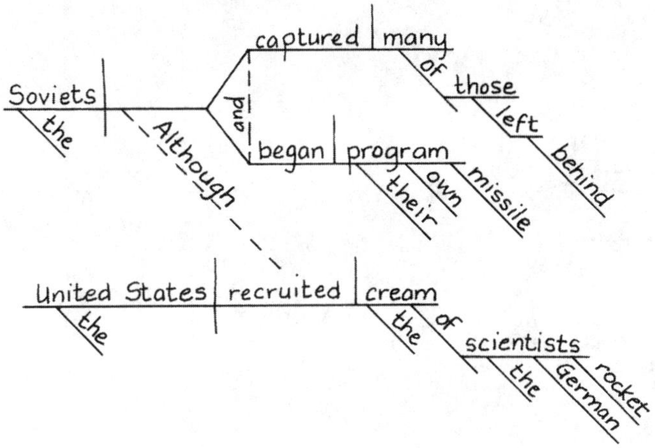

Note to Instructor: There are several legitimate ways to diagram *left behind*. I have diagrammed it as the past participle of *leave*, acting as an adjective modifying *those* and modified in turn by the adverb *behind*. It could also be treated as a single adjective modifying *those*:

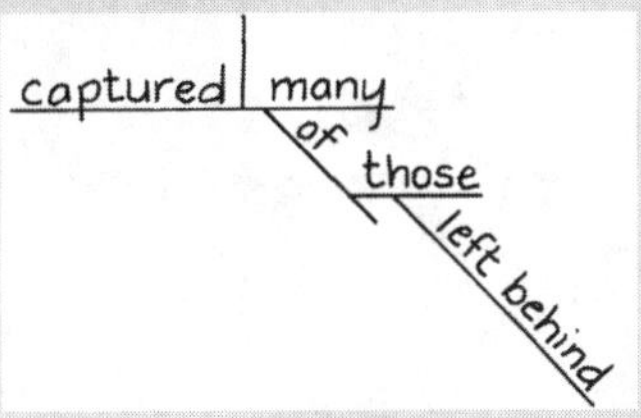

or as an adjective clause with missing elements: *those [who were] left behind*:

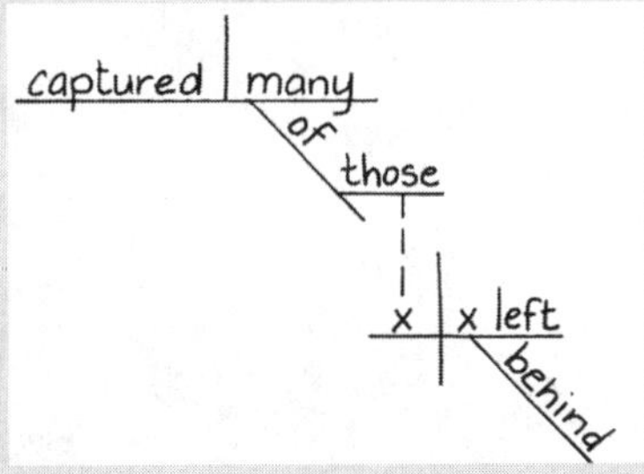

The Saturn V roared, bellowed, and shrieked, hurling out ear-stabbing sonic waves and a crackling thunder which sent birds flying and wildlife fleeing, and which slammed into people who were far away, fluttering their clothing and causing them to step back uncertainly.

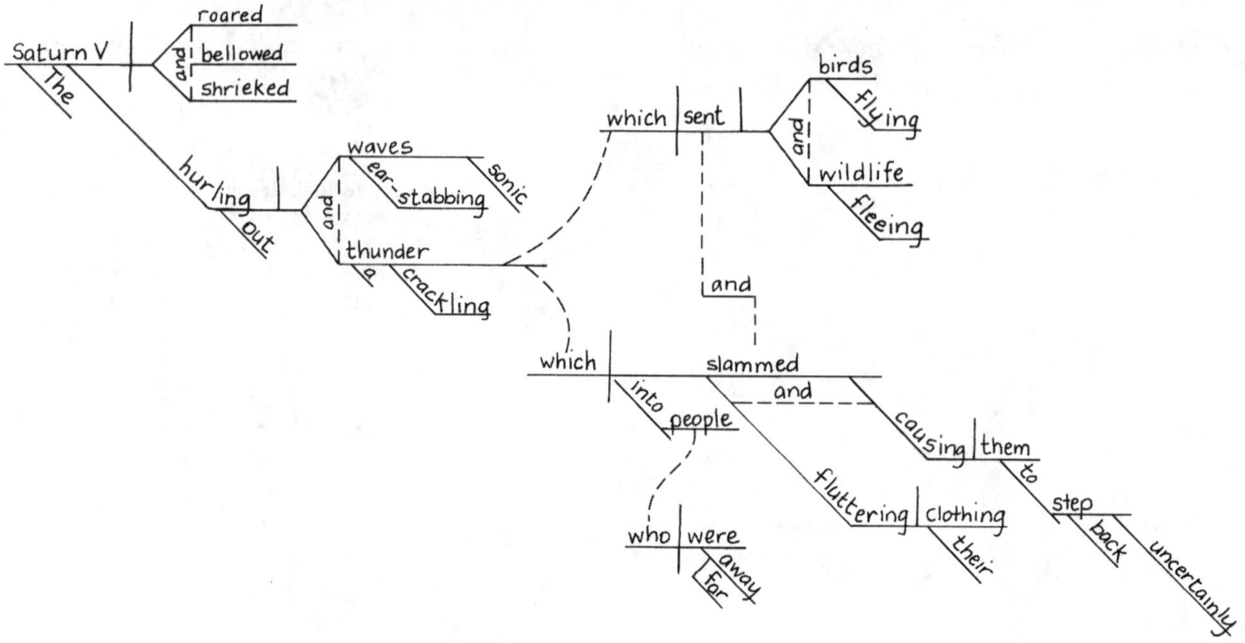

WEEK 19

More Clauses

— LESSON 73 —

Adjective and Adverb Clauses
Introduction to Noun Clauses

Exercise 73A: Identifying Clauses

In the following sentences, circle each dependent clause. Label each as *N* for noun, *ADJ* for adjective, or *ADV* for adverb. Also indicate the part of speech that each noun clause plays: subject (*S*), direct object (*DO*), predicate nominative (*PN*), or object of the preposition (*OP*). Draw a line from the subordinating word of each adjective and adverb clause to the word it modifies.

Some of these clauses may have another clause within them! Do your best to find both, and ask your instructor for help if needed.

These sentences are taken from *The Return of Tarzan* by Edgar Rice Burroughs—the 1913 sequel to Burroughs's 1912 best-seller *Tarzan of the Apes*.

ADV

Nikolas has been a bad man since I can remember.

N DO

But first I will remind you that you maligned me before the girl.

N DO N DO

Tarzan could not but wonder what manner of conspiracy was on foot, or what the scheme of the two men might be.

ADJ

It was difficult to imagine a world without a friend—without a living thing who spoke the new

ADJ

tongues which Tarzan had learned to love so well.

N PN

ADV

And so it was that before they left the amphitheater to return to their wanderings they had once more chosen him as their leader.

ADJ

They were standing on deck at a point which was temporarily deserted, and as Tarzan

ADV

came upon them they were in heated argument with a woman.

ADV

And then, as the men stood looking first at Tarzan and then at their superior the ape-man

ADJ

did the one thing which was needed to erase the last remnant of animosity which they

ADJ

might have felt for him.

N OP

From where I sat in that chair yonder I saw the reflection of it all in the mirror before me.

ADV

ADV

It was decided that although three of them would have to ride after practically no sleep, it would be best to make an early start in the morning, and attempt to ride all the way to Bou Saada in one day.

> **Note to Instructor:** The entire clause beginning with *that* can't be a direct object because the verb is passive, so it modifies *was decided*. The subject and predicate of the entire clause are *it* and *would be*. The clause *although...no sleep* modifies the predicate of the larger adverb clause.

N S

ADV

That she would have spurned Clayton once he had been stripped of both his title and his estates never for once occurred to Tarzan, for he credited to others the same honest loyalty

ADJ

that was so inherent a quality in himself.

> **Note to Instructor:** The entire noun clause *That she...his estates* serves as the subject, with *occurred* as the predicate; within the noun clause, the adverb clause *once he...his estates* modifies the predicate *would have spurned* within the noun clause. The clause *for he credited...in himself* is an independent clause linked to the first independent clause by the coordinating conjunction *for*.

Exercise 73B: Creating Noun Clauses

On your own paper, create five sentences by adding a noun clause into each of the blanks below.

If you have trouble coming up with a dependent clause, try starting out with one of the following subordinating words: *that, how, why, what/whatever, who/whoever* (these are always subjects within the dependent clause), *whom/whomever* (these are always objects within the dependent clause), *where, whether.* (This is not an exhaustive list of the possibilities—just a jumping-off place for you.)

I really wonder ______________________________.

______________________________ was unusually hard to decide.

Explain to your brother ______________________________.

______________________________ is not welcome in this house.

The most extraordinary development was ______________________________.

Note to Instructor: Answers will vary; the sentences below are examples of possible clauses. If the student has trouble with this exercise, show her the sentences below and ask her to model her answers on them.

I really wonder whether Santa Claus is a real person.

I really wonder if I should leap off that cliff into the deep seawater below.

Which movie we should go to see was unusually hard to decide.

What we wanted to eat for dinner was unusually hard to decide.

Explain to your brother that I cannot fix both fried chicken and steak.

Explain to your brother why he shouldn't jump off the roof into the swimming pool.

Whoever forgot to take his shoes off after walking through the mud is not welcome in this house.

Whichever of you dogs chewed up my sofa cushions is not welcome in this house.

The most extraordinary development was that I ran the marathon in under five hours.

The most extraordinary development was when the reindeer and the wolf snuggled up together under a tree and went to sleep.

Exercise 73C: Diagramming

On your own paper, diagram every word of the following sentences (taken from *The Return of Tarzan*).

I would not care who knew that I had killed you.

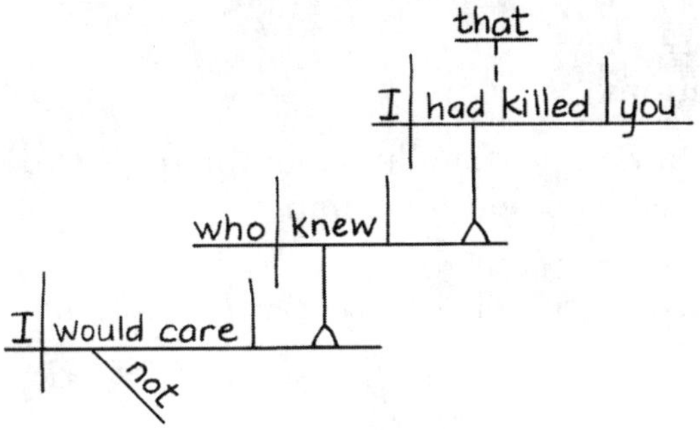

Where Tarzan stood was dark.

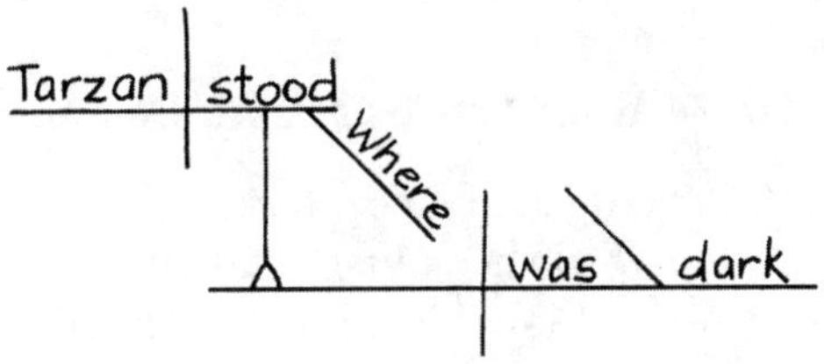

When one of the sailors had taken me out to him in another boat the professor became quite indignant at my suggestion that we return at once to land.

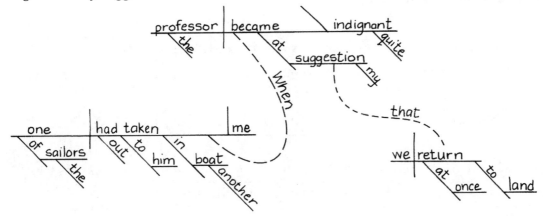

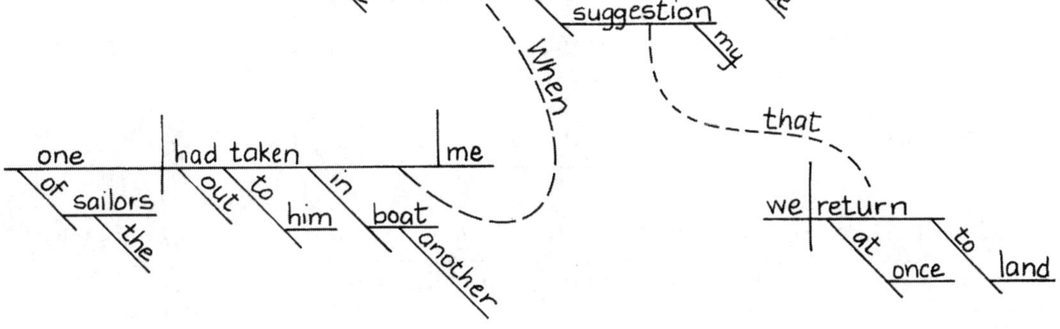

CHALLENGE SENTENCE

Note to Instructor: The student has learned to diagram each element of this sentence; encourage him to approach each phrase and clause individually, and give all necessary help.

The last few seconds of my life have taught me that it would be hideous to attempt further to deceive myself and you, or to entertain for an instant longer the possibility of ever becoming your wife, if we should regain civilization.

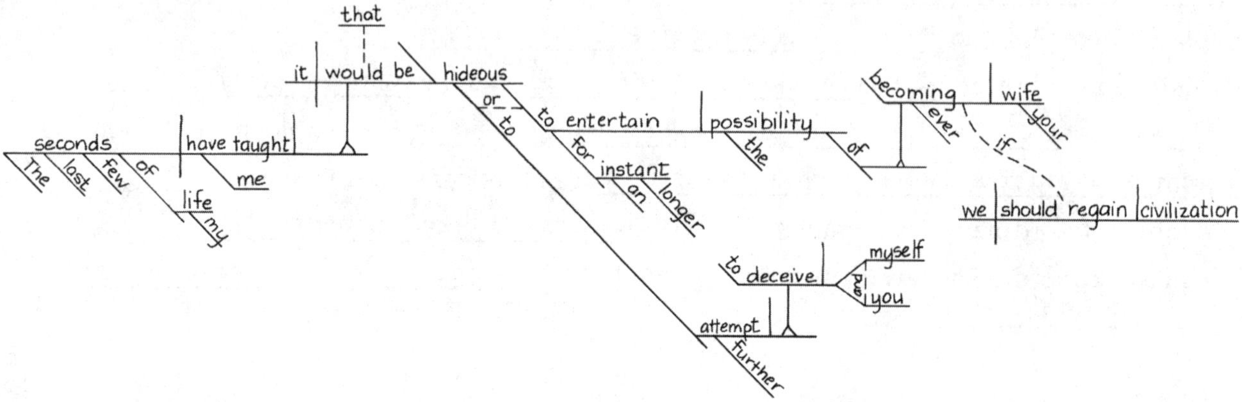

— LESSON 74 —

Clauses Beginning With Prepositions

Exercise 74A: Adjective Clauses Beginning with Prepositions

In the following sentences, circle each adjective clause. Draw a line from the subordinating word back to the word the clause modifies. If the clause begins with a preposition, underline that preposition and label its object with *OP*.

These sentences are taken from *The Clockwork Universe: Isaac Newton, the Royal Society, and the Birth of the Modern World*, by Edward Dolnick.

It means we can talk about its slope, which is a number—a regular, run-of-the-mill number, not an infinitesimal or any other colorful beast.

They make exceptions for a tiny number of geniuses whom they treat as time travelers from the present day, thinkers just like us who somehow found themselves decked out in powdered wigs.

Something is changing, and the rate at which it is changing is changing, too.

Unlike Newton, who often slept in his clothes, Leibniz was a dandy who had a weakness for showy outfits with lace-trimmed cuffs, gleaming boots, and silk cravats.

"I have done a deed which shakes the Moon in her path, which causes the Sun to be no longer the Sun, and which alters forever the destiny of the multitudinous myriads of stars that roll and glow in the majestic presence of their Creator."

"As a blind man has no idea of colors," Newton wrote, "so have we no idea of the manner by which the all-wise God perceives and understands all things."

It was Lely whom Oliver Cromwell instructed to "paint my picture truly like me," warts and all.

By paying close attention to what others had overlooked, they could find their way to utterly unexpected conclusions.

This picture of history was completely false, but Newton and many others had boundless faith in what they called "the wisdom of the ancients."

Isaac Newton was not only the supreme genius of modern times but also a man so jealous and bad-tempered that he exploded in fury at anyone who dared question him.

> **Note to Instructor:** The entire clause *that he exploded in fury at anyone who dared question him* modifies the adjectives *jealous* and *bad-tempered*, so it is an adverb clause, not an adjective clause.

Leibniz had allied himself with those scoundrels of whom it "may reasonably be suspected that they would like very well to set the king aside."

> **Note to Instructor:** The clause *that they would like very well to set the king aside* modifies the verb *may be suspected*, so it is an adverb clause, not an adjective clause.

Skeptics contended that any correct results must have been due to happy accidents in which multiple errors canceled themselves out.

> **Note to Instructor:** The entire clause *that any correct results must have been due to happy accidents in which multiple errors canceled themselves out* is a noun clause serving as the direct object of the verb *contended.*

Exercise 74B: Correct Use of *Who* and *Whom*

Choose the correct pronoun within the parentheses; cross out the incorrect pronoun.

These sentences are adapted from *Famous Men of Science*, by Sarah K. Bolton.

He returned with two gentlemen, to (~~who~~/ whom) he did not introduce me.

A woman, a princess, (who / ~~whom~~) knew about the bright boy, spoke of him to her brother.

(~~Who~~/ Whom) do the arrow heads and hatchets belong to?

He did not know a single individual from (~~who~~/ whom) he could borrow money.

Caroline, (who / ~~whom~~) loved him tenderly, was desolate.

The following year, Napoleon I, (who / ~~whom~~) was usually wise in his selection of men, appointed him one of the six inspectors-general of education.

He met Baron Humboldt, from (~~who~~/ whom) he received a large photograph.

Especially welcome were teachers, for (~~who~~/ whom) admission was free.

(~~Who~~/ Whom) should you ask?

In Rome he met a fellow painter, (who / ~~whom~~) showed him great attention, and to (~~who~~/ whom) he wrote a sonnet.

Those (who / ~~whom~~) oversee the affairs of others rarely oversee their own.

No one can be too kind to my dear wife, (who / ~~whom~~) is worth her weight in gold many times over.

(~~Who~~/ Whom) did he teach physiology to?

He gained inspiration from the young man (who / ~~whom~~) could travel four thousand miles through the marshes of Lapland, nearly barefoot and half-starved, in his study of plants.

I think he was the only man I ever knew against (~~who~~/ whom) I never heard a word said.

He brought three friends, each of (~~who~~/ whom) purchased a picture.

Exercise 74C: Formal and Informal Diction

On your own paper, rewrite the following informal sentences in formal English, placing the preposition before its object. In five sentences, you will also need to insert a relative pronoun. The first has been done for you.

Read both versions of each sentence out loud, and place a star by any sentence that sounds better in informal English.

Note to Instructor: Whether or not a sentence "sounds better" is a judgment call—accept stars by any (or no) sentences. The purpose of the exercises is to sharpen the student's ear and make her more aware of the sounds of both written and spoken English.

Whom should I speak to?

To whom should I speak?

Georges Cuvier's coffin was carried by the students at the universities which he had taught in.

Georges Cuvier's coffin was carried by the students of the universities in which he had taught.

Those students were the ones whom his books were written for.

Those students were the ones for whom his books were written.

Linnaeus discovered that the friend he had entrusted his correspondence to was hiding his letters.

Linnaeus discovered that the friend to whom he had entrusted his correspondence was hiding his letters.

Galileo asked to stand on the same level as the Aristotelian philosophers he was arguing against.

Galileo asked to stand on the same level as the Aristotelian philosophers against whom he was arguing.

The captain had no idea of the fate of the person the treasure had originally belonged to.

The captain had no idea of the fate of the person to whom the treasure had originally belonged.

The discovery of refraction was one no other scientist had laid claim to.

The discovery of refraction was one to which no other scientist had laid claim.

We are greatly influenced, for good or for evil, by those we associate with.

We are greatly influenced, for good or for evil, by those with whom we associate.

Exercise 74D: Diagramming

On your own paper, diagram every word of the following two sentences from Exercise 74A.

Something is changing, and the rate at which it is changing is changing, too.

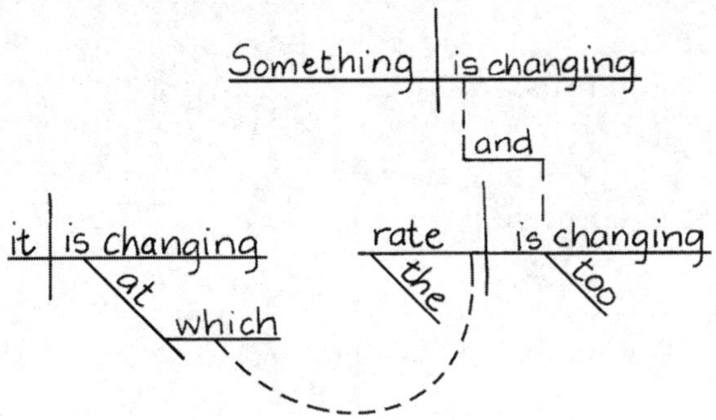

Skeptics contended that any correct results must have been due to happy accidents in which multiple errors canceled themselves out.

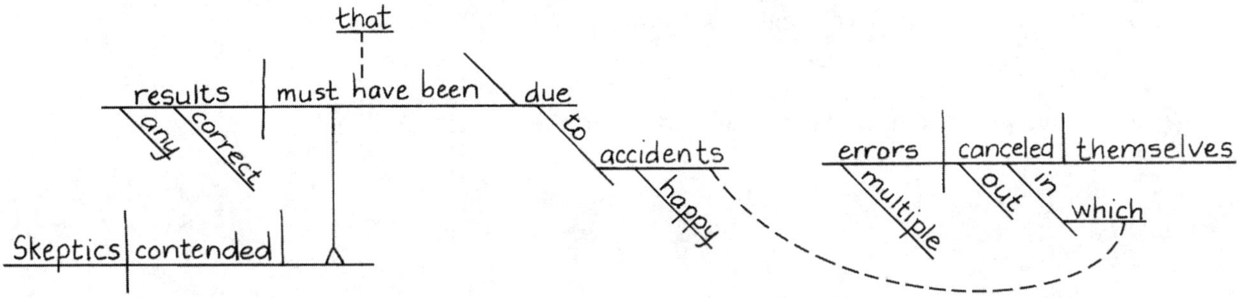

— LESSON 75 —

Clauses and Phrases
Misplaced Adjective Phrases
Misplaced Adjective Clauses

Exercise 75A: Correcting Misplaced Modifiers

Circle the misplaced adjective clauses and phrases in the following sentences. Draw an arrow to the place where each modifier should be.

The comic books were eagerly seized by the children with colorful covers.

The runners aimed for the finish line tapes that were sprinting around the track.

The black-clad man rode up to the town saloon wearing a fringed cowboy hat.

The chef filled with chives and capers drizzled the sauce over the steak.

I bought a horse from my dressage coach named Whirlaway Blaze Boy.

The bridge collapsed into the gulch with the rotting wooden rails.

The cornfield was covered in crows with three varieties of corn.

The visitors stared at the massive statue eating candy bars and swigging sodas.

I gave Jeremy a golden retriever puppy who is my best friend.

The cat finally got to the doorway that was running home.

We gathered many different kinds of fruit into our baskets that were ripe.

Exercise 75B: Diagramming

Each of the following sentences contains a misplaced clause or phrase. On your own paper, diagram each sentence correctly, and then read the corrected sentence out loud to your instructor. These sentences are taken from *Grimm's Fairy Tales*!

Sprinkled with blood, the queen gazed upon the white snow.

The queen gazed upon the white snow sprinkled with blood.

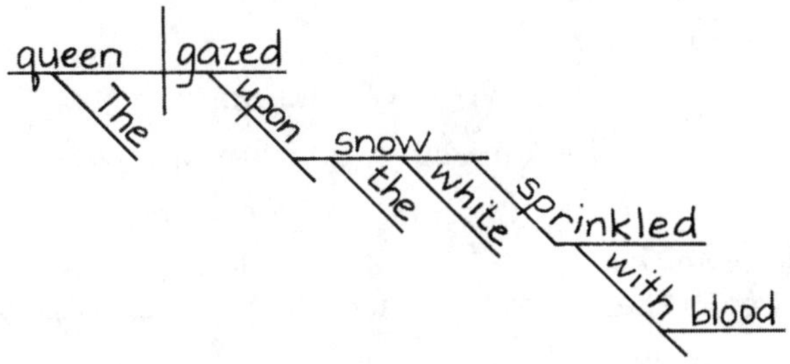

Streaming from her shoe, the older sister tried to conceal the blood from the prince.

The older sister tried to conceal the blood streaming from her shoe from the prince.

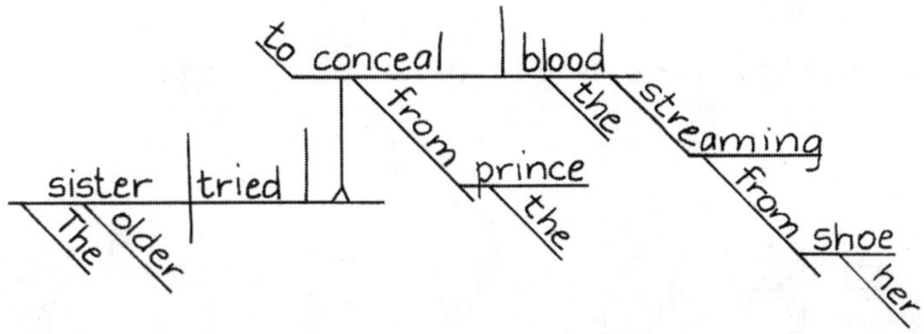

The straw stretched itself from one bank to the other, and the coal tripped quite boldly onto the newly-built bridge, who was of an impetuous disposition.

The straw stretched itself from one bank to the other, and the coal, who was of an impetuous disposition, tripped quite boldly onto the newly-built bridge.

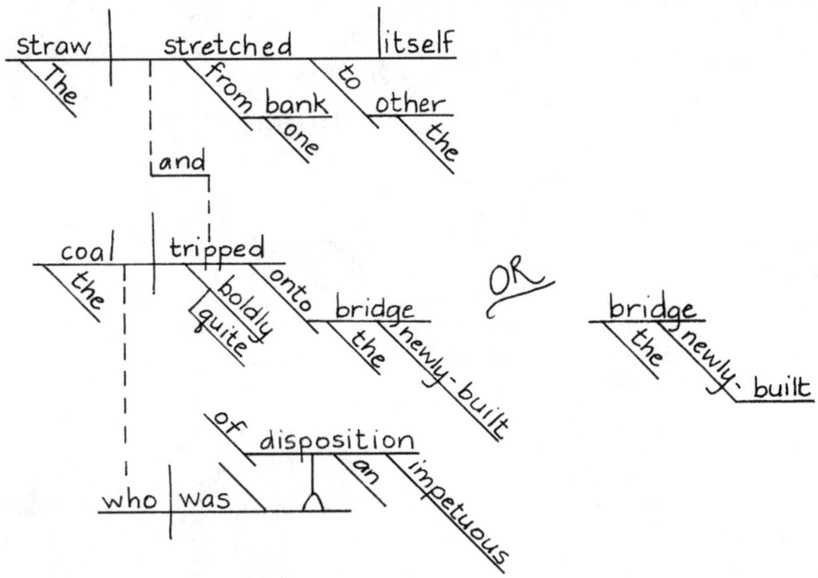

— LESSON 76 —

Noun, Adjective, and Adverb Clauses

Restrictive and Non-Restrictive Modifying Clauses

Exercise 76A: Clause Review

For each of the three sentences below, complete these steps:

1) Find and circle the dependent clauses. Label each one as adjective, adverb, or noun.
2) Identify and underline the subordinating word. (Look out for a missing subordinating word! When you find it, insert it and underline it.)
3) For the adverb and adjective clauses, draw a line from the subordinating word to the word modified. For the noun clauses, identify the part of the sentence that each clause is serving as.
4) Diagram the sentences on your own paper.

These sentences are taken from the introduction to *Women of the First Nations: Power, Wisdom, and Strength,* edited by Christine Miller and Patricia Chuchryk.

N PN

Compassion and strength are (what we are) and we have translated these into every area of

ADV

our existence (because we have had to).

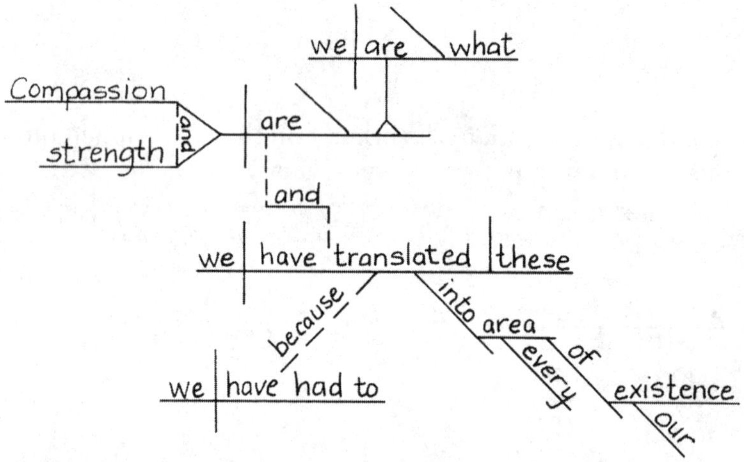

Note to Instructor: The clause *what we are* can also be diagrammed as *we are what*; the subject and predicate nominative are interchangeable.

The verb *have had to* may confuse the student; it is an idiomatic verb bearing a single meaning, so I have diagrammed *have had to* all on the predicate line. Alternately, *to* could be treated as the first part of an infinitive phrase acting as the object of the verb *had*, with understood elements: *to [translate them]*. In that case, the diagram would appear like this:

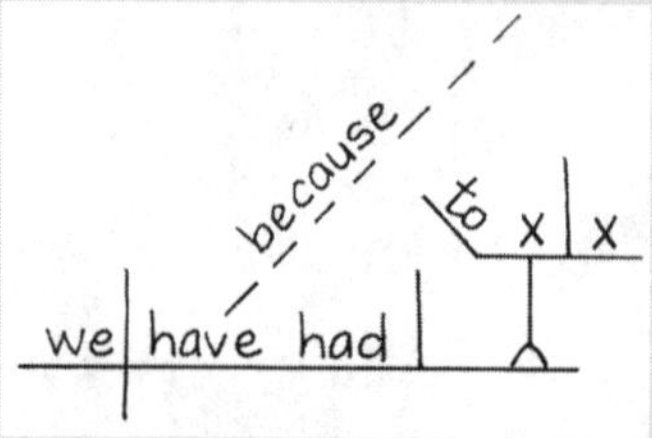

ADJ

It is a fundamental right that parents determine their own children's culture and heritage,

N DO

and what their own children learn.

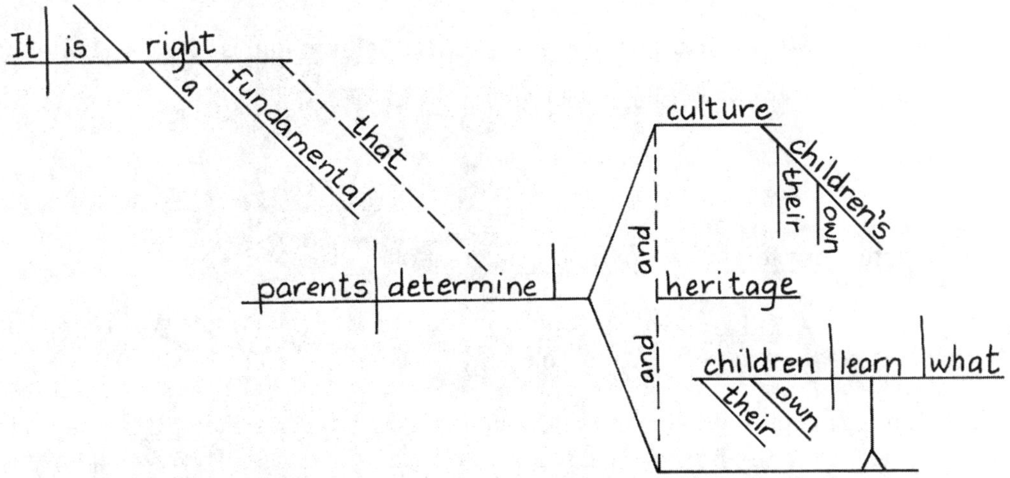

Note to Instructor: Technically, *their own children's* modifies both *culture* and *heritage*, but it is difficult to indicate this accurately on a diagram, so I have diagrammed it beneath *culture*.

ADJ

Only those who know the true nature of despair and suffering can express compassion

that ADJ

and understanding in all we do.

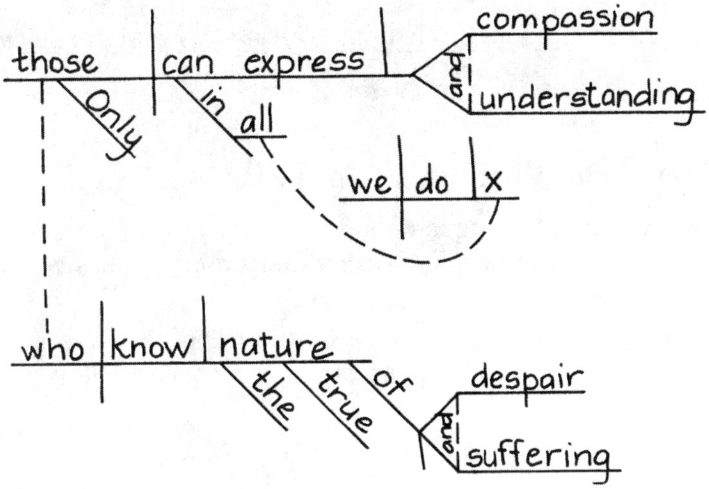

Exercise 76B: Nonrestrictive Clauses and Missing Commas

In the following sentences, taken from *The Great Circle: A History of the First Nations* by Neil Philip, underline each dependent clause. Place commas around each nonrestrictive clause. Use the proofreader's mark: ^,. Leave sentences with restrictive clauses as they are.

This was the Tree of the Great Peace, under which the Iroquoian peoples were to shelter, and beneath which they were to cast all their weapons of war.

Note to Instructor: The second comma is optional.

There was a time when our forefathers owned this great island.

When the whole tribe was united in the tribal circle, the unity of the people was represented by a sacred cottonwood pole known as the Venerable Man.

The Venerable Man was kept in one of three Sacred Tents, which contained all the sacred objects of the nation, such as the White Buffalo Hide.

The Venerable Man had a basketwork of twigs that was filled with feathers around his middle.

Although Tenskwatawa was preaching peace, his brother Tecumseh was preparing for war.

Tenskwatawa seems to have tried to obscure the fact that the Shawnee Creator was female.

But again and again his plans were disrupted by hotheads who could not wait until the agreed time before launching an attack.

While the news spread that Tecumseh was dead, the Indians melted from the battlefield.

This was the end of the long struggle in which both Tecumseh's father and his beloved brother had lost their lives.

Exercise 76C: Restrictive Clauses and Unnecessary Commas

In the following sentences, taken from John Sugden's book *Tecumseh: A Life*, underline each dependent clause. Some dependent clauses may have other dependent clauses within them—double underline clauses within clauses!

Delete the incorrect commas that have been placed around restrictive clauses. Use proofreader's marks: ℓ. Leave sentences with nonrestrictive clauses as they are.

Mill Creek was a stream, that babbled into the Cumberland through pastures, in which the cows lowed.

On the upper Wabash, far from American settlements, they might make a home, where the bounty of the earth had not been degraded.

The shadows, that hung over Tecumseh's childhood, were cast by the relationships between the Shawnees and the advancing white frontier, which tried to push them aside.

There are stories that Cheeseekau quarrelled with Watts about the propriety of the attack, but the details are hazy.

In the station the defenders fought like devils, making a defense that deservedly entered the folklore of Tennessee.

But many Indians saw this as an issue that went beyond land.

Tecumseh had gone to the Mid-Day, but Tenskwatawa remained at Prophetstown, where several hundred Kickapoos and Winnebagos camped to listen to him preach.

He hovered in the background, behind his brother, helping where he could.

These Indians had no doubt that the land on the northwestern bank of the Wabash which the Prophet had earmarked was theirs.

The implicit obedience and respect which the followers of Tecumseh pay to him is really astonishing.

In later years he took the name Tenskwatawa, which meant the Open Door.

WEEK 20

Constructing Sentences

— LESSON 77 —

Constructing Sentences

Exercise 77A: Making Sentences out of Clauses and Phrases

The independent clauses below are listed in order and make up a story—but they're missing all their supporting pieces.

On your own paper, rewrite the story by attaching the dependent clauses and phrases in Lists 2 and 3 to the independent clauses in List 1 to make complete sentences. You may insert dependent clauses that act as adjectives or adverbs into the beginning, middle, or end of independent clauses (usually by putting them right before or after the word they modify), and you may change any capitalization or punctuation necessary. But do not add or delete words.

The first sentence has been constructed for you.

Crossing out each clause or phrase as you use it will help you not to repeat yourself!

List 1. Independent Clauses

~~They grew tired~~
They thought
So they all met, and with much noise prayed
Jove and all the gods laughed
Jove threw them a log and told them
The loud fall made a great splash and frightened the Frogs
It was a long time
Some finally swam
They jumped upon it, and saw
So they asked Jove
Jove sent a Stork
The Frogs did not like this new King either
They prayed again
They told him
But Jove would not grant their prayer
He told them
They had to pay the cost
Moral: Bear the ills

List 2. Dependent Clauses

when they saw
that you have
that you do not know
that it was no King but a log
that they would like a change
that they would like
as fast as he could
before they dared
that it would be their new King
that it had been their own wish
~~when the Frogs swam at ease~~
that it did not move but lay quite still
who had some life and would move
which started to eat the Frogs
because the Frogs had been vain and foolish
rather than wishing

List 3. Phrases

to have no King at all
for new misfortunes
of course
~~through the ponds and lakes~~
to Jove
~~in old times~~
to send a King
at their new King
of the log
of the bravest
to the log
this time
to take away the Stork
to Jove, king of the gods
to send them a king
to take a peep
at the Frogs
to keep them happy
in the lake
~~of their tame mode of life~~

FIRST SENTENCE

In old times, when the Frogs swam at ease through the ponds and lakes, they grew tired of their tame mode of life.

> **Note to Instructor:** The original sentences, taken from the traditional fable "King Stork," are provided below (in chronological order). However, any sentences that the student assembles are acceptable as long as they make sense.

In old times, when the Frogs swam at ease through the ponds and lakes, they grew tired of their tame mode of life.

They thought that they would like a change.

So they all met, and with much noise prayed to Jove, king of the gods, to send them a king.

Jove and all the gods laughed at the Frogs.

To keep them happy, Jove threw them a log and told them that it would be their new King.

The loud fall of the log made a great splash in the lake and frightened the Frogs.

It was a long time before they dared to take a peep at their new King.

Some of the bravest finally swam to the log.

When they saw that it did not move but lay quite still, they jumped upon it, and saw that it was no King but a log.

So they asked Jove to send a King who had some life and would move.

Jove sent a Stork, which started to eat the Frogs as fast as he could.

Of course the Frogs did not like this new King either.

They prayed again to Jove to take away the Stork.

They told him that they would like to have no King at all.

But Jove would not grant their prayer this time.

He told them that it had been their own wish.

Because the Frogs had been vain and foolish, they had to pay the cost.

Moral: Bear the ills that you have, rather than wishing for new misfortunes that you do not know.

— LESSON 78 —

Simple Sentences
Complex Sentences

Exercise 78A: Identifying Simple and Complex Sentences

In the sentences below, underline each subject once and each predicate twice. (Find the subjects and predicates in both independent and dependent clauses.) In the blank at the end of each sentence, write *S* for simple or *C* for complex.

These sentences are taken from *A World History of Art*, by Hugh Honour and John Fleming.

The word *style* is derived from *stylus*, the writing instrument of the ancient Romans, and was first used metaphorically for the various ways of public speaking appropriate for different occasions. S

Note to Instructor: The student may choose either *word* or *style* as the subject.

The style of a group, from which that of an individual initially derives, is a visual language with a vocabulary of forms and motifs. C

Styles were the creation of painters, sculptors, architects, weavers, potters, and so on. S

The categorization of styles has, however, been the work not of artists, but of writers who have tried to impose a semblance of order on infinitely diverse expressions of creative activity. C

From the earliest times, artists used colored pigments to define images by outline. S

Flesh tones look pale against a red background but reddish against yellow. S

Painters in the West, from the fifteenth to the mid-nineteenth century, aimed for verisimilitude, an appearance of visual truth. S

The French Impressionists did their best to forget what they knew of the local color of objects and record only their optical perceptions. C

> **Note to Instructor:** The verb *record* is an infinitive with an understood *to*: they did their best to forget and [to] record.

The development of systems of perspective coincided with the emergence of the peculiarly Western concept of a painting as a window onto a real or imaginary world. S

Naturalism is usually contrasted with Idealism, which characterized the Neoclassical style of the late eighteenth century. C

Exercise 78B: Forming Complex Sentences

On your own paper, rewrite each pair of simple sentences as a single complex sentence. The first is done for you.

- You will need to add a subordinating word to one of the sentences to turn it into a dependent clause.
- There may be more than one way to rewrite each sentence, as you can see in the example.
- In the last set of sentences, try to combine all three simple sentences into one complex sentence.

These are adapted from *Byzantine Art,* by Robin Cormack.

Icons were at the center of Byzantine art. They were seen and venerated by thousands.

Icons, which were at the center of Byzantine art, were seen and venerated by thousands.

Icons, which were seen and venerated by thousands, were at the center of Byzantine art.

Icons were at the center of a burning dispute. The dispute was over imagery and the Second Commandment.

Icons were at the center of a burning dispute, which was over imagery and the Second Commandment.

Byzantine icons have a timeless quality. The timeless quality is a distinctive feature of icons.

Byzantine icons have a timeless quality that is their distinctive feature.

The Byzantines called themselves Romans. The Byzantines kept the trappings and institutions of empire.

The Byzantines called themselves Romans, because they kept the trappings and institutions of empire.

The Byzantines, who called themselves Romans, kept the trappings and institutions of empire.

There are hundreds of icons in the Monastery of St. Catherine's. Some of the icons originally belonged to hermits and other chapels.

There are hundreds of icons, some of which originally belonged to hermits and other chapels, in the Monastery of St. Catherine's.

The period around 730 marks a significant time in the history of art. Around 730, three religions held the Old Testament in common. Around 730, those three religions rejected icons as graven images.

The period around 730, when the three religions that held the Old Testament in common rejected icons as graven images, marks a significant time in the history of art.

The period around 730, when three religions held the Old Testament in common and rejected icons as graven images, marks a significant time in the history of art.

Exercise 78C: Diagramming

On your own paper, diagram the following four sentences. Beside each diagram, write the number of vertical lines dividing subjects from predicates, along with the label *S* for simple or *C* for complex.

The cat and her kittens put on their mittens to eat a Christmas pie.

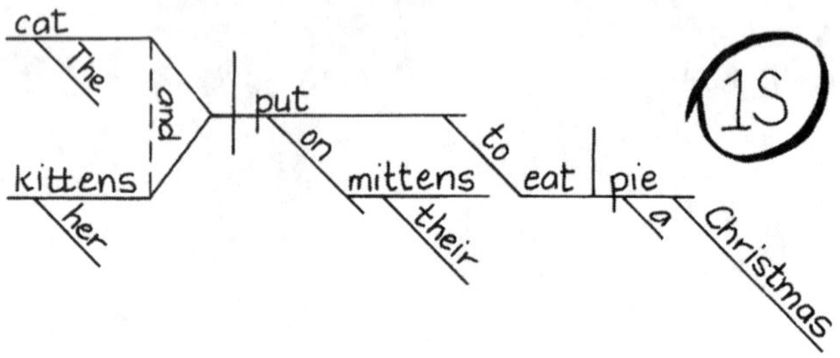

When the pie was open, the birds began to sing.

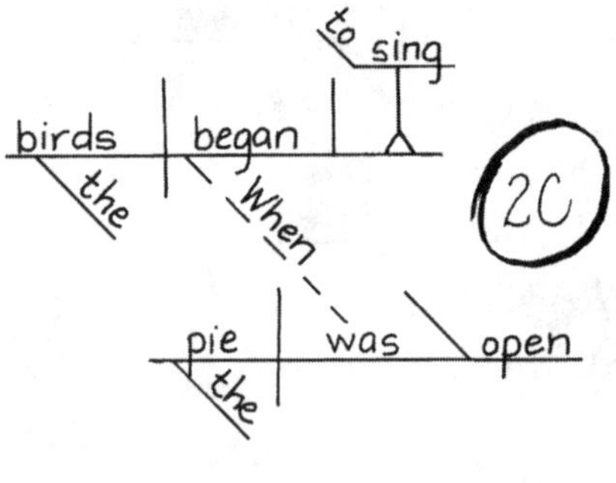

The maid was in the garden, hanging out the clothes, when down came a blackbird and pecked off her nose.

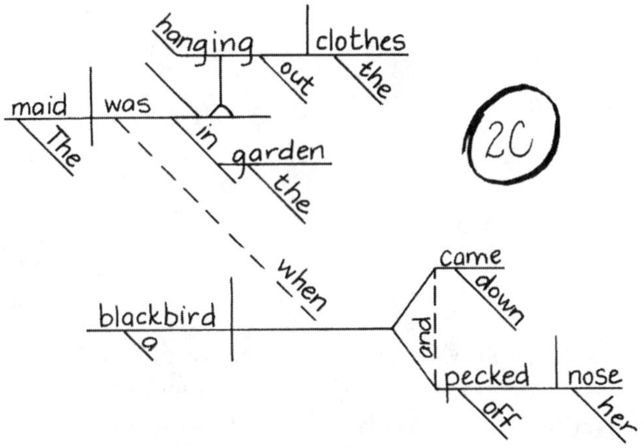

Note to Instructor: This is an interesting sentence that can be analyzed in three different ways. I have diagrammed it with *in the garden* as an adverbial phrase, since it answers the question *where*, and *hanging out the clothes* as a present participle acting as a predicate adjective. However, an argument could be made for two alternate interpretations. Both phrases could be adverbial:

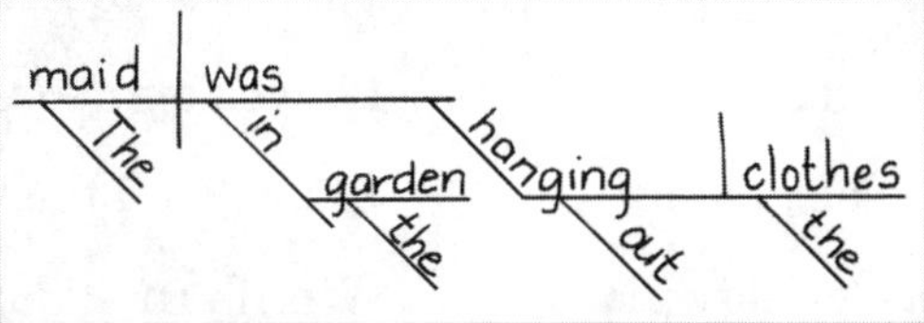

or they could be considered compound predicate adjectives:

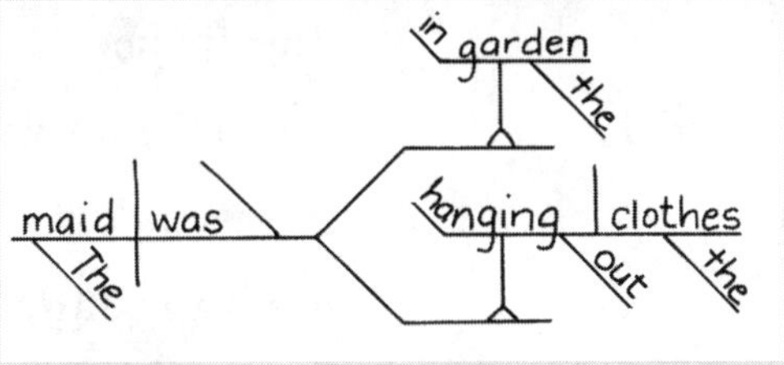

Wynken, Blynken, and Nod sailed off in a wooden shoe, sailed on a river of crystal light, into a sea of dew.

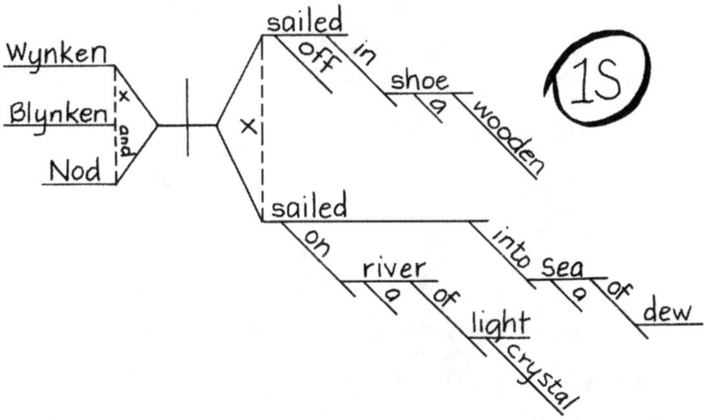

— LESSON 79 —

Compound Sentences
Run-on Sentences
Comma Splice

Exercise 79A: Forming Compound Sentences

Choose at least one independent clause from Column 1 and at least one independent clause from Column 2. Using correct punctuation and adding coordinating conjunctions as needed, combine the clauses into a compound sentence. (You may use more than two clauses, as long as your sentence makes sense!) Write your new compound sentences on your own paper. Use every clause at least once.

Column 1	Column 2
He climbed.	That will deceive them.
He put his head between his paws.	I have come to a very important decision.
I shall try to look like a small black cloud.	You missed the balloon.
Winnie-the-Pooh went to a very muddy place.	Winnie-the-Pooh floated down to the ground.
I have just been thinking.	Rabbit pulled and pulled and pulled.
You didn't exactly miss.	He climbed.
The air came slowly out of the balloon.	He thought very carefully.
Pooh Bear stretched out a paw.	He rolled until he was black all over.
	He sang a little song to himself.

Note to Instructor: The following sentences are possible answers; accept any grammatical sentences that the student offers.

He climbed and he climbed and he sang a little song to himself.

He put his head between his paws and he thought very carefully.

I shall try to look like a small black cloud; that will deceive them!

Winnie-the-Pooh went to a very muddy place and he rolled until he was black all over.

I have just been thinking, and I have come to a very important decision.

You didn't exactly *miss*, but you missed the balloon.

The air came slowly out of the balloon, so Winnie-the-Pooh floated down to the ground.

Pooh Bear stretched out a paw, and Rabbit pulled and pulled and pulled.

Exercise 79B: Correcting Run-on Sentences (Comma Splices)

Using proofreader's marks (^ to insert a coordinating conjunction, ^, to insert a comma, ^; to insert a semicolon), correct each of the run-on sentences below.

These are taken from *The Enchanted Places: A Childhood Memoir*, by Christopher Milne (the son of Winnie-the-Pooh creator A. A. Milne).

Note to Instructor: The original sentences are found below; the connecting punctuation and/or coordinating conjunctions are bolded for your reference. The student may choose to use either a semicolon, or a comma and a coordinating conjunction, in each of the bolded places.

Organ grinders always made me feel sad**, and** I used to throw them a penny.

There was a large chest by the window**, and** this was opened for me**, and** I climbed inside while my father finished his marmalade and my mother ate her apple.

We sat next to each other in class while Miss Walters did her best to teach us this and that**, and** mostly we got it wrong.

She and I inevitably drifted apart as we grew older**, but** she and my parents remained devoted to each other**, and** until I was twenty-five my mother cherished fond hopes that one day we would marry.

The Christopher Robin who appears in so many of the poems is not always me**, for** this is where my name came into its own; it was a wonderful name for writing poetry around.

Sometimes my father is using my name to describe something I did**, and** sometimes he is borrowing it to describe something he did as a child**, and** sometimes he is using it to describe something that any child might have done.

On the whole it doesn't greatly matter which of the two of us did what**;** I'm happy to accept responsibility.

Exercise 79C: Diagramming

On your own paper, diagram every word of the following sentences from A. A. Milne's stories about Winnie-the-Pooh.

The wind was behind them now, so they didn't have to shout.

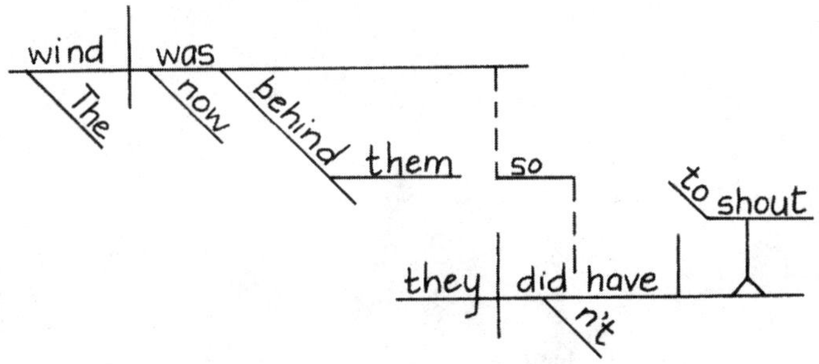

There are twelve pots of honey in my cupboard, and they've been calling to me for hours.

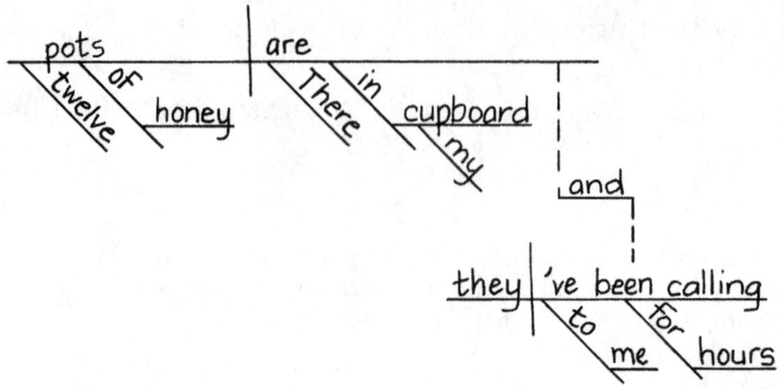

They walked off together; and for a long time Piglet said nothing, and then suddenly he made a squeaky noise.

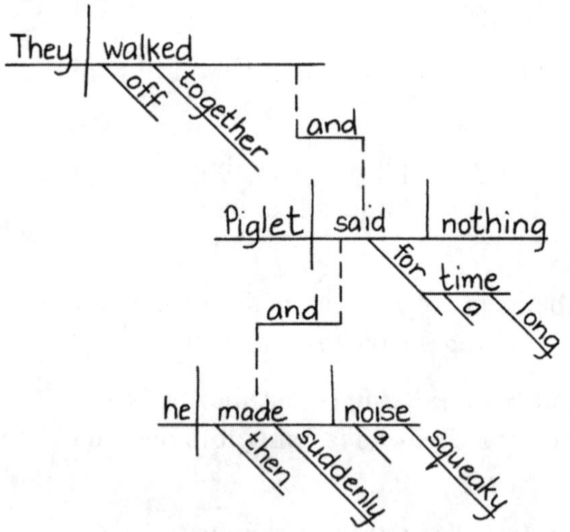

Pooh hasn't much Brain, but he never comes to any harm; he does silly things and they turn out right.

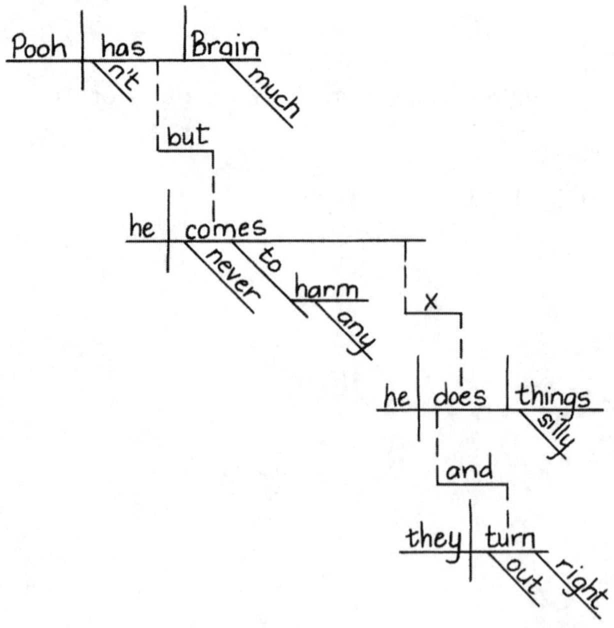

— LESSON 80 —

Compound Sentences
Compound-Complex Sentences
Clauses with Understood Elements

Exercise 80A: Analyzing Complex-Compound Sentences

The sentences below are all complex-compound sentences. For each sentence, carry out the following steps:

a) Cross out each prepositional phrase.
b) Circle any dependent clauses. Label them as *ADJ*, *ADV*, or *NOUN*. Draw a line from adjective and adverb clauses to the word modified. Label noun clauses with the part of the sentence that they function as.
c) Underline the subject of each independent clause once and the predicate twice.
d) Draw a vertical line between each simple and/or complex sentence.
e) Insert missing words (if any).

The first sentence has been done for you. Be careful—some dependent clauses may be within other dependent clauses!

These sentences are taken from a novel called *The Enchanted April*, by Elizabeth von Arnim. She was a well-known English writer, married to a Prussian nobleman, who lived in the late nineteenth and early twentieth centuries. Her books were extremely popular during her lifetime, but although they are still studied by critics, they are less read now by the general public.

NOUN DO

She had slept ~~like a baby~~, and had woken up confident; | she had found (that) there was nothing she wished to say ~~in her morning prayer~~, ~~except Thank you~~.

~~Down the stone steps on either side~~ were periwinkles ~~in full flower~~, | and she could now see what it was that had caught ~~at her~~ the night before and brushed, wet and scented, ~~across her face~~.

ADJ NOUN DO

NOUN DO

No sounds were to be heard ~~in the house~~, so she supposed | (that) it was very early | yet she felt as if she had slept a long while—so completely rested, so perfectly content.

NOUN PA

Peering out they could see that they were still ~~in the village street~~, ~~with small dark houses each side~~; and Beppo, throwing the reins ~~over the horse's back~~ as if completely confident this time that he would not go any farther, got down ~~off his box~~.

NOUN DO / ADV / ADV

Mrs. Wilkins had never yet spoken ~~to Mrs. Arbuthnot~~, who belonged ~~to one of the various church sets~~, and who analysed, classified, divided and registered the poor; she and Mr. Wilkins, when they did go out, went ~~to the parties of impressionist painters~~, ~~of whom in Hampstead~~ there were many.

ADJ / ADJ / ADV / ADJ

~~Across the bay~~ the lovely mountains, exquisitely different ~~in colour~~, were asleep too ~~in the light~~; and ~~underneath her window~~, ~~at the bottom of the flower-starred grass slope~~ ~~from which~~ the wall ~~of the castle~~ rose up, was a great cypress, cutting ~~through the delicate blues and violets and rose-colours of the mountains and the sea like a great black sword~~.

ADJ

Exercise 80B: Constructing Complex-Compound Sentences

From each set of independent clauses, construct a single complex-compound sentence. You may turn any of the clauses into dependent clauses by adding subordinating words, inserting any other words necessary, omitting unnecessary words, and making any other needed changes, but try to keep the original meaning of each clause. You must use every clause in the set!

You may turn a clause into a prepositional phrase or another form, as long as your resulting sentence has at least two independent clauses and one dependent clause and contains all of the information in the listed clauses.

Write your new sentences on your own paper. The first has been done for you.

Note to Instructor: Two possible complex/compound sentences are offered for each set of independent clauses. Others are possible—accept any grammatical answer that has at least two independent clauses and one dependent clause (and incorporates all the information!).

The Iguana Research and Breeding Station and Visitor's Center was founded in 1997.
It is on the island of Utila.
Utila is one of the Bay Islands in Honduras.
The Station helps preserve the black iguana.
The black iguana lives in mangrove forests.
It is the only iguana native to mangrove forests.

The Iguana Research and Breeding Station and Visitors Center, founded in 1997 on the Honduran Bay Island known as Utila, helps preserve the black iguana; the black iguana, which lives in mangrove forests, is the only iguana native to mangroves.

Columbus claimed Honduras for Spain in 1504.
Before 1504, the islands near Honduras were occupied by Native American groups.
Honduras did not have very much gold or other valuable minerals.
Because of the lack of minerals, the Spanish didn't pay very much attention to the islands at first.
The Spanish conquistador Cristóbal de Olid claimed Honduras for himself in 1523.
The Spanish conquistador Hernán Cortés fought against de Olid between 1524 and 1526.

Columbus claimed Honduras, which was occupied by Native American groups, for Spain in 1504; the Spanish paid little attention to the nearby islands at first, because they had little gold or minerals, but the Spanish conquistador Cristóbal de Olid claimed Honduras for himself in 1523, right before his fellow conquistador Hernán Cortés attacked him between 1524 and 1526.

Although Columbus claimed Honduras for Spain in 1504, the Spanish paid little attention to the islands, which lacked gold and minerals and were occupied by Native American groups; however, the conquistador Cristóbal de Olid claimed Honduras for himself in 1523, and then Hernán Cortés fought against him between 1524 and 1526.

In September of 1821, the people of Mexico declared independence from the Spanish Empire.
The islands of Honduras joined with the new Mexican Empire.
The emperor of this new Mexican Empire was an army officer named Augustín de Iturbide.
He became Emperor Augustín I of Mexico.
He also became the emperor of Honduras.
His empire only lasted until 1823.

In September of 1821, the people of Mexico declared independence from the Spanish Empire, and the islands of Honduras joined with the new Mexican Empire; an army officer named Augustín de Iturbide became Emperor Augustín I of Mexico and Honduras, although his empire only lasted until 1823.

When the people of Mexico declared independence from the Spanish Empire in September 1821, the islands of Honduras joined with the new Mexican Empire, under an army officer named Augustín de Iturbide who became Emperor Augustín I of Mexico; however, this Mexican-Honduran empire only lasted until 1823.

In 1969, El Salvador and Honduras fought a five-day war.
It became known as the Football War.
The two countries had disagreed about the border between them.
The president of Honduras had also objected to immigrants coming from El Salvador into Honduras.
Football (soccer) teams from the two countries played preliminary matches to qualify for the World Cup.
Fans rioted.
Then El Salvador invaded Honduras.

In 1969, El Salvador and Honduras fought a five-day war called the Football War, which began because the two countries had disagreed about the border between them, and the president of Honduras had also objected to immigrants coming from El Salvador into Honduras; when football (soccer) teams from the two countries played preliminary matches to qualify for the World Cup, fans rioted and El Salvador invaded Honduras.

> In 1969, El Salvador and Honduras fought the five-day Football War; the two countries had already disagreed about the border between them and about immigrants coming from El Salvador into Honduras, so when football (soccer) teams from the two countries played matches to qualify for the World Cup, fans rioted; afterwards, El Salvador invaded Honduras.

In 1998, Hurricane Mitch caused over 11,000 deaths in Central America.
7,000 of those deaths were in Honduras.
Hurricane Mitch was a Category 5 storm with winds of up to 180 mph.
Some areas of Honduras received 75 inches of rain.
A million Hondurans were left homeless.
According to the president of Honduras, Carlos Flores, the hurricane wiped out fifty years of progress in his country.

> In 1998, Hurricane Mitch, which was a Category 5 storm with winds of up to 180 mph, caused over 11,000 deaths in Central America, 7,000 of which were in Honduras; some areas of Honduras received 75 inches of rain, a million Hondurans were left homeless, and, according to the president of Honduras, Carlos Flores, the hurricane wiped out fifty years of progress in his country.

> When Hurricane Mitch, a Category 5 storm with winds of up to 180 mph, passed across Central America in 1998, it caused over 11,000 deaths, 7,000 of them in Honduras, which received up to 75 inches of rain; a million Hondurans were left homeless, and the president of Honduras, Carlos Flores, said that the hurricane wiped out fifty years of progress in his country.

Exercise 80C: Diagramming

On your own paper, diagram the following epigrams. (Epigram: a short, clever saying)

Next to your diagram, label each sentence as compound (*C*), complex (*CX*), or compound-complex (*CCX*).

You cannot do a kindness too soon, for you never know how soon it will be too late.
—Ralph Waldo Emerson

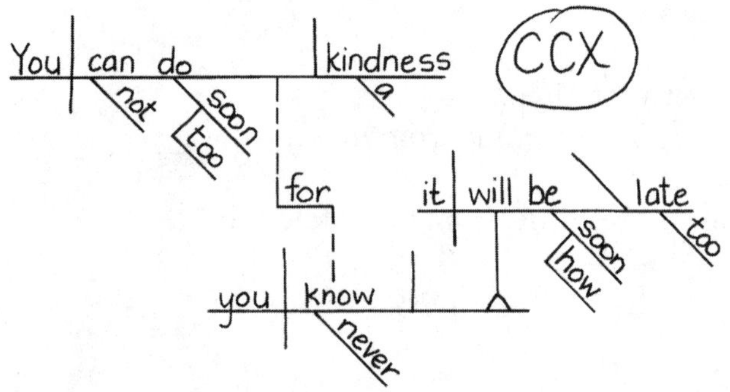

It's a recession when your neighbor loses his job; it's a depression when you lose yours.
—Harry S. Truman

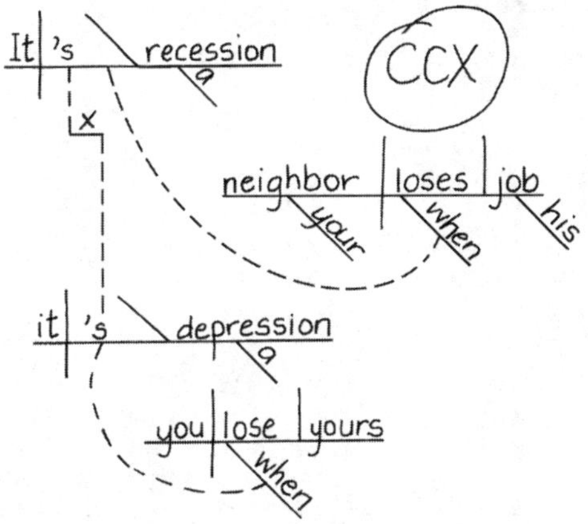

When a true genius appears, you can know him by this sign: that all the dunces are in a confederacy against him.
—Jonathan Swift

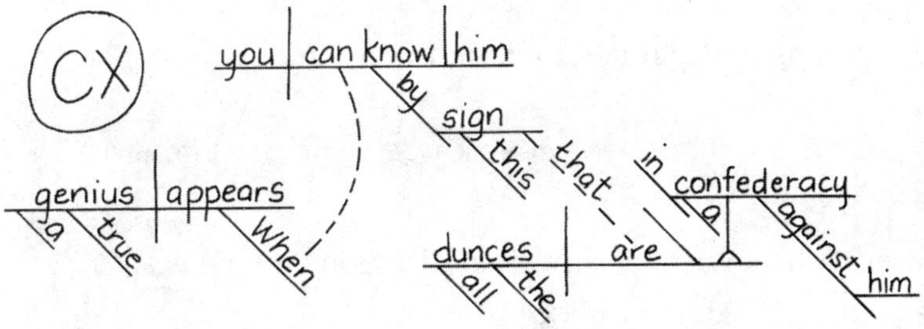

Love is the strongest force the world possesses, and yet it is the humblest imaginable.
—Mahatma Gandhi

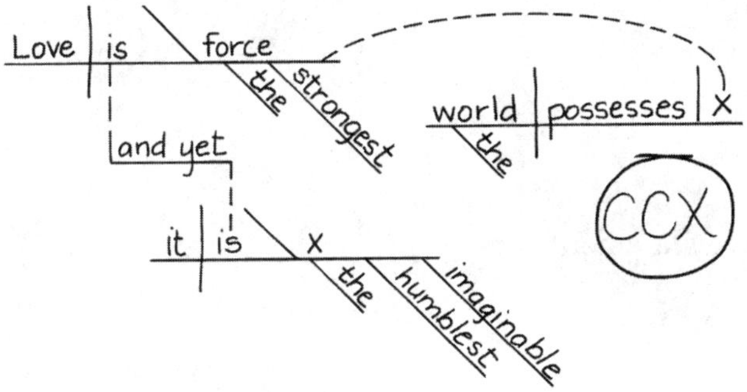

WEEK 21

Conditions

— LESSON 81 —

Helping Verbs
Tense and Voice
Modal Verbs

Exercise 81A: Using *Do, Does,* and *Did*

On your own paper, rewrite each sentence, putting it into the form described in brackets. Use the appropriate form of the helping verb along with any interrogatives or negatives necessary. Don't forget that you may have to change the form of the verb! The first one is done for you.

These sentences are taken from the alien invasion novel *The Forge of God*, by Greg Bear.

You think of the President's statement that aliens have landed and are intent on destroying earth. [Change into a question.]

What do you think of the President's statement that aliens have landed and are intent on destroying earth?

The Guest's three golden-yellow eyes stared at him without blinking. [Provide emphasis.]

The Guest's three golden-yellow eyes did stare at him without blinking.

They told you why your world was being destroyed. [Change into a question.]

Did they tell you why your world was being destroyed?

You had to call the Air Force. [Change into a question.]

Why did you have to call the Air Force?

I object. [Turn into a negative statement.]

I do not object.

We knew what was happening. [Turn into a negative statement.]

We did not know what was happening.

You had children. [Change into a question.]

Did you have children?

The spiders got through airport security. [Change into a question.]

How did the spiders get through airport security?

You have a way with words. [Provide emphasis.]

You do have a way with words.

Exercise 81B: Modal Verbs

Fill in the blanks below with an appropriate helping verb (*should, would, may, might, must, can, could*) to form a modal verb. There may be more than one correct answer for each sentence. Use each helping verb at least once.

These sentences are taken from John Wyndham's 1957 novel *The Midwich Cuckoos*—the story of a different sort of alien invasion! After you finish the exercise, be sure to read the original sentences in the Answer Key.

Note to Instructor: The original sentences are found below. Accept any helping verbs that make sense! Be sure to help the student compare her answers with the original verbs below. Ask her which sentences sound best.

And why Midwich __should__ have been singled out in preference to any one of a thousand other villages for the curious event of the 26th of September seems likely to remain a mystery for ever.

But we __must__ not simply be silent and secretive, as if we were concealing something. We __must__ make it seem that there is nothing unusual in Midwich at all.

Babies __should__ be joy and fun.

I __could__ feel my scalp prickling, and my hair beginning to rise.

Therefore you __must__ take her away without the baby. If you __can__ persuade her to that, we __can__ arrange to have it excellently looked after here.

Do your utmost to make her forget this changeling in order that she __may__ have a normal life.

That's the subconscious for you—trying to pass off the uncomfortable by telling me that the peculiarities __would__ diminish as the Children grew older.

After all, if we were to discover dangerous wild animals in our midst our duty __would__ be clear.

However interesting, scientifically, the Children __may__ have been during the first year of their lives there was little about them during that time to cause further misgiving.

The only possible compromise __would__ be for you to surrender to the baby's challenge, and come to live here, too.

I think he __might__ be able to help us, if he's willing.

We __must__ get this thing out in the open, and relieve the tension.

The only thing that __can__ beat us is something with a still better brain.

I told the Children I __could__ see very little hope of getting anyone to listen to me seriously.

No one there __could__ have been warned without the Children getting to know of it.

Exercise 81C: Verb Tense and Voice

For each sentence below, underline each verb phrase (in both dependent and independent clauses) and identify the tense and voice of the verb. For state-of-being verbs which are neither active nor passive in voice, identify the tense and write *state-of-being.* Mark modal verbs as *perfect past modal* or *simple present modal.* The first sentence is done for you.

These sentences are taken from H. G. Wells's classic science fiction novel *The First Men in the Moon.*

Perfect past, active
Why had we come to the moon?

Simple past, active / Simple past, state-of-being
But curiously enough he seemed to be labouring under a conviction that I was either dead in the moon crater or lost in the deep of space.

Perfect past, active / Perfect past modal, active
Immediately the train of thought that our conversation had suggested must have resumed its sway.

Simple present, state-of-being / Simple future, active / Perfect present, passive
Where there are minds they will have something similar—even though they have been evolved on different planets.

Simple past, active / Perfect past modal, active
I tried to imagine what could have happened to him.

Perfect present, active / Perfect past, active
I have already brought you farther than I should have done.

Perfect past, active / Perfect past, active
He had had a fever, but it had left no bad effects.

Simple present, active / Simple present, active / Simple past, passive / Simple present, active
I infer rather than learn from his narrative that he was captured by the mooncalf herds under the direction of these other Selenites who "have larger brain cases (heads?) and very much shorter legs."

Progressive past, active / Simple present, active / Simple past, active / Progressive past, passive
A wind was blowing down the shaft, and far above I fancy I heard, growing fainter and fainter, the bellowing of the mooncalves that were being driven down again from their evening pasturage on the exterior.

Simple past, state-of-being / Simple past, active / Simple past, state-of-being / Simple present, modal, active / Progressive past, active
It was quite clear to me that what I had to do was to get back to earth, but as far as I could see I was drifting away from it.

Simple past, passive / Simple present modal, active (both)
Our attention was taken up by the movements and attitudes of the Selenites immediately about us, and by the necessity of controlling our motion, lest we should startle and alarm them and ourselves by some excessive stride.

Note to Instructor: The helping verb *should* goes with both main verbs (*startle* and *alarm*) and puts both of them into the modal tense.

— LESSON 82 —

Conditional Sentences
The Condition Clause
The Consequence Clause

Exercise 82A: Identifying Conditional Sentences

Some of the sentences in this exercise are conditional sentences—and others are not! Identify each conditional sentence by writing a *C* in the margin. For each conditional sentence, label the clauses as *condition* or *consequence*.

consequence / condition
I promise you all you wish, if you will but bring my ball back again. C

The dress pleased the Bride so well that she thought it might do for her wedding-dress, and asked if it was for sale.

The little brother did not drink, although he was so thirsty.

condition / consequence
Unless he could point out the thief, he himself should be looked upon as guilty and should be executed. C

Although she was many thousand times better off here than at home, still she had a longing to be there.

As soon as the mother heard how she had come by such great riches, she was anxious for the same good fortune.

Every one wanted to have a new coat made by the little tailor, whose importance increased daily.

consequence / condition
Nothing can save you, unless you will promise to give me for mine own what first meets you on your return home. C

She remained with them while the wedding-feast lasted, and then went back again to the forest.

condition / consequence
If you forget to throw down the nut, he will let you fall into the sea. C

Exercise 82B: Tense in Conditional Sentences

Fill in each blank below with the correct tense and form of the verb in brackets. Some sentences may have more than one possible correct answer.

First conditional sentences

If I __don't study__ [negative form of *study*] a little harder for this test, I __will get__ [get] a very bad grade.

If you __don't manage__ [negative form of *manage*] to buy a ticket at the box office, __go__ [go] on home and I __will meet__ [meet] you there.

Unless he runs [run] faster, he will miss [miss] his flight to Antarctica.

If you tell [tell] me where to turn, we will find [find] the haunted corn maze much faster!

There is [state-of-being] no point in the chef putting all that chocolate frosting on the cake, unless he intends [intend] to serve it to chocolate fanatics.

Second conditional sentences

If the barn had burned OR burned [burn] down, the zombies would be [state-of-being] in flames.

If the elephant had seen [see] the mouse run across the floor, we would know [know] it.

If I knew [know] the answer, I would write [write] it down.

If the sun exploded [explode], we would be [state-of-being] very, very cold.

Third conditional sentences

If Alice had eaten [ate] more of the mushroom, she might have disappeared [disappear] altogether.

If the space lasers had destroyed [destroy] the asteroid headed for earth, we wouldn't be preparing [negative form of *prepare*] for the end of the world.

If the zombies hadn't overrun [negative of *overrun*] Atlanta, the CDC would never have exploded [negative of *explode*] into a giant fireball.

If Gollum had decided [decide] to give up the ring willingly, Frodo would have [have] ten fingers.

Exercise 82C: Diagramming

On your own paper, diagram these sentences, taken from J. R. R. Tolkien's *The Return of the King*. A conditional clause should be diagrammed like any other dependent clause.

He'd spot me, pretty quick, if I put the Ring on now, in Mordor.

Note to Student: because Sam, the speaker, is using colloquial language, *quick* is serving as an adverb. If you were writing formally, it would need to be *quickly*.

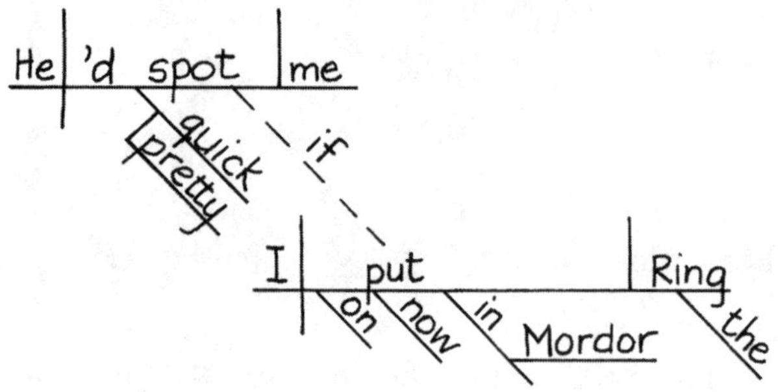

But if I should return, think better of me!

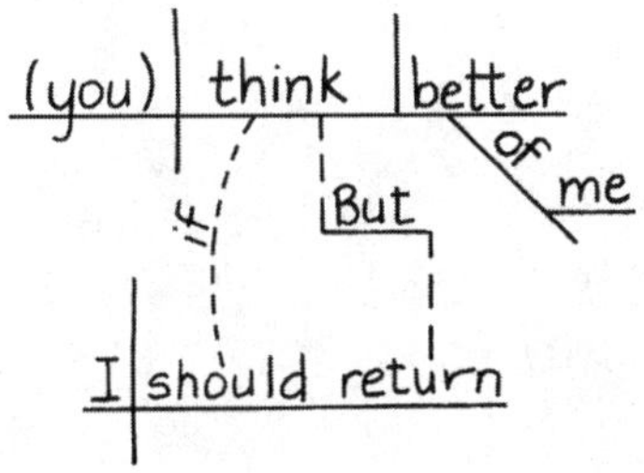

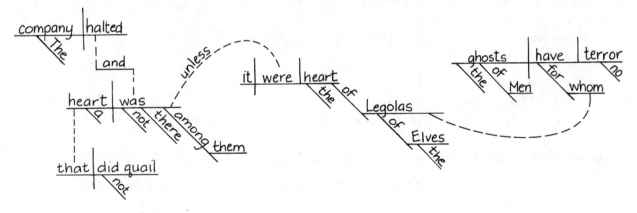

Note to Instructor: In this sentence, *better* is acting as a noun, the direct object of *think* (the thing to be thought, not a way of thinking). *But if* could also be diagrammed together on the slanted line as a compound subordinating element.

If you had waited at Orthanc, you would have seen him, and he would have shown you wisdom and mercy.

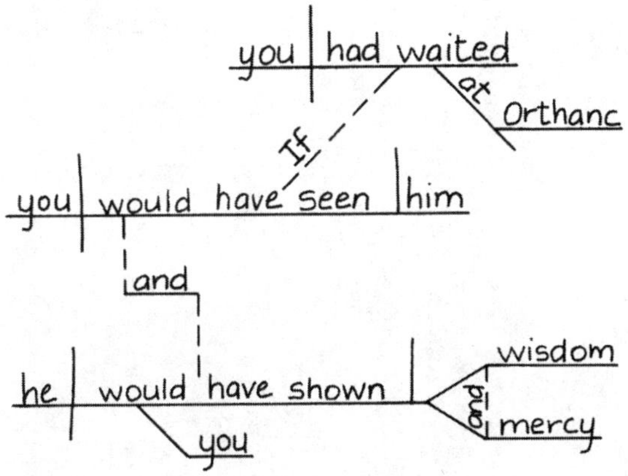

The Company halted, and there was not a heart among them that did not quail, unless it were the heart of Legolas of the Elves, for whom the ghosts of Men have no terror.

— LESSON 83 —

Conditional Sentences
The Subjunctive

Exercise 83A: Subjunctive Forms in Lines of Poetry

Fill in each blank with the correct state-of-being verb.

But O that I were young again
And held her in my arms.
  —William Butler Yeats, "Politics"

She bid me take life easy,
  as the grass grows on the weirs;
But I was young and foolish,
  and now am full of tears.
  —William Butler Yeats, "Down By the Salley Gardens"

I would I were alive again
To kiss the fingers of the rain,
  —Edna St. Vincent Millay, "Renascence"

If I were a shepherd, I would bring a lamb;
If I were a Wise Man, I would do my part;
  —Christina Rossetti, "In the Bleak Midwinter"

So I went on softly from the glade,
  And left her behind me throwing her shade,
As if she were indeed an apparition—
  —Thomas Hardy, "The Shadow on the Stone"

That's my last Duchess painted on the wall,
Looking as if she were alive.
  —Robert Browning, "My Last Duchess"

So then he asked me if I knew the Viceroy.
I said I did. And I asked the Captain,
"If he were Captain Drake himself and no other?"
  —Ernesto Cardenal, "Drake in the Southern Sea," trans. Thomas Merton

Exercise 83B: Correct Verb Forms in Complex Sentences

In each pair of verb forms, cross out the incorrect form. These sentences are from *All Creatures Great and Small,* by James Herriot.

Boardman's features seemed to soften and a light came into his eyes as though he (~~was~~/ were) talking more to himself than to me.

She (wasn't/~~weren't~~) getting to her feet in the normal way of dogs, it was as though she (~~was~~/ were) being lifted up by strings somewhere in the ceiling, the legs straightening almost imperceptibly, the body rigid, every hair bristling.

One thing (was/~~were~~) sure—she (was/~~were~~) going to come at me any second, and I blessed the luck that had made me stand right by the door.

The others followed suit immediately and though we danced about and waved our arms they ran past us as if we (~~wasn't~~/weren't) there.

Siegfried had fallen back and (was/~~were~~) staring at the ceiling with feverish eyes. His lips moved feebly as though he (~~was~~/were) praying.

When he (was/~~were~~) caught in bed he usually scored a few points by being half way through his breakfast before his brother came in.

It (was/~~were~~) old-fashioned treatment but effective. By the time I (was/~~were~~) half way down the pint pot I felt as though I (~~was~~/were) being consumed by fire.

The farmer lifted it as if it (~~was~~/were) a whippet dog and (~~lay~~/laid) it by its mother's head.

It hadn't been a happy episode but at least I did (feel/~~felt~~) a certain peace in the knowledge that there (~~was~~/were) no more doubts. I knew what (was/~~were~~) wrong, I knew that there (was/~~were~~) no hope.

As I came into the operating room I saw that Siegfried (~~has~~/had) a patient on the table. He (was/~~were~~) thoughtfully stroking the head of an elderly and rather woebegone border terrier.

— LESSON 84 —

Conditional Sentences
The Subjunctive
Moods of Verbs
Subjunctive Forms Using *Be*

Exercise 84A: Parsing Verbs

In the following sentences from *Virtuous Women: Three Classic Korean Novels* (translated by Richard Rutt and Kim Chong-un), underline each predicate, in both main clauses and dependent clauses. Above each, write the tense, voice, and mood of the verb:

Tenses: Simple past, present, future; progressive past, present, future; perfect past, present, future

Voice: Active, passive (or state-of-being)

Mood: Indicative, subjunctive, imperative, modal, subjunctive/modal

simple present, active, modal — simple present, active, imperative

A son should not go against his father's wishes. Never speak of this again.

simple past, active, indicative — simple past, active, indicative — simple present, active, subjunctive/modal

He opened his eyes and stared at her as though he could not see her, mumbling every now and

simple past, state-of-being, subjunctive

then as though he were still half asleep.

Hsing-chen stood [simple past, active, indicative] for a long while on the bridge looking in all directions, but he could [simple present, active, modal] not see where they had gone [perfect past, state-of-being, indicative], and soon the shimmering mists had dispersed [perfect past, active, indicative] and the fragrance had faded [perfect past, active, indicative] away.

simple present, state-of-being, indicative (see); perfect past, active, indicative; perfect past, state-of-being, indicative

The love of father and son is deep, but the difference between immortals and men is such that even though I should like to help you I cannot.

(is: perfect past, active, indicative; is: simple present, active, indicative; should like: simple present, active, modal; can: simple present, active, indicative)

While we have frequented [perfect present, active, indicative] this shrine where your coffin lies [simple present, active, indicative] in state, you have seemed [perfect present, active, indicative] to be with us still; when the funeral is [simple present, state-of-being, indicative] over your coffin will have left [perfect future, active, indicative] the palace for ever.

I have long been [perfect present, state-of-being, indicative] as fond of you as if you were [simple past, state-of-being, subjunctive] my own offspring. How do [simple present, active, modal] you dare [simple present, active, indicative] do this to me now?

My flesh and bones have been cremated [perfect present, passive, indicative] on the Lotus Peak, where I left [simple past, active, indicative] them. I was [simple past, state-of-being, indicative] too young to have any disciples and so there will have been [perfect future, state-of-being, indicative] nobody to collect up my relics.

Recently I am strangely troubled [simple present, passive, indicative] by a nameless fatigue, and I feel [simple present, active, indicative] as though I were [simple past, state-of-being, subjunctive] in the midst of a thick fog.

Exercise 84B: Forming Subjunctives

William Shakespeare was a fan of subjunctives!

Fill in the blanks in the following sentences from Shakespeare's plays with the correct verb form indicated in brackets. All tenses are simple.

If you __say__ [present active subjunctive of *say*] so, I __hope__ [present active indicative of *hope*] you will not kill me.

If she __be__ [present subjunctive, state-of-being] false, O, then heaven __mocks__ [present active indicative of *mock*] itself!

By heaven, he __echoes__. [present active indicative of *echo*]

As if there __were__ [present subjunctive, state-of-being] some monster in his thought,

Too hideous to be shown.

Othello

She speaks, yet she __says__ [present active indicative of *say*] nothing.

Romeo and Juliet

You __are__ [present indicative, state-of-being] plebians, if they __be__ [present subjunctive, state-of-being] senators.

Coriolanus

If I were [past subjunctive, state-of-being] Brutus now, and he were [past subjunctive, state-of-being] Cassius, he should not humour me.

Julius Caesar

I will not rise, unless your highness hear [present active subjunctive of *hear*] me.

Richard III

Unless my study and my books be [present subjunctive, state-of-being] false,
The argument you held, was [past indicative, state-of-being] wrong in you.

Henry VI, Part I

Unless I find [present active subjunctive of *find*] him guilty, he shall not die.
We intend [present active indicative of *intend*] to try his grace to-day, if he be [present subjunctive, state-of-being] guilty.

Henry VI, Part II

And, when the king comes, offer [present active imperative of *offer*] him no violence,
Unless he seek [present active subjunctive of *seek*] to put us out by force.
Is this the alliance that he seeks [present active indicative of *seek*] with France?

Henry VI, Part III

If it be [present subjunctive, state-of-being] now, 'tis not to come; if it be [present subjunctive, state-of-being] not to come, it will be [future indicative, state-of-being] now; if it be [present subjunctive, state-of-being] not now, yet it will come; the readiness is [present indicative, state-of-being] all.

Hamlet

Exercise 84C: Diagramming

On your own paper, diagram the following sentences, from Frank Herbert's classic science fiction novel *Dune*.

And if I die here, they'll say I sacrificed myself that my spirit might lead them.

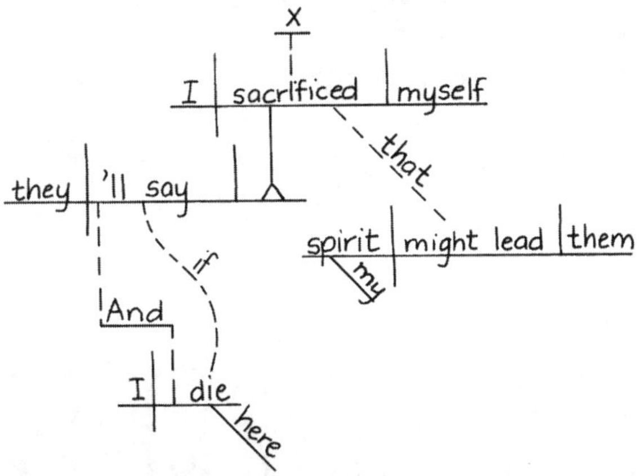

Note to Instructor: *And if* can also be diagrammed together on the slanted dotted line as a compound subordinating conjunction.

He realized that he was semi-delirious, that he should dig himself into the sand, find the relatively cool underlayer and cover himself with it.

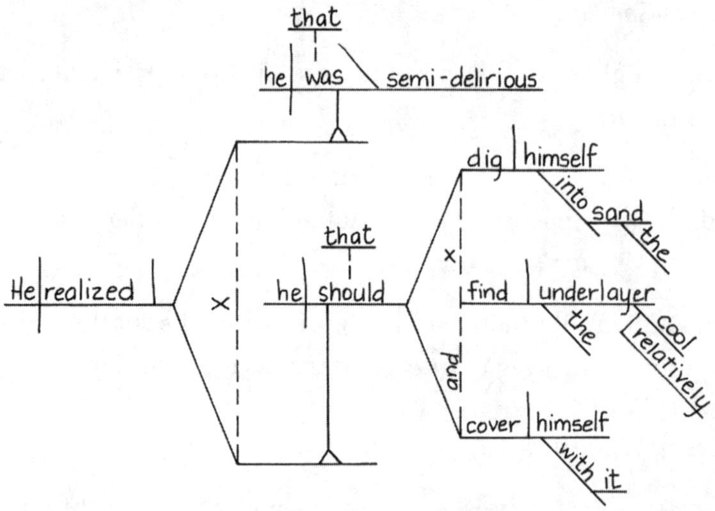

Note to Instructor: The clauses *that he was semi-delirious* and *that he should dig...himself with it* are both direct objects of *realized*. The second clause has a single subject (*he*) and three predicates, with *should* serving as the helping verb for all three (*he should dig...[should] find...[should] cover*). The student could also place *should dig* on the same line and insert Xs in front of *find* and *cover* to represent the helping verb.

Whether a thought is spoken or not it is a real thing and it has power.

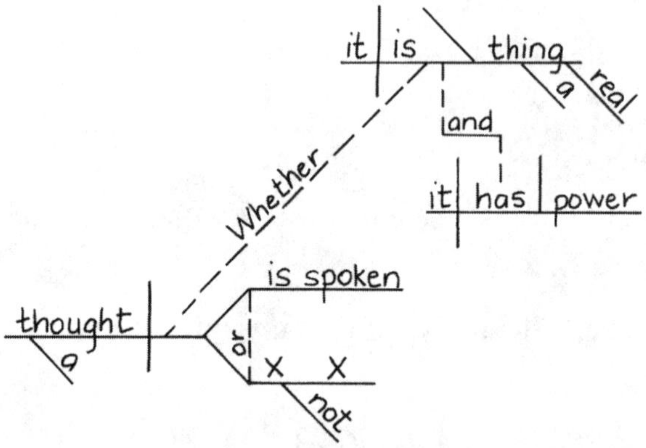

Note to Instructor: The subordinate clause *Whether a thought is spoken or not* has the understood elements *Whether a thought is spoken or [is] not [spoken]*.

— REVIEW 7 —

Weeks 19-21

Topics
Phrases and Clauses
Adjective, Adverb, and Noun Clauses
Pronouns
Mood: Modal, Subjective, Imperative, Indicative
Conditional Sentences

Review 7A: Improving Sentences with Phrases

In the blanks below, supply phrases that meet the descriptions in brackets. You may supply more than one phrase in any blank, as long as at least one phrase fulfills the requirements (often, additional prepositional phrases may be needed). The first is done for you, with explanation provided.

The original sentences are taken from James Herriot's memoir *All Things Bright and Beautiful*, about his years as a Yorkshire veterinarian.

This is a challenging assignment—prepare to spend some time on it!

When you are finished, compare your sentences with the originals in the Answer Key.

Note to Instructor: This is a difficult exercise, but it will begin to move the student toward using grammatical knowledge to construct more interesting sentences, while also giving a model from an excellent writer. If the student gets stuck, provide him with the first word or two of the original phrase.

When the student is finished, ask him to read his sentence out loud first, followed by Herriot's original sentence. Encourage him to listen carefully to both sentences.

[adverbial prepositional phrase describing the location of the archway] [adjectival participle phrase saying which archway]

Just beyond the kitchen door was a stone archway leading to the open fields and through

[adverbial prepositional phrase describing where the draught cut]

this black opening there whistled a Siberian draught which cut effortlessly through my clothes.

EXPLANATION: The phrase "beyond the kitchen door" modifies the state-of-being verb *was* and answers the question *where.*

[adverbial prepositional phrase describing where the lamb huddled]

Beside her, a tiny lamb huddled close to her flank.

They don't give vets medals for bravery, but as I pulled off my overcoat and jacket and

[adverbial present participle phrase that begins with the present participle and includes two adverbial prepositional phrases, both of them describing the present participle]

stood shivering in my shirt sleeves on that black hillside I felt I deserved one.

[adjectival present participle phrase describing the ewe] [adverbial prepositional phrase describing *trotted* and answering the question *where*]

The ewe, clearly feeling better without her uncomfortable burden, trotted behind me.

[adverbial prepositional phrase answering the question *where*]
We pushed the ewe and lambs ___into the barn___ which was piled high with hay, and [adverbial prepositional phrase answering the question *when*. Can you use a present participle as the object of a preposition?] ___before leaving___ I struck a match and looked down at the little sheep and her new family [past participle phrase acting as an adjective, describing the sheep and her family, containing a prepositional phrase acting as an adverb and answering the question *where*] ___settled comfortably among the fragrant clover___.

At the top of the grassy slope the pens, [past participle phrase acting as an adjective, describing the pens] ___built of straw bales___, formed a long row of square cubicles each [present participle phrase acting as an adjective, describing *each*] ___holding a ewe___ with her lambs and I could see Rob Benson [present participle phrase acting as an adjective, describing *Rob Benson*] ___coming round the far end___, [another present participle phrase acting as an adjective, also describing *Rob Benson*] ___carrying two feeding buckets___.

Turning, I kneeled again and began the same procedure and as I once more groped forward a tiny lamb dodged [another present participle phrase acting as an adjective, describing *dodged*] ___under my arm___ and began to suck at my patient's udder.

He was clearly enjoying it, too, if the little tail, [present participle phrase acting as an adjective, describing *tail*] ___twirling inches from my face___, meant anything.

The ewe bent over him and began [infinitive phrase acting as the object of the verb *began*] ___to lick his face and neck___ with little quick darts of her tongue; and she gave the deep chuckle [adjectival prepositional phrase describing *chuckle*] ___of satisfaction___ that you hear from a sheep only [adverbial prepositional phrase answering the question *when*] ___at this time___.

Review 7B: Improving Sentences with Clauses

Rewrite each sentence on your own paper, adding a dependent clause that meets the description in brackets. The first is done for you, with explanation provided.

The original sentences are taken from *All Things Wise and Wonderful*, by James Herriot. When you are finished, compare your sentences with the originals in the Answer Key.

That kitten grew rapidly into a sleek handsome cat with a boisterous nature [adjective clause describing *nature*] ___which earned him the name of Buster.___

EXPLANATION: The adjective clause answers the question *what kind* about the cat's nature; *which*, the subject of the clause, is a relative pronoun referring back to *nature*, and *earned* is the predicate.

That was very clever—I don't know [noun clause serving as the direct object of the verb] ___how you managed it___.

I can't remember [noun clause serving as the direct object of *can remember*] ___when I haven't had to work on Christmas Day___ because the animals have never got round to recognising it as a holiday; but with the passage of the years the vague resentment [adjective clause describing *resentment*] ___I used to feel___ has been replaced by philosophical acceptance.

The long moist furrows of the new-turned soil glittered under the pale February sun, contrasting with the gold stubble fields and the grassy pastures [adjective clause describing *pastures*] where sheep clustered around their feeding troughs.

> **Note to Instructor:** This is an unusual adjective clause because it begins with an adverb. However, it describes the pastures and answers the question *which one.*

We stood, [adverb clause describing *stood*] as we often did, eyeball to eyeball, in mutual disagreement till [noun clause acting as the object of the preposition *till* (a form of *until*)] he smiled suddenly.

[adverb clause describing *found*] When I reached the farm I found the cow comfortably ensconced in a field, in the middle of a rolling yellow ocean of buttercups.

Firstly, there was usually an anxious-faced farmer to greet me with news of [noun clause acting as the object of the preposition *of*, containing a second adverb clause modifying a verb or verb form within the noun clause] how the calf was coming when labor had started, but today I was like an unwelcome stranger.

> **Note to Instructor:** The entire clause acts as the object of the preposition. The adverb clause *when labor had started*, within the noun clause, describes the predicate of the noun clause *was coming*, and answers the question *when.*

Suddenly his teeth shone as the brown face broke into an ever-widening grin [adjective clause describing *grin*] which developed into a great shout of laughter. He was still laughing helplessly [adverb clause describing was *laughing*] when we reached the house and [adverb clause describing *leaned* and *wiped*] as I opened the kitchen door he leaned against the wall and wiped his eyes.

Review 7C: Conditional Clauses

Label the following sentences as first, second, or third conditional by writing *1*, *2*, or *3* in the blank next to each one. Underline each conditional clause. Circle each consequence clause.

These sentences are taken from *Wonder Tales from Many Lands*, by Katharine Pyle.

If you should disobey me and do this thing, you will suffer the greatest dangers, and may even pay for it with your life. 1

With the first rays of the sun, the treasure would crumble away, unless the life of a human being had been sacrificed. 2

She scarcely breathed, lest he should hear her. 1

Misfortune would come upon you if ever you entered that room. 2

> **Note to Instructor:** Within the story, it is impossible for "you" to enter the room. However, if the student answers 1, you may accept it.

If at any time I think I am going in the wrong direction, it is easy to right myself. 1

If each morning I return and find her still with you, then you shall have her for a bride after the third morning. 1

Had I known yesterday what I know to-day, I would have taken the heart of flesh out of your bosom and put in a heart of clay. 3

If no good comes of it, no harm can either. 1

If ever again you venture into my country, you shall be thrown into a dungeon and remain there as long as you live. 1

If they found anyone in the house at that time, they would surely tear him to pieces. 2

If you like, I will take you on my back and carry you down to the bottom of the sea. 1

They would have been very contented there if it had not been for a herd of buffaloes that lived on the other side of the forest. 3

If they told the ogre of the strange warrior who had come to live in their lodge, he would without doubt challenge the stranger to race with him. 2

Review 7D: Pronoun Review

The following sentences are taken from James Herriot's *The Lord God Made Them All*, the last in his four-volume memoir series.

Circle every pronoun. Label each as personal (*PER*), possessive (*POSS*), reflexive (*REF*), intensive (*INT*), demonstrative (*DEM*), interrogative (*INTER*), relative (*REL*), or indefinite (*IND*). Beside this label, add the abbreviation for the part of the sentence (or clause) that the pronoun serves as: adjective (*ADJ*), subject (*SUBJ*), predicate adjective (*PA*), direct object (*DO*), indirect object (*IO*), or object of the preposition (*OP*). (Intensive pronouns will not have one of these parts of speech—they act as appositives, which you'll cover in Lesson 94 if this is your first time through this course.)

The first has been done for you.

She (PER SUBJ) was throwing chips from a bag in her (POSS ADJ) lap to her (POSS ADJ) dog, Puppy, sitting opposite.

"But Mr. Ripley, that (DEM SUBJ)'s exactly what (REL DO) you (PER SUBJ) said last time when you (PER SUBJ) saw the blood running down my (POSS ADJ) knee. Those (DEM SUBJ) were your very words."

PER SUB · IND SUBJ · PER OP · IND ADJ · PER SUBJ · PER OP · IND SUBJ

It was difficult since neither of us spoke a word of the other's language, but I managed to get over to her that most of the sheep were of the Romney Marsh breed.

REF OP

Farmers are notoriously bad gardeners but Mr. Ripley was in a class by himself.

PER SUBJ · PER SUBJ · POSS ADJ · POSS SUBJ · PER OP · POSS ADJ

Neither Siegfried nor I suffered from insomnia, but on the rare occasions when sleep would not come we had recourse to our particular books. Mine was *The Brothers Karamazov*, a great novel, but to me, soporific in its names.

PER SUBJ · INT · PER SUBJ

I had never prescribed the stuff myself, but it was supposed to be beneficial in horses with colic and dogs with digestive troubles.

PER SUBJ · REF OP

I tipped the driving mirror down and had a look at myself.

IND ADJ · PER OP · IND ADJ · IND ADJ · POSS ADJ

There were eight strapping yearlings in there, some of them returning my stare with mild interest, others cavorting and kicking up their heels among the straw.

Note to Instructor: In this sentence, *some* and *others* are both acting as adjectives modifying *yearlings*.

INTER SUBJ · DEM PA · PER SUBJ · INTER SUBJ

"Who is this?" I asked a little breathlessly. "What on earth is the trouble?"

DEM SUBJ · PER SUBJ · PER DO · POSS ADJ

And that was a funny thing. Where was the anxious farmer? I had expected to find him pacing up and down the yard, wringing his hands, but the place seemed deserted.

Note to Instructor: The personal pronoun *him* is the direct object of the infinitive *to find*.

POSS ADJ · PER SUBJ · IND PA · IND OP · REL SUBJ · PER SUBJ

The farmer's voice thundered in my ear. He was one of the many who still thought you had to bawl lustily to cover the miles between.

Note to Instructor: The clause *you had to bawl lustily to cover the miles between* has an understood *that* introducing it and serves as the direct object of *thought*. The subject of the clause is *you* and the predicate is *had*.

Review 7E: Parsing

In the sentences below, underline every verb or verb phrase that acts as the predicate of a clause (dependent or independent). Label each verb with the correct tense, voice, and mood.

Tenses: Simple past, present, future; progressive past, present, future; perfect past, present, future

Voice: Active, passive (or state-of-being)

Mood: Indicative, subjunctive, imperative, modal, subjunctive/modal

The first is done for you.

These sentences are taken from *Seabiscuit: An American Legend*, by Laura Hillenbrand.

progressive past, active, indicative

It was raining again.

perfect past, active, indicative / perfect past, active, indicative

In 1918 he had plunked down $5,000 at an auction and walked away with the most extraordinary creature the sport had ever seen, Man o'War.

> **Note to Instructor:** The helping verb *had* belongs both to *plunked* and *walked*: he *had plunked* and *had walked*, in the same time frame.

simple present, active, subjunctive/modal / simple present, active, modal

If two track vets could confirm that the horse was really injured, Smith could scratch him.

> **Note to Instructor:** Although both verbs have the same form, *could confirm* is the main verb of the condition clause and so expresses an unreal situation.

perfect past, passive, indicative

During his sojourn in the East in 1937, Smith had been caught working Seabiscuit at night four times.

simple present, active, modal / simple present, active, modal

Hot pursuit would be Seabiscuit's downfall, but holding back might hand the race to Special Agent.

simple present, active, modal / simple present, active, modal / simple present, active, indicative / simple past, active, indicative / progressive past, active, subjunctive

Asked to run, he would drop low over the track and fall into a comical version of what horsemen call an eggbeater gait, making a spastic sideways flailing motion with his left foreleg as he swung it forward, as if he were swatting at flies.

> **Note to Instructor:** The first helping verb *would* belongs both with *drop* and with *fall* (*would drop* and *would fall*).

perfect present, active, modal

Swope must have swallowed hard.

simple future, active, indicative

I will never forget his eloquence, his wit, and his magnanimity.

progressive past, active, indicative / simple present, active, imperative

A spontaneous call was echoing over the sea of heads: "Bring on Rosemont!"

progressive past, active, indicative — progressive perfect present, active, modal

Everyone was wondering what Smith possibly could have been thinking.

simple past, passive, indicative — simple past, active, indicative — simple present, active, modal/subjunctive

Exhibit was promptly disqualified, and the stewards scheduled a meeting to determine if Pollard would have to serve a suspension for the incident.

simple past, active, indicative — simple past, active, indicative — simple past, state-of-being, indicative — perfect present, passive, modal

His jaw had a recalcitrant jut to it that implied a run-in with something—an errant hoof or an ill-placed fence post—but maybe it was the only shape in which it could have been drawn.

Review 7F: Diagramming

On your own paper, diagram every word of the following two sentences from J. R. R. Tolkien's *The Two Towers.*

Unless our enemies rest also, they will leave us far behind, if we stay to sleep.

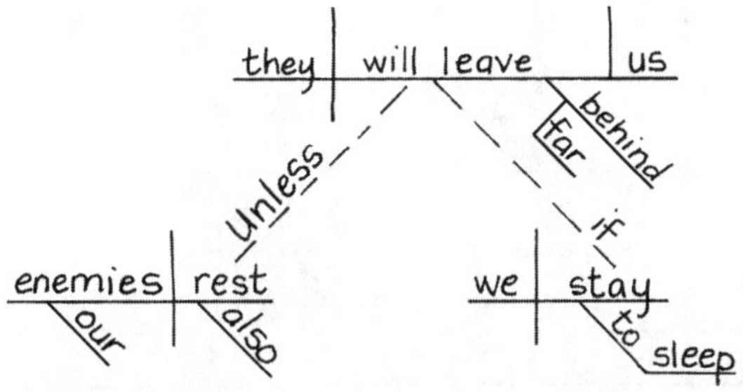

The hobbits could see that Bregalad was now listening intently, although to them, down in the dell of his ent-house, the sound of the Moot was faint.

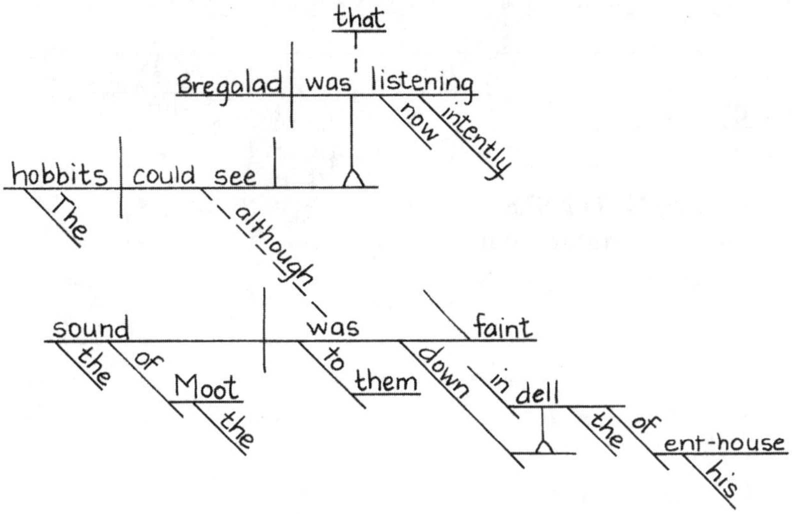

WEEK 22

Parenthetical Elements

— LESSON 85 —

Verb Review

Complete the following chart with the third-person-singular form of the verb indicated in the left-hand column. If you need help, ask your instructor.

Note to Instructor: Ask the student to make her best guess at any forms that confuse her. Then, show her the answers and have her erase (or scratch out) her incorrect answers and write in the correct ones.

INDICATIVE TENSES

		Active	Passive
SIMPLE			
betray	Past	[he, she, it] betrayed	[he, she, it] was betrayed
decorate	Present	[he, she, it] decorates	[he, she, it] is decorated
loan	Future	[he, she, it] will loan	[he, she, it] will be loaned
PROGRESSIVE			
gobble	Past	[he, she, it] was gobbling	[he, she, it] was being gobbled
sketch	Present	[he, she, it] is sketching	[he, she, it] is being sketched
prepare	Future	[he, she, it] will be preparing	[he, she, it] will be being prepared
PERFECT			
crush	Past	[he, she, it] had crushed	[he, she, it] had been crushed
stop	Present	[he, she, it] has stopped	[he, she, it] has been stopped
taunt	Future	[he, she, it] will have taunted	[he, she, it] will have been taunted

MODAL TENSES
(would OR should, may, might, must, can, could)

		Active	Passive
SIMPLE			
jump	Present	[he, she, it] would jump	
PERFECT			
yawn	Past	[he, she, it] would have yawned	

SUBJUNCTIVE TENSES

		Active	Passive
SIMPLE			
plunge	Past	[he, she, it] plunged	
terrify	Present	[he, she, it] terrify	

On your own paper, write sentences that use each of the forms above as the predicate of an independent or dependent clause. If you need help (or ideas), ask your instructor.

Note to Instructor: Model sentences using the forms in the chart are listed below. If the student needs assistance using a particular form, show him the sentence containing that form and then ask him to write a variation of it (different subject, different modifiers, etc.). Students should always be allowed to copy a model when they are confused.

Note that verbs are not used in exactly the same order as presented in the chart, since a number of them are in combination.

Elizabeth **betrayed** the hiding place of the treasure. The treasure's location **was betrayed** by Elizabeth.
A peacock feather **decorates** the hat. The hat **is decorated** by a peacock feather.
My brother **will loan** me the money. The money **will be loaned** by my brother.
The turkey **was gobbling** up the grain. The turkey dinner **was being gobbled** by our hungry family.
The artist **is sketching** the landscape. The landscape **is being sketched** by the artist.
Tomorrow, the resident chef **will be preparing** chickpea and chestnut soup. The next day, cranberry bean stew with fennel and radicchio **will be being prepared** by our guest chef.
The year before, the Roman legions **had crushed** the native British forces. The year before, the native British forces **had been crushed** by the Roman legions.
The rain has finally **stopped**. The dripping faucet **has been stopped** by the plumber.
When the first act of *Spamalot* is over, the French knights **will have taunted** King Arthur and his knights. When the first act of *Spamalot* is over, King Arthur and his knights **will have been taunted** by the French knights.
My favorite horse **would jump** any fence I put in front of him.
He was so tired that he **would have yawned**, rolled over, and gone back to sleep if the alarm had gone off.
If the temperature **plunged** that abruptly, the hikers would need to seek immediate shelter.
What if she **terrify** us with new threats?

— LESSON 86 —

Restrictive and Non-Restrictive Modifying Clauses

Parenthetical Expressions

Exercise 86A: Restrictive and Non-Restrictive Modifying Clauses

In the following sentences, mark each bolded clause as either *ADV* for adverb or *ADJ* for adjective, and draw an arrow from the clause back to the word modified. Some sentences contain more than one modifying clause.

Then, identify each adjective clause as either restrictive (*R*) or nonrestrictive (*NR*).

Finally, set off all of the nonrestrictive adjective clauses with commas. Use the proofreader's mark (^,) for comma insertion. When you are finished, compare your punctuation with the original.

These sentences are slightly condensed from *African Myths and Folk Tales,* by Carter Godwin Woodson. The original commas around the nonrestrictive clauses have been removed.

ADJ R

One of the brothers had a glass **into which he could look and find out each day everything**

ADJ R

that had happened.

ADV

While he was trying to cut through the stems a black fly began to buzz round him.

ADV

He lifted his hand to drive it away and **as he did so** he dropped the knife.

ADJ R

The place **where the rat had stopped** was near a plantain-eater's nest.

ADJ NR

This startled a monkey **which rushed forth ready for a fight**.

ADJ R

The ripe fruit fell from its stalk onto the back of an elephant **which was passing beneath**.

ADJ R

The elephant rushed away in terror and carried off a flowering creeper **which caught round his neck**.

ADJ NR

The creeper in turn pulled over an ant hill **which fell on the bush fowl's nest and broke its eggs**.

ADJ NR

Then the bush fowl stood forth and answered, "My eggs were broken by the ant hill **which**

ADJ NR ADJ NR

was pulled over by the creeper which was dragged down by the elephant which was

ADJ NR ADJ NR

knocked over by the Ntun fruit which was plucked by the monkey which was frightened

ADJ NR ADJ NR

by the plantain-eater which was startled by the rat which was scared by the serpent

ADJ NR ADJ NR

which had been jumped over by a sick woman who had been made to run by the fall of a

ADJ NR ADJ NR

knife which had been dropped by her husband who had been bitten by a black fly."

ADV

At that time, the Fangs were living on the bank of a large river, so large **that one could not see the other side.**

ADJ R

The crocodiles **that you see today** are not crocodiles any more!

ADJ R

I shall send the storm **which falls from the clouds and sweeps everything in front of him**.

ADJ R

I shall send the lightning **which flashes through the sky**.

Exercise 86B: Identifying Parenthetical Expressions

Identify each parenthetical expression as phrase, dependent clause, or sentence. These sentences are taken from John Ormsby's translation of Miguel de Cervantes Saavedra's 1605 novel *Don Quixote* (often described as the first Western novel!).

CHALLENGE EXERCISE

Provide a fuller description of each expression. What kind of phrase, clause, or sentence is it? What does it do or modify?

When you are finished, ask your instructor for the fuller explanations. Compare your descriptions to these explanations.

Note to Instructor: As long as the student is able to identify the expression as phrase, dependent clause, or sentence, you may consider the answer correct. The challenge exercise is optional. If the student has not provided the additional information included, go through each answer with her. Arrows have been inserted from adjective and adverb groups back to the words modified, in order to help you check the student's answers to the challenge exercise. You can also use this information as you go back through each answer with the student.

complete sentence,
complex sentence providing an explanation
for why there are variations on the surname

They will have it his surname was Quixada or Quesada (for here there is some difference of opinion among the authors who write on the subject), although from reasonable conjectures it seems plain that he was called Quexana.

dependent clause,
acting as an adverb, describing *was*
and answering the question *when*

You must know, then, that the above-named gentleman whenever he was at leisure (which was mostly all the year round) gave himself up to reading books of chivalry with such ardour and avidity that he almost entirely neglected the pursuit of his field-sport.

two phrases,
each one a noun renaming the curate

Many an argument did he have with the curate of his village (a learned man, and a graduate of Siguenza) as to which had been the better knight, Palmerin of England or Amadis of Gaul.

So, without giving notice of his intention to anyone, and without anybody seeing him, one

dependent clause, adjectival relative clause, describing *day*

morning before the dawning of the day (which was one of the hottest of the month of July) he donned his suit of armour, mounted Rocinante with his patched-up helmet on, braced his buckler, took his lance, and by the back door of the yard sallied forth upon the plain.

Meanwhile Don Quixote worked upon a farm labourer, a neighbour of his, an honest man

dependent clause, descriptive function; a little hard to define,
but best classified as adjectival, modifying *honest man*

(if indeed that title can be given to him who is poor), but with very little wit in his pate.

This strange spectacle at such an hour and in such a solitary place was quite enough to strike terror into Sancho's heart, and even into his master's; and (save in Don Quixote's case) did so, for all Sancho's resolution had now broken down.

phrase, adverbial, modifying *did*

All anger and gloom removed, they mounted and, without taking any fixed road (not to fix upon any being the proper thing for true knights-errant), they set out, guided by Rocinante's will.

phrase, infinitive, adverbial, modifying the participle *taking*

Therefore it seems to me it would be better (saving your worship's better judgment) if we were to go and serve some emperor or other great prince who may have some war on hand, in whose service your worship may prove the worth of your person, your great might, and greater understanding.

phrase, adverbial, participial, modifying the adjective *better*

Exercise 86C: Punctuating Sentences with Parenthetical Expressions

Correct each of the following sentences, using the proofreader's marks listed below.

delete: ℓ
insert comma: ^,
insert period: ⊙
insert exclamation point: ^!
insert question mark: ^?
move punctuation mark: ↗

If the sentence is correct, write *C* in the margin next to it.

These sentences are taken from the British best-seller *Eats, Shoots & Leaves: The Zero Tolerance Approach to Punctuation,* by Lynne Truss.

I remember, at the start of the *Two Weeks Notice* publicity campaign in the spring of 2003, emerging cheerfully from Victoria Station (was I whistling?) and stopping dead in my tracks with my fingers in my mouth.

If it were "one month's notice" there would be an apostrophe (I reasoned;), yes, and if it were "one week's notice" there would be an apostrophe.

A sign has gone up in a local charity-shop window which says, baldly, "Can you spare any old records" (no question mark) and I dither daily outside on the pavement. C

It is no accident that the word "punctilious" "(attentive to formality or etiquette)" comes from the same original root word as "punctuation."

A child sitting a County Schools exam in 1937 would be asked to punctuate the following puzzler: "Charles the First walked and talked half an hour after his head was cut off" (answer: "Charles the First walked and talked. Half an hour after, his head was cut off")⊙

Well, taking just the initial capital letters and the terminating full stop (the rest will come later.) they have not always been there.

Every time the sentence ends, there is a full stop (or a full-stop substitute such as the exclamation mark or the question mark.)

There will be those, for example, who insist that the Oxford comma is an abomination (the second comma in "ham, eggs, and chips")," whereas others are unmoved by the Oxford comma but incensed by the trend towards under-hyphenation—which the Oxford comma people have quite possibly never even noticed.

I heard from people whose work colleagues used commas instead of apostrophes; from someone rather thoughtfully recommending a restaurant called l'Apostrophe in Reims (address on request); and from a Somerset man who had cringed regularly at a sign on a market garden until he discovered that its proprietor's name was—you couldn't make it up—R. Carrott.

— LESSON 87 —

Parenthetical Expressions
Dashes

Exercise 87A: Types of Parenthetical Expressions

Identify each parenthetical expression as phrase, dependent clause, or sentence.

CHALLENGE EXERCISE

- Provide a fuller description of each expression. What kind of phrase, clause, or sentence is it? What does it do or modify?
- When you are finished, ask your instructor for the fuller explanations. Compare your descriptions to these explanations.

These sentences are taken from *The Devil's Doctor: Paracelsus and the World of Renaissance Magic and Science*, by Philip Ball.

Note to Instructor: This is a challenging assignment—give all necessary help!

phrase,
defining/explaining *Bergleute*

The hardy miners of the Harz and Saxony, known as Bergleute (mountain people), became famed throughout Europe for their skills and found employment as far afield as Serbia and Sardinia.

The Lutheran pastor Andreas Osiander explained in a sermon after an outbreak of the plague

phrase,
adverbial prepositional phrase, describing *1533* and answering the question *when*

in Nuremberg in 1533 (shortly after Paracelsus passed through the city) that "such a scourge comes perchance from the influence of the stars, from the effects of comets, from extraordinary weather conditions and changes of the air, from southerly winds, from stinking waters, or from

rotten vapours of the earth." From everything that anyone could think of, in other words—
phrase,
noun phrase, renaming/explaining the first *everything*
everything except the actual cause, a bacterium carried by fleas on the back of black rats.

Aristotle wrote very widely and was happy enough to draw analogies between disparate
dependent clause,
adjectival, modifying *topics*
phenomena, but he was conspicuously silent on some topics (such as what we would now call chemistry) and gives little impression of the need for congruence and continuity.

The central distinction between the mystical magus like Paracelsus and the academics at the universities was that, while the latter tended to believe that these rules had already been deduced by the ancients through the power of pure thought and logic, the magical adepts thought that
phrase containing a second parenthetical element, participle phrase acting as an adverb and modifying *studying*
dependent clause, occurring within the first parenthetical element, acting as an adverb and modifying *studying*
they could be found only by studying nature—crudely speaking (and I shall be more precise later), by experiment.

But much of contemporary science is itself occult in the Renaissance sense, insofar as it is
phrase,
participle phrase acting as an adverb and modifying *is "hidden."* The expression *of course* acts as a second parenthetical expression within the participle phrase.
"hidden" from our senses—that, of course, being the literal meaning of the word.

sentence,
providing additional detail about the name *Hohenheim Castle*
Hohenheim Castle stood near Stuttgart in Swabia, and it was the seat (the name means "mountain home") of Conrad Bombast, who died in 1299.

sentence,
providing additional information about the subject *Paracelsus*
Paracelsus is often credited with coining the name himself (he was fond of naming things), an
phrase,
providing the German and English names of the metals after which zinc was named
amalgam of the two metals (zinne and kupfer; tin and copper) that zinc somewhat resembles.

This scholastic tradition allowed that one might mine the "scientific" aspects of the Greek and
dependent clause,
providing further information about the "scientific" aspects mentioned
Roman world—so that Ptolemy's astronomy, Galen's medicine, and Aristotle's physics and logic were all standard components of the curriculum—but insisted that the poetry, moral philosophy, and literature of these pagans was best left untouched.

phrase, noun phrase, renaming/defining *Alpenus*
dependent clause, acting as an adjective and modifying *Alpenus*
Paracelsus takes the nickname Alpenus—a man from the Alpine slopes—which becomes corrupted to Arpenus or Arpinas, from which it is a short step to Orpinas and then to legendary Orpheus, a central character in the great tradition of natural magic, who gained victory over death.

Note to Instructor: The dependent clause *which becomes corrupted...victory over death* is the second parenthetical element, but within it are two more dependent clauses, *from which it is a short... natural magic*, and *who gained victory over death*. However, the entire clause is still a parenthetical element: the independent clause that makes up the main sentence is simply *Paracelsus takes the nickname Alpenus*.

Exercise 87B: Punctuating Parenthetical Expressions

On either side of each bolded parenthetical expression, place parentheses, dashes, or commas. There are not necessarily correct answers for these, but compare them to the originals when you have finished.

These sentences are taken from a collection of short stories by Robert Louis Stevenson.

Note to Instructor: The original versions of Stevenson's sentences are below and reflect the author's intentions; any grammatical answers are acceptable, but where the student has chosen different punctuation, ask him to read first his version, and then Stevenson's, out loud.

"Will O'the Mill"

And then the river goes out into the lowlands, and waters the great corn country, and runs through a sight of fine cities (**so they say**) where kings live all alone in great palaces, with a sentry walking up and down before the door.

It seemed like a great conspiracy of things animate and inanimate; they all went downward, fleetly and gaily downward, and only he, **it seemed**, remained behind, like a stock upon the wayside.

It scarcely seemed to have been the girl's doing—**it seemed as if things had merely so fallen out**—that she and her father took their departure that same afternoon in a farm-cart.

He hoped, **on the whole**, she would refuse him.

"The Treasure of Franchard"

We have now arrived at some idea of the composition of the gang—**for I incline to the hypothesis of more than one**—and we now leave this room, which can disclose no more, and turn our attention to the court and garden.

Besides—**and this is an argument exactly suited to your intellectual level**—many of them are English and American. Where else should we expect to find a thief?

And yet, **you will bear me out**, I supported the emotion nobly.

You have your usual flow of spirits, **I perceive**, but even less than your usual deliberation.

Some of the turtle is still left—**the most wholesome of delicacies**—and we are not a penny the worse.

"Olalla"

If they knew you were the handsomest and the most pleasant man that ever came from England (**where I am told that handsome men are common, but pleasant ones not so much so**) they would doubtless make you welcome with a better grace.

Note to Instructor: If the student uses parentheses around the bolded expression, the comma after the closing parenthesis helps to separate the opening dependent clause from the main clause. If commas or dashes are used, the comma is unnecessary.

To me, **indeed**, it seems discourteous.

Now she would speak of the warmth in which (**like her son**) she greatly delighted.

Here was a solution; and yet when I called to mind the cries (**which I never did without a shuddering chill**), it seemed altogether insufficient.

I told her you had done so—**I remembered that**—and she was pleased.

I dwell, or I think I dwell **(if I exist at all)**, somewhere apart, **an impotent prisoner**, carried about and deafened by a mob that I disown.

> **Note to Instructor:** If the student uses parentheses around the bolded expression, the comma after the closing parenthesis is optional. If commas or dashes are used, the comma is unnecessary.

When she was young–**God help me, I fear I neglected that wild lamb**–she was surely sane.

Exercise 87C: Using Dashes for Emphasis

On your own paper, rewrite the next five sentences, substituting dashes for the underlined punctuation marks and making any other capitalization or punctuation changes needed.

These sentences are taken from the classic early-twentieth-century novella (short novel, halfway between a short story and a full-length novel) *Typhoon*, by Joseph Conrad.

They are seas full of every-day, eloquent facts, such as islands, sand-banks, reefs, swift and changeable currents (tangled facts that nevertheless speak to a seaman in clear and definite language).

There were matters of duty, of course. Directions, orders, and so on; but the past being to his mind done with, and the future not there yet, the more general actualities of the day required no comment, because facts can speak for themselves with overwhelming precision.

But he had never been given a glimpse of immeasurable strength and of immoderate wrath, the wrath that passes exhausted but never appeased: the wrath and fury of the passionate sea.

There are on sea and land such men thus fortunate, or thus disdained by destiny or by the sea.

The old people ultimately became acquainted with a good many names of ships, and with the names of the skippers who commanded them: with the names of Scots and English shipowners; with the names of seas, oceans, straits, promontories; with outlandish names of lumber-ports, of rice-ports, of cotton-ports; with the names of islands; with the name of their son's young woman.

Original sentences:

They are seas full of every-day, eloquent facts, such as islands, sand-banks, reefs, swift and changeable currents—tangled facts that nevertheless speak to a seaman in clear and definite language.

There were matters of duty, of course—directions, orders, and so on; but the past being to his mind done with, and the future not there yet, the more general actualities of the day required no comment—because facts can speak for themselves with overwhelming precision.

But he had never been given a glimpse of immeasurable strength and of immoderate wrath, the wrath that passes exhausted but never appeased—the wrath and fury of the passionate sea.

There are on sea and land such men thus fortunate—or thus disdained by destiny or by the sea.

The old people ultimately became acquainted with a good many names of ships, and with the names of the skippers who commanded them—with the names of Scots and English shipowners—with the names of seas, oceans, straits, promontories—with outlandish names of lumber-ports, of rice-ports, of cotton-ports—with the names of islands—with the name of their son's young woman.

— LESSON 88 —

Parenthetical Expressions
Dashes
Diagramming Parenthetical Expressions

Exercise 88A: Diagramming Parenthetical Expressions

On your own paper, diagram each of the following sentences.

These sentences are taken from short stories written by O. Henry (the pen name of the writer William Sidney Porter). These are meant to be challenging! Do your best, and ask your instructor for help if you get frustrated. When you are finished, compare your answers to the Key. There may be more than one way to diagram these elements!

"The Skylight Room"
Your hand crept to your throat, you gasped, you looked up as from a well—and breathed once more.

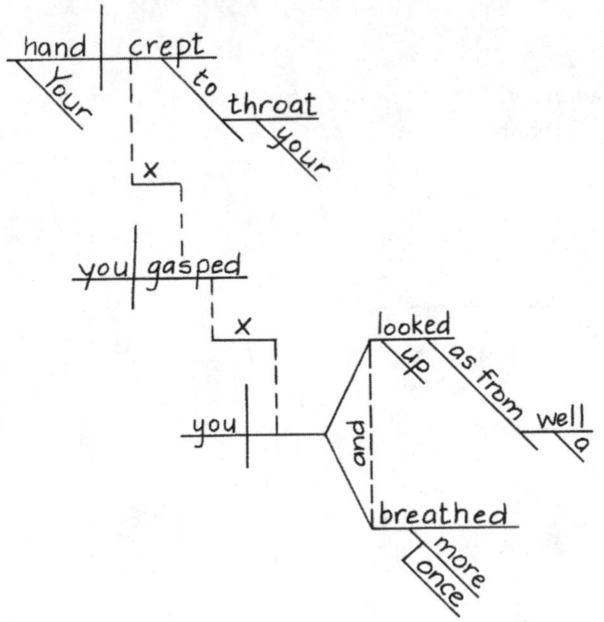

Note to Instructor: The three independent clauses (*your hand crept..., you gasped, you looked...and breathed* are connected by Xs, representing the commas. In the final clause, the parenthetical *and breathed once more* functions, grammatically, as the second predicate to the subject *you*.

In the next morning's paper I saw a little news item, and the last sentence of it may help you (as it helped me) to weld the incidents together.

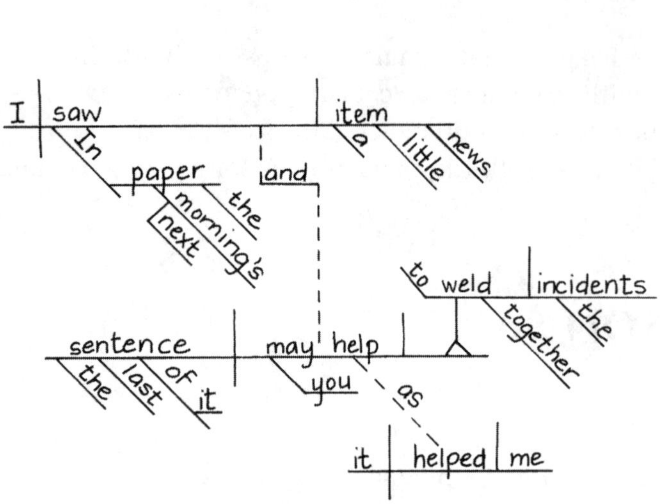

> **Note to Instructor:** The prepositional phrase *in the morning's paper* might prove difficult. Since it answers the question *where* it is adverbial, modifying the verb *saw*. The article *the* modifies *paper*; the possessive adjective *morning's* also modifies *paper*, while *next* is an adverb modifying *morning's*.
>
> The parenthetical expression *as it helped me* is a dependent clause modifying the predicate *may help*.
>
> I have diagrammed the infinitive phrase *to weld the incidents together* as the direct object of *may help* and *you* as the indirect object, on the model of a sentence such as "threw me the frisbee." But an argument also could be made for diagramming *me* as the direct object and the infinitive phrase as adverbial, describing the predicate and answering the question *how*.

"The Cop and the Anthem"

Soapy, with disgust in his heart, loafed along, twice unsuccessful.

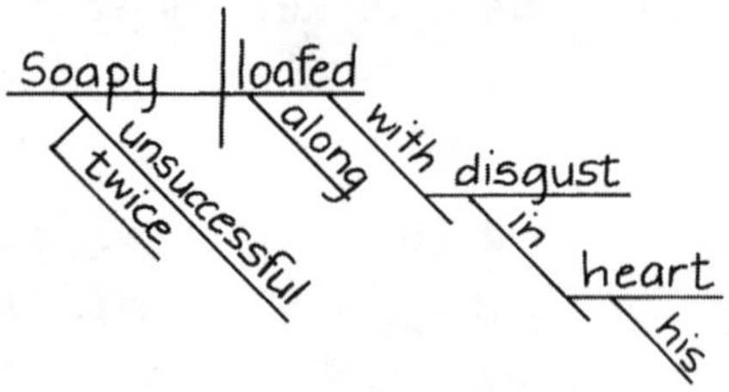

> **Note to Instructor:** *With disgust in his heart* is simply an adverbial prepositional phrase describing how Soapy loafed. *Twice unsuccessful* is a parenthetical expression that may seem to be adverbial, but it doesn't describe how Soapy loafed—it describes Soapy himself. (The adverbial form would be *unsuccessfully*.)

Through one violet-stained window a soft light glowed, where, no doubt, the organist loitered over the keys, making sure of his mastery of the coming Sabbath anthem.

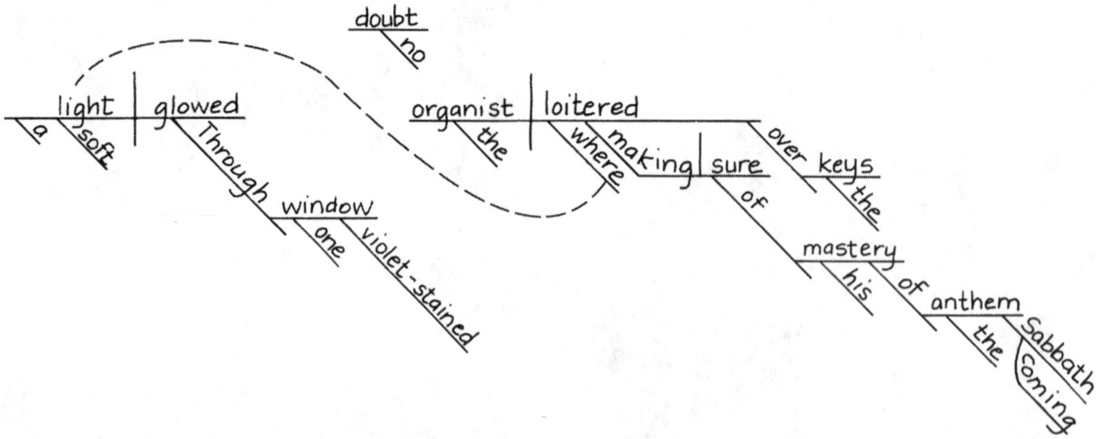

> **Note to Instructor:** The dependent clause *where...anthem* is interrupted by the parenthetical expression *no doubt*, which is diagrammed separately. The clause itself is an adjective clause introduced by a relative adverb; the adverb *where* refers back to the light, not the window (the light comes through the window, but the organist is in the light, not in the window). *Coming* modifies *Sabbath*, not *anthem*, because it is the Sabbath that is coming.

"An Adjustment of Nature"

In Cypher's she belonged—in the bacon smoke, the cabbage perfume, the grand, Wagnerian chorus of hurled ironstone china and rattling casters.

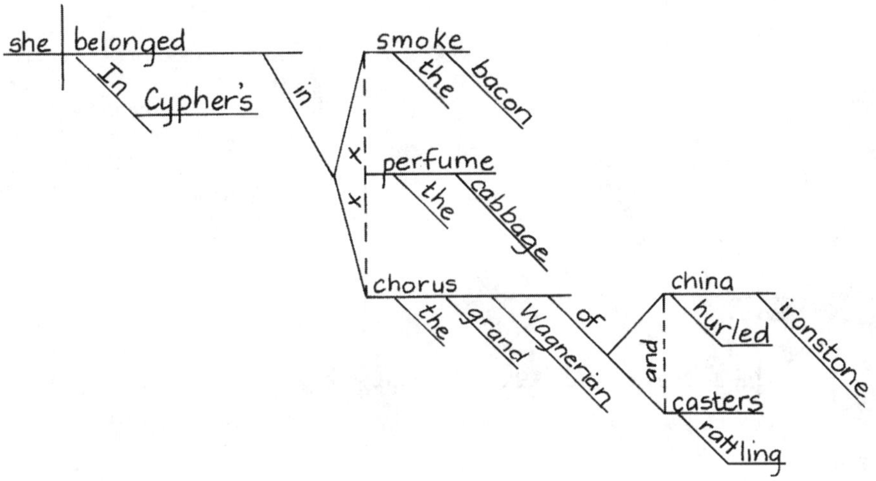

Note to Instructor: The parenthetical expression set off by the dash functions as an adverb, answering the question *where*. Notice that both *hurled* and *rattling* are verb forms serving as adjectives (past participle and present participle) and should both be diagrammed on a bent line.

And then Milly loomed up with a thousand dishes on her bare arm—loomed up big and white and pink and awful as Mount Saint Elias—with a smile like day breaking in a gulch.

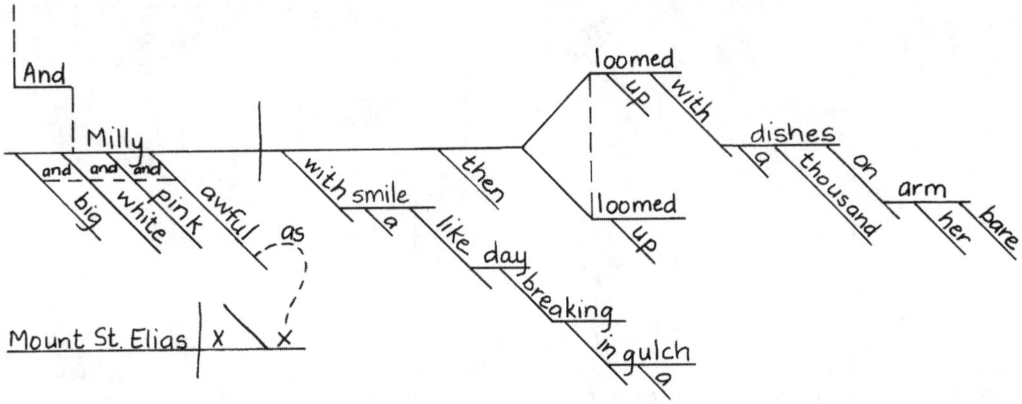

Note to Instructor: If the student diagrams the parenthetical expression as a separate unconnected element, you may accept this, but show her my alternate diagram. I have diagrammed the two occurrences of *loomed* as a compound predicate because they both have the same relationship to the subject. The adverb *then* and the adverbial phrase *with a smile...gulch* modify both occurrences of the verb *loomed*, so I have diagrammed them after the vertical divider but before the branch of the compound predicates.

In my diagram, although the adjectives *big, white, pink*, and *awful* come after *loomed*, they actually describe Milly, so are diagrammed beneath the subject. The difficulty with diagramming the parenthetical element separately is that all four of these words would have to be functioning as adverbs, not adjectives. English does occasionally use adjective forms as adverbs, but I think it is hard to argue that all four of these are modifying *loomed*.

As Mount Saint Elias is an adverbial dependent clause, modifying *awful* and containing understood elements: *awful as Mount Saint Elias [is awful]*.

"A Ramble in Aphasia"

She laughed softly, with a strange quality in the sound—it was a laugh of happiness— and of content—and of misery.

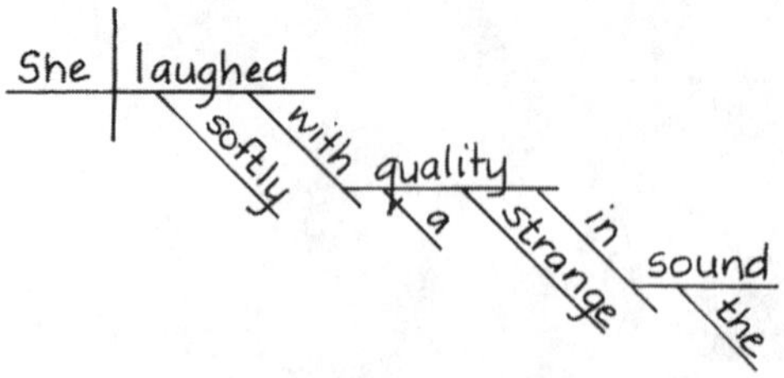

Note to Instructor: The entire parenthetical expression *it was a laugh...of misery* is an independent element. Within that expression, *and of content* and *and of misery* both function as adjectives modifying the predicate nominative *laugh*.

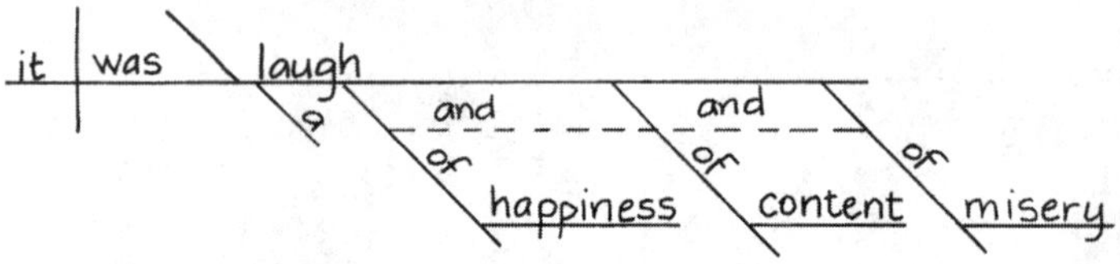

"A Municipal Report"

At nine o'clock on the next morning, after my chicken livers en brochette (try them if you can find that hotel), I strayed out into the drizzle, which was still on for an unlimited run.

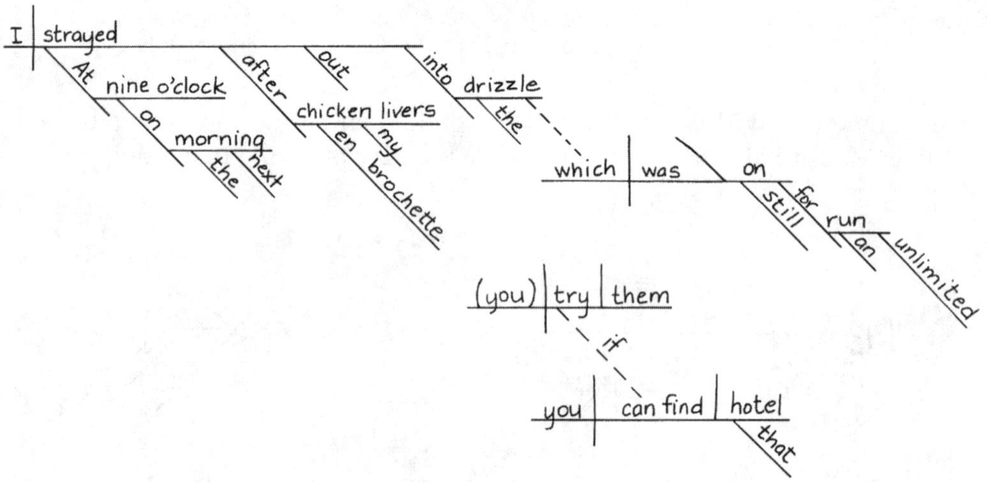

Note to Instructor: I have diagrammed *chicken livers* as a compound noun and *en brochette* ("on a skewer") as a compound adjective, but the student could also diagram *chicken* as an adjective modifying *livers*, or diagram *chicken livers en brochette* as a single compound noun all on the same line.

In the adjective clause *which was still on for an unlimited run*, the word *on* is tricky! *On* is one of those short English words that can function in several ways—as a preposition ("on the waterfront"), as an adverb answering the question *how* ("she soldiered on"), or as an adjective ("the light was on"). Here, it functions as a predicate adjective. Words with multiple functions are covered in detail in Week 27, but if this is the student's first time through the course he may not be aware of this. You might want to point out that a linking verb is much more likely to be followed by a predicate adjective than modified by an adverb!

The parenthetical expression is grammatically separate and contains an adverbial dependent clause.

WEEK 23

Dialogue and Quotations

— LESSON 89 —

Dialogue

Exercise 89A: Punctuating Dialogue

The excerpt below is from the mystery novel *The Murder of Roger Ackroyd*, by Agatha Christie. All of the dialogue is missing quotation marks, and some of it is missing ending punctuation as well. Do your best to supply the missing punctuation marks. (Don't use proofreader's marks—just write the punctuation directly into the sentences.)

When you are finished, compare your version with the original.

Note to Instructor: The original version is below. You may assign the student the task of comparing the original punctuation with her edited version. Ask her to circle any differences with a colored pencil; this will help her pay close attention to the correct punctuation.

Mrs. Ferrars' husband died just over a year ago, and Caroline has constantly asserted, without the least foundation for the assertion, that his wife poisoned him.

She scorns my invariable rejoinder that Mr. Ferrars died of acute gastritis, helped on by habitual overindulgence in alcoholic beverages. The symptoms of gastritis and arsenical poisoning are not, I agree, unlike, but Caroline bases her accusation on quite different lines.

"You've only got to look at her," I have heard her say.

Mrs. Ferrars, though not in her first youth, was a very attractive woman, and her clothes, though simple, always seemed to fit her very well, but all the same, lots of women buy their clothes in Paris, and have not, on that account, necessarily poisoned their husbands.

As I stood hesitating in the hall, with all this passing through my mind, Caroline's voice came again, with a sharper note in it.

"What on earth are you doing out there, James? Why don't you come and get your breakfast?"

"Just coming, my dear," I said hastily. "I've been hanging up my overcoat."

"You could have hung up half a dozen overcoats in this time."

She was quite right. I could have.

I walked into the dining-room, gave Caroline the accustomed peck on the cheek, and sat down to eggs and bacon. The bacon was rather cold.

"You've had an early call," remarked Caroline.

"Yes," I said. "King's Paddock. Mrs. Ferrars."

"I know," said my sister.

"How did you know?"

"Annie told me."

Annie is the house parlourmaid. A nice girl, but an inveterate talker.

There was a pause. I continued to eat eggs and bacon. My sister's nose, which is long and thin, quivered a little at the tip, as it always does when she is interested or excited over anything.

"Well?" she demanded.

"A sad business. Nothing to be done. Must have died in her sleep."

"I know," said my sister again.

This time I was annoyed.

"You can't know," I snapped. "I didn't know myself until I got there, and haven't mentioned it to a soul yet. If that girl Annie knows, she must be a clairvoyant."

"It wasn't Annie who told me. It was the milkman. He had it from the Ferrarses' cook."

As I say, there is no need for Caroline to go out to get information. She sits at home and it comes to her.

My sister continued:

"What did she die of? Heart failure?"

"Didn't the milkman tell you that?" I inquired sarcastically.

Sarcasm is wasted on Caroline. She takes it seriously and answers accordingly.

"He didn't know," she explained.

After all, Caroline was bound to hear sooner or later. She might as well hear from me.

"She died of an overdose of veronal. She's been taking it lately for sleeplessness. Must have taken too much."

"Nonsense," said Caroline immediately. "She took it on purpose. Don't tell me!"

Exercise 89B: Writing Dialogue Correctly

On your own paper, rewrite the following sentences as dialogue, using the past tense for the dialogue tags. Use the notations in parentheses to help you.

You may choose to place dialogue tags before, in the middle of, or after dialogue, or to leave the tags out completely. But you must have at least one sentence with a dialogue tag that comes before, at least one sentence with a dialogue tag that comes after, at least one speech with the dialogue tag in the middle, and at least one speech with no dialogue tag at all.

When you are finished, compare your answers with the original. The first is done for you.

This passage was taken from *Emily of New Moon*, by L. M. Montgomery. In this scene, Emily, a high school student who lives with her stern Aunt Elizabeth, her mild Aunt Laura, and her Cousin Jimmy, has offended her teacher, Miss Brownell. Miss Brownell is a vindictive teacher who doesn't like Emily, and she has come to Emily's home to tell Elizabeth, Laura, and Jimmy the worst possible version of what happened at school during the day. The farmhand, Perry, is also in high school; he saw what happened, and he's listening to the conversation from the loft above the kitchen, where he sleeps.

The text in italics is part of the scene and should be included in your final version, but it isn't dialogue.

(Aunt Elizabeth says) You have been behaving disgracefully in school. I am ashamed of you.

(Emily says, steadily) It was not as bad as that, Aunt Elizabeth. You see it was this way—

(Aunt Elizabeth says) I don't want to hear anything more about it.

(Emily cries) But you must. It isn't fair to listen only to HER side. I was a little bad—but not so bad as she says—

(Aunt Elizabeth says, grimly) Not another word! I have heard the whole story.

(Suddenly sticking his head down through the black hole, Perry says) You heard a pack of lies.

Everybody jumped—even Aunt Elizabeth, who at once became angrier than ever because she HAD jumped.

(Aunt Elizabeth commands) Perry Miller, come down out of that loft instantly!

(Perry says laconically) Can't.

(Aunt Elizabeth says) At once, I say!

(Perry repeats, winking audaciously at Miss Brownell) Can't.

(Aunt Elizabeth says) Perry Miller, come down! I WILL be obeyed. I am mistress here YET.

(Perry says cheerfully) Oh, all right. If I must.

He swung himself down until his toes touched the ladder. Aunt Laura gave a little shriek. Everybody also seemed to be stricken dumb.

(Perry is saying cheerfully, waving his legs about to get a foothold on the ladder while he hangs on to the sides of the black hole with his elbows) I've just got my wet duds off. Fell into the brook when I was watering the cows. Was going to put on dry ones—but just as you say—

(Aunt Elizabeth implores, not able to cope with the situation) Jimmy.

(Cousin Jimmy orders) Perry, get back into that loft and get your clothes on this minute!

First answer:

"You have been behaving disgracefully in school," said Aunt Elizabeth. "I am ashamed of you."

> **Note to Instructor:** Allow the student to compare his answers with the original text below, but accept any grammatical rewriting.

"You have been behaving disgracefully in school," said Aunt Elizabeth. "I am ashamed of you."

"It was not as bad as that, Aunt Elizabeth," said Emily steadily. "You see it was this way—"

Aunt Elizabeth said, "I don't want to hear anything more about it."

"But you must," cried Emily. "It isn't fair to listen only to HER side. I was a little bad—but not so bad as she says—"

"Not another word! I have heard the whole story," said Aunt Elizabeth grimly.

"You heard a pack of lies," said Perry, suddenly sticking his head down through the black hole.

Everybody jumped—even Aunt Elizabeth, who at once became angrier than ever because she HAD jumped.

"Perry Miller, come down out of that loft instantly!" she commanded.

"Can't," said Perry laconically.

"At once, I say!"

"Can't," repeated Perry, winking audaciously at Miss Brownell.

"Perry Miller, come down! I WILL be obeyed. I am mistress here YET."

"Oh, all right," said Perry cheerfully. "If I must."

He swung himself down until his toes touched the ladder. Aunt Laura gave a little shriek. Everybody also seemed to be stricken dumb.

"I've just got my wet duds off," Perry was saying cheerfully, waving his legs about to get a foothold on the ladder while he hung to the sides of the black hole with his elbows. "Fell into the brook when I was watering the cows. Was going to put on dry ones—but just as you say—"

"Jimmy," implored poor Elizabeth Murray. She could not cope with the situation.

"Perry, get back into that loft and get your clothes on this minute!" ordered Cousin Jimmy.

Exercise 89C: Proofreading

Using the following proofreader's marks, correct these incorrect sentences. The originals are from *The Hunger Games*, by Suzanne Collins.

Insert quotation marks:
insert comma:
insert period:
insert question mark:
insert exclamation point:
delete:
move punctuation mark:

"Prim"! The strangled cry comes out of my throat, and my muscles begin to move again "Prim"!

"I volunteer! I gasp "I volunteer as tribute!

Prim is screaming hysterically behind me. She's wrapped her skinny arms around me like a vise "No, Katniss! No! You can't go"!

"Prim, let go" I say harshly, because this is upsetting me and I don't want to cry.

"Well, bravo! gushes Effie Trinket, "That's the spirit of the Games!" She's pleased to finally have a district with a little action going on in it "What's your name"?

I swallow hard, "Katniss Everdeen I say.

"What an exciting day" she warbles as she attempts to straighten her wig, which has listed severely to the right "But more excitement to come! It's time to choose our boy tribute"!

— LESSON 90 —

Dialogue

Direct Quotations

Exercise 90A: Punctuating Dialogue

The passages of dialogue below, from Suzanne Collins's *Catching Fire*, are missing punctuation. Write in all of the missing punctuation marks (insert them directly rather than using proofreader's marks). When you are finished, compare your answers to the original.

Why would he paint a picture of me, Effie I ask somehow annoyed.

To show that he's going to do everything he can to defend you. That's what everyone in the Capitol's expecting, anyway Didn't he volunteer to go in with you Effie says, as if it's the most obvious thing in the world.

Actually, I painted a picture of Rue Peeta says How she looked after Katniss had covered her in flowers

There's a long pause at the table while everyone absorbs this. And what exactly were you trying to accomplish Haymitch asks in a very measured voice.

I'm not sure. I just wanted to hold them accountable, if only for a moment says Peeta...

"This is dreadful Effie sounds like she's about to cry. That sort of thinking...it's forbidden, Peeta. Absolutely. You'll only bring down more trouble on yourself and Katniss.

I have to agree with Effie on this one says Haymitch. Portia and Cinna remain silent, but their faces are very serious...

I guess this is a bad time to mention I hung a dummy and painted Seneca Crane's name on it I say.

> **Note to Instructor:** The original text is found below. You may accept grammatical variations (for example, an exclamation point at the end of a speech rather than a comma or period), but ask the student to compare his version with the original. How does the change in punctuation affect the passage?

"Why would he paint a picture of me, Effie?" I ask, somehow annoyed.

"To show that he's going to do everything he can to defend you. That's what everyone in the Capitol's expecting, anyway. Didn't he volunteer to go in with you?" Effie says, as if it's the most obvious thing in the world.

"Actually, I painted a picture of Rue," Peeta says. "How she looked after Katniss had covered her in flowers."

There's a long pause at the table while everyone absorbs this. "And what exactly were you trying to accomplish?" Haymitch asks in a very measured voice.

"I'm not sure. I just wanted to hold them accountable, if only for a moment," says Peeta...

"This is dreadful." Effie sounds like she's about to cry. "That sort of thinking...it's forbidden, Peeta. Absolutely. You'll only bring down more trouble on yourself and Katniss."

"I have to agree with Effie on this one," says Haymitch. Portia and Cinna remain silent, but their faces are very serious...

"I guess this is a bad time to mention I hung a dummy and painted Seneca Crane's name on it," I say.

Exercise 90B: Punctuating Direct Quotations

Write in all of the missing punctuation marks (insert them directly rather than using proofreader's marks). When you are finished, compare your answers to the original sentences.

These sentences have been slightly condensed from the classic study *The Common People of Ancient Rome*, by Frank Frost Abbott.

Now and then, too, a serious writer has occasion to use a bit of popular Latin, but he conveniently labels it for us with an apologetic phrase. Thus even St. Jerome, in his commentary on the Epistle to the Ephesians, says Don't look a gift horse in the mouth, as the vulgar proverb has it.

Sometimes a dramatic, lifelike touch is given by putting the inscription into the form of a dialogue between the dead and those who are left behind. Upon a stone found near Rome runs the inscription Hail, dear Stephanus, Moschis and Diodorus salute thee. To which the dead man replies Hail, chaste wife, hail Diodorus, my friend, my brother.

One tombstone reads Into nothing from nothing how quickly we go and another Once we were not, now we are as we were.

It was in these circumstances that the consul Marcellus cried out If I am prevented by the vote of the senate from taking steps for the public safety, I will take such steps on my own responsibility as consul. After saying this he darted out of the senate and presented a sword to Pompey, and said I command you to march against Cæsar in behalf of your country.

To this ill-fated campaign Cæsar devotes the latter half of the second book of his *Civil War*. In the beginning of his account of it he remarks Showing at the outset a total contempt for the military strength of his opponent, Curio crossed over from Sicily, accompanied by only two of the four legions originally given him by Cæsar, and by only five hundred cavalry.

As he himself puts it in his letter to Cicero I did not follow a Cæsar, but a friend.

Note to Instructor: The original sentences are found below.

Now and then, too, a serious writer has occasion to use a bit of popular Latin, but he conveniently labels it for us with an apologetic phrase. Thus even St. Jerome, in his commentary on the Epistle to the Ephesians, says, "Don't look a gift horse in the mouth, as the vulgar proverb has it."

Sometimes a dramatic, lifelike touch is given by putting the inscription into the form of a dialogue between the dead and those who are left behind. Upon a stone found near Rome runs the inscription, "Hail, dear Stephanus, Moschis and Diodorus salute thee." To which the dead man replies, "Hail, chaste wife, hail Diodorus, my friend, my brother."

One tombstone reads, "Into nothing from nothing how quickly we go," and another, "Once we were not, now we are as we were."

It was in these circumstances that the consul Marcellus cried out, "If I am prevented by the vote of the senate from taking steps for the public safety, I will take such steps on my own responsibility as consul." After saying this he darted out of the senate and presented a sword to Pompey, and said, "I command you to march against Cæsar in behalf of your country."

To this ill-fated campaign Cæsar devotes the latter half of the second book of his *Civil War*. In the beginning of his account of it he remarks, "Showing at the outset a total contempt for the military strength of his opponent, Curio crossed over from Sicily, accompanied by only two of the four legions originally given him by Cæsar, and by only five hundred cavalry."

As he himself puts it in his letter to Cicero, "I did not follow a Cæsar, but a friend."

Exercise 90C: Attribution Tags

In the following paragraphs, slightly condensed from *The Story of Prague*, by Count Francis Lützow, find and underline the direct quotes that are missing their attribution tags. Some sentences are not missing any attribution tags. When you are finished, ask your instructor to check your work.

Then, compare the paragraphs with the originals found in the answer key. Circle each attribution tag in the Answer Key.

Note to Instructor: The original paragraphs follow the exercise. A key below identifies the attribution tag that should be circled in each paragraph. Do not allow the student to read the key before he identifies each tag.

Libussa, though the youngest, succeeded her father as ruler of Bohemia, "<u>a wonderful woman among women, chaste in body, righteous in her morals, second to none as judge over the people</u>."

The successor of St. Wenceslas, Boleslav I, whom František Palacký calls "one of the most powerful monarchs that ever occupied the Bohemian throne," greatly extended the frontiers of his country.

Many monks, priests and Germans who had left Prague during the recent disturbances returned, believing that the hour of their triumph had come. "The Germans laughed and joyfully clapped their hands, saying, 'now these heretical Hussites and Wycliffites will perish, and there will be an end of them.'"

The old chronicler Benes of Weitmil tells us that "Charles, King of the Romans and of Bohemia, laid the first stone, and founded the new city of Prague."

The new foundation seems to have been very successful from the first. "The University became so great that nothing equal to it existed in all Germany; and students came there from all parts."

The burning of Wycliffe's works met with almost universal disapproval at Prague. "Instantly a great sedition and discord began. Some said that many other books besides those of Wycliffe had been burnt; therefore the people began to riot."

Sigismund had remained in the rear with part of his army, and returned to his camp as soon as he saw the defeat of his troops. The King "smiled—it is said—over the fate of the brave Christians who had succumbed to the heretics, who had triumphed over them."

Note to Instructor: Here are the original paragraphs for the student's reference. After completing the exercises in her workbook, she should circle each attribution tag below.

Libussa, though the youngest, succeeded her father as ruler of Bohemia. Libussa is described by the ancient chronicler Cosmas of Prague as "a wonderful woman among women, chaste in body, righteous in her morals, second to none as judge over the people."

The successor of St. Wenceslas, Boleslav I, whom František Palacký calls "one of the most powerful monarchs that ever occupied the Bohemian throne," greatly extended the frontiers of his country.

Many monks, priests and Germans who had left Prague during the recent disturbances returned, believing that the hour of their triumph had come. A contemporary chronicler tells us that "the Germans laughed and joyfully clapped their hands, saying, 'now these heretical Hussites and Wycliffites will perish, and there will be an end of them.'"

The old chronicler Benes of Weitmil tells us that "Charles, King of the Romans and of Bohemia, laid the first stone, and founded the new city of Prague."

The new foundation seems to have been very successful from the first. Benes of Weitmil writes, "The University became so great that nothing equal to it existed in all Germany; and students came there from all parts."

The burning of Wycliffe's works met with almost universal disapproval at Prague. A contemporary chronicler writes, "Instantly a great sedition and discord began. Some said that many other books besides those of Wycliffe had been burnt; therefore the people began to riot."

Sigismund had remained in the rear with part of his army, and returned to his camp as soon as he saw the defeat of his troops. According to the Austrian chronicler Ebendorf of Haselbach, the King "smiled—it is said—over the fate of the brave Christians who had succumbed to the heretics, who had triumphed over them."

Key: **The following attribution tags should be circled.**
Student: **Do not read this key until you have completed the exercise!**

Paragraph #1: Libussa is described by the ancient chronicler Cosmas of Prague as
Paragraph #2: whom František Palacký calls
Paragraph #3: A contemporary chronicler tells us that
Paragraph #4: The old chronicler Benes of Weitmil tells us that
Paragraph #5: Benes of Weitmil writes
Paragraph #6: A contemporary chronicler writes
Paragraph #7: According to the Austrian chronicler Ebendorf of Haselbach

— LESSON 91 —

Direct Quotations
Ellipses
Partial Quotations

Exercise 91A: Using Ellipses

The following six paragraphs are taken from the official Army account of the bombing of the Japanese city of Hiroshima, on August 6, 1945. It was published a year later, in the summer of 1946. The preface reads, "This report describes the effects of the atomic bombs which were dropped on the Japanese cities of Hiroshima and Nagasaki on August 6 and 9, 1945, respectively. It summarizes all the authentic information that is available on damage to structures, injuries to personnel, morale effect, etc., which can be released at this time without prejudicing the security of the United States."

The total word count is 538. Using a word processing program, retype the passage but condense it so that it has no more than 350 words. Do not cut the opening or closing words of any paragraph. Make sure that you don't end up with run-on sentences or fragments!

When you are finished, compare your version with the condensed version found in the Answer Key.

Hiroshima was the primary target of the first atomic bomb mission. The mission went smoothly in every respect. The weather was good, and the crew and equipment functioned perfectly. In every detail, the attack was carried out exactly as planned, and the bomb performed exactly as expected.

The bomb exploded over Hiroshima at 8:15 on the morning of August 6, 1945. About an hour previously, the Japanese early warning radar net had detected the approach of some American aircraft headed for the southern part of Japan. The alert had been given and radio broadcasting stopped in many cities, among them Hiroshima. The planes approached the coast at a very high altitude. At nearly 8:00 A.M., the radar operator in Hiroshima determined that the number of planes coming in was very small—probably not more than three—and the air raid alert was lifted. The normal radio broadcast warning was given to the people that it might be advisable to go to shelter if B-29's were actually sighted, but no raid was expected beyond some sort of reconnaissance. At 8:15 A.M., the bomb exploded with a blinding flash in the sky, and a great rush of air and a loud rumble of noise extended for many miles around the city; the first blast was soon followed by the sounds of falling buildings and of growing fires, and a great cloud of dust and smoke began to cast a pall of darkness over the city.

At 8:16 A.M., the Tokyo control operator of the Japanese Broadcasting Corporation noticed that the Hiroshima station had gone off the air. He tried to use another telephone line to reestablish his program, but it too had failed. About twenty minutes later the Tokyo railroad telegraph center realized that the main line telegraph had stopped working just north of Hiroshima. From some small railway stops within ten miles of the city there came unofficial and confused reports of a terrible explosion in Hiroshima. All these reports were transmitted to the Headquarters of the Japanese General Staff.

Military headquarters repeatedly tried to call the Army Control Station in Hiroshima. The complete silence from that city puzzled the men at Headquarters; they knew that no large enemy raid could have occurred, and they knew that no sizeable store of explosives was in Hiroshima at that time. A young officer of the Japanese General Staff was instructed to fly immediately to Hiroshima, to land, survey the damage, and return to Tokyo with reliable information for the staff. It was generally felt at Headquarters that nothing serious had taken place, that it was all a terrible rumor starting from a few sparks of truth.

The staff officer went to the airport and took off for the southwest. After flying for about three hours, while still nearly 100 miles from Hiroshima, he and his pilot saw a great cloud of smoke from the bomb. In the bright afternoon, the remains of Hiroshima were burning.

Their plane soon reached the city, around which they circled in disbelief. A great scar on the land, still burning, and covered by a heavy cloud of smoke, was all that was left of a great city.

Note to Instructor: A sample condensation is shown below. The student may choose to omit different parts of the passage. When she is finished, check her paragraphs for sense and readability. Ask her to read her paragraphs out loud, listening for meaning. Then, allow her to read the sample answer below.|

Each omission must be marked by ellipses.

Hiroshima was the primary target of the first atomic bomb mission...The attack was carried out exactly as planned, and the bomb performed exactly as expected.

The bomb exploded over Hiroshima at 8:15 on the morning of August 6, 1945. About an hour previously, the Japanese early warning radar net had detected the approach of some American aircraft...The alert had been given and radio broadcasting stopped...At nearly 8:00 A.M., the radar operator in Hiroshima determined that the number of planes coming in was very small...and the air raid alert was lifted...At 8:15 A.M., the bomb exploded...the first blast was soon followed by the sounds of falling buildings and of growing fires, and a great cloud of dust and smoke began to cast a pall of darkness over the city.

At 8:16 A.M., the Tokyo control operator of the Japanese Broadcasting Corporation noticed that the Hiroshima station had gone off the air. He tried to use another telephone line to reestablish his program, but it too had failed. About twenty minutes later the Tokyo railroad telegraph center realized that the main line telegraph had stopped working just north of Hiroshima. From...within ten miles of the city there came unofficial and confused reports of a terrible explosion...All these reports were transmitted to the Headquarters of the Japanese General Staff.

Military headquarters repeatedly tried to call...Hiroshima. The complete silence from that city puzzled the men at Headquarters...A young officer...was instructed to fly immediately to Hiroshima...survey the damage, and return to Tokyo...It was generally felt at Headquarters that nothing serious had taken place, that it was all a terrible rumor starting from a few sparks of truth.

The staff officer went to the airport and took off for the southwest...While still nearly 100 miles from Hiroshima, he and his pilot saw a great cloud of smoke...The remains of Hiroshima were burning.

Their plane soon reached the city...A great scar on the land...was all that was left of a great city.

Exercise 91B: Partial Quotations

On your own paper, rewrite the five statements below so that each one contains a partial quotation. Draw the partial quotation from the bolded sentences that follow each statement. The authors of the bolded sentences are provided for you—be sure to include an attribution tag for each direct quote!

You may change and adapt the statements freely.

One of your sentences should contain a very short one- to three-word quote; one should contain a preposition phrase, gerund phrase, participle phrase, or infinitive phrase; and one should quote a dependent clause.

If you need help, ask your instructor to show you sample answers.

Note to Instructor: If the student needs a jump-start, show her *one* of the three sample sentences that follow each statement.

Henry David Thoreau experimented with simple living.

For more than five years I maintained myself thus solely by the labor of my hands, and I found, that by working about six weeks in a year, I could meet all the expenses of living. The whole of my winters, as well as most of my summers, I had free and clear for study.

—Henry David Thoreau, nineteenth-century philosopher

1–3 words

The nineteenth-century philosopher Henry David Thoreau experimented with simple living, saying that he worked only "about six weeks" each year, and studied the rest of the time.

Preposition phrase

Henry David Thoreau, a nineteenth-century philosopher, wrote that "by working about six weeks in a year," he could live simply and spend the rest of the year in study.

Dependent clause

Henry David Thoreau, the nineteenth-century philosopher, wrote of his experiments in simple living "that. . . I could meet all the expenses of living" by working only six weeks out of the year.

St. Francis of Assisi was small and active.

Francis of Assisi was slight in figure with that sort of slightness which, combined with so much vivacity, gives the impression of smallness. He was probably taller than he looked; middle-sized, his biographers say; he was certainly very active and, considering what he went through, must have been tolerably tough.

—G. K. Chesterton, essayist and biographer

1–3 words

St. Francis of Assisi was "slight in figure" and active, according his biographer G. K. Chesterton.

Participle phrase

G. K. Chesterton tells us that St. Francis of Assisi was "slight," active, and, "considering what he went through. . . tolerably tough."

Dependent clause

In his biography of St. Francis of Assisi, G. K. Chesterton describes Francis as slight, active, and "probably taller than he looked."

Japanese samurai were skilled swordsmen.

The essence of a samurai's worth lay in his mastery of swordsmanship. The sword was not just a weapon but a vehicle for *seishin tanren*, a spiritual forging that enabled the user to wipe out moral stains and to achieve *satori*, spiritual perfection.

—Richard Cohen, historian

1–3 words

Japanese samurai were skilled swordsmen, as historian Richard Cohen writes, because they were attempting to achieve "spiritual perfection" through mastering the sword.

Infinitive phrase

Historian Richard Cohen explains that Japanese samurai mastered swordsmanship in order "to wipe out moral stains and to achieve. . . spiritual perfection."

Dependent clause

Richard Cohen, a historian, points out that Japanese samurai viewed their skill at swordsmanship as a spiritual discipline "that enabled the user to wipe out moral stains."

Nuclear war between the U.S. and the Soviet Union could have destroyed the entire world.

It is the smoke, after all (not the fallout, which would remain mostly limited to the northern hemisphere), that would do it worldwide: smoke and soot lofted by fierce firestorms in hundreds of burning cities into the stratosphere, where it would not rain out and would remain for a decade or more, enveloping the globe and blocking most sunlight, lowering annual global temperatures to the level of the last Ice Age, and killing all harvests worldwide, causing near-universal starvation within a year or two.

—Daniel Ellsberg, military strategist

1–3 words

The military strategist Daniel Ellsberg points out that nuclear war between the U.S. and the Soviet Union could have destroyed the entire world by causing "near-universal starvation."

Participle phrases

According to military strategist Daniel Ellsberg, nuclear war between the U.S. and the Soviet Union could have destroyed the entire world because smoke from burning cities would block the sun, "lowering annual global temperatures. . . and killing all harvests worldwide."

Dependent clause

Daniel Ellsberg, a military strategist, tells us that nuclear war between the U.S. and the Soviet Union could have destroyed the entire world because of smoke and soot rising into the stratosphere, "where it would not rain out and would remain for a decade or more."

Cows, sheep, and goats are ruminants.

The word "ruminant" comes from the Latin word *ruminare*, which means "to rechew." Food is regurgitated, rechewed, and sent to the rumen, one of the animal's stomachs, to be decomposed by fermentation before passing on to the other compartments.

—Mark Kurlansky, science writer

1–3 words

Cows, sheep, and goats, all ruminants, regurgitate and rechew their food so that it can be "decomposed by fermentation," according to science writer Mark Kurlansky.

Gerund phrase

Science writer Mark Kurlansky explains that ruminants such as cows, sheep, and goats ferment their food in the rumen "before passing it on" to other stomach compartments.

Dependent clause

Mark Kurlansky, a science writer, says that cows, goats, and sheep are known as ruminants, from ruminare, a Latin word "which means 'to rechew.'"

Exercise 91C: Diagramming

On your own paper, diagram every word of the following sentences. These are slightly adapted from *Pale Rider: The Spanish Flu of 1918 and How It Changed the World*, by Laura Spinney.

These are difficult! Do your best, and then compare your answers with the Key.

The Spanish flu infected one in three people on earth, or 500 million human beings.

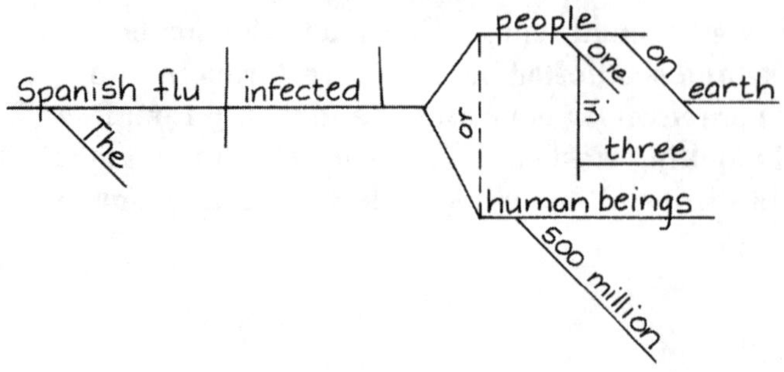

Note to Instructor: This sentence has an uncomplicated structure but multiple compounds. *Spanish flu* is a single entity and should be diagrammed in a single space. *Human beings* has been diagrammed as a single entity, but *human* could also be diagrammed beneath *beings* as an adjective. *500 million* is a single number and should be diagrammed in a single space.

There are very few cemeteries in the world that, assuming they are older than a century, don't contain a cluster of graves from the autumn of 1918—when the second and worst wave of the pandemic struck—and people's memories reflect that.

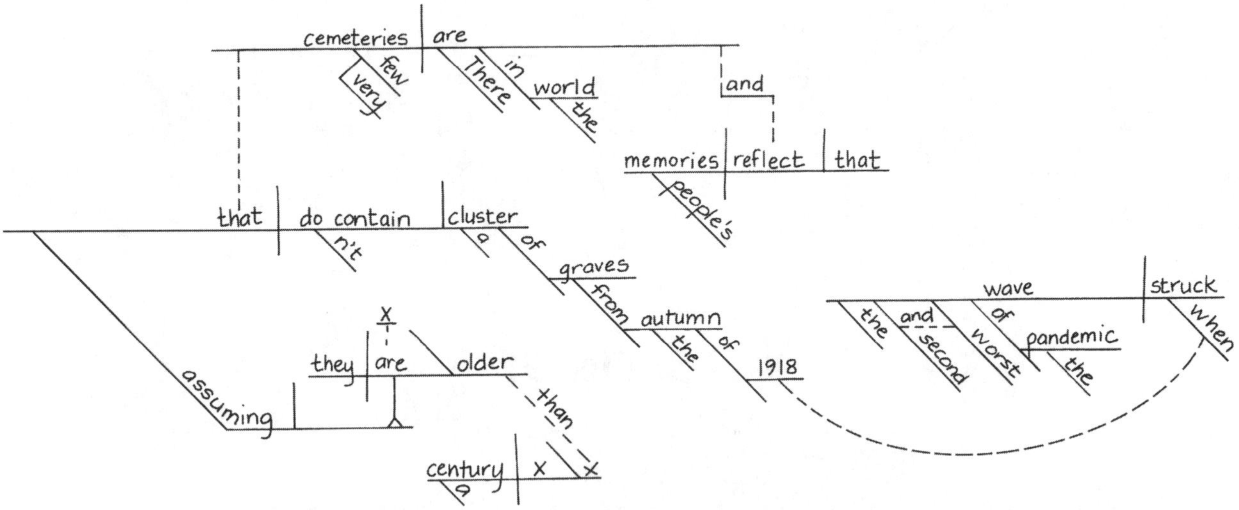

Note to Instructor: The parenthetical expression *assuming they are older than a century* is tricky! The participle *assuming* modifies the relative pronoun *that*, which itself serves as the subject of the adjectival dependent clause *that...1918*. The object of the participle is a dependent clause with an understood *that*, containing within it another dependent clause (of comparison) with additional understood elements: *assuming [that] they are older than a century [is old]*. The parenthetical expression *when the second and worst wave of the pandemic struck* is an adjective clause modifying *1918* and introduced by a relative adverb. *And people's memories reflect that* is a simple sentence, connected to the first independent clause; *that* is a demonstrative pronoun serving as a direct object.

In 1918, if you heard a neighbour or a relation coughing or saw them fall down in front of you, you knew there was a good chance that you were already sick yourself.

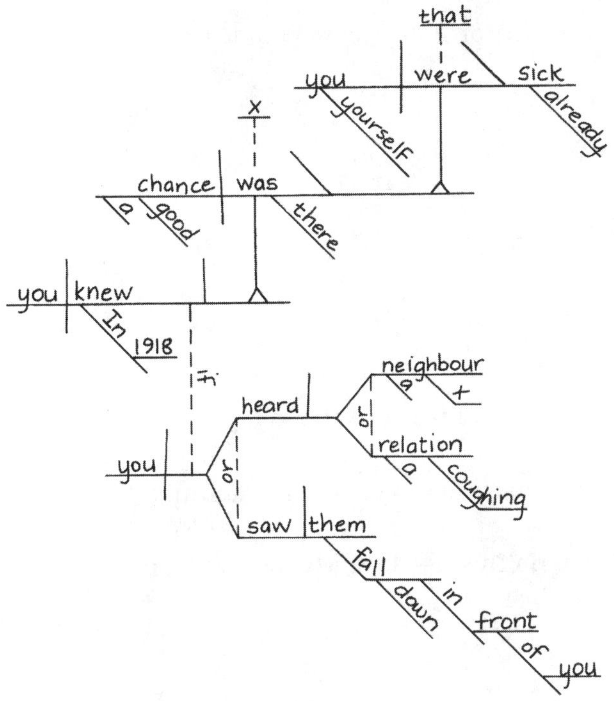

Note to Instructor: The dependent clause *[that] there was a good chance* is the direct object of the verb *knew*. The dependent clause *that you were already sick yourself* acts as a noun and is a predicate nominative renaming *chance*. The adverbial dependent clause *if you heard...in front of you* has a single subject and a compound verb, so the subordinating conjunction meets the predicate line before it divides. The student may have trouble with the phrases *hear a neighbor or a relation coughing* and *saw them fall down in front of you*. *Coughing* is a present participle that modifies both objects of *heard*. *Them* is an object pronoun and so can't be the subject of the predicate *fall*, so *fall* must be a present participle also.

There was, in other words, no warning system in place.

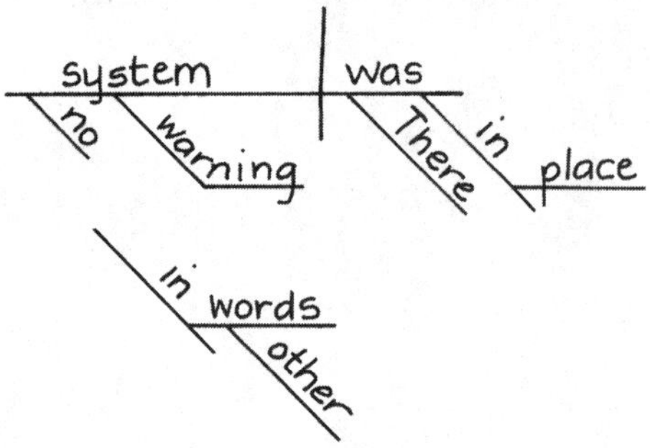

> **Note to Instructor:** The prepositional phrase *in other words* is parenthetical and has a semantic but not grammatical relationship to the rest of the sentence.

— LESSON 92 —

Partial Quotations
Ellipses
Block Quotes
Colons
Brackets

Exercise 92A: Writing Dialogue Correctly

The following speeches, from *Bambi: A Life in the Woods* by Felix Salten, are listed in the correct order, but are missing their dialogue tags. On your own paper, rewrite the speeches as dialogue, making use of the dialogue tags below. You must place at least one dialogue tag before a speech, one in the middle of a speech, and one following a speech.

A list of the rules governing dialogue follows, for your reference.

When you are finished, compare your dialogue to the original passage in the Answer Key.

List 1. Dialogue (in Correct Order)

Who are they, Mother?
Those are ants
Look, see that piece of grass jumping. Look how high it can jump!
That's not grass. That's a nice grasshopper
Why does he jump that way?
Because we're walking here; he's afraid we'll step on him
Oh; oh, you don't have to be afraid; we won't hurt you
I'm not afraid; I was only frightened for a moment when I was talking to my wife
Excuse us for disturbing you
Not at all. Since it's you, it's perfectly all right. But you never know who's coming and you have to be careful
This is the first time in my life that I've ever been on the meadow. My mother brought me

List 2. Dialogue Tags (Not in Correct Order)

said Bambi shyly
he said again politely
his mother explained
his mother answered
the grasshopper replied in a quavering voice
the grasshopper quavered
Bambi asked
he asked
cried Bambi
his mother answered
said Bambi, turning to the grasshopper, who was sitting on a daisy
Bambi explained

List 3. For Reference: Rules for Writing Dialogue

A dialogue tag identifies the person making the speech.
When a dialogue tag comes after a speech, place a comma, exclamation point, or question mark inside the closing quotation marks.
When a dialogue tag comes before a speech, place a comma after the tag. Put the dialogue's final punctuation mark inside the closing quotation marks.
Speeches do not need to be attached to a dialogue tag as long as the text clearly indicates the speaker.
Usually, a new paragraph begins with each new speaker.
When a dialogue tag comes in the middle of a speech, follow it with a comma if the following dialogue is an incomplete sentence. Follow it with a period if the following dialogue is a complete sentence.

> **Note to Instructor:** The original text is shown below. As long as the above rules are followed, the student's rewritten dialogue does not need to match the original exactly. Ask the student to point out the differences between her dialogue and the passage below.

"Who are they, Mother?" he asked.

"Those are ants," his mother answered.

"Look," cried Bambi, "see that piece of grass jumping. Look how high it can jump!"

"That's not grass," his mother explained. "That's a nice grasshopper."

Bambi asked, "Why does he jump that way?"

"Because we're walking here," his mother answered; "he's afraid we'll step on him."

"Oh," said Bambi, turning to the grasshopper, who was sitting on a daisy; "oh," he said again politely, "you don't have to be afraid; we won't hurt you."

"I'm not afraid," the grasshopper replied in a quavering voice; "I was only frightened for a moment when I was talking to my wife."

"Excuse us for disturbing you," said Bambi shyly.

"Not at all," the grasshopper quavered. "Since it's you, it's perfectly all right. But you never know who's coming and you have to be careful."

"This is the first time in my life that I've ever been on the meadow," Bambi explained. "My mother brought me."

Exercise 92B: Using Direct Quotations Correctly

On your own paper, rewrite the following three paragraphs, inserting at least one quote from each of the following three sources into the paragraph. Use the following guidelines:

a) At least one quote must be a block quote.
b) At least one quote must be a complete sentence.
c) At least one quote must be a partial sentence incorporated into your own sentence.
d) Each quote must have an attribution tag.
e) At least one quote must be condensed, using ellipses.
f) You must make at least one change or addition that needs to be put in brackets.

A list of the rules governing direct quotations follows, for your reference.

You may make whatever changes are needed to the paragraphs. When you are finished, compare your paragraphs to the sample answer in the Answer Key.

These paragraphs are adapted from Chapter Ten of *The History of the Renaissance World*, by Susan Wise Bauer.

List 1. Paragraphs

When Injong died in 1146, his oldest son Uijong was crowned in his place: the eighteenth king of his line, heir to an uneasy kingdom. Tact and wisdom were required, but Uijong had neither. His father and mother had preferred their second son, Uijong's younger brother Kyong; they thought Uijong to be a trifler, with no skill for governing.

Once on the throne, Uijong turned out to be more interested in building gorgeous gardens and writing poetry than in ruling the country. Ignoring military campaigns, he built Buddhist temples and gave them names like "Tranquillity" and "Joyful Pleasure." He wrote poetry and got drunk with his friends; he dug lily ponds, traveled from one beauty spot to another, and gave alms to the poor.

Meanwhile, he ordered soldiers to dig ditches and build walls for public projects and forced officers to act as ceremonial bodyguards to civil officials. Enlisted men found their salaries unexpectedly docked, or promised land tracts suddenly reassigned. On royal expeditions, military men were allowed to wait, cold and hungry, until civilians were well fed. Disrespect of Goryeo's military officers and scorn for their men grew more extreme.

List 2. Sources

In Uijong's twenty-fourth year [1170] the king was attending a memorial service, and again he partied with his favorite civilian officials, exchanging poems and forgetting the time. The military escorts became especially hungry.

—The contemporary history *Goryeosa*

When Uijong was still crown prince, both his father Injong and his mother Lady Im questioned his right to succeed to the throne. Injong harbored serious misgivings about Uijong's talent and ability to govern; his mother openly favored her second son, Uijong's brother Prince Kyong. Uijong won the throne only because of the staunch support of the royal tutor, Chong Supmyong, who assured the royal parents that he would personally guide and instruct Uijong once he became king. Inheriting the throne under this cloud of opposition, Uijong found his effectiveness as a monarch curbed and his ability to exercise royal prerogatives curtailed.

—Historian Edward J. Shultz, *Generals and Scholars: Military Rule in Medieval Korea*

However, it was the neglect and abuses of the military by King Uijong (1146-1170) that inspired the military revolt of 1170. An aesthetic who scorned the warrior class, he was enchanted by such peaceful arts as gardening, building a number of pavilions with names like "Tranquillity," "Joyful Pleasure," and "Beauty Attained." Around these he fashioned lily ponds and mock hillsides for his enjoyment. King Uijong's contempt for the military was blatantly exhibited by such practices as requiring distinguished commanders to serve as lowly military escorts. During this period other insults were recorded. Without suffering any consequences, Kim Ton-jung, the son of Kim Pu-sik, maliciously pulled and set fire with a candle the beard of Chong Chung-bue, a military officer.

—Author R. Barry Harmon, *5,000 Years of Korean Martial Arts: The Heritage of the Hermit Kingdom Warriors*

List 3. For Reference: Rules For Using Direct Quotations

When an attribution tag comes after a direct quote, place a comma, exclamation point, or question mark inside the closing quotation marks.

When an attribution tag comes before a direct quote, place a comma after the tag. Put the dialogue's final punctuation mark inside the closing quotation marks.

When an attribution tag comes in the middle of a direct quotation, follow it with a comma if the remaining quote is an incomplete sentence. Follow it with a period if the remaining quote is a complete sentence.

Direct quotes can be words, phrases, clauses, or sentences, as long as they are set off by quotation marks and form part of a grammatically correct original sentence.

An ellipsis shows where something has been cut out of a sentence.

Every direct quote must have an attribution tag.

If a direct quotation is longer than three lines, indent the entire quote one inch from the margin in a separate block of text and omit quotation marks.

If you change or make additions to a direct quotation, use brackets.

Note to Instructor: You will need to check the student's paragraphs against the rules above. The sample answer below is just one way to insert the direct quotations.

If the student needs prompting, allow her to read the sample answer below and then require her to use different parts of the sources in her own rewritten paragraphs.

Notice that the student has not been asked to provide footnotes or in-text citations; the focus of this lesson is on incorporating quotes properly into a piece of written work.

When Injong died in 1146, his oldest son Uijong was crowned in his place: the eighteenth king of his line, heir to an uneasy kingdom. Tact and wisdom were required, but Uijong had neither. His father and mother had preferred their second son, Uijong's younger brother Kyong; as historian Edward J. Shultz writes:

> When Uijong was still crown prince, both his father Injong and his mother Lady Im questioned his right to succeed to the throne. Injong harbored serious misgivings about Uijong's talent and ability to govern; his mother openly favored her second son. . . Inheriting the throne under this cloud of opposition, Uijong found his effectiveness as a monarch curbed and his ability to exercise royal prerogatives curtailed.

They thought Uijong to be a trifler, with no skill for governing.

Once on the throne, Uijong was more interested in building gorgeous gardens and writing poetry than in ruling the country. Ignoring military campaigns, he built Buddhist temples and gave them names like "Tranquillity" and "Joyful Pleasure." He wrote poetry and got drunk with his friends; he dug lily ponds, traveled from one beauty spot to another, and gave alms to the poor. The contemporary history *Goryeosa* tells us that the king, while attending a memorial service, spent his time "part[ying] with his favorite civilian officials, exchanging poems and forgetting the time," while the soldiers waiting for him "became especially hungry."

Meanwhile, he ordered soldiers to dig ditches and build walls for public projects and forced officers to act as ceremonial bodyguards to civil officials. Enlisted men found their salaries unexpectedly docked, or promised land tracts suddenly reassigned. On royal expeditions, military men were allowed to wait, cold and hungry, until civilians were well fed. Disrespect of Goryeo's military officers and scorn for their men grew more extreme. "During this period," the author R. Barry Harmon writes, "other insults were recorded. Without suffering any consequences, Kim Ton-jung, the son of Kim Pu-sik, maliciously pulled and set fire with a candle the beard of Chong Chung-bue, a military officer."

WEEK 24

Floating Elements

— LESSON 93 —

Interjections
Nouns of Direct Address
Parenthetical Expressions

Exercise 93A: Using Floating Elements Correctly

On your own paper, rewrite the following sentences in List 1, inserting interjections, nouns of direct address, and parenthetical expressions from List 2. You must use every item in List 2 at least once. Every sentence in List 1 must have at least one insertion.

Interjections may either come before or after sentences on their own, or may be incorporated directly into the sentence.

List 1. Sentences

I just stubbed my toe on the threshold!
Will you show me how to make your picadillo?
That piece of meat is spoiled.
Settle down or we won't be finished before recess!
I will have to leave the party early to finish my research paper.
It is so delightful to share this meal together.
Your silk scarf is exquisite.
That is the most boring movie ever made.
You sang that solo with great panache!
Climbing Mount Everest is a very stupid thing to do.
Being lazy can be a good thing.

List 2. Interjections, Nouns of Direct Address, Parenthetical Expressions

in my opinion
class
it seems to me
dear friends
Abuela
bravo
ouch
Shira
alas
after all
by the way

Note to Instructor: The answers below are samples. Any grammatical, properly punctuated versions of these sentences are acceptable.

Ouch, I just stubbed my toe on the threshold!

Will you show me how to make your picadillo, Abuela?

By the way, that piece of meat is spoiled.

Settle down, class, or we won't be finished before recess!

Alas, I will have to leave the party early to finish my research paper.

Dear friends, it is so delightful to share this meal together.

Shira, your silk scarf is exquisite.

In my opinion, that is the most boring movie ever made.

Bravo! You sang that solo with great panache!

Climbing Mount Everest, it seems to me, is a very stupid thing to do.

Being lazy can be a good thing, after all.

Exercise 93B: Parenthetical Expressions

In the following pairs of sentences, underline each subject once and each predicate twice. In each pair, cross out the parenthetical expression that is not essential to the sentences. If the expression is used as an essential part of the sentence, circle it and label it with the correct part of the sentence (e.g., *prep phrase acting as adj.*, etc.). If it acts as a modifier, draw an arrow back to the word it modifies.

The first pair is done for you.

subject and predicate

I think that I will say no more on this subject.

This subject is, ~~I think~~, one of the hardest to talk about honestly.

The knight carried, ~~to be sure~~, all the weapons he needed to slay the dragon.

infinitive phrase acting as an adverb

The knight knew it was vital to be sure of his strength.

subject and predicate

I have heard of a great and vicious monster that haunts these woods.

The monster, ~~I have heard~~, keeps the bones of its victims in a deep cave.

~~By the way~~, fifteen knights have been eaten by the monster already.

prepositional phrase acting as an adverb

A rusty suit of armor lay by the way.

conjunction, subject, and predicate of the second part of the compound sentence

The narrator of the musical cannot sing, and so he says the words instead.

The music, ~~so he says~~, is too difficult for amateurs to sing.

Exercise 93C: Diagramming

On your own paper, diagram every word of the following sentences. Several of them can be diagrammed in more than one way—when you're finished, compare your answers with the Key and look at the instructor's notes to understand the difference!

These are taken from the classic novel of the American Civil War *Gone with the Wind*, by Margaret Mitchell.

And anyway, the Yankees are too scared of us to fight.

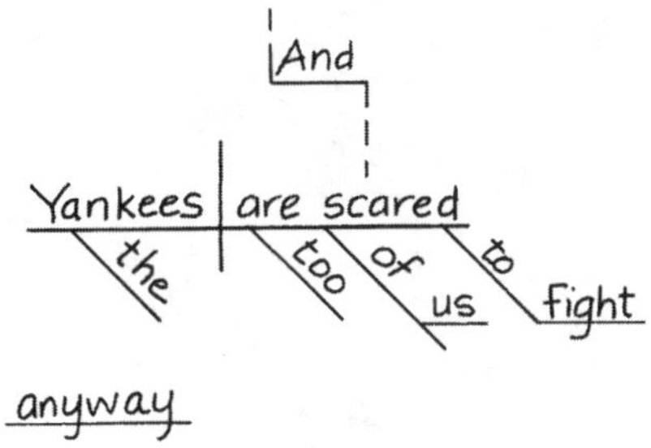

Why, honey, of course there's going to be a war.

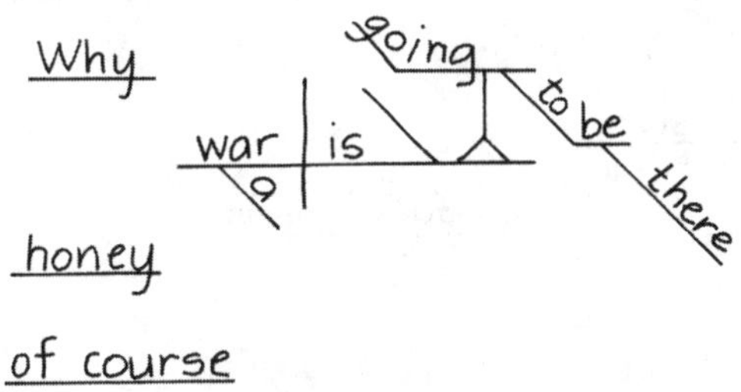

Note to Instructor: The phrase *going to be* can also be interpreted as an idiomatic verb, meaning that it could be placed all on the line elevated above the predicate nominative space, with *there* as an adverb modifying it.

I have diagrammed both *why* and *of course* as parenthetical and below the main line, but since *why* occurs alongside the direct address term *honey*, it could also be considered an interjection.

And here she had practically promised them the whole of tomorrow—seats by her at the barbecue, all the waltzes (and they'd see to it that the dances were all waltzes!) and the supper intermission.

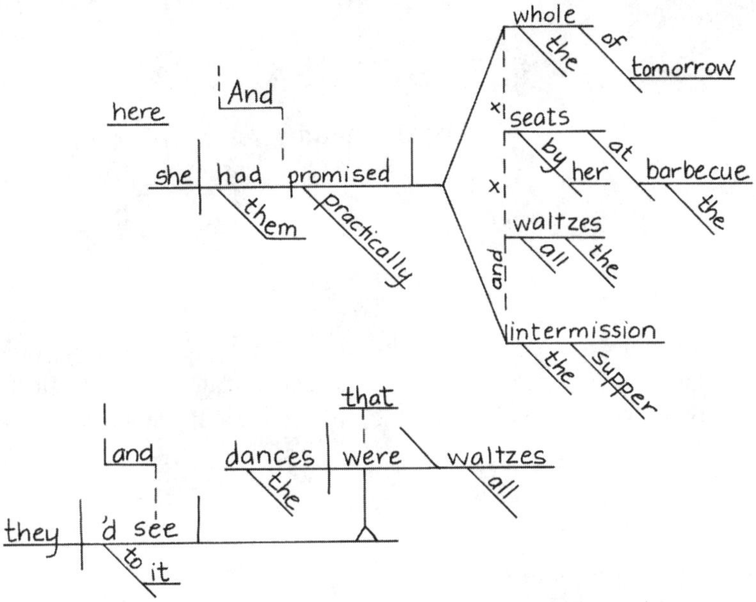

Note to Instructor: The parenthetical expression *seats by her...intermission* actually contains three of the four direct objects of *had promised*, so it has a strong grammatical relationship to the rest of the sentence. Within that expression, the second parenthetical expression *and they'd see...waltzes* has a semantic but not grammatical relationship to the rest of the sentence, so it is diagrammed separately.

The word *here* functions as a parenthetical expression, but if the student diagrams it as an adverb beneath *had promised* you may accept it. Point out, though, that it doesn't actually say *where* she *had promised*, so it is probably not functioning as an adverb.

Oh, Ashley, I love you so much that I'd walk every step of the way to Virginia just to be near you!

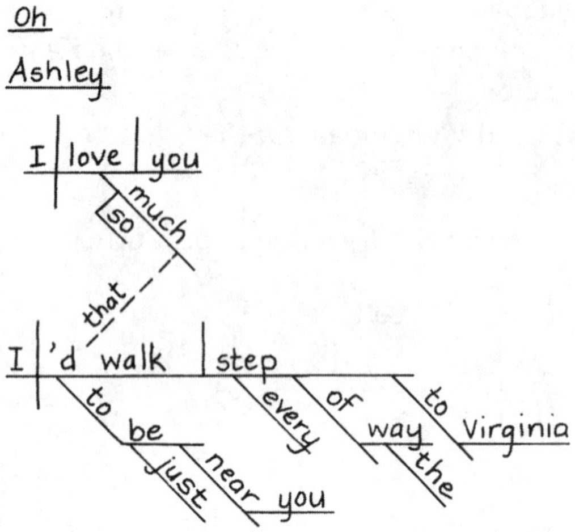

> **Note to Instructor:** The adverb clause *that I'd walk...near you* modifies *much* and answers the question *how?*

Peachtree Creek was crimson, so they say, after the Yankees crossed it.

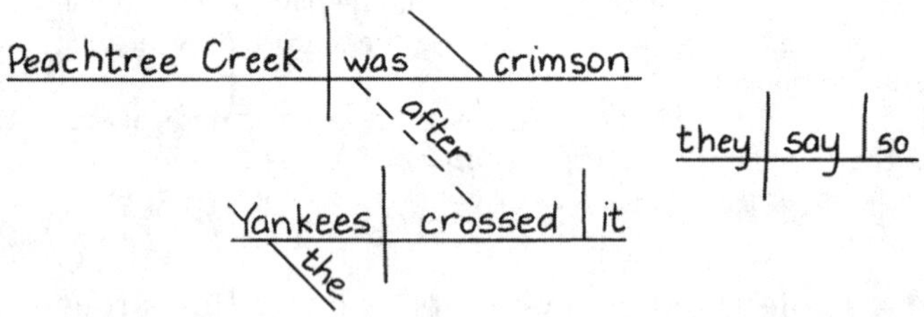

> **Note to Instructor:** In the parenthetical expression, *so* could also be diagrammed as an adverb. I have diagrammed it as a direct object because it is the *thing* that "they say."

— LESSON 94 —

Appositives

Exercise 94A: Using Appositives

Rewrite the following sentences on your own paper, inserting at least one appositive or appositive phrase from List 1 into each of the sentences in List 2, and using correct punctuation. You may insert more than one appositive into each sentence, but you must use each appositive or phrase in List 1 at least once.

List 1. Appositives

a time of unique difficulty for England and its allies

the highest mountain peak in North America

an attack that killed between 25,000 and 40,000 German civilians

a difficult target for an amateur skygazer

Sir Winston Leonard Spencer Churchill

a Class II (mid-sized) railroad bringing in over 37.4 but less than 433.2 million dollars yearly

a period of heavy bombing raids against Britain
the Red Planet
the prime minister of Britain
a century after the first attempt to reach its peak
the German military air force
two groups of Native American peoples

List 2. Sentences

The surface of Mars shows signs of water erosion.
Mars is easiest to see during the three months that it is closest to earth.
Winston Churchill exhorted the British people to "keep on" during World War II.
The Luftwaffe mounted the Blitz between 1940 and 1941; over 40,000 British civilians were killed.
Winston Churchill authorized the firebombing of Dresden.
The Inupiat and the Yup'ik held lands in the territory now known as Alaska.
The Alaska Railroad runs through Denali National Park.
Denali is also known as Mount McKinley.
By 2003, Denali had killed nearly a hundred mountaineers.

> **Note to Instructor:** The original sentences are below. The student may mix the appositives and phrases up as long as the sentences are punctuated properly.

List 3. Original Sentences

The surface of Mars, the Red Planet, shows signs of water erosion.

Mars, a difficult target for an amateur skygazer, is easiest to see during the three months that it is closest to earth.

Winston Churchill—Sir Winston Leonard Spencer Churchill—exhorted the British people to "keep on" during World War II, a time of unique difficulty for England and its allies.

The Luftwaffe, the German military air force, mounted the Blitz, a period of heavy bombing raids against Britain, between 1940 and 1941; over 40,000 British civilians were killed.

Winston Churchill, the prime minister of Britain, authorized the firebombing of Dresden, an attack that killed between 25,000 and 40,000 German civilians.

The Inupiat and the Yup'ik, two groups of Native American peoples, held lands in the territory now known as Alaska.

The Alaska Railroad, a Class II (mid-sized) railroad bringing in over 37.4 but less than 433.2 million dollars yearly, runs through Denali National Park.

Denali, the highest mountain peak in North America, is also known as Mount McKinley.

By 2003, a century after the first attempt to reach its peak, Denali had killed nearly a hundred mountaineers.

Exercise 94B: Identifying Appositives

In each of the following sentences, underline the subject once and the predicate twice. Circle each appositive or appositive phrase.

These sentences are taken from *If I Stay*, by Gayle Forman.

Adam's band, Shooting Star, is on an upward spiral, which is a great thing—mostly.

I sniff the coffee, the rich, black, oily French roast we all prefer.

We pile into the car, a rusting Buick that was already old when Gran gave it to us after Teddy was born.

Mom gives me a sidelong glance with her eyebrow arched, her version of a soul-searching stare.

I lean my head against the car window, watching the scenery zip by, a tableau of dark green fir trees dotted with snow, wispy strands of white fog, and heavy gray storm clouds up above.

The police politely offer alternate routes, back roads that will take people where they need to be.

They must have places to go, the people in these cars, but a lot of them don't turn back.

My middle school didn't have much of a music program, so Mom found me a private teacher, a college student who came over once a week.

It was at a hall in town, a place that usually showcased local bands, so the acoustics were terrible for unamplified classical.

I've never been in a hospital before. My best friend, Kim, has.

Adam played me snippets of bands he liked, a Swedish pop trio that sounded monotonous but then some Icelandic art band that was quite beautiful.

Gran tells her about the various people who are en route right now, aunts, uncles.

But eyelids are not like elbows or knees or shoulders, parts of the body accustomed to being jostled.

Exercise 94C: Diagramming (Challenge!)

On your own paper, diagram every word of the following five sentences from Exercise 94B.

NOTE: Each one of these sentences contains a slightly ambiguous element that could, possibly, be diagrammed in more than one way! Try to come up with solutions on your own—how can you make the sentence structure clear? If you get frustrated, ask your instructor for help. And when you're finished, compare your diagrams to those in the Answer Key.

Adam's band, Shooting Star, is on an upward spiral, which is a great thing—mostly.

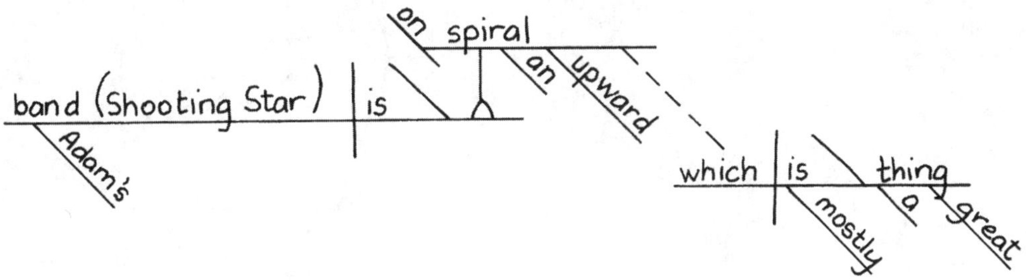

Note to Instructor: Although the student may want to diagram *on an upward spiral* as an adverb phrase, since *is* is a linking verb, it makes more sense to diagram the prepositional phrase as a predicate adjective.

We pile into the car, a rusting Buick that was already old when Gran gave it to us after Teddy was born.

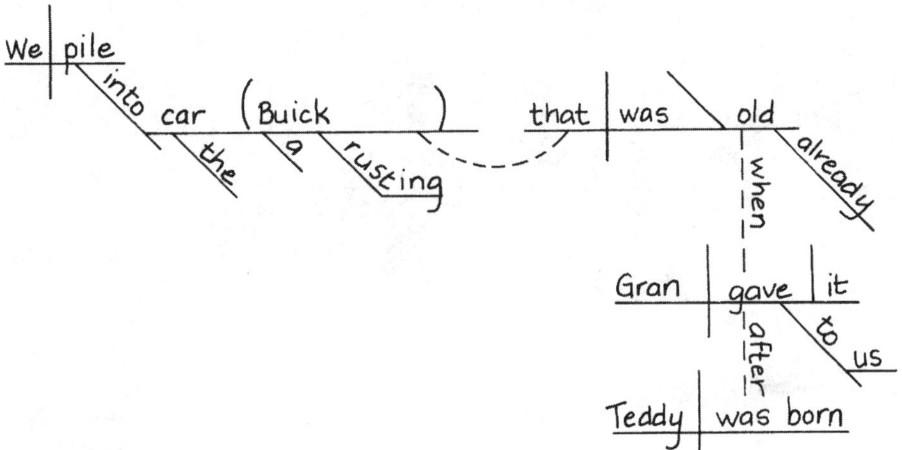

Note to Instructor: The adverb clause *when Gran gave it to us* is diagrammed as a modifier of the predicate adjective *old* (when was it old?) but could also be diagrammed as modifying *was*.

I lean my head against the car window, watching the scenery zip by, a tableau of dark green fir trees dotted with snow, wispy strands of white fog, and heavy gray storm clouds up above.

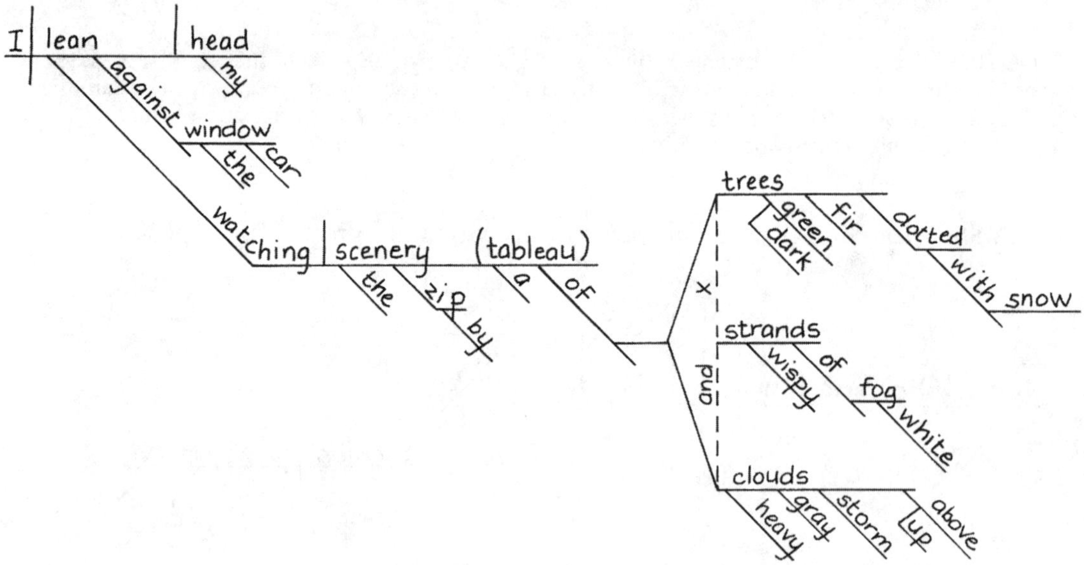

Note to Instructor: The student may be tempted to diagram *zip* as the predicate of a dependent clause serving as the object of the participle *watching*, but point out that in that case it would be *scenery zips*. *Zip* is a present participle modifying *scenery*. The appositive is *tableau*, and *trees*, *strands*, and *clouds* are all objects of the preposition *of*. Although *above* is usually an adverb, in this case it describes *clouds* (which clouds? the clouds above) and serves as an adjective.

Adam played me snippets of bands he liked, a Swedish pop trio that sounded monotonous but then some Icelandic art band that was quite beautiful.

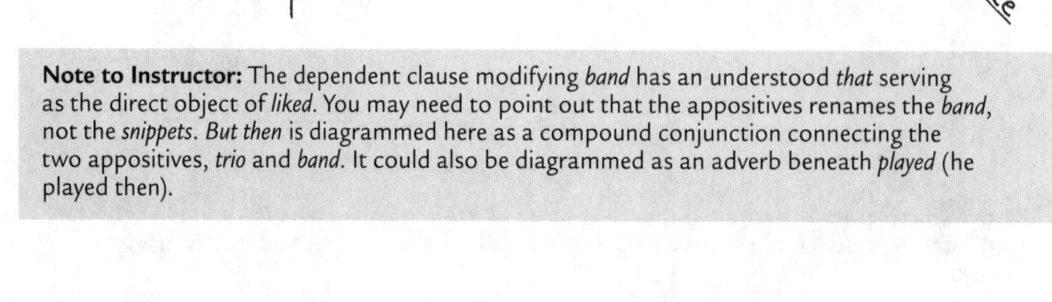

Note to Instructor: The dependent clause modifying *band* has an understood *that* serving as the direct object of *liked*. You may need to point out that the appositives renames the *band*, not the *snippets*. *But then* is diagrammed here as a compound conjunction connecting the two appositives, *trio* and *band*. It could also be diagrammed as an adverb beneath *played* (he played then).

Gran tells her about the various people who are en route right now, aunts, uncles.

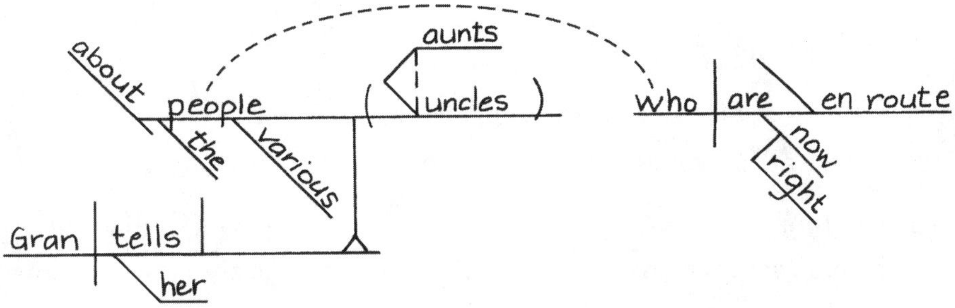

Note to Instructor: The French phrase *en route* functions in English as a single word meaning "on the way." I have diagrammed it as a predicate adjective describing who (which people? the ones *en route*), but it could also be diagrammed as a single adverb modifying *are* (where *are* they? on the way). In the same vein, *now* could be diagrammed beneath the verb or beneath *en route*.

— LESSON 95 —

Appositives
Intensive and Reflexive Pronouns
Noun Clauses in Apposition
Object Complements

Exercise 95A: Reflexive and Intensive Pronoun Review

In the following sentences from *Inkheart*, by Cornelia Funke, underline each reflexive or intensive pronoun. Put parentheses around each intensive pronoun. Label each reflexive pronoun with one of the following labels: *DO* (direct object of a verb form), *IO* (indirect object of a verb form), or *OP* (object of a preposition).

For *DO* pronouns ONLY, draw an arrow from the label back to the verb or verb form that is affecting it.

Had he ever read the name on the cover of *Inkheart* just below the title (itself)?

Suppose we're next to find ourselves (DO) on a pyre?

Perhaps I ought to catch myself (IO) one, thought Dustfinger.

She wasn't sure (herself) why she had asked the question.

And I don't suppose you think you can just help yourself (DO) to anything you want, never mind what or where.

Your innocence always amazed me—after all, you lie very cleverly to yourself (OP).

Let's try to make ourselves (DO) comfortable together.

Farid had run so fast he was gasping for breath as he flung himself down on the grass beside Dustfinger.

He (himself) had never got the knack of it.

We both know what fun it can be to get right into a book and live there for a while, but falling out of a story and suddenly finding yourself in this world doesn't seem to be much fun at all.

Sometimes Dustfinger thought Basta's constant fear of curses and sudden disaster probably arose from his terror of the darkness within himself, which made him assume that the rest of the world must be exactly the same.

I think we'd better make sure of that for ourselves, don't you?

The dog kennels lay beyond the wall, too, but when Dustfinger swung himself up and over they were empty.

They had seen for themselves that their allies knew as much about killing as their enemies.

When day dawned, she persuaded Mortimer to get a little rest (himself) while she kept watch.

Meggie bit her lip to stop herself from shaking, but she knew the fear showed in her eyes, and she knew that Capricorn saw it.

The world was as quiet as if it had spun itself into a cocoon like a moth preparing itself to slip out in the morning, young again and good as new.

The magic comes out of the books (themselves), and I have no more idea than you or any of your men how it works.

Have I made myself clear?

Exercise 95B: Clauses and Appositives

For each of the following sentences, carry out the following steps:

1) Underline every dependent clause. If a clause occurs within another clause, double underline it.
2) Label each clause as *N* for noun, *ADJ* for adjective, or *ADV* for adverb.
3) For each noun clause, identify the part of the sentence that it functions as (*S* for subject, *DO* for direct object, *IO* for indirect object, *OP* for object of the preposition, *PN* for predicate nominative, *APP* for appositive).
4) For each *ADJ* and *ADV* clause, draw an arrow from the label back to the word modified.
5) Find and circle any other noun or phrase serving as an appositive. Write *APP* above the circle. Place an *X* above every word renamed by an appositive.

These sentences have been taken (and in some cases slightly adapted) from *The Milky Way and Beyond: Stars, Nebulae, and Other Galaxies*, edited by Erik Gregersen.

The Milky Way is actually a large spiral system, (a galaxy) that consists of several billion stars.

Astronomers can determine its large-scale structure only with the aid of radio and infrared telescopes, which can detect the forms of radiation that penetrate the obscuring matter.

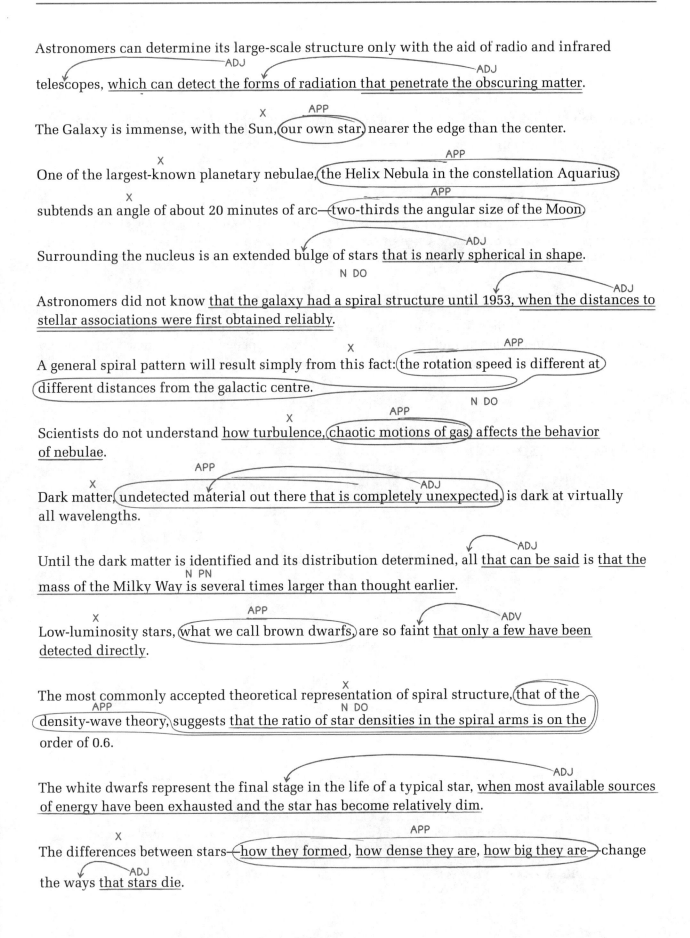

The Galaxy is immense, with the Sun, our own star, nearer the edge than the center.

One of the largest-known planetary nebulae, the Helix Nebula in the constellation Aquarius, subtends an angle of about 20 minutes of arc—two-thirds the angular size of the Moon.

Surrounding the nucleus is an extended bulge of stars that is nearly spherical in shape.

Astronomers did not know that the galaxy had a spiral structure until 1953, when the distances to stellar associations were first obtained reliably.

A general spiral pattern will result simply from this fact: the rotation speed is different at different distances from the galactic centre.

Scientists do not understand how turbulence, chaotic motions of gas, affects the behavior of nebulae.

Dark matter, undetected material out there that is completely unexpected, is dark at virtually all wavelengths.

Until the dark matter is identified and its distribution determined, all that can be said is that the mass of the Milky Way is several times larger than thought earlier.

Low-luminosity stars, what we call brown dwarfs, are so faint that only a few have been detected directly.

The most commonly accepted theoretical representation of spiral structure, that of the density-wave theory, suggests that the ratio of star densities in the spiral arms is on the order of 0.6.

The white dwarfs represent the final stage in the life of a typical star, when most available sources of energy have been exhausted and the star has become relatively dim.

The differences between stars—how they formed, how dense they are, how big they are—change the ways that stars die.

The next closest star to Earth is Proxima Centauri, which is the smallest of three stars making up the triple star Alpha Centauri.

Many models of galaxy formation have been constructed on a single basis, what we know about conditions in the early universe.

Exercise 95C: Diagramming

On your own paper, diagram every word of these two sentences from C. S. Forester's classic sea novel *Mr. Midshipman Hornblower.* Do your best to place each word on the diagram, but ask your instructor if you need help—these should be challenging!

Note to Instructor: These are complex sentences—offer the student all needed help!

There was an occasion when Mr. Bowles, the master, was holding a class in navigation for his mates and for the midshipmen, and the captain by bad luck happened by and glanced through the results of the problem the class had individually been set to solve.

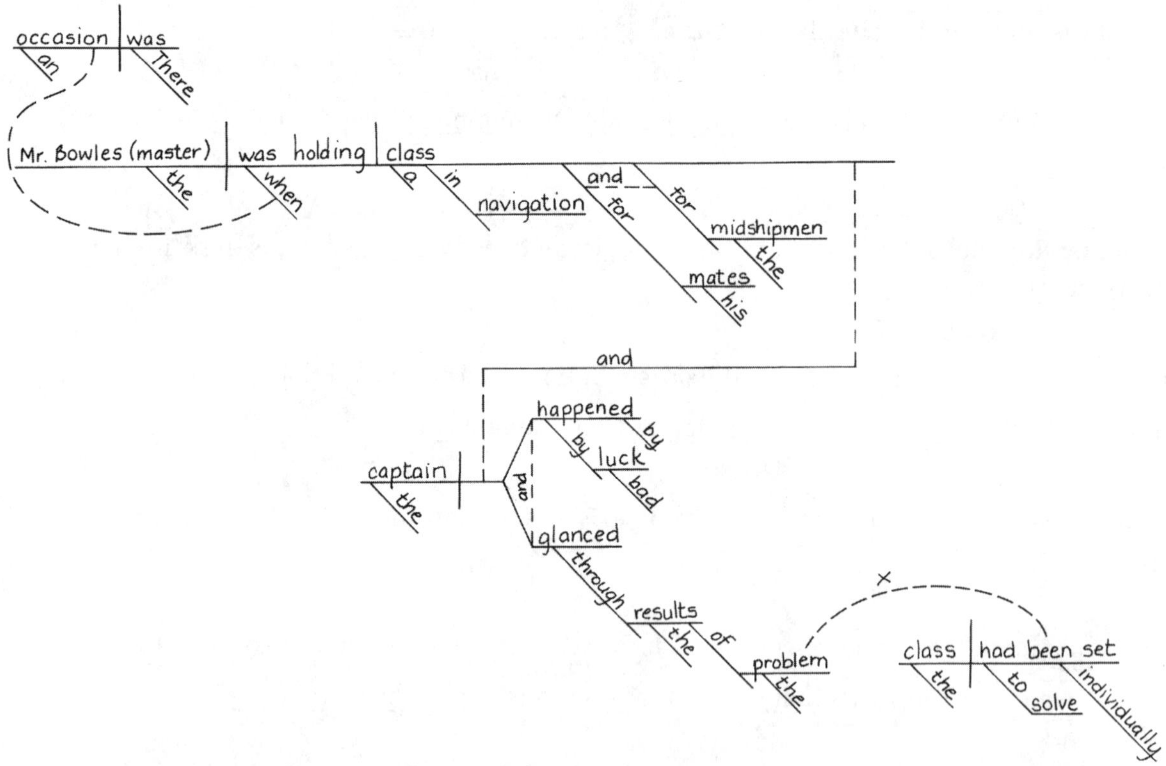

Note to Instructor: This is a compound-complex sentence; the two independent clauses, linked by the coordinating conjunction *and*, are *There was...for the midshipmen* and *the captain...set to solve.* In the first independent clause, the dependent clause *when...for the midshipmen* is an adjective clause describing a time (*occasion*) and introduced by the relative adverb *when*.

In the second independent clause, note that *by* is used both as a preposition and as an adverb. The dependent clause *[that] the class had individually been set to solve* is linked to *problem* by an understood subordinating word. Note that the understood *that* cannot be the direct object (*the class had individually been set to solve [that]*, because the verb is passive, meaning that the subject is already receiving the action of the verb.

Before and below him a British seaman was fighting a furious cutlass duel with a French officer, and he realized with vague astonishment that the kettle-mending noise he had heard was the sound of cutlass against cutlass—that clash of steel against steel that poets wrote about.

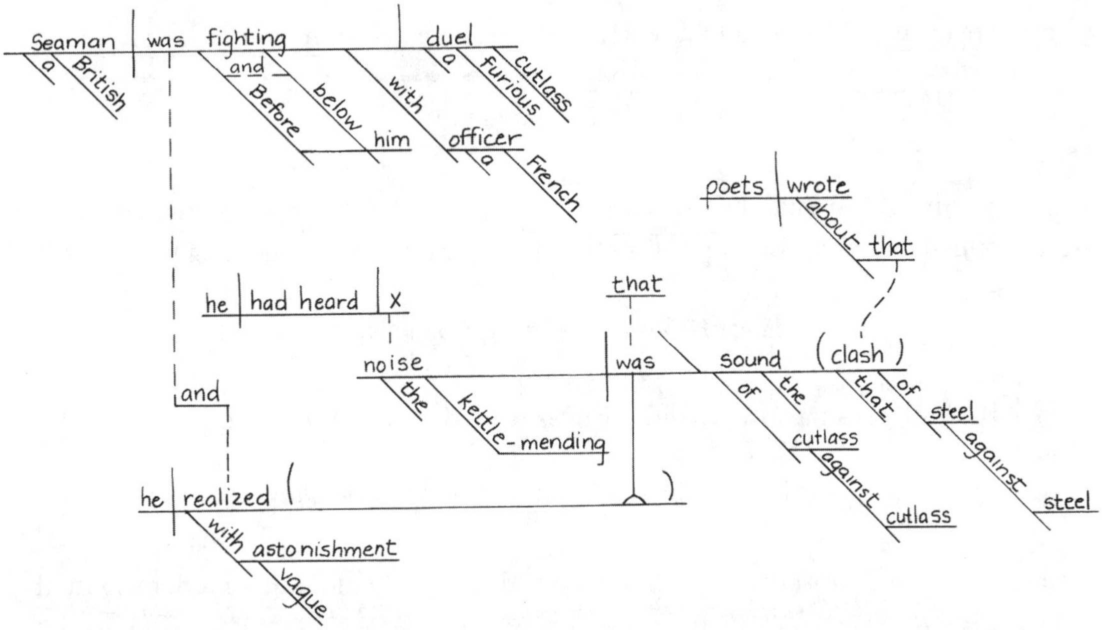

Note to Instructor: This is also a compound-complex sentence; the two independent clauses linked by the coordinating conjunction *and* are *Before* and *below...French officer*, and *he realized... poets wrote about*.

In the first independent clause, you will see the somewhat unusual case of two prepositions with the same object (*Before* and *below him*).

The second independent clause contains three dependent clauses. The first, *that the kettle-mending...wrote about* serves as the direct object of *realized*. The second and third dependent clauses are contained within the first. The adjective clause *he had heard [that]* modifies *noise* and contains an understood relative pronoun, serving as the direct object of *had heard* and referring back to *noise*. The adjective clause *that poets wrote about* refers back to *clash*, which is itself an appositive renaming *sound*.

— LESSON 96 —

Appositives
Noun Clauses in Apposition
Absolute Constructions

Exercise 96A: Identifying Absolute Constructions

In the following sentences, drawn from a whole range of novels and stories, circle the absolute constructions. Label each absolute construction as *CL* for clause or *PHR* for phrase. For clauses, underline the subject of each clause once and the predicate twice.

PHR

There was no bus in sight and Julian, his hands still jammed in his pockets and his head thrust forward, scowled down the empty street.

—Flannery O'Connor, "Everything That Rises Must Converge"

PHR

It was sitting as still as a statue, its eyes fixed unblinkingly on the far corner of Privet Drive.

—J. K. Rowling, *Harry Potter and the Sorcerer's Stone*

PHR

Six boys came over the hill half an hour early that afternoon, running hard, their heads down, their forearms working, their breath whistling.

—John Steinbeck, *The Red Pony*

PHR

Anthony jumped out of bed and, the night being cold, put on his dressing-gown and slippers; then, noiselessly, stepped on to his chair and from the chair (pushing aside the long baize curtain) to the window-ledge.

—Aldous Huxley, *Eyeless in Gaza*

PHR

I glared up at the sun, eyes narrowed, and my eyes were drawn to the moon hanging in the sky next to the sun.

—Maggie Stiefvater, *Lament: The Faerie Queen's Deception*

PHR

It was wretched weather; stormy and wet, stormy and wet; and mud, mud, mud, deep in all the streets.

—Charles Dickens, *Great Expectations*

PHR

To be fair to Patrick, he let us talk about dying, too.

—John Green, *The Fault in Our Stars*

They weren't making much sense; she decided they were having an argument as old and comfortable as an armchair, the kind of argument that no one ever really wins or loses, but which can go on for ever, if both parties are willing.

PHR

—Neil Gaiman, *Coraline*

Note to Instructor: If the student identifies this as a clause, you may accept it, but point out that it is actually not a clause, either dependent or independent; it is structured as a phrase (*the kind of argument*) that contains within it three separate dependent clauses: the adjective clause *that no one ever really wins or loses* modifying *argument*; the adjectival clause *which can go on for ever*, modifying *argument* as well; and the adverbial clause *if both parties are willing*, modifying *go*. Each one of these clauses has a grammatical relationship to the phrase *the kind of argument*, so technically they're not absolute. The phrase *the kind of argument* is absolute because it has no grammatical connection to the sentence as a whole.

CL

Immediately upon it came the thunder: a high, tearing noise, as though some huge thing were being ripped to pieces close above, which deepened and turned to enormous blows of dissolution.

—Richard Adams, *Watership Down*

Exercise 96B: Appositives, Modifiers, and Absolute Constructions

The sentences below, taken from *Whose Body?* by the British mystery novelist Dorothy Sayers, each contain phrases or clauses set off by dashes. Some are appositives, some are modifiers, and some are absolute constructions. Identify them by writing *APP, MOD,* or *AC* above each one. For appositives and modifiers, draw an arrow back to the word being renamed or modified.

AC

I believe that's his lordship just coming in again—if your Grace would kindly hold the line a moment.

> **Note to Instructor:** Although the clause set off by the dash appears to be adverbial, it doesn't clearly modify any word in the preceding clause (*kindly hold the line* doesn't tell us anything more about *I believe* or *just coming in again*).

APP AC AC

But it's been a terrible shock to me, sir—my lord, I should say, but there! my nerves are all to pieces.

APP AC MOD

But the police-inspector—Inspector Sugg, they called him, from the Yard—he was very sharp with her, poor girl.

APP

His manner as he led the way along the passage convinced Lord Peter of two things—first, that, gruesome as his exhibit was, he rejoiced in the importance it reflected upon himself and his flat, and secondly, that Inspector Sugg had forbidden him to exhibit it to anyone.

I haven't yet been able to trace the appointment, but anyhow, he returned home to his

APP

house—9 Park Lane—at twelve o'clock.

AC

No clean clothes were missing, no suit, no boots—nothing.

An important city man, on the eve of an important transaction, without a word of warning to anybody, slips off in the middle of the night, disguised down to his skin, leaving behind his

AC

watch, purse, cheque-book, and—most mysterious and important of all—his spectacles, without which he can't see a step, as he is extremely short-sighted.

> **Note to Instructor:** *Mysterious* and *important* don't modify the spectacles, which are neither; they're adjectives and can't modify the verb form *leaving*; therefore they have no grammatical relationship to the sentence.

APP AC

My client—an upright and honourable gentleman—is being tried for his life—for his life,

MOD

gentlemen—and it is the business of the prosecution to show his guilt—if they can—without a shadow of doubt.

> **Note to Instructor:** The phrase *for his life* could also be defined as a modifier, a repetition of the adverbial prepositional phrase *for his life* that comes before and modifies *being tried*. I have classified it as an absolute because *gentlemen* is a noun of direct address with no grammatical connection to the rest of the sentence. If the student identifies *for his life, gentlemen* as a modifier, accept it but ask the student what *gentlemen* is.

AC
He might have got stuck in the suburbs one night, perhaps—last train gone and no taxi—and had to walk home.

AC
Still—old bad habits die hard.

APP
We can hardly suppose that; I'm afraid this man possessed what most criminals lack—a sense of humour.

MOD
It's not an old chain—hardly worn at all.

MOD
They are very distinct on the boots—surprisingly so for gloved hands—and I deduce that the gloves were rubber ones and had recently been in water.

APP
Assigning a motive for the murder of a person without relations or antecedents or even clothes is like trying to visualize the fourth dimension—admirable exercise for the imagination, but arduous and inconclusive.

Exercise 96C: Diagramming

On your own paper, diagram every word of the following sentences, taken from the mystery novel *Gaudy Night* by Dorothy Sayers.

Her own eyes looked back at her—rather tired, rather defiant—eyes that had looked upon fear and were still wary.

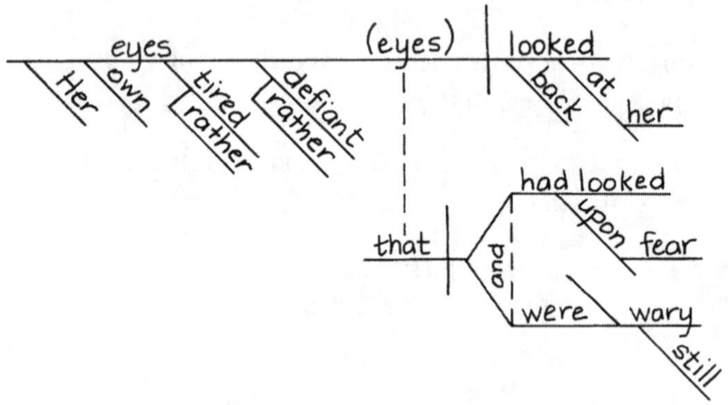

She would remain detatched, a unit in an official crowd.

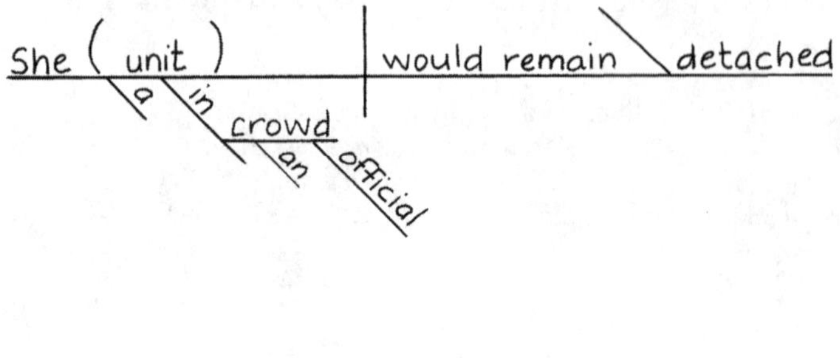

Richard—that's the eldest—is thrilled by the burial-places.

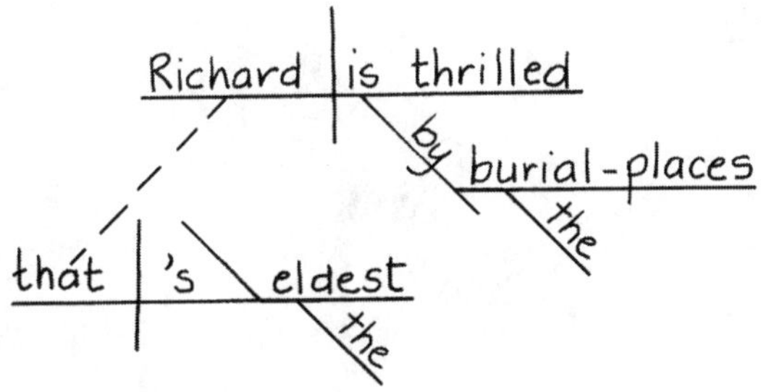

That feels much better—a marvelous sense of security.

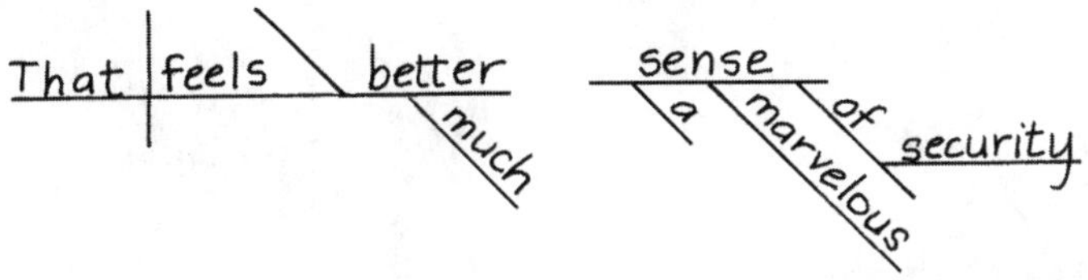

The lines swayed and lurched in her clumsy hands, uncontrollable.

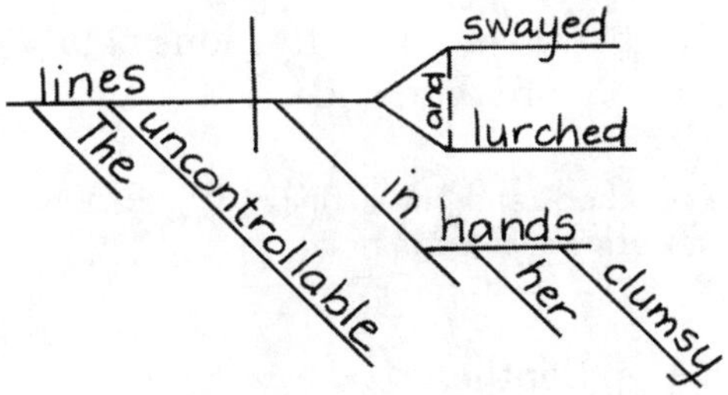

— REVIEW 8 —

Weeks 22-24

Topics
Parenthetical Expressions
Dashes, Colons, and Brackets
Dialogue and Dialogue Tags
Direct Quotations and Attribution Tags
Ellipses and Partial Quotations
Block Quotes
Interjections
Nouns of Direct Address
Appositives
Noun Clauses in Apposition
Absolute Constructions

Review 8A: Definition Fill-in-the-Blank

You learned many definitions in the past three weeks! Fill in the blanks in the definitions below with one of the terms from the list. Many of the terms will be used more than once.

Note to Instructor: Allow the student to look back through the workbook and find definitions as necessary; the value of the exercise comes in the student's completing each definition, whether from memory or not.

commas	comma	parentheses
line space	dashes	coordinating conjunction
semicolon	colon	paragraph
appositive	appositives	absolute construction
period	attribution tag	exclamation point
parenthetical expression	interjections	dialogue tag
question mark	brackets	ellipses
restrictive modifying clause	nouns of direct address	quotation marks
nonrestrictive modifying clause	closing quotation marks	short parenthetical expressions

The independent clauses of a compound sentence must be joined by a comma **and a** coordinating conjunction**, a** semicolon**, or a** semicolon **and a** coordinating conjunction**. They cannot be joined by a** comma **alone.**

Parentheses **can enclose words that are not essential to the sentence.**

A parenthetical expression **often interrupts or is irrelevant to the rest of the sentence. Punctuation goes inside the** parentheses **if it applies to the** parenthetical expression**; all other punctuation goes outside the** parentheses**.**

A parenthetical expression **only begins with a capital letter if it is a complete sentence with ending punctuation.**

A parenthetical expression **can also be set off by commas.**

Short parenthetical expressions **such as the following are usually set off by commas:** ***in short, in fact, in reality, as it were, as it happens, no doubt, in a word, to be sure, to be brief, after all, you know, of course.***

A restrictive modifying clause **defines the word that it modifies. Removing the clause changes the essential meaning of the sentence.**

A nonrestrictive modifying clause **describes the word that it modifies. Removing the clause doesn't change the essential meaning of the sentence.**

Only a nonrestrictive modifying clause **should be set off by commas.**

Dashes **can enclose words that are not essential to the sentence.**

Dashes **can also be used singly to separate parts of a sentence.**

Commas **make a parenthetical element a part of the sentence.** Dashes **emphasize a parenthetical element.**

Parentheses **minimize a parenthetical element.**

An appositive **is a noun, pronoun, or noun phrase that usually follows another noun and renames or explains it.** Appositives **are set off by** commas**.**

A dependent clause can act as an appositive **if it renames the noun that it follows.**

When a dialogue tag **comes before a speech, place a comma after the tag. Put the dialogue's final punctuation mark inside the** closing quotation marks**.**

Speeches do not need to be attached to a dialogue tag **as long as the text clearly indicates the speaker.**

Usually, a new paragraph **begins with each new speaker.**

When a dialogue tag **comes in the middle of a speech, follow it with a** comma **if the following dialogue is an incomplete sentence. Follow it with a** period **if the following dialogue is a complete sentence.**

When an attribution tag **comes after a direct quote, place a** comma**,** exclamation point**, or** question mark **inside the closing quotation marks.**

When an attribution tag **comes before a direct quote, place a** comma **after the tag. Put the dialogue's final punctuation mark inside the** closing quotation marks**.**

When an attribution tag **comes in the middle of a direct quotation, follow it with a** comma **if the remaining quote is an incomplete sentence. Follow it with a** period **if the remaining quote is a complete sentence.**

Every direct quote must have an attribution tag**.**

Ellipses **show where something has been cut out of a sentence.**

A second or third quote from the same source does not need another attribution tag**, as long as context makes the source of the quote clear.**

Direct quotes can be words, phrases, clauses, or sentences, as long as they are set off by quotation marks **and form part of a grammatically correct original sentence.**

If a direct quotation is longer than three lines, indent the entire quote one inch from the margin in a separate block of text and omit quotation marks**.**

If you change or make additions to a direct quotation, use brackets**.**

When using word processing software, leave an additional line space **before and after a block quote.**

Block quotes should be introduced by a colon **(if preceded by a complete sentence) or a** comma **(if preceded by a partial sentence).**

Interjections **express sudden feeling or emotion. They are set off with** commas **or stand alone with a closing punctuation mark.**

Nouns of direct address **name a person or thing who is being spoken to. They are set off with** commas**. They are capitalized only if they are proper names or titles.**

An absolute construction **has a strong semantic relationship but no grammatical connection to the rest of the sentence.**

Review 8B: Punctuating Restrictive and Non-Restrictive Clauses, Compound Sentences, Interjections, Parenthetical Expressions, and Nouns of Direct Address

The sentences below contain restrictive clauses, nonrestrictive clauses, interjections, parenthetical expressions, and nouns of direct address. Some are compound sentences. But all of them have lost their punctuation! Insert all necessary punctuation directly into the sentences (use the actual punctuation marks rather than proofreader's marks).

These sentences are taken from Frederick Douglass's 1845 autobiography, *Narrative of the Life of Frederick Douglass, An American Slave: Written by Himself.*

Note to Instructor: The original sentences are below; explanations have been inserted where necessary.

I do not remember to have ever met a slave who could tell of his birthday.

He that ate fastest got most; he that was strongest secured the best place; and few left the trough satisfied.

Note to Instructor: Since the three independent clauses are three items in a row, the student could use commas in place of the semicolons.

Fred, go get a fresh can of water.

He was generally called Captain Anthony—a title which, I presume, he acquired by sailing a craft on the Chesapeake Bay.

Note to Instructor: The dash could also be a comma.

They gave tongue to interesting thoughts of my own soul, which had frequently flashed through my mind, and died away for want of utterance.

> **Note to Instructor:** The comma after *mind* is optional.

O, that I were on one of your gallant decks, and under your protecting wing!

> **Note to Instructor:** The comma after *decks* is optional. The exclamation point could also be a period.

Colonel Lloyd kept a large and finely cultivated garden, which afforded almost constant employment for four men.

I sought my own employment, made my own contracts, and collected the money which I earned.

Besides, she was going to give me a pair of trousers, which I should not put on unless I got all the dirt off me.

The fact that he gave me any part of my wages was proof, to my mind, that he believed me entitled to the whole of them.

In this way I got a good many lessons in writing, which it is quite possible I should never have gotten in any other way.

They told a tale of woe which was then altogether beyond my feeble comprehension; they were tones loud, long, and deep; they breathed the prayer and complaint of souls boiling over with the bitterest anguish.

She was hired by a Mr. Stewart, who lived about twelve miles from my home.

This bread I used to bestow upon the hungry little urchins, who, in return, would give me that more valuable bread of knowledge.

He who proclaims it a religious duty to read the Bible denies me the right of learning to read the name of the God who made me.

Well, that thought has this moment struck me.

Review 8C: Dialogue

In the following two passages of dialogue from *Little Women* by Louisa May Alcott, all of the punctuation around, before, and after the lines of dialogue is missing. Insert all necessary punctuation directly into the sentences (use the actual punctuation marks rather than proofreader's marks).

There is a special challenge in the second excerpt! If you can't find it, your instructor will point it out to you.

> **Note to Instructor:** The original punctuation is below, but you may accept any appropriate ending punctuation.

By her next speech, Jo deprived herself of several years of pleasure, and received a timely lesson in the art of holding her tongue.

"I don't like favors, they oppress and make me feel like a slave. I'd rather do everything for myself, and be perfectly independent."

"Ahem!" coughed Aunt Carrol softly, with a look at Aunt March.

Note to Instructor: The exclamation point could also be a comma, but not a period.

"I told you so," said Aunt March, with a decided nod to Aunt Carrol.

Mercifully unconscious of what she had done, Jo sat with her nose in the air, and a revolutionary aspect which was anything but inviting.

"Do you speak French, dear?" asked Mrs. Carrol, laying a hand on Amy's.

"Pretty well, thanks to Aunt March, who lets Esther talk to me as often as I like," replied Amy, with a grateful look, which caused the old lady to smile affably.

"How are you about languages?" asked Mrs. Carrol of Jo.

"Don't know a word. I'm very stupid about studying anything, can't bear French, it's such a slippery, silly sort of language," was the brusque reply.

Another look passed between the ladies, and Aunt March said to Amy, "You are quite strong and well now, dear, I believe? Eyes don't trouble you any more, do they?"

"Not at all, thank you, ma'am. I'm very well, and mean to do great things next winter, so that I may be ready for Rome, whenever that joyful time arrives."

"Good girl! You deserve to go, and I'm sure you will some day," said Aunt March, with an approving pat on the head, as Amy picked up her ball for her.

*

A letter came from Aunt Carrol, and Mrs. March's face was illuminated to such a degree when she read it that Jo and Beth, who were with her, demanded what the glad tidings were.

"Aunt Carrol is going abroad next month, and wants…"

"Me to go with her!" burst in Jo, flying out of her chair in an uncontrollable rapture.

"No, dear, not you. It's Amy."

"Oh, Mother! She's too young, it's my turn first. I've wanted it so long. It would do me so much good, and be so altogether splendid. I must go!"

"I'm afraid it's impossible, Jo. Aunt says Amy, decidedly, and it is not for us to dictate when she offers such a favor."

"It's always so. Amy has all the fun and I have all the work. It isn't fair, oh, it isn't fair!" cried Jo passionately.

"I'm afraid it's partly your own fault, dear. When Aunt spoke to me the other day, she regretted your blunt manners and too independent spirit, and here she writes, as if quoting something you had said—'I planned at first to ask Jo, but as "favors burden her," and she "hates French," I think I won't venture to invite her. Amy is more docile, will make a good companion for Flo, and receive gratefully any help the trip may give her.'"

"Oh, my tongue, my abominable tongue! Why can't I learn to keep it quiet?" groaned Jo, remembering words which had been her undoing.

Note to Instructor: The student may not know that when you place a quote within another quote, you use single quotation marks to set it off—and that when you put a THIRD quote within the second quote, you go back to double quotation marks! Also note that when a quote and a quote within a quote end simultaneously, you use the single and double quotes together. If the student simply puts quote marks around the entire speech beginning "I'm afraid…", accept it but point out the original punctuation above.

Review 8D: Parenthetical Expressions, Appositives, Absolute Constructions

Each one of the sentences below contains an element not closely connected to the rest of the sentence: parenthetical, appositive, or absolute.

In each sentence, find and circle the unconnected element (word, phrase, or clause). Above it, write *PAR* for parenthetical, *APP* for appositive, or *AB* for absolute.

In the blank at the end of the sentence, note whether the element is set apart with commas (*C*), parentheses (*P*), dashes (*D*), or some other mark (*O*).

These are taken from *My First Summer in the Sierra*, by the great nineteenth-century nature writer John Muir.

APP
In the great Central Valley of California there are only two seasons—spring and summer. D

PAR
The flock, he explained, would be moved gradually higher through the successive forest belts as the snow melted, stopping for a few weeks at the best places we came to. C

APP
His master, a hunter with whom I was slightly acquainted, came to me as soon as he heard that I was going to spend the summer in the Sierra and begged me to take his favorite dog, Carlo, (APP) with me, for he feared that if he were compelled to stay all summer on the plains the fierce heat might be the death of him. C

C

APP
This morning provisions, camp-kettles, blankets, plant-press, etc., were packed on two horses, the flock headed for the tawny foothills, and away we sauntered in a cloud of dust: Mr. Delaney, (APP) bony and tall, with sharply hacked profile like Don Quixote, leading the pack-horses, Billy, the proud shepherd, and myself with notebook tied to my belt. C

O

APP
After the danger is past they call one another together with a loud piping note—Nature's beautiful mountain chickens. D

AB
Soon the whole flock seemed to be hopefully excited, the mothers calling their lambs, the lambs replying in tones wonderfully human, their fondly quavering calls interrupted now and then by hastily snatched mouthfuls of withered grass. C

In case a tired lamb, half asleep in the smothering dust, should fail to answer, its mother would come running back through the flock toward the spot whence its last response was heard, and refused to be comforted until she found it, (APP) the one of a thousand, though to our eyes and ears all seemed alike. C

AB
The meal finished, the dogs were fed, the smokers smoked by the fire, and under the influences of fullness and tobacco the calm that settled on their faces seemed almost divine, something like the mellow meditative glow portrayed on the countenances of saints. C

APP APP

The mountain quail (*Oreortyx ricta*) I often meet in my walks—a small brown partridge with a very long, slender, ornamental crest worn jauntily like a feather in a boy's cap, giving it a very marked appearance.

P

D

Review 8E: Direct Quotations

The following paragraphs have been condensed slightly from a biography of John Muir, *A Passion for Nature: The Life of John Muir*, by Donald Worster. The paragraphs contain three different direct quotations from Muir's journals and essays.

Those quotations are bolded, but they are not properly punctuated. Rewrite the paragraphs on your own paper or with your own word processor. Punctuate and space the quotations properly.

When you are finished, circle any places where words have been left out of the direct quotations. Underline any places where words have been added to the direct quotations. Then compare your answers with the original.

John Muir's last essay for the Overland Monthly magazine poked at the **soft hypocrisies** of those who congratulated themselves on having vanquished nature and all its dangers. **Man's control** he wrote **is being steadily extended over the forces of nature, but it is well, at least for the present, that storms can still make themselves heard through the thickest walls.**

No amount of magazine writing, no amount of urban planning could remedy the most serious flaw in the city—its lack of wild mountain beauty. On one dreary January day, he showed how unreconciled he was to the aesthetically impoverished cityscape. **The streets here are barren & beeless & ineffably mud[d]y & mean looking. . . A eucalyptus bush on every other corner, standing tied to a painted stick, & a geranium sprout in a pot on every tenth window sill may help heavenward a little, but how little amid so muckle downdragging mud.** Each winter he sweated over his writing, but always he dreamed of the summer day when the mountains would be free of snow and he could be among them again.

Note to Instructor: The original punctuation is shown below. Ask the student to compare her version with this one, and point out any differences.

John Muir's last essay for the Overland Monthly magazine poked at the "soft hypocrisies" of those who congratulated themselves on having vanquished nature and all its dangers. "Man's control," he wrote, "is being steadily extended over the forces of nature, but it is well, at least for the present, that storms can still make themselves heard through the thickest walls."

No amount of magazine writing, no amount of urban planning could remedy the most serious flaw in the city—its lack of wild mountain beauty. On one dreary January day, he showed how unreconciled he was to the aesthetically impoverished cityscape.

> The streets here are barren & beeless & ineffably mud[d]y & mean looking. . . A eucalyptus bush on every other corner, standing tied to a painted stick, & a geranium sprout in a pot on every tenth window sill may help heavenward a little, but how little amid so muckle downdragging mud.

Each winter he sweated over his writing, but always he dreamed of the summer day when the mountains would be free of snow and he could be among them again.

Review 8F: Diagramming

On your own paper, diagram every word of the following sentences from John Muir's *Steep Trails.*

Each sentence contains a challenge! Do your best, and ask your instructor for help if you need it!

Three fleeces were obtained—one that belonged to a large ram about four years old, another to a ewe about the same age, and another to a yearling lamb.

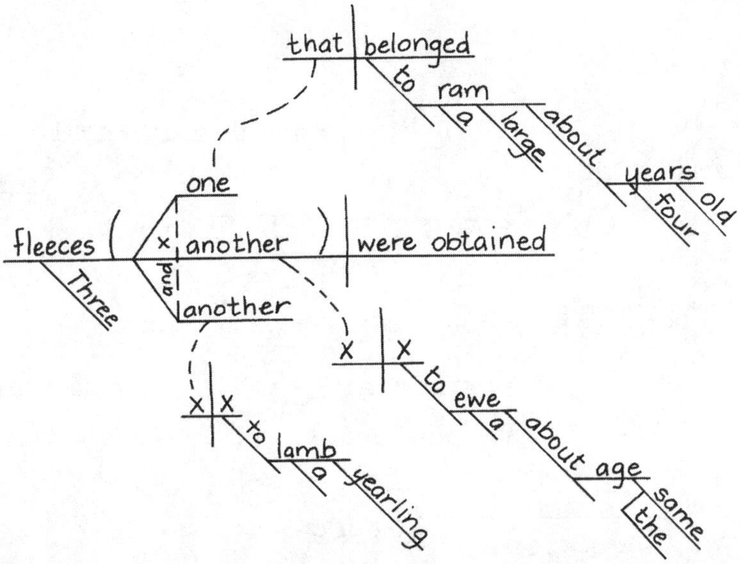

Five or six species of pines are found in the state, the most important of which, both as to lumber and as to the part they play in the general wealth and beauty of the forests, are the yellow and sugar pines (Pinus ponderosa and P. Lambertiana).

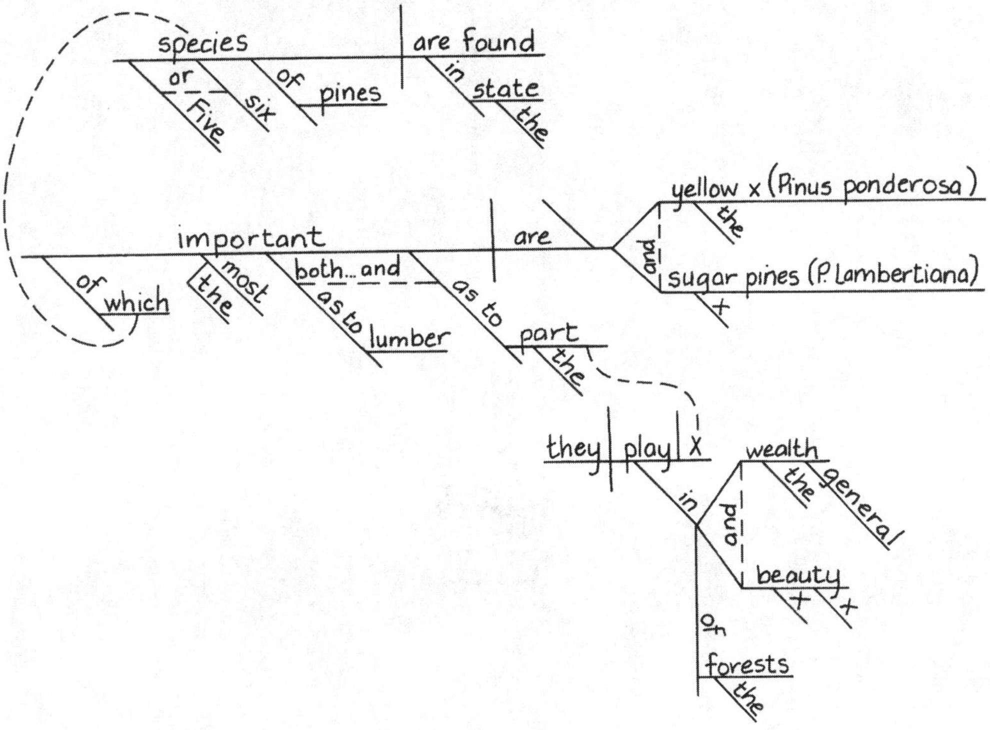

Wild wool is too fine to stand by itself, the fibers being as frail and invisible as the floating threads of spiders, while the hairs against which they lean stand erect like hazel wands; but, notwithstanding their great dissimilarity in size and appearance, the wool and hair are forms of the same thing, modified in just that way and to just that degree that renders them most perfectly subservient to the well-being of the sheep.

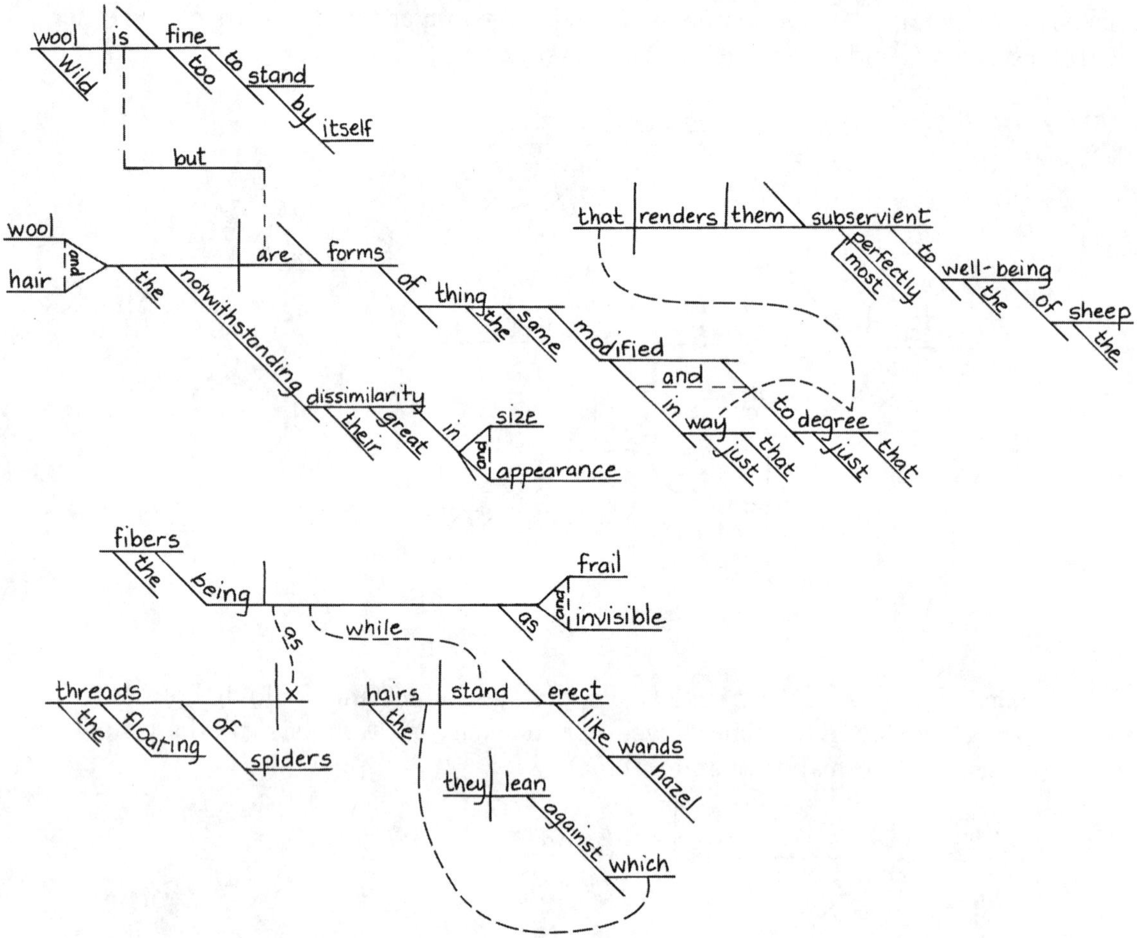

WEEK 25

Complex Verb Tenses

— LESSON 97 —

Verb Tense, Voice, and Mood
Tense Review (Indicative)
Progressive Perfect Tenses (Indicative)

Exercise 97A: Review of Indicative Tenses

The following partially completed chart shows the active and passive tenses of the regular verb *announce* (in the third-person singular), the irregular verb *fight* (in the third-person plural), and the irregular verb *feed* (in the first-person singular). Review your indicative tenses by completing the chart now.

		Active	Passive
SIMPLE TENSES			
announce *fight* *feed*	Past	he announced they fought I fed	he was announced they were fought I was fed
announce *fight* *feed*	Present	he announces they fight I feed	he is announced they are fought I am fed
announce *fight* *feed*	Future	he will announce they will fight I will feed	he will be announced they will be fought I will be fed
PROGRESSIVE TENSES			
announce *fight* *feed*	Past	he was announcing they were fighting I was feeding	he was being announced they were being fought I was being fed
announce *fight* *feed*	Present	he is announcing they are fighting I am feeding	he is being announced they are being fought I am being fed
announce *fight* *feed*	Future	he will be announcing they will be fighting I will be feeding	he will be being announced they will be being fought I will be being fed

		Active	Passive
PERFECT TENSES			
announce *fight* *feed*	Past	he had announced they had fought I had fed	he had been announced they had been fought I had been fed
announce *fight* *feed*	Present	he has announced they have fought I have fed	he has been announced they have been fought I have been fed
announce *fight* *feed*	Future	he will have announced they will have fought I will have fed	he will have been announced they will have been fought I will have been fed

Exercise 97B: Parsing Verbs

In the following sentences, underline the main verb of every clause (both independent and dependent). Above each verb, write the tense and voice. (All verbs are in the indicative mood.) You may abbreviate: *PROG, PERF, SIMP, PAST, PRES, FUT, ACT, PASS.*

These sentences are from *Hard Times*, by Charles Dickens; some have been slightly condensed.

PERF PAST, PASS / PERF PAST, ACT

He had been put through an immense variety of paces, and had answered volumes of head-breaking questions.

PERF PAST, ACT / SIMP PAST, ACT / PROG PAST, ACT

He had virtually retired from the wholesale hardware trade before he built Stone Lodge, and was now looking about for a suitable opportunity.

PROG, PERF PAST, ACT / SIMP PAST, PASS

Sissy, who all this time had been faintly excusing herself with tears in her eyes, was now waved over by the master of the house to Mr. Gradgrind.

PERF PAST, ACT / SIMP PAST, PASS

I had had the key that was found, made long before.

PROG PERF, PRES, ACT

Here, for example, I have been speaking to you this morning about tumblers.

PERF PAST, ACT / SIMP PAST, PASS

He had reached the neutral ground upon the outskirts of the town, when his ears were invaded by the sound of music.

SIMP FUT, ACT / PERF PRES, PASS

I'll recompense myself for the way in which I have been brought up.

PROG PERF, PRES, ACT / PROG PERF, PRES, ACT

But since I have been looking at it, I have been wondering about you and me, grown up.

PERF PAST, ACT — PERF PAST, PASS — SIMP PAST, ACT — SIMP PAST, ACT

When she had said this, though nothing of her had been seen but her pleasant eyes, she replaced her hood again, and they went on together.

PERF PRES PASS

I have been rather troubled with shortness of breath.

PERF PRES PASS — PERF PRES ACT — PERF PRES ACT

The emphasis was helped by the speaker's hair, which bristled on the skirts of his bald head, a plantation of firs to keep the wind from its shining surface, all covered with knobs, like the crust of a plum pie, as if the head had scarcely warehouse-room for the hard facts stored inside.

Exercise 97C: Completing Sentences

Complete the following sentences by providing an appropriate verb in the tense and voice indicated beneath each blank. (All verbs are in the indicative mood.)

Note to Instructor: As long as the verbs are in the correct tense, any verbs that make sense are acceptable.

This book __has been written__ (perfect present, passive) for readers who are passionately curious about medieval French history.

Very gradually, the balance of power between the two countries __has been shifting__ (progressive perfect present, active) to the smaller one.

For the last twenty-four hours, the butterfly __has been emerging__ (progressive perfect present, active) slowly from its chrysalis.

In ten years, huge strides __will have been made__ (perfect future, passive) in outer space exploration.

By the year 2020, I __will have been studying__ (progressive perfect future, active) medieval French history for over two decades.

If my opponent concedes defeat in the debate, an important point __will have been proved__ (perfect future, passive).

I reassured him that his lifetime of research __will__ not __have been spent__ (perfect future, passive) in vain, even if his theories __are shown__ (simple present, passive) to be false.

For a number of years before the revolution, the peasants __had been being oppressed__ (progressive perfect past, passive) at every turn.

The pass through the mountains __has been being constructed__ (progressive perfect present, passive) for years, and it still isn't ready.

The skater __is competing__ (progressive present, active) with huge confidence, since she __has been training__ (progressive perfect, present, active) with a new coach.

— LESSON 98 —

Simple Present and Perfect Present Modal Verbs

Progressive Present and Progressive Perfect Present Modal Verbs

Exercise 98A: Parsing Verbs

In the following sentences from *The Legend of Sleepy Hollow* by Washington Irving, find and underline each modal verb. Write the tense and voice of each verb above it. (For state-of-being verbs, the voice is simply state-of-being.) The first is done for you.

He was tall, but exceedingly lank, with narrow shoulders, long arms and legs, hands that dangled a mile out of his sleeves, feet that might have served [perfect present, active] for shovels, and his whole frame most loosely hung together.

The revenue arising from his school was small, and would have been [perfect present, state-of-being] scarcely sufficient to furnish him with daily bread, for he was a huge feeder, and, though lank, had the dilating powers of an anaconda; but to help out his maintenance, he was, according to country custom in those parts, boarded and lodged at the houses of the farmers whose children he instructed.

From hence the low murmur of his pupils' voices, conning over their lessons, might be heard [simple present, passive] in a drowsy summer's day, like the hum of a beehive; interrupted now and then by the authoritative voice of the master, in the tone of menace or command, or, peradventure, by the appalling sound of the birch, as he urged some tardy loiterer along the flowery path of knowledge.

He would delight [simple present, active] them equally by his anecdotes of witchcraft, and of the direful omens and portentous sights and sounds in the air, which prevailed in the earlier times of Connecticut; and would frighten [simple present, active] them woefully with speculations upon comets and shooting stars; and with the alarming fact that the world did absolutely turn round, and that they were half the time topsy-turvy!

Still he must have had [simple present, active] fire and mettle in his day, if we may judge [simple present, active] from the name he bore of Gunpowder.

He affirmed that on returning one night from the neighboring village of Sing Sing, he had been overtaken by this midnight trooper; that he had offered to race with him for a bowl of punch, and should have won [perfect present, active] it too, for Daredevil beat the goblin horse all hollow, but just as they came to the church bridge, the Hessian bolted, and vanished in a flash of fire.

She was withal a little of a coquette, as might be perceived [simple present, passive] even in her dress, which was a mixture of ancient and modern fashions, as most suited to set off her charms.

Could that girl have been playing [progressive perfect present, active] off any of her coquettish tricks?

His notable little wife, too, had enough to do to attend to her housekeeping and manage her poultry; for, as she sagely observed, ducks and geese are foolish things, and must be looked (simple present, passive) after, but girls can take (simple present, active) care of themselves.

Though the night was dark and dismal, yet the form of the unknown might (simple present, passive) now in some degree be ascertained.

"If I can but reach (simple present, active) that bridge," thought Ichabod, "I am safe."

On mounting a rising ground, which brought the figure of his fellow-traveller in relief against the sky, gigantic in height, and muffled in a cloak, Ichabod was horror-struck on perceiving that he was headless!—but his horror was still more increased on observing that the head, which should have rested (perfect present, active) on his shoulders, was carried before him on the pommel of his saddle!

The bridge became more than ever an object of superstitious awe; and that may be (simple present, state-of-being) the reason why the road has been altered of late years, so as to approach the church by the border of the millpond.

Exercise 98B: Forming Modal Verbs

Fill in the blanks with the missing modal verbs. Using the helping verbs indicated, put each action verb provided into the correct modal tense.

These sentences have been adapted from *Volcanoes of the World*, written by Lee Siebert, Tom Simkin, and Paul Kimberly.

Pyroclastic flows __can move__ down slopes at hurricane speeds, devastating all living things in their paths.

helping verb: can
simple present active of *move*

During World War II, the scientists who otherwise __could have been reporting__ volcanic activity were preoccupied with other problems.

helping verb: could
progressive perfect present active of *report*

Fatalities __may have been recorded__ from as many as 400 eruptions, with the most deadly being roughly 60,000 deaths from the 1815 Tambora eruption.

helping verb: may
perfect present passive of *record*

After a dramatic eruption, during which Tambora threw up a 33-kilometer cloud, a reasonable person __might have thought__ that the volcano was finished; but this conclusion __would have been__ wrong.

helping verb: might
perfect present active of *think*

helping verb: would
perfect present, state-of-being

Within the week, Tambora __would be erupting__ with more force than had been seen in modern history.

helping verb: would
progressive present active of *erupt*

The eruption __must have been being built__ up for over three years.
helping verb: must
progressive perfect present passive of *build*

The sound of the explosion __could be heard__ in Sumatra, over 1500 miles away.
helping verb: could
simple present passive of *hear*

Before the month was over, the effects of the eruption __would be being felt__ all around the world; global temperatures __would drop__, causing significant crop failures internationally.
helping verb: would
progressive present passive of *feel*
helping verb: would
simple present active of *drop*

— LESSON 99 —

Modal Verb Tenses
The Imperative Mood
The Subjunctive Mood
More Subjunctive Tenses

Exercise 99A: Complete the Chart

Fill in the missing forms on the following chart. Use the verbs indicated above each chart, in order. The first form on each chart is done for you.

INDICATIVE

(abandon, catch, ignite, pat, vex, wrangle, measure, extricate, describe, bite, need, swirl)

Indicative Tense	Active Formation	Examples	Passive Formation	Examples
Simple present	Add *-s* in third-person singular	I abandon he, she, it abandons	am/is/are + past participle	I am abandoned you are abandoned he, she, it is abandoned
Simple past	Add *-d* or *-ed*, or change form	I caught	was/were + past participle	I was caught you were caught
Simple future	+ will OR shall	they will ignite	will be + past participle	it will be ignited

Indicative Tense	Active Formation	Examples	Passive Formation	Examples
Progressive present	am/is/are + present participle	I am patting you are patting he, she, it is patting	am/is/are being + past participle	I am being patted you are being patted he, she, it is being patted
Progressive past	was/were + present participle	I was vexing you were vexing he, she, it was vexing	was/were being + past participle	I was being vexed you were being vexed he, she, it was being vexed
Progressive future	will be + present participle	I will be wrangling	will be being + past participle	it will be being wrangled
Perfect present	has/have + past participle	I have measured you have measured he, she, it has measured	has/have been + past participle	I have been measured you have been measured he, she, it has been measured
Perfect past	had + past participle	they had extricated	had been + past participle	you had been extricated
Perfect future	will have + past participle	we will have described	will have been + past participle	they will have been described
Progressive perfect present	have/has been + present participle	I have been biting he, she, it has been biting	have/has been being + past participle	I have been being bit he, she, it has been being bit
Progressive perfect past	had been + present participle	you had been needing	had been being + past participle	you had been being needed
Progressive perfect future	will have been + present participle	you will have been swirling	will have been being + past participle	they will have been being swirled

MODAL

(puff, promulgate, hurl, throttle)

Note to Instructor: Student's choice of modal helping verb may vary. *Should*, *would*, *may*, *might*, *must*, *can*, and *could* are all acceptable.

Modal Tense	Active Formation	Examples	Passive Formation	Examples
Simple present	modal helping verb + simple present main verb	I could puff you might puff he, she, it may puff	modal helping verb + be + past participle	I might be puffed they might be puffed
Progressive present	modal helping verb + be + present participle	I should be promulgating	modal helping verb + be + being + past participle	it may be being promulgated
Perfect present	modal helping verb + have + past participle	you could have hurled	modal helping verb + have + been + past participle	it might have been hurled
Progressive perfect present	modal helping verb + have been + present participle	I may have been throttling	modal helping verb + have been being + past participle	we should have been being throttled

IMPERATIVE

(command, fluff)

Imperative Tense	Active Formation	Examples	Passive Formation	Examples
Present	Simple present form without subject	Command! Fluff!	be + past participle	Be commanded! Be fluffed!

SUBJUNCTIVE
(pummel, yell, congratulate, relax, raise, collapse, punish, wash)

Subjunctive Tense	Active Formation	Examples	Passive Formation	Examples
Simple present	No change in any person	I pummel you pummel he, she, it pummel we pummel you pummel they pummel	be + past participle	I be pummelled they be pummelled
Simple past	**Same as indicative:** Add *-d* or *-ed*, or change form	I yelled you yelled he, she, it yelled	were + past participle	it were yelled
Progressive present	**Same as indicative:** am/is/are + present participle	I am congratulating you are congratulating he, she, it is congratulating	**Same as indicative:** am/is/are being + past participle	I am being congratulated you are being congratulated he, she, it is being congratulated
Progressive past	were + present participle	I were relaxing you were relaxing he, she, it were relaxing	were being + past participle	I were being relaxed you were being relaxed he, she, it were being relaxed
Perfect present	**Same as indicative:** has/have + past participle	I have raised he, she, it has raised they have raised	**Same as indicative:** has/have been + past participle	I have been raised he, she, it has been raised they have been raised
Perfect past	**Same as indicative:** had + past participle	we had collapsed	**Same as indicative:** had been + past participle	we had been collapsed

Subjunctive Tense	Active Formation	Examples	Passive Formation	Examples
Progressive perfect present	**Same as indicative:** have/has been + present participle	I have been punishing you have been punishing he, she, it has been punishing	**Same as indicative:** have/has been being + past participle	I have been being punished you have been being punished he, she, it has been being punished
Progressive perfect past	**Same as indicative:** had been + present participle	you had been washed	**Same as indicative:** had been being + past participle	you had been being washed

Exercise 99B: Parsing

Write the mood, tense, and voice of each underlined verb above it. The first is done for you.

These sentences are taken from Robert Louis Stevenson's classic novel *Dr. Jekyll and Mr. Hyde*. The first is done for you.

imperative present active (Mark); indicative simple future passive (will be heard)

Mark my words, he will never more be heard of.

indicative progressive perfect present active (have been wanting)

I have been wanting to speak to you, Jekyll.

imperative present passive (Be seated)

Be seated, if you please.

modal subjunctive simple present active (could set); modal simple present active (would lighten)

If he could but once set eyes on him, he thought the mystery would lighten and perhaps roll altogether away, as was the habit of mysterious things when well examined.

> **Note to Instructor:** If the student marks the first verb as either modal or subjunctive, accept the answer, but point out that this is a subjunctive verb (it represents an unreal situation) formed with a modal helping verb, so it has qualities of both moods!

modal perfect present passive (can have been disposed); modal simple present state-of-being (must be); modal perfect present active (must have fled)

He cannot have been disposed of in so short a space; he must be still alive, he must have fled!

imperative present active (Think); indicative simple future passive (shall be done)

Think before you answer, for it shall be done as you decide.

subjunctive / simple past / state-of-being

It did not seem as if the subject of his address <u>were</u> of great importance; indeed, from his pointing,

subjunctive / progressive past / active

it sometimes appeared as if he <u>were</u> only <u>inquiring</u> his way; but the moon shone on his face as he

indicative / simple past / passive

spoke, and the girl <u>was pleased</u> to watch it.

subjunctive / simple past / passive — modal / simple present / passive

I began to spy a danger that, if this <u>were</u> much <u>prolonged</u>, the balance of my nature <u>might be</u> permanently <u>overthrown</u>, the power of voluntary change be forfeited, and the character of Edward Hyde become irrevocably mine.

indicative / simple past / passive

A purse and gold watch <u>were found</u> upon the victim: but no cards or papers, except a sealed and

indicative / progressive perfect past / active

stamped envelope, which he <u>had been</u> probably <u>carrying</u> to the post, and which bore the name and address of Mr. Utterson.

subjunctive / perfect past / active — subjunctive / perfect past / active

<u>Had</u> I <u>approached</u> my discovery in a more noble spirit, <u>had</u> I <u>risked</u> the experiment while under

modal / perfect present / state-of-being

the empire of generous or pious aspirations, all <u>must have been</u> otherwise, and from these agonies of death and birth, I had come forth an angel instead of a fiend.

> **Note to Instructor:** The sense of *Had I approached* and *had I risked* is the same as *If I had approached* and *if I had risked*—both convey a situation which never happened.

— LESSON 100 —

Review of Moods and Tenses
Conditional Sentences

Exercise 100A: Conditional Sentences

Identify the following sentences (taken from *Tales of Tears and Laughter: Short Fiction of Medieval Japan*, translated by Virginia Skord) as first, second, or third conditional by writing a *1*, *2*, or *3* in the margin next to each.

If only I could have some boar, chicken, rabbit, raccoon, or badger—I'd eat it stewed. 1

I want to say my prayers, but if you don't give me something to eat, I might not be able to go on! 1

If I had asked you to spend morning and night at my side, I would indeed be hateful. 3

I may not be a dappled pony, but if I were, the more I ate, the more my limbs would grow strong. 2

Why, I'd sing a song if someone asked me to! 2

Note to Instructor: Without context, the student might mark this as a first conditional. Point out that for it to be a first conditional, the predicate of the conditional clause would need to be in the present tense. Since it is in the past tense, no one has asked the speaker to sing and the sentence represents a circumstance contrary to reality.

If I weren't worried about what people might say, I'd even walk around on stilts! 2

If you win, I will divide my domain in two and award you half, to rule just as you like. 1

He could never respond to those lines, even if he knew what they were! 2

If you learn the tales now, you will never forget them. 1

If you see your beloved too repeatedly, the blossom will wither. 1

Therefore, if your servings are too small and you want for anything, just complain bitterly and tell them that you are not used to such conditions. 1

Exercise 100B: Parsing

Write the correct mood, tense, and voice above each underlined verb. These sentences are taken from *Norse Mythology: Tales of the Gods, Sagas and Heroes*, by James Shepherd.

indicative
progressive past
active

One day Odin and his brothers were walking near the sea, when they came upon two trees, an ash and an elm.

subjunctive
simple past
state-of-being

Were it not for your keen ears that hear the grass growing and the wool thickening on the backs

modal
perfect present
active

of the sheep, our enemies might, ere this, have crossed the abyss, and have stormed Asgard.

Note to Instructor: If the student asks, this is an unusual conditional! It is a second conditional: Heimdall *does* have keen ears, and the enemies *haven't* crossed the abyss. However, while the predicate of the condition clause (*were it not*, the equivalent of *if it were not*) is simple past, the predicate of the consequence clause is perfect present rather than simple present. (These variations do occur!)

indicative
simple past
state-of-being

modal
perfect present
active

Here and there were groves in whose quiet depths a less rapid traveller might have heard the trickling of fountains.

indicative
progressive past
passive

She told Odin that a place was being made ready for his son in the lower world.

modal
simple present
active

I must go through the dark land of our enemies, the frost giants of the lower world; and then far

indicative
perfect present
active

beyond, to regions that few have visited.

indicative
perfect present
active

I fear you do not know what a mighty enemy has come to fight you.

indicative
perfect past
active

indicative
progressive past
active

Man had not learned how to control the forces of nature, and he was continually warring against them.

indicative
simple past
active

indicative
perfect past
active

She had no need of a guide to the place where her brothers had lain; for the path to the wood

indicative
perfect past
passive

had been well worn by the feet of the messenger.

Thorstein said, "Herein alone Gunnlaug pleases me not, that I find him an unsettled man; but if he

subjunctive
simple past
state-of-being

modal
simple present
active

were of a mind like thine, little would I hang back."

indicative
simple past
passive

The castle was apparently made of the same material as the bridge, and, as it rose toward the sky,

modal
perfect present
passive

might have been taken for a structure of cloud bathed in moonlight.

indicative
simple present
active

indicative
perfect present
active

modal
simple past
passive

But you still have time to escape; for you have come sooner than you were expected.

indicative
simple past
passive

modal
perfect present
state-of-being

The approach to the bridge was in this way made so clearly visible that it would have been

subjunctive
perfect past
state-of-being

impossible for anyone to get near without Heimdall's knowledge, even had his hearing been less keen.

indicative
perfect present progressive
active

I have been watching for you ever since I heard Sleipnir's eight hoofs strike the bridge.

Exercise 100C: Diagramming

On your own paper, diagram every word of the following sentences from *South African Folk Tales*, by James A. Honey.

Little Jackal wanted to attend, but there was a law made that no one should be present unless he had horns.

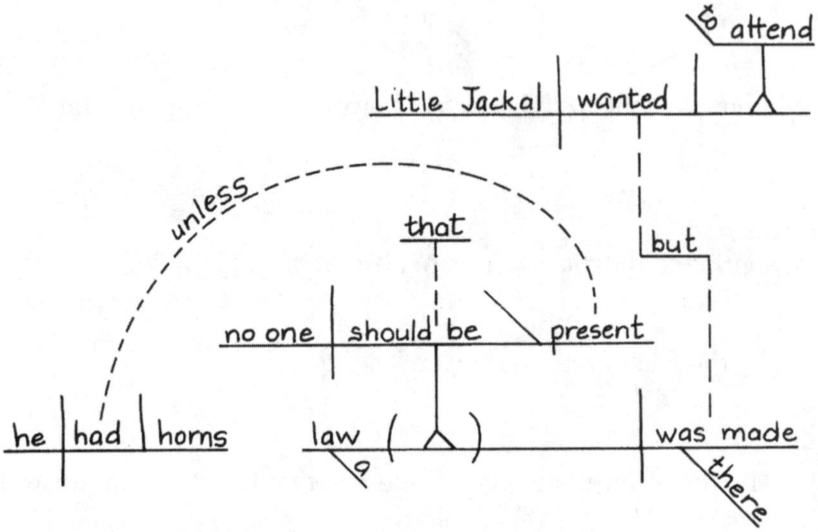

Jackal's hind feet being still free, he threatened to smash Tortoise with them if he did not release him.

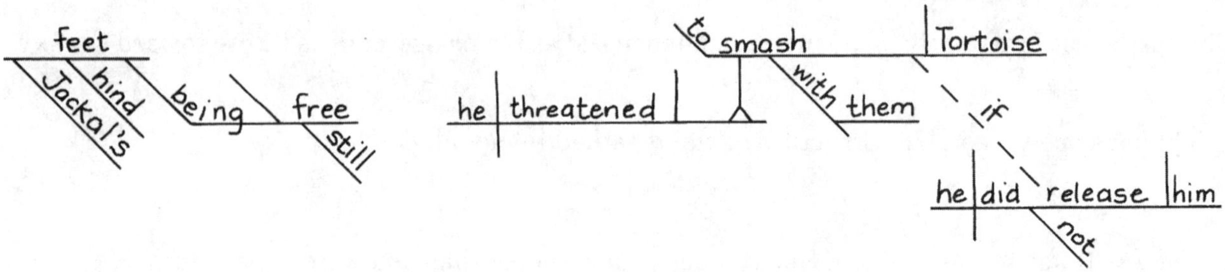

Note to Instructor: You may accept any reasonable representation of the absolute phrase *Jackal's hind feet being still free.*

Once on a time Jackal, who lived on the borders of the colony, saw a wagon returning from the seaside laden with fish; he tried to get into the wagon from behind, but he could not; he then ran on before and lay in the road as if dead.

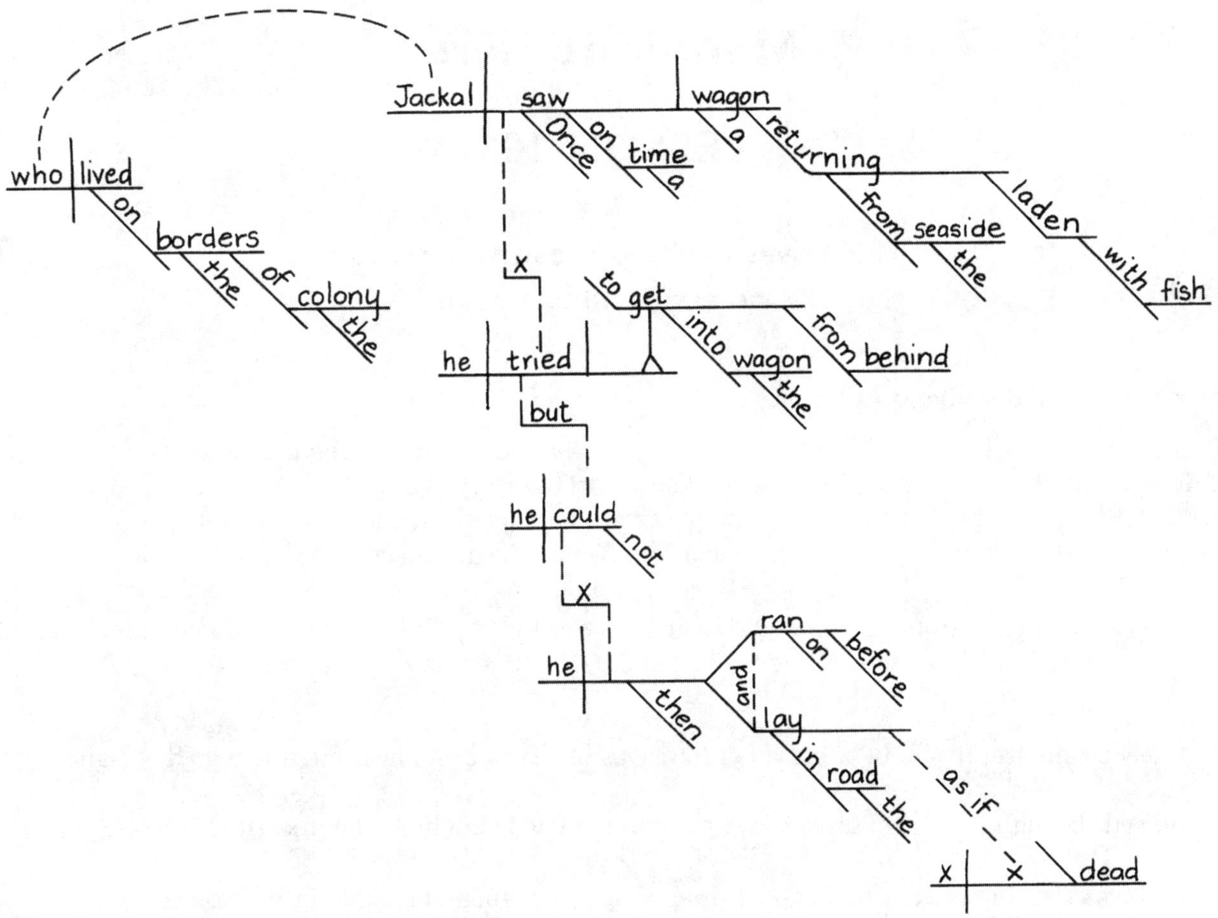

Note to Instructor: *Once on* could also be diagrammed as a single compound preposition. The final clause is adverbial and contains understood elements: *lay in the road as if [he were] dead.*

WEEK 26

More Modifiers

— LESSON 101 —

Adjective Review

Adjectives in the Appositive Position

Correct Comma Usage

Exercise 101A: Identifying Adjectives

Underline every adjective (including verb forms used as adjectives) in the following paragraph of description. Draw an arrow from each adjective to the word it modifies. Above each adjective, write *DESC* for descriptive or *POSS* for possessive. Then, label each as in the attributive (*ATT*), appositive (*APP*), or predicative (*PRED*) position. (Do not underline articles! There are just too many of them.)

This paragraph is from *Pelham*, by Edward Bulwer-Lytton. This is a very old-fashioned style of description—generally, writers today try to avoid using this many adjectives!

She was apparently about twenty; her hair was of the richest chestnut, and a golden light played through its darkness, as if a sunbeam had been caught in the luxuriant tresses, and was striving in vain to escape. Her eyes, large, deep, and shaded into softness by long and very dark lashes, were of a light hazel. Her complexion alone would have rendered her beautiful, it was so clear—so pure; like roses under a clear stream, if, in order to justify my simile, roses would have the complacency to grow in such a situation. Her nose was of a fine and accurate mould that one seldom sees, except in the Grecian statues, which unites the clearest and most decided outline with the most feminine delicacy and softness; and the short curved arch which descended from thence to her mouth, was so fine—so airily and exquisitely formed, that it seemed as if Love himself had modelled the bridge. On the right side of the mouth was one dimple, which corresponded so exactly with the smiles and movements of the rosy lips, that you might

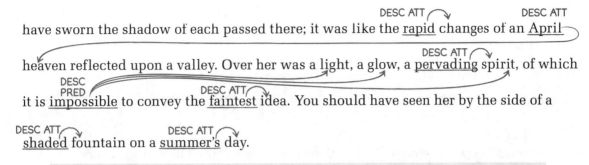

DESC ATT DESC ATT
have sworn the shadow of each passed there; it was like the rapid changes of an April heaven reflected upon a valley. Over her was a light, a glow, a pervading spirit, of which
DESC ATT
DESC PRED DESC ATT
it is impossible to convey the faintest idea. You should have seen her by the side of a
DESC ATT DESC ATT
shaded fountain on a summer's day.

> **Note to Instructor:** You may need to point out to the student that *chestnut* and *hazel* are here used as nouns—both are objects of prepositions.

Exercise 101B: Punctuation Practice

The sentences below are missing all of their punctuation marks! Using everything you have learned about punctuation, insert correct punctuation. You may simply write the punctuation marks in, rather than using proofreader's marks.

These sentences are taken from the gothic short stories of Edgar Allan Poe.

They are persevering ingenious cunning and thoroughly versed in the knowledge which their duties seem chiefly to demand

My brother was at the stern holding on to a small empty water-cask

Its discovery depends upon the mere care patience and determination of the seekers

He had singular wild full liquid eyes whose shadows varied from pure hazel to intense and brilliant jet

Through two small holes that served for nostrils the monster puffed out its thick breath with prodigious violence and with a shrieking disagreeable noise

He presently addressed us in loud harsh and disagreeable accents

The ancient time worn desks and benches were piled desperately with much bethumbed books

Boats yachts and ships have been carried away by not guarding against it before they were within its reach

Looking astern we saw the whole horizon covered with a singular copper colored cloud that rose with the most amazing velocity

They blind deafen and strangle you and take away all power of action or reflection

Never shall I forget the sensations of awe horror and admiration with which I gazed about me

Here the vast bed of the waters seamed and scarred into a thousand conflicting channels burst suddenly into frenzied convulsion heaving boiling hissing gyrating in gigantic and innumerable vortices and all whirling and plunging on to the eastward with a rapidity which water never elsewhere assumes except in precipitous descents

> **Note to Instructor:** The original sentences are found on the next page. Alternate possibilities for punctuation are noted where appropriate.

They are persevering, ingenious, cunning, and thoroughly versed in the knowledge which their duties seem chiefly to demand.

My brother was at the stern, holding on to a small empty water-cask.

> **Note to Instructor:** The comma after *stern* is needed to prevent misunderstanding (what is a "stern holding?"). The hyphen in *water-cask* is optional.

Its discovery depends upon the mere care, patience, and determination of the seekers.

He had singular, wild, full, liquid eyes, whose shadows varied from pure hazel to intense and brilliant jet.

> **Note to Instructor:** The comma after *eyes* is helpful but not necessary.

Through two small holes that served for nostrils, the monster puffed out its thick breath with prodigious violence, and with a shrieking, disagreeable noise.

> **Note to Instructor:** The comma after *violence* is optional.

He presently addressed us in loud, harsh, and disagreeable accents.

The ancient, time-worn desks and benches were piled desperately with much-bethumbed books.

> **Note to Instructor:** The hyphens in both compound adjectives are helpful but not absolutely necessary. The comma after *ancient* is necessary because the adjectives *ancient* and *time-worn* can be exchanged.

Boats, yachts, and ships have been carried away by not guarding against it before they were within its reach.

> **Note to Instructor:** It is acceptable to insert a comma after *away*.

Looking astern, we saw the whole horizon covered with a singular copper-colored cloud that rose with the most amazing velocity.

> **Note to Instructor:** The hyphen in *copper-colored* is necessary because the two adjectives that make up the compound could be considered separate (*a colored copper cloud*).

They blind, deafen, and strangle you, and take away all power of action or reflection.

> **Note to Instructor:** The comma after *you* could be omitted.

Never shall I forget the sensations of awe, horror, and admiration with which I gazed about me.

Here the vast bed of the waters, seamed and scarred into a thousand conflicting channels, burst suddenly into frenzied convulsion—heaving, boiling, hissing—gyrating in gigantic and innumerable vortices, and all whirling and plunging on to the eastward with a rapidity which water never elsewhere assumes except in precipitous descents.

> **Note to Instructor:** This is a challenge sentence! The dashes could also be commas. The comma after *vortices* is helpful but not absolutely necessary. A comma could be inserted after *eastward*. There should be no comma after *rapidity* because *which water...descents* is a restrictive clause. A comma could be inserted after *assumes*.

Exercise 101C: Diagramming

On your own paper, diagram the following sentences from *Rebecca*, a modern gothic novel by Daphne du Maurier.

Each sentence has a different variation of items in a series, separated by commas. When you're finished diagramming, try to tell your instructor what they are. (They may not be exactly parallel—look at the sense of the sentences, not just the parts of speech.)

I can feel again the wind on my face, and hear my laugh, and his that echoed it.

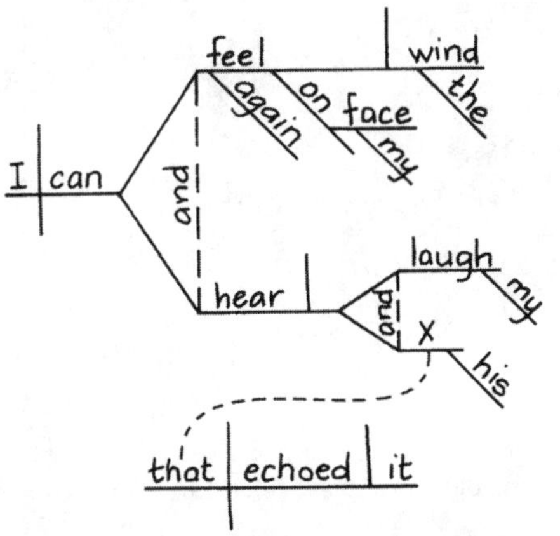

> **Note to Instructor:** The second *laugh* is understood: *his [laugh] that echoed it*. The items in the series are the three things that can be sensed: *wind, my laugh, his [laugh]*.

There was Manderley, our Manderley, secretive and silent as it had always been, the gray stone shining in the moonlight of my dreams, the mullioned windows reflecting the green lawns and the terrace.

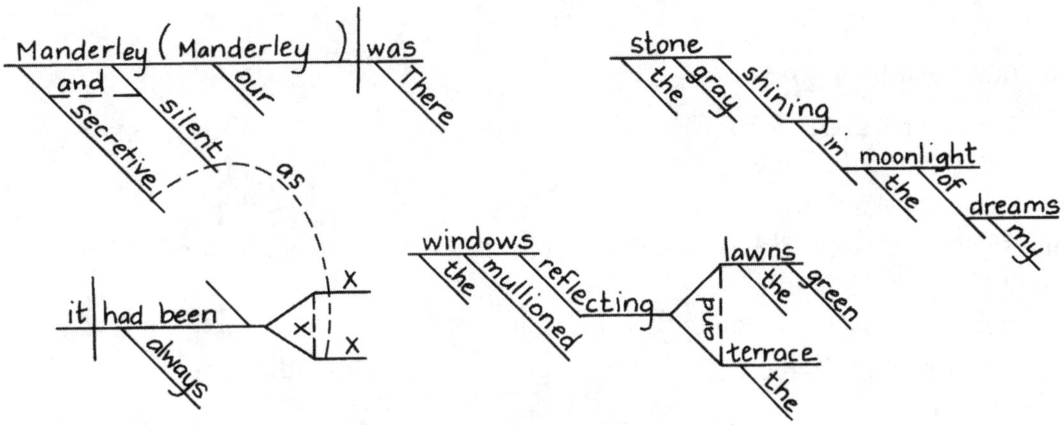

> **Note to Instructor:** This is a wonderful example of an appositive that repeats the noun it renames! The sentence also contains two different absolute phrases (*the gray stone...dreams* and *the mullioned...terrace*). In the comparison clause, the dependent clause with understood elements (*as it had always been [secretive and silent]*) connects to both adjectives (*secretive* AND *silent*), but you may accept a diagram that connects to only one.
>
> The items in the series are all of the elaborations on Manderley: the adjectives, and then the two absolutes, all filling in another detail about the lost house.

Color and scent and sound, rain and the lapping of water, even the mists of autumn and the smell of the flood tide, these are memories of Manderley that will not be denied.

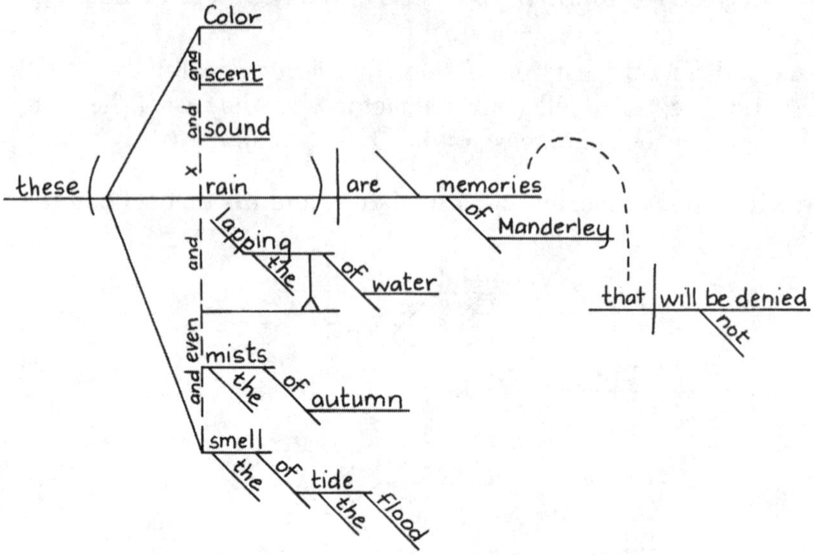

Note to Instructor: This sentence has SEVEN appositives! The student may need help identifying the actual subject (the demonstrative pronoun *these*). The appositives are (obviously) the items in a list.

— LESSON 102 —

Adjective Review
Pronoun Review
Limiting Adjectives

Exercise 102A: Identifying Adjectives

The following excerpt is taken from a ghost story called *Green Tea*, by the nineteenth-century gothic master Sheridan Le Fanu.

Underline every word that acts as an adjective.

Do not include phrases or clauses acting as adjectives. Also, do not include articles. (There are just too many!)

Label each one using the following abbreviations:

Descriptive Adjectives		**Limiting Adjectives**	
Regular	*DA-R*	Possessives	*LA-P*
Present participles	*DA-PresP*	~~Articles~~	~~*LA-A*~~
Past participles	*DA-PastP*	Demonstratives	*LA-D*
		Indefinites	*LA-IND*
		Interrogatives	*LA-INT*
		Numbers	*LA-N*

He would have been much better (DA-R) in a lodging-house, or hotel, I thought, as I drove up through a short (DA-R) double (LA-N) row of sombre (DA-R) elms to a very old-fashioned (DA-R) brick (DA-R) house, darkened (DA-PastP) by the foliage of these [LA-D] trees, which over-topped, and nearly surrounded it. It was a perverse [DA-R] choice, for nothing could be imagined more triste [DA-R] and more silent [DA-R]. The house, I found, belonged to him. He had stayed for a day or two [LA-N] in town, and, finding it for some [LA-IND] cause insupportable [DA-R], had come out here, probably because being furnished [DA-PastP] and his [LA-P], he was relieved of the thought and delay of selection, by coming here.

The sun had already set, and the red [DA-R] reflected [DA-R] light of the western [DA-R] sky illuminated the scene with the peculiar [DA-R] effect with which we are all [LA-IND] familiar [DA-R]. The hall seemed very dark [DA-R], but, getting to the back [DA-R] drawing-room, whose [LA-P] windows command the west, I was again in the same [DA-R] dusky [DA-R] light.

I sat down, looking out upon the richly-wooded [DA-R] landscape that glowed in the grand [DA-R] and melancholy [DA-R] light which was every [DA-R] moment fading. The corners of the room were already dark [DA-R]; all was growing dim [DA-R], and the gloom was insensibly toning my [LA-P] mind, already prepared [DA-PastP] for what was sinister [DA-R]. I was waiting alone for his [LA-P] arrival, which soon took place. The door communicating [DA-PresP] with the front [DA-R] room opened, and the tall [DA-R] figure of Mr. Jennings, faintly seen in the ruddy [DA-R] twilight, came, with quiet [DA-R] stealthy [DA-R] steps, into the room.

We shook hands, and, taking a chair to the window, where there was still light enough to enable us to see our [LA-P] faces, he sat down beside me, and, placing his [LA-P] hand upon my [LA-P] arm, with scarcely [DA-R] a word of preface began his [LA-P] narrative.

The faint [DA-R] glow of the west, the pomp of the lonely [DA-R] woods of Richmond, were before us, behind and about us the darkening [DA-PresP] room, and on the stony [DA-R] face of the sufferer—for the character of his [LA-P] face, though still gentle [DA-R] and sweet [DA-R], was changed—rested that [LA-D] dim [DA-R], odd [DA-R] glow which seems to descend and produce, where it touches, lights, sudden [DA-R] though faint [DA-R], which are lost, almost without gradation, in darkness. The silence, too, was utter [DA-R]; not a distant [DA-R] wheel, or bark, or whistle from without; and within the depressing [DA-PresP] stillness of an invalid's [LA-P] house.

Exercise 102B: Analysis

Note to Instructor: This exercise is intended to engage statistically inclined thinkers in a way that grammar usually doesn't. You may certainly skip it if the student finds this sort of calculation frustrating or unhelpful.

The passage above shows you how a good writer uses adjectives: a mix of colorful descriptive adjectives and sparer, simpler limiting adjectives.

The total word count of the excerpt is 384 words. Now count each type of adjective and fill out the following chart:

Descriptive Adjectives		**Limiting Adjectives**	
Regular	42	Possessives	10
Present participles	3	~~Articles~~	
Past participles	2	Demonstratives	2
		Indefinites	2
		Interrogatives	0
		Numbers	2
Total Descriptive Adjectives	47	Total Limiting Adjectives	16

Total Adjectives Used 63

Good prose can't be reduced to *just* formulas—but formulas can give you some extra help in writing well. The total word count of the excerpt is 384 words. You can figure out what fraction of the total word count is taken up by adjectives by dividing the total word count by the total number of adjectives used. Determine that quotient now, and ask your instructor for help if necessary.

63 ⟌ 384 = 6r.6

The quotient above tells you that 1 out of every 6 [insert answer to division problem!] words in this passage is an adjective. In other words, adjectives do not make up more than about 1/6 of this descriptive writing.

Now let's look at the relationship between limiting and descriptive adjectives. Complete the following division problem:

[number of limiting adjectives] 16 ⟌ 47 [number of descriptive adjectives] = 2 r. 15

The calculation above tells you that 1 out of every 2 - 3 [insert answer to second division problem!] adjectives used is a limiting adjective.

Ask your instructor to share the last part of this exercise with you.

Note to Instructor: Share the following conclusion with the student.

So, about 1/6 of Le Fanu's words are adjectives (1 out of every 6 words). Of those adjectives, between 1/3 and 1/2 are limiting (1 out of every 2 or 3 adjectives). The rest are descriptive.

Exercise 102C: Using Adjectives

On your own paper, rewrite the passage below. It is taken from Sheridan Le Fanu's short story "The Watcher"—but all of the adjectives (except for articles) have been removed.

- Where adjectives could be removed without making the sentence ungrammatical, they have simply been deleted without a trace. Where removing an adjective made the sentence unreasonable, a blank has been inserted instead. So you know that adjectives go in the blanks—but you'll have to find a lot of other places to put them as well!
- You can also insert adverbs, additional articles, and conjunctions as necessary to make your insertions work.
- Aim to use the same proportions as the passage in Exercise 102B. This excerpt originally had 375 words, so use 60 to 62 total adjectives, not including articles.
- Use no more than 17 limiting adjectives. Use at least 3 different kinds of limiting adjectives (your choice!).
- The remainder should be descriptive adjectives. Use at least 3 participles (present or past) as adjectives.

When you are finished, compare your work with the original passage in the Answer Key.

The stranger stopped at the door of the room, and displayed ________ form and face completely. He wore a cloak, which was ________ and ________, not ________ quite to the knees; ________ legs were cased in stockings, and ________ shoes were adorned with roses of the ________ colour. The opening of the cloak in front showed the under-suit to consist of ________ very ________, perhaps ________ material, and ________ hands were enclosed in a pair of gloves which ran up considerably above the wrist, in the manner of a gauntlet. In ________ hand he carried ________ walking-stick and ________ hat, which he had removed, and the other hung heavily by ________ side. A quantity of hair descended in tresses from ________ head, and ________ folds rested upon the plaits of a ruff, which effectually concealed ________ neck.

So far all was ________; but the face!—all the flesh of the face was coloured with the hue which is sometimes produced by the operation of medicines administered in quantities; the eyes were ________, and the white appeared both above and below the iris, which gave to them an expression of insanity, which was heightened by ________ fixedness; the mouth was writhed considerably to ________ side, where it opened in order to give egress to fangs, which projected from the jaw, far below the lip; the hue of the lips themselves bore the ________ relation to that of the face, and was consequently nearly ________. The character of the face was ________ to the ________ degree; and, indeed, such a combination of horror could hardly be accounted for.

There was something indescribably ________, even ________ about ________ motions, something ________, something ________—it was as if the limbs were guided and directed by a spirit ________ to the management of ________ machinery. During ________ stay he did not once suffer ________ eyelids to close, nor even to move in the ________ degree; and further, there was a stillness in ________ person, owing to the absence of the motion of the chest ________ by the process of respiration.

Notes to Instructor: The original passage, found below, actually had 64 adjectives, of which 18 were limiting adjectives—almost exactly the proportions found in the first passage! Le Fanu's style is very consistent.

When the student has finished, show her the original.

You may need to remind her that she can add more than one descriptive adjective to any given noun or pronoun.

If she gets frustrated, show her one or more lines of the original and encourage her to use a thesaurus.

The stranger stopped at the door of the room, and displayed his form and face completely. He wore a dark-coloured cloth cloak, which was short and full, not falling quite to the knees; his legs were cased in dark purple silk stockings, and his shoes were adorned with roses of the same colour. The opening of the cloak in front showed the under-suit to consist of some very dark, perhaps sable material, and his hands were enclosed in a pair of heavy leather gloves which ran up considerably above the wrist, in the manner of a gauntlet. In one hand he carried his walking-stick and his hat, which he had removed, and the other hung heavily by his side. A quantity of grizzled hair descended in long tresses from his head, and its folds rested upon the plaits of a stiff ruff, which effectually concealed his neck.

So far all was well; but the face!—all the flesh of the face was coloured with the bluish leaden hue which is sometimes produced by the operation of metallic medicines administered in excessive quantities; the eyes were enormous, and the white appeared both above and below the iris, which gave to them an expression of insanity, which was heightened by their glassy fixedness; the mouth was writhed considerably to one side, where it opened in order to give egress to two long, discoloured fangs, which projected from the upper jaw, far below the lower lip; the hue of the lips themselves bore the usual relation to that of the face, and was consequently nearly black. The character of the face was malignant to the last degree; and, indeed, such a combination of horror could hardly be accounted for.

There was something indescribably odd, even horrible about all his motions, something undefinable, something unnatural, unhuman—it was as if the limbs were guided and directed by a spirit unused to the management of bodily machinery. During his stay he did not once suffer his eyelids to close, nor even to move in the slightest degree; and further, there was a death-like stillness in his whole person, owing to the total absence of the heaving motion of the chest caused by the process of respiration.

— LESSON 103 —

Misplaced Modifiers
Squinting Modifiers
Dangling Modifiers

Exercise 103A: Correcting Misplaced Modifiers

Circle each misplaced modifier and draw an arrow to the place in the sentence that it should occupy.

He stood in the doorway with a startled expression.

The sun on the bright water shone pleasantly.

The chef handed out after-dinner treats to all his guests in paper bags.

Nell sat in the fishing boat with a smile.

Without getting permission, the chocolate frosted brownie was consumed by the hungry boy.

I decided to go home for Thanksgiving in July.

The golden brown turkey sat on the china platter steaming gently.

Running through the haunted countryside, scared and afraid, I watched the scary movie about the fleeing woman.

One morning, I spotted an elephant in my pajamas.

Exercise 103B: Clarifying Squinting Modifiers

Circle each squinting modifier. On your own paper, rewrite each sentence twice, eliminating the ambiguity by moving the squinting modifier to produce sentences with two different meanings. Insert commas and change capitalization/punctuation as needed. (And be aware—you might be able to eliminate the ambiguity by simply changing punctuation!)

The first is done for you.

Note to Instructor: Explanatory notes in italics follow each set of sentences. Use these to help the student understand as needed.

The cow that was in the back pasture recently had twin calves.

The cow that was recently in the back pasture had twin calves.
The cow that was in the back pasture had twin calves recently.

The calves only seemed interested in eating more hay.

Only the calves seemed interested in eating more hay.
The calves seemed interested only in eating more hay.
The calves seemed interested in eating only more hay.

There are actually three options here—accept any two! First: The calves, not the cow, were interesting in eating more hay. Second: The calves were interested in eating and nothing else. Third: The calves were interested in eating, but only hay, no other food.

I told the farmer when the storm ended we should put all the cows back outside.

When the storm ended, I told the farmer we should put all the cows back outside.
I told the farmer we should put all the cows back outside when the storm ended.

First: The storm ended, and then I told the farmer what to do with the cows.
Second: The cows go back outside after the storm.

Farmers who move their cows from pasture to pasture often have healthier livestock.

Farmers who move their cows from pasture to pasture have healthier livestock often.
Often, farmers who move their cows from pasture to pasture have healthier livestock.
Farmers who often move their cows from pasture to pasture have healthier livestock.

There are actually three options here—accept any two! The first and second sentences have the same meaning: When farmers move their cows, their livestock are frequently healthy.
The third sentence means: When farmers move their cows regularly, they are healthier.

The farm manager decided after two weeks to sell the belligerent bull.

After two weeks, the farm manager decided to sell the belligerent bull.

The farm manager decided to sell the belligerent bull after two weeks.

First: Two weeks went by and the farm manager decided to sell the bull.
Second: The farm manager decided to wait two weeks and then sell the bull.

When cows calve often they will give enough milk for more than two calves.

When cows calve often, they will give enough milk for more than two calves.

When cows calve, they will often give enough milk for more than two calves.

First: Inserting a comma clarifies the ambiguity! When cows have calves frequently, they give more milk.
Second: When cows calve, whenever they do it, they often give more milk than they need.

We agreed at the eight month mark to wean the calves onto grass and grain.

At the eight month mark, we agreed to wean the calves onto grass and grain.

We agreed to wean the calves onto grass and grain at the eight month mark.

First: When the calves were eight months old, we agreed to wean them.
Second: We agreed (beforehand, probably) that the calves would be weaned at eight months.

Feeding calf pellets rapidly produces very strong, hearty calves.

Rapidly feeding calf pellets produces very strong, hearty calves.

Feeding calf pellets produces very strong, hearty calves rapidly.

First: When the pellets are fed quickly, the calves grow strong and hearty.
Second: When the pellets are fed, the calves get strong and hearty rapidly.

The farmer decided during calving season to spend nights at the barn.

During calving season, the farmer decided to spend nights at the barn.

The farmer decided to spend nights at the barn during calving season.

First: While calving season was going on, the farmer decided to spend nights at the barn.
Second: At some undetermined point, the farmer decided that when calving season was underway, he/she would spend nights at the barn.

Exercise 103C: Rewriting Dangling Modifiers

On your own paper, rewrite each of these sentences twice, using each of the strategies described in the lesson. You should feel free to change verbs and other words, as long as the sentence remains grammatical and has the same meaning as the original.

These have been adapted from *Chasing New Horizons: Inside the Epic First Mission to Pluto*, by Alan Stern and David Grinspoon. When you've finished rewriting your sentences, your instructor will show you the originals!

Note to Instructor: Answers may vary; as long as they follow the rules in the How to Fix a Dangling Modifier section in this lesson, you may accept different versions.

After you have checked the student's versions, show her the original sentences.

Reading everything he could find in the local library relating to astronomy and planets, the debate about the controversial "canals" on Mars "discovered" and promoted by the wealthy and charismatic Boston astronomer Percival Lowell absorbed him.

Reading everything he could find in the local library relating to astronomy and planets, he was absorbed in the debate about the controversial "canals" on Mars "discovered" and promoted by the wealthy and charismatic Boston astronomer Percival Lowell.

As he read everything he could find in the local library relating to astronomy and planets, the debate about the controversial "canals" on Mars "discovered" and promoted by the wealthy and charismatic Boston astronomer Percival Lowell absorbed him.

ORIGINAL

He read everything he could find in the local library relating to astronomy and planets, and he followed the debates about the controversial "canals" on Mars "discovered" and promoted by the wealthy and charismatic Boston astronomer Percival Lowell.

Meanwhile, out there on its own, deep in the Pluto system, the team was watching New Horizons do what it had been designed and built to do a dozen years before.

Meanwhile, out there on its own, deep in the Pluto system, New Horizons, watched by the team, was doing what it had been designed and built to do a dozen years before.

Meanwhile, even though New Horizons was out there on its own, deep in the Pluto system, the team was watching it do what it had been designed and built to do a dozen years before.

ORIGINAL

Meanwhile, out there on its own, deep in the Pluto system, New Horizons was doing what it had been designed and built to do a dozen years before.

As it flashed past Pluto and its five moons that day, a library of data was being gathered, so vast that it would take sixteen months to send it all back to Earth.

As it flashed past Pluto and its five moons that day, New Horizons was gathering a library of data, so vast that it would take sixteen months to send it all back to Earth.

As New Horizons flashed past Pluto and its five moons that day, it was gathering a library of data so vast that it would take sixteen months to send it all back to Earth.

ORIGINAL

As it flashed past Pluto and its five moons that day, it was gathering a library of data so vast that it would take sixteen months to send it all back to Earth.

Having traveled four hours at the speed of light from Pluto 3 billion miles away, Alice Bowman beamed and gave a thumbs-up at the expected time, when the signal reached Earth.

Having traveled four hours at the speed of light from Pluto 3 billion miles away, the signal reached Earth and Alice Bowman beamed and gave a thumbs-up at the expected time.

After the signal traveled four hours at the speed of light from Pluto 3 billion miles away, Alice Bowman beamed and gave a thumbs-up at the expected time, when it reached Earth.

ORIGINAL

At the expected time, when the signal reached Earth—having traveled four hours at the speed of light from Pluto 3 billion miles away—Alice Bowman beamed and gave a thumbs-up.

— LESSON 104 —

Degrees of Adjectives

Comparisons Using *More, Fewer,* and *Less*

Exercise 104A: Positive, Comparative, and Superlative Adjectives

Use the following chart to review spelling rules for forming degrees of adjectives. Fill in the missing forms. Then, fill in the blank in each sentence with each adjective indicated in brackets (properly spelled!).

The sentences are all drawn from Charlotte Brontë's classic novel *Villette.*

Spelling Rules:

If the adjective ends in *e* already, add only *–r* or *–st.*

noble	nobler	noblest
pure	purer	purest
true	truer	truest

If the adjective ends in a short vowel sound and a consonant, double the consonant and add *–er* or *–est.*

red	redder	reddest
thin	thinner	thinnest
hot	hotter	hottest

If the adjective ends in *–y*, change the *y* to *i* and add *–er* or *–est.*

hazy	hazier	haziest
tiny	tinier	tiniest

And Graham once more snatched her aloft, and she again punished him; and while she pulled his lion's locks, termed him—"The naughtiest, rudest, worst, untruest person that ever was." [in order, the superlatives of *naughty, rude, bad, untrue*]

Mr. Jones, a dried-in man of business, stood behind his desk: he seemed one of the greatest, and I one of the happiest of beings. [in order, the superlatives of *great* and *happy*]

I took off my pink dress and lace mantle with happier feelings than I had experienced in putting them on. [the comparative of *happy*]

He did not grow gayer—no raillery, no levity sparkled across his aspect—but his position seemed to become one of more pleasure to himself, and he spoke his augmented comfort in readier language, in tones more suave. [in order, the comparatives of *gay* and *ready*]

The afternoon hours were over, and the stiller time of evening shaded the quiet faubourg. [the comparative of *still*]

I believe, if some of you were thrown into Nebuchadnezzar's hottest furnace you would issue forth untraversed by the smell of fire. [the superlative of *hot*]

A handsome middle-aged lady in dark velvet; a gentleman who might be her son—the best face, the finest figure, I thought, I had ever seen; a third person in a pink dress and black lace mantle. [in order, the superlatives of *good* and *fine*]

Those eyes had looked on the visits of a certain ghost—had long waited the comings and goings of that __strangest__ spectre, Hypochondria. [the superlative of *strange*]

I think I should have declined had I been __poorer__ than I was, and with __scantier__ fund of resource, more stinted narrowness of future prospect. [in order, the comparatives of *poor* and *scanty*]

The Queen's eye, however, was her own; and pity, goodness, sweet sympathy, blessed it with __divinest__ light. [the superlative of *divine*]

The __smaller__ room was __better__ furnished and more habitable than the __larger__; thither he introduced me. [in order, the comparatives of *small*, *good*, and *large*]

As she passed me to-night, triumphant in beauty, my emotions did her homage; but for one luckless sneer, I should yet be the __humblest__ of her servants. [the superlative of *humble*]

There is the wonderful Great Wall of China; here is a Chinese lady, with a foot __littler__ than mine. [the comparative of *little*]

Exercise 104B: Forming Comparisons

Rewrite each set of independent clauses so that they form a comparative sentence making use of *more*, *less*, *fewer*, and/or comparative forms of the adjectives indicated. The first is done for you.

When you are finished, ask your instructor to show you the original sentences, which are taken from the novel *Anna Karenina*, by Leo Tolstoy, translated by Constance Garnett.

Note to Instructor: This may be a challenging assignment for some students; give all help needed. If necessary, read the first part of the sentence out loud and encourage the student to try to finish it. When the student is finished, show her the original sentences. Her sentences do not need to be identical as long as they incorporate a comparison.

One lives longer.
One learns.

The longer one lives the more one learns.

He tried to compose himself.
He found himself breathless.

The more he tried to compose himself, the more breathless he found himself.

He told her.
He did nothing.
He had less time to do anything.

As he told her, the more he did nothing, the less time he had to do anything.

He listened to the fantasia of King Lear.
He felt further from forming any definite opinion of it.

The more he listened to the fantasia of King Lear the further he felt from forming any definite opinion of it.

His behavior was externally obedient and respectful.
In his heart, he respected and loved her less.

The more externally obedient and respectful his behavior, the less in his heart he respected and loved her.

He read and thought.
He read more.
He thought more.
He felt further from the aim he was pursuing.

He read and thought, and the more he read and the more he thought, the further he felt from the aim he was pursuing.

Exercise 104C: Using *Fewer* and *Less*

Complete the sentences by filling in each blank with either *fewer* or *less*.

The original sentences are taken from Jane Austen's novel *Emma.*

As she thought __less__ of his inebriety, she thought more of his inconstancy and presumption; and with __fewer__ struggles for politeness, replied, "It is impossible for me to doubt any longer."

When first sounded on the subject, he was so miserable, that they were almost hopeless—a second allusion, indeed, gave __less__ pain.

A woman with __fewer__ resources than I have need not have been at a loss.

But Harriet was __less__ humble, had __fewer__ scruples than formerly.

Nothing should tempt her to go, if they did; and she regretted that her father's known habits would be giving her refusal __less__ meaning than she could wish.

She saw that with all the deep blush of consciousness, there had been a smile of secret delight, she had __less__ scruple in the amusement, and much __less__ compunction with respect to her.

Exercise 104D: Diagramming

On your own paper, diagram every word of the following sentences from *Watership Down*, by Richard Adams.

Each sentence has at least one understood element! If you can't find it, ask your instructor to show you the sentences with the understood elements spelled out.

Note to Instructor: Each sentence is followed by a version with the understood elements spelled out, and a diagram of the sentence. If the student has difficulty, show him the spelled-out version of the sentence, but cover the diagram until he makes an attempt at it himself.

The slower the journey, the more dangerous it would be, and stragglers would attract elil and discourage the rest.

The slower the journey [was], the more dangerous it would be, and stragglers would attract elil and [would] discourage the rest.

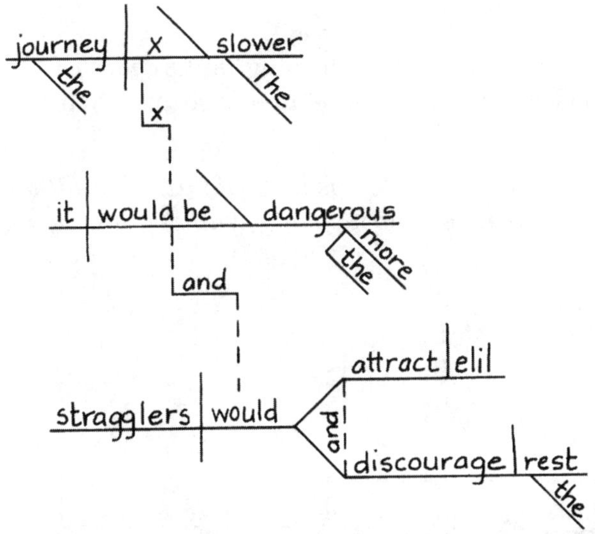

Note to Instructor: In this sentence, both terms of comparison (*slower* and *more dangerous*) are predicate adjectives that follow linking verbs. In the last independent clause, the helping verb *would* goes with both action verbs. It could also be diagrammed on the same line as *attract* with an *x* coming before *discourage* to represent the repeated helping verb.

She knew what to do, and the less they were seen together the better.

She knew what to do, and the less they were seen together, the better [it would be].

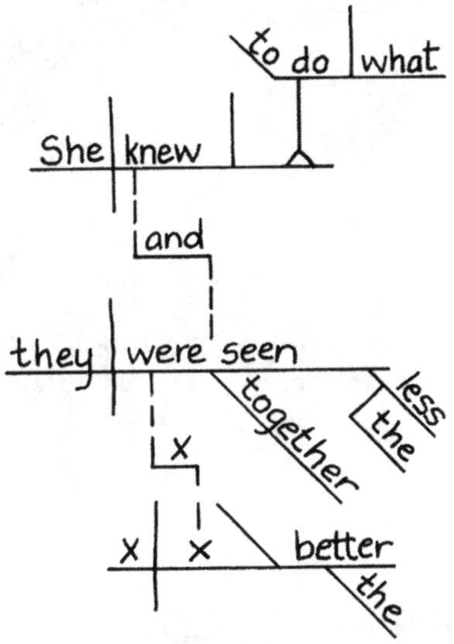

Note to Instructor: In the diagram, the infinitive phrase *to do what* is diagrammed as the object of the verb *knew*. The student could also diagram *what* as the direct object of the verb, and diagram *to do* on a tree as an object complement (see Lesson 40).

The final clause has an understood subject and predicate.

Together here functions as an adverb, answering the question *how/where*.

CHALLENGE SENTENCE

Try to figure out the understood elements and diagram them yourself (but if you get stuck, ask for help!).

But the more he thought about it—as well as he could for hunger and fear and the trance that comes upon rabbits face to face with death—the more it seemed to him that there was at least a chance of success.

But the more he thought about it—as well as he could [think well] for hunger and fear and the trance that comes upon rabbits [who are] face to face with death—the more it seemed to him that there was at least a chance of success.

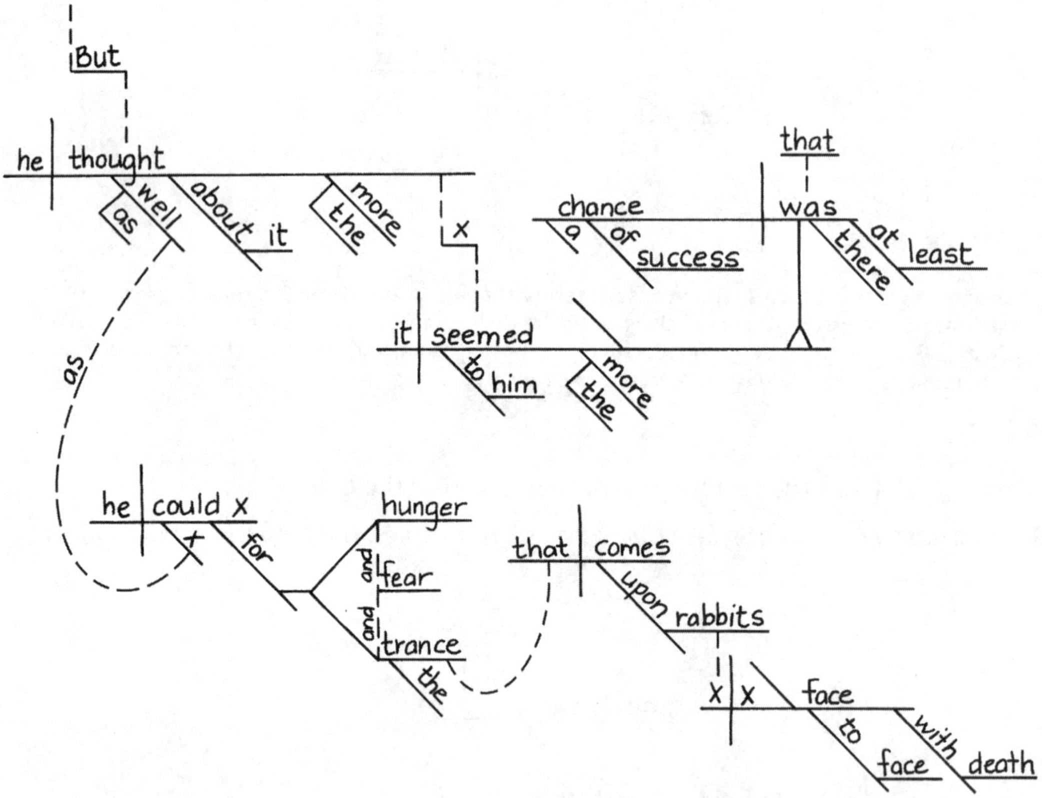

Note to Instructor: In the subordinate clause *as well as he could...*, the first *as* modifies *well*, while the second acts as a subordinating conjunction connecting *well* with the understood repetition of *well* modifying *could [think]*.

WEEK 27

Double Identities

— LESSON 105 —

Clauses with Understood Elements

Than as Conjunction, Preposition, and Adverb

Quasi-Coordinators

Exercise 105A: Comparisons Using *Than*

Each of the following sentences, taken from *The History of the Peloponnesian War* by the ancient Greek historian Thucydides, contains a comparison clause introduced by *than* and missing some of its words. Using carets, do your best to insert the missing words.

Note to Instructor: The student's phrasing may differ.

Each comparison clause must have a subject and predicate. Words in brackets fill the clauses out; if the student does not include them, do not mark the answer wrong. However, when the student is finished, ask him to compare his work to the answers below.

Thucydides, an Athenian, wrote the history of the war between the Peloponnesians and the Athenians, beginning at the moment that it broke out, and believing that it would be a great war and more worthy of relation than any that had preceded it ^were [worthy of relation].

And so the power of the descendants of Pelops came to be greater than that of the descendants of Perseus ^was [great].

He had also a navy far stronger than ^the navy of his contemporaries ^was [strong].

An examination of the facts will show that it was much greater than the wars which preceded it ^were [great].

To them, laborious occupation is less of a misfortune than the peace of a quiet life ^is [a misfortune].

Thus it happens that the vast experience of Athens has carried her further than you ^have gone on the path of innovation.

And none care to inquire why this reproach is not brought against other imperial powers, who treat their subjects with less moderation than we do ^treat [our subjects].

Exercise 105B: Identifying Parts of the Sentence

In the following sentences, also drawn from *The History of the Peloponnesian War*, identify each bolded word or phrase as *SC* for subordinating conjunction, *QC* for quasi-coordinator, *PREP* for preposition, *ADJ* for adjective, or *ADV* for adverb.

Note to Instructor: The student only needs to insert the labels below. Additional notes are for your reference; use them to help the student as needed.

What enabled Agamemnon to raise the armament was more, in my opinion, his superiority in strength, **than** [SC] the oaths of Tyndareus^ [, enabled him]; which bound the suitors to follow him .

It has possessed the same form of government for **more than** [ADV] four hundred years, reckoning to the end of the late war, and has thus been in a position to arrange the affairs of the other states. [*four hundred* is an adjective modifying *years, more than* modifies *four hundred*]

Accordingly they suddenly attacked and took Iasus, whose inhabitants never imagined that the ships could be **other than** [PREP] Athenian. [*Athenian* is the object of the preposition; the prepositional phrase *other than Athenian* serves as a predicate nominative renaming *ships.*]

For kindness opportunely shown has a greater power of removing old grievances **than** [SC] the facts of the case may warrant. [This subordinate clause has no missing elements!]

They chose to prosecute their complaints by war, **rather than** [QC] prosecuting them by a fair trial. [the quasi-coordinator links an infinitive phrase to a participle phrase, so the parts of the sentence are unequal]

The Corinthians had been victorious in the sea-fight until night; and having thus been enabled to carry off most wrecks and dead, they were in possession of no **fewer than** [ADV] a thousand prisoners of war. [*thousand* is an adjective modifying *prisoners, fewer than* is an adverb modifying the adjective *thousand*]

And yet the world used to say that you were to be depended upon; but in your case, we fear, it said **more than** [ADJ] the truth. [*more than* modifies the noun *truth*]

Against Athens you prefer to act on the defensive instead of on the offensive, and to make it an affair of chances by deferring the struggle till she has grown far stronger **than** [SC]^ [she was] at first.

And indeed, in spite of the time occupied with the necessary arrangements, **less than** [ADJ] a year elapsed before Attica was invaded, and the war openly began. [*less than* modifies the noun *year*]

Exercise 105C: Diagramming

On your own paper, diagram every word of the following three sentences, also taken from *The History of the Peloponnesian War.*

Less than a year elapsed before Attica was invaded, and the war openly began.

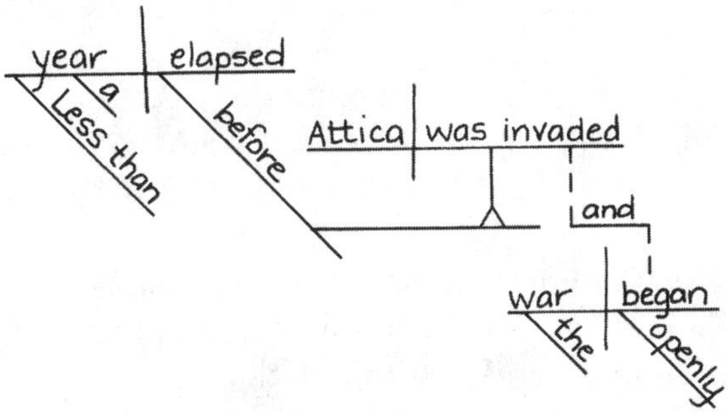

Farmers are a class of men that are always more ready to serve in person than in purse.

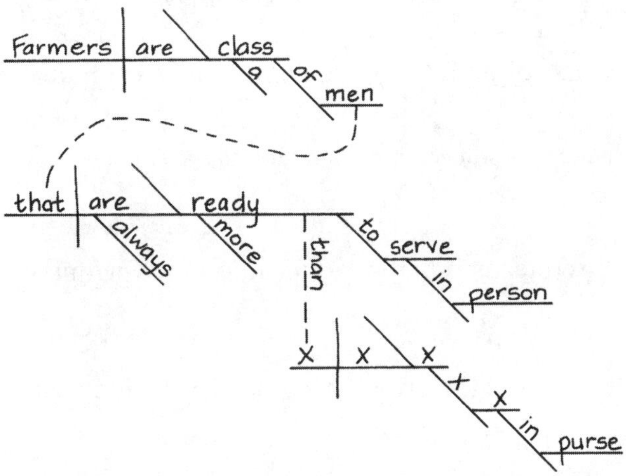

Note to Instructor: The understood words in the subordinate clause are *to serve in person than [they are ready to serve] in purse.*

Accordingly they suddenly attacked and took Iasus, whose inhabitants never imagined that the ships could be other than Athenian.

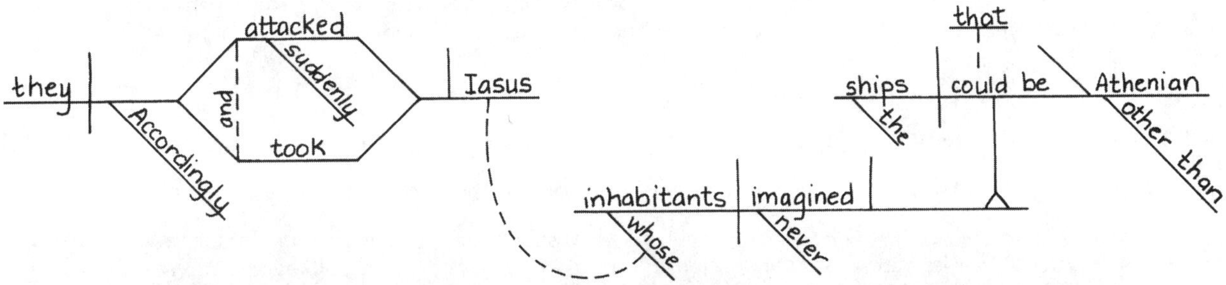

Note to Instructor: Technically, *Iasus* is the direct object of both *attacked* and *took*, but you may accept it as a direct object of either verb. *Suddenly* could also be diagrammed beside *Accordingly* as modifying both verbs.

— LESSON 106 —

The Word *As*

Quasi-Coordinators

Exercise 106A: Identifying Parts of the Sentence

In the following sentences, find and underline every adverb, preposition, conjunction, and quasi-coordinator. Then label each as *ADV* for adverb, *PREP* for preposition, *CC* for coordinating conjunction, *SC* for subordinating conjunction, and *QC* for quasi-coordinator. Remember that a quasi-coordinator can be a short phrase as well as a single word.

These sentences are taken from *The Poison Squad: One Chemist's Single-Minded Crusade for Food Safety at the Turn of the Twentieth Century*, by Deborah Blum, an account of food chemist Harvey Wiley's fight for laws that would regulate how food and drink are sold to the public.

Some of these are tricky—be careful, and ask your instructor for help if you need it!

Note to Instructor: Explanations have been added for more difficult sentences—share with the student as needed.

PREP ADV PREP ADV ADV PREP
Faced with hostility, he became more rigid in his stance, often refusing to compromise even on small details.

Note to Instructor: The placement of *even* might confuse the student: it modifies the adjective *small* (*refusing to compromise on even small details*).

PREP SC PREP PREP
"The cry 'Poisoned Milk'" rings through the land, he wrote, as it had over decades of government
CC
inaction and corruption.

SC ADV PREP
He estimated that corn-derived glucose had about two-thirds the sweetening power of cane sugar;
ADV ADV PREP
it was also far cheaper, produced for less than half the cost.

Note to Instructor: *Also* is an adverb modifying *was* and answering the question *to what extent*. *Far* is an adverb modifying *cheaper*. *For* is a preposition; its object is *half*, here serving as a noun ("a half"), and so *less than* here is acting as an adjective modifying *half*!

SC PREP PREP ADV ADV SC
He urged that copper be banned as an additive from American food products as soon as possible.

Note to Instructor: *As* serves three different functions in this sentence. The prepositional phrase *as an additive* modifies *copper*. The adverb *soon* modifies the verb *be banned*; the *as* before it modifies *soon*; the *as* after it introduces the subordinate clause with understood elements *as [it was] possible*.

PREP ADV PREP PREP
In the year 1904, Dodge noted, more than twenty thousand children under the age of two had died
PREP CC PREP
in New York City and that milk was considered a major contributor to those fatalities.

Note to Instructor: The word *that* is a trick! It is not a subordinating conjunction—if *that milk was considered...fatalities* were a subordinate clause acting as a direct object, it would have to receive the action of the verb *noted* (*Dodge noted that...*). But *Dodge noted* is a parenthetical expression, not the main clause of the sentence. The subject and predicate of the first independent clause are *children had died*. The second independent clause, *that milk was considered a major contributor to those fatalities*, is linked to the first by a coordinating conjunction—and *that* is a demonstrative adjective modifying *milk*.

ADV SC SC PREP PREP
La Follette conveniently overlooked the fact that butter itself, when produced in the winter from
PREP QC ADV ADV SC
cows fed on hay rather than pasture grass, turns out more white than yellow.

> **Note to Instructor:** This sentence contains two clauses with understood elements: *when [it is] produced...* and *than [it turns out] yellow.*

PREP QC PREP
Those with a healthy stomach, as he put it, were unlikely to be harmed by an occasional exposure
PREP CC
to copper or zinc.

SC ADV CC ADV ADV PREP
If risks were clearly and methodically identified, then those compounds should be removed from
CC
all food and drink.

> **Note to Instructor:** *Then* cannot be a subordinating conjunction, because *If risks...identified* is a dependent clause—nothing can be subordinated to it! Instead, *then* modifies *should be removed* and answers the question *when.*

Exercise 106B: Diagramming

On your own paper, diagram every word of the following sentences, very slightly adapted from *Swindled: The Dark History of Food Fraud, from Poisoned Candy to Counterfeit Coffee*, by Bee Wilson. Ask for help if you need it!

> **Note to Instructor:** Provide all necessary help.

White bread was always more expensive than brown bread, because the bran was wasted and because the bread was made from wheat rather than the cheaper barley and rye.

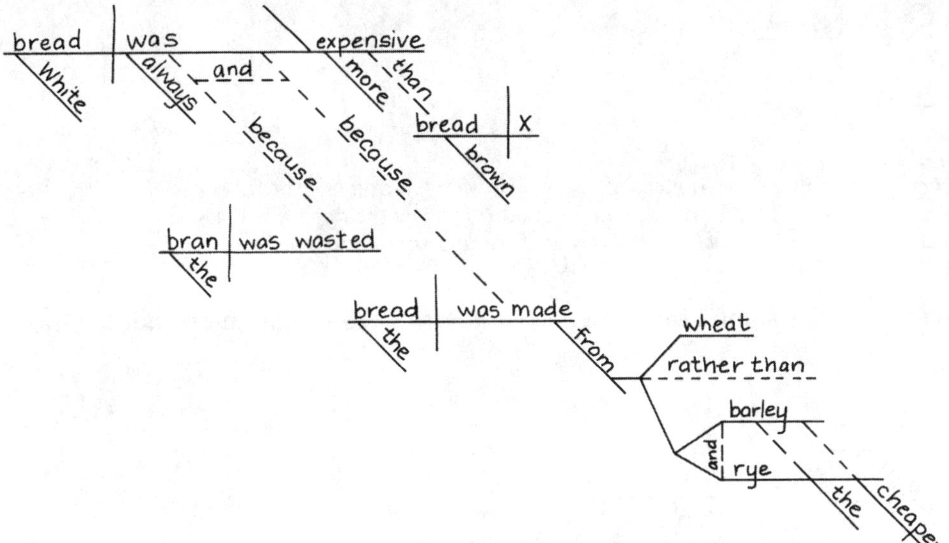

> **Note to Instructor:** This is an unusual sentence—the coordinating conjunction *and* connects two dependent clauses, both introduced by *because. Than* is a subordinating conjunction connecting a dependent clause with understood elements to the term of comparison: *more expensive than brown bread [was].* The phrase *from wheat rather than the cheaper barley and rye* contains both a quasi-coordinator and a coordinating conjunction—accept any effort by the student to show this! In that phrase, *the* and *cheaper* modify both *barley* and *rye,* but if the student simply puts them beneath *barley,* accept the answer and show the student the version in this Key.

Given the poor, sour grain, bakers used more alum than usual, which resulted in a "harsh" crumb and acrid taste.

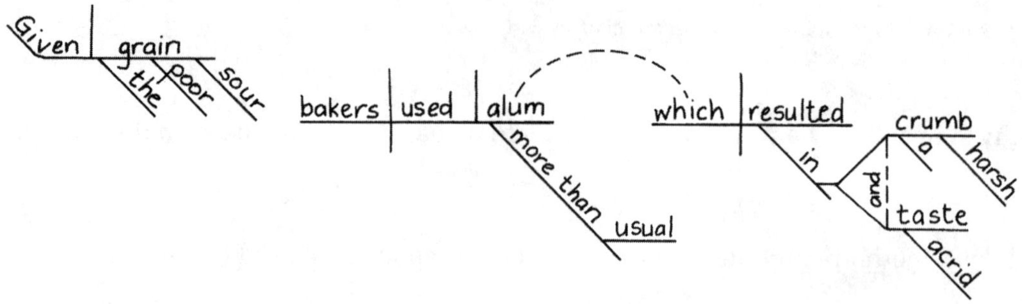

Note to Instructor: *Given the poor, sour grain* is an absolute construction—it connects to the rest of the sentence in meaning, but not grammatically. *More than* acts here not to connect a dependent clause to the main clause, but as a compound preposition, with *usual* acting as a noun: *more than [the] usual.* Some students may decide that *more than* is a compound subordinating conjunction connecting a dependent clause with understood elements (*more than [it is] usual*); you may accept this answer.

But shouldn't all food be as safe and as pure and as fresh as possible?

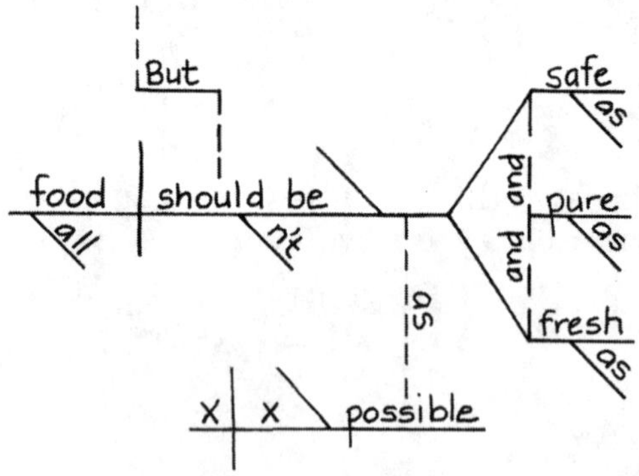

Note to Instructor: The first three occurrences of *as* are all adverbs, modifying the three predicate adjectives; the fourth is a subordinating conjunction, linking the dependent clause with understood elements (*as [it is] possible*) to the terms of comparison in the main clause.

The swindlers still have roughly the same kind of expertise to draw on—legal and scientific—as the antiswindlers.

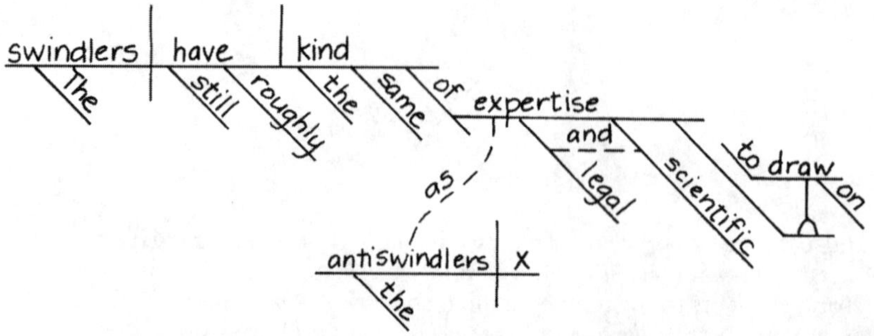

Note to Instructor: In this sentence, *as* links the quality being compared (*expertise*) to the subject of the subordinate clause.

Just as false and exaggerated dangers swarm everywhere, real dangers may become invisible.

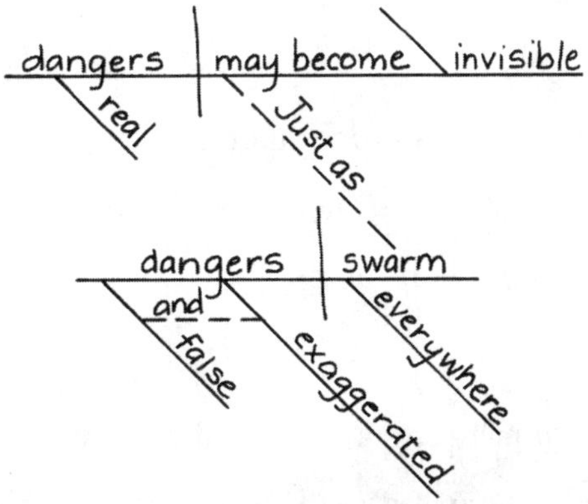

Note to Instructor: *Just as* here functions as a compound subordinator, linking the dependent clause to the main clause *real dangers may become invisible.*

— LESSON 107 —

Words That Can Be Multiple Parts of Speech

Exercise 107A: Identifying Parts of Speech

Identify the part of speech of each underlined word (adapted from *The Old Curiosity Shop*, by Charles Dickens) by writing the correct abbreviation above it: *N* (noun), *PRO* (pronoun), *V* (verb), *ADJ* (adjective), *ADV* (adverb), *PREP* (preposition), *CC* (coordinating conjunction), or *SC* (subordinating conjunction).

SC PREP
Although I am an old man, night is generally my time for walking.

PRO ADJ SC PREP N
"I know that, sir," she replied timidly. "I am afraid it is a very long way, for I came from there to-night."

Note to Instructor: In the phrase *from there, there* functions as a noun: the place that is a very long way.

ADV PREP N SC
She walked on as before, growing more familiar with me as we proceeded and talking cheerfully
PREP PRO PREP PREP
by the way, but she said no more about her home, beyond remarking that we were going quite a
SC PRO
new road and asking if it were a short one.

Note to Instructor: In the phrase *as before, before* is a noun because it is the name of a point in time: *a thing.*

ADV SC SC ADJ
There's a friend of mine waiting <u>outside</u>, and <u>as</u> it seems <u>that</u> I may have to wait <u>some</u> time, I'll call
ADV
him <u>in</u>, with your leave.

PREP
Now, just as Mr Quilp laid his hand <u>upon</u> the lock, and saw with great astonishment that the
ADV
fastenings were undone, the knocking came <u>again</u> with the most irritating violence, and the
PREP N
daylight which had been shining <u>through</u> the key-hole was intercepted on the <u>outside</u> by a
human eye.

ADV PRO SC PREP
<u>There</u> were <u>none</u> to see the frail, perishable figure, <u>as</u> it glided <u>from</u> the fire and leaned pensively
PREP PRO PREP PREP
<u>at</u> the open casement; <u>none</u> <u>but</u> the stars, to look <u>into</u> the upturned face and read its history.

ADJ ADJ
<u>Full</u> of <u>these</u> meditations, she reached the church.

ADV PRO
I called <u>up</u> <u>all</u> the strange tales I had ever heard of dark and secret deeds committed in great
SC ADJ
towns and escaping detection for a long series of years; wild <u>as</u> many of <u>these</u> stories were, I could
PRO ADV ADV SC
not find <u>one</u> adapted to this mystery, which <u>only</u> became <u>the</u> more impenetrable, in proportion <u>as</u>
I sought to solve it.

> **Note to Instructor:** In the phrase *all the strange tales*, the object of *called* is the pronoun *all*, and *the strange tales* is the object of an understood preposition: *all [of] the strange tales*. If the student labels *all* as an adjective, accept it, but point out the understood preposition.

ADV PRO PREP
"It's <u>as</u> well not to say <u>more</u> than one can help <u>before</u> our worthy friend," said Quilp, making a
PREP
grimace <u>towards</u> the slumbering Dick.

SC N ADV SC
<u>As</u> it grew <u>dusk</u>, the wind fell; its distant moanings were <u>more</u> low and mournful; and, <u>as</u> it came
PREP ADJ
creeping <u>up</u> the road, and rattling covertly among the dry brambles on <u>either</u> hand, it seemed like
ADJ ADV
<u>some</u> great phantom for whom the way was narrow, whose garments rustled as it stalked <u>along</u>.

PREP ADV ADV
In a small dull yard <u>below</u> his window, <u>there</u> was a tree—green and flourishing <u>enough</u>, for such
SC PREP
a place—and <u>as</u> the air stirred <u>among</u> its leaves, it threw a rippling shadow on the white wall.

ADV PREP ADJ
He was <u>soon</u> calmed and fell asleep, singing to himself in a low voice, <u>like</u> a <u>little</u> child.

PREP SC
My boat is <u>on</u> the shore and my bark is on the sea, but <u>before</u> I pass this door I will say farewell
to thee.

PREP
But these fears vanished <u>before</u> a well-trimmed lamp and the familiar aspect of her own room.

Exercise 107B: Diagramming

On your own paper, diagram every word of the following sentences from *The Old Curiosity Shop*.
If you need help, ask your instructor!

Man wants but little here below, nor wants that little long!

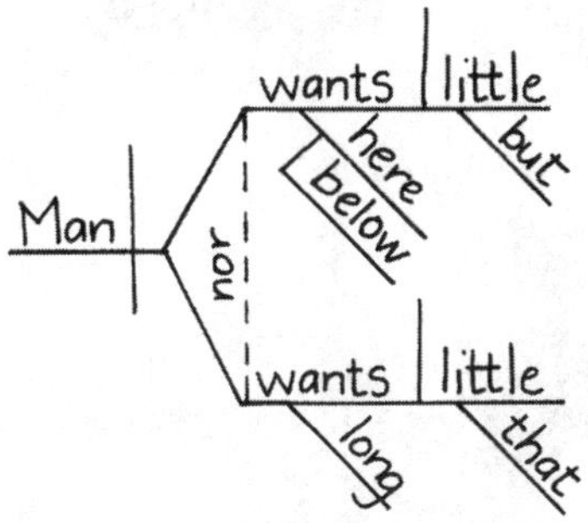

Note to Instructor: The structure of this sentence is straightforward, but it contains several words acting in odd roles: *below* modifying another adverb, *little* as a noun acting as a direct object, *but* as an adjective, and *long* as an adverb (as opposed to an adjective).

Of these Mr Quilp delivered himself with the utmost animation and rapidity, and with so many distortions of limb and feature, that even his wife, although tolerably well accustomed to his proficiency in these respects, was well-nigh beside herself with alarm.

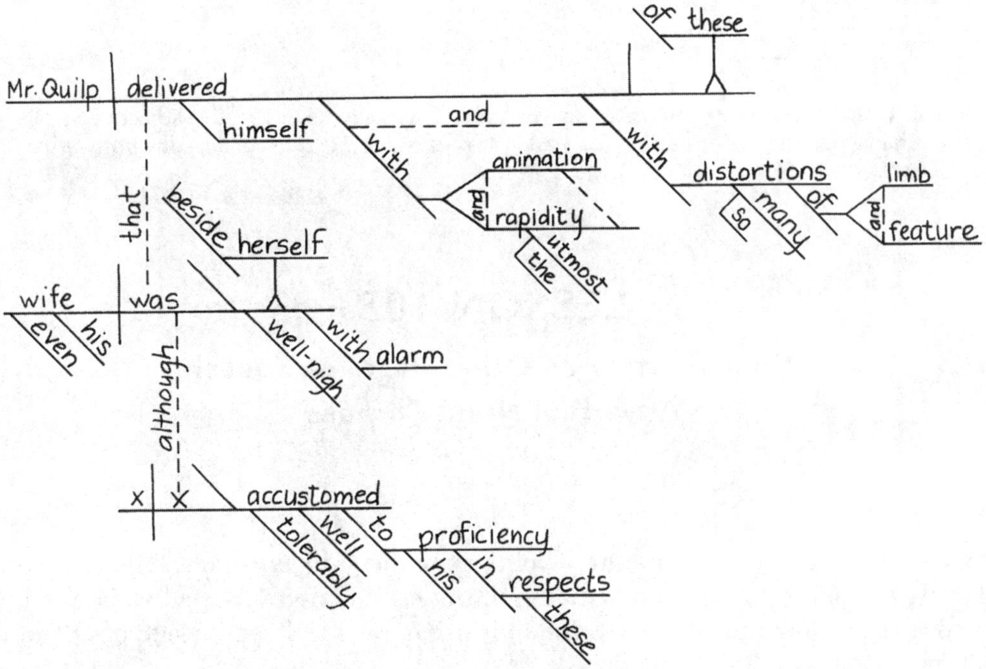

Note to Instructor: The prepositional phrase *of these* acts as the direct object of the verb *delivered*: it represents the things delivered. *Utmost* describes both *animation* and *rapidity* and could also be diagrammed just before the diagram branches into the compound objects of the preposition *with*. The modifiers *well-nigh* and *with alarm* modify the entire prepositional phrase *beside herself*, which acts as a predicate adjective; if the student does not know where to place them, point out that *herself* is neither *well-nigh* nor *with alarm*, and prepositions can't be modified.

I have diagrammed the phrase *although tolerably well accustomed...respects* as a subordinate clause with understood elements: *although [she was] tolerably well accustomed...respects*. If the student diagrams *accustomed* as a past participle modifying *wife*, accept the answer, but point out that this leaves the student with a problem: *although* then has to act as an adverb modifying the participle, and *although* doesn't answer any of the adverb questions (*where, when, how, how often, to what extent*).

There was but one lady who seemed to understand the child, and she was one who sat alone in a handsome carriage, while two young men in dashing clothes, who had just dismounted from it, talked and laughed loudly at a little distance.

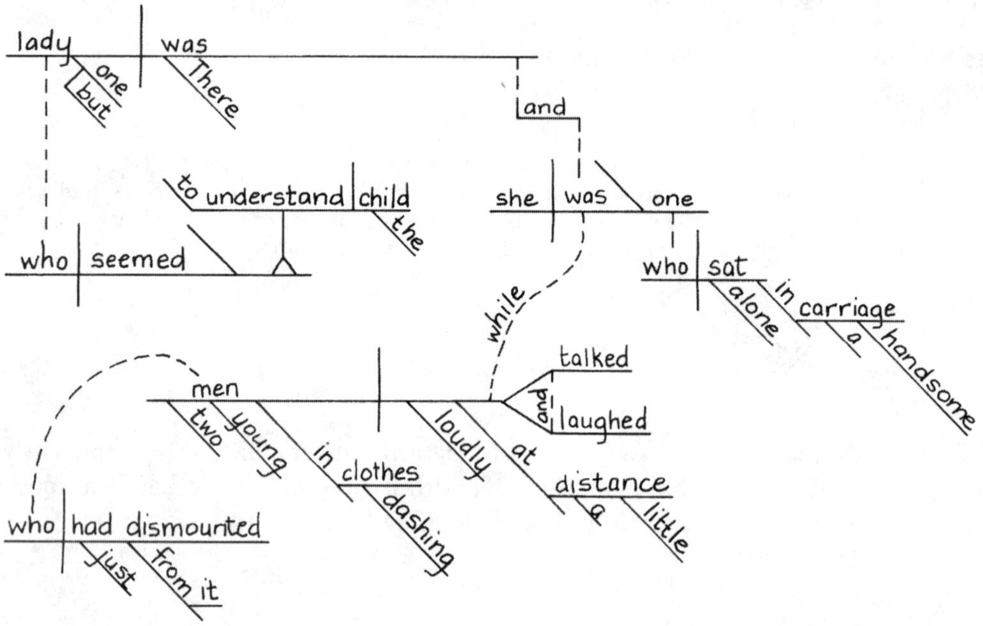

Note to Instructor: *Dashing* could also be diagrammed as a simple descriptive adjective rather than a participle. The adverb *loudly* and the phrase *at a little distance* describe both *talked* and *laughed.*

— LESSON 108 —

Nouns Acting as Other Parts of Speech
Adverbial Noun Phrases

Exercise 108A: Nouns

These sentences are all taken from the three volumes of the *Hunger Games* trilogy, by Suzanne Collins. Identify the part of the sentence that each underlined noun plays by labeling it as *S* for subject, *PN* for predicate nominative, *APP* for appositive, *DO* for direct object, or *OP* for object of the preposition.

OP
We're on a flat, open stretch of ground.

OP OP
If the Gamemakers want us in the open, then in the open we will be.

S
The red blinking light on one of the cameras catches my eye.

DO OP
I can see her tallying the cost of my ultimatum, weighing it against my possible worth.

PN
Prim was one slip of paper in thousands!

PN
And whatever Peeta wants, it's his turn to be saved.

S
After days of inactivity, the hunt has taken its toll.

OP
Whatever the opposite of fine is, that's what I am.

APP
Prim is in my first reaping outfit, a skirt and ruffled blouse.

DO
But my mind seems foggy and forming a plan is hard.

OP
He got a knife in the back at the Cornucopia.

Exercise 108B: Nouns as Other Parts of Speech

Each of the following sentences is missing one of the nouns from the exercise above—but the noun is functioning as another part of speech!

Your task: figure out which noun can fill every blank.

These sentences are also from the *Hunger Games* trilogy.

___Fine___ bread like this is for special occasions.

Most of the Peacekeepers ___turn___ a blind eye to the few of us who ___hunt___ because they're as hungry for fresh meat as anybody is.

It's this detail, the untucked blouse forming a ducktail, that brings me ___back___ to myself.

Then his eyes ___open___, unmistakably blue in the brown mud and green leaves.

He's got Peeta's nose blocked off but his mouth tilted ___open___, and he's blowing air into his lungs.

"Don't ___light___ a fire," he says.

But there are other people who'd make your life ___worth___ living.

I put the cheese carefully in my pocket as I ___slip___ outside.

We're on a flat, ___open___ stretch of ground.

My fingers ___stretch___ out, seeking Prim's warmth but finding only the rough canvas cover of the mattress.

I chop them very ___fine___ and add them to the pot, switch out the rocks again, put on the lid, and let the whole thing stew.

Each tessera is ___worth___ a meager year's supply of grain and oil for one person.

I ___plan___ for us to ___skirt___ around the corner and then detonate the Meat Grinder, but another unmarked pod lies in wait.

I ___back___ away, panting, turn on my heel, and take off again.

Effie's having a ___fine___ time ordering everybody around, keeping us all on schedule.

"What did you ___cost___ me again?" I ask.

Exercise 108C: Identifying Parts of Speech

Identify the part of speech of each underlined word by writing the correct abbreviation above it: *N* (noun), *ADV-N* (adverbial noun), *PRO* (pronoun), *V* (verb), *ADJ* (adjective), *ADV* (adverb), *PREP* (preposition), *CC* (coordinating conjunction), *CorrC* (correlative conjunctions), *SC* (subordinating conjunction), or *QC* (quasi-coordinator).

These sentences are taken from *The Devil's Doctor: Paracelsus and the World of Renaissance Magic and Science*, by Philip Ball.

Some of these are very difficult—ask for help if you need it!

Note to Instructor: Explanations are provided in brackets; provide all necessary help to the student.

ADV CC N ADJ N

The Black Death swept <u>out</u> of Asia in late 1347, <u>and</u> in the following two <u>years</u> it killed <u>as much as</u> a <u>third</u> of the population.

[The adverb *out* modifies *swept*, and the adverbial prepositional phrase *of Asia* modifies *out*. (If you were diagramming this sentence, you could also classify *out of* as a single compound preposition introducing the adverbial prepositional phrase *out of Asia*.) *Years* is the object of the preposition *in*. *As much as* is a single compound adjective modifying the noun *third*, which is the direct object of *killed*.]

PREP ADJ CC

<u>As for</u> the <u>third</u> item in your diagnosis, I cannot understand it, <u>but</u> it seems likely to me.

[The compound preposition *As for* introduces a prepositional phrase which serves as an absolute construction, with *item* as the object of the preposition and *third* modifying *item*.]

ADV-N PREP ADJ

Agricola died a <u>year</u> <u>before</u> *De re Metallica* was published, to the dismay of learned men of <u>every</u> persuasion.

[The adverbial noun *year* modifies *died*. The clause *De re Metallica was published* serves as the direct object of the prepositional phrase *before...published*, which itself functions as an adverb modifying the adverbial noun! If the student is confused by this, point out that if the sentence read *Agricola died a year before his brother*, it would be very clear that *before* is a preposition.]

CC ADV

This was fortunate, <u>for</u> a student was expected to travel a <u>lot</u>, and the roads were seldom safe.

[The noun *lot* here modifies the infinitive *to travel* and answers the question *how much*. The student may confused by the fact that *a* here acts as an adverb, modifying another adverb!]

SC N

It would be wrong to imagine <u>that</u> the surgeon's <u>lot</u> was, in comparison to the physician's, necessarily humble.

[The subordinating conjunction *that* introduces the subordinate clause *that the surgeon's lot...humble*, which itself serves as the object of the infinitive *to imagine*. The noun *lot* is the subject of the subordinate clause.]

ADV QC

Forty of Paracelsus's theological monographs <u>still</u> survive, <u>as well as</u> sixteen Bible commentaries, twenty sermons, twenty works on the Eucharist, and seven on the Virgin Mary.

[The quasi-coordinator connects the subject *Forty* with the additional subjects *commentaries*, *sermons*, *works*, and *seven*. Note that of the five subjects (all of them go with the predicate *survive*), two are numbers and three are objects!]

ADV ADJ
Luther and Paracelsus never met, and it is probably just as well.
[The adjective *well* serves as a predicate adjective describing *it*, and the compound adverb *just as* modifies *well*. If the student were diagramming this sentence, *as* could be diagrammed as an adverb modifying *well*, and *just* could be diagrammed as an adverb modifying *as*.]

ADV
The students gather round to watch the dissection.

ADJ CC
For Thales, there was but a single element—water—but his successors postulated a variety of elemental schemes.
[The prepositional phrase *for Thales* modifies *was* and answers the question *how* (or, possibly, *where*!). The adjective *but* modifies the noun *element*.]

CorrC ADJ
"I am neither the author nor the executor of that Philosopher's Stone, which is differently described
ADV SC ADV
by others," he wrote in 1526, even as he worked alongside Kilian in their alchemical laboratory.
[The subordinating conjunction *as* introduces the subordinate clause *as he worked alongside...laboratory*. The adverb *even* modifies the verb *worked*. If the student were diagramming this sentence, *even as* could serve as a compound subordinating conjunction introducing the subordinate clause.]

ADV
"I do not take my medicines from the apothecaries," he once insisted, "their shops are just foul
PREP
sculleries which produce nothing but foul broths."
[The adverb *just* modifies the state-of-being verb *are* and answers the question *to what extent*—if the student labels it as an adjective modifying *sculleries*, do not mark the answer wrong, but point out that it does not answer any of the adjective questions. The prepositional phrase *but foul broths* is adjectival and modifies *nothing*.]

CC
But in prescientific times there was no clear division between the inorganic and the vital worlds,
CC ADJ N
for even metals were thought to have a kind of sluggish, unresponsive "life."

ADJ PREP N PREP
They bleed their patients in more ways than one, while confining them to a bleak and joyless life.
[The prepositional phrase *than one* modifies *ways* and acts as an adjective. *While*, most frequently an adverb, here acts as a preposition with the object *confining*, and the prepositional phrase *while...life* is adverbial and modifies *bleed*.]

ADV
Perhaps it was hard for him to imagine that anyone could find his way to the heart of medicine by
QC N
a path other than the one he himself had taken.
[The adverb *Perhaps* here modifies *was*. *Other than* may appear to be a subordinating conjunction, but it actually connects the two objects of the preposition *by*: *path* and *one*. The subordinate clause *he himself had taken* has an understood subordinating conjunction and modifies *one*: *a path other than the one [that] he himself had taken*.]

Exercise 108D: Adverbial Noun Phrases

Circle each adverbial noun or noun phrase, and draw an arrow from the circle to the word modified.

These sentences are taken from *The Devil's Doctor: Paracelsus and the World of Renaissance Magic and Science*, by Philip Ball.

At the University of Paris, work began at six in the morning in winter and an hour earlier in summer.

As if that were not bad enough, the student found himself confronted by such gnomic questions as "Is the loud voice warm?" and "Is it healthy to get drunk once a month?"

CHALLENGE ASSIGNMENT! Can you deduce from context what *gnomic* means? Tell your instructor and see how close you are!

Note to Instructor: *Gnome* is an English noun derived from the Greek gnṓmē, which means "judgment, opinion." A *gnome* is an aphorism, the brief expression of a thought; *gnomic* means "having to do with an aphorism." A gnomic question is one that leads you to formulate an aphorism. (It is very unlikely the student will come up with this answer!)

Citizens of almost any town could consider themselves highly fortunate if they experienced no outbreak for two decades, and sometimes the plague returned every year.

When I returned home my first care was to procure the whole works of this author, and afterwards of Paracelsus and Albertus Magnus.

Agrippa met Faust, probably in Paris in 1528, when Francis I sent for him and saw him conjure the royal princes out of thin air even though they were many miles away.

One moment he exhibits robust skepticism and contempt for superstition; the next, he comes across as the most credulous dupe.

Note to Instructor: This is a trick sentence! There is an understood adverbial noun in the second independent clause: *The next [moment], he comes across as the most credulous dupe.* If the student misses the understood adverbial noun, don't mark the sentence wrong, but show her this explanation.

Becher saw many strange things on his restless travels—geese that lived in trees, stones of invisibility, bottles that captured spoken words so that they sounded again when the vessel was opened hours later.

He became abbot of the Benedictine monastery at Sponheim aged only twenty-two, barely a year after entering the order and before he had even been ordained.

Note to Instructor: If the student circles *barely a year* instead of *barely a year after entering the order*, accept the answer, but point out that the prepositional phrase *after entering the order* modifies *year.*

The following day, the patients who had received this soothing balm were in far better shape than those cauterized with hot oil.

Exercise 108E: Diagramming

On your own paper, diagram every word of the following sentences, taken from a collection of Paracelsus's writings selected and translated (and with an introduction by) Nicholas Goodrick-Clarke.

Note to Instructor: Give all necessary help—particularly with the last sentence!

The work was an immediate success and was reprinted a year later.

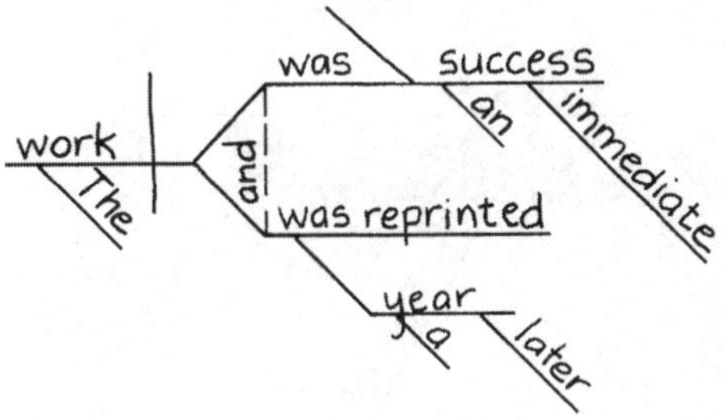

All things are created as far as we know them, but not as far as they should be.

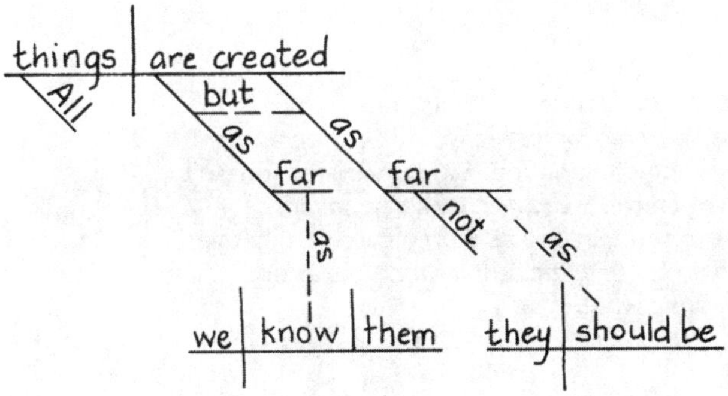

Note to Instructor: In the two occurrences of *as far as*, the first *as* functions as a preposition introducing an adverbial prepositional phrase answering the question *how*, while the second *as* is a subordinating conjunction.

If nature enables one to hear a voice a hundred paces away, this species enables one to hear it a hundred German miles off.

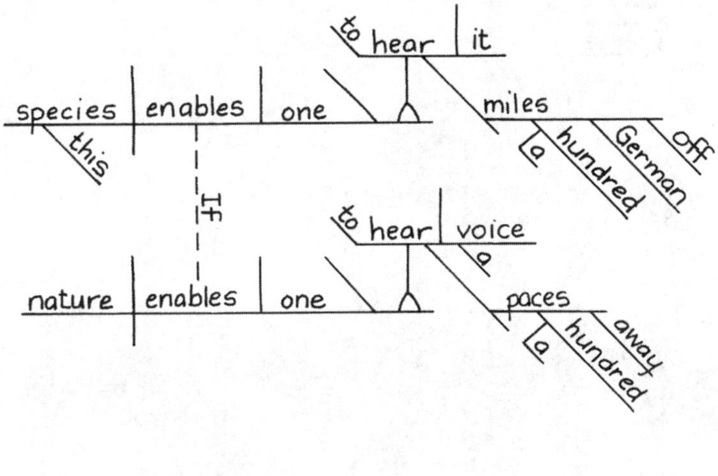

Note to Instructor: I have diagrammed the two infinitive phrases as object complements because they follow and describe the direct objects (see Lesson 40), and because the predicates are causing the description to happen to the direct objects. However, the student could also diagram them beneath the direct objects as adjectival phrases. Point out both options to the student and remind her there is sometimes more than one way to represent a sentence in a diagram.

So it was that after the Creation he gave its own proper name to everything, to animals, trees, roots, stones, minerals, metals, waters, and the like, as well as to other fruits of the earth, of the water, of the air, and of the fire.

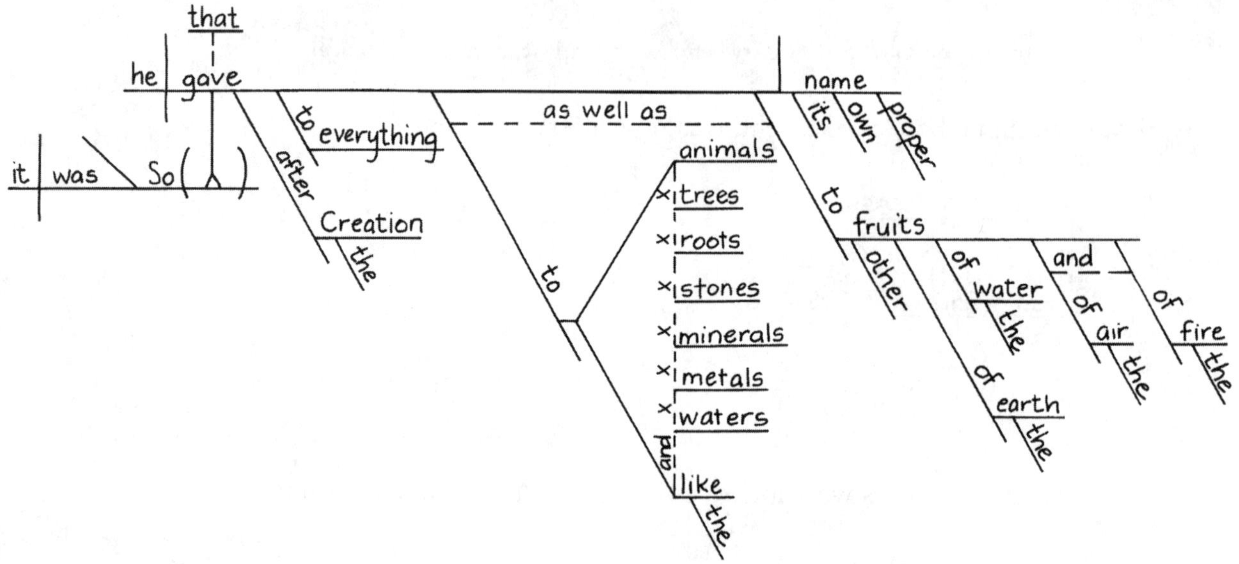

Note to Instructor: The main clause is simply *So it was*. The student may assume that *So* is an adverb, in which case the entire subordinate clause *that after...of the fire* would be diagrammed as an adverbial clause linked to *was* by the subordinating conjunction *that*. However, *so* doesn't make sense as an adverb modifying a linking verb (when this word occurs as an adverb, it modifies an action verb: Do it so!). Instead, it is a pronoun, acting as a predicate nominative, standing in for the meaning of the entire subordinate clause, which then functions as an appositive renaming the pronoun (and so also renaming what it is).

WEEK 28

— REVIEW 9 —

Weeks 25-27

Topics
Progressive Perfect Indicative Tenses
Progressive Present and Progressive Perfect Present Modal Verbs
Conditional Sentences
Adjectives in the Appositive Position
Correct Comma Usage
Limiting Adjectives
Misplaced, Squinting, and Dangling Modifier Comparisons
Using "More," "Fewer," and "Less" Quasi-Coordinators
Words That Can Be Multiple Parts of Speech
Nouns Acting as Other Parts of Speech
Adverbial Nouns

Review 9A: Definition Fill-in-the-Blank

In the last three weeks, you learned (and reviewed) even *more* definitions than in Weeks 22, 23, and 24! Fill in the blanks in the definitions below with one of the terms from the list. Many of the terms will be used more than once.

Note to Instructor: Allow the student to look back through the workbook and find definitions as necessary; the value of the exercise comes in the student's completing each definition, whether from memory or not.

abstract noun
adjectives
adverbs
attributive
comma
compound modifiers
dangling modifier
descriptive adjective
imperative
indicative
less
noun
past
perfect past
positive
present
progressive present
simple
squinting modifier
subordinating conjunction
active
adverb
apostrophe
cardinal numbers
commas
compound preposition
demonstrative adjectives
fewer
indefinite adjectives
interrogative adjectives
misplaced modifier
ordinal numbers
past participle
perfect present
possessive adjective
progressive
quasi-coordinators
simple present
state-of-being
superlative
adjective
adverbial noun
appositive
clause
comparative
coordinating conjunction
demonstrative pronouns
first conditional
indefinite pronouns
interrogative pronouns
modal
passive
perfect
plural
predicative
progressive perfect
second conditional
singular
subjunctive
third conditional

In a sentence with an __active__ verb, the subject performs the action. In a sentence with a __passive__ verb, the subject receives the action.

A __simple__ verb simply tells whether an action takes place in the past, present, or future.

A __progressive__ verb describes an ongoing or continuous action.

A __perfect__ verb describes an action which has been completed before another action takes place.

A __progressive perfect__ verb describes an ongoing or continuous action that has a definite end.

__Cardinal numbers__ represent quantities (one, two, three, four . . .).

__Ordinal numbers__ represent order (first, second, third, fourth . . .).

The present passive imperative is formed by adding the helping verb *be* to the __past participle__ of the verb.

The present passive subjunctive is formed by pairing *be* with the __past participle__ of a verb.

Use the simple past subjunctive __state-of-being__ verb, plus an infinitive, to express a future unreal action.

__First conditional__ sentences express circumstances that might actually happen. The predicate of the condition clause is in a __present__ tense. The predicate of the consequence clause is an __imperative__ or is in a __present__ or __future__ tense.

__Second conditional__ sentences express circumstances that are contrary to reality. The predicate of the condition clause is in a __past__ tense. The predicate of the consequence clause is in the __simple__ or __progressive present__ modal tense.

__Third conditional__ sentences express past circumstances that never happened. The predicate of the condition clause is in the __perfect past__ tense. The predicate of the consequence clause is in the __perfect present__ modal or __simple present__ modal tense.

__Demonstrative pronouns__ demonstrate or point out something. They take the place of a single word or a group of words.

__Demonstrative adjectives__ modify nouns and answer the question *which one.*

__Indefinite pronouns__ are pronouns without antecedents.

__Indefinite adjectives__ modify nouns and answer the questions *which one* and *how many.*

A __descriptive adjective__ tells what kind.

A __descriptive adjective__ becomes an __abstract noun__ when you add *-ness* to it.

A __possessive adjective__ tells whose.

A __noun__ becomes an __adjective__ when it is made possessive.

Form the possessive of a __singular__ noun by adding an __apostrophe__ and the letter *s.*

Form the possessive of a __plural__ noun ending in *-s* by adding an __apostrophe__ only.

Form the possessive of a plural noun that does not end in *-s* as if it were a singular noun.

Indicative verbs express real actions.

Subjunctive verbs express situations that are unreal, wished for, or uncertain.

Imperative verbs express intended actions.

Modal verbs express possible actions and situations that have not actually happened.

An adjective that comes right before the noun it modifies is in the attributive position.

An adjective that follows the noun it modifies is in the predicative position.

Appositive adjectives directly follow the word they modify.

When three or more nouns, adjectives, verbs, or adverbs appear in a series, they should be separated by commas.

Quasi-coordinators link compound parts of a sentence that are unequal.

Quasi-coordinators include *rather than*, *sooner than*, *let alone*, *as well as*, and *not to mention.*

When three or more items are in a list, a coordinating conjunction before the last term is usual but not necessary.

When three or more items are in a list and a coordinating conjunction is used, a comma should still follow the next to last item in the list.

When two or more adjectives are in the attributive position, they are only separated by commas if they are equally important in meaning.

Interrogative pronouns take the place of nouns in questions.

Interrogative adjectives modify nouns.

The positive degree of an adjective describes only one thing. The comparative degree of an adjective compares two things.

The superlative degree of an adjective compares three or more things. Most regular adjectives form the comparative by adding *-r* or *-er.*

Most regular adjectives form the superlative by adding *-st* or *-est.*

Many adjectives form their comparative and superlative forms by adding the word *more* or *most* before the adjective instead of using *–er* or *–est.*

In comparative and superlative adjective forms, the words *more* and *most* are used as adverbs.

Use *fewer* for concrete items and *less* for abstractions. In comparisons using *more . . . fewer* and *more . . . less*, *more* and *less* can act as either adverbs or adjectives and *the* can act as an adverb.

In comparisons using two comparative forms, the forms may act as either adverbs or adjectives, and *the* can act as an adverb. A coordinating conjunction joins equal words or groups of words together.

A subordinating conjunction joins unequal words or groups of words together.

When *than* is used in a comparison and introduces a clause with understood elements, it is acting as a subordinating conjunction.

Other than is a compound preposition that means "besides" or "except."

More than and *less than* are compound modifiers.

An adverbial noun tells the time or place of an action, or explains how long, how far, how deep, how thick, or how much. It can modify a verb, adjective, or adverb.

An adverbial noun plus its modifiers is an adverbial noun phrase.

A misplaced modifier is an adjective, adjective phrase, adverb, or adverb phrase in the wrong place.

A squinting modifier can belong either to the sentence element preceding or the element following.

A dangling modifier has no noun or verb to modify.

Review 9B: Parsing

Above each underlined verb, write the complete tense, the voice (or note state-of-being), and the mood. The first verb is done for you.

These sentences are from *The Jamestown Project*, by Karen Ordahl Kupperman.

progressive past, active, indicative

What they were experiencing was the difference between a maritime climate, seen in countries

simple present, active, indicative

lying to the east of great oceans, and the continental regime that prevails in lands to their west.

perfect past, passive, indicative — simple past, active, indicative

The Roanoke colonists had been cut loose, and their successors in Jamestown never doubted

simple present, active, modal

that the same could happen to them through the vagaries of ocean travel or changes in European politics.

perfect past, state-of-being, modal — simple present, active, modal

It would have been extremely difficult to predict in 1617 that the colony would grow so dramatically in the coming years.

But without the hope of riches or access to the eastern trades, it is doubtful that colonies

perfect present, passive, modal

would have been undertaken in this period.

simple past, active, indicative — progressive past, passive, indicative

In 1621 the company complained about the poor quality of the tobacco they were being sent.

simple past, active, indicative

She refused the presents Smith offered her; with "teares running downe her cheekes, shee said

simple present, active, modal — simple past, state-of-being, subjunctive

shee durst not be seene to have any: for if Powhatan should know it, she were but dead."

perfect past, active, indicative

Thomas Harriot, deeply troubled by the diseases that had struck so many coastal Carolina

simple past, active, indicative

Algonquians while he was there with the first Roanoke colony in 1585-86, wrote that some of

perfect past, active, indicative

the English had pointed to a comet that had appeared just a few days before "the said sicknesse"

perfect present, active, modal

broke out, and they also thought that a solar eclipse the previous year might have played a role.

progressive past, active, indicative

They claimed that as he was dying, he begged to be buried in an English graveyard so his people

simple present, active, modal — perfect past, passive, indicative

would not know he had been killed by a bullet.

simple past, active, indicative

But Pory attested that they did not dare to "call Poole to account" because of the damage he

simple present, active, modal

could do to their relationship with Opechancanough.

perfect past, active, subjunctive — perfect present, passive, modal

Had the ships not fired their ordnance, the colony would have been overwhelmed.

> **Note to Instructor:** This is a third conditional sentence written as a formal conditional: *If the ships had not fired their ordnance, then the colony would have been overwhelmed.* The verb of the first clause is subjunctive because it represents an unreal condition (the ships *did* fire their ordnance!).

simple past, active, indicative

He brought an Indian man home to Cape Cod from England; Smith identified him as Tantum, and

perfect present, active, indicative — perfect present, state-of-being, modal

some have speculated that he might have been the Squanto (or Squantum) who lived with the later Pilgrim colony.

Setting the beginning and end of the Little Ice Age is difficult because even a generally colder

simple future, passive, indicative

period will be interrupted by warmer decades.

perfect past, active, indicative — simple past, passive, indicative

Many had emigrated to the Netherlands, but now that Protestant country was threatened by the

progressive past, active, indicative

European war, and they were willing to consider the possibility of recreating English society in a completely new setting.

simple past, active, indicative

It spoke of the company's "great griefe" in learning of the deaths of "hundreds, and almost the utter destruction of some particular Plantations," and acknowledged that such catastrophe

simple present, passive, modal

must be seen as the "chastisement" of God to draw people on both sides of the Atlantic away from sin.

simple present, active, modal
Nemattanew said that his men would carry the Englishmen's armor and weapons for them and
simple present, passive, modal
they would be furnished with moccasins for the march.

Review 9C: Provide the Verb

Complete each poem stanza by providing an appropriate verb in the tense indicated. You may want to use the chart in Lesson 99 for reference.

If there are two blanks for a single verb, the helping verb is divided from the main verb by another part of the sentence.

If you can't think of a verb, ask your instructor for help.

When you are finished, compare your answers to the original lines.

Note to Instructor: The original verbs are inserted below. You may accept any answers that make sense. Show the student the original poems after she completes the exercise.

The sun is warm, the sky is clear,
progressive present, active, indicative
The waves are dancing fast and bright,
simple present, active, indicative
Blue isles and snowy mountains wear
The purple noon's transparent light.

Percy Bysshe Shelley, "Stanzas Written in Dejection Near Naples"

perfect present progressive, active, indicative / perfect present progressive, active, indicative
I have been laughing, I have been carousing,
Drinking late, sitting late, with my bosom cronies;
simple present, passive, indicative
All, all are gone, the old familiar faces.

Charles Lamb, "The Old Familiar Faces"

"My days, my friend, are almost gone,
perfect present, passive, indicative
My life has been approved,
And many love me; but by none
Am I enough beloved."

William Wordsworth, "The Fountain"

So when the last and dreadful hour
simple future, active, indicative
This crumbling pageant shall devour,
simple future, passive, indicative
The trumpet shall be heard on high,
The dead shall live, the living die,
simple future, active, indicative
And Music shall untune the sky.

John Dryden, "Song for St. Cecelia's Day"

simple present, active, imperative
__Gather__ ye rose-buds while ye may,
Old Time is still a-flying:
And this same flower that smiles to-day,
progressive future, active, indicative
To-morrow __will be dying__.
Robert Herrick, "Counsel to Girls"

simple present, active, modal
And I __do tremble__ when I think
simple present, state-of-being, modal subjunctive
Heigh ho, __would__ she __were__ mine!
Thomas Lodge, "Rosaline"

simple present, state-of-being, subjunctive
__Were__ I as high as heaven above the plain,
And you, my Love, as humble and as low
As are the deepest bottoms of the main,
simple present, active, modal
Whereso'er you were, with you my love __should go__.
Joshua Sylvester, "Love's Omnipresence"

The vernal leaves—she loved them still,
Nor ever tax'd them with the ill
perfect past, passive, indicative
Which __had been done__ to her.
William Wordsworth, "Ruth: Or the Influences of Nature"

simple past, passive, indicative
Those are Grecian ghosts, that in battle __were slain__
And unburied remain
Inglorious on the plain.
John Dryden, "Alexander's Feast, or, The Power of Music"

simple present, passive, subjunctive
My Son, if thou __be humbled__, poor,
Hopeless of honour and of gain,
O! do not dread thy mother's door,
simple present, active, imperative
__Think__ not of me with grief and pain:
William Wordsworth, "The Affliction of Margaret"

simple present, active, modal
For __should__ he __find__ us in the glen,
simple present, active, modal
My blood __would stain__ the heather.
Thomas Campbell, "Lord Ullin's Daughter"

"The morn is merry June, I trow,
progressive present, active, indicative
The rose is budding fain;
simple future, active, indicative
But she shall bloom in winter snow
Ere we two meet again."
Sir Walter Scott, "The Rover"

Review 9D: Identifying Adjectives and Punctuating Items in a Series

In the following description, from *Ivanhoe,* by Sir Walter Scott, carry out the following three steps:

a) Underline once and label all adjectives (except for articles), using the following abbreviations:

Descriptive Adjectives		Limiting Adjectives	
Regular	DA-R	Possessives	LA-P
Present participles	DA-PresP	~~Articles~~	~~LA-A~~
Past participles	DA-PastP	Demonstratives	LA-D
		Indefinites	LA-IND
		Interrogatives	LA-INT
		Numbers	LA-N

b) Circle all adjectives that are in the predicate or in the predicative position and draw an arrow from each back to the noun it modifies.

c) The passage contains five indefinite pronouns. Find each, underline them twice, and identify them as part of the sentence (*SUBJ* for subject, *DO* for direct object, *IO* for indirect object, *OP* for object of the preposition).

d) Draw a star in the margin next to any items of three or more in a series.

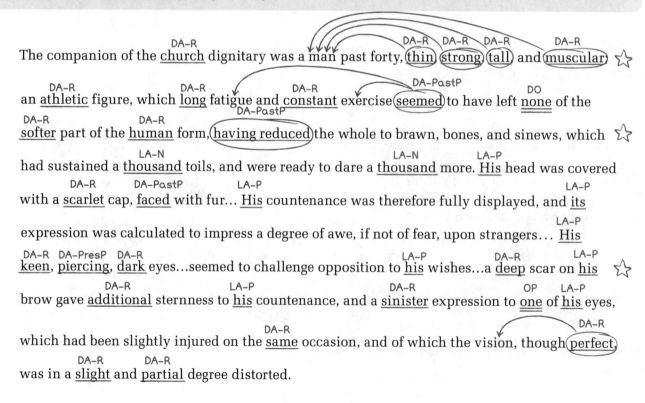

The companion of the church [DA-R] dignitary was a man past forty, thin [DA-R], strong [DA-R], tall [DA-R] and muscular [DA-R] ☆ an athletic [DA-R] figure, which long [DA-R] fatigue and constant [DA-R] exercise seemed [DA-PastP] to have left none [DO] of the softer [DA-R] part of the human [DA-R] form, having reduced [DA-PastP] the whole to brawn, bones, and sinews, which ☆ had sustained a thousand [LA-N] toils, and were ready to dare a thousand [LA-N] more. His [LA-P] head was covered with a scarlet [DA-R] cap, faced [DA-PastP] with fur... His [LA-P] countenance was therefore fully displayed, and its [LA-P] expression was calculated to impress a degree of awe, if not of fear, upon strangers... His [LA-P] keen [DA-R], piercing [DA-PresP], dark [DA-R] eyes...seemed to challenge opposition to his [LA-P] wishes...a deep [DA-R] scar on his [LA-P] ☆ brow gave additional [DA-R] sternness to his [LA-P] countenance, and a sinister [DA-R] expression to one [OP] of his [LA-P] eyes, which had been slightly injured on the same [DA-R] occasion, and of which the vision, though perfect [DA-R], was in a slight [DA-R] and partial [DA-R] degree distorted.

The upper [DA-R] dress of this [LA-D] personage resembled that [DO] of his [LA-P] companion in shape...but the colour, being [DA-PresP] scarlet, showed that he did not belong to any [OP] of the four [LA-N] regular [DA-R] orders of monks. On the right [DA-R] shoulder of the mantle there was cut, in white [DA-R] cloth, a cross of a peculiar [DA-R] form....He rode, not a mule, like his [LA-P] companion, but a strong [DA-R] hackney for the road, to save his [LA-P] gallant [DA-R] war-horse, which a squire led behind, fully accoutred [DA-PastP] for battle, with a chamfron or plaited [DA-PastP] head-piece upon his [LA-P] head, having [DA-PresP] a short [DA-R] spike projecting [DA-PresP] from the front. On one [LA-N] side of the saddle hung a short [DA-R] battle-axe, richly inlaid [DA-PastP] with Damascene [DA-R] carving; on the other [OP] the rider's [LA-P] plumed [DA-PastP] head-piece and hood of mail, with a long [DA-R] two-handed [DA-R] sword.

Review 9E: Correcting Modifiers

The following sentences all have modifier problems!

Rewrite each sentence correctly on your own paper, and be ready to explain the solution out loud to your instructor. You may need to add or delete words or phrases—as long as the sentence makes sense, that's fine. There may be more than one way to fix each sentence.

The first is done for you.

Exploring the maze of cobblestone streets, the farmers were setting up their booths for the farmer's market.

While I was exploring the maze of cobblestone streets, the farmers were setting up their booths for the farmer's market.

Exploring the maze of cobblestone streets, I saw the farmers setting up their booths for the farmer's market.

Explanation: The present participle phrase *Exploring the maze of cobblestone streets* is dangling because it doesn't modify anything in the independent clause that follows. It needs either a subject and predicate of its own (the first answer), or it needs to relate to the subject of the independent clause (the second answer).

Eggplants, artichokes, tomatoes, and zucchini waited for buyers picked that very morning to gather them up.

Eggplants, artichokes, tomatoes, and zucchini, picked that very morning, waited for buyers to gather them up.

Explanation: The past participle phrase *picked that very morning* is misplaced—it should modify the four vegetables, not *buyers*.

I bought the amazingest tarte tatin I have ever tasted.

I bought the most amazing tarte tatin I have ever tasted.

Explanation: The adjective *amazing* uses *more* and *most* rather than *-er* and *-est* to form the comparative and superlative.

I find that organic elephant garlic is deliciouser than any other variety.

I find that organic elephant garlic is more delicious than any other variety.

> **Explanation:** The adjective *delicious* uses *more* and *most* rather than *-er* and *-est* to form the comparative and superlative.

Getting to the cheese merchant's stall, the Camembert de Normandie and the fromage blanc were all gone, but there was plenty of Brie de Melun and Roquefort left.

When I got to the cheese merchant's stall, the Camembert de Normandie and the fromage blanc were all gone, but there was plenty of Brie de Melun and Roquefort left.

Getting to the cheese merchant's stall, I saw that the Camembert de Normandie and the fromage blanc were all gone, but there was plenty of Brie de Melun and Roquefort left.

> **Explanation:** The present participle phrase *Getting to the cheese merchant's stall* is dangling because it doesn't modify anything in the independent clause that follows. It needs either a subject and predicate of its own (the first answer), or it needs to relate to the subject of the independent clause (the second answer).

Cheeses are rich, creamy, and lend a unique taste to carefully prepared dinners that are not refrigerated.

Cheeses that are not refrigerated are rich, creamy, and lend a unique taste to carefully prepared dinners.

> **Explanation:** The subordinate adjective clause *that are not refrigerated* is misplaced—it should modify *cheeses*, not *dinners.*

Seeing that the jam merchant had a long line at his table, checking out the olive oil table instead seemed like a good idea.

When I saw that the jam merchant had a long line at his table, checking out the olive oil table instead seemed like a good idea.

Seeing that the jam merchant had a long line at his table, I decided to go check out the olive oil table instead.

> **Explanation:** The present participle phrase *Seeing that the jam merchant had a long line at his table* is dangling because it doesn't modify anything in the independent clause that follows. It needs either a subject and predicate of its own (the first answer), or it needs to relate to the subject of the independent clause (the second answer).

My favorite fruits to eat that I bought at the market with the Muscat wine are peaches, plums, cherries, and melon.

My favorite fruits to eat with the Muscat wine that I bought at the market are peaches, plums, cherries, and melon.

My favorite fruits to eat with the Muscat wine are peaches, plums, cherries, and melon that I bought at the market.

> **Explanation:** The subordinate adjective clause *that I bought at the market* is squinting—it isn't clear whether the Muscat wine was bought at the market (the first answer) or the fruits were bought there (the second answer).

The artichoke salad and the celeri remoulade look much temptinger than the chickpea salad.

The artichoke salad and the celeri remoulade look much more tempting than the chickpea salad.

> **Explanation:** The adjective *tempting* uses *more* and *most* rather than *-er* and *-est* to form the comparative and superlative.

Surveying all of the market stalls, my favorite was the one selling spices: persillade, herbes de Provence, fines herbes, nutmeg, saffron, chervil, and chives.

After I surveyed all of the market stalls, my favorite was the one selling spices: persillade, herbes de Provence, fines herbes, nutmeg, saffron, chervil, and chives.

Surveying all of the market stalls, I decided that my favorite was the one selling spices: persillade, herbes de Provence, fines herbes, nutmeg, saffron, chervil, and chives.

> **Explanation:** The present participle phrase *Surveying all of the market stalls* is dangling because it doesn't modify anything in the independent clause that follows. It needs either a subject and predicate of its own (the first answer), or it needs to relate to the subject of the independent clause (the second answer).

Before preparing for dinner, a farmer's market might offer fresh vegetables and local meats.

Before preparing for dinner, a French cook might go to the farmer's market and see what fresh vegetables and local meats are available.

Before she prepares for dinner, a French cook might go to the farmer's market and see what fresh vegetables and local meats are available.

> **Explanation:** The prepositional phrase *Before preparing for dinner* is dangling because it doesn't modify anything in the main clause. Because the phrase does not refer to the farmer's market, a noun capable of performing the action of preparing dinner has to be inserted. This can be put in the main clause only (the first answer) or in both the prepositional phrase (turning it into a subordinate clause) and the main clause (the second answer).

If you shop at a market in the middle of the week, you'll get more low prices and find less tourists.

If you shop at a market in the middle of the week, you'll get lower prices and find fewer tourists.

> **Explanation:** The adjective *low* uses *-er* and *-est*, not *more* and *most*, to form the comparative and superlative. Because *tourists* is a concrete noun, not an abstract one, it should be modified by *fewer* rather than *less*.

The Christmas markets not only sell food, hot wine, chocolates, and cheese, but also offer entertainments that are held in the north of France!

The Christmas markets that are held in the north of France not only sell food, hot wine, chocolates, and cheese, but also offer entertainments!

> **Explanation:** The subordinate clause *that are held in the north of France* is misplaced—it describes the markets, not the entertainments. (As written, the sentence could describe Christmas markets in any country that offers entertainments that are held in the north of France—which is silly.)

There are 246 varieties of French cheese, and fifty six kinds are protected by French law.

There are 246 varieties of French cheese, and fifty-six kinds are protected by French law.

> **Explanation:** Compound adjectives in the attributive position must be hyphenated.

A yard sale, where everyone cleans out their attic and sells the random things they find there in France, is known as a vide-grenier.

In France, a yard sale, when everyone cleans out their attic and sells the random things they find there, is known as a vide-grenier.

A yard sale in France, when everyone cleans out their attic and sells the random things they find there, is known as a vide-grenier.

> **Explanation:** The prepositional phrase *In France* describes the location of the yard sale, not the things sold. (As written, the sentence could describe people all over the world cleaning out their attics and then selling the objects in France—again, silly.)

Review 9F: Identifying Adverbs

In the following sentences, taken from *Mars: Our Future on the Red Planet*, by Leonard David (a companion book to the National Geographic TV series *Mars*), carry out the following steps:

a) Underline each word, phrase, or clause that is acting as an adverb.

b) Draw a line from the word/phrase/clause to the verb, adjective, or adverb modified.

c) Above the word or phrase, note whether it is a regular adverb (*ADV*), an adverbial noun or noun phrase (*AN*), a prepositional phrase (*PrepP*), an infinitive phrase (*INF*), a present participle phrase (*PresP*), a past participle phrase (*PastP*), or an adverbial clause (*C*).

Remember: within a phrase or clause acting as an adverb, there might also be an adverb modifying an adjective or verb form within the phrase or clause. Underline these adverbs a second time.

C; ADV; ADV; PrepP

Buzz Aldrin was adamant when he told me that the next dream to work toward was putting humans on Mars.

PrepP; PrepP

In 2010 President Barack Obama declared that the United States was going to Mars.

ADV; PrepP; INF

Four decades have now passed since the touchdown on Mars of America's Viking 1 and Viking 2 landers, sent to probe the prospect of Martian life, extinct or extant.

ADV; PrepP; AN; PrepP; C; ADV; ADV; ADV

Decades later and billions of dollars in Mars spacecraft costs borne by several nations, the inquiry about past or present life on the planet remains alive and well—even if life on Mars is long gone or never even existed.

> **Note to Instructor:** *Decades* and *billions* are both nouns acting as adverbs; the entire adverbial noun phrase *Decades later...several nations* modifies *remains*, answering the questions *when* and *how*. Within that adverbial noun phrase, *later* and *of dollars* modify the adverbial nouns themselves. The predicate adjectives *alive* and *well* describe *inquiry* and follow *remains*, which is acting as a linking verb. The clause *even if...even existed* as a whole modifies *remains* and has three other adverbs within it.

ADV; PrepP; ADV; ADV; PrepP

The now orbiting International Space Station is acknowledged as the most complex scientific and technological endeavor ever undertaken to date.

> **Note to Instructor:** The student may label *as the most...to date* as a clause, rather than a prepositional phrase, but *endeavor undertaken* is not a subject and predicate—it is a noun and a past participle acting as an adjective. In this case, *as* acts as a preposition and *endeavor* is the object of the preposition.

While the International Space Station is seen as a starting point for undertaking 21st-century deep space travel, a number of analog sites on Earth are also prompting advisory notes before humans congregate in the harsh climes of Mars.

If you want mortal danger go to Antarctica.

Other Mars Society findings are that small, nimble field mobility systems like all-terrain vehicles are much more useful for a Mars crew than large pressurized rovers.

The pattern continues even as spacecraft bring human cargo as well.

Will humans on Mars, by their very presence, introduce Earth life into places on the Red Planet where it could potentially prosper, and perhaps taint the very signs of life we are looking for?

Review 9G: Comma Use

The following sentences have lost all of their commas. Insert commas directly into the text (no need to use proofreader's marks) wherever needed.

These sentences were taken from the 1934 science fiction adventure *A Martian Odyssey*, by Stanley G. Weinbaum.

> **Note to Instructor:** The original sentences are below; you may accept variations as long as they follow the rules of comma use.

The other three stared at him sympathetically—Putz, the engineer, Leroy, the biologist, and Harrison, the astronomer and captain of the expedition.

There was a racket like a flock of crows eating a bunch of canaries—whistles, cackles, caws, trills, and what have you.

It had four-toed feet, and four-fingered things—hands, you'd have to call them—and a little roundish body, and a long neck ending in a tiny head—and that beak.

There was a flurry of tentacles and a spurt of black corruption, and then the thing, with a disgusting sucking noise, pulled itself and its arms into a hole in the ground.

The Martian wasn't a bird, really.

It had a beak, all right, and a few feathery appendages, but the beak wasn't really a beak.

The top tiers of bricks were heaving, shaking, and suddenly slid down the sides with a thin crash.

Well, we stared at the fire a while and I decided to attempt some sort of communication with the Martian.

Then I sketched in Mercury, and Venus, and Mother Earth, and Mars, and finally, pointing to Mars, I swept my hand around in a sort of inclusive gesture to indicate that Mars was our current environment.

It was just before twilight that I reached the edge of Thyle, and looked down over the gray Mare Chronium. And I knew there was seventy-five miles of that to be walked over, and then a couple of hundred miles of that Xanthus desert, and about as much more Mare Cimmerium.

"In the morning," resumed Jarvis, "we started off again."

A long, silvery-grey arm appeared, dragging after it an armored body. Armored, I mean, with scales, silver-grey and dull-shining.

It didn't look like a flame or torch, you understand, but more like a civilized light, and I thought that I might get some clue as to the creatures' development.

There was something beyond the wheel, something shining on a sort of low pedestal.

Review 9H: Conjunctions

In the following sentences from H. G. Wells's *The War of the Worlds*, find and circle every conjunction. Label each as coordinating (*C*), subordinating (*SUB*), coordinating correlative (*CC*), subordinating correlative (*SC*), or quasi-coordinator (*QC*).

SUB QC
My brother, very luckily for him as it chanced, preferred to push on at once to the coast rather
SUB
than wait for food, although all three of them were very hungry.

SUB SUB
I defied him, although I felt no assurance that he might not do this thing.

SUB C
At that time it was quite clear in my own mind that the Thing had come from the planet Mars, but
SUB
I judged it improbable that it contained any living creature.

SUB C
Then I saw through a sort of glass plate near the edge of the body the face, as we may call it, and
C
the large dark eyes of a Martian, peering, and then a long metallic snake of tentacle came feeling slowly through the hole.

QC
In the darkness I could just see the thing—like an elephant's trunk more than anything else—waving towards me and touching and examining the wall, coals, wood and ceiling.

> **Note to Instructor:** The quasi-coordinator *more than* connections the prepositional phrase *like an elephant's trunk* to the prepositional phrase (with understood preposition) *[like] anything else*. The student could, however, also interpret it as a subordinating conjunction introducing a subordinate clause with understood elements: *more than [it was like] anything else*. Point out that either answer is acceptable.

In Sunbury, and (C) at intervals along the road, were dead bodies lying in contorted attitudes, horses as well as (QC) men, overturned carts and (C) luggage, all covered thickly with black dust.

But (C) he was one of those weak creatures, void of pride, timorous, anæmic, hateful souls, full of shifty cunning, who face neither (CC) God nor (CC) man, who face not even themselves.

Certainly, unless (SC) death had overtaken them suddenly, my cousins and (C) she would have fled thence; but (C) it seemed to me I might find or (C) learn there whither the Surrey people had fled.

I knew I wanted to find my wife, that (C) my heart ached for her and (C) the world of men, but (C) I had no clear idea how the finding might be done.

Review 91: Identifying Independent Elements

The following sentences, taken from two novels by Shannon Hale, all contain independent elements: absolutes (*ABS*), parenthetical expressions (*PE*), interjections (*INT*), nouns of direct address (*NDA*), appositives (*APP*), and/or noun clauses in apposition (*NCA*).

Locate, underline, and label each one.

From *The Goose Girl*

She was born Anidori-Kiladra Talianna Isilee, Crown Princess of Kildenree (APP), and she did not open her eyes for three days.

The baby in her crib dreamed of milk, her round, perfect lips nursing in sleep (ABS).

In cold weather or spring rain, the aunt sat on the nursery floor and told Ani stories of fantastic and faraway things: a land where mares pawed gold nuggets from the earth and chewed them in order to breathe out music (NCA); a baker who baked birds from dough and sent them out the window in search of a treasured pot of apricot preserves (NCA); a mother who loved her baby so fiercely, she put him in a tight locket around her neck so that he might never grow up (NCA).

> **Note to Instructor:** Three separate noun clauses (*a land where...music, a baker...preserves*, and a *mother...grow up*) follow and rename *things*: these are three of the things that Ani heard the stories of.

The aunt sang songs again and again until Ani learned the words, her toddler's voice as dry and delicate as a sparrow's call (ABS).

APP

The key-mistress and her daughter, Seliak, passed by the pond on the walk to the garden.

NCA

The view from the window tugged at her attention, teasing her with indistinct movements in the direction of the stables, brown spots that might have been horses running.

> **Note to Instructor:** The noun clause *brown spots...running* renames the noun *movements* but is, unusually, separated from it by a preposition phrase. However, it clearly renames the noun (so is not an absolute) and cannot be an adjective phrase (since *spots* is a noun).

INT

You have grown as tall as your mother, save her, though not quite as pretty, and I wonder, since you seem to always be quite busy, if you have yet learned what duties are most important to your station?

> **Note to Instructor:** The clause *since you seem to always be quite busy* is adverbial: it modifies the verb *wonder* and answers the question *why?*

From *Book of a Thousand Days*

INT

These past meals have been as hearty as I ever had, and if being a lady's maid means I get to eat the same food as my lady — with spices even! — then you'll never hear me complain.

PE

It isn't allowed for a commoner, of course, to speak to gentry first.

NDA

"Swear you'll serve me, Dashti. Swear you won't abandon me."

ABS

I led her back to the bed and had her sit while I combed the muddle of her hair and bound it in a braid, every hair criscrossing so the smarts wouldn't wander out of her head.

APP

Qadan taught me the names of other cloths — brocade, satin, damask, silk.

ABS

And now that her hair was fixed and her face washed, I saw just how lovely she was, the glory of the Ancestors shining through her.

ABS

Surely she had a wise and profound reason for her stubbornness, one blessed by the Ancestors.

> **Note to Instructor:** Like the appositive above, this one is separated from the noun it renames (*reason*) by a prepositional phrase.

Review 9J: Words with Multiple Identities

In the following sentences, taken from *T. Rex and the Crater of Doom,* by Walter Alvarez, identify each bolded word as a noun (*N*), verb (*V*), adverb (*ADV*), adjective (*ADJ*), pronoun (*PRO*), preposition (*PREP*), subordinating conjunction (*SC*), or coordinating conjunction (*CC*).

PRO / N / PRO / ADJ

Canadian geologist Richard Grieve had compiled a list of authenticated impact craters, and **many** of us studied the list with great **care**, looking for **one** that might be the KT **impact** site.

ADJ / ADJ

Dating ancient **impact** craters is difficult, and the ages of **many** craters on the list were very uncertain.

V
You might ask why anyone would **care** about concentrations that low, but geochemists have found
ADJ
that rare **trace** elements, like rare fingerprints at a crime scene, can reveal the most interesting
N
things about events in the **past**.

ADJ
Volcanism has always been of **prime** interest to geologists.

ADV ADJ PRO
Meteors are **so** frequent that **almost** anyone who lives away from bright lights can see **one** every few minutes in the dark night sky.

Maybe the extraterrestrial event responsible for the iridium and the extinction had been a
N
giant **impact**.

N
We had been wrong in thinking there was no **trace** of the crater at the surface.

ADJ
Scholars of human history have two ways of identifying times **past**.

PRO SC
Iridium was **one** such element, **so** maybe our anomalous iridium came from a supernova.

ADV ADJ ADJ ADJ
Chuck Officer disagreed intensely and often—**not only** with me, but with **almost** everyone **else**
N
who favored **impact**.

Note to Instructor: In the prepositional phrase *with me*, *only* modifies the pronoun *me* (and so serves as an adjective), while *not* modifies the adjective *only* (and *so* serves as an adverb).

SC
Although a microscope was required for studying them, microfossils became the dating material of choice by the middle of the twentieth century.

CC ADV
But Nature seemed to be showing us something **quite** different.

ADJ
Only places which happened to be shielded by thick storm clouds would have avoided this lethal heat.

ADJ
What **else** might have caused the KT extinction?

Review 9K: Phrases, Clauses, and Absolutes

The following paragraph—the first in Zane Grey's classic western *The U. P. Trail*—is made up of one single sentence!

First, read the sentence as it was written, in paragraph form. (You might want to read it out loud.)

> In the early sixties a trail led from the broad Missouri, swirling yellow and turgid between its green-groved borders, for miles and miles out upon the grassy Nebraska plains, turning westward over the undulating prairie, with its swales and billows and long, winding lines of cottonwoods, to a slow, vast heave of rising ground—Wyoming—where the herds of buffalo grazed and the wolf was lord and the camp-fire of the trapper sent up its curling blue smoke from beside some lonely stream; on and on over the barren lands of eternal monotony, all so gray and wide and solemn and silent under the endless sky; on, ever on, up to the bleak, black hills and into the waterless gullies and through the rocky gorges where the deer browsed; then slowly rising to the pass between the great bold peaks, and across the windy uplands into Utah, with its verdant valleys, green as emeralds, and its haze-filled cañons and wonderful wind-worn cliffs and walls, and its pale salt lakes, veiled in the shadows of stark and lofty rocks, dim, lilac-colored, austere, and isolated; ever onward across Nevada, and ever westward, up from desert to mountain, up into California, where the white streams rushed and roared and the stately pines towered, and seen from craggy heights, deep down, the little blue lakes gleamed like gems; finally sloping to the great descent, where the mountain world ceased and where, out beyond the golden land, asleep and peaceful, stretched the illimitable Pacific, vague and grand beneath the setting sun.

Then, look at the version of the sentence that follows. Each part of the sentence has been placed on a separate line. For each part, point out the following:

- Identity: Is it a phrase, clause, independent element (*ind*)—or other?
- Type: If it's a phrase, is it prepositional (*prep*), present participle (*pres part*), or past participle (*past part*)? If it's a clause, is it independent (*ind*) or subordinate (*sub*)? And if it's "other," how would you describe it?
- Part of speech: Then, identify whether the part serves as an adjective (*adj*), adverb (*adv*), appositive (*app*), noun—or something else.
- Finally, in the last blank, if the part modifies, renames, or otherwise relates to another word in the sentence, list that word.

The first two are done for you.

Take some time over this. Ask your instructor for help if necessary. And if you get frustrated, just remember—we could have asked you to diagram this sentence!

This exercise should give you a sense of just how an accomplished writer can string together MANY different sentence elements to create a vivid scene.

Note to Instructor: Offer all help and accept any reasonable answers! This is an exploration into the ways that English grammar can help writers paint a vivid scene.

	Identity	Type	Part of Speech	Related to (if any) (modifies or renames)
In the early sixties	phrase	prep	adv	led
a trail led	clause	ind	main	none
from the broad Missouri,	phrase	prep	adv	led
swirling yellow and turgid between its green-groved borders,	phrase	pres part	adj	Missouri
for miles and miles out upon the grassy Nebraska plains,	phrase	prep	adv	led
turning westward over the undulating prairie,	phrase	pres part	adj	trail
with its swales and billows and long, winding lines of cottonwoods,	phrase	prep	adj	prairie
to a slow, vast heave of rising ground—	phrase	prep	adv	turning
Wyoming—	ind	app	noun	heave
where the herds of buffalo grazed and the wolf was lord and the camp-fire of the trapper sent up its curling blue smoke	clause	sub	adj	Wyoming
from beside some lonely stream;	phrase	prep	adv	sent
on and on	phrase	adv	adv	led

Note to Instructor: Accept any effort of the student to define *on and on*, as long as they are identified as adverbs. Together, the two adverbs form a phrase, but they are also separate adverbs connected with a coordinating conjunction.

	Identity	Type	Part of Speech	Related to (if any) (modifies or renames)
over the barren lands of eternal monotony,	phrase	prep	adv	led
all so gray and wide and solemn and silent under the endless sky;	ind	adj	noun	lands

Note to Instructor: This is an absolute—an independent element with a noun leading (*all*) which, although it does not grammatically link back to *lands*, nevertheless connects to it in meaning.

	Identity	Type	Part of Speech	Related to (if any) (modifies or renames)
on, ever on,	phrase	adv	adv	led

Note to Instructor: As with *on and on* above, these are two separate adverbs joined in a phrase, except that *ever* is now serving as a coordinating conjunction in the place of *and.*

	Identity	Type	Part of Speech	Related to (if any) (modifies or renames)
up to the bleak, black hills	phrase	prep	adv	led
and into the waterless gullies	phrase	prep	adv	led

	Identity	Type	Part of Speech	Related to (if any) (modifies or renames)
and through the rocky gorges	phrase	prep	adv	led
where the deer browsed;	clause	sub	adj	gorges
then slowly rising to the pass between the great bold peaks,	phrase	pres part	adj	trail

Note to Instructor: Despite the semicolon, the descriptors now refer back to the trail itself, from the beginning of the sentence.

	Identity	Type	Part of Speech	Related to (if any) (modifies or renames)
and across the windy uplands into Utah,	phrase	prep	adv	rising
with its verdant valleys, green as emeralds, and its haze-filled cañons and wonderful wind-worn cliffs and walls, and its pale salt lakes,	phrase	prep	adj	Utah
veiled in the shadows of stark and lofty rocks, dim, lilac-colored, austere, and isolated;	phrase	past part	adj	lakes
ever onward across Nevada, and ever westward,	phrase	prep	adv	rising
up from desert to mountain,	phrase	prep	adv	rising
up into California,	phrase	prep	adv	rising
where the white streams rushed and roared and the stately pines towered,	clause	sub	adj	California
and seen from craggy heights, deep down,	phrase	past part	adj	lakes
the little blue lakes gleamed like gems;	clause	sub	adj	California
finally sloping to the great descent,	phrase	pres part	adj	trail
where the mountain world ceased	clause	sub	adj	descent
and where, out beyond the golden land, asleep and peaceful, stretched the illimitable Pacific, vague and grand	clause	sub	adj	descent
beneath the setting sun.	phrase	prep	adv	vague and grand

WEEK 29

Still More Verbs

— LESSON 109 —

Hortative Verbs

Subjunctive Verbs

Exercise 109A: Identifying Hortative Verbs

Speechmakers are often exhorting their readers—so they tend to use many hortative verbs! In the following sentences, underline twice every element of each hortative verb (*let* or *may*, any other helping verbs, and the main verb). Above the verb, identify it as state-of-being (*SB*), active (*A*), or passive (*P*). If the person or thing being exhorted is present in the sentence, circle the noun or pronoun that identifies him/her/it, and identify it as *S* for subject or *O* for object.

Be careful—some sentences may not include any hortative verbs!

The first is done for you.

O A
Let him set to work to procure a better assemblyman or better alderman before he tries his hand at making a mayor, a governor, or a president.

O A O A O A
Let him make up his mind to do his duty in politics without regard to holding office at all, and let him know that often the men in this country who have done the best work for our public life have not been the men in office. If, on the other hand, he attains public position, let him not strive to plan out for himself a career.

O A
Do not let him think about the matter at all.

—"Duties of American Citizenship," by Theodore Roosevelt

O A O P
Do not let him wrong any one, and do not let him be wronged.

—"Speech Given at the Grand Canyon," by Theodore Roosevelt

S SB
May it not also be that the cause of civilization itself will be defended by the skill and devotion of a few thousand airmen?

Even though large tracts of Europe and many old and famous States have fallen or may fall into the grip of the Gestapo and all the odious apparatus of Nazi rule, we shall not flag or fail.

> **Note to Instructor:** The verb may *fall* is modal, not hortative.

—"We Shall Fight on the Beaches," by Winston Churchill

S A
May (you) never find yourselves, men of Athens, in such a position!

And I pray to all the gods that whatever be the decision that you are about to make, it may be for your good.

> **Note to Instructor:** The verb *may* be is modal, not hortative.

And I beg you, men of Athens, if I tell you certain truths outspokenly, to let no resentment on your part fall upon me on this account.

> **Note to Instructor:** The verb form *to let* is infinitive, not hortative.

O A
And let (no one) ask, What do these things amount to?

O A
And when we have made all these preparations ourselves, then let (us) call upon the other states for aid, and send envoys to carry our message in all directions, to the Peloponnese, to Rhodes, to Chios, to the king.

O A A
But if any one has a better proposal to make, let (him) make it, and give us his advice.

> **Note to Instructor:** This is a compound hortative verb, with *let* serving as the helping verb for both *make* and *give*, and *him* as the object of both. The pronouns *it* and *us* serve as indirect objects.

—"The Third Philippic," by Demosthenes

S SB
May all the (competition) between the two countries be the competition of industry, civilization,
S
and peace! May the foolish (sentiments) of individual hostility entertained by some in both
A
countries, gradually vanish before the influence of good sense and right feeling; and, as both
S P
nations possess a common language, and are derived from a common source, may (they) be united in lasting relations of good will and amity!

— "Address on the King's Speech," by Sir Robert Peel

O A
So, first of all, let (me) assert my firm belief that the only thing we have to fear is fear itself—nameless, unreasoning, unjustified terror which paralyzes needed efforts to convert retreat into advance.

We may now restore that temple to the ancient truths.

> **Note to Instructor:** The verb *may restore* is modal, not hortative.

S A
May He protect each and every one of us.

—"First Inaugural Address," by Franklin D. Roosevelt

O A
Let us not deceive ourselves, sir.

O A
The war is inevitable–and let it come!

Gentlemen may cry, Peace, Peace—but there is no peace.

Note to Instructor: The verb *may cry* is modal, not hortative.

—"Give Me Liberty or Give Me Death," by Patrick Henry

Exercise 109B: Rewriting Indicative Verbs as Hortative Verbs

Hortative verbs also appear frequently in poetry! In the lines below, the statements and commands in bold type originally contained hortative verbs. On your own paper, rewrite each bolded clause so that the main verbs are hortative. Then, compare your answers with the original.

If you need help, ask your instructor.

The rhymes and meters of the poems might give you a hint or two!

Note to Instructor: Each excerpt with bolded clauses is followed by the original, hortative version. Accept any reasonable answers, but ask the student to read both her rewritten sentences and the originals out loud, listening carefully to both.

If the student needs help, give her the first three or four words of the original poem and ask her to continue rewriting from there.

We will go then, you and I,
When the evening is spread out against the sky.
—T. S. Eliot, "The Love Song of J. Alfred Prufrock"

Let us go then, you and I,
When the evening is spread out against the sky.
—T. S. Eliot, "The Love Song of J. Alfred Prufrock"

Come, said my soul,
Write such verses for my Body (for we are one).
—Walt Whitman, "Leaves of Grass"

Come, said my soul,
Such verses for my Body let us write (for we are one).
—Walt Whitman, "Leaves of Grass"

Turn the bed-clothes toward the foot of the bed,
Physician and priest, go home.
—Walt Whitman, "Song of Myself"

Turn the bed-clothes toward the foot of the bed,
Let the physician and the priest go home.
—Walt Whitman, "Song of Myself"

And I say to any man or woman,
Your soul stands cool and composed
before a million universes.
—Walt Whitman, "Song of Myself"

And I say to any man or woman,
Let your soul stand cool and composed
before a million universes.
—Walt Whitman, "Song of Myself"

Here's to the Dove of Peace!
She will find a mate some day,
And her tribe will increase
As fast as she can lay!
—Oliver Herford, "The Dove of Peace"

Here's to the Dove of Peace!
May she find a mate some day,
And may her tribe increase
As fast as she can lay!
—Oliver Herford, "The Dove of Peace"

Exercise 109C: Diagramming

On your own paper, diagram every word of each sentence. These come from the collected writings and speeches of the nineteenth-century writer and speaker Robert G. Ingersoll.

Give us good money—the life-blood of business—and let it flow through the veins and arteries of commerce.

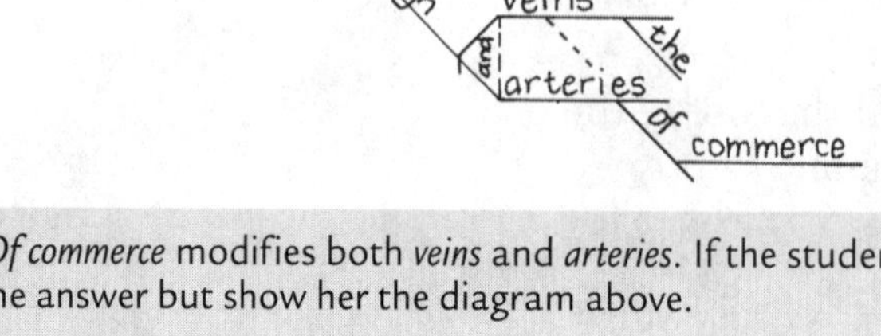

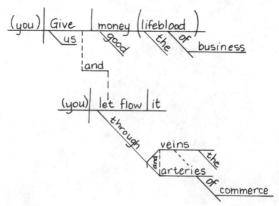

Note to Instructor: *Of commerce* modifies both *veins* and *arteries*. If the student diagrams it below *arteries* only, accept the answer but show her the diagram above.

May you live long in the land you helped to save; may the winter of your age be as green as spring, as full of blossoms as summer, as generous as autumn, and may you, surrounded by plenty, with your wives at your sides and your grandchildren on your knees, live long.

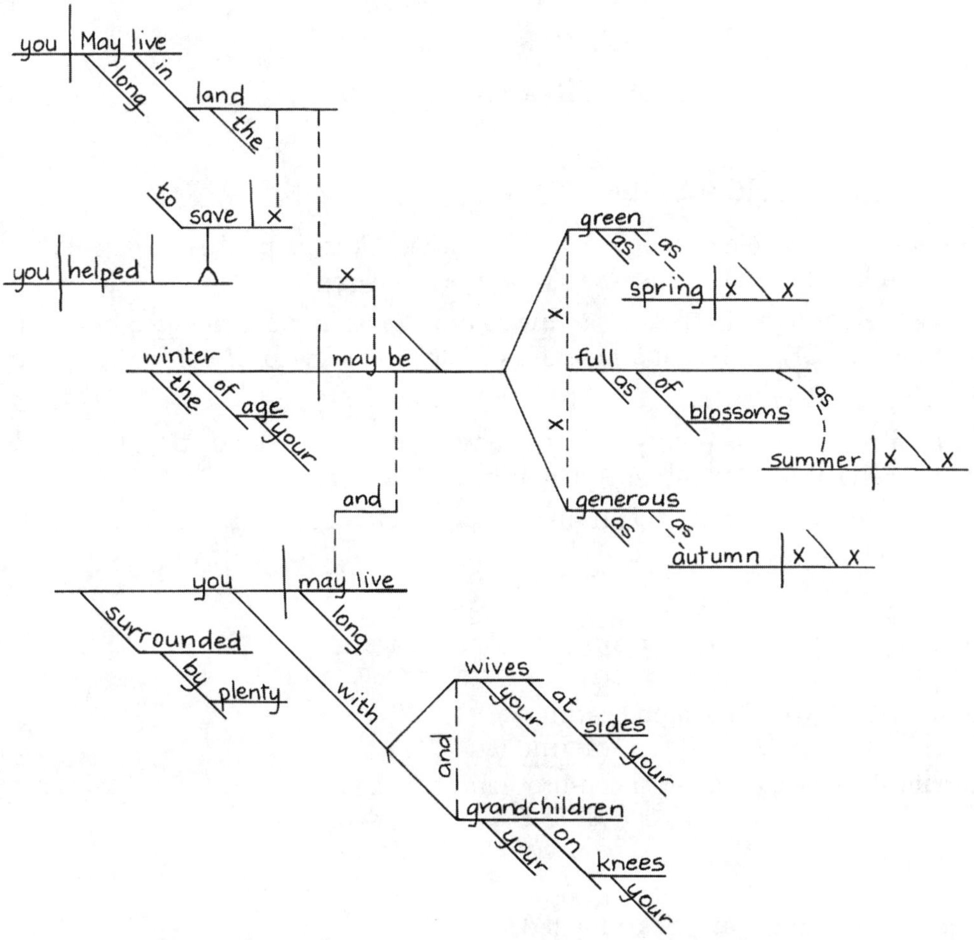

Note to Instructor: If the student is confused by the three comparative clauses with understood elements (as green as spring [is green], as full of blossoms as summer [is full], as generous as autumn [is generous]), ask her to review Lesson 106.

— LESSON 110 —

Transitive Verbs
Intransitive Verbs
Sit/Set, Lie/Lay, Rise/Raise
Ambitransitive Verbs

Exercise 110A: Ambitransitive Verbs

Each one of the sentences below (adapted from traditional Mexican folk tales) contains at least one ambitransitive verb. For each sentence, carry out the following steps:

a) Underline the action verbs that are acting as predicates (in both independent and subordinate clauses), and label each one as *TR* for transitive or *INTR* for intransitive.
b) Label each transitive verb as *A* for active or *P* for passive.
c) Circle the direct object of each active transitive verb and label it as *DO* (*TR*). Circle the subject of each passive transitive verb and label it as *S* (*TR*).
d) Choose two sentences with active transitive verbs. On your own paper, rewrite them so that the verb becomes passive.

Whenever Pedro got [INTR] into trouble, he managed [TR A] to get out again [DO (TR)].

Pedro got [TR A] a drum [DO (TR)] that would not stop [TR A] beating [DO (TR)].

The unfortunate sister managed [TR A] her sheep-brothers [DO (TR)] with care.

She never beat [TR A] them [DO (TR)].

At the very idea, the young man's heart melted [INTR].

The sun shouted [TR A], "Mama! Mama! There is a man! I will melt [TR A] him [DO (TR)]!" [DO (TR)]

The old woman stood [INTR] at the window, weeping and crying to be let in.

Pedro stood [TR A] the statue [DO (TR)] back up again and pretended [TR A] that it had never fallen [INTR] down [DO (TR)].

He pretended [INTR] very convincingly!

The old witch broke [TR A] a horn [DO (TR)] of each of the oxen.

As the waves broke [INTR] against the shore, the young woman began [TR A] to walk into the deepening water [DO (TR)].

The poor boy breathed [INTR] in and out, in and out.

The Devil breathed [TR A] fire [DO (TR)] and brimstone [DO (TR)] at the unfortunate tailor.

The tailor threaded [TR A] his needle [DO (TR)] with a short thread and sewed [INTR] so fast that the Devil [S (TR)] was amazed [TR P].

The Devil sewed (TR A) his cloth (DO (TR)) with a long thread that tangled (INTR) constantly.

The tailor's daughters threaded (INTR) between the pillars to reach him where he sat (INTR).

The sheep ate (INTR) and drank (INTR) in peace.

The oldest sheep ate (TR A) the finest grass (DO (TR)) and drank (TR A) the clearest water (DO (TR)).

Note to Instructor: The student's two rewritten sentences should resemble two of the following.

Whenever Pedro got into trouble, he was managed back out of trouble again.

A drum was gotten by Pedro that would not stop being beat.

The sheep-brothers were managed with care by the unfortunate sister.

They were never beaten by her.

The words "Mama! Mama! There is a man! He will be melted by me!" were shouted by the sun.

The statue was stood back up again by Pedro, and it was pretended by Pedro that the statue had never fallen down.

A horn of each of the oxen was broken by the old witch.

As the waves broke against the shore, walking into the deepening water was begun by the young woman.

Fire and brimstone was breathed by the Devil at the unfortunate tailor.

The needle was threaded with a short thread by the tailor, who sewed so fast that the Devil was amazed.

The cloth was sewed by the Devil with a long thread that tangled constantly.

The finest grass was eaten by the oldest sheep, and the clearest water was drunk by them.

Exercise 110B: The Prefix *Ambi-*

Using a dictionary or thesaurus, find two more words using the prefix *ambi-* where the prefix carries the meaning of "both." On your own paper, write the words and their definitions, and then use each correctly in a sentence. If the word is too technical for you to write an original sentence, you may locate a sentence using an Internet search and write it down.

Note to Instructor: These are sample answers; the student's answers may vary. Make sure that the words the student chooses carry the meaning of *both* rather than *around*, another possible meaning of the prefix *ambi-* (so: *ambivalent*, but not *ambiance* or *ambition*).

ambidextrous: able to use the right and left hands equally well
The ambidextrous tennis player confused her opponent by using both hands on the racket.

ambilateral: affecting both sides
The patient's muscle weakness was ambilateral.

ambilevous: having awkwardness at completing manual tasks with both right and left hands
The ambilevous child couldn't open the toy box with either hand.

ambiloquent: regularly speaking to both sides at once, "double tongued"
That politician is the most ambiloquent leader since Machiavelli.

ambipolar: having both positive and negative charge carriers
"Ambipolar diffusion is important in redistributing magnetic flux." (From *Issues in Astronomy and Astrophysics*)

ambisinister: equally clumsy with both hands
The ambisinister cook dropped the tureen of soup, cut both hands with his paring knife, and burned his left elbow while trying to turn on the burner with his right hand.

ambisyllabic: a word with a single sound that is shared by two different syllables
The word apple is ambisyllabic, because the "p" sound belongs to both the first and the last syllable.

ambitendency: contradictory behaviors rising out of conflicting thoughts or impulses
Her ambitendency appeared when she put out her hand for a handshake, drew it away, put it back out, and then withdrew it again.

ambivalent: having mixed feelings or more than one feeling, having trouble choosing between two different options
The six-year-old felt ambivalent about the family's enormous new dog.

ambivert: someone who is both introverted and extroverted
Ambiverts make good salespeople because they enjoy talking to customers but don't overwhelm them with too much attention.

Exercise 110C: Diagramming

On your own paper, diagram every word of the following quotations.

When you forgive, you in no way change the past—but you change the future.
—Bernard Meltzer

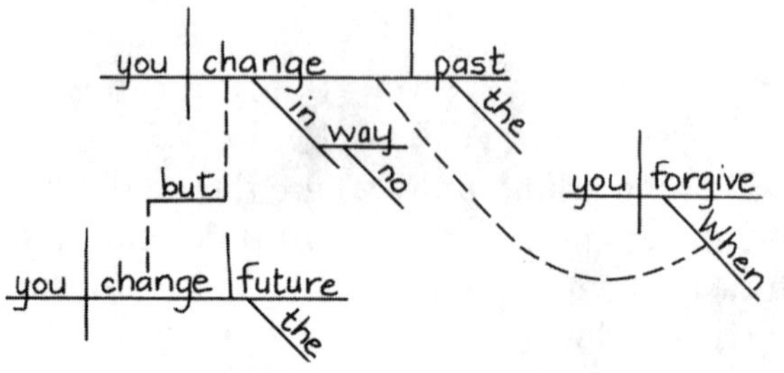

Only the wisest and stupidest of men never change.
—Confucius

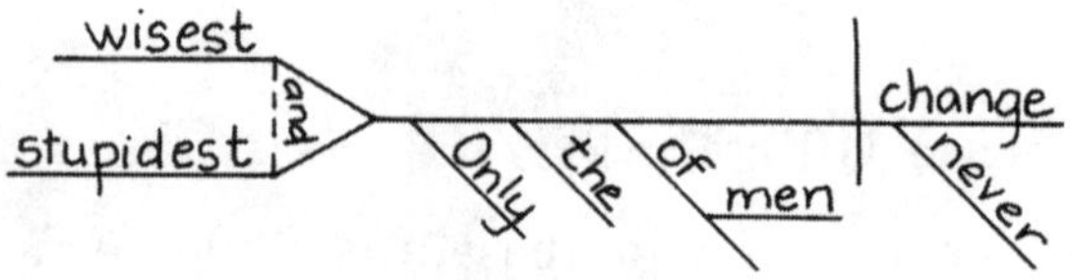

Not everything that is faced can be changed, but nothing can be changed until it is faced.
—James Baldwin

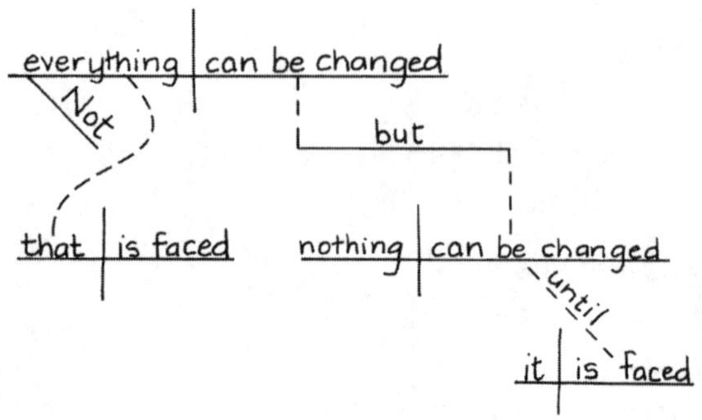

If you cannot forgive and forget, pick one.
–Robert Brault

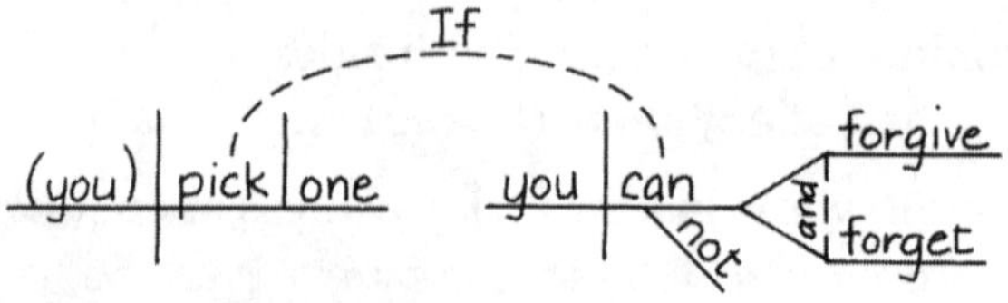

The mind, once stretched by a new idea, never returns to its original dimensions.
—Ralph Waldo Emerson

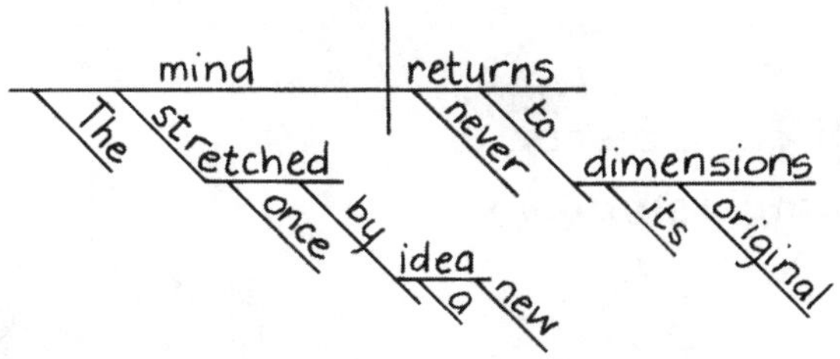

And yet, when I look up at the sky, I somehow feel that everything will change for the better, that this cruelty too shall end, that peace and tranquility will return once more.
—Anne Frank

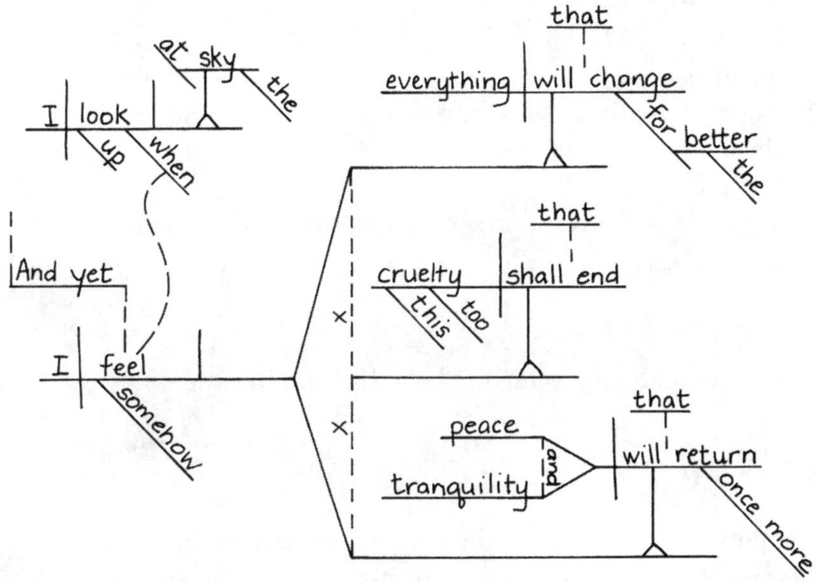

Beware of the man who does not return your blow: he neither forgives you nor allows you to forgive yourself.
—George Bernard Shaw

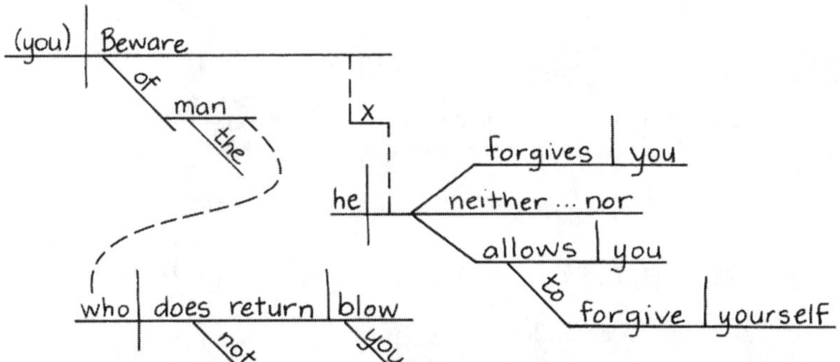

— LESSON 111 —

Ambitransitive Verbs
Gerunds and Infinitives
Infinitive Phrases as Direct Objects
Infinitive Phrases With Understood *To*

Exercise 111A: Infinitives and Other Uses of *To*

In the following sentences from Thomas Hardy's classic novel *The Return of the Native*, underline every phrase that incorporates the word *to*. For infinitives, underline just the infinitive itself; for prepositional phrases, underline just the preposition and its object (and any words that come between); for verb phrases, underline the entire verb.

- Label each phrase as *INF* for infinitive, *PREP* for prepositional, or *V* for verb.
- For infinitives, further identify the phrase as *S* for subject, *DO* for direct object, *PA* for predicate adjective, *PN* for predicate nominative, *ADJ* for adjective, or *ADV* for adverb.
- For prepositional phrases, label the object of the preposition as *OP*. For verb phrases, parse the verb, giving tense, voice, and mood.
- For infinitive adjective and adverb phrases, draw an arrow back to the word modified.

The first is done for you. Some of these are tricky—ask for help if you need it!

INF PA

The distant rims of the world and .of the firmament seemed to be a division in time no less than a division in matter.

INF DO INF DO

He wished to marry me, and I wish to marry him.

PREP OP INF DO

The face of the heath by its mere complexion added half an hour to evening; it could in like manner retard the dawn, sadden noon, anticipate the frowning of storms scarcely generated, and intensify the opacity of a moonless midnight to a cause of shaking and dread.

PREP OP INF ADJ INF PA

After replying to the old man's greeting he showed no inclination to continue in talk, although they still walked side by side, for the elder traveller seemed to desire company.

INF ADV INF ADV

Now, sir, I am sorry to say that my ponies are tired, and I have further to go.

> **Note to Instructor:** The infinitive *to say* modifies the predicate adjective *sorry* and answers the question *how.* The infinitive *to go* modifies the adverb *further* and answers the question *to what extent.*

V present active modal PREP OP INF ADJ

I don't know if I ought to complain to you about this, but I am not quite sure what to do.

> **Note to Instructor:** The pronoun *what* is the object of an understood preposition: *I am not quite sure [of] what to do.* The prepositional phrase *[of] what* modifies the predicate adjective *sure,* and the infinitive phrase *to do* modifies *what.*

INF S

Moreover to light a fire is the instinctive and resistant act of man when, at the winter ingress, the curfew is sounded throughout Nature.

PREP INF PN
The beaming sight, and the penetrating warmth, seemed to breed in him a cumulative
PREP OP
cheerfulness, which soon amounted to delight.

The audience cleared their throats and tossed a few stalks into the fire, not because
INF ADV INF ADJ
these deeds were urgent, but to give themselves time to weigh the moral of the story.

INF ADV INF PA
When Mrs. Yeobright had drawn near to the inn, and was about to enter, she saw a horse and vehicle some two hundred yards beyond it, coming towards her, a man walking alongside with a lantern in his hand.

Yeobright went down the back staircase and into the heath by another path than that
INF DO
in front, intending to walk in the open air till the party was over, when he would
INF ADV
return to wish Thomasin and her husband good-bye as they departed.

Note to Instructor: The infinitive *to walk* is the object of the adverbial participle *intending*; *return* is intransitive, so *to wish* is a modifier, not a direct object.

INF DO
Red suns and tufts of fire one by one began to arise, flecking the whole country round.

INF S
To recline on a stump of thorn in the central valley of Egdon, between afternoon and night, as now, where the eye could reach nothing of the world outside the summits and shoulders of heathland
INF S
which filled the whole circumference of its glance, and to know that everything around and underneath had been from prehistoric times as unaltered as the stars overhead, gave ballast
PREP OP
to the mind adrift on change, and harassed by the irrepressible New.

Note to Instructor: This is a long and complicated sentence! The subjects and predicate are *To recline* and *to know gave*. The noun *ballast* is the direct object of the action verb *gave*.

Exercise 111B: Diagramming

On your own paper, diagram every word of the following sentences from *The Return of the Native*.

I tried to get her to eat something, but she couldn't; and she fell asleep.

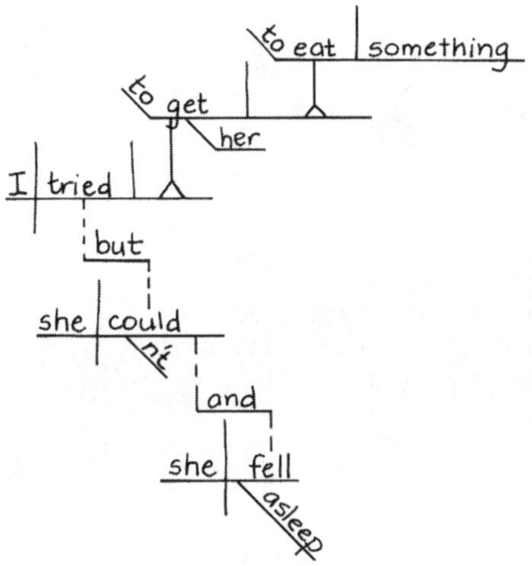

On the Sunday after this wedding an unusual sight was to be seen on Rainbarrow.

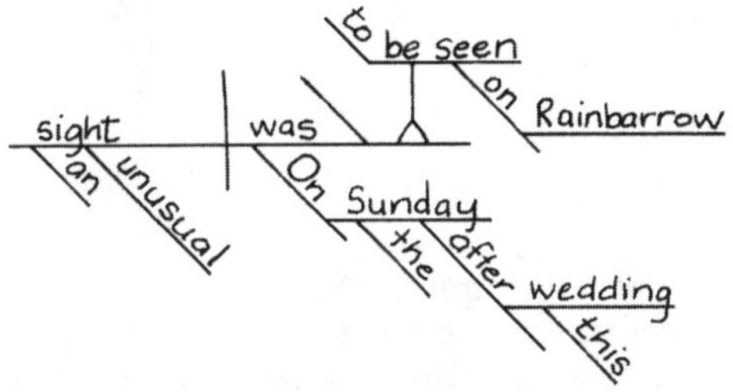

I have thought of your sufferings that morning on which I parted from you; I know they were genuine, and they are as much as you ought to bear.

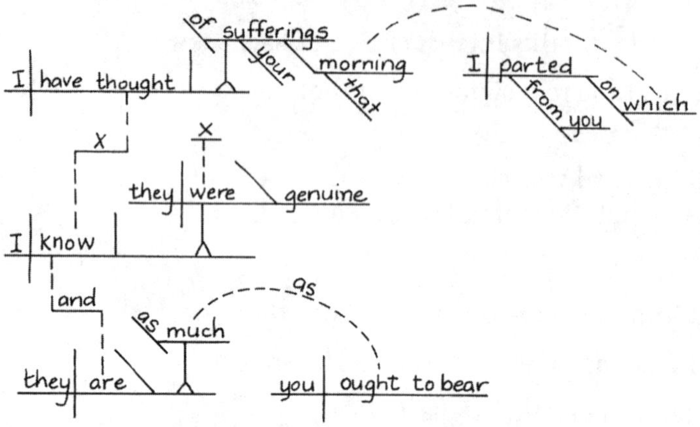

Note to Instructor: The clause *as much as you ought to bear* is difficult. I have interpreted *as much* as a preposition phrase acting as a predicate nominative, with the second *as* functioning as a subordinating conjunction linking *much* to *ought to bear.* If the student chooses another arrangement, do not mark it wrong, but show her the diagram above.

The commanding elevation of Rainbarrow had been chosen for two reasons: first, that it occupied a central position among the remote cottages around; secondly, that the preacher thereon could be seen from all adjacent points as soon as he arrived at his post, the view of him being thus a convenient signal to those stragglers who wished to draw near.

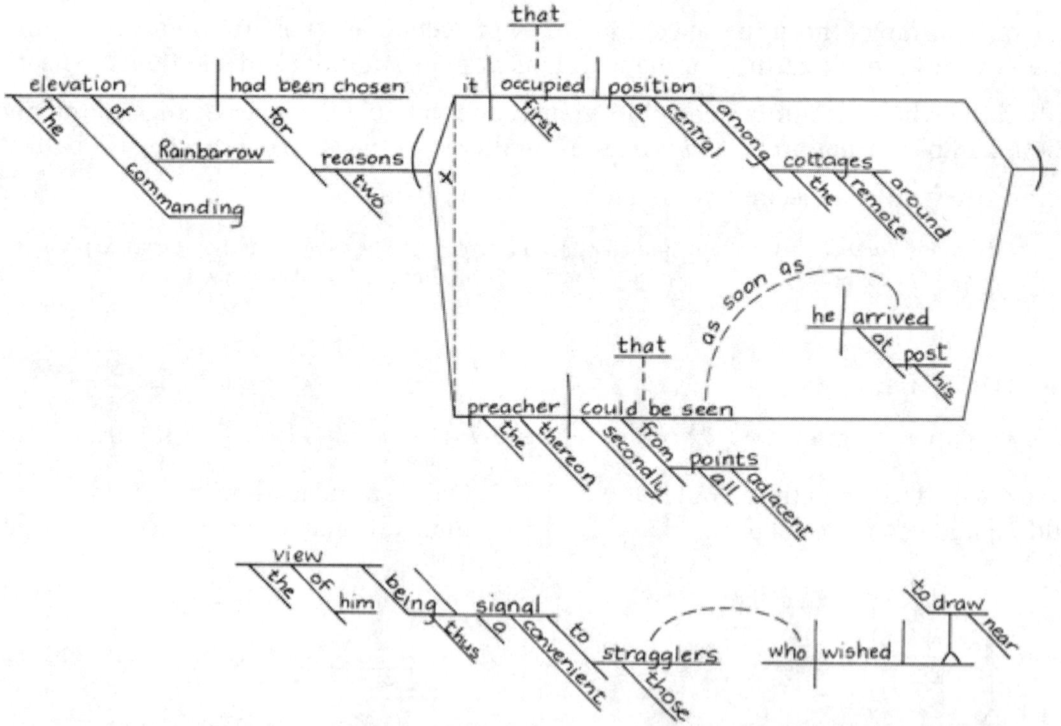

Note to Instructor: The adjective *commanding* could also be diagrammed as a regular adjective rather than a present participle. The two subordinate clauses (*first...around* and *secondly...near*) are both appositives renaming *reason.* In this diagram, there is no closing parenthesis because of the branching lines, but the student could also bring the branches back together and insert a closing parenthesis, or else diagram one appositive on the same line as *reasons* and the other above or below it.

The modifier *thereon* could also be interpreted as an adverb modifying *could be seen. As soon as* is a compound subordinating conjunction (see Lesson 72). The final phrase, *the view of him...to draw near,* is an absolute, with semantic but not grammatical connection to the rest of the sentence.

— LESSON 112 —

Principal Parts

Yet More Troublesome Verbs

EExercise 112A: Verb Definitions

Match the terms on the left with the definitions on the right by drawing lines between them.

progressive verb
imperative
transitive verb
indicative
gerund
subjunctive
present participle
ambitransitive verb
first principal part
modal
perfect verb
second principal part
hortative
intransitive verb
infinitive
simple verb
third principal part

the perfect past verb form, minus helping verbs
expresses possible actions
describes an ongoing or continuous action
present participle acting as a noun
describes an action which has been completed before another action takes place
expresses action that is received by some person or thing
the simple present (first-person singular)
formed by combining *to* and the first-person-singular present form of a verb
the same as the simple past verb form
encourages or recommends an action
expresses situations that are unreal, wished for, or uncertain
simply tells whether an action takes place in the past, present, or future
can be either transitive or intransitive
expresses intended actions
affirms or declares what actually is
expresses action that is not received by any person or thing
a verb form ending in *-ing*

Exercise 112B: Using Troublesome Verbs Correctly

In the following sentences from *Korean Folk Tales: Imps, Ghosts and Fairies*, by Im Bang and Yi Ryuk, translated by James S. Gale, fill in the blanks.

The first blank (above the sentence) should be filled in with the first principal part of the correct verb: *lie* or *lay* in the first set of sentences, *sit* or *set* in the second set, and *rise* or *raise* in the third set of sentences.

You will be able to tell from the context of the sentence whether you should use the transitive verbs *lay, set,* and raise (if the verb is passive, or has a direct object), or the intransitive verbs *lie, sit,* and *rise* (if the action of the verb is not passed on to any other word in the sentence).

The second blank (in the sentence itself) should be filled in with the correct form of that verb.

The first sentence in each section is done for you.

active indicative of lay
I have something very important to say, a private matter to lay before your Excellency.

They arrived at the gate, and the spirits who had him in hand led him in, and when they
simple past active indicative of lay
entered the inner courtyard they laid him down on his face.

simple past active indicative of lie
The dogs lay as they were all day long, and neither ate nor moved.

simple past active indicative of lay
Thus he laid aside his weather-beaten clothes and donned the vestments of the genii.

simple present active indicative of lie
They followed the road that leads toward the mountains that lie between Yang-tok and Maing-san counties.

simple past active indicative of lie
When he took to sea the waters lay quiet before him, and all his path was peace.

simple past active modal of lay
He would awake at first cock-crow of the morning, wash, dress, and never lay aside his book.

After drinking it he uttered the most gruesome and awful noises; his face grew very red
simple past active indicative of lie
and he lay down and slept.

perfect past active indicative of lie
A few days later, at night, I had lain down, when suddenly there was a sound of crackling paper overhead from above the ceiling.

simple past active indicative of lie
I lay motionless at the foot of the terrace till the following morning, when my father found me and had me taken in hand and cared for, so that I came to, and we all left the haunted house, never to go back.

simple past active indicative of sit
The Minister sat down, comforted him, and then sent him away.

Here I found the master himself, an old gentleman, who put me through my humble
active infinitive of sit
exercises, and then ordered me gently to come up and sit beside him.

simple past active indicative of sit
In the night he studied by candle-light, while she sat by his side and did silk-spinning.

simple past passive indicative of set
The pair of worn shoes were set aside.

simple past active indicative of sit
The stranger and the people with him sat the day through without any harm overtaking them, even though they were in the midst of the enemy's camp, as it were.

simple past passive indicative of set
After this he brought an armful of wood, which was set in the middle of the courtyard.

simple past active indicative of sit
A little later he came and sat on the bank and roared his threatenings at us.

progressive past active indicative of sit
One day he was sitting with a friend playing chess, when they agreed that the loser in each case was to pay a fine in drink.

simple past active indicative of set
He set them all aside and fixed his affections on this one only.

His cap was made of metal, which he used to cook his food in, and which he then washed
simple past active indicative of set
and set back on his head again.

The priest, however, beat him with his stick, and when others went to help, he beat them also,
active infinitive of rise
so that they were completely worsted and unable to rise or walk.

simple past active indicative of raise
Kim raised his eyes to see, and there was the exact duplicate of his wife, with a basket in her hand and roasted chestnuts.

simple past active indicative of rise
Vile fumes rose up and filled the house.

simple past active indicative of raise
In a little the quilt began to move, and she in alarm raised it to see what had happened, when lo! beneath it the child was gone and there lay coiled a huge snake instead.

simple past active indicative of rise
I rose to take her by the hand, when she began walking backwards, so that my hand never reached her.

simple past passive indicative of raise
He was raised to the rank of Prince and became, later, Prime Minister.

simple past active indicative of rise
Then both rose, came down to the entrance, and vaulted off into mid-air, where they disappeared from sight.

simple past active indicative of raise
But the host smiled upon him, raised his hands and asked, "Do you not know me? Look now."

simple past active indicative of raise
They raised him up in order to prepare him for burial, when suddenly he came to life, looked at them in anger, and asked what they meant.

Exercise 112C: More Irregular Principal Parts

Fill in the chart below with the missing principal parts of each verb. (You may use a dictionary if necessary.) Then, in the sentences (from Samuel Butler's classic translation of Homer's *Odyssey*), fill in the blanks with the correct verb, in the tense, mood, and voice indicated in brackets at the end of each sentence. Each verb is used one time.

	First Principal Part **Present**	Second Principal Part **Past**	Third Principal Part **Past Participle**
I	overtake	overtook	overtaken
	bind	bound	bound
	pay	paid	paid
	drive	drove	driven
	lie	lay	lain
	give	gave	given
	hear	heard	heard
	leap	leaped/leapt	leaped/leapt
	spill	spilled/spilt	spilled/spilt
	say	said	said
	light	lit/lighted	lit/lighted
	weep	wept	wept
	mean	meant	meant
	show	showed	shown
	go	went	gone
	strike	struck	struck
	bid	bid	bid

She had been nurse to Nausicaa, and had now lit the fire for her, and brought her supper for her into her own room. [perfect past active indicative]

"Vulcan," said Neptune, "if Mars goes away without paying his damages, I will pay you myself." [simple present active subjunctive] [simple future active indicative]

Mars and Minerva made me doughty in war; when I had picked my men to surprise the enemy with an ambush I never gave death so much as a thought, but was the first to leap forward and spear all whom I could overtake. [simple past active indicative] [active infinitive] [simple present active modal]

There it was that I heard news of Ulysses, for the king told me he had entertained him, and had shown him much hospitality while he was on his homeward journey. [simple past active indicative] [perfect past active indicative]

In the end, however, he escaped with his life, drove the cattle from Phylace to Pylos, avenged the wrong that had been done him, and gave the daughter of Neleus to his brother. [simple past active indicative]

The chief men among the suitors are lying in wait for you in the Strait between Ithaca and Samos, and they mean to kill you before you can reach home. [progressive present active indicative] [simple present active indicative]

Here was a bard also to sing to them and play his lyre, while two tumblers went about performing in the midst of them when the man struck up with his tune. [simple past active indicative]

The bath was overturned, so that all the water was spilt on the ground. [simple past passive indicative]

The sons of Autolycus busied themselves with the carcass of the boar, and bound Ulysses' wound; then, after saying a spell to stop the bleeding, they went home as fast as they could. [simple past active indicative] [present participle]

As she spoke, she told Eumaeus to set the bow and the pieces of iron before the suitors, and Eumaeus wept as he took them to do as she had bidden him. [simple past active indicative] [perfect past active indicative]

WEEK 30

Still More About Clauses

— LESSON 113 —

Clauses and Phrases

Exercise 113A: Phrases and Clauses

Identify each underlined set of words as *PH* for phrase or *CL* for clause.

- Then, identify the part of the sentence (*S, DO, IO, OP, PN, PA, ADV, ADJ*) that each set of words functions as.
- For phrases, further identify the phrase as *PREP* (prepositional), *INF* (infinitive), *PresP* (present participle), or *PP* (past participle).
- For clauses, write *S* above the subject of the clause and *P* above the predicate.
- For adjective and adverb phrases and clauses, draw an arrow to the word modified.
- If words are double-underlined, be careful—a phrase or clause is within another phrase or clause! Be sure to carry out the instructions above for both the larger phrase/clause and the phrase/clause within it.

The first is done for you. All of these sentences are taken from *Mariel of Redwall* by Brian Jacques.

CL ADV
S P PH ADV PREP
As sleep descended upon her weary body, strange thoughts flooded her mind.

PH ADV PresP
PH ADV PREP PH ADV PREP
He was back in a while, splashing water over his sleeping friend.

CL ADJ
PH ADV PREP S P PH ADV PREP
They sat around the bright flames, which provided an island of golden light against the gloomy vault of the forest in front of them.

PH ADV PREP
CL ADJ
S P
The two mice made their way between the flowerbeds which dotted the dark greensward.

CL ADV
S P
When she looked down, the lizard had gone.

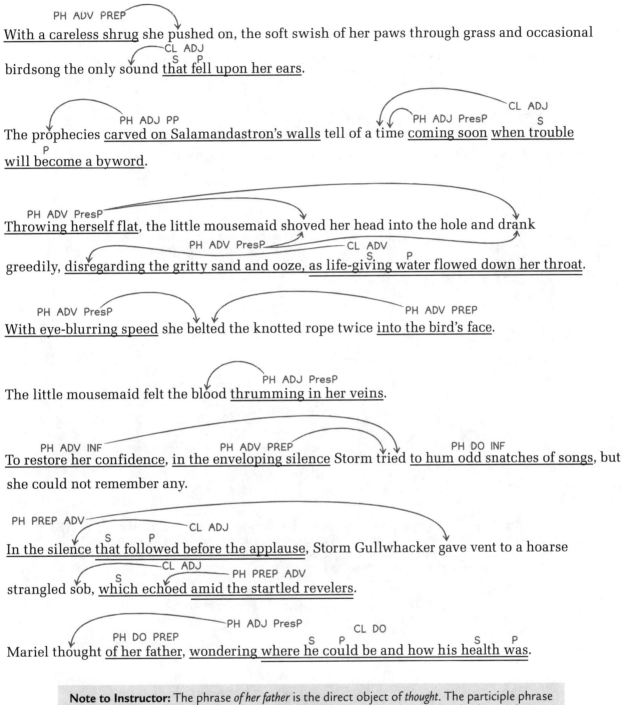

PH ADV PREP

CL ADJ S P

With a careless shrug she pushed on, the soft swish of her paws through grass and occasional birdsong the only sound that fell upon her ears.

PH ADJ PP PH ADJ PresP CL ADJ S P

The prophecies carved on Salamandastron's walls tell of a time coming soon when trouble will become a byword.

PH ADV PresP PH ADV PresP CL ADV S P

Throwing herself flat, the little mousemaid shoved her head into the hole and drank greedily, disregarding the gritty sand and ooze, as life-giving water flowed down her throat.

PH ADV PresP PH ADV PREP

With eye-blurring speed she belted the knotted rope twice into the bird's face.

PH ADJ PresP

The little mousemaid felt the blood thrumming in her veins.

PH ADV INF PH ADV PREP PH DO INF

To restore her confidence, in the enveloping silence Storm tried to hum odd snatches of songs, but she could not remember any.

PH PREP ADV CL ADJ S P

In the silence that followed before the applause, Storm Gullwhacker gave vent to a hoarse strangled sob, which echoed amid the startled revelers.

CL ADJ S PH PREP ADV

PH ADJ PresP PH DO PREP CL DO S P S P

Mariel thought of her father, wondering where he could be and how his health was.

Note to Instructor: The phrase *of her father* is the direct object of *thought*. The participle phrase *wondering where...health was*, as a whole, modifies *thought*. Within that participle phrase, the clauses *where he could be* and *how his health was* are both direct objects of the participle *wondering*.

PH ADV PresP CL DO S P

All around them, searats squatted, cooking whatever they had found during the day.

Exercise 113B: Diagramming

On your own paper, diagram every word of the following sentences, taken from *Doomwyte* by Brian Jacques.

Note to Instructor: Give all necessary help!

There were creatures inside, young mice, moles, squirrels, and hedgehogs.

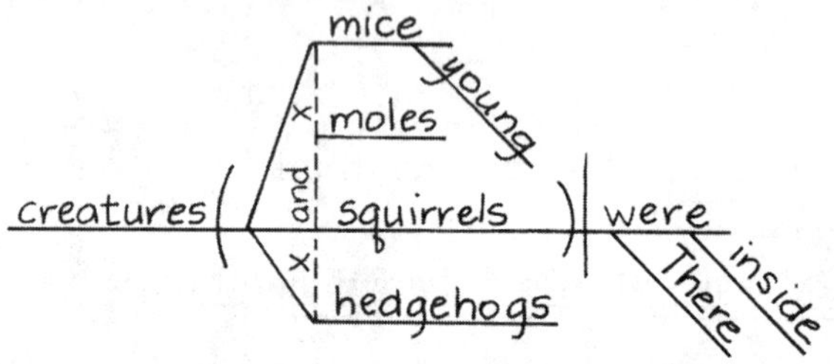

Note to Instructor: As long as the student indicates that *mice, moles, squirrels,* and *hedgehogs* are all appositives renaming *creatures*, her diagram does not need to match the answer exactly.

Back at the dormitory, the pillow fight was at its height, as was the noise.

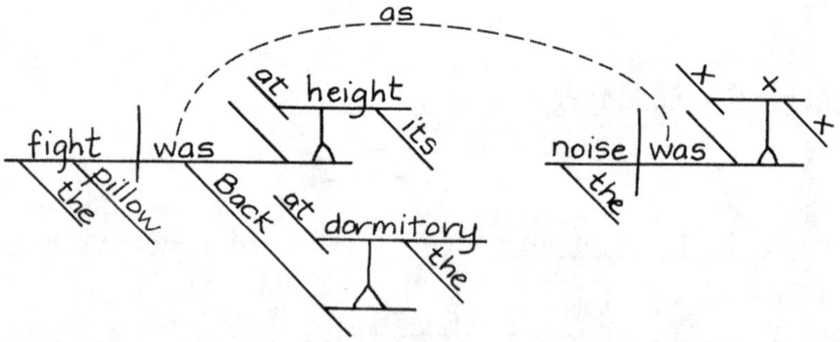

Note to Instructor: The prepositional phrase *at the dormitory* serves as the object of the preposition *Back*. If the student diagrams *Back* as an adverb and *at the dormitory* as a separate prepositional phrase modifying *was*, accept the answer, but show her the diagram above and point out that *at the dormitory* is *where* the Back *was*!

It is acceptable to diagram *pillow fight* as a single compound noun.

I have diagrammed the adverbial clause *the noise was [at its height]* with the understood predicate adjective phrase *at its height* indicated, but the student does not need to do this as long as she diagrams the clause correctly.

Brother Torilis, the Herbalist and Infirmary Keeper, did not bother to knock.

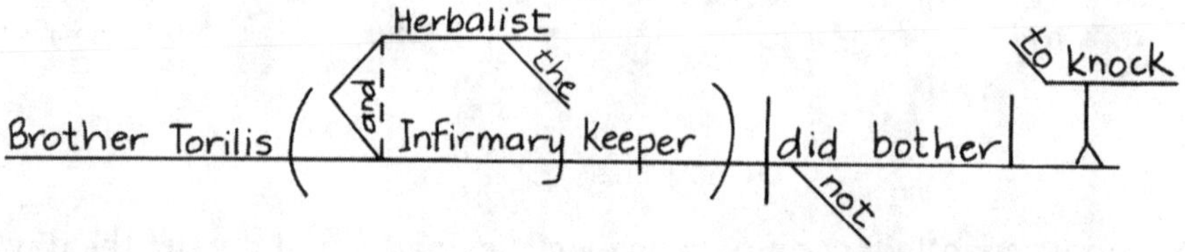

Note to Instructor: The student can indicate the compound appositive in whatever way makes the relationship of *Herbalist* and *Infirmary Keeper* clear. The infinitive phrase *to knock* is the direct object of the transitive verb *did bother*.

Flinging the door open, he strode straight into the scene of chaos.

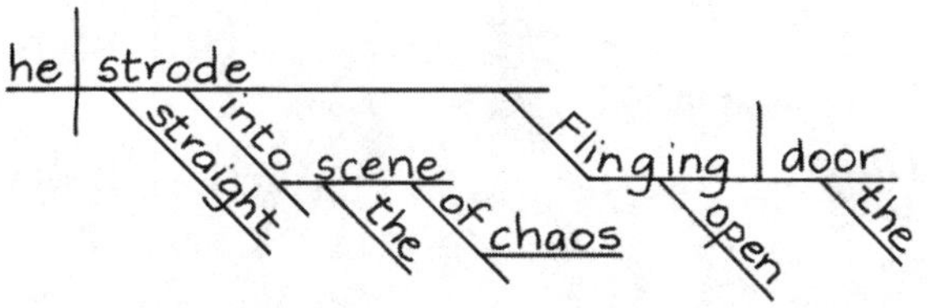

> **Note to Instructor:** The student could also diagram the prepositional phrase *into the scene of chaos* as the direct object of *straight*, which would turn *straight* into a preposition rather than an adverb.

A hush fell over the entire chamber, broken only by a volebabe falling from the top of a wardrobe onto a bed, where he lay at rigid attention.

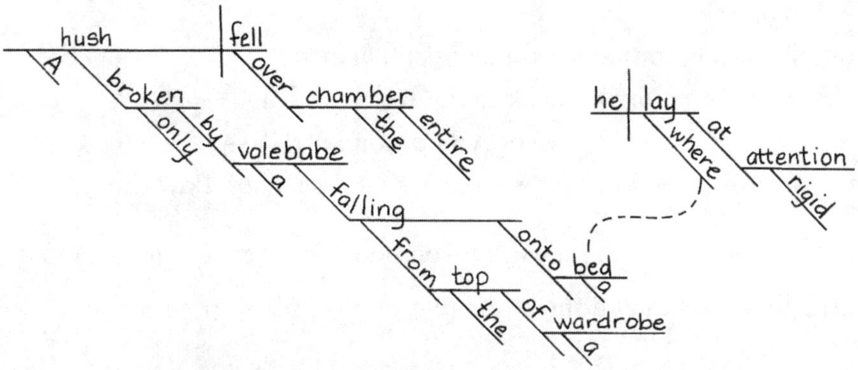

> **Note to Instructor:** The clause *where he lay at rigid attention* is an adjective clause introduced by a relative adverb (see Lesson 71).

Tossed about on the dark skies, like a scrap of black-and-white rag, the magpie caught sight of the imposing building as she was swept high over the swaying green of Mossflower woodlands.

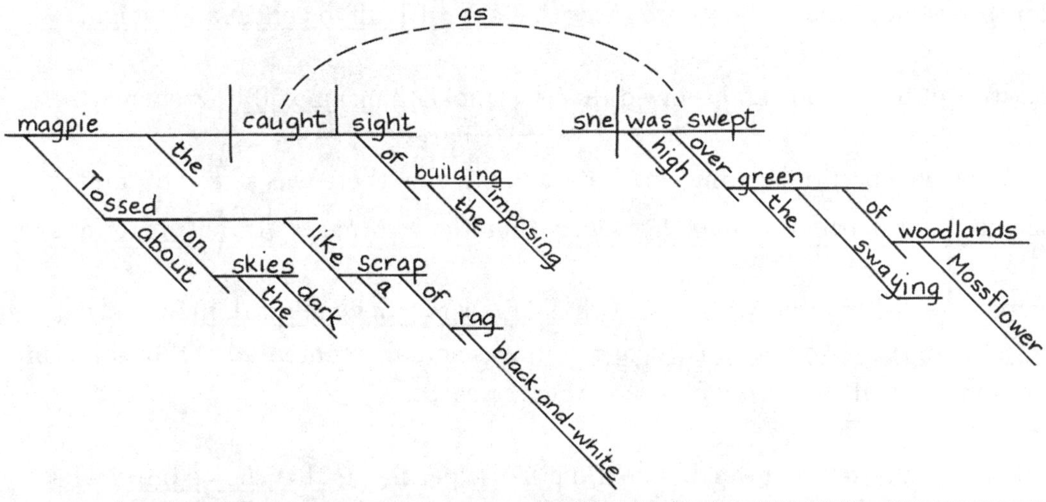

> **Note to Instructor:** The prepositional phrase *like a scrap of black-and-white-rag* modifies *Tossed*, not *magpie*, because it expresses *how* the magpie was tossed. You may accept the student's diagram if she places the phrase below *magpie*, but show her the answer above.
>
> *Imposing* can be diagrammed either as a regular adjective, as above, or on a bent line as a present participle.

— LESSON 114 —

Restrictive and Non-Restrictive Modifying Clauses
Punctuating Modifying Clauses
Which* and *That

Exercise 114A: Restrictive and Non-Restrictive Adjective Clauses

Find every adjective clause in the following sentences, taken from *A Little History of Science* by William Bynum, and then follow these steps:

a) Underline each adjective clause.
b) Circle the relative pronoun that introduces each clause.
c) Draw an arrow from the pronoun back to the word modified.
d) Label each clause as *R* for restrictive or *NR* for nonrestrictive.
e) Draw an asterisk or star next to each sentence that does not follow the which/that rule.

Ancient astronomers thought that there were seven planets: Mercury, Venus, Mars, Jupiter, and Saturn, plus the sun and the moon, which they also called planets. NR

He was also very interested in eclipses, which occur when the sun, moon, or one of the planets gets in the way of another planet and becomes partly or wholly covered from our sight. NR

* Another planet, Saturn, had two big blobs which didn't look like moons and which we now call its "rings." R R

When most things burn, the products are gases that are difficult to collect and weigh. R

He burnt a stick of fresh wood and showed that the smoke that came off it was not air. R

He knew air played a part in burning, and he also knew that there was a kind of "air" (a gas) that made things burn even more vigorously than the "ordinary" air that surrounds us. R R

His telescope revealed that the Milky Way, which appears as a wonderful, fuzzy blur of light when looking with the naked eye on a clear night, was actually composed of thousands and thousands of individual stars, very far away from the earth. NR

In fact, Galileo didn't use the tower, but he did other experiments that showed him what the result would be, and he found that a ten-pound ball and a one-pound ball would hit the ground at the same time. R

* Second, Aristotle insisted on the central role that the heart and blood play in our lives, after observing the tiny beating heart which was the first sign of life in the speck of a chick in an egg. R R

NR
The heart, which has long been associated with blood, was also fascinating to Harvey.

Anaesthesia was a triumph for chemistry in the service of medicine, since the compounds that
R
were shown to put people to sleep—ether and chloroform—were chemicals made in the laboratory.

Exercise 114B: Dependent Clauses within Dependent Clauses

The following sentences all contain dependent clauses that have other dependent clauses within them.

Underline the whole of each one of these dependent clauses (including additional dependent clauses that act as nouns or modifiers within it). Draw a box around the subject of the main dependent clause, and underline its predicate twice. In the right-hand margin, write the abbreviation for the part of the sentence that the main dependent clause is fulfilling: *N-SUB* for a noun clause acting as subject, *N-PN* for predicate nominative, *N-DO* for direct object, *N-OP* for object of the preposition, *N-APP* for appositive, and then *ADJ* for adjective and *ADV* for adverb. For adjective and adverb clauses, draw a line from the label back to the word in the main dependent clause modified.

Then, circle any additional clauses that fall within the main dependent clause. Label each clause, above the circle, in the same way: *N-SUB* for a noun clause acting as subject, *N-PN* for predicate nominative, *N-DO* for direct object, *N-OP* for object of the preposition, *N-APP* for appositive, and then *ADJ* for adjective and *ADV* for adverb. For adjective and adverb clauses, draw a line from the label back to the word in the main dependent clause modified.

The first sentence is done for you.

These are all taken from *Science and Modern India: An Institutional History, c. 1784–1947*, edited by Uma Das Gupta.

When we deal with such small or such large objects we must expect that their N-DO
ADJ
behaviour will be very different from that of the objects of medium size to which
we are used on the surface of this earth.

Note to Student: The first dependent clause, *When we deal with such small or such large objects*, is not underlined because it does not contain another clause within it. It acts as an adverb modifying the modal verb *must expect*.

In the world of the atom, however, we meet with the principle of complementarity, which ADJ
ADV
expresses, as Bohr has said, "the fundamental limitations, met with in atomic physics, of
ADJ
our ingrained idea of phenomena as existing independently of the means by which they
are observed."

Note to Instructor: The student may also draw an arrow from the first *ADJ* back to *principle*. *Complementarity* is the specific principle described by the dependent clause, but it also describes *principle*, so can be said to modify either word.

This equation holds for all arithmetical numbers and we can express all such statements in the general equation a x b=b x a, which forms the foundation of the mathematics which is taught at school. ADJ ADJ

Note to Instructor: The student may also draw an arrow from the first *ADJ* back to *a x b=b x a*, the appositive of *equation*.

During the 33 years which have elapsed since the instruments now in use in the observatory were ordered, astronomy has advanced so rapidly along certain lines that the instrumental equipment is again found very defective. ADJ ADJ

Note to Student: Don't forget—only underline the dependent clause that contains another dependent clause!

One might wonder why, of all places, Roorkee was chosen by the colonial rulers when it came to opening an engineering college. ADV N-DO

These observations consisted of the computed elements for the comets of 1843 and 1845 and of the solar eclipse of 21 December 1843, which he observed near the source of the Mah River, where the eclipse fell just short of totality but offered a beautiful view of Baily's beads. ADJ ADJ

Note to Student: For extra credit, find out what Baily's beads are!

Note to Instructor: Baily's beads are the glimpses of the sun visible during a total eclipse, produced by the mountainous edge of the lunar disk which allows tiny "beads" or "diamonds" of light through. They were explained by the astronomer Francis Baily in 1836.

The clause *where the eclipse...beads* is an adjective clause describing a place and introduced by a relative adverb.

He also believed that the clause which made it mandatory for an alumnus to return the sum of money spent on him by the university if he refused to join the College of Science was downright unjust. ADJ ADV N-DO

Note to Student: Be careful—the sentence above has a clause within a clause within a clause!

Exercise 114C: Diagramming

On your own paper, diagram every word of the following sentence(s). If you need help, ask your instructor. You'll need a very large piece of paper!

These are from *A Short History of Science*, by W. T. Sedgwick and H. W. Tyler.

Note to Instructor: Give all necessary help!

The following sentence has seven separate clauses!

Hicetas of Syracuse, according to Theophrastus, believes that the heavens, the sun, moon, stars, and all heavenly bodies are standing still, and that nothing in the universe is moving except the earth, which, while it turns and twists itself with the greatest velocity round its axis, produces all the same phenomena as if the heavens were moved and the earth were standing still.

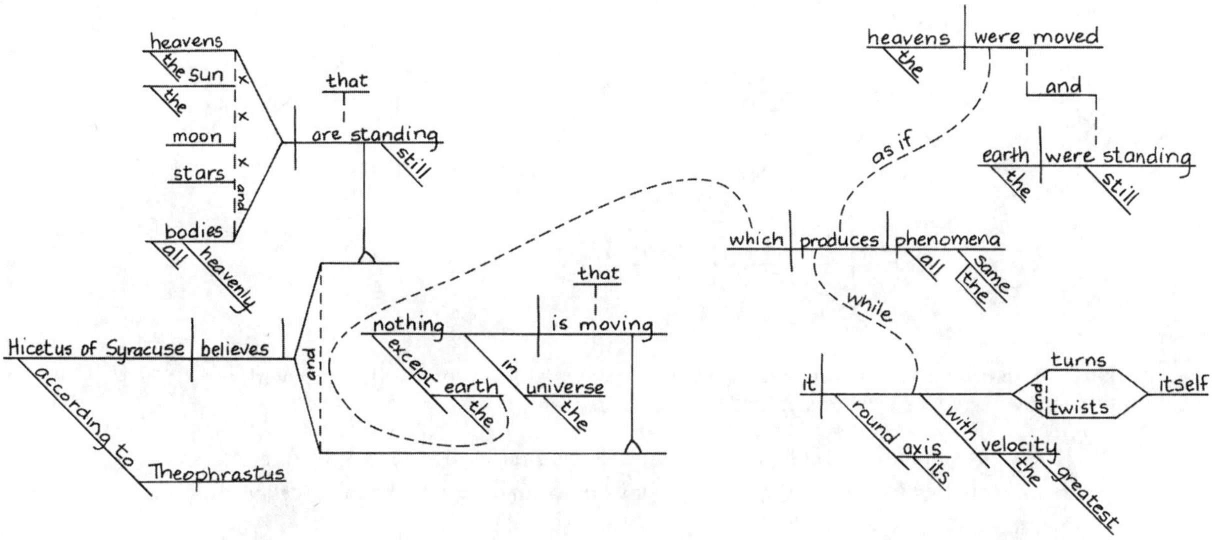

Note to Instructor: *According to* is a single compound preposition; *as if* is a compound subordinate conjunction. The prepositional phrases *round its axis* and *with the greatest velocity* modify both verbs *turns* and *twists*.

The following sentence has one main and three subordinate clauses—but they're hiding in plain view. Can you find them?

Pliny the Elder, sometimes called Pliny the Naturalist, is another Roman of scientific attainments, whose work entitled *Natural History,* although more an encyclopedia of miscellaneous information than a scientific treatise, is nevertheless, like the works of Herodotus, a landmark in the history of civilization.

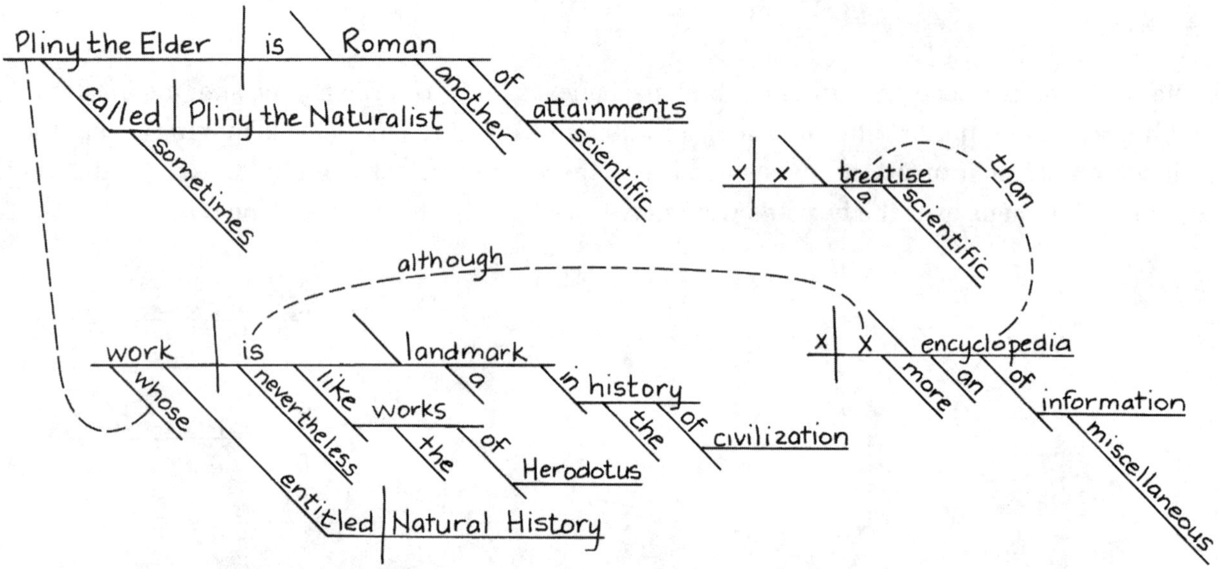

Note to Instructor: You may need to show the following version of the sentence, with the understood sentence elements spelled out, to the student:

Pliny the Elder, sometimes called Pliny the Naturalist, is another Roman of scientific attainments, whose work entitled *Natural History*, although [it is] more an encyclopedia of miscellaneous information than [it is] a scientific treatise, is nevertheless, like the works of Herodotus, a landmark in the history of civilization.

I have linked *encyclopedia* and *treatise* with the comparative *than*, because those seem to be the terms that are being compared, but an argument could be made for linking *more* and *treatise* (see the diagrams in Lesson 105).

— LESSON 115 —

Conditional Sentences
Conditional Sentences as Dependent Clauses
Conditional Sentences with Missing Words
Formal *If* Clauses

Exercise 115A: Conditional Clauses

In the following sentences from *Persuasion*, by Jane Austen (no zombies in *Persuasion*, alas!), circle every conditional sentence. This may mean circling the entire sentence, or circling simply the part of it that makes up the conditional-consequence clause set, or circling the conditional and consequence clauses separately if they are divided by other words.

After you have circled the conditional sentences, underline twice and then parse the predicate in each conditional and consequence clause.

Finally, write a *1*, *2*, or *3* in the blank to indicate first, second, or third conditional.

The first is done for you.

Note to Instructor: You may need to remind the student that predicates expressing unreal past or present circumstances are subjunctive, even if the form is the same as the indicative.

simple present, state-of-being, modal subjunctive
If Louisa Musgrove would be beautiful and happy in her November of life,
simple future, active, indicative
she will cherish all her present powers of mind. 1

simple present, active, modal subjunctive
Should he ever propose to me (which I have very little reason to imagine
simple future, active, indicative
he has any thought of doing), I shall not accept him. 1

simple past, active, subjunctive
These valuable pictures of yours, Sir Walter, if you chose to leave them,
simple present, state-of-being, modal
would be perfectly safe. 2

perfect present, state-of-being, modal — perfect past, active, subjunctive
It would have been strange if I had not gone. 3

perfect past, active, subjunctive — perfect past, active, subjunctive
I do believe if Charles were to see me dying, he would not think there was anything the matter with me. 2

Note to Instructor: The conditional sentence is the direct object of the verb *do believe*. The last part of the conditional sentence, the clause *there was anything the matter with me*, has an understood introductory *that* and is the direct object of the verb *would think*.

simple past, active, subjunctive — simple present, state-of-being, modal

If Louisa recovered, it would all be well again. 2

simple future, active, indicative — simple present, state-of-being, indicative

Anne will send for me if anything is the matter. 1

simple present, state-of-being, indicative — simple present, state-of-being, indicative

If there is anything disagreeable going on men are always sure to get out of it, and Charles is as bad as any of them. 1

simple present, active, indicative — simple present, active, imperative

Charles, if you see Captain Harville anywhere, remember to give Miss Anne's message. 1

simple present, active, modal — simple past, active, modal

I should not go, you may be sure, if I did not feel quite at ease about my dear child. 2

simple present, active, indicative — simple past, active, modal

If a man has not a wife, he soon wants to be afloat again. 1

perfect present, state-of-being, modal — perfect past, active, subjunctive

Everybody is always supposing that I am not a good walker; and yet they would not have been pleased, if we had refused to join them. 3

simple present, active, indicative — simple present, active, imperative

If you value her conduct or happiness, infuse as much of your own spirit into her as you can. 1

simple present, active, indicative — simple present, active, indicative

I have no scruple of observing to you, how nonsensical some persons are about their place, because all the world knows how easy and indifferent you are about it; but I wish anybody could give Mary a hint that it would be a great deal better if she were not so very tenacious. 2

Note to Student: The last sentence in this exercise does not completely follow the rules! Try to identify the type of conditional it contains, and then check with your instructor.

Anne talked of being perfectly ready, and tried to look it; but she felt that could Henrietta have known the regret and reluctance of her heart in quitting that chair, in preparing to quit the room, she would have found, in all her own sensations for her cousin, in the very security of his affection, wherewith to pity her. 3

perfect present, active, modal subjunctive (have known)

perfect present, active, modal (would have found)

Note to Instructor: In the sentence above, the verb of the formal condition clause is in the perfect present rather than the perfect past because it is modal subjunctive rather than simply subjunctive, expressing Henrietta's ability to know, not just her lack of knowledge. Show the student these three variations, and point out that in the first two, the perfect past verb does not express ability.

...if Henrietta had known the regret...she would have found...
...had Henrietta known the regret...she would have found...
...if Henrietta could have known the regret...she would have found...

Exercise 115B: Diagramming

On your own paper, diagram every word of the following two sentences from Exercise 115A.

Both of these sentences have challenging elements! Do your best, and ask your instructor for help if you need it. (You might want to use some scratch paper as well.)

Should he ever propose to me (which I have very little reason to imagine he has any thought of doing), I shall not accept him.

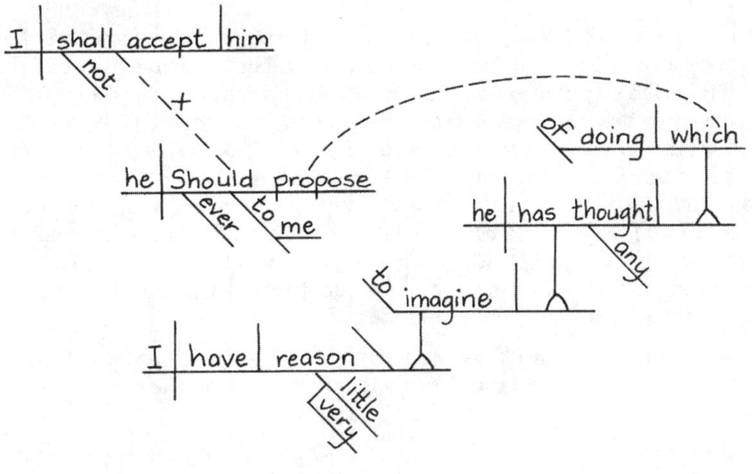

Note to Instructor: The formal conditional clause is linked to the consequent clause by an understood *if.* This sentence has an unusual construction: the relative pronoun *which* here actually links to the predicate *should propose.* (You will probably need to show this to the student—and remind her that English is a flexible and not completely rational language!)

The infinitive *to imagine* serves as the object complement to *reason* (it renames *reason*), and itself has the prepositional phrase of *doing* as its object. The relative pronoun *which* serves as the direct object of the participle *doing.*

Anne talked of being perfectly ready, and tried to look it; but she felt that could Henrietta have known the regret and reluctance of her heart in quitting that chair, in preparing to quit the room, she would have found, in all her own sensations for her cousin, in the very security of his affection, wherewith to pity her.

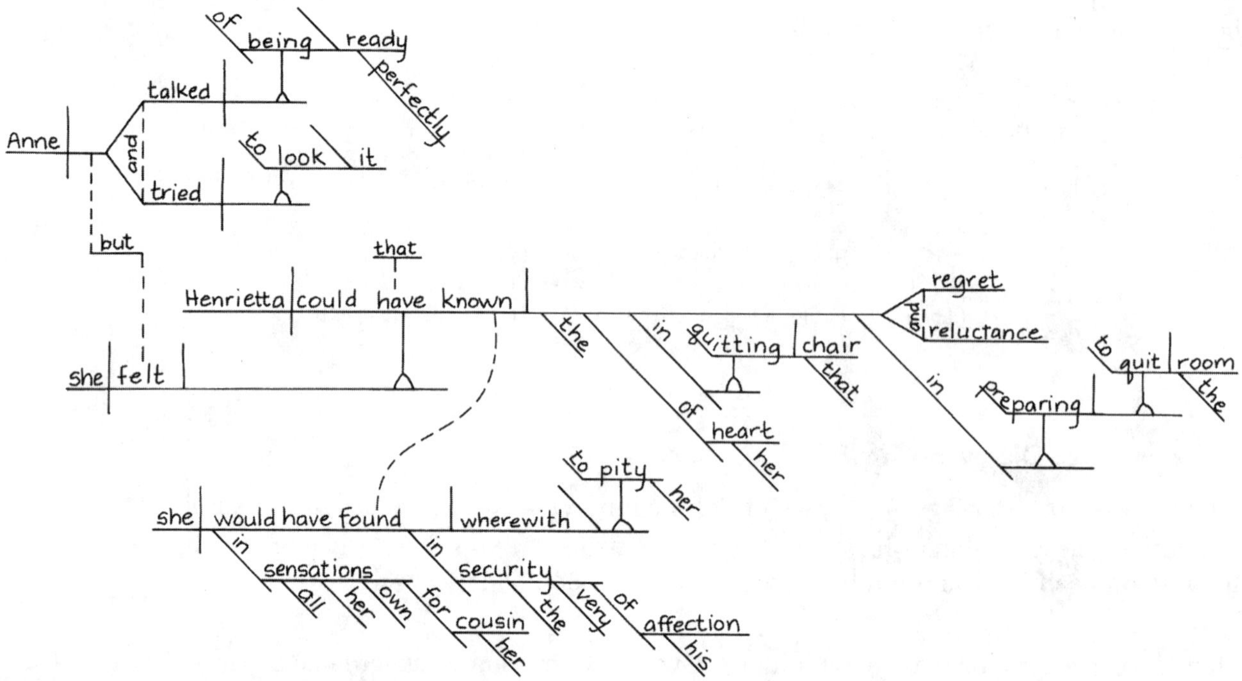

Note to Instructor: In the first main clause, the prepositional phrase *of being perfectly ready* and *to look it* both serve as objects for the verbs *talked* and *tried*. The participle *being* and the infinitive *to look* are both followed by puzzling constructions! You may reassure the student that there is no clear correct way to diagram these. (Remember, English is not completely rational!) I have diagrammed *ready* as a predicate adjective because it refers back to *Anne* and follows a linking verb form, and *it* as a predicate nominative because *it* follows a linking verb (*look* here does not function as an action verb—she is not looking at anything). However, *ready* could be diagrammed as an adverb beneath *of being*, and *to look it* could be diagrammed as a single idiomatic expression. If the student comes up with another solution, you may accept it! It's important that she continue to recognize diagramming as a useful tool for analyzing how sentences work, rather than an assignment with black and white solutions.

The words and phrases *the*, *of her heart*, *in quitting that chair*, and *in preparing to quit the room* all modify both *regret* and *reluctance*, and so they are diagrammed after the direct object line but before the branch in the diagram.

The pronoun *wherewith* is the direct object of *would have found*, and the infinitive phrase *to pity her* is an object complement. If the student diagrams it as an adjective phrase modifying *wherewith*, you may accept the answer, but show her the alternative diagram in this Key.

—LESSON 116—

Words That Can Be Multiple Parts of Speech
Interrogatives
Demonstratives
Relative Adverbs and Subordinating Conjunctions

Exercise 116A: Words Acting as Multiple Parts of Speech

Use these sentences, taken from Zane Grey's classic western novel *The Light of Western Stars*, to identify the parts of speech that the bolded words can serve as. The first blank is filled in for you. Fill in the blanks with the correct labels from the following list:

conjunction	interjection	preposition	adverb
adjective	noun	pronoun	verb

Which pronoun (twice) adjective

As she sat down to wait she reviewed the causes which accounted for the remarkable situation in which she found herself.

Well, if your memory for faces is so good, maybe you can tell me which one of these cowboys wasn't clean-shaven.

One adjective pronoun (twice)

One afternoon, however, Edith appeared prone to talk seriously.

Then, gradually, one by one they tired and went to bed.

Along adverb preposition

A huge cloud of dust went along over our heads.

Upon the drive in to the ranch, as she was passing the lower lake, she saw Stewart walking listlessly along the shore.

Forever noun adverb

He was somewhat wild and sudden and—sentimental in his demand to protect me—and it was not clear whether he meant his protection for last night or forever; but I am happy to say he offered me no word that was not honorable.

I cannot stay out here forever.

Clear adjective adverb verb noun

But Madeline detected a merry twinkle in her clear eyes.

Lastly, the fact standing clear of all others in its relation to her interest was that he had been almost ruined, almost lost, and she had saved him.

Ten thousand dollars would clear me and give me another start.

One look at him at close range in the clear was enough for Madeline to award him a blue ribbon over all horses, even her prize-winner, White Stockings.

Warm adjective verb

When she did slip her bare feet out upon the stone floor she very quickly put them back under the warm blankets.

It'll warm up directly.

Unless conjunction preposition

But don't yell in his ear unless you want Florence and me to see you disappear on the horizon.

Human life is not for any man to sacrifice unless in self-defense or in protecting those dependent upon him.

> **Note to Instructor:** The prepositional phrases *in self-defense* and *in protecting those dependent upon him* serve as compound objects of the preposition *unless*.

Even adverb conjunction adjective

Madeline did not faint or even shut her eyes, but she felt as if she were fast in a cold vise.

Still, even had he not replied at all she would have gone on with him.

Majesty heaved upward with a snort, the wet saddle creaked, and an even motion told Madeline she was on level ground.

For preposition conjunction

Perhaps the station agent will return soon, or Alfred will come for me.

We'll have to go, whether we want to or not, for when Bill learns you are here he'll just pack us all off.

Since preposition conjunction adverb

Madeline's personal opinion of Stewart had not changed in the least since the night it had been formed.

I have never had a day's worry since I bought the ranch.

I long since separated from love.

Back noun adjective adverb

From the back of the house sounded the tramp of boots and voices of men, and from outside came a dull thump of hoofs, the rattle of harness, and creak of wheels.

Alfred bundled her up into the back seat, and Florence after her, and wrapped them with robes.

Nothing could have turned her back then.

Exercise 116B: Words Introducing Clauses

In the following sentences, taken from *American Indian Stories* by the nineteenth-century Sioux writer Zitkala-Sa, underline every subordinate clause. Then, carry out the following steps:

a) Circle the introductory word of the clause. (NOTE: When the introductory word is the object of a preposition, circle the word itself, not the preposition that precedes it. See the sample sentence.) If the introductory word is understood, insert it with a caret and then circle it.

b) Label the clause as *N* (for noun), *ADJ* (for adjective), or *ADV* (for adverb).

c) For noun clauses, further identify them as *S* for subject, *O* for object, or *PN* for predicate nominative.

d) For adjective or adverb clauses, draw an arrow to the word modified.

e) Finally, label the introductory word as one of the following: *RP* for relative pronoun, *P* for a pronoun introducing a noun clause that does not refer back to a word in the main clause, *RAdj* for relative adjective (a relative pronoun functioning as an adjective and introducing an adjective clause), *RAdv* for relative adverb, *SC* for subordinating conjunction, or *A-SC* for adverb functioning as a subordinating conjunction.

The first is done for you.

ADJ RP

An invisible power passed from her outstretched fingers to the evil at which she aimed.

A-SC ADV

Always, when my mother started for the river, I stopped my play to run along with her.

P N O

Then I clung to her hand and begged to know what made the tears fall.

Loosely clad in a slip of brown buckskin, and light-footed with a pair of soft moccasins on my feet,

ADJ RP

I was as free as the wind that blew my hair.

Having gone many paces ahead I stopped, panting for breath, and laughing with glee

SC ADV

as my mother watched my every movement.

N PN

SC

It was as if I were the activity, and my hands and feet were only experiments for my spirit to work upon.

RP that

Returning from the river, I tugged beside my mother, with my hand upon the bucket ^

ADJ

she was carrying.

Setting the pail of water on the ground, my mother stooped, and stretching her left hand out on

ADJ RAdv

the level with my eyes, she placed her other arm about me; she pointed to the hill where my uncle and my only sister lay buried.

ADV SC

My poor child, how I cried with her because the Great Spirit had forgotten us!

A-SC ADV

At last, when we reached this western country, on the first weary night your sister died.

ADJ RAdv

The morning meal was our quiet hour, when we two were entirely alone.

ADJ RAdj

My uncle, whose death my mother ever lamented, was one of our nation's bravest warriors.

Though I heard many strange experiences related by these wayfarers, I loved best the evening meal, for that was the time (that) old legends were told.

> **Note to Instructor:** If the student identifies the entire clause *that was the time old legends were told* as a subordinate clause, point out that the clause can stand on its own as a complete sentence. The conjunction *for* is a coordinating conjunction linking the independent clause to the independent clause that precedes it.

I ate my supper in quiet, listening patiently to the talk of the old people, wishing all the time that they would begin the stories.

As each in turn began to tell a legend, I pillowed my head in my mother's lap.

The glare of the fire shone on a tattooed star upon the brow of the old warrior who was telling a story.

Then followed a long silence in which he clasped tighter and unclasped again his interlocked fingers.

After the warrior's story was finished, I asked the old woman the meaning of the blue lines on her chin, looking all the while out of the corners of my eyes at the warrior with the star on his forehead.

I was a little afraid that he would rebuke me for my boldness.

It was a long story of a woman whose magic power lay hidden behind the marks upon her face.

It took many trials before I learned how to knot my sinew thread on the point of my finger.

Exercise 116C: Diagramming

(You didn't think you'd escape diagramming, did you?)

On your own paper, diagram every word of the following sentences from *North American Legends*, as retold by Zitkala-Sa.

If you need help, ask your instructor.

The fat ducks waddled in through a small opening, which was the only entrance way.

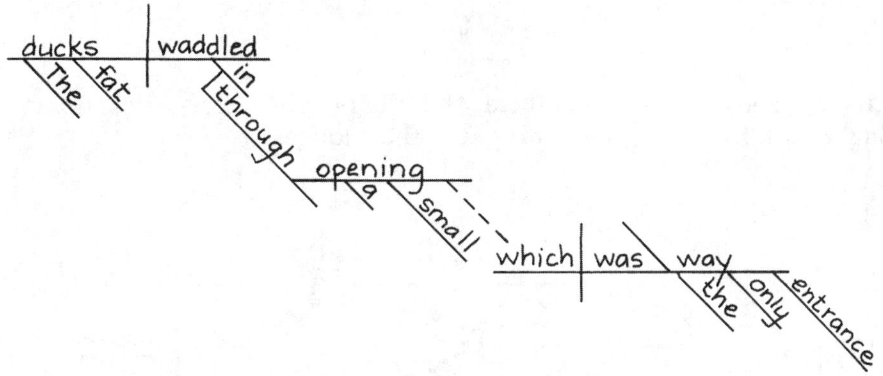

Note to Instructor: I have diagrammed *through a small opening* as a prepositional phrase modifying the adverb *in*, but it could also be diagrammed as a separate adverbial phrase modifying *waddled* directly.

They were talking of a strange young man whom they spied while out upon a hunt for deer beyond the bluffs.

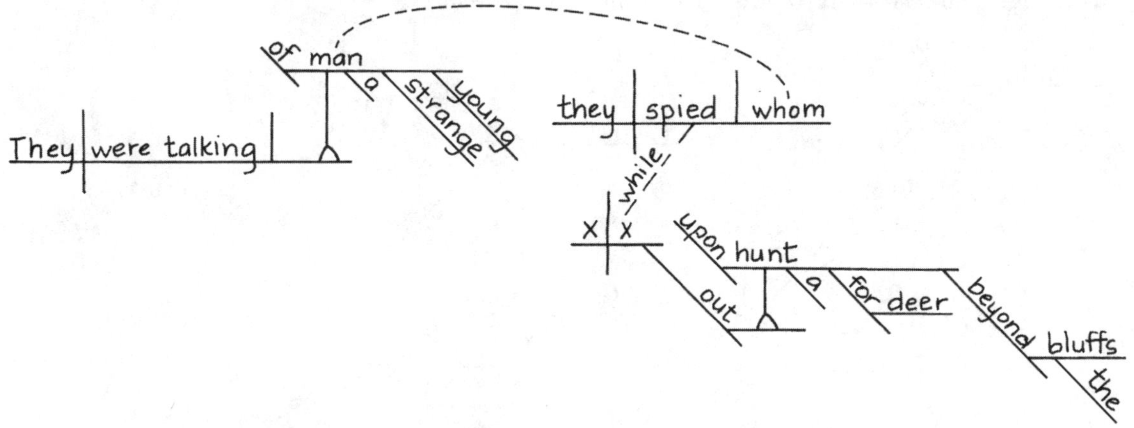

Note to Instructor: The phrase *while out upon a hunt for deer beyond the bluffs* is actually a clause with understood elements: *whom they spied while [they were] out...*

I have diagrammed *beyond the bluffs* as modifying *hunt* (the *hunt* was *beyond the bluffs*), but if the student diagrams *beyond the bluffs* as modifying *deer*, accept the answer (since the deer were also beyond the bluffs)

He who dares to open his eyes, forever red eyes shall have.

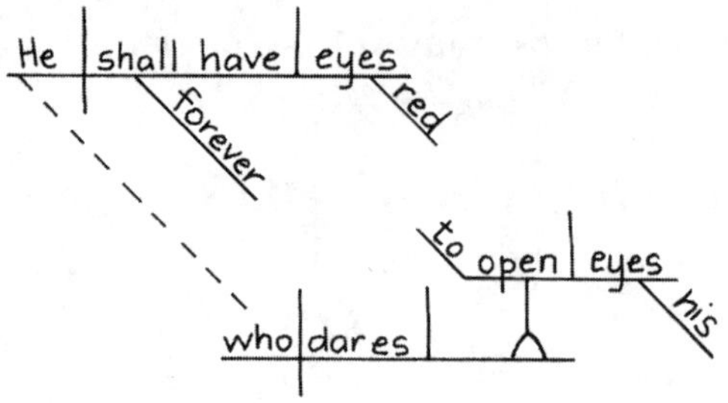

They poked their noses at him trying to know who he was.

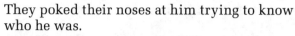

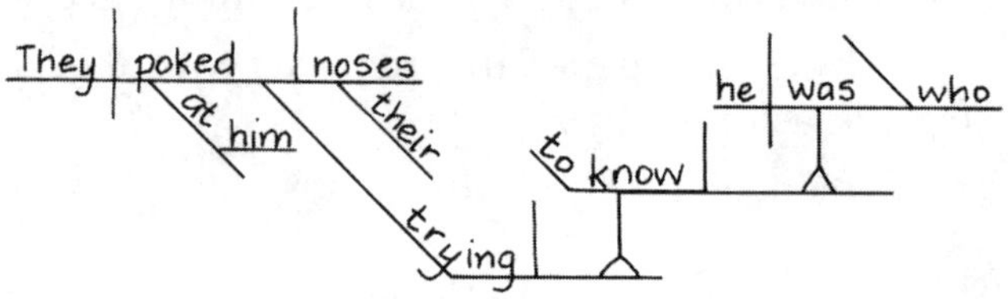

As the badger stood there unrecognized, he saw that the bear had brought with him his whole family.

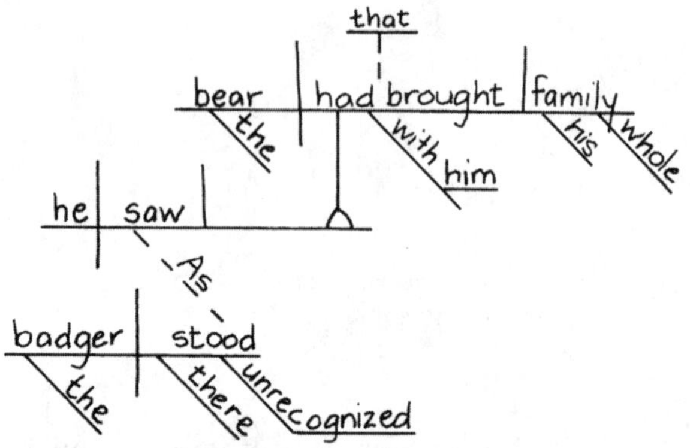

Then it was that the people, terror-stricken, ran screaming into their lodges.

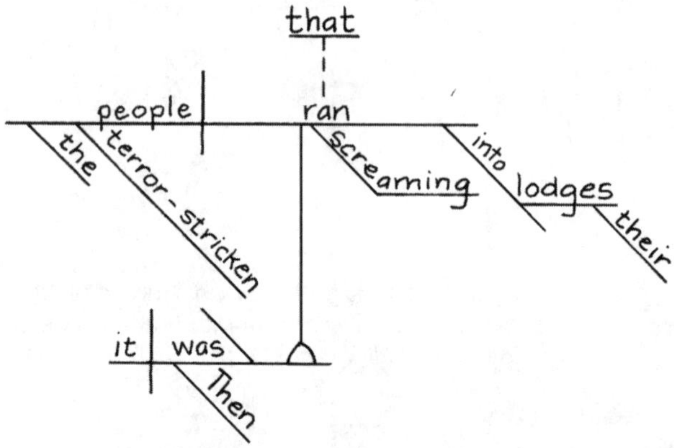

When you see the black coals rise to the surface of the water, clap your hands and shout aloud, for soon after that sign I shall return to you with some tender meat.

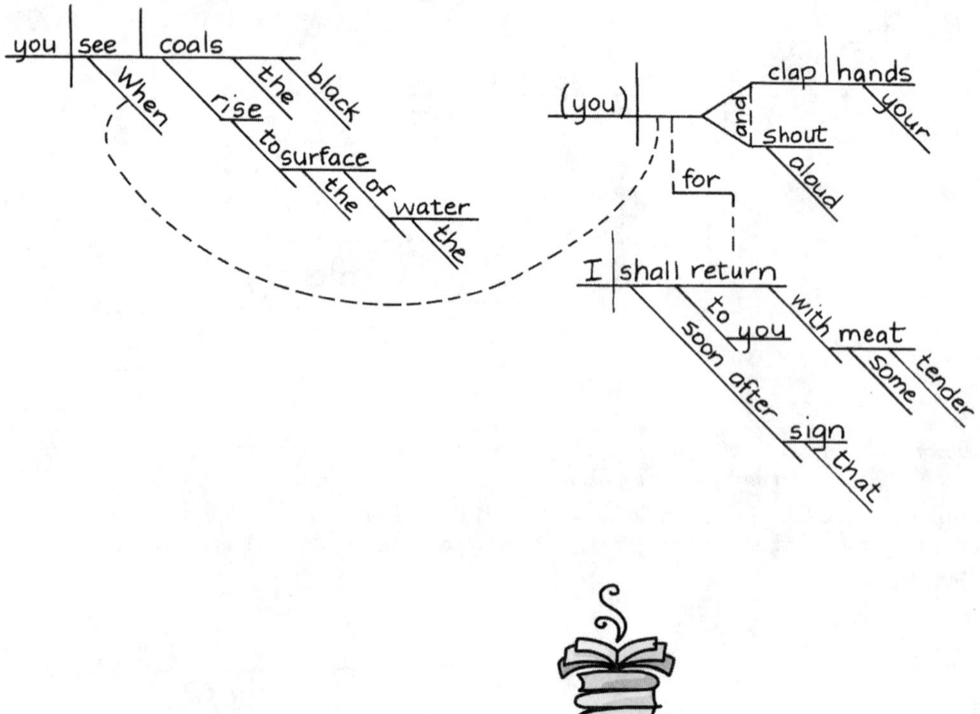

WEEK 31

Filling Up the Corners

— LESSON 117 —

Interrogative Adverbs
Noun Clauses
Forming Questions
Affirmations and Negations
Double Negatives

Exercise 117A: Identifying Adverbs, Interrogative and Demonstrative Pronouns and Adjectives, and Relatives

In the following sentences from Mort Rosenblum's *Chocolate: A Bittersweet Saga of Dark and Light*, follow these steps:

a) Label each bolded word as one of the following:

ADV for adverb

Draw an arrow from the adverb to the word modified.

If the adverb also introduces a clause, underline the clause.

PRO for pronoun

If the pronoun has an antecedent, label the antecedent as *ANT.* If the pronoun introduces a clause, underline the clause.

Label each pronoun as *S* for subject, *PN* for predicate nominative, *DO* for direct object, *IO* for indirect object, *OP* for object of the preposition, or *ADJ* (see below).

ADJ for adjective

Draw an arrow from the adjective to the word modified. If the adjective introduces a clause, underline the clause.

b) Label each underlined clause as *ADV-C* for adverb clause, *ADJ-C* for adjective clause, or *N-C* for noun clause.

c) Draw an arrow from each *ADV-C* and *ADJ-C* clause back to the word modified. Label each *N-C* noun clause as *S* for subject, *APP* for appositive, *PN* for predicate nominative, *DO* for direct object, *IO* for indirect object, or *OP* for object of the preposition.

The first is done for you. Notice that *whose* has two labels because it is both an adjective and a relative pronoun.

ANT PRO ADJ ADJ-C

She also brought her own Viennese chocolatier, **whose** specialty was a brew mixed with orchid powder, orange blossoms, and almond milk.

ANT PRO S ADJ-C

Marie-Antoinette, she of let-them-eat-cake fame, was yet another Austrian **who** came to France with chocolate in her baggage train.

ADJ

From my first day on the chocolate trail, I was obsessed by **this** obvious and overriding question:

N-C APP

PRO-S

Who does make the best chocolate?

> **Note to Instructor:** *Who does make the best chocolate* is set off by a colon, so it could be considered a parenthetical element, but it has a direct grammatical relationship to the rest of the sentence because it renames the noun *question*.

ADV N-C PN

This is **how** you heat water for chocolate.

ADV N-C DO

I could see **why** marauding monkeys and bush rats could be a worse scourge to cacao growers than armed rebels.

ANT PRO-S N-C PN

This seemingly simple step is **what** marshals the molecules so the finished chocolate ends up creamy-smooth and shining.

ADV-C

ADV

By 2002, **when** the great chocolate tremor shook central Pennsylvania, Hershey had spent thirteen years as the largest candy-maker in the United States.

ANT PRO-S ADJ-C

The Kiss, **which** dates back generations, is a major seller, as are Hershey's chocolate morsels, its

ADJ ANT PRO-DO ADJ-C

baking chocolate, and **those** same cans of Hershey's Syrup **that** our grandparents used.

Together they introduced the aging, stately Hershey Chocolate Corp. to the cut-throat

ANT PRO-DO ADJ-C ADV ADJ-C

world of candy **that** Forrest Mars had created, **where** Willy Wonka is motivated by greed, rivalry, secrecy and paranoia.

> **Note to Instructor:** The adjective clause *where Willy Wonka...paranoia* is introduced by the relative adverb *where*.

ADJ

This last step—the addition of sugary chocolate—is crucial for the right balance.

ANT ANT PRO-S ADJ-C

Someone is obviously enjoying all the Hershey bars and Kisses **that** after all these years continue to sell in the millions.

> **Note to Instructor:** The adjective clause modifies both *Hershey bars* and *Kisses*, as can be seen from the plural verb *continue*, which shows that the relative pronoun *that* is plural and references both nouns (remember, *it continues*, or *they continue*).

ADV

Why would you depend on someone else?

ANT

Mexico's army is great, Flores explained, because it has so many Oaxacan soldiers

PRO ADJ ADJ-C

whose diet is corn and chocolate.

Exercise 117B: Forming Questions

On your own paper, rewrite the following statements as questions.

Use each of the three methods for forming questions (adding an interrogative pronoun, reversing the subject and helping verb, adding the helping verb *do, does,* or *did* in front of the subject and adjusting the tense of the main verb) at least once. You may change tenses, add or subtract words, or alter the statements in any other necessary ways, as long as the meaning remains the same.

These statements are all adapted from famous questions in books and movies. When you have transformed your statements into questions, compare them with the originals.

Note to Instructor: The student's questions do not need to be identical to the originals, but each question should be grammatically correct, and each method should be used at least once.

STATEMENT	QUESTION
My super suit is somewhere.	Where's my super suit? *The Incredibles*
Your king is this.	Is this your king? *Black Panther*
You are not entertained.	Are you not entertained? *Gladiator*
You judge me by my size.	Judge me by my size, do you? *Star Wars Episode V: The Empire Strikes Back*
Your damage is something.	What's your damage? *Heathers*
The net amount of entropy of the universe can somehow be massively decreased.	How can the net amount of entropy of the universe be massively decreased? *"The Last Question," Isaac Asimov*
A raven is like a writing desk.	Why is a raven like a writing desk? *Alice's Adventures in Wonderland,* Lewis Carroll
We three shall meet again.	When shall we three meet again? *Macbeth,* William Shakespeare
I am too late for Alexander's panic attack.	Am I too late for Alexander's panic attack? *Galaxy Quest*

This corn is hand shucked.	Is this corn hand shucked? *What About Bob?*
Andy might get another dinosaur, a mean one.	But what if Andy gets another dinosaur, a mean one? *Toy Story*

Exercise 117C: Affirmations and Negations

On your own paper,

- Rewrite each of the following affirmative statements as a negation, using one adverb or adjective of negation. You may add or subtract words or change tenses as necessary.
- Rewrite each of the following negative statements as an affirmative, using at least one adverb of affirmation.
- Rewrite any double negation as an affirmative, also using at least one adverb of affirmation.

When you are finished, compare your answers with the original sentences, slightly adapted from *The Captain of the Polestar and Other Tales*, by Sir Arthur Conan Doyle (the author of the Sherlock Holmes stories—but these are all tales of adventure and seafaring!).

Note to Instructor: The student's answers do not need to be identical to the original sentences, as long as the guidelines above are followed. Check to see that the student has included adverbs or adjectives of affirmation and negation in each sentence; these are bolded in the original sentences below.

ASSIGNED SENTENCES	ORIGINAL VERSIONS
Talk to me more, please.	Do**n't** talk to me any more, please.
It wasn't a strange coincidence.	It was **certainly** a strange coincidence.
The night wasn't not dark.	The night was **very** dark.
I thought of it often before.	I **never** thought of it before.
At last it occurred to him that by a daring and original experiment the question might never be decided.	At last it occurred to him that by a daring and original experiment the question might be **definitely** decided.
There were many people for many miles in each direction.	There were **no** other people for many miles in each direction.
The man's memory of his whole life before the fatal blow was not erased.	The man's memory of his whole life before the fatal blow was **entirely** and **absolutely** erased.

Note to Instructor: The original sentence has two adverbs of affirmation, but one is sufficient!

It was long before I discovered that her suspicions were not well founded.	It was **not** long before I discovered that her suspicions were well founded.

Kick me under the table, Flannigan.	Do**n't** you kick me under the table, Flannigan.
You will surely desert me.	Surely you will **not** desert me.

> **Note to Instructor:** The student will probably write "You will not desert me," rather than *Surely you will not desert me.* This is a correct answer, but you may want to point out that the presence of the adverb of negation *not* applies to *surely* as well as *will desert*, converting *surely* from an affirmative to a negative meaning!

— LESSON 118 —

Diagramming Affirmations and Negations
Yet More Words That Can Be Multiple Parts of Speech
Comparisons Using *Than*
Comparisons Using *As*

Exercise 118A: Identifying Parts of Speech

Label each of the bolded words in these sentences (from *Jewish Fairy Tales and Legends*, by Gertrude Landa) with one of the following abbreviations.

ADJ: adjective	ADV: adverb
ADV-N: adverb of negation	ADV-A: adverb of affirmation
ADV-R: relative adverb	SC: subordinating conjunction
PREP: preposition	RP: relative pronoun
DP: demonstrative pronoun	IP: indefinite pronoun
N: noun	P: plain ol' pronoun

Where a subordinating conjunction introduces a comparison clause with missing words, draw a caret and insert the missing words.

ADV SC ADV PREP
Scarcely a word was spoken **as** the king and his hunters made their way **back to** the land East of the Rising Sun.

> **Note to Instructor:** If the student marks *scarcely* as an adjective modifying *word*, point out that it isn't a "scarcely word" – instead, the word "was scarcely spoken."

ADV-N ADV-N ADV-N ADV ADV PREP N
"**No**, **no**, I know **not**," she repeated **again** and **again**, and **at length** the man departed.

PREP PREP
With trembling hands the high priest placed it **before** his majesty.

SC (ADV) PREP ADV PREP ADV
Before King Hagag could recover **from** his surprise the youth ran **back to** the river and swam **across**.

> **Note to Instructor:** *Before* is an adverb acting as a subordinating conjunction; point out this dual identity to the student.

PREP PREP
Across the desolate plain and **through** the forest the chase continued.

Noting the direction of the sun, he bored a tiny hole in the wall, and a thin sunbeam gleamed
ADV
through.

PREP N SC is radiant
In their **midst** stood the princess, a dazzling vision, radiant **as** the dawn^.

ADV-A ADV ADJ
Hanina and his wife followed the giant frog to the woods **very early one** morning, and a comical
SC ADV
figure it presented **as** it hobbled **along**.

ADV ADJ
There they spent **quite** an hour.

PREP
The king regarded the task of governing his subjects **as** a big nuisance.

PREP SC
Deal **with** affairs **as** you think best.

IP PREP P ADV-A ADV
One of them, **indeed**, was **unduly** interested in him.

ADV ADV-R PREP
He endured agonies, **especially when** the friend invited Ben Maslia to dine **with** him, and Ben
PREP ADV
Maslia, **after** a few moments' hesitation, **firmly** declined.

ADV ADV PREP
He clapped his hands, and **immediately**, in **quite** startling fashion, a dozen servants stepped **from**
PREP RP PREP
behind the hangings **which** had hidden them and bowed **before** their master.

ADV ADV SC ADV ADJ ADV ADV
As well as the hunters could make **out, no** foot had **ever** trodden the region **before**.

Exercise 118B: Diagramming

On your own paper, diagram every word of the following sentences from *A Book of Giants: Tales of Very Tall Men of Myth, Legend, History, and Science*, by Henry Wysham Lanier. Ask your instructor for help if you need it.

Heave and strain as he might, Thor could only get one paw off the floor.

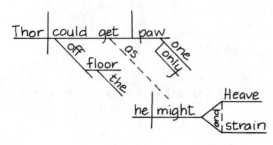

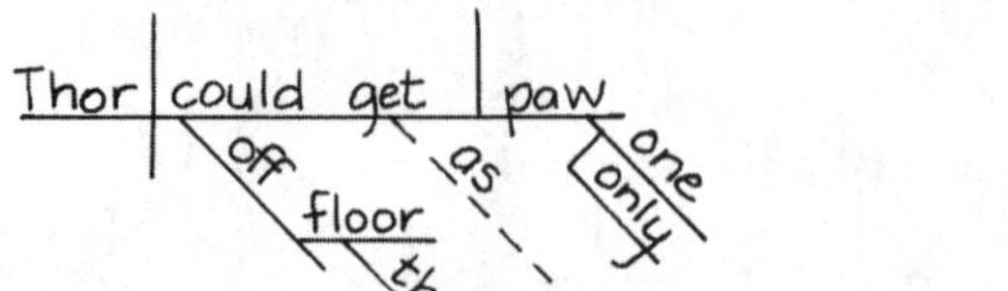

Nurse Elli was in fact old age—and never yet has man wrestled with her as have you.

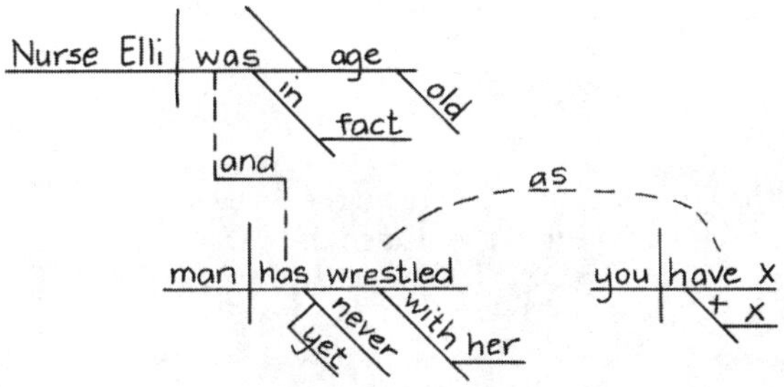

> **Note to Instructor:** The understood words of the comparative clause are *as have you* (*wrestled with her*).

So lofty were its walls and buildings that their heads bent back on their necks as they gazed up to the pinnacles of the towers.

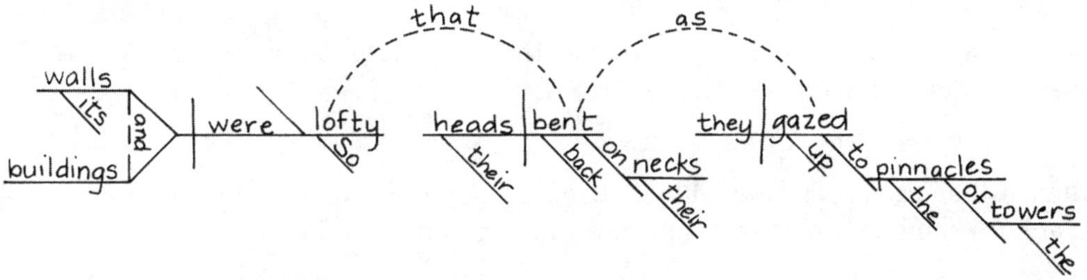

Yes, the Giant was ready to do that, and he turned the six brothers into king's sons again, and their brides into king's daughters.

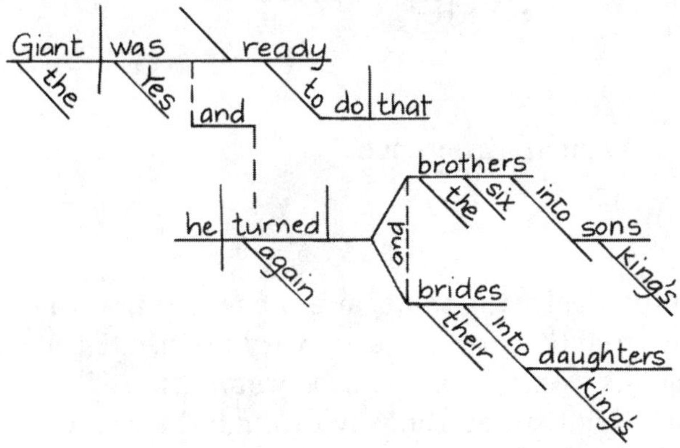

Yet amid this charming serenity Kronos could never forget the curse of his father Uranus whom he had overthrown, and the prophecy that he himself should in his turn be cast down by his own children.

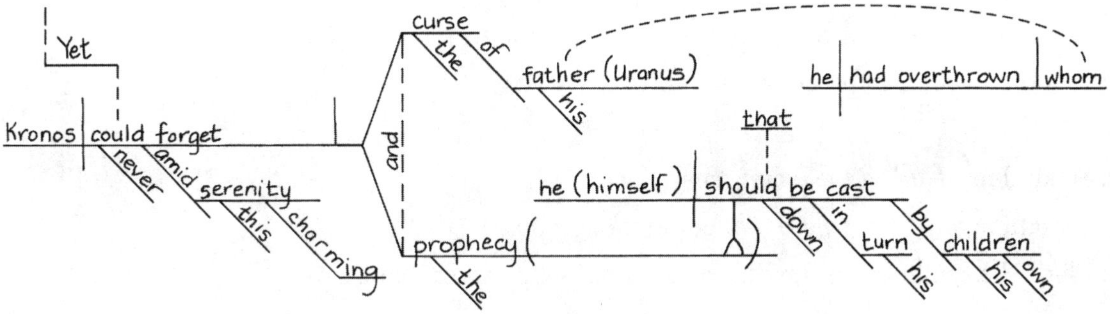

— LESSON 119 —

Idioms

Note to Instructor: The dialogue from the Core Instructor Text is continued here, in the Answer Key, so that instructor and student can study different idioms each year. If the student is unfamiliar with any idiom covered, provide the meaning.

Instructor: We can divide idioms into two types. In the first type, all of the words in the idiom are serving a clear, familiar grammatical function—but the idiom itself means something completely different than its literal meaning. The next sentences in your workbook are this type of idiom. Read me the first sentence, spoken by someone who is very, very tired.

Student: I have been burning the candle at both ends!

Instructor: This sentence means exactly the same thing as the next sentence in your workbook—also spoken by someone who is extremely tired.

Student: I have been overworking myself for many days!

Instructor: Both sentences have a verb, followed by a direct object and modified by a prepositional phrase. Put both sentences on the diagram frames in your workbook now.

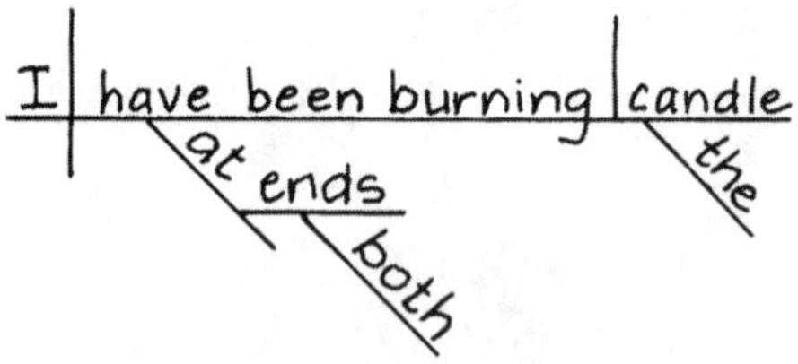

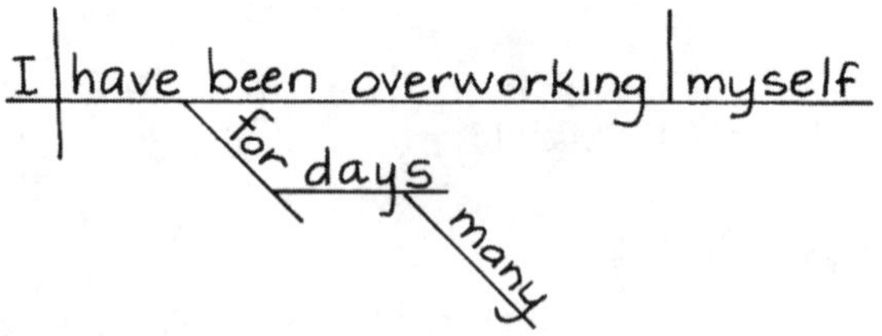

Instructor: Look at these two diagrams. What is the only small difference?

Student: There is an extra adjective in the first diagram.

Instructor: Otherwise, the sentences are identical!

Even though these sentences are grammatically the same, and the meaning is the same, the words used to express just how tired the speaker is are very different! The idiom *burning the candle at both ends* means *working much harder than usual.* The wick of a candle is a braided cotton thread that runs all the way through the wax of the candle. If you light the wick on just the top of the candle, it will burn at a normal speed—but if you scrape away the wax at the bottom to reveal the wick, and also light it there, the candle will burn at twice the usual speed. So *burning the candle at both ends* is an idiom for *wearing yourself out unusually quickly.* Read me the next sentence.

Student: Alas, our Labor Day party plans are dead in the water.

Instructor: Are the Labor Day party plans floating in water?

Student: No.

Instructor: What does *dead in the water* mean?

Student: Over, not going anywhere, not going to happen.

Instructor: Place the sentence on the diagram frame in your workbook now.

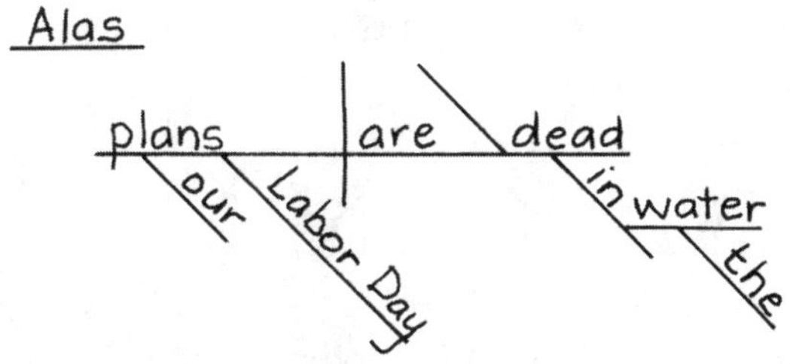

Instructor: None of those parts of speech are unusual! If you can diagram an idiom without any trouble, you know that it has regular grammar—even if it has an unexpected meaning.

The second type of idiom uses combinations of words that might not fit into the patterns you've already learned. Read me the next sentence.

Student: The little girl will be taken care of while her mother is sleeping.

Instructor: What part of speech is *of*?

Student: Preposition.

Instructor: Does the preposition *of* have an object?

Student: No.

Instructor: There's no way to diagram *of* as a preposition, since there's no prepositional phrase. And how about *care*? What part of speech is *care*?

Student: A noun.

Instructor: It looks like a direct object—but there's a reason why it can't be a direct object, and it has to do with the verb *will be taken*. Do you know the reason?

Note to Instructor: Prompt the student for the following answer if necessary.

Student: It is a passive verb.

Instructor: The subject of the passive verb is *the little girl*. It can't have a direct object!

The verb *take care of* is an idiom, meaning to *tend*, *keep*, or *watch*. But there's no way to diagram *care* or *of* separately from *will be taken*. When you can sum up the meaning of an idiom with one word, it should always go on a single line in your diagram. Diagram this sentence onto the frame in your workbook.

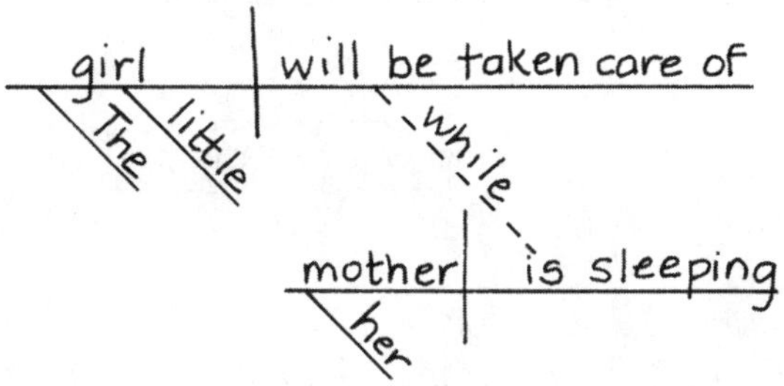

Instructor: English has many idioms that use multiple words to express a single meaning—and others that use just a few words to express a much longer meaning! The next sentence is a simple one. Read it out loud.

Student: I'm all ears.

Instructor: What part of speech is *ears*?

Student: A noun.

Instructor: Look at the diagram that follows. What part of the sentence is *ears* diagrammed as?

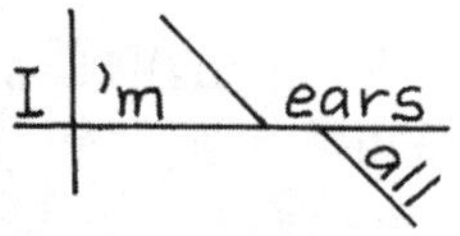

Student: Ears is a predicate nominative.

Instructor: That's just silly. People aren't ears! And *ears* can't rename *I*. Try to place the sentence on the next diagram frame.

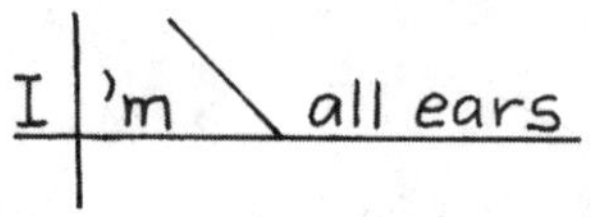

Instructor: Now, the idiom *all ears* has become a predicative adjective, describing *I*. Try to put the idiom *all ears* into other words. What is the speaker saying about herself?

> **Note to Instructor:** Give the student as much help as she needs to formulate the following answer.

Student: "I am anxious to hear what you have to say" OR "I can't wait to hear this!" OR "I am paying very close attention" [or a similar answer].

Instructor: "All ears" is a short, easy way to express something that otherwise needs many more words. That's one of the strengths of idioms—they boil something complicated down into something simple.

The following sentences are all taken from *Pirates: The Complete History from 1300 BC to the Present Day*, by Angus Konstam. Circle each idiom. Then, try to rephrase the sentence out loud, replacing the idiom with the literal meaning. After each rephrasing, we'll discuss which sentence works the best—the original, or your paraphrase!

> **Note to Instructor:** Suggested rephrasings and explanations are found in italics below, but accept any reasonable (and grammatical!) literal interpretation. Which sentence works best is a judgment call—there are no right or wrong answers, but the student should be able to articulate her reasoning to you!

By 1585, the rivalry between England and Spain was heating up.

had grown stronger
was becoming worse

The idiom "was heating up" isn't shorter or more concise, but it is more colorful and active.

Carleille's troops were sent ashore under cover of darkness.

once it was too dark for the enemy to see them
after dark so that they could not be seen

The idiom "under cover of darkness" is briefer and more elegant.

The die was now cast.

The situation could not now be changed.
The conflict was inevitable and could not be avoided.

The idiom "The die was now cast" is briefer and more energetic.

They waged a low-key war that lasted well into the fourteenth century.

not very energetic
slow and not very intense

The idiom "low-key" is both concise and clear.

The Barbary beys had to make sure that reports of such attacks did not reach the ears of the sultan in Constantinople.

needed to be certain
needed to guarantee
had to be certain

The idiom "had to make sure" isn't noticeably better, but it is more colloquial and conversational.

were kept away from

The idiom "did not reach the ears of" isn't noticeably better, but it is more colloquial and conversational. Another option would be to rephrase the whole second part of the sentence as "that the sultan in Constantinople did not find out about the reports..."

When the governor came aboard to pay his respects, he was kidnapped.

to show proper respect to the pirates
to demonstrate that he respected the pirates

The idiom "to pay his respects" is more concise.

He was not pleased by the compliment, though he put up with it for the present.

tolerated it
endured it

The idiom "put up with it" is more colloquial and a little more vivid

As he stood beside the executioner's block he reputedly struck a deal—pardons would be granted to all of the crewmen whom he could walk past after his head was cut off.

made an agreement
negotiated a compromise

The idiom "struck a deal" is more active and vivid.

Instructor: Complete your exercises now.

Exercise 119A: Explaining Idioms

The following direct quotes are all by James Cameron, the film director of *Terminator*, *Titanic*, *Avatar*, and many other movies.

Mr. Cameron likes idioms! Circle each complete idiom. Write its meaning above it in your own words. (You can use more than one word—in fact, you may need several sentences!)

These are taken from the biography *The Futurist: The Life and Films of James Cameron*, by Rebecca Keegan.

Note to Instructor: The explanations below are suggestions. Accept any reasonable explanations that the student offers.

pay the price for what we took
"We have taken from nature without giving back, and the time to pay the piper is coming."

resolving all the problems for the audience
"I began to think that the message of the film might be better served by not letting the audience off the hook so easily."

answer all the questions
"We decided not to tie it all up with a bow but to suggest that the struggle was ongoing, and in fact
adjust to, understand
might even be an unending one for us flawed creatures trying to come to terms with technology and our own violent demons."

resolve to do the job
"You roll up your sleeves and you get to work."

to go away alone
"I still need to bunker completely to get anything good written."

carefully plan out your story
"It forces you to really have your narrative ducks in a row."

the final end
"It wasn't full stop, just leave Hollywood like J. D. Salinger or something."

liked each other
"Stan and I clicked early on because we both respect the artist."

good/intelligent workers
"There were a few bright lights amongst the younger art-department people, but for the most part, we despised them and they despised us."

Exercise 119B: Diagramming

On your own paper, diagram every word of the following sentences, taken from Charles Dickens's classic novel *The Old Curiosity Shop.*

When you are finished, tell your instructor what each idiom means! Several sentences have more than one idiom—and almost all of them can be diagrammed in more than one way. Do your best, and ask for help when you need it.

Note to Instructor: These are difficult—give the student all necessary help.

The old man and I will remain at daggers drawn to the end of our lives.

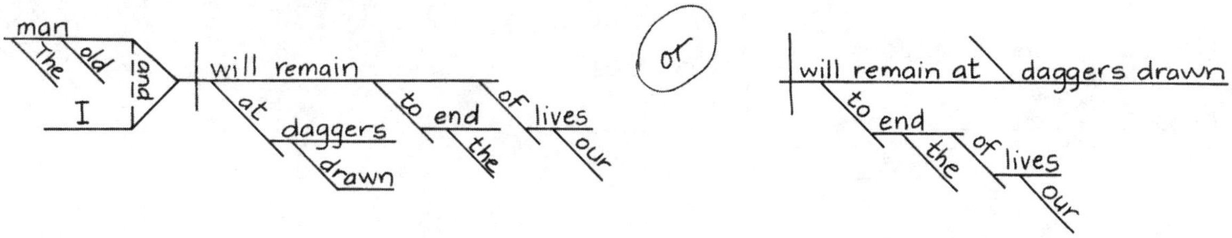

Note to Instructor: The complete predicate can be diagrammed in two different ways—both are correct. In the first, *at daggers drawn* is an adverb phrase modifying the verb and answering the question *how.* In the second, *will remain at* functions as a linking verb and the phrase *daggers drawn* is a predicate adjective modifying the compound subject. The phrase *daggers drawn* can be diagrammed either as a compound noun or as a noun modified by a past participle, in either diagram.

The idiom "will remain at daggers drawn" means "will remain enemies."

You mark me, sir?

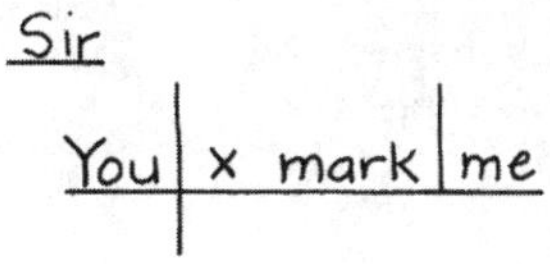

Note to Instructor: Since this is a question, the helping verb *do* is understood ("Do you mark me, sir?"). If the student does not insert it, do not mark the diagram as incorrect, but show her the answer above.

The idiom "mark me" means "understand me."

Beyond that, I don't know him from Adam.

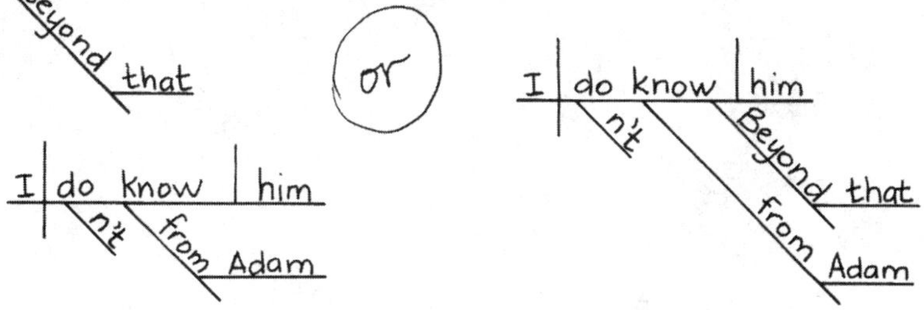

Note to Instructor: The phrase *Beyond that* can be diagrammed either as an absolute construction, or as a prepositional phrase modifying the verb.

This sentence contains two idioms. "Beyond that" means "In addition to everything I've just said," and "I don't know him from Adam" means "I don't know him at all."

You shall not be permitted to fly in the face of your superiors in this exceedingly gross manner.

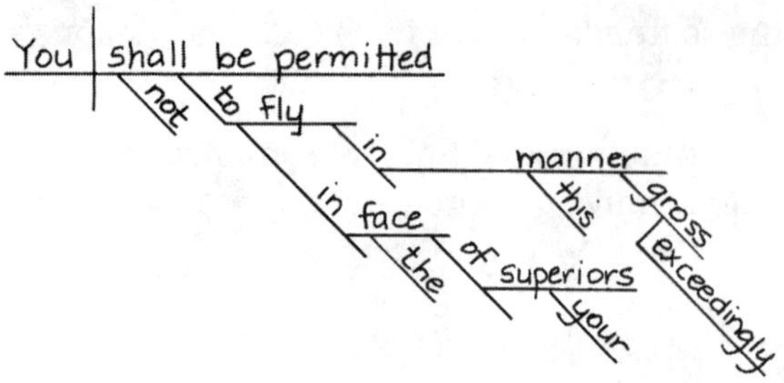

Note to Instructor: The idiom "to fly in the face of" means "to defy."

Nell felt as if her heart would break when she saw them meet.

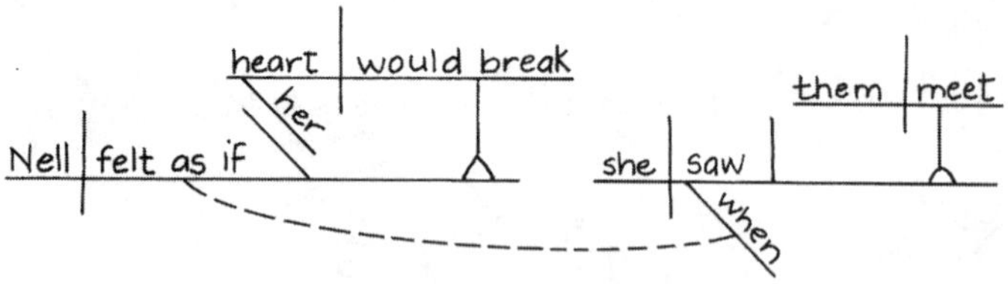

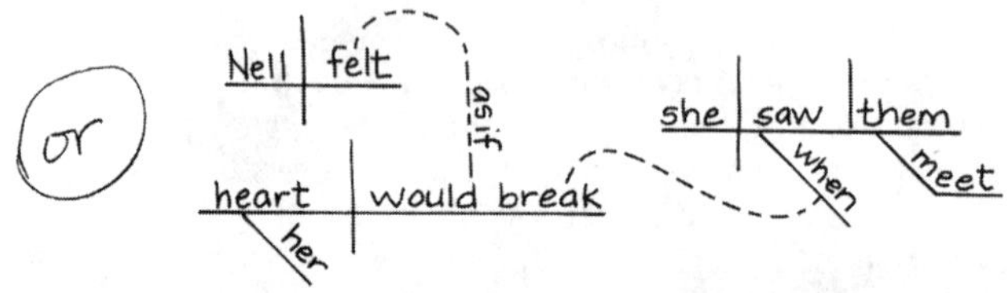

Note to Instructor: The idiom *felt as if her heart would break* can be diagrammed as a linking verb followed by a clause acting as a predicate adjective (as in the first diagram), or as a verb with a clause introduced by a compound subordinating conjunction, acting as an adverb describing the verb (the second diagram). In addition, you can make an argument for the adverbial clause *when she saw them meet* modifying either predicate (*felt* or *would break*).

The phrase *them meet* is also difficult. It acts as the direct object of the verb *saw*, but since *them* is an object rather than subject pronoun, it can be diagrammed either as an unusual subject/verb noun clause (the first diagram), or else *meet* can be diagrammed as an unusual form of the past participle acting as an adjective (the second diagram).

The idiom itself means "felt unutterably sad."

Take my word for it, the feller that came back to work out that shilling will show himself one of these days in his true colours.

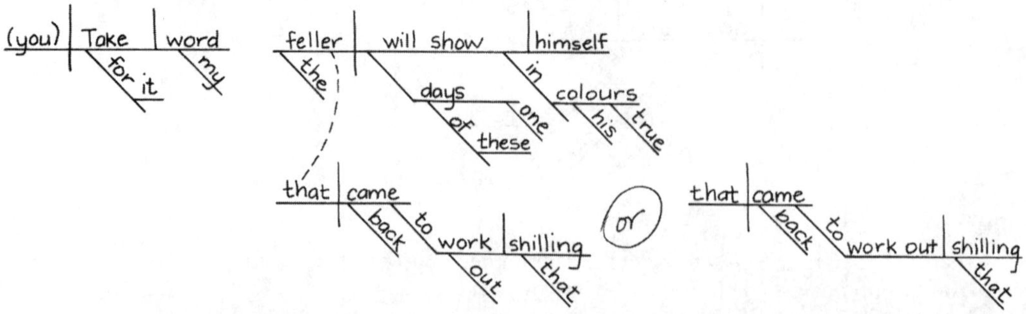

Note to Instructor: *To work out* can be diagrammed as a single infinitive, or as an infinitive modified by an adverb.

The idiom "Take my word for it" is diagrammed as an absolute and means "Believe me."

The idiom "show his true colours" means "his true character will become obvious."

The idiom "to work out that shilling" means "to do the work that is worth a shilling's pay."

Exercise 119C: Finding Idioms

On your own paper, rewrite the following four sentences, replacing the bolded words in each with an idiom that means the same thing.

If you need help, ask your instructor.

Note to Instructor: Accept any reasonable idiom. If the student cannot think of an idiom, give him the first and last word of the bolded italicized answer.

I was just tired of being **the one who was unlike everyone else.**

I was just tired of being ***the odd man out****.*

You've worked very hard this year, but don't **stop trying because you've already worked hard**!

You've worked very hard this year, but don't ***rest on your laurels****!*

The hiker escaped from the mountain lion **but only just barely**.

The hiker escaped from the mountain lion ***by the skin of his teeth****.*

When the fraud was discovered, the embezzler **confessed** his wrongdoings.

When the fraud was discovered, the embezzler ***made a clean breast of*** *his wrongdoings.*

— LESSON 120 —

Troublesome Sentences

Exercise 120A: A Selection of Oddly Constructed Sentences

After your instructor discusses each sentence with you, diagram it on your own paper.

These sentences are taken from the novel *Passing*, by Nella Larsen. Larsen, who was born in Chicago in 1891, was the child of an Afro-Caribbean father and a Danish mother. Because of her African blood, she was considered to be black by early twentieth-century American culture, and so was unable to enter white-only areas or take part in white-only privileges as she was growing up. *Passing* is the story of an early twentieth-century woman who has African blood but, because of her light skin, has concealed the fact—and knows that if her husband and social circles find out that she is "black," she will lose everything.

Note to Instructor: For each sentence, go through the dialogue provided and then ask the student to diagram the sentence before moving on to the next. Prompt the student for answers as necessary.

Instructor: Each one of these sentences has a slightly odd element—and we'll have to figure out how to diagram each one! Read me the first sentence now.

Student: She got out, and thanking him smilingly as well as in a more substantial manner for his kind helpfulness and understanding, went in through the Drayton's wide doors.

Instructor: What is the subject?

Student: She.

Instructor: The subject has a compound predicate. The first is *got*. The second may be harder to find. What is it?

Student: Went.

Instructor: She got out and went in. That is the skeleton of the sentence. *Went* is modified by the adverb *in*, but also by a prepositional phrase acting as an adverb. What is the phrase telling you where she went in?

Student: Through the Drayton's wide doors.

Instructor: Now let's look at that phrase in the middle: *thanking him smilingly as well as in a more substantial manner for his kind helpfulness and understanding.* "He" is the doorman. Do you know what "in a more substantial manner" means?

Student: She gave him a tip.

Instructor: So there are two ways she thanked the doorman. First, "smilingly." What part of speech is that?

Student: An adverb.

Instructor: It modifies the present participle *thanking*. She thanked him smilingly, and she thanked him *in a more substantial manner*. That prepositional phrase also modifies *thanking*. The words *as well as* connect the adverb to the adverbial prepositional phrase, so here, *as well as* acts as a coordinating conjunction, like and.

Try diagramming the sentence now.

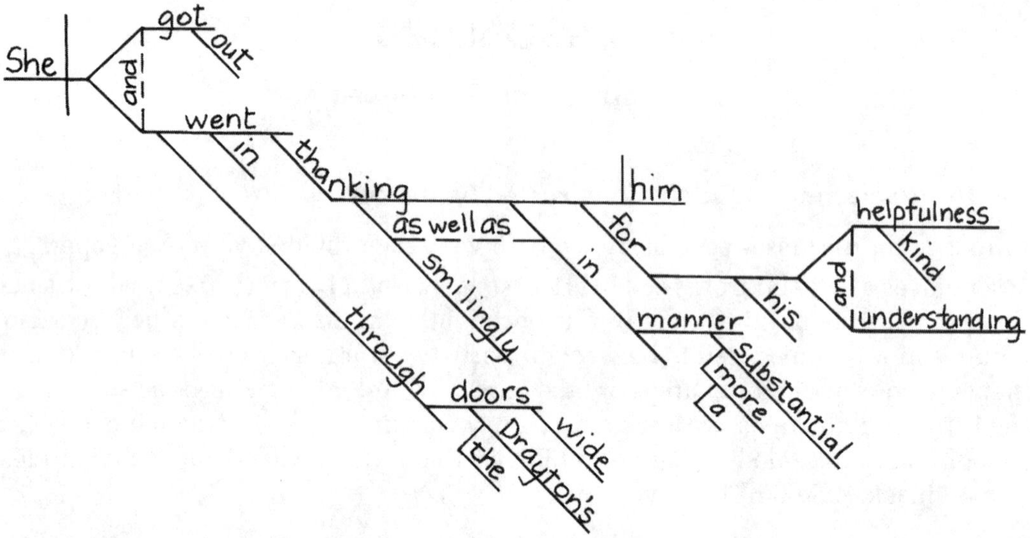

Note to Instructor: The article *a* here modifies the adverb *more*, but the student could also choose to place it beneath *manner* (its placement is ambiguous). *His* is diagrammed before the split of the compound object of the preposition *for*, since both the understanding and the helpfulness are modified by *his*. The student could also choose to put *kind* before the split, since it could be interpreted as modifying *understanding* as well as *helpfulness*.

Instructor: Read me the second sentence.

Student: Did that woman, could that woman, somehow know that here before her very eyes on the roof of the Drayton sat a Negro?

Instructor: Even though there's only one actual woman who's the subject of this sentence, grammatically speaking there is a compound subject! What is the compound subject?

Student: That woman, that woman.

Instructor: The compound subject has a single predicate. What is the single action verb that acts as the predicate?

Student: Know.

Instructor: That one action verb has two different helping verbs! What are they?

Student: Did, could.

Instructor: When you diagram this sentence, you'll need to try to figure out how to give the single action verb two different helping verbs. Do your best, and then I'll show you the answer.

The object of the action verb *know* is the noun clause beginning with *that here* and ending with *sat a Negro.* One adverb and two adverb phrases modify the verb *sat.* Diagram the sentence now.

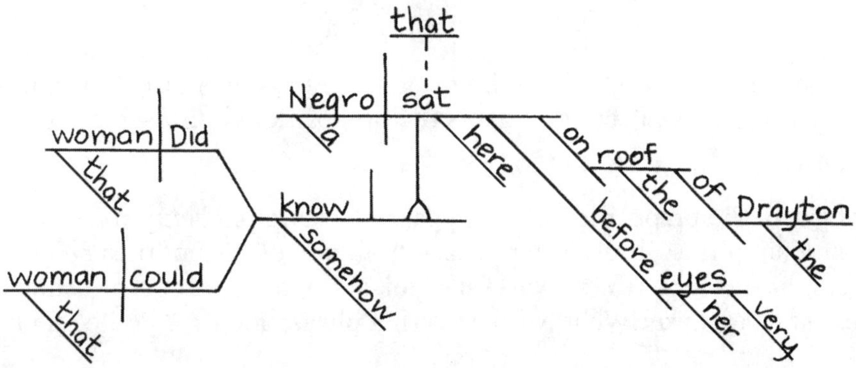

Instructor: Read me the third sentence.

Student: Suppose the woman did know or suspect her race.

Instructor: What part of speech is *suppose*?

Student: A verb.

Instructor: Do you see a subject that goes with *suppose*?

Student: No.

Instructor: Usually, when you have a verb without a subject, you have a command—a sentence with the understood subject *you*. But this sentence isn't exactly a command. It's more of a reflection! So rather than diagramming this as a command, with the understood subject "you" in parentheses, it makes more sense to simply represent the understood subject with an X—since we don't know who the subject is!

What's the direct object? What is the subject supposing?

Student: That the woman did know or suspect her race.

Instructor: This is a noun clause with an understood subordinating *that*, acting as the direct object of the verb *suppose.* When you diagram it, note that there's a compound predicate—*know* or *suspect*—but only one object. Diagram that sentence now.

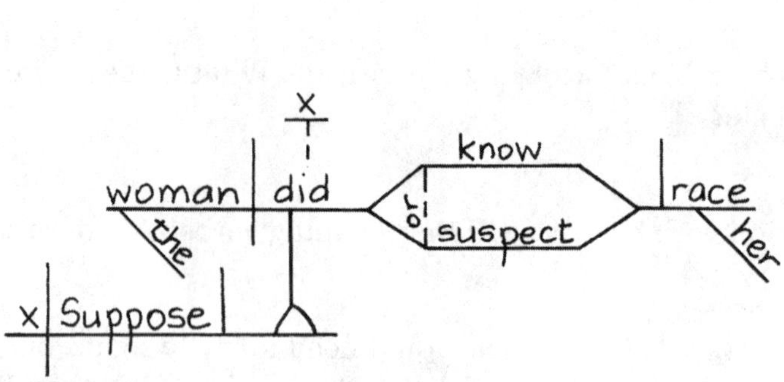

Instructor: Read your next sentence out loud.

Student: *It was the idea of being ejected from any place, even in the polite and tactful way in which the Drayton would probably do it, that disturbed her.*

Instructor: What is the main independent clause?

Student: *It was the idea of behind ejected from any place.*

Instructor: The subject *it* is followed by a linking verb, a predicate nominative, and a prepositional phrase acting as an adjective. What is the prepositional phrase? It describes *idea.*

Student: *Of being ejected from any place.*

Instructor: The object of the preposition *of* is the passive participle *being objected*, and within that prepositional phrase, the shorter phrase *from any place* modifies *being ejected* and answers the question *where.* Now let's look at the next part of the sentence, *even in the polite and tactful way.* What word does that phrase modify? Polite and tactful way to do what?

Student: *Being ejected* OR *Ejecting her.*

Instructor: The prepositional phrase *in the polite and tactful way* is another adverb phrase modifying *being ejected.* Now—where would you put *even*?

Note to Instructor: Let the student come up with an answer. If he student suggests that *even* modifies *in*, point out prepositions generally do not take modifiers.

Even has two possible placements. It can modify *way*—"*in even the way.*" Or, it can be considered part of a compound preposition: "*even in.*" The diagram below shows *even* as modifying *way*, but the student could also place it on the same preposition line as *in.*

Instructor: Finally, the clause in *which the Drayton would probably do it* modifies what word?

Student: *Way.*

Instructor: *Way* is a noun, so this must be an adjective clause. Diagram it by connecting the relative adverb *which* to the noun *way,* and then compare your diagram to the answer.

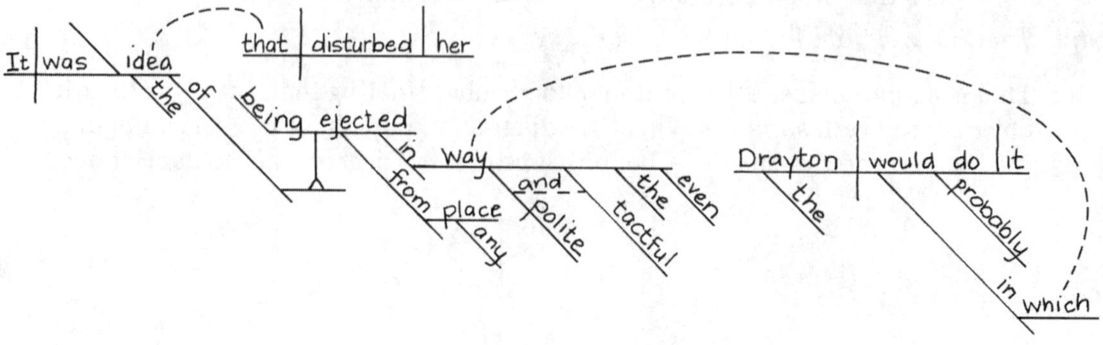

Instructor: Read me the next sentence out loud.

Student: *It was as if, in a house long dim, a match had been struck, showing ghastly shapes where had been only blurred shadows.*

Instructor: The subject and predicate are very simple. What are they?

Student: *It was.*

Instructor: Everything else in the sentence describes *it*. All of the words from *as if, in a house,* all the way through *only blurred shadows*, are a single predicate nominative! That predicate nominative has a noun clause at its center. What are the subject and verb of that noun clause?

Student: *Match had been struck.*

Instructor: The first words of the predicate nominative are a subordinating conjunction with two words in it. What are they?

Student: *As if.*

Instructor: Because this is a noun clause, you'll diagram it up on a tree in the predicate nominative space, and *as if* will go in the same place as *that*, if *that* were introducing the noun clause.

Try to diagram the rest of the sentence now, and then compare it with the answer.

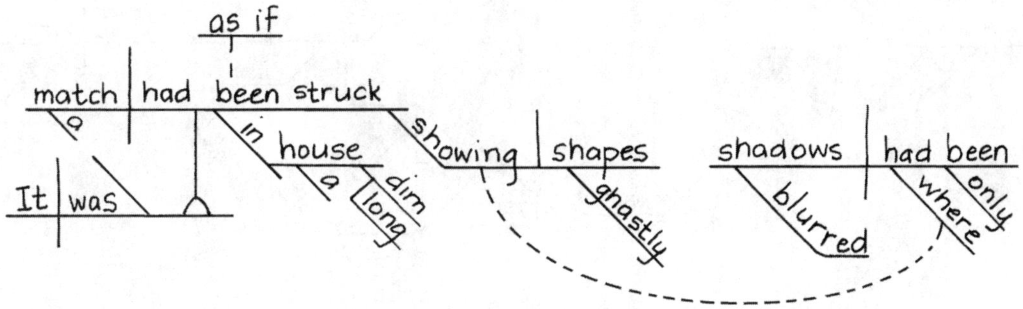

Instructor: Let's do one last sentence. Read it out loud for me now.

Student: *It was that very thing which, in a way, finally decided me not to go out and see you one last time before I went away to stay.*

Instructor: The first part of this sentence is simple: a subject, linking verb, and predicate nominative. What are those three words?

Student: *It was thing.*

Instructor: The adjectives *that* and *very* modify *thing*. The relative clause beginning *which, in a way, finally decided me* also modifies *thing*. What are the subject and predicate of the relative clause?

Student: *Which decided.*

Instructor: The verb *decided* is usually intransitive—but not always! Here, it has a direct object. What is the direct object?

Student: *Me.*

Instructor: And that's not all! The object pronoun *me* also has an object complement—a compound infinitive that describes *me*. What are those two infinitives?

Student: To go and to see.

Instructor: You'll need to diagram "to go" and "to see" together on top of a tree in the object complement space on the diagram. Here's one more complicating factor: they have the same object! What is it?

Student: You.

Instructor: The adverb *not* and the adverbial noun phrase *one last time* modify both infinitives, so you'll need to diagram them *before* the vertical object line that comes before *you*. And there's one more complicated part of this sentence—the adverb clause *before I went away to stay*! The line connecting that clause with the infinitives *to see* and *to go* will also need to come before the vertical object line.

Try to diagram the sentence now.

Note to Instructor: If the student is confused, show him the diagram below, allow him to study it, and then remove it and ask him to diagram the sentence himself. Remember: diagramming is an exercise in thinking through the logic of sentences, not a test!

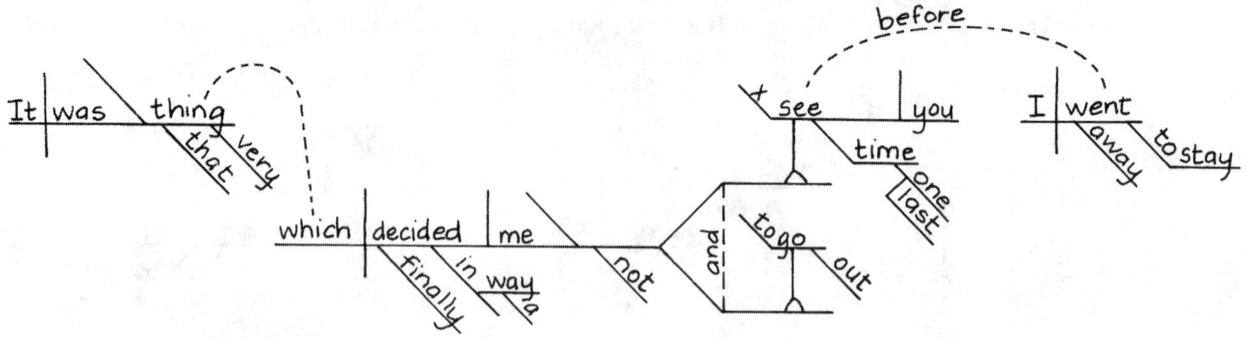

WEEK 32

—REVIEW 10—

Weeks 29-31

Topics
Hortative Verbs
Ambitransitive Verbs
Infinitive Phrases as Objects
Infinitive Phrases With Understood "To"
Principal Parts of Irregular Verbs
Noun Clauses as Appositives
Which/That in Restrictive and Non-Restrictive Clauses
Formal Conditionals
Words Acting as Multiple Parts of Speech
Affirmations and Negations
Idioms

Review 10A: The Missing Words Game

Fill in each blank below with the exact form described—but choose your own words!

Show your answers to your instructor, who will insert them into the matching blanks in the short essay in the Answer Key.

Your instructor will then show you the original essay—and your version.

Here's the only information I'm going to give you before you fill in your forms—everything in this review has to do with *food* and *farming*.

Note to Instructor: Write the student's answers into the blanks below. The fill-in-the-blank version of the text is followed by the original. You may decide which version to show the student first.

The following excerpt is from a 1915 book that combined memoir, fiction, and recipes. It was called *Mary at the Farm: And the Book of Recipes Compiled During Her Visit among the Pennsylvania Germans*. The author, Edith M. Thomas, took actual details about a young Philadelphia woman's visit to see her relatives in Amish country, combined it with storytelling, and added traditional Amish recipes.

Almost before Mary realized it, the farm house ________________ (modal active simple passive verb (third-person singular)) in the distance, and her uncle called her attention to his ________________ (adjective), red barn, which ________________ (indicative past perfect passive verb (third-person singular)) since her last visit ______________ (three-word prepositional phrase), and which, in her Uncle's estimation, was of much ______________ (comparative form of an adjective) importance than the house.

Mary ____________ with pleasure the old landmarks ________ familiar to her on former
indicative active simple past verb (third-person singular) adverb

visits. They passed the small, ____________ school house at the ____________ , and in a
adjective compound concrete noun

short time the horses turned ______________ into the lane ______________ to the barn,
adverb present active participle

a country lane in __________ truth, a ______________ of ______________ vines, wild
adjective that can also be an adverb concrete noun adjective that can also be a noun

rose bushes, by farmers called "Pasture Roses," ______________ with bushes of sumach, ____
past active participle adjective

carrots and golden rod.

Mary insisted ______________ her uncle drive ______________ to the barn, as was his
subordinating conjunction adverb

______________ custom, __________ she ____________________ at the farm house gate by
adjective subordinating adverb indicative simple past passive verb plus adverb (third-person singular)

her Aunt. As her Uncle led away the horses, he said, "I will ______________ join you, Mary,
adverb of time

'______________ of our bread and eat of our ____________,' as they say in the 'Shrine.'"
active infinitive verb concrete noun

On their way to the house, Mary remarked: "I am so glad we reached __________ before
adverb of place

dusk. The country is simply beautiful! Have you ever noticed, Aunt Sarah, __________ a
demonstrative adjective

symphony in green is the yard? ____________ at the buds on the maples and lilacs—a
active present imperative verb

faint yellow green—and the ______________ pine tree near by; the ____________ of
compound adjective plural concrete noun

the ______________ iris are another shade; the grass, dotted with yellow dandelions, and
proper adjective

blue violets; the straight, __________, reddish-brown stalks of the peonies before the leaves
adjective

____________ , all roofed over with the ________________ branches of pear, apple and
indicative present perfect active verb (third-person plural) compound adjective that includes a past participle

'German Prune' trees. Truly, this ______________ Paradise!"
modal simple present active verb (third-person singular)

"Yes," assented her Aunt, "I ____________ knew blossoms to remain on the pear trees ____
adverb of negation adverb

long a ______________. We ______________ no 'blossom shower' as yet to scatter them,
adverbial noun indicative perfect present active verb (first-person plural)

but there ____________ (indicative simple future state-of-being verb) ____________ (concrete plural noun) tonight, I think, ________ (conjunction) I am ________ (adjective of negation) prophet. I feel rain in the atmosphere, and Sibylla said a few moments ago she heard a 'rain bird' in the mulberry tree."

"Aunt Sarah," ____________ (indicative simple past active verb (third-person singular)) Mary, "is the rhubarb ____________ (predicate adjective) enough to use?"

"________ (adverb of affirmation), ____________ (adverb of affirmation), we ____________ (indicative perfect present active verb (first-person plural)) rhubarb pies and have had a ____________ (abstract singular noun) of dandelion salad or 'Salat,' ________ (subordinating conjunction) our neighbors designate it. ________ (possessive pronoun) uncle calls 'dandelion greens' the ____________ (possessive plural noun acting as an adjective) spring tonic; that and 'celadine,' ________ (demonstrative adjective) plant you see growing by the side of the house. ____________ (adverb of time) in the season it bears small, yellow flowers ____________ (adverb of negation) unlike a very ________ (adjective) buttercup blossom, and it ____________ (indicative simple present passive verb (third-person singular)) to be an ____________ (adjective) remedy for chills and fevers, and it tastes almost ____________________ (comparison using as...as...). There are bushels of dandelion blossoms, some of ____________ (demonstrative pronoun) we shall pick tomorrow, and from them make dandelion ________ (concrete singular noun)."

"And what use will my ____________ (adjective) Aunt make of the blue violets?" ____________ (adverb) inquired Mary.

"The violets," replied her Aunt, "I ____________ (indicative simple future active verb (first-person singular)) up ____________ (adverb) with some earth ____________ (present active participle) to their roots and place them in a ________ (adjective that can also be a noun) bowl for a centrepiece on the table for my artistic and ____________ (hyphenated compound adjective) niece; and if ____________ (past active participle) moist, you ____________ (indicative simple future passive verb (second-person singular)) at the length of time they will remain 'a thing of beauty' if not a '____________ (singular abstract noun) forever.' And later, Mary, from them I'll teach you ____________ (active infinitive) ____________ (color adjective) ____________ (concrete plural noun)."

Almost before Mary realized it, the farm house could be seen in the distance, and her uncle called her attention to his new, red barn, which had been built since her last visit to the farm, and which, in her Uncle's estimation, was of much greater importance than the house.

Mary greeted with pleasure the old landmarks so familiar to her on former visits. They passed the small, stone school house at the crossroads, and in a short time the horses turned obediently into the lane leading to the barn, a country lane in very truth, a tangle of blackberry vines, wild rose bushes, by farmers called "Pasture Roses," interwoven with bushes of sumach, wild carrots and golden rod.

Mary insisted that her uncle drive directly to the barn, as was his usual custom, while she was warmly welcomed at the farm house gate by her Aunt. As her Uncle led away the horses, he said, "I will soon join you, Mary, 'to break of our bread and eat of our salt,' as they say in the 'Shrine.'"

On their way to the house, Mary remarked: "I am so glad we reached here before dusk. The country is simply beautiful! Have you ever noticed, Aunt Sarah, what a symphony in green is the yard? Look at the buds on the maples and lilacs—a faint yellow green—and the blue-green pine tree near by; the leaves of the German iris are another shade; the grass, dotted with yellow dandelions, and blue violets; the straight, grim, reddish-brown stalks of the peonies before the leaves have unfolded, all roofed over with the blossom-covered branches of pear, apple and 'German Prune' trees. Truly, this must resemble Paradise!"

"Yes," assented her Aunt, "I never knew blossoms to remain on the pear trees so long a time. We have had no 'blossom shower' as yet to scatter them, but there will be showers tonight, I think, or I am no prophet. I feel rain in the atmosphere, and Sibylla said a few moments ago she heard a 'rain bird' in the mulberry tree."

"Aunt Sarah," inquired Mary, "is the rhubarb large enough to use?"

"Yes, indeed, we have baked rhubarb pies and have had a surfeit of dandelion salad or 'Salat,' as our neighbors designate it. Your uncle calls 'dandelion greens' the farmers' spring tonic; that and 'celadine,' that plant you see growing by the side of the house. Later in the season it bears small, yellow flowers not unlike a very small buttercup blossom, and it is said to be an excellent remedy for chills and fevers, and it tastes almost as bitter as quinine. There are bushels of dandelion blossoms, some of which we shall pick tomorrow, and from them make dandelion wine."

"And what use will my thrifty Aunt make of the blue violets?" mischievously inquired Mary.

"The violets," replied her Aunt, "I shall dig up carefully with some earth adhering to their roots and place them in a glass bowl for a centrepiece on the table for my artistic and beauty-loving niece; and if kept moist, you will be surprised at the length of time they will remain 'a thing of beauty' if not a 'joy forever.' And later, Mary, from them I'll teach you to make violet beads."

Review 10B: Identifying Infinitive Phrases, Noun Clauses, and Modifying Clauses

In the following sets of sentences, follow these four steps:

a) Identify every set of underlined words as *INF* for infinitive phrase, *PREP* for prepositional phrase, or *CL* for clause.

b) Label each phrase or clause as *ADV* for adverb, *ADJ* for adjective, or *N* for noun.

c) For adjective and adverb phrases and clauses, draw an arrow from the label to the word modified.

d) For noun phrases and clauses, add the appropriate part of the sentence label: *S* for subject, *DO* for direct object, *IO* for indirect object, *OP* for object of a preposition, *PN* for predicate nominative, *APP* for appositive.

Notice: Some sets of words are within other sets of words, so you'll see some double underlining! If you see double underlining, be sure to follow the instructions for both sets of underlined words.

The first sentence is done for you.

Another sentence has an unexpected twist—look out for it!

INF N S CL N DO
To say Hamilton Brothers is old school would be a serious understatement.

Note: The entire infinitive phrase is the subject. Within that phrase, the clause (introduced by an understood "that") is the direct object of the infinitive verb *To say*.

CL ADJ
Our farm is proof that small-scale, sustainable farming is a viable alternative.

INF N DO INF N DO
We wanted to raise our own food, to have animals and a big garden, but we didn't really know
CL N DO
what we were doing.

CL ADV CL N PN
The salient point when it comes to coop construction is that varmints will find and exploit any weakness, no matter how small.

The New Farm: Our Ten Years on the Front Lines of the Good Food Revolution, by Brent Preston

INF N S PREP ADJ
To have the two of them there, at opposite corners of the table, with their long endurance in their faces, and their present affection and pleasure, was a blessing of another kind.

CL ADJ
INF N DO INF N DO
Perhaps the most urgent task for all of us who want to eat well and to keep eating is to
INF N PN INF ADV
encourage farm-raised children to take up farming.

Note to Instructor: The adjective clause *who want...eating* can also be marked as modifying *us*. The two infinitive phrases in this clause are the compound direct object of *want*. The student may wonder why the infinitive phrase *to take up farming* isn't an adjective modifying *children*; point out that it answers the adverb question *how* (how do we encourage them? we encourage them to take up farming) and not any of the adjective questions (which one? what kind? how many? whose?).

CL ADJ INF N PN
The goal of intelligent farmers, who desire the long-term success of farming, is to adapt their work
PREP ADV
to their places.

Bringing It to the Table: On Farming and Food, by Wendell Berry

PREP ADJ CL ADJ
We have the right to convenient food that is healthy. We want healthy options in corner
CL ADV INF ADV
stores while empowering the community to make better food choices.

INF N S CL N DO INF N S
To acknowledge that we as humans are not the most powerful force in nature and to act accordingly is not always roses and sunshine.

> **Note to Instructor:** The two infinitive phrases are the compound subjects of the verb *is*. The first infinitive phrase contains within it a clause acting as the direct object of *acknowledge*.

CL ADJ CL N DO
In Haiti the farmers say, "*Sonje lapli ki level mayi ou,*" which means, "Remember the rain
CL ADJ
that made your corn grow."

> **Note to Instructor:** This is the "twist" sentence mentioned in the instructions—there are three clauses all in one! The adjective clause *which...corn grow* modifies the italicized quote. Within that clause, *Remember the rain that made your corn grow* follows the action verb *means* and serves as its direct object. The last clause within the second clause, *that...grow*, modifies *rain*.

Farming While Black: Soul Fire Farm's Practical Guide to Liberation on the Land, by Leah Penniman

CL N DO
Until a few years ago I wouldn't say I was a particularly enlightened consumer.

CL N DO
I knew potato chips contained an artery-clogging dose of partially hydrogenated oil and
CL N DO
that eating steak every day would give me a heart attack.

> **Note to Instructor:** The first noun clause is introduced by an understood subordinating *that*, while in the second clause, *that* is written out. Point this interesting style choice out to the student. Ask her to read the sentence out loud, listening to the rhythm. Then have her read it eliminating the *that*. How does the added *that* change the sentence?
>
> The author includes it because the first clause has a noun, *potato chips*, for its subject, and the second has the gerund *eating*. Putting *that* before the second clause prepares the student's ear to hear a different kind of subject.

PREP ADV
CL N OP CL N OP
I was utterly disconnected from who made my food and how it ended up in my grocery store.

Local: The New Face of Food and Farming in America, by Douglas Gayeton

Review 10C: Parsing

Parse every bolded verb in the following sentences.

Provide the following information:

Person: First, second, or third
Number: Sing. or pl.
Tense: Simple past, present, or future; perfect past, present, or future; progressive past, present, or future; or progressive perfect present
Voice: Active, passive, or state-of-being
Mood: Indicative, subjunctive, imperative, hortatory, or modal
If the verb is also emphatic, add this label to the mood.

The first is done for you.

3rd sing., simple past, active, indicative
Gillian **planted** another tray of broccoli that afternoon to replace the plants that
3rd pl., perfect passive, active, indicative
had been lost.

3rd pl., simple present, active, modal — 3rd pl., progressive present, active, modal
Consumers **would feel** good about themselves because they **would be helping** increase access to organic food, as well as supporting local farmers.

1st sing., simple present, active, indicative emphatic — 1st sing., perfect present, active, subjunctive
I **don't know** if I **have** ever **seen** an animal run so fast.

3rd pl., simple present, active, modal — 1st pl., perfect past, active, indicative
They **would delight** in running back to the house to tell us what kind of animals we **had caught** that day.

The New Farm: Our Ten Years on the Front Lines of the Good Food Revolution, by Brent Preston

3rd sing., simple future, passive, indicative — 3rd sing., simple present, active, modal
Even the levee, only a man-made mound, **will be breached** one day so the river **can reclaim**
3rd sing., simple past, state-of-being, indicative
what **was** once naturally hers.

3rd pl., simple past, passive, indicative
The inside walls **were planked** with pine 1x8s.

3rd sing., simple past, active, indicative
A life-long bachelor, Howard the Dairyman, as I called him, **worked** December 25 as
3rd sing., simple past, state-of-being, subjunctive
if it **were** June 25.

3rd sing., perfect present, active, modal
Uncle Honey **must have had** a hand in that, too.

The Land of Milk and Uncle Honey: Memories from the Farm of My Youth, by Alan Guebert with Mary Grace Foxwell

3rd sing., perfect present, passive, indicative

It is fork-tender and **has been transformed** from the tough cut that it was this morning to an easily enjoyed piece of beef later this afternoon.

3rd pl., progressive present, active, indicative

Each week the cucumber plants are a bit larger, the winter squash vines **are beginning** to hit the edges of the raised beds, but everything is far from robust.

1st pl., simple past, state-of-being, subjunctive — 3rd sing., simple present, state-of-being, modal

If we **were** to serve a squash soup, then the squash **should be** visible as a piece of squash.

On this winter day it is hard to believe that the eventual milk of this young calf Alice

3rd sing., simple future, passive, indicative

will be used in the dinner.

3rd sing., perfect present progressive, active, indicative

The yeast **has** slowly **been expanding** and growing, puffing out the rolls.

3rd sing., perfect past, active, subjunctive — 3rd sing., perfect present, passive, modal

If they **had dried** too much on the surface and crusted over, the rising **would have been hindered.**

Growing a Feast: The Chronicle of a Farm-to-Table Meal, by Kurt Timmermeister

3rd pl., perfect present, passive, indicative

Those carefully stacked pyramids of fruit in the produce aisle **have been placed** there

3rd sing., simple present, state-of-being, subjunctive — 3rd pl., simple present, active, subjunctive

just for you. If your allegiance **is** elsewhere, if the miles your food travels **matter** and

2nd sing., simple present, active, subjunctive modal

you'**d prefer** instead to buy your food from a local farmer, the entire distribution apparatus

3rd sing., simple future, active, indicative

will change.

Local: The New Face of Food and Farming in America, by Douglas Gayeton

3rd sing., simple present, active, subjunctive modal

He's certainly well on his way, **should** he **choose** to put down the whisk and pick up a pen.

3rd pl., perfect present progressive, active, indicative

Most of our waiters **have been working** with us for at least five years, many of them for ten, and some for fifteen.

Away from the Kitchen: Untold Stories, Private Menus, Guarded Recipes, and Insider Tips, by Dawn Blume Hawkes

Review 10D: *Which* and *That* Clauses

In the following sentences, underline each clause introduced by *which* or *that*. If *that* is understood, use a caret to insert it. If a *which* or *that* clause falls within another clause, underline the entire larger clause once, and the clause-within-a-clause a second time.

- Label each clause as *ADJ* for adjective, *ADV* for adverb, or *N* for noun.
- For adjective and adverb clauses, draw an arrow back to the word modified.
- For noun clauses, label the part of the sentence that the clause fulfills (*S*, *PN*, *DO*, *IO*, *APP*).
- Finally, label each adjective clause as *R* for restrictive or *NON-R* for nonrestrictive.

The first sentence is done for you.

ADJ NON-R

The sheep is one of the most efficient machines for converting sun and water and nutrients into protein and energy, which we use in the form of meat, milk, leather, and wool.

N S

That four ewes all decide to give birth at the same time seems like a really bad idea.

ADJ R

Sometimes it's a lamb that has been born overnight and is too weak or cold to stand up and nurse.

N DO

She knows which lambs are hers and she takes good care of them.

Sheepish: Two Women, Fifty Sheep, and Enough Wool to Save the Planet, by Catherine Friend

ADJ R

This struggle of animal against nature was a yearly childhood event, one that connected me, even as a young boy, to the mysterious natural world around me.

Local: The New Face of Food and Farming in America, by Douglas Gayeton

ADJ NON-R

Urban farming is a new term for growing a kitchen garden (or, to use the French term, *potager*), which has been practiced since the advent of cities.

Your Farm in the City: An Urban Dweller's Guide to Growing Food and Raising Animals, by Lisa Taylor and the Gardeners of Seattle Tilth

N APP

I had that feeling I sometimes get when I'm up by myself in the early morning, that I'm lucky to be in this place, at this moment.

Note to Instructor: The appositive renames *feeling* and is in an unusual position (at the end of the sentence).

ADJ NON-R

We even tried something called forage radishes, which grew enormous tubers that burrowed six feet down into the subsoil, bringing copious nutrients up to the surface.

ADV

Rather than being grumpy, they were grateful that we had come out in such terrible weather.

ADJ NON-R

I had built a sturdy door that locked with heavy slide bolts, leaving a gap at the bottom of less than a quarter of an inch. Nothing could get in there that didn't have opposable thumbs.

ADJ R

The New Farm: Our Ten Years on the Front Lines of the Good Food Revolution, by Brent Preston

ADJ NON-R

I cut a cedar tree that filled a corner of the parlor, reached to the ceiling, and gave its fragrance to the whole room.

Bringing It to the Table: On Farming and Food, by Wendell Berry

that N DO N DO

I thought^this place would be mine for years, that I could live here until I was ready to move on to the next big thing and plan my life around that.

N DO

As I clicked through, I saw that the man had litters available a few times a year.

ADJ NON-R

Inside it was an old dog crate, which I'd lined with fresh straw.

Barnheart: The Incurable Longing for a Farm of One's Own, by Jenna Woginrich

ADJ NON-R

The bulky stockpot straddles two of the burners on the gas range, which I turn up to high, the flames hitting two sides of the heavy-bottomed stainless steel pot.

ADV

By six in the morning I was relieved that I could get out of bed and head over to the kitchen to begin the day's work.

Note to Instructor: You may need to remind the student that the clause cannot be a direct object because *was relieved* is a passive verb, so the subject is already receiving the action.

ADJ R

The goal is a thick, almost sticky paste that, once cooled, will set into a jelly—rigid, and with the ability to be cut.

Growing a Feast: The Chronicle of a Farm-to-Table Meal, by Kurt Timmermeister

Review 10E: Words Acting as Multiple Parts of Speech

In each set of sentences below, underline the repeated word. Label each occurrence as *N* for noun, *V* for verb, *PRO* for pronoun, *ADV* for adverb, *ADJ* for adjective, *PREP* for preposition, *CC* for coordinating conjunction, or *SC* for subordinating conjunction.

Do not mark repeated articles or common pronouns such as *it*—all of the words you're looking for are 4 letters or longer!

Besides, the selling season was pretty nearly over [ADJ].

When the grass had all been once mowed over [ADV], we resorted to the clover.

Long before I had gone over [PREP] it once, the portion first mowed was up high enough to be mowed again.

This is more than one-third of the quantity estimated as above [N].

> **Note to Instructor:** Here, *above* acts as the object of the preposition *as*. The prepositional phrase is adverbial and modifies *estimated*.

I cut off the canes six inches above [PREP] the root.

That moisture exists not only in the skies above [ADJ], but in the earth beneath our plants.

I prefer removing the old wood in the autumn, for the reasons above [ADV] given.

> **Note to Instructor:** Here, *above* modifies the past participle *given*, which itself acts as an adjective modifying *reasons*.

The green and fertile tracts that lay beyond [ADV] were unseen.

Over the run of four years there has been no profit beyond [PREP] the manure.

Ten Acres Enough: How a Very Small Farm May Be Made to Keep a Very Large Family, by Edmund Morris

Still [ADJ] others, such as lettuce and onions, produce seeds after they flower.

If the seedlings are still [ADV] too young to go out into the garden, you will need to throw these in the garbage and start over.

Start [V] with good soil and keep improving on it.

It can be more economical, especially if you have a large garden, and it gives you a head start [N].

The Everything Grow Your Own Vegetables Book: Your Complete Guide to Planting, Tending, and Harvesting Vegetables, by Catherine Abbott

The barns protect the babies from the snow, wind, and ice, and can be warm inside (ADV) from all the body heat that the sheep give off.

Mary caught the lamb and tucked it inside (PREP) her jacket to warm it up.

I like (V) patting their heads and scratching behind their ears.

Do you know what a Blue-faced Leicester looks like (ADV)?

Merinos are so wrinkly they look like (PREP) huge Shar Pei dogs with a seven-inch-long fleece.

Sheepish: Two Women, Fifty Sheep, and Enough Wool to Save the Planet, by Catherine Friend

The juice ran down my face (N) and chin.

Here was Eduardo, the representation of two centuries' worth of free-ranging fowl, face (ADJ) to face (ADJ) with the insult.

> **Note to Instructor:** If the student marks the above words as nouns, accept the answer but point out that the idiom *face to face* (meaning "looking directly at" or "suddenly presented with") modifies the proper noun *Eduardo.*

Others argue that Haber's science has saturated the planet with excess nitrogen, creating a profound chemical dependence in agriculture and, in the process, precipitating many of the most vexing environmental problems we face (V) today.

The Third Plate: Field Notes on the Future of Food, by Dan Barber

Humans are good at making our dreams manifest and we do, historically speaking, get what we wish (V) for.

We had all shared this wish (N), in some way or another: that it wouldn't rain on our day off.

Animal, Vegetable, Miracle: A Year of Food Life, by Barbara Kingsolver

Review 10F: Idioms

Circle each idiom in the following sentences. Above each one, write its meaning within the sentence. The first is done for you.

> **Note to Instructor:** Accept any answer that approximates the explanations below.

These farmers paid close attention (carefully examined) to things like germination percentages, and they were especially vigilant about disease, weeds, and any contamination possibilities.

continually talk about, be very explicit about supporting
You don't wear the high ideals of sustainability on your sleeve—you don't gloat about saving old, forgotten seeds of lettuce—and then serve a plate of bluefin.

The Third Plate: Field Notes on the Future of Food, by Dan Barber

something I have always been involved in
With farming in my blood, I have traveled back and forth across the country for the past 17 years, helping people create the outdoor spaces of their dreams.

to want, to be inclined towards
Many of us (me included) have been feeling a pull toward becoming more self-sufficient in sourcing our own food and are looking at how we can use our own spaces to grow that food.

to start
Whatever the reason, if you're keen to jump on board, my advice can help you ease into this way of life as smoothly as possible.

guideline, instruction
Here is my rule of thumb for what works best.

Vegetables, Chickens & Bees: An Honest Guide to Growing Your Own Food Anywhere, by Carson Arthur

appropriate consequences
What are the just deserts for a species too selfish or preoccupied to hope for rain when the land outside is dying?

too brief, too short
Returning now would allow my kids more than just a hit-and-run, holiday acquaintance with grandparents and cousins.

taught me lessons about, made me understand; lots, many
Tucson had opened my eyes to the world and given me a writing career, legions of friends, and a
amazing, spectacular
taste for the sensory extravagance of red hot chiles and five-alarm sunsets.

Note to Instructor: As long as the student identifies at least one of the three idioms above, accept his answer, but point out the other two.

Animal, Vegetable, Miracle: A Year of Food Life, by Barbara Kingsolver

Review 10G: Ambitransitive Verbs

In the following sentences, underline each action verb that acts as a predicate. Mark each of these verbs as *T* for transitive or *IT* for intransitive. For transitive verbs, draw an arrow from the label *T* to the word that receives the action of the verb.

The first is done for you.

T T
Goats have a curiosity that is often misunderstood.

T
They eat a little here and a little there, acquiring a variety of plants to meet their dietary needs.

T T
Bring goats into your life, and you will quickly learn many lessons both about goats and yourself.

IT
Learn by assisting your goat mentor with a few births before tackling this on your own.

The Dairy Goat Handbook: For Backyard, Homestead, and Small Farm, by Ann Starbard

IT IT
When I grew up and moved away from the apple trees and into the city, growing things stayed with me.

T T IT T
We ate what we grew and put away for the winter so that we'd have our own supply all year long.

T T T
Hanging baskets can be moved and rotated if one side of the plant is getting all the sunlight.

Vegetables, Chickens & Bees: An Honest Guide to Growing Your Own Food Anywhere, by Carson Arthur

T that IT
But you could argue^it really began a few years earlier, when my brother David and I

T
began to notice the forest encroaching on Blue Hill's pastureland.

Note to Instructor: The direct object of the verb *could argue* is the clause *[that] it really...earlier.* The next verb, *began,* is intransitive, while the third verb, *began* again, is transitive; its direct object is the infinitive *to notice.*

IT
It was two decades after my grandmother Ann had passed away.

T
Laws were passed to protect the grazing areas.

T
They are large enough to allow smaller tuna, the ones that haven't reached maturity, to escape and

T
forge on to the Mediterranean, where they continue the cycle.

Note to Instructor: In the phrase *to escape and forge,* the verb *forge* is an infinitive that shares *to* with *to escape,* not a predicate.

IT IT
As he turned to walk back to his car, he stopped and reached into his pocket for his cell phone.

IT T
It went on so long that it stopped conversations in the dining room.

T
He turned over another infected leaf, and then another.

The Third Plate: Field Notes on the Future of Food, by Dan Barber

IT IT IT IT
The work of adaptation must go on because the world changes; our places change and we change;

T T
we change our places and our places change us.

IT
And his words fell upon the table like a blessing.

IT
Unlike cow manure, which is heavy and chunky, horse manure is light and breaks up well coming out of the spreader.

T T
Reading a few lines at random will often do the trick, break the knot.

Wendell Berry, *Bringing It to the Table: On Farming and Food*

Review 10H: Hunt and Find

In the following essay, find, underline, and label each of the following:

Infinitive phrase acting as a noun	Noun clause in apposition
Noun clause acting as a predicate nominative	Adverbial noun
Infinitive phrase acting as an adjective	Indirect object
Infinitive phrase acting as an adverb	Clause with an understood *that*
To as a preposition	Comparison
Hortative verb	Participle or participle phrase acting as a noun
That acting as a demonstrative pronoun	Compound subordinating conjunction
Restrictive clause introduced by *which*	*Which* acting as a demonstrative pronoun
Nonrestrictive clause introduced by *which*	Noun clause acting as a direct object

adverbial noun / participle phrase acting as a noun [direct object of *started*] / infinitive phrase acting as a noun [direct object of *decided*]

A couple of years ago, when we started growing cut flowers from seed inside, we decided to try

infinitive phrase acting as a noun [direct object of *to try*] / indirect object

to grow our own tomatoes from seed. Not only did this give us a greater selection of tomato

which acting as a demonstrative pronoun / infinitive phrase acting as an adjective [modifying *which*] / infinitive phrase acting as a noun [direct object of *allowed*] / noun clause acting as a direct object [of *to control*] / *to* as a preposition

varieties from which to choose, but it also allowed us to control exactly what contributed to our

to as a preposition

seedling's growth. . . . Now we grow all of our own starts and take the extras to the farmer's market.

The Joy of Hobby Farming: Grow Food, Raise Animals, and Enjoy a Sustainable Life, by Michael Levatino and Audrey Levatino

participle phrase acting as a noun [subject of *has been*]

Iowa leads the United States in pork production, and for many years raising hogs has been one of

infinitive phrase acting as a noun [direct object of *sought*]

comparison

the main ways Iowa's farmers have sought to do something more profitable with their grain than

to as a preposition

selling it to the local elevator as a raw commodity.

noun clause acting as a predicate nominative

to as a preposition

The country is home, we fantasize, our real home, our natural home. It is what we go back to, and it

compound subordinating conjunction

is supposed to be still there when we return, even if, as the historian Bill Malone has observed, we

clause with an understood *that*

[also] noun clause acting as a direct object

that

know^it really isn't.

Farming for Us All: Practical Agriculture and the Cultivation of Sustainability, by Michael Mayerfeld Bell

noun clause in apposition

infinitive phrase acting as an adverb [modifying *respectable*]

participle phrase acting as a noun [object of the preposition *of*]

The feeling that it is not quite respectable to go into debt has grown out of the old habit of borrowing

infinitive phrase acting as an adverb [modifying *borrowing*]

that acting as a demonstrative pronoun

to pay living expenses. That was regarded, perhaps rightly, as a sign of incompetency....But

infinitive phrase acting as a noun [subject of *is*]

restrictive clause introduced by *which*

to borrow for a genuinely productive purpose, for a purpose which will bring you in more than

infinitive phrase acting as an adjective [modifying *enough*]

enough to pay off your debt, principal and interest, is a profitable enterprise.

Note to Instructor: If the student marks the clause *that it is...into debt* as adjectival, accept the answer but point out that it renames *feeling* so could equally well be classified as appositive.

Farm Knowledge: A Complete Manual of Successful Farming, ed. by Edward Loomis Davenport Seymour

nonrestrictive clause introduced by "which"

Partially wilted cherry leaves produce cyanide, which can cause breathing difficulty, spasms, coma, and death in humans and livestock.

hortative verb

[participle acting as a noun]

[participle acting as a noun]

infinitive phrase acting as an adjective [modifying *world*]

Let us combine hunting with farming for our world to be better.

Farming While Black: Soul Fire Farm's Practical Guide to Liberation on the Land, by Leah Penniman

Review 10I: Conditionals and Formal Conditionals

In each of the following conditional sentences, parse the underlined verbs, giving tense, voice (*active, passive*, or *state-of-being*), and mood. Then, classify the sentences as first, second, or third conditional by placing a *1, 2*, or *3* in the blank at the end.

The first verb is parsed for you.

progressive present, active, subjunctive — simple present, state-of-being, indicative — simple present, active, modal

If your llama is foaming at the mouth, it's overheating and you should take steps to cool it off, including running fans on it and shearing it immediately. 1

The Joy of Hobby Farming: Grow Food, Raise Animals, and Enjoy a Sustainable Life, by Michael Levatino and Audrey Levatino

perfect past, active, subjunctive — perfect present, active, modal

I suspected that if we'd met at a different time in our lives we would have run as fast as possible away from each other. 3

The Dirty Life: A Memoir of Farming, Food, and and Love, by Kristin Kimball

simple present, passive, subjunctive — simple future, active, indicative

If we mean to reclaim it, asparagus seems like a place to start. 1

simple present, passive, subjunctive — simple future, active, indicative

If the spears are allowed to proceed beyond their first exploratory six inches, they'll green

simple future, active, subjunctive

out and grow tall and feathery like the houseplant known as asparagus fern, which is the next of kin. 1

simple present, active, modal subjunctive — simple present, active, indicative

If the Europeans could make a big deal of its arrival, we could too: we

progressive past, active, indicative

were waiting for asparagus. 1

simple present, active, subjunctive

For most of us, if we see asparagus in any month far removed from April,

progressive present, active, indicative

we're looking at some hard traveling. 1

Animal, Vegetable, Miracle: A Year of Food Life, by Barbara Kingsolver

simple present, state-of-being, indicative — simple present, active, subjunctive — simple future, state-of-being, indicative

Land is the only real wealth in this country, and if we don't have any of it, we'll be out of the picture. 1

Farming While Black: Soul Fire Farm's Practical Guide to Liberation on the Land, by Leah Penniman

perfect past, state-of-being, subjunctive — simple present, state-of-being, modal

If it had only been a matter of moving myself and the dogs, it wouldn't even be cause to blink. 3

Barnheart: The Incurable Longing for a Farm of One's Own, by Jenna Woginrich

simple present, state-of-being, subjunctive / simple future, passive, indicative / simple future, passive, indicative

If a chicken's coop is too small, the chicken will be pecked and harassed by its coop-mates. 1

The New Farm: Our Ten Years on the Front Lines of the Good Food Revolution, by Brent Preston

simple present, active, subjunctive / simple present, active, modal

Thus, if we choose, we may sandwich in the poetry with the prose of life. 1

simple present, state-of-being, subjunctive / simple present, active, subjunctive / simple present, active, subjunctive / simple present, active, subjunctive

Should the milker be too impetuous; should he swear, speak loud and sharp, scold

simple present, active, subjunctive / simple present, active, subjunctive / simple present, active, subjunctive / simple future, active, indicative

or kick, or otherwise abuse or frighten the cow, she will probably prove refractory

simple present, active, modal

as a mule, and may give the uncouth and unfeeling milker the benefit of her heels,—

simple present, state-of-being, indicative

a very pertinent reward, to which he, the uncouth milker, is justly entitled. 1

Ten Acres Enough: How a Very Small Farm May Be Made to Keep a Very Large Family, by Edmund Morris

simple past, active, subjunctive / simple present, state-of-being, modal

So even if we wanted to go back to hunting and gathering wild species, it cannot be an option: There are far too many of us and not nearly enough of them. 2

The Omnivore's Dilemma: A Natural History of Four Meals, by Michael Pollan (sentence slightly adapted)

Review 10J: Affirmations and Negations

The following sentences all contain adverbs of affirmation and negation. Circle each one, and label them as *AFF* or *NEG.*

Then, choose three sentences and rewrite them on your own paper, turning affirmatives into negatives and vice versa. Show your sentences to your instructor.

Note to Instructor: Sample rewritten sentences follow each original sentence. Accept any reasonable rephrasings. (Some rewritten sentences will not make good sense, but that's fine—the student is merely being encouraged to pay attention to the presence of the affirmatives and negations.)

NEG

Farmers are not us even as they are us.

Farmers are definitely us, even as they are us.

NEG / AFF

Well, I don't put on any more spray, or anything like that, than I feel I absolutely have to.

Well, I do put on more spray, and anything like that, than I feel I don't have to.

Farming for Us All: Practical Agriculture and the Cultivation of Sustainability, by Michael Mayerfeld Bell

NEG
I (never) set out to become a gardener; it was on my list of skills to learn because growing my own food was important to me.

I absolutely set out to become a gardener

AFF
I told her I (absolutely) wanted them but I needed to get permission from my landlady first and set up a shed and pen for them.

I told her I never wanted them

AFF
For some, this is (surely) the only cure.

For some, this is not the only cure.

NEG
The animals were (not) concerned.

The animals were certainly concerned.

Barnheart: The Incurable Longing for a Farm of One's Own, by Jenna Woginrich

NEG AFF NEG
It was(n't) supposed to be nearly this big, or this remote. And it was (definitely) (not) supposed to be swampy.

It was definitely supposed to be this big, and this remote. But it was never surely supposed to be swampy.

NEG
I had (never) in my life been so dirty.

I had definitely in my life been so dirty.

NEG
There is (no) better lesson in commitment than the cow. Her udder knows no exceptions or excuses.

> **Note to Instructor:** This is a trick sentence—the second *no* is an adjective of negation, not an adverb, because it modifies the noun *exceptions*. The first *no* is adverbial because it modifies an adjective.

There is absolutely a better lesson in commitment than the cow.

AFF
I'd forgotten how (very) clean my mother's world is until we walked in with those boxes, which were smudged with field dirt, a few limp leaves clinging to their bottoms.

I'd forgotten how not clean my mother's world is

The Dirty Life: A Memoir of Farming, Food, and Love, by Kristin Kimball

AFF NEG
The fungi (surely) have a syntax of their own, but we do(n't) know all its rules, especially the ones that govern the creation of a mushroom, which can take three years or thirty, depending.

The fungi never have a syntax of their own, but we certainly know all its rules

The Omnivore's Dilemma: A Natural History of Four Meals, by Michael Pollan

Review 10K: Diagramming

On your own paper, diagram every word of the following sentences.

Greens (spinach, lettuce, kale, etc.), cucumbers, and squash also germinate and grow well when direct seeded.

The Joy of Hobby Farming: Grow Food, Raise Animals, and Enjoy a Sustainable Life, by Michael Levatino and Audrey Levatino

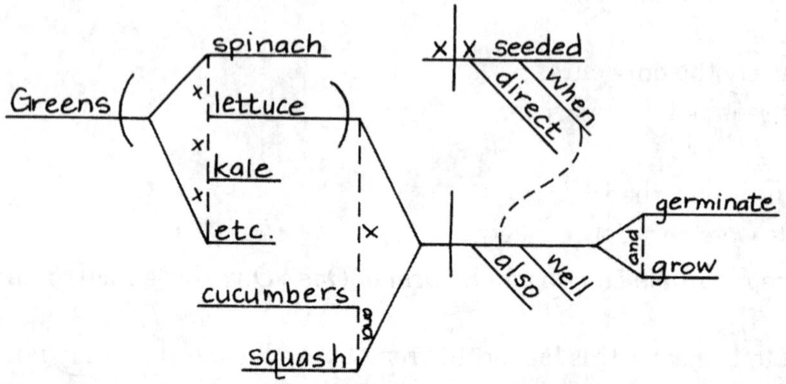

Note to Instructor: In this sentence, *etc.* acts as a noun, one of the four appositives following *Greens*. The adverbs *all* and *well* modify both verbs so are placed after the subject/verb divider but before the compound verb. The clause *when direct seeded* is adverbial and contains understood elements: *when [they are] direct seeded.*

Eighty dollars an acre, they told me, was the current average price in the county, with some land fetching up to double that in recent months.

Farming for Us All: Practical Agriculture and the Cultivation of Sustainability, by Michael Mayerfeld Bell

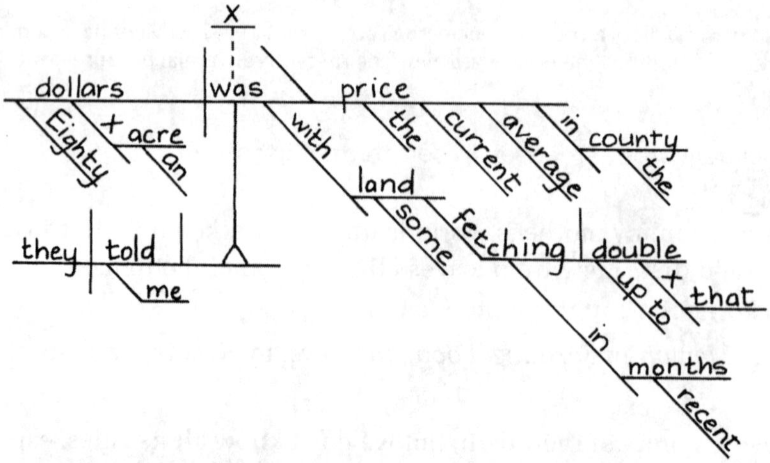

Note to Instructor: The noun clause with understood *that* is the direct object of the predicate *told*, with *me* as the indirect object: *they told me [that] eighty dollars an acre was...*

Eighty dollars is modified by the prepositional phrase, with understood preposition, *[for] an acre.*

The adjective *double* here serves as a noun, the direct object of the adjectival participle *fetching*. The phrase *up* to serves as a compound preposition (together, the words have a single meaning).

The small family farm is one of the last places—they are getting rarer every day—where men and women (and girls and boys, too) can answer that call to be an artist, to learn to give love to the work of their hands.

Bringing It to the Table: On Farming and Food, by Wendell Berry

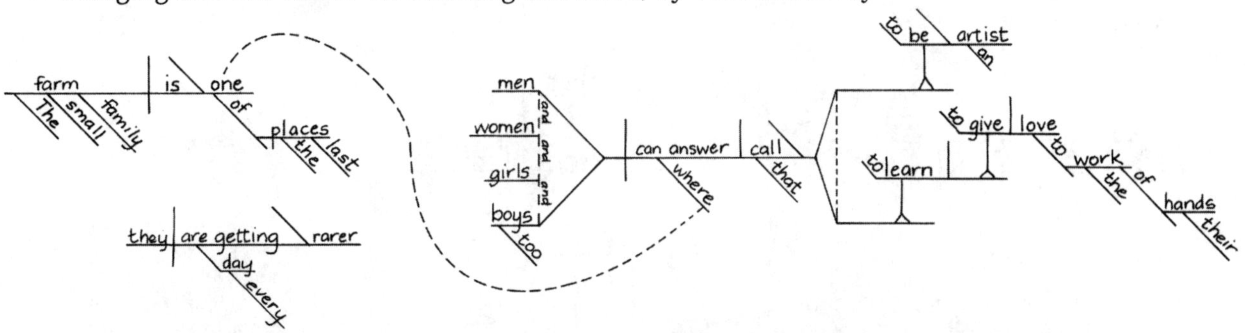

Note to Instructor: The floating element *they are getting rarer every day* has a semantic, but not grammatical relationship to the rest of the sentence, and so is diagrammed separately to the left.

The clause *where men and women...hands* is an adjective clause describing a place, introduced by a relative adverb. The dotted line could also connect *where* to *places.*

Within the adjective clause, the infinitive phrases *to be an artist* and *to learn to give love to the work of their hands* serve as compound object complements, renaming the direct object *call.* Within the second phrase, the infinitive *to give love* serves as the direct object of the infinitive *to learn.*

Note that *to the work* is a prepositional phrase, so *to* should have a slight tail on its preposition line, while the other *to* phrases are infinitive and should not have tails on the *to* lines.

The more questions this new knowledge forces us to ask, the more we start understanding that every purchase we make is a vote to support one system over another.

Local: The New Face of Food and Farming in America, by Douglas Gayeton

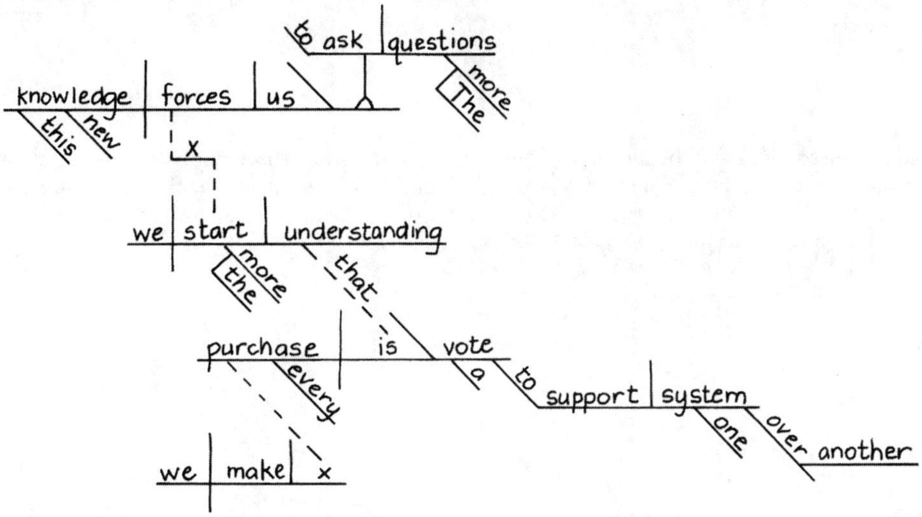

Note to Instructor: In this sentence, *forces* acts as an ambitransitive verb, with the infinitive phrase *to ask the more questions* as the direct object and *us* as the indirect object (on the model of *they threw us the ball*).

The participle *understanding* acts as a noun, receiving the action of the verb *start.* The clause *that every purchase...over another* describes *understanding* and answers the question *what kind.* (What kind of understanding? The understanding that every purchase...) Within the clause, the clause with understood element *[that] we make* modifies *purchase.* The understood *that* is the relative pronoun, with *purchase* as its antecedent.

We had been living on the farm for almost a year, and I was suddenly struck by the wondrous realization that we actually owned this place, that all this land was ours—a realization that struck me on a regular basis back then, and sometimes still does.

The New Farm: Our Ten Years on the Front Lines of the Good Food Revolution, by Brent Preston

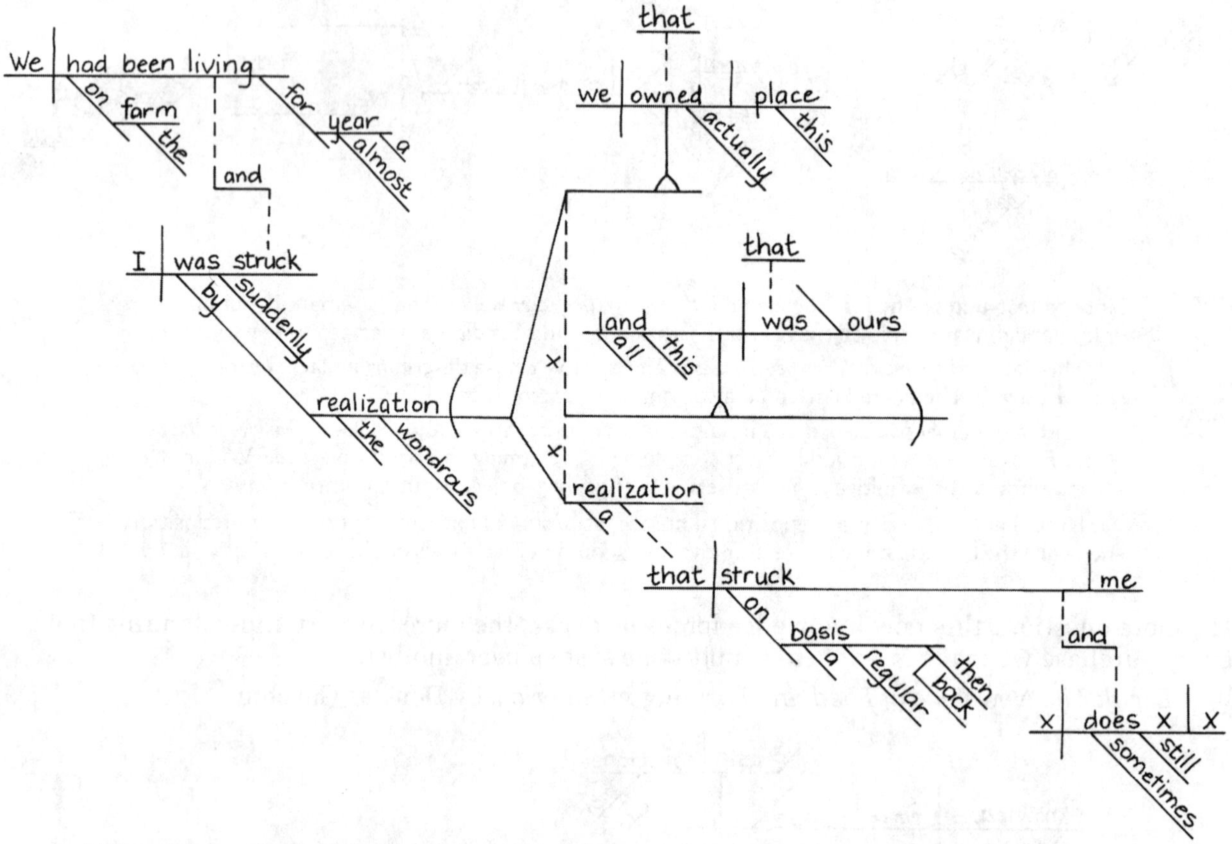

Note to Instructor: The first occurrence of *realization* is followed by three appositives—two clauses (*that we...place, that all...ours*) and a repetition of the noun, the last modified by the adjective clause *that struck...does*. The phrase *and sometimes still does* is actually a second independent clause with understood elements: *and [that] sometimes still does [strike me]*.

Review 10L: Explaining Sentences

Tell your instructor every possible piece of grammatical information about the following sentences. Follow these steps:

a) Underline each clause. Describe the identity and function of each clause and give any other useful information (introductory word, relationship to the rest of the sentence, etc.)

b) Circle each phrase. Describe the identity and function of each phrase and give any other useful information.

c) Parse all verbs acting as predicates.

d) Describe the identity and function of each individual remaining word.

If you need help, ask your instructor.

Note to Instructor: Use the information in the Notes, below, to prompt the student as necessary. The purpose of this exercise is to build the student's confidence in defining and explaining sentences out loud. Give all necessary help and encourage the student to answer loudly and in complete sentences.

I retreated to the house, not sure what I should do and completely mystified as to what had happened.

The New Farm: Our Ten Years on the Front Lines of the Good Food Revolution, by Brent Preston

a) I retreated to the house, not sure what I should do and completely mystified as to what had happened.

Note to Instructor: The main independent clause *I retreated...had happened* contains within it the dependent clauses *what I should do* and *what had happened.*

The clause *what I should do* modifies *sure*, which is itself an idiom: the meaning is *I retreated...[I was] not sure*. The introductory demonstrative pronoun *what* serves as the direct object of the clause. Grammatically, *sure* is an adjective, so the clause *what I should do* is adverbial.

The clause *what had happened* serves as a noun, the object of the compound preposition *as to.* The demonstrative pronoun *what* serves as the subject of the clause.

b) I retreated (to the house), not sure what I should do and completely mystified (as to what had happened.)

Note to Instructor: The sentence contains two prepositional phrases, *to the house* (adverbial, modifying the verb *retreated*), and *as to what had happened*, introduced by the compound preposition *as to*, with the clause *what had happened* as the object of the preposition (adverbial, modifying the past participle *mystified*).

c) The predicate *retreated* is simple past, active, indicative.

The predicate *should do* is simple present, active, modal.

The predicate *had happened* is past perfect, active, indicative.

d) The pronoun *I* is the subject of the independent clause.

The noun *house* is the object of the preposition *to* and is modified by the article *the*.

The adverb of negation *not* modifies the adjective *sure*.

The second pronoun *I* is the subject of the first dependent clause.

The conjunction *and* links the idiomatic phrase *not sure* with the past participle *mystified*.

Completely is an adverb modifying the past participle *mystified*.

The past participle *mystified* acts as an adjective modifying *I*.

Feeling the heartbeat of a warm young animal as he sits in your lap, stroking his head, and giggling as his tail tickles your legs...it was like living in a storybook.

Barnheart: The Incurable Longing for a Farm of One's Own, by Jenna Woginrich

a) Feeling the heartbeat of a warm young animal as he sits in your lap, stroking his head, and giggling as his tail tickles your legs...it was like living in a storybook.

> **Note to Instructor:** The main independent clause is *it was like living in a storybook*. Everything in front of the ellipses is "floating"—semantically but not grammatically related to the independent clause.
>
> Within those floating elements are two dependent clauses, *as he sits in your lap* and *as his tail tickles your legs*. Both of these clauses are adverbial, and both are introduced by the subordinating conjunction *as*. The first clause modifies the participle *Feeling*, and the second modifies the participle *giggling*.

b) Feeling the heartbeat of a warm young animal as he sits in your lap, stroking his head, and giggling as his tail tickles your legs...it was like living in a storybook.

> **Note to Instructor:** This sentence contains four participle phrases. The phrases beginning with *Feeling*, *stroking*, and *giggling* are all floating elements which are semantically but not grammatically related to the main clause *It was like living in a storybook*.
>
> Within the first participle phrase, the prepositional phrase of *a warm young animal* is adjectival and modifies the noun *heartbeat*, and the prepositional phrase *in your lap* is adverbial and modifies the noun *sits*.
>
> The fourth participle phrase, *like living in a storybook*, acts as a noun and serves as the predicate nominative renaming *it*. Within that fourth participle phrase, the prepositional phrase *in a storybook* is adverbial and modifies *living*.

c) The predicate *sits* is simple present, active, indicative.

The predicate *tickles* is simple present, active, indicative.

The predicate *was* is simple past, state-of-being, indicative.

d) The noun *heartbeat* is the subject of the participle *Feeling* and is modified by the article *the*.

Animal is the object of the preposition *of*, and is modified by the adjectives *warm* and *young*.

The pronoun *he* is the subject of the predicate *sits*. Its antecedent is *animal*.

The noun *lap* is the object of the preposition *in* and is modified by the possessive pronoun *your.*

The noun *head* is the object of the participle *stroking* and is modified by the possessive pronoun *his.*

The noun *tail* is the subject of the dependent clause *as his tail tickles your legs* and is modified by the possessive pronoun *his.* The noun *legs* is the direct object of the verb *tickles* and is modified by the possessive pronoun *your.*

The pronoun *it* is the subject of the independent clause.

The adverb *like* modifies the present participle *living.*

The noun *storybook* is the object of the preposition *in* and is modified by the article *a.*

As we walked, I fell into a dark mood, which I tried to blame on the weather and the fact that I hadn't yet had any coffee, but the truth was I'd gotten my hopes up, and the farm, under the filtered morning light, was disappointing.

The Dirty Life: A Memoir of Farming, Food, and Love, by Kristin Kimball

a) As we walked, I fell into a dark mood, which I tried to blame on the weather and the fact that I hadn't yet had any coffee, but the truth was I'd gotten my hopes up, and the farm, under the filtered morning light, was disappointing.

Note to Instructor: This sentence is made up of three independent clauses (*As we...coffee, the truth...hopes up, the farm...was disappointing*), linked by the coordinating conjunctions *but* and *and.*

The first independent clause contains two dependent clauses, *As we walked* (adverbial, modifying the predicate *fell* and introduced by the subordinate conjunction *As*), and *which I tried... any coffee* (adjectival, modifying the noun *mood* and introduced by the relative pronoun *which,* referring back to *mood.* Within the dependent clause, which serves as the direct object of the infinitive *to blame*). Within the second dependent clause, the clause *that I...coffee* is adjectival and modifies *fact,* with *that* serving as a subordinating conjunction.

The second independent clause, *the truth...hopes up* is linked to the first by the subordinating conjunction *but.* Within that clause, the noun clause *I'd gotten my hopes up* serves as a predicate nominative renaming *truth* and is introduced by an understood subordinating *that.*

The third independent clause, *the farm...was disappointing,* is linked to the second by the coordinating conjunction *and,* and contains no subordinate clauses.

b) As we walked, I fell into a dark mood, which I tried to blame on the weather and the fact that I hadn't yet had any coffee, but the truth was I'd gotten my hopes up, and the farm, under the filtered morning light, was disappointing.

Note to Instructor: The prepositional phrase *into a dark mood* is adverbial and describes the predicate *fell.*

The infinitive phrase *to blame on the weather...any coffee* is adverbial and modifies the verb *tried.* (*Try* is, in this usage, intransitive.) Within the infinitive phrase, the prepositional phrase *on the weather and the fact that I hadn't yet had any coffee* modifies the infinitive *to blame. Weather* and *fact* are the compound objects of the preposition *on.*

In the third independent clause, the prepositional phrase *under the filtered morning light* is adjectival and modifies *farm.*

c) The predicate *walked* is simple past, active, indicative.

The predicate *fell* is simple past, active, indicative.

The predicate *tried* is simple past, active, indicative.

The predicate *had had* is perfect past, active, indicative.

The predicate *had gotten* is perfect past, active, indicative.

The predicate *was* is simple past, state-of-being, indicative.

d) The pronoun *we* is the subject of the first dependent clause.

The pronoun *I* is the subject of the first independent clause.

The noun *mood* is the object of the pronoun *into* and is modified by the adjective *dark* and the article *a*.

The next pronoun *I* is the subject of the second dependent clause.

The noun *weather* is the object of the preposition *on* and is modified by the article *the*.

The conjunction *and* links the compound objects of the preposition, *weather* and *fact*. *Fact* is also modified by the article *the*.

The third occurrence of the pronoun *I* is the subject of the third dependent clause, contained within the second.

The adverbs *not* and *yet* both modify the predicate *had had*.

The noun *coffee* is the object of the predicate *had had* and is modified by the adjective *any*.

The noun *truth* is the subject of the second independent clause and is modified by the article *the*.

The fourth occurrence of the pronoun *I* is the subject of the noun clause.

The noun *hopes* is the direct object of the verb *had gotten* and is modified by the personal pronoun *my*.

The adverb *up* modifies the verb *had gotten*.

The noun *farm* is the subject of the third independent clause and is modified by the article *the*.

The noun *light* is the object of the preposition *under* and is modified by the article *the*, the past participle *filtered*, and the adjective *morning*.

The predicate adjective *disappointing* modifies *farm*.

WEEK 33

Mechanics

— LESSON 121 —

Capitalization Review
Additional Capitalization Rules
Formal and Informal Letter Format
Ending Punctuation

Exercise 121A: Proofreading

Use proofreader's marks to insert the missing capital letters and punctuation marks into the following sentences. They are all taken from mystery novels written by the great English novelist Agatha Christie.

capitalize letter: ≡	make letter lowercase: /
insert period: ⊙	insert exclamation point: ^!
insert comma: ^,	insert question mark: ^?
insert apostrophe: ˅'	

If a word or phrase should be italicized, indicate this by underlining.

Note to Instructor: The original sentences are below. Where alternative corrections are acceptable, notes are inserted. However, be sure to show the student the original sentences for comparison.

This is a very pleasant meeting for me, Miss Cynthia.

This is my old friend, Monsieur Poirot, whom I have not seen for years.

Note to Instructor: The comma after *Poirot* is necessary, but since this is a short appositive, the comma before *Monsieur* is optional.

No one but I, Hercule Poirot, would attempt it!

Note to Instructor: A period at the end of the sentence is also acceptable.

On Tuesday, the 17th July, you went, I believe, with another guest, to visit the dispensary at the Red Cross Hospital in Tadminster?

Note to Instructor: Since *the 17th July* is a short appositive, the commas are optional, but preferable. The comma after *guest* is optional. The sentence may also be followed by a period.

The Mysterious Affair at Styles

Can I speak to Detective Inspector Hardcastle?

A thoroughfare uncompromisingly labelled Albany Road barred my way.

He knew a little about Miss Pebmarsh, though their paths had never crossed professionally.

The Clocks

Besides, there was something very cosy and English about old ladies like this old lady and his Aunt Mildred. They could be classed with plum pudding on Christmas Day and village cricket and open fireplaces with wood fires.

> **Note to Instructor:** The period after *Mildred* could also be a semicolon.

Then he opened *The Times* and became absorbed in more serious matters.

> **Note to Instructor:** *The Times* should be underlined. You may need to tell the student that the article *The* is part of the newspaper's title.

Murder Is Easy

Through all Gwenda's plans and preoccupations, the voice of Mrs. Hengrave droned thinly on recounting the details of the late Major Hengrave's last illness.

> **Note to Instructor:** The comma after *preoccupations* is preferable, but optional. A comma could also follow *on*. At least one of these commas should be inserted to prevent confusion.

She flinched slightly at the prospect of *They Walked without Feet*, but supposed she might enjoy it—only the point about "significant" plays was that you usually didn't.

> **Note to Instructor:** The student should be able to tell from context that *They Walked without Feet* (which should be underlined) is a play. The preposition *without* could also be capitalized. The dash after *it* could be a comma, and the comma after *Feet* is optional.

Sleeping Murder

Before God, I didn't know what it was, sir.

Indian Island had really been bought by Miss Gabrielle Turl, the Hollywood film star!

> **Note to Instructor:** The sentence could also end with a period.

The train is the 12:40 from Paddington and you will be met at Oakridge station.

> **Note to Instructor:** A comma could follow *Paddington. Station* could also be capitalized.

We were together at Bellhaven Guest House in August some years ago, and we seemed to have so much in common.

> **Note to Instructor:** A comma could also follow *August*.

And Then There Were None

A big scarlet Rolls-Royce had just stopped in front of the local post office.

> **Note to Instructor:** Although the name of the company is *Rolls-Royce*, the name is often incorrectly written as *Rolls Royce*. If the student does not hyphenate the name, accept the answer but show her the original sentence.

Instead, he seemed to see a more imposing Elizabethan mansion, a long sweep of park, a more bleak background.

> **Note to Instructor:** The comma after *Instead* is optional.

M. Gaston Blondin, the proprietor of that modish little restaurant Chez Ma Tante, was not a man who delighted to honour many of his clientele.

> **Note to Instructor:** You may need to explain that *M.* is the French abbreviation for *Monsieur.*

Dr. Bessner read sonorously in German from a Baedeker, pausing every now and then to translate for the benefit of Cornelia, who walked in a docile manner beside him.

> **Note to Instructor:** You may need to explain that Baedeker is the name of a German publisher that put out well-known travel guidebooks. The books themselves became known as Baedekers.

The *Normandie*, I remember, sailed two days after the *Carmanic.*

Mr. Fanthorp turned a page of *Europe from Within.*

Death on the Nile

I'm American born, but I've spent most of my life in England.

I must be right, therefore this new murder is impossible unless—unless—Oh, wait, I implore you.

> **Note to Instructor:** The comma after *right* could be a semicolon, as long as a comma follows *therefore.* The dashes cannot be commas, but *Oh, wait, I* could also be punctuated as *Oh! Wait, I* or *Oh wait, I...*

Murder on the Links

Exercise 121B: Correct Letter Mechanics

The following text is a letter written by Agatha Christie to an American fan who asked her for an interview. On your own paper (or with your own word processing program), rewrite or retype the text so that it is properly formatted, punctuated, and capitalized. You may choose either letter format from this lesson.

The address of the sender (Agatha Christie) is in England. Churston Ferrers is the town, and South Devon is the county.

Notice that there are no ZIP codes in the address of the recipient, because ZIP codes were only created by the U.S. Post Office in 1963.

The first two sentences in the letter are one paragraph, while the last sentence is its own separate paragraph.

The abbreviation "Esq." follows the name of the recipient, and tells you that the recipient is a lawyer.

When you are finished, compare your letter with the two versions in the Answer Key.

greenway house churston ferrers south devon england may 15 1961 homer hall esq 123 john street de kalb illinois usa dear mr. hall thank you very much for your letter and for sending me the somewhat gruesome photograph i am glad to have it to keep among my mementoes of crime i am so glad you enjoy my stories yours sincerely agatha christie

Note to Instructor: Two correct versions of the letter are shown below. The letter itself has been very slightly adapted—Christie's original letter had no date. Mr. Hall's original letter was dated April 21, 1961. Accept any reasonable punctuation of the text of the letter, as long as the paragraphing is properly done.

Greenway House
Churston Ferrers
South Devon
England

May 15, 1961

Homer Hall, Esq.
123 John Street
De Kalb, Illinois
USA

Dear Mr. Hall,

Thank you very much for your letter and for sending me the somewhat gruesome photograph. I am glad to have it to keep among my mementoes of crime!

I am so glad you enjoy my stories.

Yours sincerely,

Agatha Christie

Greenway House
Churston Ferrers
South Devon
England

May 15, 1961

Homer Hall, Esq.
123 John Street
De Kalb, Illinois
USA

Dear Mr. Hall,

Thank you very much for your letter and for sending me the somewhat gruesome photograph. I am glad to have it to keep among my mementoes of crime!

I am so glad you enjoy my stories.

Yours sincerely,

Agatha Christie

— LESSON 122 —

Commas
Semicolons
Additional Semicolon Rules
Colons
Additional Colon Rules

Exercise 122A: Comma Use

In the blank at the end of each sentence, write the number from the list above that describes the comma use. If more than one number seems to fit equally well, write all suitable numbers.

These sentences are from *The House of Mirth*, by Edith Wharton.

Note to Instructor: As long as the student writes at least one number, accept the answer. However, ask him if there is a second (or third) rule that could be applied. After the student answers, point out the additional numbers that could have been referenced.

As she entered her bedroom, with its softly-shaded lights, her lace dressing-gown lying across the silken bedspread, her little embroidered slippers before the fire, a vase of carnations filling the air with perfume, and the last novels and magazines lying uncut on a table beside the reading-lamp, she had a vision of Miss Farish's cramped flat, with its cheap conveniences and hideous wall-papers. 2, 4, 11, 19

Oh, Lily, do look at this diamond pendant—it's as big as a dinner-plate! 5, 9

Really, Lily, I don't see why you took the trouble to go to the wedding, if you don't remember what happened or whom you saw there. 7, 5, 19

Gerty hid her face from the light, but it pierced to the crannies of her soul. 1

Here was, after all, something that her charming listless hands could really do; she had no doubt of their capacity for knotting a ribbon or placing a flower to advantage. 7

And of course only these finishing touches would be expected of her: subordinate fingers, blunt, grey, needle-pricked fingers, would prepare the shapes and stitch the linings, while she presided over the charming little front shop—a shop all white panels, mirrors, and moss-green hangings—where her finished creations, hats, wreaths, aigrettes and the rest, perched on their stands like birds just poising for flight. 2, 4, 8

Note to Instructor: The words *hats, wreaths, aigrettes and the rest* are all appositives renaming *creations*. This series does not use the Oxford comma, but the series above (*white panels, mirrors, and moss-green hangings*) does.

Mr. Bry, a short pale man, with a business face and leisure clothes, met the dilemma hilariously. 8, 19

She rose and handed the hat to Miss Kilroy, who took it with a suppressed smile. 6

No, that's rather out of my line. 10

"I came here because I couldn't bear to be alone," she said. 17

In her stuffy room at the hotel to which she had gone on landing, Lily Bart that evening reviewed her situation. 11

On and on it flowed, a current of meaningless sound, on which, startlingly enough, a familiar name now and then floated to the surface. 8, 6, 7

> **Note to Instructor:** The phrase *a current of meaningless sound* is an appositive renaming *it*; *on which... floated to the surface* is a nonrestrictive adjective clause, and *startlingly enough* is a parenthetical expression.

The row of budding trees, the new brick and limestone house-fronts, the Georgian flat-house with flowerboxes on its balconies, were merged together into the setting of a familiar scene. 4

Exercise 122B: Capitalization and Punctuation

Insert all missing punctuation and correct all capitalization in the text that follows. Use these proofreader's marks:

capitalize letter: ≡ | make letter lowercase: /
insert period: ⊙ | insert exclamation point: ^!
insert comma: ^, | insert question mark: ^?
insert colon: ^: | insert semicolon: ^;
insert dash: (—) | insert quotation marks: ^"
insert hyphen: ^-

If a word or phrase should be italicized, indicate this by underlining.

> **Note to Instructor:** The original sentences are found below. Where there is a legitimate judgment call over which punctuation mark to admit, a note has been inserted. Make sure that the student looks at the original sentences once the exercise is finished, so that she can be familiar with the different ways in which these punctuation marks may be used.
>
> Be sure to check the student's proofing of the citations as well as the sentences themselves.

122B.1: Sentences

The photograph, by Herbert Mason, of St. Paul's Cathedral on December 29–30, 1940, expresses an unalterable historical truth and a tragically false prophecy.

> **Note to Instructor:** The commas around *by Herbert Mason* prevent misunderstanding but could also be eliminated.

Since September, London had been the chief, almost the exclusive, target of a relentless series of raids by German bombers: 27,500 high-explosive bombs and innumerable incendiaries were dropped, on average 160 bombers attacking nightly, between September 7 and November 13.

> **Note to Instructor:** The comma after *September* is optional. The colon could also be a semicolon or a period (but not a comma, since there is no coordinating conjunction).

The docks were a prime target, often in flames; the dwellings of the poor who lived nearby were reduced to street after street of smoking rubble.

> **Note to Instructor:** The semicolon after *flames* could also be a period, with the following *the* capitalized.

Of 147,000 serious or fatal casualties caused by bombardment in Britain, 80,000 were in London (29,890 killed and 50,000 badly injured), and 1.5 million homes were destroyed.

> **Note to Instructor:** The parentheses could also be dashes, in which case the comma after the closing parenthesis should be eliminated.

London: A History, by A. N. Wilson

The Battle of Britain was over and the attack on Coventry wasn't till mid-November.

> **Note to Instructor:** A comma could also follow *over.* Because the two sentences are short, a comma does not necessarily need to accompany the coordinating conjunction.

"What are you doing?" she shouted over the drone of the bombers.

> **Note to Instructor:** A comma could also follow *shouted.*

She was exactly where she'd told the lab—and Colin—she'd be: working in a department store on Oxford Street and sleeping in a tube station that had never been hit.

> **Note to Instructor:** The dashes could also be commas or parentheses. To have no punctuation surrounding *and Colin* is grammatically correct, but makes the sentence harder to read. The colon after *be* could also be a comma or a dash.

He'd set the net so he'd come through at 7 p.m. on September 16, 1940.

> **Note to Instructor:** The time can be represented as *7 p.m.* or *7 PM*, but not as *7 pm.*

"London Damaged by Bombs," the headline read.

> **Note to Instructor:** The headline could also be underlined (italicized) rather than placed in quotation marks.

Blackout, by Connie Willis

She forced the cough back, holding her breath, and looked up the nave toward the dome—and saw flames.

> **Note to Instructor:** The dash is optional.

They must be blowing in through the shattered stained-glass windows from the fires in Paternoster Row.

The sixpenny print of The Light of the World caught fire, the edges curling up, the shut door in the picture burning away to black, to ash.

All Clear, by Connie Willis

122B.2: Letter Format

The following letters were written by Londoners who lived through the World War II bombing of London by German planes (the Blitz).

The first letter, slightly adapted, is from a mother in London to her six-year-old son, who had been sent away from the city into the country so that he would be safe from the bombing.[1] Roddy is the child's dog, and Bob is his cat. "Anderson" is the brand name of a type of bomb shelter used during the war. "Combinations" were warm underwear that had both pants and a vest.

The second letter is a shortened version of a letter written by Queen Elizabeth The Queen Mother to her mother-in-law, describing a bombing raid on London in 1940.[2] East Ham and West Ham are districts in London.

---

[1]http://www.bbc.co.uk/history/ww2peopleswar/stories/40/a8917040.shtml

[2]https://www.telegraph.co.uk/news/uknews/theroyalfamily/6179312/Queen-Mother-Blitz-letter-in-full.html

59 St. Asaph Road
Brockley, London SE4

Wednesday, August 23, 1944

Dear Francis,

We arrived home safely. The scullery ceiling was down. A bomb had fallen very near the allotment. We now sleep in the public shelter because it is wet in the Anderson. It has rained a lot this past few days.

I hope you are well and happy. Roddy and Bob are all right and the tortoise is still in his box.

I have sent two cakes, one for you and one for Norman and some chocolate, done in two different papers. Have one each. They are both the same inside.

If you feel cold, put on your combinations.

Lots of love,

Mummy

Windsor Castle
September 13, 1940

My darling Mama,

I hardly know how to begin to tell you of the horrible attack on Buckingham Palace this morning. We heard the unmistakable whirr-whirr of a German plane. We said, "Ah! A German!" and before anything else could be said, there was the noise of aircraft diving at great speed, and then the scream of a bomb. It all happened so quickly that we had only time to look foolishly at each other, when the scream hurtled past us, and exploded with a tremendous crash in the quadrangle.

I saw a great column of smoke and earth thrown up into the air, and then we all ducked like lightning into the corridor. My knees trembled a little bit for a minute or two after the explosions!

Luckily at about 1:30 the all-clear sounded, so we were able to set out on our tour of East and West Ham – the damage there is ghastly. I really felt as if I was walking in a dead city, when we walked down a little empty street. All the houses evacuated, and yet through the broken windows one saw all the poor little possessions, photographs, beds, just as they were left.

At the end of the street is a school which was hit, and collapsed on the top of 500 people waiting to be evacuated – about 20 are still under the ruins. It does affect me seeing this terrible and senseless destruction – I think that really I mind it much more than being bombed myself.

Your loving daughter-in-law,

Elizabeth

122B.3: Quotes

Bertrand Russell wrote in 1936 that when London was bombed it would be "one vast raving bedlam, the hospitals will be stormed, traffic will cease, the homeless will shriek for help, the city will be a pandemonium."

The First Day of the Blitz: September 7, 1940, by Peter Stansky

So much for the historical truth. The photograph also, by implication, speaks a prophecy that

This England never did, nor never shall,
Lie at the proud foot of a conqueror.

London: A History, by A. N. Wilson

Bomb disposal teams were taking no chances. Henry Beckingham wrote afterwards:

There had been a heavy air raid on the 17th/18th August '43 in the Hull, Hedon, and Hornsea areas, when a large number of butterfly bombs were dropped, causing havoc. For weeks we were still searching in the hedgerows and ditches for these lethal fragmentation bombs.

Blitz Diary: Life Under Fire in World War II, by Carol Harris

— LESSON 123 —

Colons
Dashes
Hyphens
Parentheses
Brackets

Exercise 123A: Hyphens

Some (but not all) of the following sentences—each taken from an essay in the classic 1914 collection *The Oxford Book of American Essays*—contain words that should be hyphenated. Insert a hyphen into each word that needs one.

At last, the long-expected day arrived, preceded by a very restless night.

He is a busy-minded personage, who thinks not merely for himself and family, but for all the country round, and is most generously disposed to be everybody's champion.

Though really a good-hearted, good-tempered old fellow at bottom, yet he is singularly fond of being in the midst of contention.

His family mansion is an old castellated manor-house, gray with age, and of a most venerable, though weather-beaten appearance.

Note to Instructor: *manor house* is also correct.

There are, however, complete suites of rooms apparently deserted and time-worn; and towers and turrets that are tottering to decay; so that in high winds there is danger of their tumbling about the ears of the household.

A certain fashion of thought prevailed half a century ago; another is popular today.

We wish to be self-sustained.

The civilized nations—Greece, Rome, England—have been sustained by the primitive forests which anciently rotted where they stand.

Such companions befit the season of frosted window-panes and crackling fires, when the blast howls through the black-ash trees of our avenue, and the drifting snowstorm chokes up the wood paths and fills the highway from stone wall to stone wall.

Note to Instructor: *window panes* is also correct.

There is a kind of ludicrous unfitness in the idea of a time–stricken and grandfatherly lilac-bush.

Note to Instructor: *lilac bush* is also correct.

To judge from your physiognomy, you are now well stricken in years.

The escape of genius from the cloud-covered mountain–tops of the unknown into human society has not yet been accounted for.

The learned shook their heads at him, for he was a poor half–educated varlet, that knew little of Latin, and nothing of Greek, and had been obliged to run the country for deer–stealing.

In two respects the absorption of large numbers of immigrants from many nations into the American commonwealth has been of great service to mankind. In the first place, it has demonstrated that people who at home have been subject to every sort of aristocratic or despotic or military oppression become within less than a generation serviceable citizens of a republic; and, in the second place, the United States have thus educated to freedom many millions of men.

Exercise 123B: Parenthetical Elements

The following sentences, also taken from *The Oxford Book of American Essays*, each contain parenthetical elements. Set off each bolded set of words with commas, dashes, or parentheses. Choose the punctuation marks that seem to fit best. Then, compare your answers with the original punctuation in the Answer Key.

Note to Instructor: Unless otherwise noted, parentheses, dashes, and commas are interchangeable. However, ask the student to compare her answers with the originals below. How do the different choices of punctuation affect the relationship of the parenthetical element to the rest of the sentence? How do they change the rhythm of the sentence?

My first object (as usual) was originality.

All possible encouragement, therefore, should be given to the growth of critics, good or bad.

Note to Instructor: One-word parenthetical elements should generally be set off with commas only.

The blackbirds—three species of which consort together—are the noisiest of all our feathered citizens.

For all that American literature is—in the apt phrase of Mr. Howells—"a condition of English literature," nevertheless it is also distinctively American.

There are no richer parterres to my eyes than the dense beds of dwarf andromeda (Cassandra calyculata) which cover these tender places on the earth's surface.

We were, of course, very open to satire and attack.

But, above all, I discovered around me—it was near the end of June—on the ends of the topmost branches only, a few minute and delicate red cone-like blossoms, the fertile flower of the white pine looking heavenward.

> **Note to Instructor:** Since the parenthetical element is an independent clause, it should be set off with dashes or parentheses, not merely commas.

After a few such experiences, I, for one, have felt as if I were merely one of those horrid things preserved in spirits (and very bad spirits, too) in a cabinet.

I think that I cannot preserve my health and spirits, unless I spend four hours a day at least—and it is commonly more than that—sauntering through the woods and over the hills and fields, absolutely free from all worldly engagements.

> **Note to Instructor:** Since the parenthetical element is an independent clause, it should be set off with dashes or parentheses, not merely commas.

One sunny morning, he rose from his rug, went into the conservatory (he was very thin then), walked around it deliberately, looking at all the plants he knew, and then went to the bay-window in the dining-room, and stood a long time looking out upon the little field, now brown and sere, and toward the garden, where perhaps the happiest hours of his life had been spent.

> **Note to Instructor:** Since the parenthetical element is an independent clause, it should be set off with dashes or parentheses, not merely commas.

The neighbors—and I am convinced that the advice of neighbors is never good for anything—suggested catnip.

> **Note to Instructor:** Since the parenthetical element is an independent clause, it should be set off with dashes or parentheses, not merely commas.

Balmy Spring—weeks later than we expected, and months later than we longed for her—comes at last to revive the moss on the roof and walls of our old mansion.

Popular education is another great field in which public activity should be indefinitely enlarged, not so much through the action of the Federal government, though even there a much more effective supervision should be provided than now exists, but through the action of states, cities, and towns.

— LESSON 124 —

Italics

Quotation Marks

Ellipses

Single Quotation Marks

Apostrophes

Exercise 124A: Proofreading Practice

The sentences below have lost most punctuation and capitalization. Insert all missing punctuation marks, and correct all capitalization errors. When you are finished, compare your sentences with the originals.

Use these proofreader's marks:

capitalize letter: ≡	make letter lowercase: /
insert period: ⊙	insert exclamation point: ^!
insert comma: ^,	insert question mark: ^?
insert colon: ^:	insert semicolon: ^;
insert apostrophe: ∨'	insert quotation marks: ∨“
insert dash: (—)	insert hyphen: ≙

If a word or phrase should be italicized, indicate this by underlining.

Note to Instructor: The original sentences are found below. Additional notes have been inserted where there can be differences of interpretation. If the student punctuates correctly but veers from the original, ask him to first read aloud his version of the sentence, and then the original version. Do they sound different? (There is no right answer to this question—it's intended to continue to train the student's ability to "hear" punctuation marks.)

The following sentences below are from the trilogy by Suzanne Collins. The trilogy contains three titles; it begins with *The Hunger Games*, and then includes two additions to the series, *Catching Fire* and *The Mockingjay*. The first book, *The Hunger Games*, has three parts: "The Tributes," "The Games," and "The Victor."

Note to Instructor: The semicolon could also be a period, followed by a capitalized *It*. The colon following *parts* could be a dash, but the colon is less confusing.

Prim named him Buttercup, insisting that his muddy yellow coat matched the bright flowers.

Effie Trinket says as she always does, "Ladies first!" and crosses to the glass ball with the girls' names.

Note to Instructor: An additional comma could follow *says*.

"I volunteer!" I gasp. "I volunteer as tribute!"

The Hunger Games

But he did his job—more than his job—because for the first time in history, two tributes were allowed to win.

> **Note to Instructor:** The dashes could also be parentheses. An additional comma could also follow *because*.

"I have a problem, Miss Everdeen," says President Snow. "A problem that began the moment you pulled out those poisonous berries in the arena."

> **Note to Instructor:** The period after *Snow* could also be a comma, with the article *A* lowercase (*Snow, "a problem that...*)

Now he's arranging things around my living room: clothing, fabrics, and sketchbooks with designs he's drawn.

> **Note to Instructor:** The colon could also be a dash.

The rest of the day is a blur of getting to the station, bidding everyone good-bye, the train pulling out, the old team—Peeta and me, Effie and Haymitch, Cinna and Portia, Peeta's stylist—dining on an indescribably delicious meal I don't remember.

> **Note to Instructor:** The dashes could also be parentheses, but not commas, because the parenthetical (appositive) element itself contains so many commas.

The Hunger Games: Catching Fire

> **Note to Instructor:** This should be challenging! If the student cannot figure out the punctuation of the title from context, tell her that *The Hunger Games* is the title of the series (the main title), while *Catching Fire* is the individual title within the series (the subtitle), and colons separate titles from subtitles. (This also applies to the title below, *The Hunger Games: The Mockingjay.*)

Finally, Plutarch Heavensbee, the Head Gamemaker who had organized the rebels in the Capitol, threw up his hands.

> **Note to Instructor:** The comma after *Finally* is optional. The adjective clause *who had organized the rebels in the Capitol* is restrictive because there is more than one Head Gamemaker in the series—and Plutarch is the only Gamemaker to organize rebels.

Music plays them out, and then there's a woman reading a list of expected shortages in the Capitol—fresh fruit, solar batteries, soap.

> **Note to Instructor:** The dash could also be a colon.

Somewhere in District 13, Beetee hits a switch, because now it's not President Snow but President Coin who's looking at us.

> **Note to Instructor:** The comma after *13* is preferable (to avoid confusion) but not necessary. Commas could also surround *but President Coin*. The comma after *switch* is preferable but not necessary.

The words *traitor*, *liar*, and *enemy* bounce off the walls.

> **Note to Instructor:** You may need to remind the student that words are italicized if they are the subject of discussion.

The Hunger Games: Mockingjay

Exercise 124B: Foreign Phrases That Are Now English Words

The following phrases and words are now part of English and are usually not italicized. Using a dictionary, look up each one. In the blank, write the original language that the word belongs to, the meaning in English, and the meaning in the original language. The first is done for you.

> **Note to Instructor:** The most common meanings are listed below, but the student may choose others as long as they are in the dictionary.

cul-de-sac	French, a dead-end street, "bottom of the sack"
glitch	Yiddish, a problem or error, "slip, skate, nose-dive"
kindergarten	German, the year before first grade, "children's garden"
cafe	French, a small informal restaurant, "coffee"
karaoke	Japanese, the act of singing along to a recording, "empty orchestra"
klutz	Yiddish, a clumsy person, "a block of wood"
guru	Sanskrit (Hindi), an expert or guide, "venerable, weighty"
en masse	French, overwhelmingly, as a majority, "in a crowd"
genre	French, a category of book, movie, or music, "kind, style"
zebra	Portuguese, an African mammal of the genus *Equus*, "wild ass"

WEEK 34

Advanced Quotations & Dialogue

LESSONS 125 and 126

No exercises in these lessons.

— LESSON 127 —

Practicing Direct Quotations and Correct Documentation

Note to Instructor: The student's instructions and the resources given are provided below for your reference. You will need to check the paper for each of the five required elements and compare the student's formatting to the rules in the workbook.

A simple retelling of each story is all that's necessary. The essay may be any length, as long as it is over 250 words.

A sample essay is provided at the end of this lesson for your reference. If the student has trouble getting started, read her the first paragraph of the sample essay (don't let her look at it, since formatting the quotes properly is part of the challenge) and tell her she can use it as a model for the first paragraph of her own essay.

The student's Works Cited section should be identical to the Works Cited section of the sample essay.

The student may write an introduction and conclusion, but since the focus of this assignment is on documentation, four paragraphs that just retell important parts of the four stories are perfectly acceptable.

After the assignment is completed, ask the student to read the sample essay and the explanatory notes.

Additional Note to Instructor: The student's resources include two books by Logan Marshall. The student has instructions about how to write repeated citations of two books by the same author. However, in this case, because Logan Marshall is the author of one book and the editor of the other, the student can simply write "Marshall, p. #" for the authored book, and "Marshall, ed., p. #" for the edited book, as illustrated in the sample composition below.

Your assignment: Write a short essay called "Four Disasters at Sea." It should be at least 250 words, although it will probably need to be longer.

You must quote directly from all four of the sources listed below, footnote each direct quote, and put all four on your Works Cited page.

Your essay must include the following:

a) A brief quote that comes before its attribution tag.
b) A brief quote that comes after its attribution tag.
c) A brief quote divided by its attribution tag.
d) A block quote.
e) A quote that is incorporated into a complete sentence and serves a grammatical function within that sentence.
f) A quote that has been altered with either brackets or ellipses.
g) A second quote from the same source.

One quote can fulfill more than one of these requirements. If you need help, ask your instructor.

Note to Student: There's a challenge below you haven't seen yet—two books by the same author, Logan Marshall!

You've learned that your first reference to a book should be a full listing of author, title, publisher, date, and page number, but that the second time, you can simply list the author's last name and the page number.

If the author has written *two* books that you reference, you have to add a little more information! If Julia Smith wrote *A Guide to Giant Owls* and *Handbook of Pygmy Owls* and you quote both, you still give a full citation for the first time you quote each book, but then the second time you need to specify which book you're citing—so, instead of

Smith, 42

you would write

Smith, *A Guide to Giant Owls*, 42

or

Smith, *Handbook of Pygmy Owls*, 42

Note that you don't have to provide any other information, because that all came in your first citation of each book.

The books below are a little different, though! Tell your instructor what the difference is now. (If you can't figure it out, ask for help!)

Note to Instructor: See the answer above in Additional Note to Instructor.

Author: Logan Marshall, ed.
Title of Book: *The Sinking of the Titanic and Great Sea Disasters: Thrilling Stories of Survivors*
City of Publication: New York
Publisher: L. T. Myers
Date: 1912

The story begins a short while after the Titanic *hit an iceberg and began to sink.*

41

Once on the deck, many hesitated to enter the swinging life-boats. The glassy sea, the starlit sky, the absence, in the first few moments, of intense excitement, gave them the feeling that there was only some slight mishap; that those who got into the boats would have a chilly half hour below and might, later, be laughed at.

It was such a feeling as this, from all accounts, which caused John Jacob Astor and his wife to refuse the places offered them in the first boat, and to retire to the gymnasium. In the same way H. J. Allison, a Montreal banker, laughed at the warning, and his wife, reassured by him, took her time dressing. They and their daughter did not reach the Carpathia. Their son, less than two years old, was carried into a life-boat by his nurse, and was taken in charge by Major Arthur Peuchen.

42

The admiration felt by the passengers and crew for the matchlessly appointed vessel was translated, in those first few moments, into a confidence which for some proved deadly. The pulsing of the engines had ceased, and the steamship lay just as though she were awaiting the order to go on again after some trifling matter had been adjusted. But in a few minutes the canvas covers were lifted from the life-boats and the crews allotted to each standing by, ready to lower them to the water.

Nearly all the boats that were lowered on the port side of the ship touched the water without capsizing. Four of the others lowered to starboard, including one collapsible, were capsized. All, however, who were in the collapsible boats that practically went to pieces, were rescued by the other boats.

Presently the order was heard: "All men stand back and all women retire to the deck below." That was the smoking-room deck, or the B deck. The men stood away and remained in absolute silence, leaning against the rail or pacing up and down the deck slowly. Many of them lighted cigars or cigarettes and began to smoke.

The boats were swung out and lowered from the A deck above. The women were marshaled quietly in lines along the B deck, and when the boats were lowered down to the level of the latter the women were assisted to climb into them.

As each of the boats was filled with its quota of passengers the word was given and it was carefully lowered down to the dark surface of the water…

64

The captain and officers behaved with superb gallantry, and there was perfect order and discipline among those who were aboard, even after all hope had been abandoned for the salvation of the ship.

65

Many women went down, steerage women who were unable to get to the upper decks where the boats were launched, maids who were overlooked in the confusion, cabin passengers who refused to desert their husbands or who reached the decks after the last of the life-boats was gone and the ship was settling for her final plunge to the bottom of the Atlantic.

Narratives of survivors do not bear out the supposition that the final hours upon the vessel's decks were passed in darkness. They say the electric lighting plant held out until the last, and that even as they watched the ship sink, from their places in the floating life-boats, her lights were gleaming in long rows as she plunged under by the head. Just before she sank, some of the refugees say, the ship broke in two abaft the engine room after the bulkhead explosions had occurred...

67

The bearded admiral of the White Star Line fleet, with every life-saving device launched from the decks, was returning to the deck to perform the sacred office of going down with his ship when a wave dashed over the side and tore him from the ladder.

The Titanic was sinking rapidly by the head, with the twisting sidelong motion that was soon to aim her on her course two miles down. Murdock saw the skipper swept out; but did not move. Captain Smith was but one of a multitude of lost at that moment....

The wave that swept the skipper out bore him almost to the thwart of a crowded life-boat. Hands reached out, but he wrenched himself away, turned and swam back toward the ship.

Some say that he said, "Good-bye, I'm going back to the ship."

He disappeared for a moment, then reappeared where a rail was slipping under water. Cool and courageous to the end, loyal to his duty under the most difficult circumstances, he showed himself a noble captain, and he died a noble death.

Author/Editor/Sponsoring Organization: Time
Name of Web Article: The Forgotten Maritime Tragedy That Was 6 Times Deadlier Than the Titanic
URL: https://time.com/4198914/wilhelm-gustloff-salt-to-the-sea/
Date of access: Use the date on which you are writing your essay

...*the Wilhelm Gustloff,* a German ocean liner...was taken down by a Soviet sub on Jan. 30, 1945, killing 9,343 people—most of them war refugees...

The victims of the worst maritime tragedy in history were not only Germans, but also Prussians, Lithuanians, Latvians, Poles, Estonians and Croatians. World War II was drawing to an end, and the Soviet army was advancing. Though it would be months before the final fall of the Nazi regime, it was clear the end was coming—and they were desperate to escape before things came to a head. As a result, 10,582 people were packed onto a cruise ship that was meant to accommodate only about 1,900. Though some on the ship were Nazis themselves, others had been the victims of Nazi aggression. When three torpedoes hit the ship, there weren't nearly enough lifeboats, and many of the those that did exist were frozen to the deck. The majority of the passengers drowned.

Author: Logan Marshall
Title of Book: *The Tragic Story of the Empress of Ireland and Other Great Sea Disasters*
City of Publication: New York
Publisher: L. T. Myers
Date: 1914

The account below tells of the collision of the Canadian ship the Empress of Ireland *and the Norwegian ship* Storstad *on May 28, 1914.*

19

The horrible fact, about which there can be no dispute, is that the *Storstad* crashed bow on into the side of the big Canadian liner, striking it on the starboard side about midway of its length. The steel-sheathed bow of the collier cut through the plates and shell of the *Empress* and penetrated the hull for a distance of about twelve feet, according to the best testimony.

The water didn't flow in. It rushed in. From such stories as could be gathered from survivors and from members of the crew, it appears that Captain Kendall and his officers did all that was humanly possible in the fourteen minutes that the *Empress* hung on the river.

Captain Kendall said that he rang to the engine-room for

20

full speed ahead, with the object of trying to run ashore and save the passengers, but almost immediately after the engines stopped and the ship began to list rapidly...All lights went out almost at once. More than 1,400 persons were fighting for life in the black dark; yet, for the most part the flight was not one of panic, but grim determination to find, if possible, some means of safety.

Wireless operator Bomford and others who managed to win a way to the top deck saw scores leap into the sea. They saw hundreds trying to crawl up decks that were sloping precipitously, lose their balance and fall backward into the rising water. Passengers who couldn't get to the few life-boats in time seized chairs, anything loose they could find, and leaped into the river. Very many persons perished in the cold water while clinging to bits of wreckage and praying for help...

21

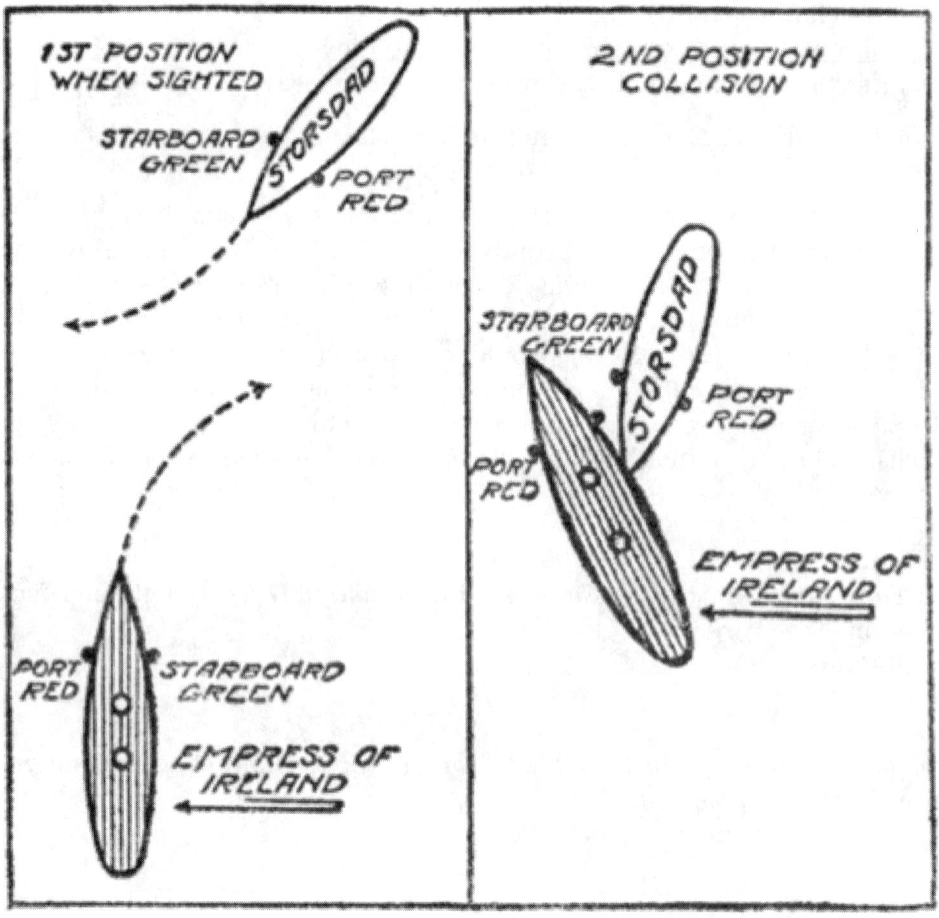

22

In a moment the fate of the *Empress* was known to all. The one smashing blow had done for her and the great bull-nose of the 3,500-ton freighter had crashed through the ribs and bulkheads...The S. O. S. call was ticked out by Edward Bomford, the junior wireless operator...

23

Many steamships picked up the call, but they were hours away. They started for the position given, but long before they had made any progress the *Empress* and two-thirds of her ship's company were under fifteen fathoms of water. Fourteen minutes is too brief a time for much rescue work...

24

The stewards did not have time to rouse the people from their berths. Those who heard the frenzied calls of the officers for the passengers to hurry on deck lost no time in obeying them, rushing up from their cabins in scanty attire. They piled into the boats, which were rapidly lowered, and were rowed away. Many who waited to dress were drowned.

The horror of the interval during which the *Empress of Ireland* was rapidly filling and the frightened throngs on board her were hurrying every effort to escape before she sank was added to by what seemed like an explosion, which quickly followed the ripping and tearing given the liner by the *Storstad*'s bow. As Captain Kendall afterwards explained, this supposed explosion was in reality the pressure of air caused by the in-rushing water. The ship's heavy list as the water pouring in weighted her on the side she was struck, made the work of launching boats increasingly difficult from moment to moment, and when she finally took her plunge to the bottom scores still left on her decks were carried down in the vortex, only a few being able to clear her sides and find support on pieces of wreckage.

Name of Article: Adventures of Men and Ships
Author: James Michener
Magazine: *Life*
Date: December 21, 1962
Volume and issue number: Volume 53, No. 25 Page range of article: 96–98, 111–114

Early in 1942, during World War II, the American ship U.S.S. Houston *was crippled by bombing near Java, and then was trapped by a convoy of Japanese ships.*

113

The U.S. cruiser lay trapped just northwest of Sunda Strait, and the Japanese fleet swarmed in for the kill. Searchlights brilliantly outlined the target. Eight-inch shells were lobbed into her from minimum range. Torpedoes were launched in groups of salvos. At times enemy destroyers came so close that gunners aboard *Houston* fired at them with machine guns.

Miraculously *Houston* withstood this assault for more than an hour. Her skipper, Albert H. Rooks, kept headway and somehow she managed to evade the torpedoes—until after midnight when she took her final blows. The shells that

114

raked her from stem to stern still did not put her out of commission...

Somehow the bridge remained operative most of the time and here Captain Rooks directed the last stages of the defense. That he kept his ship afloat was remarkable enough, but that he could still drive the enemy back with only one remaining turret was astonishing. Every available shell was fired...Finally there was literally nothing left to throw at the enemy. And now no amount of gallantry could prolong the life of the cruiser.

A salvo smashed directly into the bridge, killing Captain Rooks. The captain's Chinese cook sat on the deck beside his body and announced that he, too, would go down with the ship. When *Houston* finally died, the cook went with her.

> **Note to Instructor:** The numbers of the required elements are in marginal brackets below.
> Remember: don't expect deathless prose! This exercise is about proper citation, so although the essay should be grammatical, don't worry too much about transitions, thesis statements, etc.

SAMPLE ESSAY

The sinking of the *Titanic* is probably the most famous sea disaster. Some of the passengers thought that the collision with the iceberg was only a "slight mishap"[1] and that e) the boat couldn't sink, so they didn't go into the lifeboats. When they did start to leave the *Titanic,* the women got into the lifeboats first. According to the book *The Sinking of the Titanic and Great Sea Disasters,*

> The captain and officers behaved with superb gallantry, and there was perfect order and discipline among those who were aboard, even after all hope had been abandoned for the salvation of the ship.[2] d, g)

> Even though many women were saved in the lifeboats, many others "went down, steerage women...maids...[and] cabin passengers."[3] e, f, g)

Most people have heard of the *Titanic,* but many more passengers were killed when the German ship *Wilhelm Gustloff* sank at the end of World War II. *Time* says, "The victims...were not only Germans but also Prussians, Lithuanians, Latvians, Poles, Estonians and Croatians."[4] b)

Another little-known disaster happened in 1914, when *The Empress of Ireland* collided with a Norwegian ship called the *Storstad.* Water poured into the ship. An SOS was sent. "Many steamships were called," author Logan Marshall writes, "but they were hours away."[5] a,b,c)

None of them could rescue the passengers. Marshall adds that when the ship finally sank, "scores...were carried down in the vortex."[6] f, g)

These three disasters all involved passenger ships. But early in 1942, an American warship called the *Houston* was sunk by Japanese fire. Her captain, Albert H. Rooks, managed to keep the ship afloat and fighting until "[a] salvo smashed directly into the bridge,"[7] killing him instantly. He and his cook both went down with the ship.

---

[1] Logan Marshall, ed., *The Sinking of the Titanic and Great Sea Disasters: Thrilling Stories of Survivors* (L. T. Myers, 1912), p. 41.

[2] Marshall, ed., p. 64.

[3] Marshall, ed., p. 65.

[4] *Time,* "The Forgotten Maritime Tragedy That Was 6 Times Deadlier Than the Titanic," https://time.com/4198914/wilhelm-gustloff-salt-to-the-sea/ (accessed November 21, 2019).

[5] Logan Marshall, *The Tragic Story of the Empress of Ireland and Other Great Sea Disasters* (L. T. Myers, 1914), p. 23.

[6] Marshall, p. 24.

[7] James Michener, "Adventures of Men and Ships." *Life*, December 21, 1962, p. 114.

WORKS CITED

Marshall, Logan, ed. *The Sinking of the Titanic and Great Sea Disasters: Thrilling Stories of Survivors.* New York: L. T. Myers, 1912.

Marshall, Logan. *The Tragic Story of the Empress of Ireland and Other Great Sea Disasters.* New York: L. T. Myers, 1914.

Michener, James. "Adventures of Men and Ships." *Life* 53:25 (December 21, 1962), pp. 96–98, 111–114.

Time. "The Forgotten Maritime Tragedy That Was 6 Times Deadlier Than the Titanic," https://time.com/4198914/wilhelm-gustloff-salt-to-the-sea/ (accessed November 21, 2019).

WEEK 35

Introduction to Sentence Style

— LESSON 128 —

Sentence Style: Equal and Subordinating
Sentences with Equal Elements: Segregating, Freight-Train, and Balanced

Exercise 128A: Identifying Sentence Types

In the blank that follows each sentence or set of sentences, write *S* for segregating, *FT* for freight-train, or *B* for balanced.

I now quit altogether public affairs, and I lay down my burden.
—Edward VIII, December 11, 1936 B

And the rain descended, and the flood came, and the winds blew, and they beat on that house, and it did not fall.
—Matthew 7:25 FT

Anne had been too little from home, too little seen. Her spirits were not high. A larger society would improve them. She wanted her to be more known.
—Jane Austen, *Persuasion* S

The old man leaned the mast with its wrapped sail against the wall and the boy put the box and the other gear beside it.
—Ernest Hemingway, *The Old Man and the Sea* B

Moon, stars, and street lamps burst back into life. A warm breeze swept the alleyway. Trees rustled in neighbouring gardens and the mundane rumble of cars in Magnolia Crescent filled the air again.
—J. K. Rowling, *Harry Potter and the Order of the Phoenix* S, B

The storm had raged for full three hours; the lightning had grown fainter and less frequent; the thunder, from seeming to roll and break above their heads, had gradually died away into a deep hoarse distance; and still the game went on, and still the anxious child was quite forgotten.
—Charles Dickens, *The Old Curiosity Shop* FT

They wanted more land. They wanted our country. Our eyes were opened. Our minds became uneasy. Wars took place.
—Red Jacket of the Seneca People, "Brother, the Great Spirit Has Made Us All" S

One day when he was out walking, he came to an open place in the middle of the forest, and in the middle of this place was a large oak-tree, and, from the top of the tree, there came a loud buzzing noise.
—A. A. Milne, *Winnie-the-Pooh* FT

We had left the damp fog of the great city behind us, and the night was fairly fine.
—A. Conan Doyle, *The Sign of Four* B

He was invited to Kellynch Hall; he was talked of and expected all the rest of the year; but he never came.
—Jane Austen, *Persuasion* S

The robot left with a disconsolate step and Gloria choked back a sob.
—Isaac Asimov, *I, Robot* B

We've looked and we've looked and we've looked for him, but we can't find him.
—Isaac Asimov, *I, Robot* FT

I think that there is no more to be said; and I suggest that you now disperse quietly to your homes.
—T. S. Eliot, *Murder in the Cathedral* B

The cellar door opened out of the kitchen. There were five wooden steps leading down. A bacon-rack hung under its ceiling. There was wood in it, and coal.
—E. Nesbit, *The Railway Children* S

Then the arm of the Station Master was raised, the hand of the Station Master fell on a collar, and there was Peter firmly held by the jacket, with an old carpenter's bag full of coal in his trembling clutch.
—E. Nesbit, *The Railway Children* FT

— LESSON 129 —

Subordinating Sentences:
Loose, Periodic, Cumulative, Convoluted, and Centered

Exercise 129A: Identifying Subordinating Sentences

In each sentence, underline the subject(s) of the main clause once and the predicate twice.

Label each sentence in the blank that follows it as *L* for loose, *P* for periodic, *CUMUL* for cumulative, *CONV* for convoluted, or *CENT* for centered. For the purpose of this exercise, any sentence with three or more phrases and dependent clauses before or after the main clause should be considered cumulative. If two or fewer phrases or dependent clauses come before or after the main clause, the sentence should be classified as loose or periodic. Don't worry too much about figuring out exactly how many phrases or clauses are in the sentence—just do your best.

If phrases or clauses come before and after the main clause, the sentence is centered, no matter how many other phrases or clauses there are.

If any phrases or clauses come between the subject, predicate, and any essential parts of the main clause (objects, predicate nominatives, or predicate adjectives), the sentence is convoluted, no matter how many other phrases and clauses there are.

More precision was needed, to define what had caused the outbreak and to find the contaminated food in time to shut the outbreak down. L

— Maryn McKenna, *Beating Back the Devil: On the Front Lines with the Disease Detectives of the Epidemic Intelligence Service*

But for many reasons—the difficulty of organizing yet another pediatrician's visit for kids already getting many childhood vaccines, the lack of a clear message that children were themselves at risk—the recommendation was not effective. CUMUL

—Maryn McKenna, *Superbug: The Fatal Menace of MRSA*

And then, critically, from time to time they would exchange microbes. P

—Nathan Wolfe, *The Viral Storm: The Dawn of a New Pandemic Age*

The retrovirus class of viruses begins with RNA genetic code, which is translated into DNA before it can insert itself into the DNA of its host. L

—Nathan Wolfe, *The Viral Storm: The Dawn of a New Pandemic Age*

On New Year's morning, sometime after breakfast—a cold morning, air temperature in the forties, the grass wet and cold—they drove up the mountain along a muddy track. CUMUL

—Richard Preston, *The Hot Zone*

In 1918, if you heard a neighbour or a relation coughing, or saw them fall down in front of you, you knew there was a good chance that you were already sick yourself. CENT

—Laura Spinney, *Pale Rider: The Spanish Flu of 1918 and How It Changed the World*

It is tempting to imagine a single chimpanzee hunter as patient zero—an individual, the first of its species to harbor the novel virus—acquiring these viruses in short order from the monkeys it hunted, possibly on the same day. CUMUL

—Nathan Wolfe, *The Viral Storm: The Dawn of a New Pandemic Age*

While most viruses are ball-shaped particles that look like peppercorns, the thread viruses have been compared to strands of tangled rope, to hair, to worms, to snakes. CENT

—Richard Preston, *The Hot Zone*

On the other hand, names the current guidelines would rule out, such as monkey pox, arguably contain useful information about the disease's animal host and hence a potential source of infection. CONV

—Laura Spinney, *Pale Rider: The Spanish Flu of 1918 and How It Changed the World*

Perhaps the single most devastating infectious disease that afflicts humans today is malaria. CONV

—Nathan Wolfe, *The Viral Storm: The Dawn of a New Pandemic Age*

I was able in my mind's eye to zero in on the little fleshy crevices around Tom's and Jenny's teeth as they ate their meal and to see the turmoil of microbic life there, the spirochetes and vibratos in furious movement, the thicker corkscrewlike spirilla and vibrios gliding back and forth and the more sluggish or quiet chains and clusters and colonies of bacilli and cocci, massed around or boiling between detached epithelial scales and the fibers and debris of cells and food particles. CUMUL

—Theodor Rosebury, *Life on Man*

People who are afflicted with sickle cell have their origins almost exclusively in one of the world's most intensely malaria affected areas—west central Africa. CONV

—Nathan Wolfe, *The Viral Storm: The Dawn of a New Pandemic Age*

Ebola virus is named for the Ebola River, which is the headstream of the Mongala River, a tributary of the Congo, or Zaire, River. L

—Richard Preston, *The Hot Zone*

The smallpox was always present, filling the churchyard with corpses, tormenting with constant fear all whom it had not yet stricken, leaving on those whose lives it spared the hideous traces of its power. CUMUL

—Thomas Babington Macaulay, *History of England*

The Level 4 air lock is a gray area, a place where two worlds meet, where the hot zone touches the normal world. L

—Richard Preston, *The Hot Zone*

The close relationship we have with dogs, whether as companions, work animals, dinner guests, or a source of food, should not surprise us. CONV

—Nathan Wolfe, *The Viral Storm: The Dawn of a New Pandemic Age*

Staph aureus, a spherical bacterium that under a microscope bunches together like clusters of grapes, is everywhere in the environment. CONV

— Maryn McKenna, *Beating Back the Devil: On the Front Lines with the Disease Detectives of the Epidemic Intelligence Service*

Cut through the center by a river flowing from a rain forest some hundred or so miles away, it provides a unique microclimate—a well-hydrated strip in an otherwise dry landscape. CENT

—Nathan Wolfe, *The Viral Storm: The Dawn of a New Pandemic Age*

The blood culture the doctors had ordered that morning came back positive for methicillin-resistant *Staphylococcus aureus*, MRSA, a bug that could shrug off not only the methicillin family of antibiotics but also a half dozen others. CONV

—Jessica Sachs, *Good Germs, Bad Germs: Health and Survival in a Bacterial World*

The holism movement within medicine was never more than a minority voice, and its influence quickly evaporated after World War II, partly because it had been espoused by a number of leading Nazi doctors, and partly because the new range of biologicals and miracle drugs, above all, insulin, penicillin, and cortisone, promised that experimental research might indeed cure all ills. CUMUL

—William Bynum, *The History of Medicine: A Very Short Introduction*

Note to Instructor: The student may find this sentence challenging because it begins with two independent clauses. The second independent clause is followed by three subordinate elements: the clause *partly because it...Nazi doctors*, the clause *partly because the new...cure all ills*, and within the second clause, the parenthetical element *above all, insulin, penicillin, and cortisone.* Because the parenthetical element stands out from the clause that contains it, I have listed this as a cumulative sentence, but it is also acceptable to list it as a loose sentence (taking only the two subordinate clauses themselves into account).

The case of Charles Monet emerges in a cold geometry of clinical fact mixed with flashes of horror so brilliant and disturbing that we draw back and blink, as if we are staring into a discolored alien sun. CUMUL

—Richard Preston, *The Hot Zone*

Dr. Musoke was widely considered to be one of the best young physicians at the hospital, an energetic man with a warm sense of humour, who worked long hours and had a good feel for emergencies. L

—Richard Preston, *The Hot Zone*

What modern medicine needed, the German pathologist Paul Ehrlich concluded in 1885, was a "magic bullet" that would destroy bacterial cells but leave human cells unscathed. CONV

—Jessica Sachs, *Good Germs, Bad Germs: Health and Survival in a Bacterial World*

The quintessential early laboratory, and the one most frequently illustrated, was that of the alchemist, as natural philosophers sought to learn how to turn base metals into gold. CONV

—William Bynum, *The History of Medicine: A Very Short Introduction*

In areas where malaria-carrying mosquitoes bite year-round, people develop some immunity to the disease, though the protection takes years to build up and is never absolute. CENT

— Maryn McKenna, *Beating Back the Devil: On the Front Lines with the Disease Detectives of the Epidemic Intelligence Service*

Late in the afternoon, near sunset, the clouds thickened and boiled up into an anvil thunderhead that flickered with silent lightning. CENT

—Richard Preston, *The Hot Zone*

When a hot virus multiplies in a host, it can saturate the body with virus particles, from the brain to the skin. CENT

—Richard Preston, *The Hot Zone*

But that Saturday morning at home, as he laid out his tools and the pieces on an antique clock that needed fixing, he could not stop thinking about the monkeys. P

—Richard Preston, *The Hot Zone*

Note to Instructor: Since the participle phrase *thinking about the monkeys* acts as the direct object of the verb *could stop*, I have not counted it as a subordinate element following the verb.

But all four children had initially been given the beta-lactam cephalosporin when they were first hospitalized, because it was the first drug on the list for treating childhood infections suspected to be caused by staph. CUMUL

— Maryn McKenna, *Beating Back the Devil: On the Front Lines with the Disease Detectives of the Epidemic Intelligence Service*

Koch and Pasteur's proof that specific microbes cause specific diseases spurred a new generation of medical researchers to launch an all-out war on the world of bacteria with the goal of eradicating them. CONV

—Jessica Sachs, *Good Germs, Bad Germs: Health and Survival in a Bacterial World*

Around the hospital and the church stood the beautiful ferocious trees, a complex of camphors and teaks. CENT

—Richard Preston, *The Hot Zone*

He liked termites so much that he refrigerated them with his blood samples, to keep the termites fresh all day so that he could snack on them like peanuts with his evening gin as the sun went down over the African plains. CUMUL

—Richard Preston, *The Hot Zone*

The danger lies in the possibility that discovering such infections will set off a call to arms that brings about a historic increase in antibiotic use before we have applied the hard-won lessons of our first Hundred Years War on germs. CUMUL

—Jessica Sachs, *Good Germs, Bad Germs: Health and Survival in a Bacterial World*

The gorge, while not the only one of its kind, is unusual. CONV

—Nathan Wolfe, *The Viral Storm: The Dawn of a New Pandemic Age*

Having had centuries of experience with the smallpox virus, the village elders had instituted their own methods for controlling the virus, according to their received wisdom, which was to cut their villages off from the world, to protect their people from a raging plague. CENT

—Richard Preston, *The Hot Zone*

— LESSON 130 —

Practicing Sentence Style

Note to Instructor: The student may choose one of the assignments below. The first (rewriting) will suit students who do not easily come up with creative ideas; the second is intended for students who find creative writing natural.

A sample composition, along with the original Grimm tale, has been provided for the first, but there is no way to provide a sample or rubric for the second.

Choose one of the following assignments:

Exercise 130A: Rewriting

The following list of events, from the very old Norse fairy tale "The Three Billy Goats Gruff," needs to be rewritten as a story.

Think this is an easy task? Just remember that this story must have at least one of each of the following types of sentences:

Segregating (at least three sentences in a row)
Freight-Train
Balanced
Loose
Periodic
Cumulative (with four or more subordinate phrases/clauses; main clause can come either first or last)
Convoluted
Centered

AND the story must be at least 400 words long and make good sense.

So you can't simply write out the story you remember from your childhood picture books—you're going to have to put some brainpower into this assignment!

there were three billy goats (male goats)
they lived at the bottom of a hill
all three of them had the surname "Gruff"
they wanted to go up the hillside
they needed to eat grass and make themselves fat
there was a bridge on the way up the hill
the bridge went over a creek (also called a "burn")
a troll lived under the bridge
the troll had eyes as big as saucers
the troll had a nose as long as a poker
the first billy goat to cross the bridge was the youngest
his hooves went "trip, trap" on the bridge

the troll roared, "who is on my bridge"
the youngest goat said, "it is the tiniest billy goat Gruff"
the youngest goat said, "I am going up to make myself fat"
the youngest goat said this in a small voice
the troll said, "I am coming to gobble you up"
the youngest goat said, "oh, no, don't eat me"
the youngest goat said, "I am too little"
the youngest goat said, "wait for the second billy goat Gruff"
the youngest goat said, "he is much bigger"
the troll told him to go
a little while passed
the second billy goat started to cross the bridge
his hooves went "trip, trap" on the bridge
the troll roared, "who is on my bridge"
the second billy goat said, "it is the second billy goat Gruff"
the second billy goat said," I am going up to make myself fat"
the second billy goat had a louder voice
the troll said, "I am coming to gobble you up"
the second goat said, "oh, no, don't eat me"
the second goat said, "wait for the big billy goat Gruff"
the second goat said, "he is much bigger"
the troll told him to go
just then the biggest billy goat Gruff arrived
his hooves made the sound TRIP TRAP on the bridge
he was large and heavy
the bridge creaked and groaned
the troll roared, "who is on my bridge"
the biggest billy goat said, "it is the biggest billy goat Gruff"
the biggest goat had an ugly loud hoarse voice
the troll said, "I am coming to gobble you up"
the biggest billy goat said, "come along"
he said, "I have two spears"
he said, "I will poke out your eyeballs"
he said, "I've got two curling-stones"
he said, "I will crush you to bits"
the biggest billy goat charged the troll
he poked out the troll's eyes
he crushed the troll to bits
he tossed the troll into the creek
he went up the hill
all three billy goats got fat
they were so fat they could hardly walk home again
they are still fat now
the end of the tale

Note to Instructor: This sample composition shows one way in which the assignment could be completed. Each sentence fulfilling one of the required elements is underlined, with the label of the required element written in the margin next to the line where the sentence ends.

The original tale, which does not meet the requirements for sentence styles, is also included. If the student has trouble rewriting, allow her to read the original tale.

SAMPLE COMPOSITION

Once upon a time, in a valley beneath a hill, there were three billy goats, all called Gruff, all wanting to go eat grass. (centered) To get to the good grass on the hillside above them, they had to cross a bridge over a creek. But a troll lived there. He was huge. He was ugly. He had eyes like saucers. His nose was like a poker. (segregating)

The youngest billy goat Gruff, tiny and dainty and with a very small voice, crossed the bridge first. (convoluted) His hooves made the noise "trip, trap, trip, trap," on the bridge. When the troll, who was under the bridge, heard the noise, which echoed down to him, he emerged. (periodic)

"Who's that crossing my bridge?" the troll shouted. "I'll eat you!"

"No one important is here, it's just me, I am crossing the bridge, and I am going to eat grass, but I am very tiny, the second billy goat Gruff is much bigger, you should wait for him, just let me go!" (freight-train) said the youngest billy goat Gruff in a tiny little voice.

"Well, that seems fair, and you should go, little goat," said the troll.

So the tiny goat ran across the bridge and up the hillside. (balanced)

Not long after, the second billy goat Gruff came walking along and stepped on the bridge. He was heavier than the littlest billy goat, with a curly beard that blew in the wind, and bigger hooves, which made a louder trip trap noise on the bridge, a sound that brought the troll out from underneath at once. (loose)

"Who's that crossing my bridge?" the troll shouted for a second time. "I'll eat you!"

"Well, you could eat me," said the second billy goat Gruff. "But I'm not very fat. It's hardly worth your time. The biggest billy goat Gruff is coming. He's so much bigger. Eat him instead!" (segregating)

"Oh, fine," said the troll. "Go on and eat your grass."

Just as soon as the second billy goat Gruff was across the bridge, the biggest billy goat Gruff appeared. He was huge and he was heavy, and his beard reached his knees, and his feet tromped on the bridge, and the bridge creaked, and the bridge groaned. (freight-train)

"Who's that crossing my bridge?" the troll shouted for a third time.

"IT IS I!" the biggest billy goat Gruff shouted back, in his own big loud voice.

"I'll eat you!" the troll roared.

"Well, come along then!" the biggest billy goat Gruff roared back.

"My horns are spears, the better to poke out your eyes, and I'll crush you to bits, body and bones and all!" balanced

So the troll climbed up on the bridge. And the biggest billy goat Gruff charged at him, horns at the ready, to poke out his eyes, and to crush him to bits, body and bones, and to toss him out into the stream under the bridge, where he could never hurt another goat who wanted to cross the bridge and go up to the grass on the hillside, ever again. cumulative

Then the biggest billy goat Gruff went up the hillside, where he met up with the littlest billy goat and the second billy goat, who were eating grass until they were so fat that they could barely walk home again. loose

ORIGINAL STORY

"The Three Billy Goats Gruff," from *East of the Sun and West of the Moon: Old Tales from the North*, by Peter Christen Asbjørnsen and Jørgen Engebretsen Moe.

Once upon a time there were three Billy-goats, who were to go up to the hill-side to make themselves fat, and the name of all three was "Gruff."

On the way up was a bridge over a burn they had to cross; and under the bridge lived a great ugly Troll, with eyes as big as saucers, and a nose as long as a poker.

So first of all came the youngest billy-goat Gruff to cross the bridge.

"Trip, trap! trip, trap!" went the bridge.

"Who's that tripping over my bridge?" roared the Troll.

"Oh! it is only I, the tiniest billy-goat Gruff; and I'm going up to the hill-side to make myself fat," said the billy-goat, with such a small voice.

"Now, I'm coming to gobble you up," said the Troll.

"Oh, no! pray don't take me. I'm too little, that I am," said the billy-goat; "wait a bit till the second billy-goat Gruff comes, he's much bigger."

"Well! be off with you," said the Troll.

A little while after came the second billy-goat Gruff to cross the bridge.

"Trip, trap! trip, trap! trip, trap!" went the bridge.

"WHO'S THAT tripping over my bridge?" roared the Troll.

"Oh! It's the second billy-goat Gruff, and I'm going up to the hill-side to make myself fat," said the billy-goat, who hadn't such a small voice.

"Now, I'm coming to gobble you up," said the Troll.

"Oh, no! don't take me, wait a little till the big billy-goat Gruff comes, he's much bigger."

"Very well! be off with you," said the Troll.

But just then up came the big billy-goat Gruff.

"TRIP, TRAP! TRIP, TRAP! TRIP, TRAP!" went the bridge, for the billy-goat was so heavy that the bridge creaked and groaned under him.

"WHO'S THAT tramping over my bridge?" roared the Troll.

"IT'S I! THE BIG BILLY-GOAT GRUFF," said the billy-goat, who had an ugly hoarse voice of his own.

"Now, I'm coming to gobble you up," roared the Troll.

"Well, come along! I've got two spears,
And I'll poke your eyeballs out at your ears;
I've got besides two curling-stones,
And I'll crush you to bits, body and bones."

That was what the big billy-goat said; and so he flew at the Troll and poked his eyes out with his horns, and crushed him to bits, body and bones, and tossed him out into the burn, and after that he went up to the hill-side. There the billy-goats got so fat they were scarce able to walk home again; and if the fat hasn't fallen off them, why they're still fat; and so:

Snip, snap, snout,
This tale's told out.

Exercise 130B: Original Composition

Write an original composition of at least 400 words, with at least one of each of the following types of sentences:

Segregating (at least three sentences in a row)
Freight-Train
Balanced
Loose
Periodic
Cumulative (with four or more subordinate phrases/clauses; main clause can come either first or last)
Convoluted
Centered

This composition may be one of the following:

a) A plot summary of one of your favorite books or movies,

b) A narrative of some event, happening, trip, or great memory from your past,

c) A scene from a story that you create yourself, or

d) Any other topic you choose.

WEEK 36

— REVIEW 11 —

Final Review

Note to Instructor: This is not a "test"—it is a review and a challenge to the student to use the knowledge acquired. Give all necessary assistance.

Review 11A: Explaining Sentences

Tell your instructor every possible piece of grammatical information about the following sentences. Follow these steps (notice that these are slightly different than the instructions in your previous "explaining" exercise):

1) Identify the sentence type and write it in the left-hand margin.
2) Underline each subordinate clause. Describe the identity and function of each clause and give any other useful information (introductory word, relationship to the rest of the sentence, etc.)
3) Label each preposition as *P* and each object of the preposition as *OP*. Describe the identity and function of each prepositional phrase.
4) Parse, out loud, all verbs acting as predicates.
5) Describe the identity and function of each individual remaining word. Don't worry about the articles and coordinating conjunctions, though.
6) Provide any other useful information that you might be able to think of.

Note to Instructor: Use the information below to prompt the student as necessary. (Numbered information sections correspond to instruction steps above.) Give all necessary help. Encourage the student to answer loudly and in complete sentences.

The feeling which beset the child was one of dim uncertain horror.
—Charles Dickens, *The Old Curiosity Shop*

1) convoluted **The feeling which beset the child was one of dim uncertain horror.**

2) **The feeling <u>which beset the child</u> was one of dim uncertain horror.**

Note to Instructor: The single subordinate clause, introduced by the relative pronoun *which*, acts as an adjective modifying *feeling*.

3) **The feeling <u>which beset the child</u> was one of (P) dim uncertain horror (OP).**

Note to Instructor: The prepositional phrase is adjectival and modifies the indefinite pronoun *one*.

4) *Beset* is simple past, active, indicative. (The simple present would be *besets*.) The verb *was* is simple past, linking, indicative.

5) *Feeling* is a singular noun serving as the subject of the main clause, with *was* as the predicate. Within the subordinate clause, the relative pronoun *which* serves as the subject, *beset* is the predicate, and *child* is a singular noun serving as the direct object of *beset*.
In the main clause, the predicate nominative *one* (an indefinite pronoun standing in for a noun) renames *feeling* and is modified by the adjectival prepositional phrase *of dim uncertain horror*.
The adjectives *dim* and *uncertain* both modify the noun *horror*.

6) The subordinate clause *which beset the child* is a restrictive adjective clause modifying *feeling*.

If there's a buzzing-noise, somebody's making a buzzing-noise, and the only reason for making a buzzing-noise that I know of is because you're a bee.
—A. A. Milne, *Winnie-the-Pooh*

1) periodic *and* convoluted **If there's a buzzing-noise, somebody's making a buzzing-noise, and the only reason for making a buzzing-noise that I know of is because you're a bee.**

Note to Instructor: This is a compound sentence—two independent sentences connected with a comma and coordinating conjunction (*and*). The first sentence is periodic, with the subordinate clause *If there's a buzzing noise* preceding the main clause, and the second is convoluted, with the prepositional phrase and subordinate clause *for making...know of* coming between the subject (*reason*) and predicate (*is*).

2) **If there's a buzzing-noise, somebody's making a buzzing-noise, and the only reason for making a buzzing-noise that I know of is because you're a bee.**

Note to Instructor: *If there's a buzzing noise* is an adverb clause modifying the predicate *[i]s making* and introduced by the subordinating conjunction *if*. The subordinate clause *that I know of* is an adjective clause modifying *reason* and introduced by the relative pronoun *that*, which refers back to *reason*; within the clause, *that* is the object of the preposition *of*.

The subordinate clause *because you're a bee* is a noun clause serving as a predicate nominative and renaming *reason*. In this clause, *because* serves as a subordinating conjunction, not an adverb. This usage of *because* is slightly idiomatic—it would also be acceptable for the student to classify *because* as a preposition with the noun clause *you're a bee* as its object (see below).

3) **If there's a buzzing-noise, somebody's making a buzzing-noise, and the only reason for (P) making (OP) a buzzing-noise that (OP) I know of (P) is because you're a bee.**

Note to Instructor: The prepositional phrase *for making a buzzing-noise* is adjectival and modifies the noun *reason*. The present participle *making* is a gerund (acting as a noun) and is the object of the preposition; it also has its own object, *buzzing-noise*. The subordinate clause *that I know of* contains the prepositional phrase *of that*, which serves as the direct object of the predicate *know*. Finally, as noted above, it is possible to classify *because* as a preposition, with the noun clause *you're a bee* serving as the object of the preposition; in this case, the entire prepositional phrase *because you're a bee* serves as a predicate nominative renaming *reason*.

4) *'s* is the contraction for *is*, simple present, state-of-being, indicative.
's making is the contraction for *is making*, progressive present, active, indicative.
know is simple present, active, indicative.
is is simple present, linking, indicative.
're is the contraction for *are*, simple present, state-of-being, indicative.

5) The first *there* is an adverb modifying the first predicate, *'s*.
The indefinite pronoun *somebody* is the subject of the first independent clause.
The adjective *only* describes the noun *reason*, which is the subject of the second independent clause.
The personal pronoun *I* is the subject of the subordinate clause.
The personal pronoun *you* is the subject of the subordinate clause.
The noun *bee* is a predicate nominative renaming *you*.

6) No additional information is necessary.

So, first of all, let me assert my firm belief that the only thing we have to fear is fear itself— nameless, unreasoning, unjustified terror which paralyses needed efforts to convert retreat into advance.

—Franklin D. Roosevelt, speech given March 4, 1933

1) loose **So, first of all, let me assert my firm belief that the only thing we have to fear is fear itself— nameless, unreasoning, unjustified terror which paralyses needed efforts to convert retreat into advance.**

2) **So, first of all, let me assert my firm belief that the only thing we have to fear is fear itself— nameless, unreasoning, unjustified terror which paralyses needed efforts to convert retreat into advance.**

Note to Instructor: The subordinate clause *that the only thing we have to fear is fear itself* acts as a noun and is an appositive renaming *belief.* It is introduced by the subordinating conjunction *that.* Within that subordinate clause, the clause with understood subordinating element *[that] we have to fear* is adjectival and describes *thing.* It is linked to *thing* by the understood *that*, which is a relative pronoun renaming *thing* and serves as the understood object of the infinitive *to fear.*

The clause *which paralyses needed efforts to convert retreat into advance* is adjectival and describes *terror.* The relative pronoun *which* serves as the subject of the clause and renames *terror.*

3) **So, first of (P) all (OP), let me assert my firm belief that the only thing we have to fear is fear itself— nameless, unreasoning, unjustified terror which paralyses needed efforts to convert retreat into (P) advance (OP).**

Note to Instructor: The prepositional phrase *of all* is adverbial because it describes the adverb *first*, which itself modifies the hortative verb *let* (see below). The object of the preposition, *all*, is an indefinite pronoun. The prepositional phrase *into advance* is adverbial and modifies the infinitive *to convert.* (It doesn't describe *retreat* because the retreat isn't *into advance*—rather, it answers the adverb question *how* and describes *how* the conversion will take place.)

4) The hortative verb *let* is simple present, active, hortative. (The understood subject of *let* is the pronoun *you*. The personal pronoun *me* is the object of *let*, and the verb *assert* is an objective complement. See Lesson 109 to review hortative verbs.)
The predicate *have* is simple present, active, indicative.
The predicate *paralyses* is simple present, active, indicative.

5) The introductory *So* is an adverb modifying the hortative verb *let*. (See Lesson 109).
The adverb *first* modifies the hortative verb *let*.
The verb form *assert* is an objective complement that follows and describes the object pronoun *me*.
The noun *belief* is the object of the verb form *assert*. The possessive pronoun *my* and the adjective *firm* both describe *belief*.
Within the first subordinate clause, *thing* is the subject and *only* is an adjective describing it.
Within the clause *[that] we have to fear*, the personal pronoun *we* serves as the subject of the predicate *have*, and the infinitive *to fear* is adverbial and describes *have*. (The understood *that* is the object: *We have [that] to fear*.)
The noun *fear* following the predicate *is* is a predicate nominative renaming *thing*. The reflexive pronoun *itself* renames the noun *fear*.
The entire phrase *nameless, unreasoning, unjustified terror which paralyses needed efforts to convert retreat into advance* is an appositive renaming *fear*. Within that phrase, *terror* is the actual appositive noun. *Nameless, unreasoning*, and *unjustified* are all adjectives describing *terror*.
Within the adjectival subordinate clause *which paralyses needed efforts to convert retreat into advance*, the noun *effort* is the direct object of *paralyses*. The past participle *needed* is an adjective modifying *efforts*. The infinitive phrase to *convert retreat into advance* is adjectival and modifies *efforts*. The noun *retreat* is the direct object of the infinitive.

6) The verb phrase *have to fear* could also be classified as an idiom with a single meaning.

When they first went to live at Three Chimneys, the children had talked a great deal about their Father, and had asked a great many questions about him, and what he was doing and where he was and when he would come home.

—E. Nesbit, *The Railway Children*

1) centered **When they first went to live at Three Chimneys, the children had talked a great deal about their Father, and had asked a great many questions about him, and what he was doing and where he was and when he would come home.**

> **Note to Instructor:** The main clause *the children had talked...and had asked* is preceded by a subordinate clause and followed by three more subordinate clauses, as described below.

2) **When they first went to live at Three Chimneys, the children had talked a great deal about their Father, and had asked a great many questions about him, and what he was doing and where he was and when he would come home.**

> **Note to Instructor:** The first subordinate clause is adverbial and modifies both the predicate *had talked* and the predicate *had asked*. The subordinating adverb *when* links the predicate *went* to both other predicates.
>
> The three subordinate clauses *what he was doing* and *where he was* and *when he would come home* are all noun clauses and are all objects of the preposition *about*. (The fourth object is *him*—see below.) In the first clause, the introductory word *what* is the object of the predicate *was doing*. In the second clause, the introductory word *where* is an adverb modifying *was*. In the third clause, the introductory word *when* is an adverb modifying *would come*.

3)

P OP

When they first went to live at Three Chimneys, the children had

P OP

talked a great deal about their Father, and had asked a great many

P OP OP OP

questions about him, and what he was doing and where he was and

OP

when he would come home.

> **Note to Instructor:** The prepositional phrase *at Three Chimneys* is adverbial and modifies the infinitive *to live*. *Three Chimneys* is a compound proper noun.
>
> The prepositional phrase *about their Father* is adverbial and modifies the predicate *had talked*.
>
> The last prepositional phrase is adverbial and modifies the predicate *had asked*. The objective personal pronoun *him* is the first object of the preposition, followed by the three noun clauses.

4) The predicate *went* is simple past, active, indicative.
The predicates *had talked* and *had asked* are both perfect past, active, indicative.
The predicate *was doing* is progressive past, active, indicative.
The predicate *was* is simple past, state of being, indicative.
The predicate *would come* is simple present, active, modal.

5) In the first subordinate clause, the personal pronoun *they* serves as the subject. The infinitive *to live* is adverbial and modifies *went*.
In the main clause, the plural noun *children* serves as the subject. The noun *deal* is the direct object of the first predicate *had talked*, and is modified by the adjective *great*. The noun *questions* is the direct object of the second predicate *had asked* and is modified by the adjective *many*; *great* is an adverb that modifies *many*.
In the three noun clauses that serve as objects of the preposition, *he* serves as the subject of each. In the second noun clause, *where* modifies the predicate *was*. In the third noun clause, *when* modifies the predicate *would come*, and *home* is an adverbial noun also modifying *would come*.

6) Although the sentence is technically centered, with subordinate constructions both before and after the main clause, it has the feel of a loose sentence because of the number of subordinate constructions that follow the predicate.

He whipped out his lens and a tape measure, and hurried about the room on his knees, measuring, comparing, examining, with his long thin nose only a few inches from the planks, and his beady eyes gleaming and deep-set like those of a bird.

—Arthur Conan Doyle, *The Sign of Four*

1) loose **He whipped out his lens and a tape measure, and hurried about the room on his knees, measuring, comparing, examining, with his long thin nose only a few inches from the planks, and his beady eyes gleaming and deep-set like those of a bird.**

2) **He whipped out his lens and a tape measure, and hurried about the room on his knees, measuring, comparing, examining, with his long thin nose only a few inches from the planks, and his beady eyes gleaming and deep-set like those of a bird.**

> **Note to Instructor:** Unusually, for a sentence of this length, there are no subordinate clauses—only participle phrases!

3) **He whipped out his lens and a tape measure, and hurried about (P) the room (OP) on (P) his knees (OP), measuring, comparing, examining, with (P) his long thin nose (OP) only a few inches from (P) the planks (OP), and his beady eyes (OP) gleaming and deep-set like (P) those (OP) of (P) a bird (OP).**

> **Note to Instructor:** The prepositional phrases *about the room* and *on his knees* are both adverbial and both modify the predicate *hurried.*
>
> The preposition *with* has two objects: *nose* and *eyes*. The prepositional phrase *with his long...of a bird* is adverbial and modifies the present participle *examining*, which is itself an adjective describing the pronoun *He*. (See below for other options.)
>
> Within the longer prepositional phrase, *from the planks* is another prepositional phrase; it is adverbial because it describes *inches*, which here acts as an adjective describing the noun *nose*. (See below.) The prepositional phrase *like those of a bird* is adverbial because it modifies the two adjective forms *gleaming* and *deep-set*. Within that phrase, *of a bird* is adjectival and modifies the pronoun *those*, which itself is the object of the preposition *like*.

4) The predicates *whipped* and *hurried* both belong in the main clause, and both are simple past, active, indicative.

5) The adverb *out* modifies *whipped* (the word *out* can also serve as a preposition, but here it is an adverb). The noun *lens* and the compound noun *tape measure* are the direct objects of *whipped.* The possessive pronoun *his* describes *lens.*

The noun *room* is the object of the preposition *about.*

The noun *knees* is the object of the preposition *on*, and is modified by the possessive pronoun *his.*

The present participles *measuring, comparing*, and *examining* are all adverbial and all describe the predicate *hurried* (they are all actions that he took, as he was hurrying). You may also accept *measuring, comparing,* and *examining* as adjectival and describing *He.*

The noun *nose* is the object of the preposition *with*, and is modified by the adjectives *long* and *thin* and the possessive pronoun *his.*

Although *inches* normally appears as either a noun or an adverbial noun, here it seems to modify *nose* so is serving as an adjective. *Few* is an adverb modifying *inches*, and *only* is an adverb modifying *few.*

The plural noun *planks* is the object of the preposition *from.*

The possessive pronoun *his* and the adjective *beady* both modify the noun *eyes.*

The present participle *gleaming* and the compound adjective *deep-set* both modify the noun *eyes* and are in the predicative, rather than attributive, position.

6) It is possible to interpret the phrase *with his long thin nose [held] only a few inches from the planks, and his beady eyes gleaming and deep-set like those of a bird,* in which case *inches* could be functioning as an adverbial noun modifying the understood past participle, rather than as an adjective describing *nose.*

Had I known it, I would have had the pleasure of talking to him about you.
—Jane Austen, *Persuasion*

1) centered **Had I known it, I would have had the pleasure of talking to him about you.**

Note to Instructor: The main clause *I would have had the pleasure* is preceded by the formal condition clause *Had I known it,* which is subordinate, and is followed by three prepositional phrases.

2) **<u>Had I known it</u>, I would have had the pleasure of talking to him about you.**

Note to Instructor: The formal condition clause *Had I known it* is a form of *If I had known it* and so is subordinate (see 6, below).

3) **<u>Had I known it</u>, I would have had the pleasure of (P) talking (OP) to (P) him (OP) about (P) you (OP).**

Note to Instructor: The phrase *of talking* is adjectival and modifies *pleasure.* The phrases *to him* and *about you* are both adverbial and modify the present participle *talking.*

4) The predicate *Had known* is perfect past, active, subjunctive.
The predicate *would have had* is perfect present, active, modal.

5) In the first subordinate clause, the personal pronoun *I* is the subject and the pronoun *it* is the object.
In the main clause, the personal pronoun *I* is once again the subject. The noun *pleasure* is the direct object of the predicate.
The present participle *talking* is a gerund (a verb form functioning as a noun) and serves as the object of the preposition *of.*
The object pronoun *him* is the object of the preposition *to.*
The personal pronoun *you* is the object of the preposition *about.*

6) This sentence is a formal third conditional sentence—it expresses past circumstance that never happened, and also drops if from the condition clause and reverses the order of the subject and helping verb. See Lesson 115 to review.

Review 11B: Correcting Errors

Rewrite the following sets of sentences on your own paper (or with a word-processing program), inserting all necessary punctuation and capitalization.

Include the citations in your corrections!

Note to Instructor: The original sentences are listed below. In some cases, there are multiple correct options for punctuation. As many acceptable alternatives as possible are listed below, but if the student chooses an option not listed and it appears to follow the rules, you may choose to accept it.

When the student is finished, show him the original sentences for comparison.

Ah, of course, here is a hole in the roof.

"Away, is he?" said Holmes, in a disappointed voice. "I am sorry for that, for I wanted to speak to Mr. Smith."

—Arthur Conan Doyle, *The Sign of Four*

Note to Instructor: The comma after *Holmes* is optional. The period after *voice* could also be a comma. The comma after *that* is optional.

The Sign of Four is generally italicized because it is closer to novel than short story in length, but you may accept quotation marks around the title instead.

Tecumseh was killed in battle on the Thames River, near Chatham, Ontario, on October 5, 1813.

—W. C. Vanderwerth and William R. Carmack, eds., *Indian Oratory: Famous Speeches by Noted Indian Chiefs*

Note to Instructor: The comma after *River* is necessary because the river as a whole is not near Chatham—just the place where Tecumseh was killed is near Chatham.

Lighting her candle, she retreated as silently as she had come, and, gaining her own room once more, sat up during the remainder of that long, long, miserable night.

—Charles Dickens, *The Old Curiosity Shop*

Note to Instructor: The comma after *come* is optional.

Then he climbed a little further...and a little further...and then just a little further. By that time he had thought of another song:

It's a very funny thought that, if Bears were Bees,
They'd build their nests at the bottom of trees.

—A. A. Milne, *Winnie-the-Pooh*

Note to Instructor: The ellipses after both occurrences of *further* can also be commas (or even dashes). The punctuation marks could also be eliminated entirely, although this will make the sentence a little harder to read.

The period after the final *further* could also be a semicolon.

The colon after *song* cannot be a period, but could be a comma.

The capitalization of *Bears* and *Bees* is author's choice, and is not necessary. The comma after *Bees* is optional, but both lines of the song must be capitalized.

All of Harry's spellbooks, his wand, robes, cauldron, and top-of-the-line Nimbus Two Thousand broomstick had been locked in a cupboard under the stairs by Uncle Vern on the instant Harry had come home.

—J. K. Rowling, *Harry Potter and the Chamber of Secrets*

So they all sat down on a great flat grey stone that had pushed itself up out of the grass; it was one of many that lay about on the hillside, and when Mother came out to look for them at eight o'clock, she found them deeply asleep in a contented, sun-warmed bunch.

—E. Nesbit, *The Railway Children*

Note to Instructor: The semicolon could be a period, with *it* capitalized.
The comma after *o'clock* is optional but prevents misunderstanding.
There are no commas in *great flat grey* because the order of the adjectives cannot be changed.
There are commas in *contented, sun-warmed* because the order of the adjectives *can* be changed.
Mother is capitalized because it is here used as a proper name.

Gloria emerged sulkily. "You peeked!" she exclaimed, with gross unfairness. "Besides I'm tired of playing hide-and-seek. I want a ride."

—Isaac Asimov, *I, Robot*

Note to Instructor: The period after *seek* can also be a semicolon. The name *hide-and-seek* is generally written with hyphens, but can also be written simply as *hide and seek*.

With the exception, perhaps, of Admiral and Mrs. Croft, who seemed particularly attached and happy (Anne could allow no other exceptions even among the married couples), there could have been no two hearts so open, no tastes so similar, no feelings so in unison, no countenances so beloved.

—Jane Austen, *Persuasion*

Note to Instructor: The parentheses could also be dashes, in which case the comma after the final parenthesis should be eliminated. A comma could also follow *exceptions*.
Alternately, a comma could follow *happy*, a period could follow *couples*, and *there* could be capitalized. This is grammatical but does not flow as freely as the original.

Review 11C: Fill in the Blank

Each of the following sentences is missing one of the elements listed. Provide the correct required form of a word that seems appropriate to you. When you are finished, compare your sentences with the originals.

Fetching (present participle) a cloth and wiping (present participle) up the spilt (past participle) milk helped Bobbie a little (adverb).

They all (indefinite adjective) climbed on to the top (singular noun) of the fence, and then (adverb) suddenly (adverb) there was a rumbling (present participle) sound that made them look along (preposition) the line to the right, where (subordinating adverb) the dark (adjective) mouth of a tunnel opened (past participle) itself (reflexive pronoun) in the face of a rocky cliff; next (adjective) moment a train had rushed (perfect past, active, indicative, action verb) out of the tunnel with a shriek (singular noun) and a snort (singular noun), and had slid (perfect past, active, indicative, action verb) noisily (adverb) past them.

—E. Nesbit, *The Railway Children*

Little soft clouds played happily in a blue sky, skipping from time

adjective adjective adverb present participle

to time in front of the sun as if they had come to put it out, and

subordinating compound conjunction present active infinitive adverb

then sliding away suddenly so that the next might have his turn.

present participle adverb simple present active, modal action verb singular noun

—A. A. Milne, *Winnie-the-Pooh*

Anne kept her appointment; the others kept theirs, and of course

singular noun plural indefinite pronoun plural possessive pronoun short parenthetical expression

she heard the next morning that they had had a delightful evening.

adverbial noun perfect past, active, indicative action verb adjective noun

If he were a little spoilt by such universal, such

simple past, state-of-being, subjunctive verb adverb predicate adjective adjective

eager admiration, who could wonder?

adjective noun simple present, active, modal action verb

—Jane Austen, *Persuasion*

Give me problems, give me work, give me the

present active imperative action verb plural noun present active imperative action verb singular noun present active imperative action verb

most abtruse cryptogram or the most intricate analysis, and I am

adjective singular noun adjective singular noun

in my own proper atmosphere.

prepositional phrase acting as a predicate adjective

Then came rows of two-storied villas, each with a fronting of miniature

plural noun compound adjective adjective

garden, and then again interminable lines of new staring brick

singular noun adjective adjective present participle

buildings— the monster tentacles which the giant city was throwing out into the country.

appositive, containing adjectival clause, renaming the lines of brick buildings

—Arthur Conan Doyle, *The Sign of Four*

His action shows convincingly that there is no chance of expecting that

single noun adverb adjective of negation present participle acting as a noun

this man will ever give up his practice of using force to gain

simple future, active, indicative action verb adverb present participle acting as a noun present active infinitive

his will. He can only be stopped by force.

simple present, passive, modal action verb

—Neville Chamberlain, "This country is now at war with Germany," September 3, 1939 (referring to Hitler and his invasion of Poland two days before)

A cheerful fire was blazing (progressive present, active, indicative action verb) on the hearth (singular noun), the lamp (singular noun) burnt brightly (adverb), my clock (singular noun) received (simple past, active, indicative action verb) me with its old (adjective) familiar (adjective) welcome (singular noun); everything (indefinite pronoun) was quiet, warm and cheering, and in happy (adjective) contrast (singular noun) to the gloom and darkness I had quitted (adjective clause describing gloom and darkness).

—Charles Dickens, *The Old Curiosity Shop*

Review 11D: Diagramming

On your own paper, diagram every word of the following sentences.

Note to Instructor: As always, give all necessary help.

It was a September evening, and not yet seven o'clock, but the day had been a dreary one, and a dense drizzly fog lay low upon the great city.

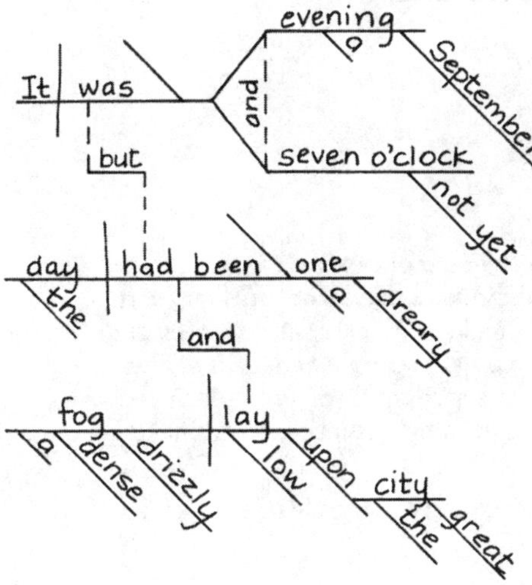

Note to Instructor: The compound noun *seven o'clock* cannot be separated into *o'clock* and *seven*, since this substantially changes the meaning. I have diagrammed *not yet* as a single adverb because it conveys a single meaning, but *not* could also be diagrammed as an adverb modifying *yet*, with *yet* modifying *seven o'clock*.

There was, to my mind, something eerie and ghost-like in the endless procession of faces which flitted across these narrow bars of light,—sad faces and glad, haggard and merry.

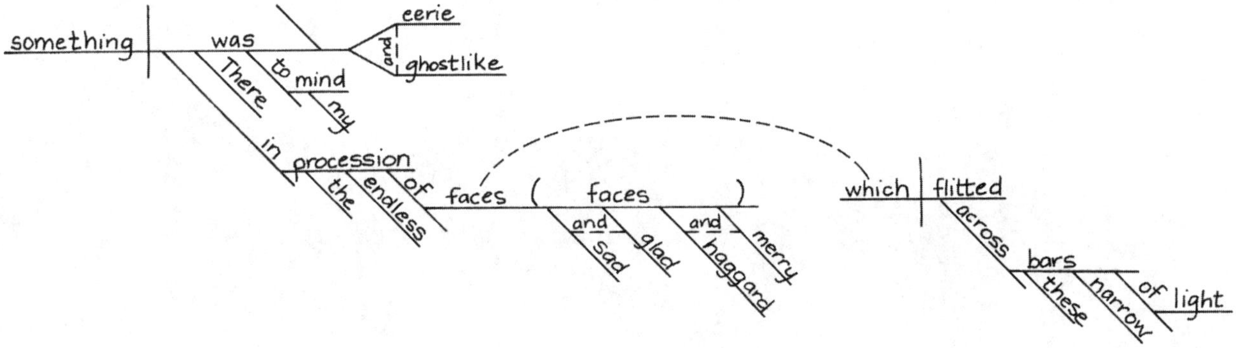

—Arthur Conan Doyle, *The Sign of Four*

King Henry— God bless him— will have to say, for reasons of state, that he never meant this to happen; and there is going to be an awful row; and at the best we shall have to spend the rest of our lives abroad.

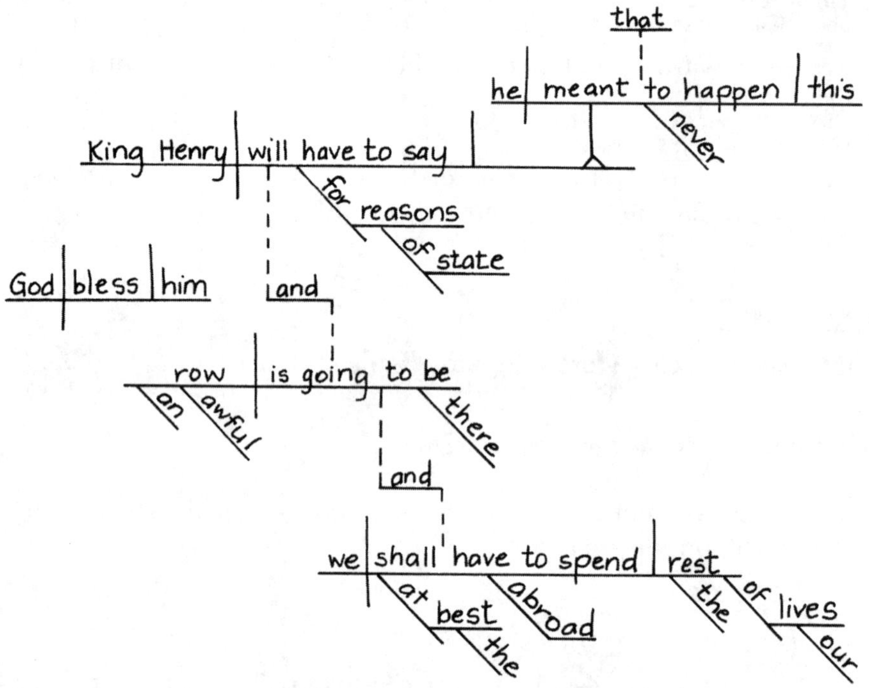

—T. S. Eliot, *Murder in the Cathedral*

Note to Instructor: This is a challenging sentence because of the verb phrases *will have to say, meant to happen, is going to be*, and *shall have to spend.* Each of these makes use of an "auxiliary verb," a verb combined with an infinitive to produce a meaning. In the diagram, *to say* and *to spend* are diagrammed as adverbial, while *to happen* is diagrammed as an object complement and *to be* is diagrammed as a predicate adjective. It is also acceptable for the student to diagram each verb phrase on a single predicate line, as below. Remember that diagramming is intended to make sentence structure clear—it isn't a test!

Note that the parenthetical expression *God bless him* is diagrammed separately to the left, and that *abroad* is an adverbial noun.

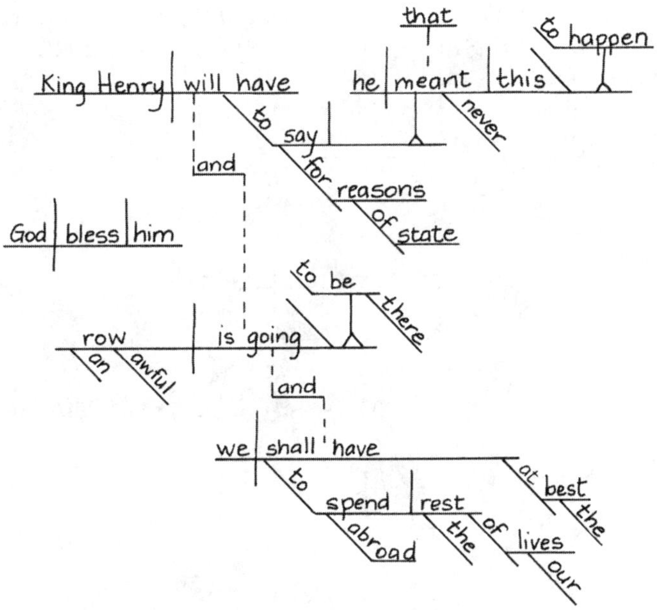

In the field of world policy I would dedicate this nation to the policy of the good neighbour—the neighbour who resolutely respects himself and, because he does so, respects the rights of others; the neighbour who respects his obligations and respects the sanctity of his agreements in and with a world of neighbors.

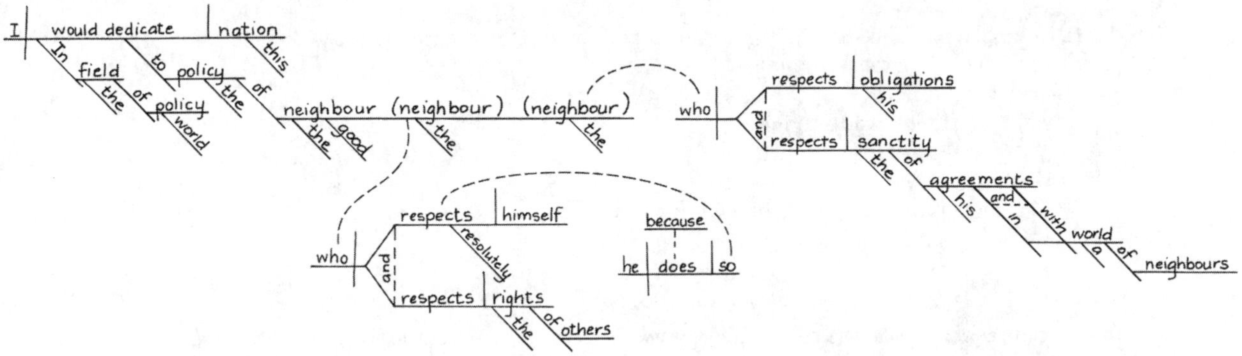

—Franklin D. Roosevelt, "The only thing we have to fear is fear itself," March 4, 1933, Washington, DC, USA

Note to Instructor: In the subordinate clause *Because he does so*, the word *so* has an unusual function—it acts as a pronoun standing in for the phrase *resolutely respects himself!* I have represented this on the diagram by linking *so* to *respects*. However, it is acceptable for the student to diagram *because* as the subordinating adverb on the dotted line; in this case, the dotted line would link the verb *respect* and *does*, and *so* could be diagrammed beneath *does* as an adverb (answering the question *how*).

Also note that the prepositions *in* and *with* have the same object, *world*. This could also be represented as below:

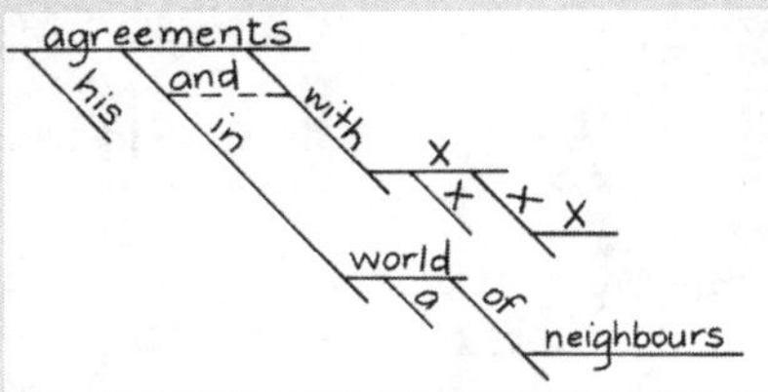

You can imagine what a bitter blow it is to me that all my long struggle to win peace has failed, yet I cannot believe that there is anything more, or anything different, that I could have done and that would have been more successful.

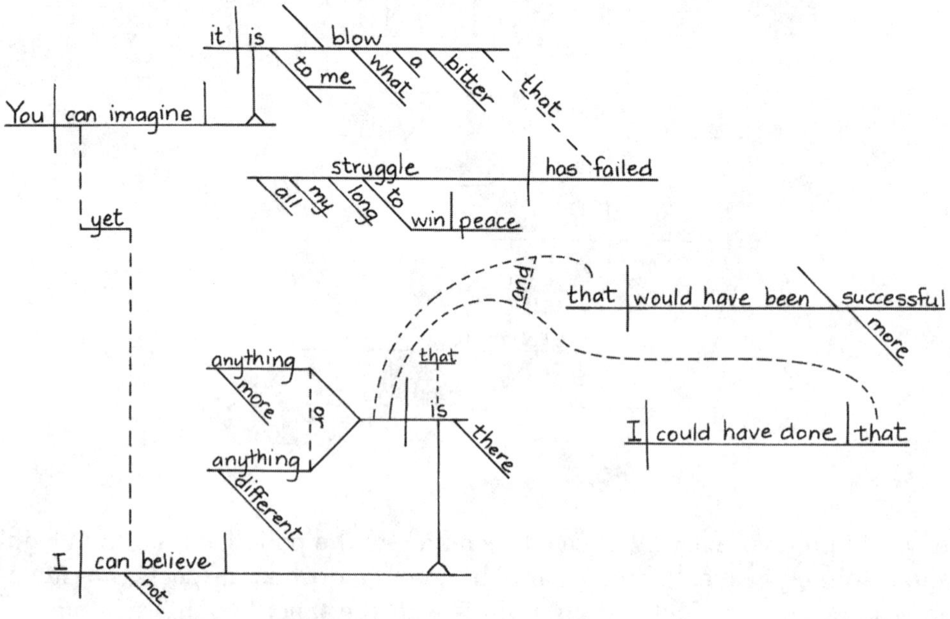

—Neville Chamberlain, "This country is now at war with Germany," September 3, 1939

Note to Instructor: The student may find it useful to write this sentence out with each clause on a different line before diagramming it:

You can imagine
what a bitter blow it is to me
that all my long struggle to win peace has failed
yet I cannot believe
that there is anything more or anything different
that I could have done
and
that would have been more successful

In the clauses *that I could have done* and *that would have been more successful*, the word *that* serves as a relative pronoun, both of them referring back to the double occurrence of *everything*. The student will have to be creative in order to get *and* on the diagram—accept any reasonable arrangement!

The berries, when they come, are bright scarlet, but if you pick them, they disappoint you by turning black before you get them home.

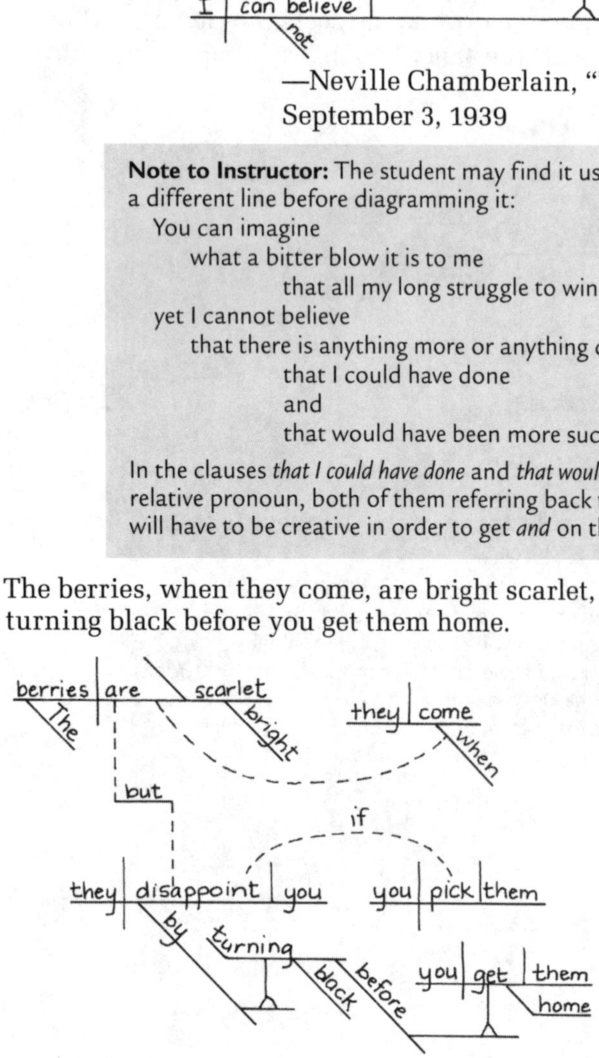

Note to Instructor: This is an unusual occurrence of *black* as an adverb, modifying the present participle *turning* and answering the question *how.*

At the end of the field, among the thin gold spikes of grass and the harebells and Gipsy roses and St. John's Wort, we may just take one last look, over our shoulders, at the white house where neither we nor anyone else is wanted now.

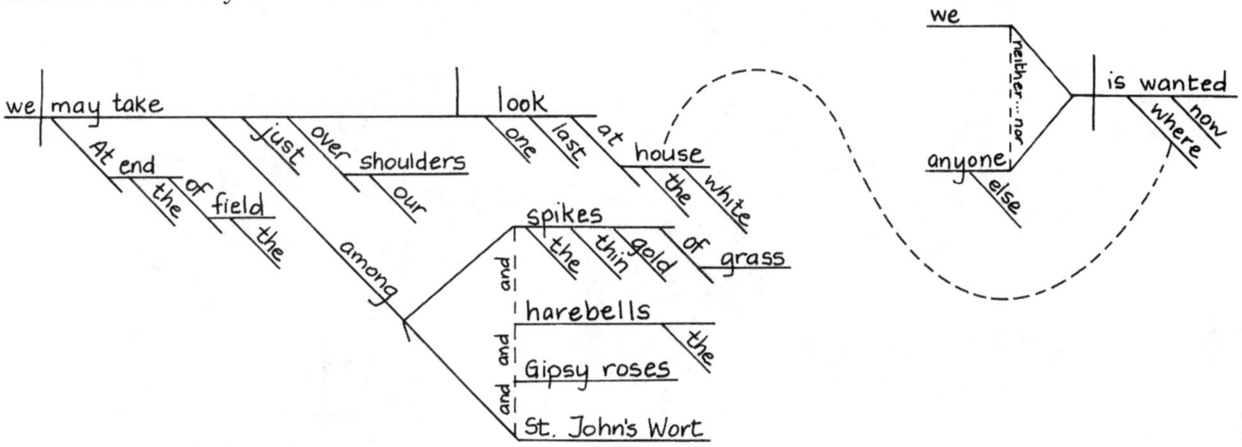

—E. Nesbit, *The Railway Children*

In the summer I often leave home early in the morning, and roam about fields and lanes all day, or even escape for days or weeks together; but, saving in the country, I seldom go out until after dark, though, Heaven be thanked, I love its light and feel the cheerfulness it sheds upon the earth, as much as any creature living.

—Charles Dickens, *The Old Curiosity Shop*

Note to Student: The word *saving* is an archaic preposition meaning *except for.*

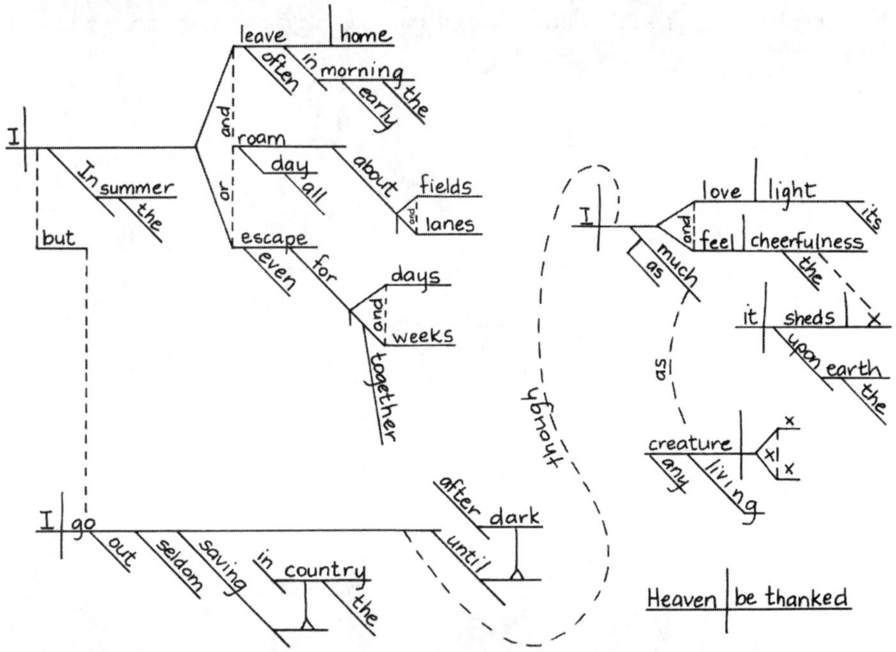

Note to Instructor: The word *early* could also be diagrammed beneath *leave* as an adverb. The adjective *together* modifies both *days* and *weeks.*

If the student needs to review how to diagram *as much as any creature living,* this is covered in Lesson 118. The full clause with understood elements is *as much as any creature living [loves and feels].*

There they returned again into the past, more exquisitely happy, perhaps, in their re-union, than when it had been first projected; more tender, more tried, more fixed in a knowledge of each other's character, truth, and attachment; more equal to act, more justified in acting.

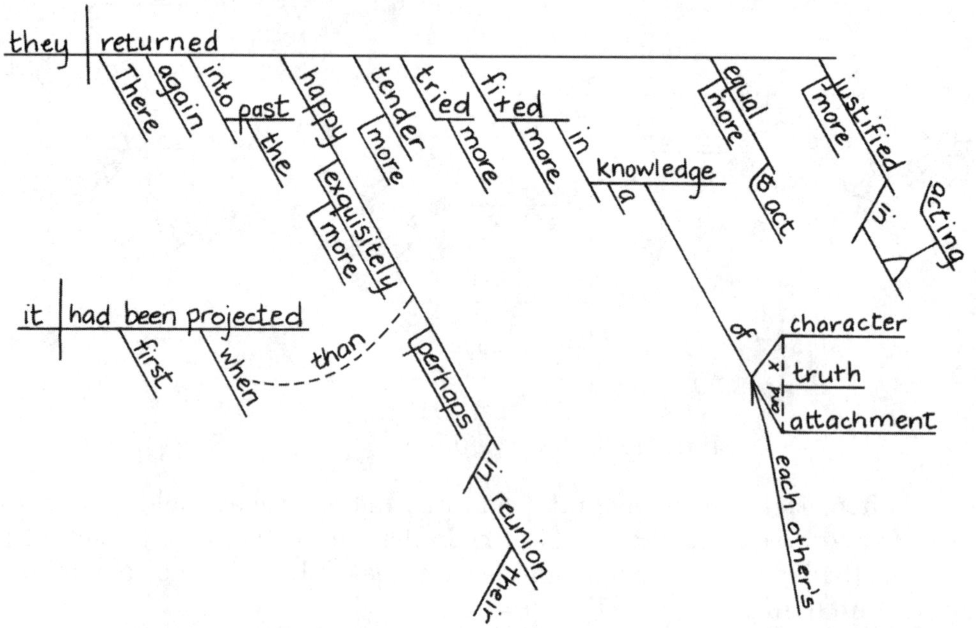

—Jane Austen, *Persuasion*

Note to Instructor: The student may need to review Lesson 66 in order to diagram the comparison *than when it had been first projected*. The comparison is between the happiness felt now and the happiness felt *when*, so the dotted line links the quality (*happy*) to the adverb representing the previous time.